THE CRAFT OF PUBLIC HISTORY

An Annotated Select Bibliography

David F. Trask

and

Robert W. Pomeroy III,

General Editors

Prepared under the Auspices of
the National Council on Public History

Greenwood Press
Westport, Connecticut • London, England

Library of Congress Cataloging in Publication Data

Main entry under title:

The Craft of public history.

"Prepared under the auspices of the National Council
on Public History."
  Includes bibliographies and index.
  1. Historiography—United States—Bibliography.
2. United States—Historiography—Bibliography.
3. Archives—United States—Bibliography. 4. Archives—
Bibliography. 5. Library science—Bibliography.
6. Libraries—United States—Bibliography. I. Trask,
David F. II. Pomeroy, Robert W. III. National Council
on Public History (U.S.) IV. Title: Public History.
Z6208.H5C73 1983   016.9072   83-1505
[D13.5.U6]
ISBN 0-313-23687-9 (lib. bdg.)

Library of Congress Catalog Card Number: 83-1505
ISBN: 0-313-23687-9

First published in 1983

Greenwood Press
A division of Congressional Information Service, Inc.
88 Post Road West
Westport, Connecticut 06881

Printed in the United States of America

10 9 8 7 6 5 4 3 2 1

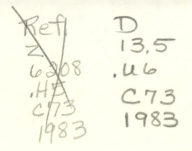
CONTENTS

PREFACE

Public history is an ancient approach to the study of past processes that has recently attracted renewed attention, so much so that it is undergoing dynamic redefinition. The term "public history" denotes the practice of history and history-related disciplines in settings elsewhere than in educational institutions— schools, colleges, and universities.

Historical activities *per se* include, *inter alia*, those of historians in the service of government at all levels—federal, state, regional, and local—and in the service of diverse private organizations, notably historical societies, museums, libraries, private businesses, research groups, and firms of historical consultants.

History-related activities include, *inter alia*, those of archivists, librarians, museum curators, preservationists, directors of institutional history offices, staff members of historical societies, and makers of audiovisual forms that present historical content.

The word "public" does not mean "official" or governmental, although it certainly encompasses history and history-related activities within governments. Rather, the term refers to the larger blessings that flow through the society from the activities of all public historians—for whom this mission is fundamental, the *raison d'être* of their practice.

The Craft of Public History: An Annotated Select Bibliography, commissioned by the National Council on Public History, provides a basic guide to the literature of public history. It is the first book-length reference work on the subject. The citations of information are indeed highly selective; the various chapters include those materials considered most representative drawn from the larger body of information useful to the public historian. As the title of this work suggests, emphasis is placed on "how-to-do-it"—*on the craft*—but theoretical works are included, and so are examples of various forms. The general editors hope that this volume alerts all interested users not only to the present state of the art but to the bright future of public history.

The annotated citations are presented in eleven chapters, each edited by distinguished practitioners who assume responsibility for their contributions. Each chapter treats a topic of major concern in the field of public history. Earlier chapters consider general matters of interest to all historians. Later chapters consider types of practice in public history. Individual chapters usually begin with general works, continue with listings on specific aspects, and conclude with guidance on reference materials. Each editor introduces his or her chapter with a brief description and guide.

Chapter 1, "Public History: Research and Writing," edited by Lawrence B. de Graaf, cites fundamental reference works of special utility to public historians and also research applications in the practice of public history.

Chapter 2, "Public History: Training," edited by David A. Johnson, guides the user to information concerning educational opportunities in the field, stressing academic programs and topical themes that have developed in recent years as part of the broad reawakening now in progress.

Chapter 3, "Public History: Business Management," edited by Robert W. Pomeroy III, provides guidance on the direction or leadership of activity in public history, a unique dimension of this bibliography.

Chapter 4, "Archives, Records, and Information Management," edited by Richard M. Kesner, provides comprehensive guidance to a history-related activity of the greatest importance to all practitioners.

Chapter 5, "Genealogy and Family History," edited by Glen M. Leonard, lists sources and authorities, many of them interdisciplinary in nature, for what is at once among the oldest fields of historical practice and one of the most popular present-day interests.

Chapter 6, "Historical Editing," edited by Suellen Hoy, considers its subject as both a basic professional activity and a skill of special importance in the field of public history.

Chapter 7, "Historical Resource Management," edited by Theodore J. Karamanski, presents the literature dealing with historic preservation and cultural resource management, including museums, as practiced in nonacademic settings, much more the rule than the exception.

Chapter 8, "Library Science," edited by Richard Hume Werking and Boyd Keith Swigger, is, like historical editing, a subject to be mastered as a professional discipline and as a field of professional practice.

Chapter 9, "Media and History," edited by Gerald H. Herman, introduces an area that has come to prominence only in very recent times. The topic, another unique contribution, is treated in terms of material available for research and as a means for disseminating nonprint information.

Chapter 10, "Oral History," edited by Enid H. Douglass, lists materials in an activity now considered more than a technique but less than a full-fledged discipline. This chapter stresses basic works on the art of interviewing, and information on evaluation and teaching, and applications made in specific areas, ranging from women's studies to the arts.

Chapter 11, "Policy History," edited by Peter N. Stearns, concentrates on material relating to the uses of history in policy making, both in the public sector and the private sector. Policy-related history is of interest in some way to large numbers of public historians, a circumstance that distinguishes them from their academic colleagues.

The general editors recognize that users may detect errors and omissions, despite every effort to avoid them. For these defects the general editors offer apology, accepting the risk of imperfections in order to provide the first comprehensive presentation of the most useful literature extant on public history without further delay. We respectfully request that users draw our attention to helpful corrections and additions so that we may use them in preparing supplements or new editions.

How to Use This Bibliography

Presentation. Citations of references in sections within each chapter are listed in alphabetical order by author or, if there is no author, by the first work in the title. Each citation is numbered in sequence to provide a convenient means of locating items by use of the author index.

Cross-Reference. Coded references, with a few exceptions, are assigned only one number. A relatively small number of references are annotated in more than one chapter when they have special importance for more than one subject. In such cases the full citation, numbered and annotated, usually appears in the most convenient chapter, and a short title, often followed by a second annotation, appears in another place. Note the following example:

Evans, Frank B., and Harold T. Pinkett, eds. *Research in the Administration of Public Policy*. See no. *51*.

Users are urged to consult the table of contents carefully so that they may locate all the sections that might list desired information.

Method of Citation. The form for the citation of references generally follows the prescriptions in the *Manual of Style*, 12th ed., rev., published by the University of Chicago Press. Citations for books and comparable publications include the first name, middle initial, and last name of the author(s), the title and subtitle in italics, the volume number if appropriate, and the place of publication, the publisher, and the year of publication. When feasible shortened names are used to identify publishers. Citations for articles and comparable publications include first name, middle initial, and last name of the author(s), title, journal title, volume number of the journal, the month and year of the issue, and the pagination. Note the following examples:

864. Schlereth, Thomas J. *Artifacts and the American Past*. Nashville: American Association for State and Local History, 1980.

1011. Schad, Jasper G., and Ruth L. Adams. "Book Selection in Academic Libraries: A New Approach." *College and Research Libraries*, Vol. XXX (September 1969), 437-442.

Annotation. Annotations stress description. Given the selectivity of this bibliography, all listed items are presumed to be of high quality and significant utility to users. Annotations provide information about content, but they do not include qualitative judgments. The editors leave this decision to the readers. The contributor of each annotation is identified by initials. The full names and affiliations of the contributors are provided in a list, alphabetized by initials, that follows the preface.

Author Index. The author index lists authors of references cited in the bibliography. Each index entry gives the first name, middle initial, and last name of the author, and the number assigned to the citation. These citations are easily located because all entries are numbered sequentially in the volume.

A large number of individuals and their institutions, other than those named in the list of contributors, lent generous assistance. We much appreciate their guidance concerning areas to which attention should be given and their advice on specific citations. We list them, with our sincere thanks, below.

Chapter 1, "Public History: Research and Writing": Joseph P. Harahan (U.S. Air Force), Edie Hedlin (National Historical Records and Publications Commission), Suellen Hoy (North Carolina Division of Archives), John Howell (California State University, Fullerton), G. Wesley Johnson (University of California, Santa Barbara), Theodore J. Karamanski (Loyola University of Chicago), Richard M. Kesner (F. W. Faxon Company, Inc.), David E. Kyvig (University of Akron), Glen M. Leonard (The Church of Jesus Christ of Latter-day Saints), Roy Lopata (City of Newark, Delaware), Ernest R. May (Harvard University), Patricia Melvin Mooney (University of Arkansas, Little Rock), Jackson K. Putnam (California State University, Fullerton), Glenda Riley (University of Northern Iowa), Noel J. Stowe (Arizona State University), and David Van Deventer (California State University, Fullerton).

Chapter 3, "Public History: Business Management": American Bankers Association (Washington, D.C.), *Harvard Business Review* (Boston, Massachusetts), Albro Martin (Bradley University), and U.S. Small Business Administration (Washington, D.C.).

The three institutions listed above, the American Bankers Association, the *Harvard Business Review*, and the U.S. Small Business Administration, generously permitted us to quote or paraphrase their own material. Whenever this is the case, the institution's initials are shown, along with those of the particular citation's author.

Chapter 4, "Archives, Records and Information Management": Francis X. Blouin, Jr. (University of Michigan).

Chapter 11, "Policy History": Andrew Achenbaum (Carnegie-Mellon University), Mary Benbenek (Carnegie-Mellon University), Edward Berkowitz (George Washington University), Jay Harper (Carnegie-Mellon University), Suellen Hoy (North Carolina Division of Archives and History), David Kaiser (Carnegie-Mellon University), Richard Kohn (Office of Air Force History), Susan Lewis (Carnegie-Mellon University), Rachel Maines (Carnegie-Mellon University), Scott Martin (Carnegie-Mellon University), Ernest R. May (Harvard University), Alex Roland (National Space and Aeronautical Agency), Todd Shallat (U.S. Army Corps of Engineers), Joel Tarr (Carnegie-Mellon University), Charles Van Ryn (Carnegie-Mellon University), Steve Weber (Carnegie-Mellon University), and Samuel Wells, Jr. (Woodrow Wilson Center).

In assembling and producing this bibliography, we are most grateful for the able participation of our indexer, Laurence R. Trask, and editorial assistant, Noel H. Trask, as well as the excellent typing and manuscript preparation provided by Diane Bayer and Susan McGee and the copyediting of Sharon Skowronski. Finally, our most sincere thanks to our families, for their support, patience and understanding throughout the two years needed to complete this work.

CONTRIBUTORS

ABA	American Bankers Association
AEW	A. Elizabeth Watson (National Trust for Historic Preservation)
AMH	Alice M. Hoffman (Pennsylvania State University, Radnor)
AOM	Andrew O. Manzini (EBASCO Services Inc.)
BCC	Ballard C. Campbell (Northeastern University)
BEB	Barbara E. Benson (Historical Society of Delaware)
BG	Bernard Galm (University of California, Los Angeles)
BMK	Betty McKeever Key (The Maryland Historical Society)
BKS	Boyd Keith Swigger (Texas Woman's University)
CD	Cullom Davis (Sangamon State University)
CHS	Charles H. Shultz (Alfred University)
CK	Carol Krucoff (Chicago Historical Society)
CMG	Charles M. Getchell, Jr. (University of Kansas)
CTM	Charles T. Morrissey (*Vermont Life*)
DAJ	David A. Johnson (Portland State University)
DFT	David F. Trask (U.S. Army Center of Military History)
DJK	David J. Keene (Loyola University of Chicago)
DKD	David King Dunaway (University of New Mexico)
EBM	Elizabeth B. Mason (Columbia University)
EDH	Edward D. Hendricks (The Association of Management Consulting Firms)
EHD	Enid H. Douglass (Claremont Graduate School)
FCS	Fay C. Schreibman (National Jewish Archive of Broadcasting, The Jewish Museum)
GHH	Gerald H. Herman (Northeastern University)
GML	Glen M. Leonard (The Church of Jesus Christ of Latter-day Saints)
GPW	Gordon P. Watts, Jr. (East Carolina University)
HBR	*Harvard Business Review*

HH	Hope Headley (National Trust for Historic Preservation)
JAM	Joe A. Mobley (North Carolina Division of Archives and History)
JAN	John A. Neuenschwander (Carthage College)
JCP	J. Carlyle Parker (California State College, Stanislaus)
JDF	Joyce Duncan Falk (University of California, Irvine)
JEO	John E. O'Connor (New Jersey Institute of Technology)
JES	James E. Smith (Brigham Young University)
JFD	James F. Dinwiddie (George Washington University)
JG	Joel Gardner (Louisiana State Archives)
JHM	James H. Madison (Indiana University)
JJ	Jill Jeskin (Chicago Historical Society)
JJC	Jeffrey J. Crow (North Carolina Division of Archives and History)
JMC	Judy M. Cato (University of Virginia)
JW	Judy Weisman (Chicago Historical Society)
KS	Kip Sperry (The Church of Jesus Christ of Latter-day Saints)
LB	Lotte Bailyn (Massachusetts Institute of Technology)
LBD	Lawrence B. de Graaf (California State University, Fullerton)
LJM	Linda J. Martin (Arizona State University)
LMD	Lorna M. Daniells (Harvard University)
MKP	Marion K. Pinsdorf (Amfac, Inc.)
MVC	Mary V. Chatfield (*Harvard Business Review*)
NCB	Nancy Comfort Bowen (*Harvard Business Review*)
NJS	Noel J. Stowe (Arizona State University)
NL	Nancy Lace (Chicago Historical Society)
PA	Polly Athan (Chicago Historical Society)
PGWK	Peter G. W. Keen (Decision Support Systems)
PJT	Paul J. Tedesco (Northeastern University)
PMH	Pamela M. Hanson (Smithsonian Institution)
PMS	Philip M. Smith (Citibank)
PNS	Peter N. Stearns (Carnegie-Mellon University)
RHL	Roy H. Lopata (Newark, Delaware)
RHW	Richard Hume Werking (Trinity University)
RJG	Ronald J. Grele (University of California at Los Angeles)
RJM	Robert J. Mitchell (Maine Council on Economic Education)
RJR	Richard J. Roddewig (Chicago, Illinois)
RMK	Richard M. Kesner (F. W. Faxon Company, Inc.)
RMS	Roger M. Scanland (Brigham Young University)
RPC	Rodney P. Carlisle (Rutgers University)
RSJ	Rebecca S. Jimenez (Baylor University)
RWP	Robert W. Pomeroy III (Inter-American Development Bank)
SAA	Sheila A. Adams (Arizona State University)
SBA	U.S. Small Business Administration
SBH	Samuel B. Hand (University of Vermont)

SC   Scott Cline (Jewish History Collection, Western Reserve Historical Society)

SH   Suellen Hoy (North Carolina Division of Archives and History)

SS   Susan Shearer (National Trust for Historic Preservation)

TJK   Theodore J. Karamanski (Loyola University of Chicago)

TLC   Thomas L. Charlton (Baylor University)

WKB   Willa K. Baum (University of California at Berkeley)

WKK   William K. Klingaman (Corporate Historical Services)

WWM   William W. Moss (John F. Kennedy Library)

THE CRAFT
OF PUBLIC
HISTORY

———————————

CHAPTER 1

PUBLIC HISTORY: RESEARCH AND WRITING

Lawrence B. de Graaf, editor

The statement of C.V. Wedgewood that History's mansion has enough rooms to accommodate all of us is put to a serious test in the case of public history, particularly when applied to the wide array of research and writing that characterizes it. Far from being a discrete field, public history broadly defined encompasses virtually all the methodologies of academic history and analytical, descriptive, and narrative modes of writing. It has expanded sources and formats into areas rarely utilized by historians at the academy. Even in one arena of public history, the agencies of the federal government, the public historian's research and writing range from analytical studies of public policies, calling for models and methodologies from other disciplines, to more traditional narrative accounts of agency activities, to the evaluation and description of archival documents, material culture, and historical sites, to the writing of reports and memoranda that are part of the operations of an organization.

The definitions of public history are only of limited assistance in ascertaining relevant forms of research and writing. One reason is that most definitions advanced to date have described the conditions of research and writing but not their actual content or method. Public historians tend to work in teams; they are usually held to shorter and less flexible deadlines; and they must be prepared to tailor their work to the specifications of clients. Such descriptions suggest some forms of research that are likely *not* to be appropriate, for example, the extensively documented monograph on a topic of the historian's choosing completed over a period of years that addresses historiographical and methodological questions raised by academic peers. However, even this often-repeated description can be misleading: Public historians do conduct extensive research; they may find need for a wide variety of methodologies; and they are increasingly incorporating recent historical trends into such activities as preservation and site interpretation. For this reason, a bibliography of writing and research in public history must include a cross-section of the works that might be consulted by historians in universities as well as those that address other types of historical work.

The very word "public" further broadens the potential scope of this bibliography for it can be interpreted to mean several different audiences and hence different styles, modes of writing, and formats. Insofar as the general public is one audience, public historians must look beyond the types of documents conventionally used in academic writings, indeed beyond the document altogether, and make greater use of photographs and material objects. Public historians working for corporations or government agencies also find themselves drawn into source materials not commonly used by historians in the past. All of these considerations have been acknowledged aspects of the public history movement, but their combined consequences for the task of compiling a bibliography of public history are only now being realized.

Given the potential vastness of this chapter, several presumptions have governed the editor's selection. First, it is an exceedingly select bibliography, designed to provide an idea of the variety of sources that might be used in public history research and writing rather than an extensive listing of the works in any category. As partial compensation, one criterion of selection is that, when feasible, the work listed is one that is most recent and that possesses an extensive bibliography of further writings in its field. Another consequence of selectivity is the decision to use only works that either describe how research or writing is carried out or discuss issues or concepts related to research and writing. The editor is aware that a well-written book or article employing a particular methodology or style can be the best teacher of all, but given the many different examples of such literature that would have to be shown, this approach is deemed unfeasible within the limits of this chapter and is left to later chapters. The final concession to the need for selectivity is that this chapter is for beginners. It is aimed primarily at the student or lay historian desiring to become acquainted with an area of research or writing. Individual chapters dealing with a specific sector of public history contain works more oriented toward professionals in that field.

The final presumption that governed the compilation of this chapter is in many respects most significant: no dichotomy exists between public history and much of the scholarship that has long comprised the discipline of history in academic institutions. In some areas of research and writing, for example, history of technology or public policy, the two are almost indistinguishable. In nearly all sectors good research and writing cannot result without making use of concepts of evidence, causation, generalization, and criticism that have been central to the traditional historical craft. Therefore this chapter begins with a section largely devoted to general academic works on research and writing. The second section is devoted to historical thinking. Research and writing in specific areas of public history comprise the third section. The fourth section lists manuals and guides to research and writing. Reference tools conclude the chapter.

Items in the first section, entitled "General Works on Research and Writing," cover several categories. A few works treat the nature of history, methods of historical research, and techniques of writing. Others focus on evidence and historical criticism.

The selections under "Historical Thinking" represent various views on major issues within the discipline of history. Some works treat methodology and generalizations in history, and others dwell on social science methods. Finally, a number of citations cover quantitative resources and methods, verbal resources, and nonverbal resources.

Section III, "Varieties of Research and Writing in Public History," presents works expressly oriented toward one or more sectors of public history. Given the eclectic nature of this field, the items represent a potpourri of representative materials. This section lists a few general definitions of public history, works describing research and writing in one or more of its sectors, and observations on differences between public and academic historical research and writing. Also included are works on areas that are not covered in other chapters, such as local history, and a few samples of historians' works that are quite different from traditional forms of exposition.

Whereas the earlier sections are weighted toward research, the section "Manuals and Guides to Research and Writing" concentrates on texts, handbooks, and aids to writing history. A few college-level texts describe the organization and composition of research papers as well as writing and style. Also included are widely used works on grammar, usage, style, and mechanics; some standard aids to vocabulary; and more specialized writing and research guides designed for specific fields of public history. A few items cover a neglected topic, indexing, and others treat copyright law, libel, and means of obtaining grants in support of research and writing.

The last section, "Reference Tools," provides highly selective lists that cover the entire discipline of history. The items fall into three broad categories: bibliographical, continuing references, and informational. Within the bibliographical category are guides to reference works, bibliographies of American history and special subjects, and guides to public documents and other specialized sources. The section on continuing references contains periodicals and other works that regularly report recent literature, regularly issue indexes to serial literature, documents, and data, and tools that periodically update reference works. The items in this section will provide historians with a means of keeping other reference tools up-to-date. The last part, informational tools, includes such convenient sources of data as encyclopedias, biographical dictionaries, yearbooks of political data, statistical sources, and various directories. Reference tools specifically designed for one area of public history may be found in later chapters of this bibliography.

All entries in this chapter are designed to convey one theme: research and writing in public history marries the concepts, techniques, and tools long used in scholarly writing with the subjects and formats appropriate to various public audiences. Perhaps these suggested sources will contribute to synthetic works that will display this combination, serving as guides to future research and writing in public history.

I. General Works on Research and Writing

1. Barzun, Jacques, and Henry F. Graff. *The Modern Researcher*. 3d ed. New York: Harcourt Brace Jovanovich, 1977.

This work on research and report writing first appeared in 1957. It interweaves some basic historiographical questions with a step-by-step progression from thinking out a topic to note-taking through several phases and problems of research and writing. It is one of the few works that combine questions central to historical research—verification, truth and causation, pattern and bias—with guides to writing that are applicable to a wide variety of fields. It is skeptical about social science methods, particularly quantification, and gives little attention to methodology or theorizing. (LBD)

2. Becker, Carl. "Everyman His Own Historian." *American Historical Review*, Vol. XXXVII (January 1932), pp. 221-236. This article is also included in Carl Becker, *Everyman His Own Historian*. Chicago: Quadrangle, 1966.

Becker sets forth a simple definition of history as the memory of things said and done and postulates from it that everyone is a historian. Becker asserts the relativism of the professional historian to the climate of opinion in which he writes. Often overlooked is the fact that he grounded this view on the necessity of professional historians to relate to the general public. (LBD)

3. Bloch, Marc. *The Historian's Craft*. Translated by Peter Putnam. New York: Knopf, 1953.

These essays treat the methods of historical science. Emphasizing critical techniques and the uses of language, Bloch provides illustrations from European history. (LBD)

4. Carr, Edward Hallett. *What Is History?* New York: Knopf, 1964.

This series of lectures discusses key concepts in the discipline of history. These include the nature of facts, the role of individual motives and social forces, determinism and accident, objectivity and moral judgment, and history as progress. (LBD)

5. Davidson, James West, and Mark Hamilton Lytle. *After the Fact: The Art of Historical Detection*. New York: Knopf, 1982.

This work combines a text on selected subjects in American history and a book on various aspects of historical research and writing. It discusses such methodologies as psychohistory, community as microcosm, theory in history, oral history, political history, policy models, and some basic issues in the craft of history, such as selecting evidence, pictoral evidence, document analysis, great man, and contemporary history with a narrative account of a topic. The result is an "apprentice approach" to history in which the reader learns how to research and write while learning the substance. (LBD)

6. Dray, William H. *Philosophy of History*. Englewood Cliffs, N.J.: Prentice-Hall, 1964.

This book is one of the simpler and shorter comprehensive works on the philosophy of history. Its contents mirror the general topics of most works of this genre such as historical understanding; facts and explanation and law; historical objectivity: relativism, positivism, past and present values; causal judgement, nature of cause, theory of cause; and major philosophical schools. (LBD)

7. Gottschalk, Louis. *Understanding History: A Primer of Historical Method*. 2d ed. New York: Knopf, 1969.

This comprehensive text on the nature and method of historical research and writing is aimed mainly at university students. Part of the book goes through the process of research with particular emphasis on external and internal criticism. Another part discusses some theoretical issues in history such as arrangement, cause, and uses of history. (LBD)

8. Handlin, Oscar. *Truth in History*. Cambridge, Mass.: Harvard University Press, 1979.

Handlin offers a personal summation of his philosophy of history and a running criticism of numerous trends in recent historical studies. He considers the use of history to be the preservation of truth for posterity and denounces all efforts to make history relevant to the present. There are essays on use of words, numbers, pictorial evidence. The essay on "History in a World of Knowledge" summarizes the many facets of life that history touches. All essays are heavily footnoted, providing references to recent scholarship. (LBD)

9. Hewlett, Richard G. "Government History: Writing from the Inside." In Frank B. Evans and Harold T. Pinkett, eds. *Research in the Administration of Public Policy*. Washington: Howard University Press, 1975.

Historians in the government can preserve independence and freedom by (1) getting support from the highest levels of their agencies; (2) assuring themselves of full access to records; and (3) working at the highest professional level. A historical advisory committee strengthens the hand of the government historian. (RPC)

10. Hughes, H. Stuart. *History as Art and as Science: Twin Vistas on the Past*. New York: Harper and Row, 1964.

This short collection of essays offers the general message that the issue of whether history is an art or science is an unnecessary one. The two modes of learning have much in common. The first essay critically summarizes philosophical schools of history. Others set out the impact of some natural science and social science scholarship on broadening the interpretation of history. The final essays discuss writing narrative history and contemporary history. (LBD)

11. Iggers, Georg G., and Harold T. Parker, eds. *International Handbook of Historical Studies: Contemporary Research and Theory*. Westport, Conn.: Greenwood, 1979.

This anthology discusses recent developments in the discipline of history. The first section covers philosophy of history and major topical areas; the second covers regional and national developments. Each chapter has an extensive bibliography. Collectively, this work provides an overview of changes in the writing of history in the past thirty years. While heavily oriented to conceptual models of the meaning of history (Annales, Marxist), it provides a background of theoretical considerations in writing history within which to place public history. (LBD)

12. Kammen, Michael, ed. *The Past before Us: Contemporary Historical Writing in the United States*. Ithaca, N.Y.: Cornell University Press, 1980.

This work is the most recent of a series of anthologies on the state of historical writing. This circumstance and the extensive footnotes, which serve in lieu of a bibliography, make it of use to public historians seeking information on recent scholarship in geographical areas, topical areas, or select methodologies. Like most earlier anthologies, this work neglects public history and most component sectors, for example, preservation, archives, public policy, business history. Exceptions are the articles "Community Studies, Urban History, and Local History" and "Oral History." All articles summarize ideas and characteristics of recent historical writing and offer critical evaluations of the state of such. (LBD)

13. Kent, Sherman. *Writing History*. 2d ed. New York: Appleton Century Crofts, 1967.

First written in 1941 by a historian who subsequently spent years in the federal government, this guide for undergraduate students of history treats the whole process of research and writing from topic selection to preparing an index. Sections on writing and index preparation should be useful to public historians. (LBD)

14. Mandelbaum, Maurice. *The Anatomy of Historical Knowledge*. Baltimore: Johns Hopkins University Press, 1977.

This recent work on philosophical issues in history is by a veteran scholar of that field. A chapter on structures of historical accounts sets forth comparisons between expository, narrative, and interpretative accounts. Treatment of classical issues of cause and objectivity reviews and often criticizes prior scholarship on these issues and thus provides public historians with recent writings on those questions. Extensive footnotes provide both many sources and frequent commentary on these sources. (LBD)

15. Meyerhoff, Hans, ed. *The Philosophy of History in Our Time*. Garden City, N.Y.: Doubleday, 1959.

This anthology of writings is organized around what the editor, a philosopher, sees as the central issues concerning the meaning and nature of history. The introduction synthesizes philosophic debate from medieval times to the early twentieth century, stressing the decline of religious and positivistic philosophies of history and the rise of doubts about the ultimate purpose, nature, and method in history. Several historians and philosophers treat historicism, history as art or science, morality and history, and meaning in history. (LBD)

16. Rundell, Walter, Jr. *In Pursuit of American History: Research and Training in the United States*. Norman: University of Oklahoma Press, 1970.

This study of the education of American historians is based on extensive interviews made in the mid-1960s. Rundell notes the decline of training in historical method and the simultaneous rise of social science tools. Many interviews were with public historians, chiefly archivists, librarians, and heads of historical societies. Several chapters are devoted expressly to use of public history tools, for example, archives and local sources, or training in areas of public history, particularly document editing. (LBD)

17. Schlesinger, Arthur M., Jr. "The Historian as Participant." In Felix Gilbert and Stephen Graubard, eds. *Historical Studies Today*. New York: Norton, 1971.

The author argues that "eyewitness historians" should be considered as objective and professional as are "technical historians" writing with the advantage of time. He contends that recent developments in communication render "instant history" more insightful and necessary and refutes the long-held view that truth is only possible with the passage of time. While not directly referring to public historians, this article provides an intellectual foundation for the contemporary topics that often are the product of public historians. (LBD)

18. Shafer, Robert Jones. *A Guide to Historical Method*. 3d ed. Homewood, Ill.: Dorsey, 1980.

This undergraduate text on the method of researching and writing academic history places particular emphasis on the external and internal criticism of evidence. It is organized to follow step by step the process of research and, to a lesser extent, of writing. (LBD)

19. Social Science Research Council, Committee on Historiography. *Historical Study*. Bulletin 64. New York: Social Science Research Council, 1954.

This publication offers an overview of social science disciplines and methodologies in history and comments on social science versus narrative synthesis. (LBD)

20. Stephens, Lester D. *Probing the Past: A Guide to the Study and Teaching of History*. Boston: Allyn and Bacon, 1974.

The book is divided into two parts. Stephens first provides a brief introduction to most basic components of the discipline of history: evidence, bias and judgment, explanation, speculation, related disciplines, and issues in the application of history. Quoting widely from well-known sources in each area, he provides a primer on these topics and sources for further reading. The second part considers the teaching of history, primarily in public schools. (LBD)

21. Stone, Lawrence. "Revival of Narrative: Reflections on a New Old History." *Past and Present,* no. 85 (November 1979), pp. 13-24.

Stone argues that structured analytical history (Marxist, Annales, cliometric) is declining and that historians are returning to the narrative mode. He links this shift to growing interest in personal motives and values, predicting that this mode enables historians to reach broader audiences. (LBD)

22. *Theory and Practice in Historical Study: A Report of the Committee on Historiography*. Bulletin 54. New York: Social Science Research Council, 1946.

This report sets forth a set of principles for the practice of historical research and writing. The initial chapter by Charles Beard reads like writings that bemoan the prevalent attitude that history is of little use while citing historical events as "the ultimate source of knowledge and 'laws' for demonstrating the invincible validity of policies proposed or already in practice." The last two chapters define key terms in historical writing, for example, cause and analogy, and also sets forth propositions for the practice of history that anticipate some recent presumptions of public history. (LBD)

23. Tuchman, Barbara. *Practicing History*. New York: Knopf, 1981.

Tuchman, a prominent free-lance historian, presents her views on the writing of history. The first part offers ideas on the writing of narrative history, the use of fiction for generalizations and style, and the writing of popular history. She views history as potentially replacing fiction as narrator of "great themes." (LBD)

24. Turner, James. "Recovering the Uses of History." *Yale Review,* Vol. LXX (Winter 1981), pp. 221-233.

Turner gives reasons why academic history has lost popularity and makes suggestions on how to regain it. He advocates that historians concentrate on providing an integrated meaning for an overspecialized world and help shape a moral view of the world. Both activities should be aimed at general audiences. While not referring specifically to public history, this article summarizes some of its broadest ideals in the context of how historians should conduct research and writing. (LBD)

25. Wise, Gene. *American Historical Explanations: A Strategy for Grounded Inquiry*. 2d ed. Minneapolis: University of Minnesota Press, 1980.

Wise, writing primarily for intellectual historians, challenges historians to make their methods more explicit: He proposes that history, like natural science, has undergone "paradigms" of explanation-forms. The first chapters explore different forms of historical understanding used by academic American historians. The second portion puts forth strategies for "grounded inquiry" into interpretations of historians. The last section is a synthesis of three main schools of American historiography. (LBD)

26. Zinn, Howard. *The Politics of History*. Boston: Beacon, 1970.

Three sets of essays urge that historians base their work on moral values and become actively engaged in contemporary issues, particularly those embraced by liberals and radicals. The first urges that historians orient their writing toward contemporary causes and takes issue with the idea of objective truth as the sole aim of the historian. The second group provides examples of such history. The final group makes a philosophical defense of this approach to history. (LBD)

II. Historical Thinking

27. Beringer, Richard E. *Historical Analysis: Contemporary Approaches to Clio's Craft*. New York: Wiley, 1978.

This introductory text treats recent techniques in historical research and analysis. Three groups of techniques are covered: intellectual history, psychosociological history, and quantitative history, encompassing nineteen different chapters. Each chapter is a short essay, describing the technique, its evolution and rationale, and how and when it might be used in academic writing, followed by an example of that technique in the writing of another historian. (LBD)

28. Berkhofer, Robert F., Jr. *A Behavioral Approach to Historical Analysis*. New York: Free Press, 1969.

Berkhofer advocates a conceptual framework for the research and writing of history that incorporates theoretical and methodological developments in the social sciences and recognizes the complexity of human society. Particularly oriented toward dealing with broad concepts like culture and society, the work cites social science literature extensively, providing historians with a synthesis of many key ideas of related disciplines through the late 1960s. (LBD)

29. Bogue, Allan G., and Jerome M. Clubb, eds. "History and the Social Sciences: Progress and Prospects." *American Behavioral Scientist*, Vol. XXI (November-December 1977).

The authors review twenty years of "new" history "designed to contribute to the development of scientific knowledge of human behavior." Articles cover quantification, economic history, political behavior, urban history, demography, family history, and modernization. (LBD)

30. Brooks, Philip C. *Research in Archives: The Use of Unpublished Primary Sources.* Chicago: University of Chicago Press, 1969.

This manual for graduate students and researchers describes the use of any repository of primary sources, with special emphasis on the National Archives and the Library of Congress. It discusses finding aids, relations between researcher and archivist, limits on access and use, note-taking and copying, and new techniques in archival research. (LBD)

31. Dollar, Charles M., and Richard J. Jensen. *Historian's Guide to Statistics: Quantitative Analysis and Historical Research.* New York: Holt, Rinehart, and Winston, 1971.

The authors describe statistical methods and data processing, especially as used in academic historical work. (LBD)

32. Drake, Michael, ed. *Applied Historical Studies: An Introductory Reader.* London: Methuen, 1973.

Applied historical studies are defined as "explorations of the past undertaken with the explicit purpose of advancing social scientific enquiries." Essentially a collection of essays on historical topics, ranging from education and the idea of achievement to Robert Fogel's analogy between railroads and space program and Stephen Thernstrom's essay on social mobility. (LBD)

33. Fischer, David Hackett. *Historian's Fallacies: Toward a Logic of Historical Thought.* New York: Harper and Row, 1970.

Despite the author's contention to the contrary, this work is essentially a compilation of historical fallacies, grouped under three major divisions: inquiry, explanation, and argument. (LBD)

34. Gottschalk, Louis, ed. *Generalization in the Writing of History: A Report of the Committee on Historical Analysis of the Social Science Research Council.* Chicago: University of Chicago Press, 1963.

This series of essays by academic historians treats generalization in different periods and the generic problem of generalization. (LBD)

35. Gottschalk, Louis. "The Historian and the Historical Document." In Social Science Research Council. *The Use of Personal Documents in History, Anthropology, and Sociology.* Bulletin 53. New York: Social Science Research Council, 1945.

This work discusses different forms of personal documents encountered by historians, problems inherent in their use, and techniques of internal and external criticism employed to determine validity and authenticity. Examples are almost entirely concerned with elites and political history. (LBD)

36. Hollingsworth, Thomas Henry. *Historical Demography.* Ithaca, N.Y.: Cornell University Press, 1969.

This text covers techniques of demography, historical sources on population, and important work in historical demography. Three appendices present sample essays, and a bibliographic essay summarizes work in the field through the late 1960s. (LBD)

37. Hughes, H. Stuart. "The Historian and the Social Scientist." In Alexander Riasanovsky and Barnes Riznik, eds. *Generalizations in Historical Writing.* Philadelphia: University of Pennsylvania Press, 1963.

This essay considers similarities and differences between history and the social sciences, noting where they can profitably learn from each other and where they pursue different objectives. Hughes notes four levels of generalization (semantic, structural, procedural, and metahistorical) and some ways in which social science theories and concepts can help historians make broader, more accurate, and more meaningful generalizations. (LBD)

38. Kaplan, Abraham. *The Conduct of Inquiry: Methodology for Behavioral Science.* San Francisco: Chandler, 1964.

This work on social science concepts and methods provides basic definitions of concept, law, and theory as well as basic methodologies such as models and measurement. (LBD)

39. Nie, Norman H., C. Hadlai Hall, Jean G. Jenkins, Karin Steinbrenner, and Dale H. Bent. *SPSS: Statistical Package for the Social Sciences.* New York: McGraw-Hill, 1975.

This is a guide for both newcomers to the field and experts on computer-based research in the social sciences. The authors describe in considerable detail the SPSS system of computer programs, originally developed at Stanford University and now widely available for data analysis. (See also no. *344*). (LBD)

40. Noël Hume, Ivor. *Historical Archaeology.* New York: Knopf, 1969.

This text presents methods of conducting archaeology on postaboriginal sites of importance in American history, offering a step-by-step explanation of planning, excavation, and recording processes. (LBD)

Quimby, Ian M. G., ed. *Material Culture and the Study of American Life.* See no. *960.*

This work is an anthology of essays on the role of material culture in American studies. Essays cover various types of material objects, photographs, historical preservation, and some techniques of museum work, especially exhibit design. Most articles attempt to show interrelationships between museum persons and historians, particularly the contributions that material culture can make to "New History." (LBD)

41. Saveth, Edward N., ed. *American History and the Social Sciences.* New York: Free Press, 1964.

This anthology presents articles on the use of social science concepts in research and writing American history. The several sections include articles by social scientists about the use of history in their disciplines, articles by historians illustrating different concepts as they were applied to specific topics, and articles on some limitations of social science concepts in history. (LBD)

Schlereth, Thomas J. *Artifacts and the American Past.* See no. *864.*

Ten essays treat various types of nonverbal sources and their use in historical study and writing. Essays cover photographs, mail-order catalogs, maps, historic houses and sites, vegetation, regional studies, and above-ground archaeology. The final essay is a critique of both written history and museums. (LBD)

42. Shorter, Edward. *The Historian and the Computer: A Practical Guide.* New York: Norton, 1975.

First published in 1971, this short work remains the only guidebook to the process of computer operation that is specifically oriented toward research in history. (LBD)

43. Simon, Julian L. *Basic Research Methods in Social Science.* New York: Random House, 1969.

This text considers structure of social science research methods, tracing the process of social science research step by step with commentary on obstacles. Simon emphasizes nonquantitative research. (LBD)

44. Swierenga, Robert P. "Computers and American History: The Impact of the 'New Generation.' " *Journal of American History*, Vol. LX (March, 1974), pp. 1045-1070.

Swierenga reviews the early years of computerized research by historians. He includes some issues concerning the effects of computers on the discipline and a discussion of major problems to greater use of computers. (LBD)

45. Trachtenberg, Alan. "Introduction: Photographs on Symbolic History." In *The American Image: Photographs from the National Archives, 1860-1960.* New York: Pantheon, 1979.

This essay comments on reading and interpreting still photographs, describing the means of extracting both literal content and symbolic meaning from photographs. Trachtenberg makes numerous references to photographs, providing illustrations to follow the analysis. (LBD)

Weinstein, Robert A., and Larry Booth. *Collection, Use, and Care of Historical Photographs*. See no. *456.*
Early chapters in this introductory work review potential uses of historic photos and the methods of finding, identifying, reproducing them. Later chapters consider more technical areas of legal rights, cataloging, preservation, and restoration. The authors append a bibliography of technical and historical literature. (LBD)

46. Williamson, John B., David B. Karp, and John R. Dalphin. *The Research Craft: An Introduction to Social Science Methods*. Boston: Little, Brown, 1977.
This text is designed for the introductory course in social research methods in several social science disciplines. Most of the book describes specific research methodologies, for which there are annotated bibliographies and sample literature. (LBD)

47. Winks, Robin W., ed. *The Historian as Detective: Essays on Evidence*. New York: Harper and Row, 1968.
This anthology raises various issues of historical evidence, each cleverly presented as a mystery analogous to a detective story. Some are essays on historical method; others examine specific problems, involving forgeries, missing documents, and fictitious persons. Other selections deal with questions of doubt and relevance of history. (LBD)

III. Varieties of Research and Writing in Public History

48. Brumberg, G. David. "The Case for Reunion: Academic Historians, Public Historical Agencies, and the New York Historians-in-Residence Program." *Public Historian*, Vol. IV (Spring 1982), pp. 71-91.
Brumberg summarizes the divergence of academic historical research and writing from local history and recent professional trends in each area. He sees the New York program as designed to bring the two groups together on exhibition-interpretation projects as an example of the potential for reunion between these groups. (LBD)

49. Burchell, Robert W., and David Listkokin. *The Fiscal Impact Handbook*. New Brunswick, N.J.: Center for Urban Policy Research, 1978.
This "how-to" book provides a step-by-step methodology for accurately estimating municipal costs and revenues generated by land development. While the authors may not have thought about it, theirs is a study based on historical as well as statistical analysis. That is, one cannot predict the revenue potential or the cost of future growth without measuring the existing built environment,

a task that requires relatively sophisticated studies of trends over time. The authors also provide brief historical summaries of the origins of various fiscal impact methodologies. (RHL)

Burnette, O. Lawrence, Jr. *Beneath the Footnote: A Guide to the Use and Preservation of American Historical Resources*. See no. *428*.

This comprehensive description covers most types of primary source materials in the United States, including archives of various types, manuscript collections, newspapers, public records, and oral and visual sources. Designed for "neophyte, fledgling, and amateur historians," it is neither a finding aid nor a manual for professional archivists and librarians but an introduction to the variety of historical resources and their use in historical research. It includes an extensive bibliography of finding aids, books, and articles. (LBD)

50. Craig, Gordon A. "On the Nature of Diplomatic History: The Relevance of Some Old Books." In Paul Gordon Lauren, ed. *Diplomacy: New Approaches in History, Theory, and Policy*. New York: Free Press, 1979.

Craig offers an example of historians finding clues to a policy process (diplomacy) by study of old books on that subject. By extension, he suggests the possibility of extracting policy-relevant material from many historical resources. (LBD)

51. Evans, Frank B., and Harold T. Pinkett, eds. *Research in the Administration of Public Policy*. National Archives Conferences, Vol. VII. Washington: Howard University Press, 1975.

These are the papers and proceedings of a 1970 conference of historians, political scientists, public administrators, and archivists held to encourage the use of the National Archives. The volume has several essays treating research and writing on histories of federal agencies, historical policy issues, and administrative reform, and it contains Louis Morton's proposal for a government-wide historical office. (LBD)

52. Felt, Thomas E. *Researching, Writing, and Publishing Local History*. Nashville: American Association for State and Local History, 1966.

This layperson's handbook is particularly aimed at those who write popular history for commercial sale. It focuses on types of materials in research and on legal and mechanical points in writing. The last chapter deals with design and publication. (LBD)

53. Finberg, H.P.R. "How Not to Write Local History." In H.P.R. Finberg and V.H.T. Skipp. *Local History: Objective and Pursuit*. Newton Abbot: David & Charles, 1967.

An English writer provides a humorous critique of much local history. (LBD)

54. Foreman, Richard. "History inside Business." *The Public Historian*, Vol. III (Summer 1981), pp. 41-61.

Foreman analyzes changing trends in the writing of business history, the problems likely to be encountered by historians writing histories of corporations, and some issues of professionalism involved in business history. He includes suggestions on the relationship historians ought to make with corporate personnel to write a history of such an organization. (LBD)

55. George, Alexander L. "Case Studies and Theory Development: The Method of Structured, Focused Comparision." In Paul Gordon Lauren, ed. *Diplomacy: New Approaches in History, Theory, and Policy*. New York: Free Press, 1979.

Acknowledging that "lessons of history" are an unreliable basis for policy, this article sets forth a methodology of deriving historically grounded theory by cooperative efforts between historians and political scientists. It lays out a research design involving case studies and theory. It is one of the most explicit descriptions of how historical research and writing might be changed to make them more adaptable to policy. (LBD)

56. Gerber, David A. "Local and Community History: Some Cautionary Remarks on an Idea Whose Time Has Returned." *History Teacher*. Vol. XIII (November 1979), pp. 7-30.

Gerber comments on the recent popularity of local history, viewing it as both an opportunity and a potential problem. He warns against undue emphasis on ethnic distinctions and evocative accounts, especially oral history, and advocates a merger of scholarly analysis and popular interest. (LBD)

57. Goldfield, David R. "Living History: The Physical City as Artifact and Teaching Tool." *History Teacher*, Vol. VIII (August 1975), pp. 535-556.

Goldfield provides an introduction to the interpretation of buildings and urban landscapes, correlating various physical components of the city to periods, trends, and issues in urban history. (LBD)

58. Grable, Stephen W. "Applying Urban History to City Planning: A Case Study of Atlanta." *Public Historian*, Vol. I (Summer 1979), pp. 45-59.

The author reviews various approaches to urban history and finds the urban structure approach the best one for linking urban history to planning. While the data is confined to the case of an Atlanta housing development, this article provides insights to the differences between practitioners and academic historians in their approaches to problem solving and urban planning analysis. (LBD)

59. Graham, Otis L. "Historians and the World of (Off-Campus) Power." *Public Historian*, Vol. I (Winter 1979), pp. 34-40.

Graham discusses the employment of historians in government, chiefly the federal government, setting forth difficulties to be faced in such positions but arguing that historians have key skills to offer. Chief among these are memory, synthesis, and literary capacity. He suggests additional training that public historians may need. (LBD)

60. Hewlett, Richard G. "The Practice of History in the Federal Government." *Public Historian,* Vol. I (Fall 1978), pp. 29-36.

Hewlett discusses the evolution of historians' offices in several federal agencies and the requirements for the profession to fill out such positions. He finds that academic historical training often fails to provide potential federal historians with skills needed for that work, and he outlines several issues in defining and training the professional historian. (LBD)

61. Hoy, Suellen, and Michael C. Robinson. "Historical Analysis: A New Management Tool for Public Works Administrators." *Public Works,* Vol. CVIII (June 1977), pp. 88-89.

The authors propose that historical analysis, that is, the historical method of analyzing issues, can be an important asset to officials dealing with public works. By extension, they suggest its utility throughout the profession of management, viewing historical analysis as particularly useful in developing alternatives to technologies and policies, in providing expert testimony in legal cases, and in boosting employee morale. (LBD)

62. Johnson, Ronald W. "The Historian and Cultural Resource Management." *Public Historian*, Vol. III (Spring 1981), pp. 43-51.

Johnson provides an introduction to the research and writing functions of public historians in the area of cultural resources management (CRM). He gives the legal background of CRM work and runs through the process of researching and writing a CRM report, even to the offices contacted and main sources checked, and gives a brief outline of the mitigation process. (LBD)

Kyvig, David, and Myron Marty. *Nearby History.* See no. *958.*

The authors combine research and writing of local history with historic preservation, material culture study, and archives as they pertain to localities. They also include chapters on family history and oral history. Primarily oriented to techniques for using a wide variety of historical resources, this work provides bibliographies on the literature of these techniques. (LBD)

63. Lauren, Paul Gordon. "Diplomacy: History, Theory, and Policy." In Paul Gordon Lauren, ed. *Diplomacy: New Approaches in History, Theory, and Policy.* New York: Free Press, 1979.

Lauren contends that history, political theory, and foreign policy have a necessary interrelationship in forming policy. History provides a check on theoretical models and offers a study of processes, people, and a selection of facts all vital to policy making. He acknowledges difficulties in adapting history to policy and suggests new approaches for doing so. (LBD)

64. Lewis, W. David, and Wesley Phillips Newton. "The Writing of Corporate History." *Public Historian*, Vol. III (Summer 1981), pp. 63-74.

The authors make observations on the writing of corporate history with suggestions on its importance and on how to conduct the process of research and writing in different stages. Footnotes provide numerous examples of corporate histories. (LBD)

65. Lopata, Roy H. "Small Cities Planning from an Historic Perspective: A Case Study of the Municipal Response to Tax Exempt Landholdings." *Public Historian*, Vol. IV (Winter 1982), pp. 53-64.

This article describes a municipal planning study and report directed and coauthored by a historically trained city planner. The issue is presented from a planning rather than strictly historical perspective, illustrating the nature of contemporary small city problems while at the same time suggesting that historians operating in a public sector have talents and perspectives relevant in municipal government administration. (RHL)

66. Lubove, Roy. "The Urbanization Process: An Approach to Historical Research." *Journal of the American Institute of Planners*, Vol. XXXIII (January 1967), pp. 33-39.

Lubove calls for urban historians to approach history of the city from the perspective of "city-building," utilizing the historical site and all institutions, organizations, and developments associated with the city. (LBD)

67. *Managing the Modern City*. Washington: International City Management Association, 1971.

This text is issued by the ICMA as part of its Municipal Management Series of "green books." It provides a general overview of the administration of the modern city. The text reflects the city management form of government approach to municipal affairs. (RHL)

68. Mehnig, D.W., ed. *The Interpretation of Ordinary Landscapes: Geographical Essays*. New York: Oxford University Press, 1979.

A series of essays by geographers, much of this book deals with the historical landscape, how to interpret it, and how its interpretation might affect historic preservation, cultural history, and historic symbolism. As such it is a source of ideas and approaches for site interpreters, preservationists, and local historians. (LBD)

69. Moore, Jamie W. "History, the Historian, and the Corps of Engineers." *Public Historian*, Vol. III (Winter 1981), pp. 64-74.

Moore gives an overview of historical research and writing in the Army Corps of Engineers, covering the evolution of its historian's office, writing and research activities, sample monographs and projects. Footnotes provide extensive specific examples of published works. (LBD)

70. Scheips, Paul J., et al. "What Is a Federal Historian?" *Public Historian*, Vol. II (Summer 1980), pp. 84-100.

Contributors offer descriptions of the organization and function of historians employed by the federal government. There are comments by an archivist, museum curator, preservationist, military historian, and historical editor. Each gives some idea of the nature of research and writing in his respective area of public history. (LBD)

71. Schlereth, Thomas. "A Perspective on Criticism: Guidelines for History Museum Exhibition Reviews." *History News*, Vol. XXXV (August 1980), pp. 18-19.

Schlereth provides a model outline of the criteria and questions that should be asked in reviewing museum exhibits, much as historians have long reviewed books. (LBD)

72. Sharlin, Harold Issadore. "What's Historical about Science and Technology Policy?" *Public Historian*, Vol. II (Spring 1980), pp. 20-38.

Here is an argument for the use of history in analysis of scientific and technological policies. Sharlin notes the lack of awareness by most public officials of the use of history in policy. He sets forth two strategies for use of history: the principle of substitution in the technological paradigm and history as a presenter of alternatives to advocacy. (LBD)

73. Stearns, Peter N. "Applied History and Social History." *Journal of Social History*, Vol. III (Summer 1981), pp. 533-537.

This clarification of "applied history" demonstrates its link with academic social history in policy analysis. Stearns argues that social history-applied history can improve policy analysis in several specific areas. (LBD)

Stearns, Peter N. "History and Policy Analysis: Toward Maturity." See no. *1551*.

Stearns defines the "applied history" branch of public history as the application of history to policy analysis. He summarizes the weaknesses of policy analysis by social sciences that historians might correct and notes some unique contributions that historians can make to public policy. Some comparisons of academic and applied historical writing and research are included. (LBD)

Stearns, Peter N., and Joel A. Tarr. "Applied History: A New-Old Departure." See no. *1552*.

This description of the program in applied history at Carnegie-Mellon University covers purposes, structure of both undergraduate and graduate programs, and methods used in the applied history approach to public policy issues. The last section offers an introduction to research methods in public history, particularly use of analogies, trend assessment, and case studies. (LBD)

74. *The Practice of Government Planning*. Washington: International City Management Association, 1979.

This "green book" is part of the ICMA's Municipal Management Series. According to the Association, the various editions of this volume have had the "widest recognition and greatest professional impact." The latest effort, published in cooperation with the American Planning Association, provides an overview in considerable detail of the present state of the city planning profession and contemporary urban planning issues and controversies. (RHL)

Trask, David F. "A Reflection on Historians and Policymakers." See no. *1553*.

This short overview of the importance of history to policy making at the federal level notes some reasons why historians have played a limited role in it. Trask suggests unique contributions historians can make as opposed to social scientists. He recommends that historians end their misgivings about contemporary history and equip themselves better to play an active role in policy making. (LBD)

75. Weitzman, David. *Underfoot: An Everyday Guide to Exploring the American Past*. New York: Scribner's, 1976.

This guide to a wide variety of historical resources can be used in family history, local history, and historical archaeology. It includes oral history, photography, census archives, structures, artifacts, and old books. Extensively illustrated with photographs, old sketches, and samples of historical sources, it is aimed at the popular historian and historical societies. (LBD)

76. White, Gerald T. "The Business Historian and His Sources." *American Archivist*, Vol. XXX (1967), pp. 19-31.

This overview of research and writing in business history discusses several problems inherent in writing a corporate biography. The major portion of the article sets forth various types of business records with comments on their prospective availability and uses. (LBD)

77. Wood, Elizabeth B. "Pots and Pans History: Relating Manuscripts and Printed Sources to the Study of Domestic Art Objects." *American Archivist*, Vol. XXX (July 1967), pp. 431-442.

This overview of the study of household items and art objects distinguishes between the art historian and the cultural historian. The latter is viewed as serving diverse audiences. Wood lays out a sample research project to demonstrate the use of printed reference tools. She ends with suggestions for archivists and librarians on how to serve this type of research. (LBD)

IV. Manuals and Guides to Research and Writing

78. The Chicago Manual of Style for Authors, Editors, and Copywriters. 13th ed., rev. and exp. Chicago: University of Chicago Press, 1982.

This comprehensive guide for writers, editors, and typesetters is in three parts. The first section covers parts of a book, manuscript preparation, proofs, and rights. The second offers a guide to mechanics, quotations, and specialized forms of expression. The final section covers production. Each point is separately numbered, allowing easy reference to specific questions. (LBD)

79. Alderson, William T. *Securing Grant Support: Effective Planning and Preparation.* Technical Leaflet 62. Nashville: American Association for State and Local History, 1972.

Ultimately much research in public history depends on securing financial support. This short leaflet, an insert in the December 1972 issue of *History News*, concisely sets forth the basic requirements of successful grant procurement. It concludes with a checklist of essential elements, a sample budget, and a few directories and foundation or agency addresses. (LBD)

80. Ashley, Paul P. *Say It Safely: Legal Limits in Publishing, Radio, and Television.* 5th ed. Seattle: University of Washington Press, 1976.

This layperson's handbook on libel is designed mainly for the news industry, but it may be of use to public historians whose work might be scrutinized for libelous statements. (LBD)

81. Baker, Sheridan. *The Practical Stylist.* 5th ed. New York: Harper and Row, 1981.

This undergraduate text in rhetoric proceeds from the structure of a whole essay through paragraph and sentence to mechanics, vocabulary, and usage. It briefly sets forth what the author believes to be the most essential points in writing. (LBD)

82. Bartlett, John. *Familiar Quotations.* Edited by Emily Morison Beck. 15th ed. Boston: Little, Brown, 1980.

This extensive collection is arranged chronologically, with author and extensive subject index. Sources are worldwide but with emphasis on Americans. (LBD)

83. Barzun, Jacques. *Simple and Direct: A Rhetoric for Writers.* New York: Harper and Row, 1975.

Aimed at changing the common notion of historians and students that facts and research are all-important and writing can be taken for granted, this book presents a guide to the elements of rhetoric. It proceeds from diction (selecting words) to linking (forming sentences), tone, meaning, composition, and revision. Numerous exercises and examples of good writing appear in the book. (LBD)

84. Cohen, Morris L. *Legal Research in a Nutshell.* 3d ed. St. Paul, Minn.: West, 1978.

This introductory guide discusses all forms of legal documents and major reference aids. Each chapter begins with explanation and history of a given type of document. There are illustrations of pages from basic sources and occasional tracings of a single bill or case. (LBD)

85. Collison, Robert L. *Abstracts and Abstracting Services.* Santa Barbara, Calif.: ABC-Clio, 1971.

The author provides an introduction to the technique of writing abstracts, dealing also with the history of abstracting and current abstracting services. Appendices list all abstracting services as of 1970 and provide a basic bibliography on abstracting. (LBD)

86. Collison, Robert L. *Indexes and Indexing.* 4th ed. London: Ernest Benn, 1972.

This text on indexing treats both books and nonverbal materials. The first part goes from basic to more specific aspects of book indexing. The second section treats indexing of nonverbal materials, covering the use of computers in indexing. The final section has appendices of sample indexes and summary principles of indexing. (LBD)

87. Crews, Frederick. *The Random House Handbook.* 3d ed. New York: Random House, 1980.

Crews treats both "rhetoric," organizing and composing an essay, and grammar, usage, and mechanics. He describes several modes of writing and the principles of logical reasoning. The last portion covers library use and footnotes. (LBD)

88. Emory, C. William. *Business Research Methods.* Homewood, Ill.: Richard D. Irwin, 1976.

Emory brings together research problems from diverse areas of business and a scientific problem-solving framework of research. He covers scientific research method, elements of research design, data collection, and analysis and reporting, and includes a bibliography of reference works. (LBD)

89. Ewing, David W. *Writing for Results in Business, Government, and the Professions.* New York: Wiley, 1974.

This guide to effective communication for managers, staff persons, and professionals takes the reader through the process of beginning, organizing, and composing for maximum persuasiveness. The last portion deals with coherence and style. Ewing includes sample problems and numerous examples of both external and internal reports and memos.

90. Fowler, Henry W. *A Dictionary of Modern English Usage*. Rev. ed. Oxford: Oxford University Press, 1965.

The 1926 edition, reprinted in 1959, is a dictionary-form collection of misused words, grammatical problems, punctuation and other mechanical questions in the English language. Frequently two or more commonly confused words are treated together. Fowler often makes witty criticisms of common misuse of words, grammar, or style. (LBD)

91. Hartman, Hedy A., comp. *Funding Sources and Technical Assistance for Museums and Historical Agencies*. Nashville: American Association for State and Local History, 1979.

This list covers agencies and some foundations, museums, and associations that give assistance to historical museums and related projects. It is arranged by type of assistance, such as funding, technical, and exhibition. Private sources are less thoroughly developed. Each agency listing contains relevant information to help users determine whether it can be of help to a particular project. (LBD)

92. Henn, Harry G. *Copyright Primer*. New York: Practising Law Institute, 1979.

This work treats the copyright law of 1976 that took effect in 1978. Written for lawyers, it examines the act section by section. Extensive appendices form the bulk of the book; they provide the full text of both old and new copyright laws, rules, and regulations at the copyright office, select copyright office circulars, excerpts from congressional hearings, and a bibliography. (LBD)

93. Knight, G. Norman. *Training in Indexing*. Cambridge, Mass.: M.I.T. Press, 1969.

This series of lectures given by the British Society of Indexers seeks to train both professional indexers and authors desiring to make their own indexes. Early lectures go through the basics of any index; later ones discuss composition of specialized types of indexes. A few exercises with answers are included. (LBD)

94. Lester, James D. *Writing Research Papers: A Complete Guide*. 3d ed. Glenview, Ill.: Scott, Foresman, 1980.

Definitely aimed at the undergraduate student, this guide takes the reader step by step from topic selection through the bibliography. Frequent headings, illustrations, and margin comments facilitate its educational mission. While aimed at a general readership, most of this guide is suitable for history students. It has a bibliography of reference works and periodicals. (LBD)

95. Lottinville, Savoie. *The Rhetoric of History*. Norman: University of Oklahoma Press, 1976.

This is a guide to would-be publishers of rhetorical works written by a university press editor. It follows production of a historical work from conceptualization to opening paragraphs, narrative, character portrayal, time and setting, to bibliography criticism, rhetoric, and publishing. (LBD)

96. Murray, James A. H., et al. *The Oxford English Dictionary*. Rev. ed. Oxford: Clarendon Press, 1961. Burchfield, R. W., ed. *Supplement to the Oxford English Dictionary*. Vol. I, A-G; Vol. II, H-Z. Oxford: Clarendon Press, 1972, 1976.

The most extensive dictionary of the English language stresses the historical evolution of each word with examples of its use over the centuries. Supplements add new meanings and further examples. Not intended to be used to ascertain simple definitions, this work is useful to historians who wish to clarify nuances and precise usage of words in a particular time period. (LBD)

97. Perrin, Porter G. *Writer's Guide and Index to English*. 5th ed. Glenview, Ill.: Scott, Foresman, 1972.

Originally published in 1939 and periodically revised, this is a combined text in English rhetoric and an alphabetized guide to English usage. The first part largely treats the development of various types of written papers: personal experience, explanation, and persuasion. The second portion has articles on misused words, revisions, grammar, and varieties of English. (LBD)

98. Ross, Robert. *Research: An Introduction*. New York: Barnes and Noble, 1974.

While basically oriented toward the undergraduate student, this guide has sections designed for advanced students and professionals. General emphasis is on problems rather than strictly on academic topics. The majority of the work is a step-by-step guide to the research process. The later chapters treat writing of reports for business or public agencies and use of visual materials. (LBD)

99. Sherman, Theodore A., and Simon S. Johnson. *Modern Technical Writing*. 3d ed. Englewood Cliffs, N.J.: Prentice-Hall, 1975.

This text treats technical report writing and business correspondence. It covers organization, style, mechanics, and special presentation forms for technical writing in general and then goes through the process of writing both informal and formal reports. It offers a long section on letters and a concluding portion on fundamentals of English. (LBD)

100. Strong, William S. *The Copyright Book: A Practical Guide*. Cambridge, Mass.: M.I.T. Press, 1981.

This guide to the new copyright law that took effect in 1978, written for the layperson, is organized by main components of copyright rather than sections of the statute. Marginal headings and index help to find specific information. Appendices illustrate a few specialized areas of copyright, and notes cite sections of the statute or court cases. (LBD)

101. Strunk, William, Jr., and Elwyn B. White. *The Elements of Style*. 3d ed. New York: Macmillan, 1978.

This brief handbook of elementary rules of usage, composition, and style compiles rules on each of these areas with a short dictionary of commonly misused words. (LBD)

102. Turabian, Kate L. *A Manual for Writers of Term Papers, Theses, and Dissertations*. 4th ed. Chicago: University of Chicago Press, 1973.

This abridgment of the University of Chicago Press *Manual of Style*, 12th ed., rev., has utility for professionals as well as students. Early chapters summarize correct usage in abbreviations, capitalization and style, and quotations. Later chapters summarize various footnote and bibliography forms. Separate chapters treat table format and illustrating. Each rule or example is given a separate number to assist reference and cross-reference. (LBD)

103. U.S. Department of the Air Force. *Air Force Regulation 210-1*. Washington, 10 October 1980.

This regulation describes the Air Force Historical Program, lists its publications, and gives brief instructions on preparation of histories and other publications. It is illustrative of guides for several organizations, detailing publication policies and procedures for historians. (LBD)

104. U.S. Government Printing Office. *Style Manual*. Rev. ed. Washington: Government Printing Office, 1973.

This official manual of the Public Printer for all U.S. government publications is designed to standardize all federal documents. It stresses technical details and format rather than style and English. Primarily designed for printers, it is of interest to historians writing for the federal government. (LBD)

105. U.S. Office of Air Force History. *Editorial Style Guide*. n.p., 1981.

This brief guide to format and particulars of style, punctuation, and mechanics for writers of Air Force publications emphasizes samples of citation forms and portions of a publication. It provides an example of the numerous specialized style guides for various agencies and institutions that the historian may consult. (LBD)

106. Wittenberg, Philip. *The Protection of Literary Property*. 2d rev. ed. Boston: The Writer, 1978.

This is a legal work on copyright and literary property, revised to take account of the new copyright law. It has a chapter on the history of copyright and sections that go beyond copyright, for example, right of privacy, censorship, and contracts for publication. (LBD)

107. Zinsser, William. *On Writing Well: An Informal Guide to Writing Non-fiction.* New York: Harper and Row, 1976.

A veteran writer for newspapers and popular magazines offers personal suggestions on clear and effective writing. Primarily oriented to journalism, its advice on simplicity, clutter, and other basic problems of clear writing is applicable to historical writing. (LBD)

V. Reference Tools

108. Akey, Denise S., ed. *Encyclopedia of Associations.* 17th ed. 3 vols. Detroit: Gale, 1982.

This directory lists volunteer groups, including professional associations, trade associations, labor unions, fraternal groups. Most are in the United States, but it includes some international and some for-profit groups. Volume I is a directory categorized by type of organization, with a combined title and keyword index. Volume II is a geographical and executive index. Volume III lists new associations and projects not cited in Volume I. (LBD)

109. America: History and Life: A Guide to Periodical Literature. Santa Barbara, Calif.: Clio Press, 1964-.

This publication provides periodical abstracts and a general bibliography on U.S. and Canadian history. Part A, abstracts of periodical literature, is heavily weighted toward recent U.S. history. Part B indexes book reviews. Part C is an unannotated bibliography of books, articles, and dissertations. Part D is an index to the other three components. The final section of part A contains works on public history and methodology of research and writing. (LBD)

110. American Association of Museums. *The Official Museum Directory 1982: United States, Canada.* Skokie, Ill.: National Register Publishing Co., 1981.

This directory, reissued annually, lists all museums in the United States and Canada by state and city. It contains descriptions of scope and operations. Special sections list accredited museums and museum organizations, and there are indexes to personnel and categories of museums. (LBD)

111. American Association for State and Local History. *Directory of Historical Societies and Agencies in the United States and Canada.* 12th ed. Nashville: American Association for State and Local History, 1982.

This directory of historical societies, national archives and records centers, and historical sites operated as agencies provides information on location, size, membership, major programs, and chief officers for each organization. Periodically updated, it is indexed by areas of special interest. (LBD)

112. American Statistics Index. Washington: Congressional Information Service, 1973-.

This reference service is available in loose-leaf, machine-readable, and annual bound formats. It provides access to data published in several thousand federal agency reports. The *Index* portion uses twenty geographic, economic, and demographic categories and a variety of policy headings to trace data. The *Abstracts* volume gives complete bibliographic data and a narrative of the contents. A retrospective volume covers statistical publications back to 1960. On-line computer searching is available through the facilities of Systems Development Corporation. A companion set, *Statistical Reference Index*, appeared in 1980, aiming at similar access to nongovernmental data. (LBD)

113. Andriot, John L. *Guide to U.S. Government Publications*. McLean, Va.: Documents Index, 1959-.

Originally the *Guide to U.S. Government Serials and Periodicals*, this work has been revised at different intervals and in various formats. It endeavors to list all serial publications by agency, often with annotations. It includes an agency and a title index. (LBD)

114. Beers, Henry P., ed. *Bibliographies in American History*. 2d ed. New York: Wilson, 1942. *Bibliographies in American History, 1942-1978*. 2 vols. Woodbridge, Conn.: Research Publications, 1982.

This bibliography of bibliographies includes books, articles, pamphlets, and many catalogs of archival and manuscript collections. It is not annotated, but the first edition is organized chronologically and topically and the update by topic and by state. (LBD)

115. Bibliographic Index: A Cumulative Bibliography of Bibliographies. New York: Wilson, 1938-.

This index of bibliographical literature appears semiannually in a format similar to periodical indexes. It covers books, articles, pamphlets, and extensive bibliographies in books otherwise not of that nature. It permits updating of existing bibliographies. (LBD)

116. Brown, Edna T. *Union List of Serials Located in Libraries of United States and Canada*. 3d ed. 5 vols. New York: Wilson, 1965.
New Serial Titles: A Union List of Serials Commencing Publication after December 31, 1949, 1950-1970, Cumulative. 4 vols. New York: Bowker, 1973.
New Serial Titles. 3d ed. *1971-75 Cumulation*. 2 vols. Washington: Library of Congress, 1976.
New Serial Titles. 3d ed. *1976-79 Cumulation*. 2 vols. Washington: Library of Congress, 1980.

The *Union List* is a basic list for locating periodicals in libraries. It is organized alphabetically by serial title, with select library holdings and respective dates below. Succeeding volumes do not include all titles in earlier ones; therefore a thorough search for periodicals several decades old may require the use of some or all of the cumulations. (LBD)

116a. Burns, Richard D., ed. *Guide to American Foreign Relations Since 1700.* Santa Barbara, Calif.: ABC-Clio, 1983.

This comprehensive bibliography cites works on American foreign policy and diplomacy, covering the subject across the entire span of American colonial and national history. It does not include citations to collections of unpublished manuscripts, but it covers published manuscript collections. It updates the work of Samuel Flagg Bemis and Grace Gardner Griffin, *Guide to the Diplomatic History of the United States, 1775-1921* (Washington: Government Printing Office, 1935). (DFT)

116b. Chase, Harold, Thomas C. Cochran, Jacob Cooke, Robert Daly, Wendell Garrett, and Robert Multhauf, eds. *Dictionary of American History.* Rev. ed. 8 vols. New York: Charles Scribner's Sons, 1976-1978.

This reference work treats events, organizations, and broad topics, such as city planning and preservation movement, in American history. Each article has a brief bibliography. The final volume is an index to the set. (LBD)

117. CIS Annual Index to Congressional Publications and Public Laws and *CIS Annual Abstracts of Congressional Publications and Legislative Histories.* Washington: Congressional Information Service, 1970-.

These publications include hearings, reports, committee prints, and other congressional publications from 1970 on. Indexing is by name of author, agency, or subject. Abstracts are arranged by house and committee. It is cumulated in loose-leaf monthly editions and bound in annual volumes. Nearly all documents indexed are available from CIS on microfilm. (LBD)

118. CIS U.S. Serial Set Index. 36 vols. Washington: Congressional Information Service, 1975.

This multivolume index covers select government publications that appeared between 1787 and 1969. It complements the *CIS Annual* (see no. *117*). It is the only comprehensive index to the Serial Set (congressional journals, internal publications, reports, and outside reports received by Congress). It is organized in twelve parts by chronology, each part including a topical subject index and policy/document-type finding lists. (LBD)

Daniells, Lorna M. *Business Information Sources.* See no. *402.*

This bibliography lists a wide variety of reference works, periodicals, statistical sources, and services arranged mainly by area of business. The opening and closing chapters single out most basic reference works. (LBD)

119. Evans, Frank B. "The National Archives and Records Service and Its Research Resources—a Select Bibliography." In Frank B. Evans and Harold T. Pinkett, eds. *Research in the Administration of Public Policy*. National Archives Conference, Vol. VII. Washington: Howard University Press, 1975.

Evans lists bibliographies of records of the National Archives and Records Service to 1973, categorized by topic and period. He includes both bibliographic publications of the National Archives and articles in scholarly journals and books. (LBD)

120. Facts on File Yearbook. New York: Facts-on File, 1940-.

This service provides a weekly summary of national and world news and binds them into annual volumes. The result is a journalistic chronicle of that year's events. Stories are much like those in a weekly news magazine, but they are usually more compact. An extensive subject index is available for each annual volume, and there are five-year cumulative indexes. (LBD)

121. Freidel, Frank, ed. *Harvard Guide to American History*. Rev. ed. 2 vols. Cambridge, Mass.: Harvard University Press, 1974.

This book is a comprehensive reference guide and bibliography to United States history. Volume I includes a series of topical bibliographic essays, a few dealing with areas of public history, especially state and local history. Volume II is organized chronologically; it emphasizes secondary works. Citations are not annotated, but chapter introductions provide an indication of the nature of works in each unit. (LBD)

122. Hamer, Philip M., ed. *A Guide to Archives and Manuscripts in the United States*. New Haven, Conn.: Yale University Press, 1961.

Hamer provides a selective guide to manuscript holdings of leading libraries in the United States. Organized by state, city, and institution, it is indexed by person or organization whose papers are collected. It lists collections rather than individual holdings. (LBD)

123. Higham, Robin, ed. *A Guide to the Sources of United States Military History*. Hamden, Conn.: Archon, 1975.

This series of bibliographic essays by academic and military historians is arranged both topically and chronologically. It includes several chapters on defense policy and diplomacy to 1973, aimed at policy analysts as well as military historians. (LBD)

124. History News. American Association for State and Local History, 1940-.

History News, a monthly, carries no bibliographic feature and only a few book reviews, but its articles cover several sectors of public history and often serve to bring readers up to date on publications and trends. Most issues contain a "Technical Leaflet"; often these are guides to executing specific functions, particularly in historical preservation, exhibition, and interpretation. (LBD)

125. Holler, Frederick L. *Information Sources of Political Science.* 3d ed. Santa Barbara, Calif.: ABC-Clio, 1981.

Holler provides a bibliography of reference works in all social sciences, including history, followed by more extensive listing of works on American government and international relations. There are lengthy annotations and frequent references to machine-readable counterparts of printed works. (LBD)

126. Hoy, Suellen M., and Michael C. Robinson, comps. and eds. *Public Works History in the United States: A Guide to the Literature by the Public Works Historical Society.* Nashville: American Association for State and Local History, 1982.

This work provides a guide to documentary sources and historical scholarship on the history of public works in the United States. It cites more than five thousand items. (DFT)

127. Johnson, Allen, and Dumas Malone, eds. *Dictionary of American Biography.* 10 vols. New York: Scribner, 1946.
Garraty, John, Edward T. Jones, Robert L. Schuyler, and Harris Starr, eds. *Supplements.* 7 vols. New York: Charles Scribner's Sons, 1958-1981.
Dictionary of American Biography: Complete Index Guide, Vols. I-X, Supplements 1-7. New York: Charles Scribner's Sons, 1981.

This national biography contains lengthy articles by prominent scholars on leading Americans who died prior to 1966. The original ten volumes, each supplement, and the separate recent volume all provide indexes, and each article has a brief bibliography. (LBD)

128. Journal of American History. Bloomington, Ind.: Organization of American Historians, 1914-.

Originally the *Mississippi Valley Historical Review,* each issue of this journal contains scholarly reviews, a bibliography of recent periodical literature, and book notes. (LBD)

129. Kaminkow, Marion J., ed. *United States Local Histories in the Library of Congress: A Bibliography.* 5 vols. Baltimore: Magna Carta Book, 1975.

This oversize bibliography lists all books classified under local history in the Library of Congress as of mid-1972. The first four volumes are organized by region and state. The fifth volume provides a supplement of all cards filed from 1972 to 1975 on local history and an index to all volumes. (LBD).

130. Kreslins, Janis A., ed. *Foreign Affairs Bibliography.* 5 vols. New York: Bowker, 1976.

This bibliography was first published in 1933, and it has been updated periodically, providing a comprehensive bibliography of English language books on international relations and foreign policy. It is updated by bibliographic lists in the journal *Foreign Affairs*. (LBD)

Kruzas, Anthony T., and John Schmittroth, Jr. *Encyclopedia of Information Systems and Services.* See no. *411.*
This work provides a comprehensive listing of information centers, computerized systems and services, networks and cooperative programs, data bases, clearinghouses, and other computer services. Listings are arranged alphabetically by name of system or service, followed by a description. It contains twelve indexes. (LBD)

131. La Beau, Dennis, and Gary C. Tarbert. *Biographical Dictionaries Master Index, 1975-76.* 3 vols. Detroit: Gale, 1975.
This tool provides a guide to biographical information on over 700,000 persons in various *Who's Who*s and other current biographical reference books. Alphabetically arranged, the index gives full name and abbreviation for the biographical work, year, and page that describes a given person. The *First Supplement* appeared in 1979. (LBD)

132. Lewis, Mariana O., ed. *The Foundation Directory.* 7th ed. New York: Foundation Center, 1979.
This select listing of nongovernmental grant-making foundations in the U.S. is organized alphabetically by state. It indexes foundations by location, donors, and field of interest. Most entries give information on application procedures. (LBD)

133. Newsome, Walter L., comp. *Government Reference Books: A Biennial Guide to U.S. Government Publications.* Littleton, Colo.: Libraries Unlimited, 1968/69-.
This guide updates the federal government's output of bibliographies, guides, manuals, and handbooks every two years. Organized generally by academic disciplines in social science, science and technology, and humanities categories. (LBD)

134. National Archives and Records Service, Office of the Federal Register. *United States Government Organization Manual.* Washington: Government Printing Office, 1935-.
This official handbook of all agencies of the federal government provides a directory of major officials. It appears annually in two volumes, the larger being a complete listing of all legislative, judicial, and executive offices in Washington. The second volume, *Directory of Federal Regional Structures*, sets forth the regional offices of various agencies, their addresses and chief officers, and frequently maps of the boundaries of various agency structures. All agencies are

described in terms of their creation, purpose, organization, and current activities. (LBD)

135. Palumbo, Dennis James, and George A. Taylor. *Urban Policy: A Guide to Information Sources*. Detroit: Gale, 1979.

This short work is presented from both an academic and applied perspective. It is one of a twelve-volume series entitled *Urban Studies Information Guide Series* on topics such as suburbia, urban community, decision making, and urban planning. This series is one of the most recent guides to these areas. (LBD)

136. Poulton, Helen J. *The Historian's Handbook: A Descriptive Guide to Reference Works*. Norman: University of Oklahoma Press, 1972.

This guide to both bibliographic and informational reference works in history is organized by type of reference work. Each chapter is a bibliographic essay on major reference sources. Critical elements illuminate shortcomings of some works. (LBD)

137. *Public Affairs Information Service Bulletin*. New York: Public Affairs Information Service, 1915-.
Foreign Language Index . . . , 1972-.
Cumulative Subject Index to the Public Affairs Information Service Bulletin, 1915-1974. Arlington, Va.: Carrollton, 1977.

This select guide to periodical literature, books, public documents, and institutional publications in economics and public policy treats economic and social conditions, public administration, and international relations. Most citations are contemporary, not historical. The *Foreign Language Index* offers English subject access to works in five European languages. The *Cumulative Subject Index* compresses sixty years of older issues into a few volumes. (LBD)

138. Schmeckebier, Laurence F., and Roy S. Eastin, eds. *Government Publications and Their Use*. Rev. ed. Washington: Brookings Institution, 1969.

This text on various types of federal and state documents covers the ways to use them in research. Organization is by type of document. This is not as much a reference work as a book to help understand the nature, scope, applicability, and limitations of various types of government documents. (LBD)

139. Sheehy, Eugene P., comp. *Guide to Reference Works*. 9th ed. Chicago: American Library Association, 1976.

This comprehensive guide to reference works in all fields is periodically revised or supplemented to keep it reasonably up to date. It includes bibliographies, directories, encyclopedias, and handbooks. It is organized in five basic sections, one of which is wholly given to history and area studies. A *Supplement* (1980) for the first time contains data banks. (LBD)

140. Sills, David L., *International Encyclopedia of the Social Sciences*. 17 vols. New York: Macmillan, 1968.
Biographical Supplement. . . . New York: Macmillan, 1979.

This encyclopedia of essays covers social science disciplines, concepts, methods, and major historical trends. It is a complete revision of the original *ESS*. All essays are by leading scholars, usually with substantial bibliographies. (LBD)

141. *Social Science Index*. New York: Wilson, 1974-.

Originally the *International Index*, later the *Social Sciences and Humanities Index*, this work lists articles from academic journals on various subjects in the social sciences. (LBD)

142. *Statemen's Yearbook*. London, New York: Macmillan, 1863-.

This work is the oldest of the several annual summaries of political, economic, and demographic information on all nations. Arranged alphabetically by nation, it presents current government structure and officials; data on internal economy and trade; and select social and demographic data. Each nation is treated in essay form. (LBD)

143. *Technology and Culture*. Quarterly Journal of the Society for the History of Technology. Chicago: University of Chicago Press, 1961-.

This publication offers an annual bibliography, "Current Bibliography in the History of Technology." It is categorized by period and subcategorized by type of work or area of technology. Besides technology, it treats architecture and related areas such as transportation, agriculture, communications, and military technology. (LBD)

144. *The American Archivist*. Chicago: Society of American Archivists, 1943-.

This quarterly periodical carries an annual "Writings on Archives, Current Records, and Historical Manuscripts." This is the most complete continuing update on literature not only in archives and records management but in related areas of public history, particularly editing, and on research collections and policies of interest to all historians. (LBD)

145. *The Federal Index*. Cleveland: Predicasts, 1976-.

This unofficial guide covers current legal and political outputs of the federal government, such as bills, public laws, court decisions, hearings, and reports. It includes the *Federal Register*, the *Congressional Record*, and the *Commerce Business Daily*, along with a few nongovernmental publications such as the *Washington Post*. The *PTS Federal Index* and the *PTS Federal Index Weekly* are machine-readable versions covering current month only. (LBD)

146. *The Public Historian*. Berkeley: University of California Press, 1978-.

A comprehensive journal of public history, each issue is a potential update of some aspects of this field. Articles include examples of research, substantive reports, and descriptions of training programs and courses. (LBD)

147. U.N. Statistical Office. *Statistical Yearbook.* New York: United Nations Statistical Office, 1948-.

This compilation provides economic and select social statistics for the world, continents, and nations. A continuation of the League of Nations publications, early volumes contain retrospective data back to the 1920s. It is bilingual in French and English. Most data lag at least a year; more contemporary data may be found in this office's *Monthly Bulletin of Statistics.* Demographic data may be found in the regularly published *Demographic Yearbook.* (LBD)

148. U.S. Bureau of the Census. *Historical Statistics of the United States, Colonial Times to 1970.* Washington: Government Printing Office, 1975.

This compilation of select statistics, usually in decennial units, reaches as far back as colonial times in a few cases. It is organized in topical chapters, each of which is a bibliographical essay giving the source of each column, guiding the researcher to other sources of more detailed statistics, and commenting on the reliability of various sources. All tables are for the nation only; for local and state data, one must consult various decennial censuses or other sources. (LBD)

149. U.S. Bureau of the Census. *Statistical Abstract of the United States.* Washington: Government Printing Office, 1878-.

This annual compilation reports select data on social, economic, and political trends and conditions in the United States. Most tables are retrospective for at least a decade, although only for select years. Most data are at national level only. Each table carries a citation, making it a guide to further statistical sources. (LBD)

150. U.S. Library of Congress. *National Union Catalog of Manuscript Collections.* Washington: Government Printing Office, 1959-.

This annual listing describes the holdings of all manuscript collections in the United States. The basic unit is the individual collection, grouped by institution. Annotations describe chief papers in each collection and their size. The index relates these items to subject. (LBD)

151. U.S. Superintendent of Documents. *Monthly Catalog of United States Government Publications.* Washington: Government Printing Office, 1895-.
Buchanan, William W., and Edna Kanely, comps. *Cumulative Subject Index to the Monthly Catalog of U.S. Government Publications, 1900-1971.* 15 vols. Arlington, Va.: Carrollton, 1973-1975.

Long the basic comprehensive listing of federal documents, the *Monthly Catalog* is issued monthly and bound in annual editions. The extensive subject index has recently been augmented with a keyword index and an index to serials. The organization of each volume is archival. The subject index is extensive but largely limited to words appearing in titles. Each item is given an accession number, which is the key to linking the *Monthly Catalog* with the *Cumulative Subject Index*. The index is unannotated; it simply gives the year of the monthly catalog and the accession number after each subject entry. (LBD)

152. Wasserman, Paul, and Esther Herman. *Catalog of Museum Publications and Media*. 2d ed. Detroit: Gale, 1980.

This catalog lists books, serials, pamphlets, films, videotapes, and other media produced by United States and Canadian museums. Oriented to museum personnel and general researchers, the first part is organized by museums, listing all publications currently available. Later sections are indexed by title and keyword, periodicals, subject, and geographic location. (LBD)

153. Wasserman, Paul, and Jacqueline Bernero. *Statistics Sources*. 5th ed. Detroit: Gale, 1977.

This publication provides a dictionary guide to organizations and titles that put out regular data. It is primarily oriented toward business statistics and has alphabetized entries by industry, company, and product. (LBD)

154. Williams, Martha E., and Sandra H. Rouse. *Computer-Readable Bibliographic Data Bases: A Directory and Data Sourcebook*. Washington: American Society for Information Science, 1976-.

This loose-leaf reference work provides updates on machine-readable data bases composed mainly of bibliographic information that is publicly available. Most listed data bases are in the United States. It is alphabetically arranged by name of data base, with annotations categorized to show such things as the main intended user. It is indexed by subject, name, acronym, producer, and data element codes. (LBD)

155. Wynar, Bohdan S., ed. *American Reference Book Annual*. Littleton, Colo.: Libraries Unlimited, 1970-.

This annual review of recently published reference works is categorized largely by academic disciplines, but author and subject indexes allow retrieval from public history sectors. It permits updating of existing bibliographies or obtaining evaluation on new works. (LBD)

CHAPTER 2

PUBLIC HISTORY: TRAINING

David A. Johnson, editor

Over the past five years, formal training programs in public history have pro-
liferated across the United States and the world. The articles, essays, interviews,
guidelines and statements, and books included below only begin to identify the
vast, and growing, literature on training programs for "public historians"—
archivists, museum curators, historical society staff members, historic preservation and cultural resource management specialists, consultants in the public
and private sectors, and others.

As a sample of the writing currently available on public history training
programs, these essays testify to the embryonic and multifaceted nature of the
field, to its vitality, and to the controversies surrounding its development. Together, they give a glimpse—a historical snapshot if you will—of training in
public history in the late 1970s and early 1980s. Thus over time they will provide
historians with a referent from which to measure the successes, and failures, in
the development of history as a professional public enterprise.

I. General Works

156. Clary, David H. "Write When You Find Work: Advice to Graduate Faculty
on Training Employable Historians." *History Teacher*, Vol. XII (November
1978), pp. 65-85.

The author, formerly the chief historian of the History Division of the Forest
Section, U.S. Department of Agriculture, reviews the current job crisis in history
and argues that university faculty must look beyond training their students for
academic careers to the training needed by historians whose careers will be spent
in the public sector. Opportunities for historians outside of college and university
teaching exist, but preparation is necessary. Therefore, training should emphasize
working with deadlines, efficiency, understanding the policy process, and the
nature of organizational decision making. Further, public historians must be

prepared to write for administrators and to do broad-based research in the types of records relevant to concerns such as public health, environmental protection, urban planning, epidemiology, and land use. Clary includes an afterword on advice for unemployed historians. (DAJ)

157. Green, Howard. "A Critique of the Professional Public History Movement." *Radical History Review*, no. 25 (October 1981), pp. 164-171.

The author critiques "three overlapping tendencies" in the professional public history movement and the training programs developed as part of this movement. The first encompasses attempts to train historians for employment as archivists, records managers, editors, museum directors and curators, historic preservation and cultural resource management specialists. The second emphasizes the production of historian-consultants who can play central roles in public and private policy making, primarily as consultants. The third, tending to relate to the second, is committed to forging an integral place for historians in the policy making apparatus, joining him with "economists, political scientists, and sociologists as members of the 'brain trust.' " According to the author, each of these approaches fails to advance a truly public history, in turn denying the importance of amateurism and community commitment in local history, obscuring the political nature of policy making and the ethical difficulties associated with commissioned public history, and abdicating the historian's independent critical stance. The author concludes with a discussion of an alternative conception of public history, community based, openly political, and committed to a "sense of the possible in the collective recreation of the past." (DAJ)

158. Hyman, Harold M. "The Uses of History: Job Alternatives at the Bicentennial." *History Teacher*, Vol. XI (May 1978), pp. 393-399.

Rice University's Department of History, in response to employment and enrollment problems confronting history departments across the nation, has designed and sponsored two projects. First is the Houston Metropolitan Archives and Research Center Project. Under the umbrella of the South West Center for Urban Research and with funding support from the National Endowment for the Humanities, faculty, graduate students, and archivists were involved in the location, retrieval, accessioning, and cataloging of manuscript materials related to urban legal history in metropolitan Houston. Through this project, graduate fellows and graduate field researchers were introduced to archival theory and practice, oral history, and project design and administration. At the same time that important historical materials were preserved and made accessible, the project introduced historians to new areas of potential employment. The second project introduces law students to the history of the law. In cooperation with the local law schools, the Rice Department of History offers a one-year M.A. program, open to law students between their first and second, or second and third, years of legal training. The article describes the design, development, and implementation of this program, and its positive effects on graduate enrollment, departmental alumni relations, and the vitality of the department's graduate program. (DAJ)

159. Johnson, G. Wesley, Jr. "Editor's Preface." *Public Historian*, Vol. I (Fall 1978), pp. 4-10.

In introducing this new journal, the editor discusses the need for historical expertise outside of colleges and universities. In post industrial society, when continuity is obscured, the services of the historian as interpreter are essential. Therefore, historians must make the transition from academy to public arena, as have journalists, political scientists, and sociologists. Potential areas for historical careers include government, business, research organizations, the media, archives, records management, and the teaching of a new generation of public historians. The *Public Historian* provides a forum for exchange upon ideas, opportunities, methods, and ethical questions related to public history, as history emerges as a profession encompassing more than teaching in schools and colleges. (DAJ)

160. Johnson, G. Wesley, Peter Stearns, and Joel A. Tarr. "Public History: A New Area of Teaching, Research, and Employment." *AHA Newsletter*, Vol. XVIII (March 1980), pp. 8-10.

The article provides an early description of the emerging field of public history from the perspectives of the directors of two graduate-level training programs, those at the University of California, Santa Barbara, and at Carnegie-Mellon University. The authors provide an overview of development in the 1970s, curricular adjustments made in light of their first year of actual operation, and the resulting core requirements and elective opportunities. At UCSB and Carnegie-Mellon, public history is distinguished from older public history programs that emphasize museology, archival administration, and historical editing. Rather, they intend to "train a new kind of professional person," able to translate the historian's skills to policy making in the public and private spheres. (DAJ)

161. Jones, Arnita. "The National Coordinating Committee: Programs and Possibilities." *Public Historian*, Vol. I (Fall 1978), pp. 49-60.

The National Coordinating Committee was established in response to the current crisis in the historical discipline—the decline in the demand for teachers and the increased desire to find employment for historians outside teaching. The NCC intends to provide a structure for making this transition through promoting history and through research on relevant uses of history in government and business. As an example, the author describes the University of California, Berkeley, Career Seminar Series and Resource Center, which served to expose students to historians outside of teaching and provided information about skills, résumé writing, and employment searches. (DAJ)

162. Kelley, Robert. "A Note on Teaching: The Graduate Program in Public Historical Studies." *History Teacher*, Vol. XI (February 1978), pp. 227-228.

The University of California, Santa Barbara, Graduate Program in Public Historical Studies is one attempt to make a positive response to the question, "Do historians have a legitimate role to play in the task of policy making?" raised by David F. Trask in no. *1553*. Through the training of public historians, the Santa Barbara program intends to open up state and local government to the potential contributions that historians can make as policy makers, building on the notion that history is invaluable to understanding the problems decision makers confront. As a corollary, the program will open the doors to a new professional role for historians. Kelley describes the UCSB program curriculum, its emphasis upon team research in a problem-oriented core seminar, internship requirements, and M.A. thesis and Ph.D. dissertation. Policy areas investigated by program students include noise pollution and airport expansion, water rights, historic surveying, corporate policy making, and electric power supply. (DAJ)

163. Kelley, Robert. "Public History: Its Origins, Nature, and Prospects." *Public Historian*, Vol. I (Fall 1978), pp. 16-28.

An early discussion of the emerging field of public history, this article discusses (1) the value of the *historian's perspective* to the world beyond the classroom; (2) the *practical value* of history to public life; (3) new directions in *historical training* undertaken at the University of California, Santa Barbara, where historians are trained to meet the demands of nonacademic careers; (4) the presence and need to make visible existing *role models*, those historians who currently practice their craft in a wide range of nonacademic settings; and (5) the *curriculum* developed at Santa Barbara for training in public history. The author describes the Santa Barbara core seminar, its emphasis on team research, mission-oriented projects, meeting deadlines, and fulfilling the requirements of a research contract with a public client. Also outlined are program electives, student areas of emphasis, the program internship, and the M.A. thesis and Ph.D. dissertation. (DAJ)

164. Kelley, Robert. "Team Research in History Graduate Study." *AHA Newsletter*, Vol. XIX (November 1981), pp. 4-5.

The author, a member of the University of California, Santa Barbara, Graduate Program in Public History Studies, reports on the organization and operation of this program's core team research seminar. Emphasizing client-oriented and deadline-constrained contract research, the seminar in 1979-1980 contracted with the Santa Barbara County Environmental Resources Office for a history of the county's environmental review process. Kelley reviews the seminar's progress over the term and the faculty director's responsibility for coordinating the various aspects of the research, meeting deadlines, and editing the final report to the client. For a companion piece which discusses the use of historians in teams dealing with crisis management, see David F. Trask, "Historians and Teamwork:

The Case of Crisis Management," *AHA Newsletter*, Vol. XIX (November 1981), pp. 6-7. (DAJ)

165. Liebs, Chester. "Preservation and Conservation: Perspectives, Programs, Projects." *Journal of Architectural Education*, Vol. XXX (November 1976).

The author, director of the Historic Preservation Graduate Curriculum at the University of Vermont, describes the philosophy and curriculum of the Vermont program. Professional preservationists, according to Liebs, need to "develop their own common value system to replace the subjectivity, prejudice, pat answers, and preference for action over action guided concept. . . . " During the two years students spend in the Vermont Graduate Curriculum in Historic Preservation, emphasis is placed upon the development of perspective and the acquisition of requisite skills through courses related to a wide variety of design solutions, preservation techniques, institutional programs, and a student-directed preservation advocacy project. (DAJ)

166. "New Graduate Program in Public Historical Studies." *AHA Newsletter*, Vol. XIII (October 1975), p. 2.

In the Fall of 1976, the University of California, Santa Barbara, Program in Public Historical Studies was initiated. The program intends to train historians to serve as research historians for the community at large. Curriculum of the program emphasizes public-oriented research for government and business organizations, using as models the training provided professional sociologists, political scientists, economists, and statisticians. A basic premise of the program is that the historian's skills are important to policy making and provide an antidote to policy made in ignorance of the "essentially human story that explains why things are the way they are." Training at UCSB begins with a core seminar on an issue of concern to government agencies in the city and county of Santa Barbara. Students choosing this option in their graduate program are expected, through course work provided by the history department and related disciplines and through practical experience, to develop expertise in areas such as water resources, housing, race relations, transportation, energy, land use, industrial development, zoning, or crime prevention. (DAJ)

167. Roddy, Joseph. "Historians Go Public." *Rockefeller Foundation Illustrated*, Vol. IV (September 1979), p. 18.

Based on an interview with Robert Kelley and G. Wesley Johnson, of the University of California, Santa Barbara, Roddy describes the origins, development, and aspirations of the UCSB Graduate Program in Public Historical Studies. (DAJ)

168. Salisbury, Karen. "Is There a Future in the Study of the Past?" *Humanities*, Vol. II (October 1981), pp. 3-4.

As part of a collection of essays on public history, this essay reviews the new field of public history and its development in the context of declining university enrollments and academic opportunities. Public and applied history training programs—at the University of California, Santa Barbara; Harvard; and New York University—are briefly described. (DAJ)

169. "Scholars in Transition Program." *AHA Newsletter*, Vol. XIX (March 1981), p. 15.

This article describes the program, sponsored by the Institute for Research in History and financed by the Fund for the Improvement of Post Secondary Education (FIPSE), for college and university faculty who wish to leave teaching for other careers. The program is organized around workshops on skills assessment, job sector identification, résumé writing, interviewing, and the necessity of a realistic evaluation of one's prospects for specific careers outside of teaching. (DAJ)

170. Sitton, Thad. "Public Schools and Public History." *Educational Forum*, March 1980, pp. 277-280.

This is a rare article in a growing field. Sitton suggests a model to focus public history in the classroom. It includes adaptations of document collection, a photographic archives, oral history, and the use of a single-concept publication. Sitton reports on a survey of 1977 that revealed a large number of publications modeled after *Foxfire*. (PJT)

171. "Standards for Historical Agency Training Programs." *History News*, Vol. XXXVI (July 1981), centerfold.

In response to the proliferation of college and university training programs related to historical agencies, a committee of the American Association for State and Local History was appointed in 1980 to develop a set of minimal program standards. This committee reported to the annual meeting of the AASLH in September, 1980, and the proposed standards were approved, "to be advocated by the Association as an organization." The standards are intended to complement those adopted by the American Association of Museums and published in *Museum News* (November-December 1978). The AASLH will publish a list of training programs that submit evidence of meeting AASLH standards. While the standards do not constitute accreditation, they will help guide students in choosing between programs and colleges/universities in developing their curriculum. The standards relate to (1) program direction; (2) core curriculum; (3) internships. Copies of the complete standards are available from the American Association for State and Local History, 1400 Eighth Avenue, South Nashville, Tennessee 37103. (DAJ)

172. "University of Connecticut Program in Public History." *AHA Newsletter*, Vol. XVIII (February 1980), p. 9.

This notice describes the University of Connecticut Program in Public History and Archival Management. Established in September 1980, it emphasizes training for employment in public, business, and labor archives. The curriculum includes training in archival management and organization, management information systems, archives-related computer technology, practicums, and a fifteen-week internship in a public agency, business, or labor archive. (DAJ)

173. "What's Going On." *History News*. Published monthly by the American Association for State and Local History in *History News*.

"What's Going On" is a monthly department of *History News*, the official publication of the American Association for State and Local History. In it is current information about activities related to state and local historical societies, conferences, local and national training seminars and sessions. Under the category "Educational Opportunities" are listings of history-related programs leading to graduate degrees and fellowships for historical training. Under "On the Horizon" are schedules of upcoming national, regional, and local workshops, seminars, and conferences. (DAJ)

174. Wills, John. "History and Its Audience: A Course and a Concept." *AHA Newsletter*, Vol. XVI (February 1979), pp. 5-8.

The current employment crisis, according to the author, reveals the dangers inherent in the overspecialization plaguing the historical discipline. Historians must learn to communicate with a broader audience than the profession itself. One attempt to address the problem is found in a course, "History and Its Audience," which trains both undergraduates and beginning graduate students to communicate historical knowledge relevant to policy making in the public and private spheres, journalism, the mass media, and education in the schools. The course introduces students to history as a public concern, opportunities for historians outside of college and university teaching, and, in the form of a term project, to the practice of history for particular, nonacademic audiences. (DAJ)

II. Historic and Cultural Resource Preservation

175. Bronitsky, Gordon. "Amateur Certification in Archaeology: Retrospect and Prospect." *Plains Anthropologist*, Vol. XXV (November 1980), pp. 269-278.

The destruction of archaeological sites across the United States has raised the need for education and training of amateur archaeologists. The author reviews six programs designed to give short-term, basic training to amateurs and related professionals in site selection, surveying, excavation, field skills, and laboratory analysis of archaeological materials. He also discusses rationales for and against certification of amateurs, based upon the varied experience of such public training programs in Arkansas, Kansas, New Mexico, California, Iowa, and New York. (DAJ)

176. Floyd, Candace. "Coming Full Circle: A Master Restorationist Trains a New Generation of Craftsmen." *History News*, Vol. XXXV (July 1980), pp. 9-10.

Joseph Lewes, a professional historic restorationist since 1956, retired in 1977 and then joined the National Trust for Historic Preservation's Restoration Workshop. As the Workshop's master restorationist, he oversees as many as ten restoration apprentices in preservation, restoration, renovation, and maintenance projects. The Workshop is housed at Lyndhurst, in Tarrytown, New York, and its staff provides services for members of the National Trust and owners of National Register Buildings. Since 1973, sixteen apprentices have completed the restoration training program. Applicants must have one year of experience in the building trades and intend to follow careers in restoration. (DAJ)

177. "Higher Education Supplement." *Preservation News* (October 1981).

In this four-page supplement to the October 1981 issue of *Preservation News* are found (1) a description of special preservation programs funded by the National Trust for Historic Trust Education Grants; (2) a report on special programs in preservation sponsored by Kansas State University, the University of New Orleans, and Cornell University; (3) a preliminary listing of programs listed in the NTHP's *Guide to Undergraduate and Graduate Education in Historic Preservation;* and (4) a report on the National Council for Preservation Education's efforts to establish standards for training programs in preservation education. (DAJ)

178. Holmes, Kay. "Learning about the Real World." *Historic Preservation*, Vol. XXXII (July-August 1980), pp. 20-25.

The Columbia University Graduate Program in Historic Preservation has transformed the Jasper Ward House into the "Center for Building Conservation" to serve professional conservationists, preservation students, and the general public. The center grew out of the Columbia graduate historic preservation program, and the building's restoration provides a laboratory for students' artifact-centered projects. The article includes a description of the graduate curriculum in historic preservation at Columbia. (DAJ)

179. Huhta, James. "Organizing for Better Education." *Preservation News*, Vol. XIX (October 1979), pp. 7-9.

The author reviews the efforts of the National Trust for Historic Preservation's Higher Education Study Group, begun in 1978, to advise on the development of historic preservation training programs. The National Council for Preservation Education, formed on the recommendation of the Study Group, intends to serve the needs of a higher education constituency by encouraging communication between educators, preservationists, and government, by voicing the collective concerns of preservationists about training programs, and by promoting public awareness of historic preservation education. The article includes a chart describing eighteen programs in preservation education, including the date established, degrees offered, sponsoring department, emphases, course and internship requirements, thesis (if required), summer programs, workshops, special activities, average program enrollment, and time to completion of degree. (DAJ)

180. Kilstrom, Richard G. "Post Graduate Education in Conservation of the Built Environment." Masters Degree Dissertation, Edinburgh College of Art/ Heriott-Watt University (Edinburgh, Scotland), 1981.

This dissertation intends to provide a single source of information on the field of architectural and urban conservation worldwide. Part I "surveys, analyzes, and compares conservation education programs . . . in the context of three geographic areas: Great Britain, the United States, and Europe." Part II constitutes a case study of the conservation education program at Heriott-Watt University in the context of the analysis contained in Part I. (DAJ)

181. Lee, Antoinette. "A Field Open to Specialists." *Preservation News*, Vol. XIX (October 1979), pp. 7-9.

This article describes preservation education programs in universities from 1959, when the University of Virginia initiated courses in American Architectural History and Architectural Preservation, to 1979. The author reviews the growth of programs at Virginia, Cornell, Columbia, Florida, and Middle Tennessee and briefly describes the different emphases and requirements of graduate preservation education programs existing in 1979. The article includes a chart describing preservation education programs, including information on curriculum, emphases, internships, special projects, and related fields available for elective training. (DAJ)

182. Lee, Antoinette, ed. *Guide to Undergraduate and Graduate Education in Historic Preservation*. Washington: National Trust for Historic Preservation, 1981.

This book provides an enlarged descriptive guide to universities that offer undergraduate and graduate preservation *degree programs* and to individual departments of architecture, history, law, planning, American Studies, business and management, anthropology, landscape architecture, and interior design that offer *courses* related to historic preservation. (DAJ)

183. Lee, Antoinette. "Sorting History-Related Programs and Careers." Higher Education Supplement, *Preservation News*, Vol. XX (October 1980).

The author describes, for prospective students, the available types of preservation-related programs leading to the M.A. or M.S. in historic preservation or to a professional degree in architecture, planning, or landscape architecture. She discusses what to look for in a program *vis-à-vis* curriculum, laboratory facilities, and special opportunities, and how, through correspondence with recent graduates, to evaluate a program's overall quality. The article also reviews training programs in museology, archival management, archaeology, and public history. (DAJ)

184. Longacre, William A., and J. Jefferson Reid. "The University of Arizona Archaeological Field School at Grasshopper: Eleven Years of Multidisciplinary Research and Teaching." *Kiva*, Vol. XL (Fall-Winter 1974), pp. 3-38.

The authors offer a historical review of the University of Arizona Archeological Field School at Grasshopper Run. They summarize the teaching and research carried out between 1963 and 1974 at the field school, with particular emphasis on how students have been involved in an ongoing, multidisciplinary research program. The reconstruction of the archaeological site is discussed, annual accomplishments reviewed, and plans for the future outlined. (DAJ)

185. Melnick, Robert. "Landscape Architecture: Kansas State University." *Preservation News*, Vol. XIX (October 1979), p. 10.

The author discusses the importance of landscape architecture to historic preservation. Landscape architecture, concerned as it is with "everything that is out of doors"—the built environment generally conceived, including neighborhoods, towns, cities, and regions—offers a broad perspective toward the landscape that needs to be included in historic preservation programs. At Kansas State University, an attempt to integrate architecture, landscape architecture, and planning is underway, emphasizing neighborhood and small-town preservation, historic trails, farmsteads, ranches, and the tall-grass prairie. (DAJ)

186. National Conservation Advisory Council. *Suggested Guidelines for Training in Architectural Conservation: A Supplement to the Report of the Study Committee on Architectural Conservation.* Washington: NCAC, 1980.

An outgrowth of the *Report of the Study Committee on Architectural Conservation* (1977), this pamphlet defines the roles and skills of the architectural conservator; proposes the scope and content for a sample curriculum in architectural conservation; outlines facility requirements; and suggests procedures for the accreditation of such programs. (DAJ)

187. "Public History Curriculum." *Public Historian*, Vol. II (Fall 1979), pp. 20-41.

This is a panel discussion at the First National Symposium on Public History (Montecito, California, April 1979), on Public History Curriculum. The panel discusses, among other topics, the case study method, requirements for internships, and the need for interdisciplinary training in public history programs. The participants were: Corrine Gelb (Wayne State University), Garrett Weaver (Jackson State), Dennis Harris (Sonoma State), Gerald Herman (Northeastern University), Lawrence de Graaf (Fullerton State), Carl Becker (Wright State), and Ernest May (Harvard University). (DAJ)

188. "Public History in the Academy: An Overview of University and College Offerings." *Public Historian,* Vol. II (Fall 1979), pp. 85-116.

This article includes information on thirty-six graduate and ten undergraduate programs in public history. The programs are divided into graduate and undergraduate and described in terms of (1) definition of fields, (2) course requirements, (3) suggested electives, (4) internships, and (5) complementary options. (DAJ)

189. Sheppard, Nathaniel, Jr. "Practicing What They Teach: In the Field, in the Museum, and in the Classroom." *Change,* Vol. X (January 1978), pp. 8-11.

Sheppard describes the Beloit College (Wisconsin) archaeological field school, an effort to introduce undergraduates to training usually reserved for graduate school. Emphasis in the program is on "learning by doing," and students find the program valuable as a guide to deciding whether or not they wish to pursue careers in archaeology. (DAJ)

190. "Standards for Graduate Programs in Preservation." *National Council for Preservation Education Newsletter*, Vol. I (Fall 1981).

In this first issue of the *NCPE Newsletter*, the events leading to the appointment of the Committee on Standards are reviewed, in particular the growing concern about the proliferation in the 1970s of graduate programs related to preservation, and a concern that "some such programs are opportunistic ventures of dubious value, and may be of potential harm to students, employers, and historic resources." As a result, a draft report on standards was presented to, and adopted by, the annual meeting of the NCPE in October 1981. The text of the standards, meant "to encourage truly different approaches," rather than demand a "model curriculum," is included in this issue of the *Newsletter.* (DAJ)

191. Stephenson, Robert L. "New Degree Focused on Contract Archaeology." Higher Education Supplement, *Preservation News,* Vol. XX (October 1980).

The author describes the University of South Carolina program in contract archaeology, which provides specialized training in the methods and theory of conservation archaeology. The program offers both a certificate program in conservation archaeology and a masters of arts degree in public service archaeology. The certificate program is primarily addressed to federal agency administrators who desire an introduction to contract archaeology, and the MA program to graduate students seeking professional training in public archaeology. (DAJ)

192. Tishler, William H. "The University of Wisconsin." *Preservation News,* Vol. XIX (October 1979), p. 10.

At the University of Wisconsin, the Department of Landscape Architecture has expanded its training program to address historic and cultural resource management and preservation. This field constitutes one of four areas of emphasis within the department and draws upon an interdisciplinary faculty from architecture, urban planning, regional planning, geography, art, psychology, communication, ecology, and computer science. (DAJ)

193. William, James C. "So You've Got Some Old Ruins—Now What?" *AHA Newsletter*, Vol. XVIII (January 1980), pp. 6-10.

This article describes the experience of a junior college instructor who had returned to graduate study in the University of California, Santa Barbara, Graduate Program in Public Historical Studies, and then returned to his teaching position at Gavilan College. While at UCSB, the author had observed an undergraduate historical methods seminar in which students had completed original local history research projects focusing on a historic building survey. The article describes the author's experience in applying the same approach of team-based, client-oriented research to history education at the junior college level. (DAJ)

194. Wolkomin, Richard. "Old McDonalds Have a Friend: His Name Is Leibs." *Smithsonian*, Vol. XII (1981), pp. 62-69.

Wolkomin offers a portrait of Chester Leibs, director of the University of Vermont Program in Historic Preservation, and founder, American Association for Industrial Archaeology and American Society for Commercial Archaeology. The article discusses Leibs's efforts to preserve the American-built environment, techniques used in preservation instruction at the University of Vermont, successful preservation projects, and the work done by the University of Vermont Preservation Laboratory (director, Phillip Marshall). (DAJ)

III. Archival Administration

195. Bemis, Samuel Flagg. "The Training of Archivists in the United States." *American Archivist*, Vol. II (July 1939), pp. 154-161.

This article constitutes the first formal attempt to address archival training. Bemis argues for the European tradition of archival education, in which historians are provided with technical archival training. Two types of training are identified, one at the Ph.D. level for archival administrators and one at the M.A. level for archivists in smaller governmental institutions, businesses, and historical agencies. (SC)

196. Blouin, Francis X., Jr. "The Relevance of the Case Method to Archival Education and Training." *American Archivist*, Vol. XLI (January 1978), pp. 37-44.

The training of archivists is compared to the training of lawyers, and the use of the casebook method of instruction is promoted. The archival profession, like the law, rests on principles that are often in conflict and demand heuristic judgment by the professional. In this respect, the archivist is required to make decisions on a case-by-case basis. The application of the case method in archival training, therefore, provides future professionals with a clear sense of what the archivist actually does and how he or she thinks. It provides a pragmatic, scientific approach and would, if adopted, lead to innovative practices. The author, in this respect, criticizes the education guidelines of the Society of American Archivists for not addressing the complex matters of modern archival administration. (SC)

197. Breck, Allen du Pont. "New Dimensions in the Education of American Archivists." *American Archivist*, Vol. XXIX (April 1966), pp. 173-186.

The education of archivists, according to the author, should not be based exclusively on library schools or history departments. On the contrary, the broadest possible training should be sought. At the M.A. level, a solid program should emphasize the range of archival procedures and require a thesis on a subject related to archives. A Ph.D. program in American studies that includes archives methodology would provide a good education for the upper-level archivist. An archivist, according to the author, must be able to instruct and publish scholarly works. The article also traces the development of training programs and reviews the ways in which the post-World War II data explosion has changed the requirements of archival education. (SC)

198. Buck, Solon. "The Training of American Archivists." *American Archivist*, Vol. IV (April 1941), pp. 84-90.

In this article, the author describes a graduate-level program in archival science. In concert with graduate historical education, archival training should include courses on the nature and value of archives, appraisal, arrangement, description, preservation, reprographics, reference, internal organization, and special handling of certain record types. The article argues for education in history rather than library science. (SC)

199. Colson, John C. "On the Education of Archivists and Librarians." *American Archivist*, Vol. XXXI (April 1968), pp. 167-174.

This article notes the common ground shared by archivists and librarians and supports archival education located in library schools. Both professions are concerned with recorded matter, reference, and preservation. Training programs should stress joint concerns. The daily function of archival institutions is more like libraries than history departments. Education of prospective archivists should be at the graduate level, not the undergraduate level, because the latter would dilute general education. Curriculum must be broadly based in order to meet the needs of archives with different emphases. (SC)

200. Cook, Michael. *The Education and Training of Archivists—Status Report of Archival Training Programmes and Assessment of Manpower Needs*. Paris: UNESCO, 1979.

This monograph evaluates archival education around the world. It argues that archival training in the United States consists of little more than part-time introductions that are too often simply an element in programs that emphasize other disciplines. American programs, in this respect, do not provide models for substantive archival training, despite their relative economies of organization and operation. The author argues in favor of the European model of archival education. (SC)

Evans, Frank B. "Postappointment Archival Training: A Proposed Solution for a Basic Problem." See no. *490.*

The article discusses, from a historical perspective, three approaches to archival education. Two were first proposed in the nineteenth century—training centered in library schools and history departments—while the third, of more recent vintage, is categorized as "self help." Evans argues that neither library schools nor history departments fully meet the educational needs of archivists. Currently, most archival training is in-service or post-appointment. This job-related training is necessary, and, therefore, the Society of American Archivists should provide a series of short institutes throughout the United States. Advanced-level post-appointment training should also be provided as a supplement to the archivists' in-service institutes. Certifying examinations, similar to those available to records managers, are also discussed. (SC)

201. Hansen, James E., and John Newman. "Training History Students in Working Archives." *History Teacher*, Vol. XIII (February 1980), pp. 211-221.

The Colorado State University Archival Training Option was established for graduate students in history in 1975. It stemmed from a project, begun in the early 1970s, to organize an archive related to the university's history. With this archive, and the university's special collections library serving as a laboratory, the archival option was established, drawing also upon the Colorado State Archive Director as a consultant and practicum supervisor. From 1975 to the present, the university's course on archival management and related opportunities for practical experience in the university library and State Archive were refined in order to center on instruction in basic archival skills and student projects that integrate experience in inventorying, appraising, processing, arranging, and description. The article includes a copy of the introductory course syllabus. (DAJ)

202. Helmuth, Ruth. "Education for American Archivists: A View from the Trenches." *American Archivist*, Vol. XLIV (Fall 1981), pp. 295-303.

Archival training must look to the future and not merely attempt to consolidate the gains of the past. Formal graduate education gives a greater opportunity for professional advancement than in-service training. Archivists, according to the author, must be scholars who understand the process of research in order to appraise, arrange, describe, and provide reference services. Moreover, training in records management, administration, and legal issues should be integrated into archival training programs. The article reviews the guidelines of the Society of American Archivists issued in 1977 for archival education and discusses the curricular controversies that have subsequently arisen. (SC)

203. Jones, Houston G. "Archival Training in American Universities, 1938-1968." *American Archivist*, Vol. XXXI (April 1968), pp. 135-154.

This article, based upon a paper delivered at the 1967 meeting of the Society of American Archivists, challenges Theodore Schellenburg's argument for library-school-based archival training. It describes, among others, early programs at American University, the University of Denver, Wayne State University, and the North Carolina Department of Archives and History, as well as summer institutes at several colleges and universities. Archivists can arrange, describe, and appraise records only if they have an advanced grasp of history. Training, therefore, should be in graduate history programs and should include courses on record making and record keeping, archival procedures and techniques, and an internship. (SC)

204. Lamb, W. Kaye. "The Modern Archivist: Formally Trained or Self-educated." *American Archivist*, Vol. XXXI (April 1968), pp. 175-177.

Archival training is best served by sound historical education in concert with practical experience. Before an effective training program can be instituted, professional archivists must establish basic training standards and principles and a consistent terminology. Archival education must be at the graduate level and centered in an archival institution. The article takes exception to the claim that libraries and archives share a common interest. Library schools present library techniques to archivists, and these techniques do not necessarily meet the needs of the archival repository. Most library material is replaceable, whereas archival records are unique. Therefore, archivists require training that is relevant to the particular character of an archival repository. (SC)

205. LeFurgy, William G. "The Practicum: A Repository View." *American Archivist*, Vol. XLIV (Spring 1981), pp. 153-155.

The article describes the need for the practicum (or internship) in archival training and cautions that the proper organization and direction of the practicum is difficult even in the best of circumstances. Presently, there are no basic standards for practicums. Since repositories differ from one another, guidelines must be sufficiently broad so that different institutions can adapt them to their particular needs. Solid classroom instruction must precede the practicum. The repository that sponsors a practicum must be able to provide professional staff time to supervise student work. Close cooperation and coordination, therefore, must exist between universities and archival institutions in the design of practicums. (SC)

206. Mariz, George. "Multiple Uses of a Survey: Training, Guides, Records Management." *American Archivist*, Vol. XLII (Fall 1979), pp. 301-306.

The author describes a records survey in which student interns were used. Students from Western Washington University with classroom training in archives or records management, and with a practicum already completed, were employed as interns. The article describes the Pacific Northwest Power Records Survey and the role of the interns. It concludes that such on-the-job experience is essential to the training of archivists but that interns must have preliminary knowledge gained in the classroom. (SC)

207. McCrank, Lawrence. "Prospects for Integrating Historical and Information Studies in Archival Education." *American Archivist*, Vol. XLII (October 1979), pp. 443-455.

This article laments the apparently irresolvable controversy over the relative merits of historical or library education as the basis of archival training. The shortcomings of both models are reviewed, and a proposal for a joint MA/MLS program is presented. Modeled after an example provided by Case Western Reserve University, such a joint degree program would cross departmental lines and provide a grounding in information science as well as history or American studies. Another alternative is a two-year MLS program in which the first year entails work in library science while the second year emphasizes specialization in an academic discipline. Cooperation with Ph.D. programs could grow from this approach. Above all, archivists should insist that one- and two-course approaches to archival training be recognized for what they are: little more than introductions to "archival appreciation." (SC)

208. "Minutes: Council Meeting, 28 January 1980." *American Archivist*, Vol. XLIII (Summer 1980), pp. 411-423.

Pages 420-422 include the guidelines adopted by the Society of American Archivists for the practical experience component of archival training programs. Entitled "Program Standards for Archival Education, The Practicum," the guidelines amplify and supplement the "Laboratory Elements" section of the SAA "Guidelines for Graduate Archival Education Programs." In the "Minutes," the practicum is distinguished from the internship. The latter is defined as on-the-job training while the former is described in terms of laboratory classroom education. The guidelines provide a detailed definition of the practicum structure and staffing, course content, required resources, and procedures for evaluation. Generally speaking, the guidelines state that the practicum should provide students with experience in acquisition procedures, processing, preservation, and reference services. (SC)

209. Orr, William. "Archival Training in Europe." *American Archivist*, Vol. XLIV (Winter 1981), pp. 27-39.

Orr describes the development of archival education in Europe and compares training standards in different countries. The debate over archival education in the United States has dismissed European models because of their emphasis upon research as opposed to basic arrangement and description. In general, European archivists stress a dual archival role: custodian *and* interpreter. There, local history is viewed as the preserve of the archivist because it is central to the needs of local archive users. Most countries provide separate education for senior archivists and mid-grade archivists. The latter generally receive more extensive training than American archivists. Based upon his review of European training, the author argues that archival education in the United States should be separate from both history departments and library schools in order to avoid the debate over where, institutionally, archival training should be located. (SC)

210. Peace, Nancy, and Nancy Fisher Chudcoff. "Archivists and Librarians: A Common Mission, a Common Education." *American Archivist*, Vol. XLII (October 1979), pp. 456-462.

This article argues in favor of archival training based upon MLS programs. Archives and libraries share a common goal—the control and dissemination of information. Thus they are basically the same profession and share educational needs. Most archival training is centered on one instructor, but one person cannot teach all the courses archivists need, such as cataloging, reference, administration, reprographics, and preservation. Library schools, with their extensive resources, provide the framework for a standardized archival education. The article describes a format for archival training within the larger context of library education. (SC)

211. Prince, Carl E., and Michael Lutzker. "Career Training Offered by NYU Archival Management/Historical Editing Program." *AHA Newsletter*, Vol. XVIII (April 1980), pp. 12-13.

The authors describe the development of the New York University Management/Historical Editing Program. The article reviews the current controversy over the proper institutional location of archival education programs and the efforts of the NYU program to provide a "proper mix" of training in history, archival theory, and hands-on experience. Also described are the phases of the program's development; the available resources for archival and editing education provided by the NYU archives, special collections library, and resident editing programs; the basic requirements students must meet in history, archival management, and historical editing; and the areas, such as oral history, conservation and micrographics, historical societies and local history, photo analysis and conservation, that are covered by the program. (DAJ)

212. Schellenburg, Theodore R. "Archival Training in Library Schools," *American Archivist*, Vol. XXXI (April 1968), pp. 155-165.

The author argues that library science and archival science are complementary. The European model of archival training, in which historians are provided with supplementary training, is not applicable to the United States because archivists deal with largely organic records. Schellenburg notes that library schools reach the majority of records custodians—namely librarians. This is important because many libraries hold archival records. The article discusses the relative advantages and disadvantages of archival education in library schools versus history departments. (SC)

213. Society of American Archivists. *Education Directory.* Chicago: Society of American Archivists, 1978.

This, the third edition of the *SAA Education Directory*, contains (1) general information on careers in archives (the work of the archivist, types of archival agencies, qualifications for employment, salaries, placement, education and training); (2) the SAA Guidelines for Graduate Archival Education, organized in terms of *theory* (nature of archives, acquisitions, processing, use of archives, administration of archives), *laboratory elements*, and *independent study*; (3) a listing of multicourse and single-course archival programs and archival institutes; and (4) a listing of SAA publicationss. (DAJ)

214. Taylor, Hugh A. "The Discipline of History and the Education of the Archivist." *American Archivist*, Vol. XL (October 1977), pp. 395-402.

Archivists are described as a combination of museum curators, librarians, and historians. Currently, archivists are collecting more media-related materials than in the past, and, therefore, greater training and professionalism have become mandatory. In another generation, the author believes, archival training will include one year of library science, information science, and archival science, with a second-year specialization in archives. Archivists need a "badge," and while advanced degrees do not necessarily indicate better qualifications, they generally are advantageous. Archivists must be attuned to the latest developments in research methodology and would be well served by an institute of advanced archival studies at the Ph.D. or postgraduate level. (SC)

215. Warner, Robert M. "Historians and Archivists." *AHA Newsletter*, Vol. XVIII (November 1980), pp. 4-5.

This article, written by the Archivist of the United States, addresses the need for cooperation between archivists and historians in the training of archivists. The author reviews the recent history-department-based training programs in archival management that have emerged in response to the employment crisis in academic history. Often designed with little forethought, these programs have had mixed results, and historians as well as archivists must take responsibility for insuring that students receive quality training. (DAJ)

IV. Other Areas

216. Bracken, Alexander E., and E. Bruce Geelhoed. "Clio and the Marketplace: Teaching American Business History." *History Teacher*, Vol. XIV (February 1981), pp. 209-222.

The authors call for a more systematic integration of business history into the college/university history curriculum. Citing the "new vocationalism," they propose that business history offers a means of communicating literary skills and liberal learning to the business professional. Included are descriptions of five models for presenting business history (business leaders, family businesses, American business development, conflict in American business, and the social basis of particular businesses). Also reviewed are available texts and supplementary readings. (DAJ)

217. "Careers in Business Program Enters Second Year." *AHA Newsletter*, Vol. XVI (November 1978), pp. 3-4.

This article describes a summer program at the New York University School of Business "designed to open pathways to business and management careers for recent ABD's and Ph.D.'s in the humanities and related social sciences." The program, an intensive summer orientation, includes workshops, lectures, and assignments designed to introduce participants to the corporate setting, its language, managerial tools, and professional expectations. Of fifty participants in the 1978 program, seven had received offers of employment within two weeks of the session's conclusion. (DAJ)

218. Dailey, Charles A. "Bringing a Unique Perspective to Museum Work." *Museum News*, Vol. LV (May-June 1977), pp. 53-54.

The article describes the museum training program developed at the Institute of American Indian Arts in Santa Fe, New Mexico. The IAIA program, begun in 1971, was developed with the specific needs of Indian students and the problems of small museums in mind. The author reviews the program's teaching philosophy, curriculum, and operation. (DAJ)

219. Flanders, Robert. "The Center for Ozark Studies: Regional Public History." *Public Historian*, Vol. I (Fall 1978), pp. 42-48.

This article describes the Center for Ozark Studies at Southwest Missouri State University, the purpose of which is to increase public understanding of the history, culture, geography, and economy of the region through (1) location of relevant information in libraries and archives, and the production of a bibliographic finding aid; (2) promotion of interdisciplinary cultural resource management projects; (3) multimedia productions about the region; and (4) sponsorship of conferences and public education programs, monographs, a journal, and documentaries. (DAJ)

220. Eisler, Colin. "Curatorian Training for Today's Art Museum." *Curator*, Vol. IX (March 1966), pp. 51-61.

The author reviews the changing nature of the American art museum over the last fifty years and the similarly changing demands confronting curators and aspiring curators. He reviews a variety of museum training programs, historical and contemporary; discusses the necessary balance between academic and experiential preparation; and notes the pitfalls confronting the curator who must be adept at dealing with a bewildering array of subordinates, superordinates, clients, and publics. (DAJ)

221. Graves, Helen. "Comparative Political Internships: Assuring Academic Validity." *Teaching Political Science*, Vol. VII (January 1980), pp. 219-230.

Through the placement of American students in foreign government agencies, future policy professionals gain a valuable perspective on their careers. Students from the University of Michigan, Dearborn, who had completed internships in government agencies in Toronto and Ottawa, were forced to confront their ethnocentrism and inexperience, were exposed to different definitions and expectations about the policy process, and gained a broader understanding of solutions to policy problems and potential role models. (DAJ)

222. Hogan, Patricia, and Carol Stapp. "The Best of All Possible Internships." *Museum News*, Vol. LVII (November-December 1978), pp. 59-63.

The authors, a museum intern and a museum intern supervisor, discuss their experience (from "different sides of the fence") of the role, structure, and evaluation of the internship in museum education. (DAJ)

Luey, Beth. "Teaching for Nonteaching Careers." See no. *836.*

Morrissey, Charles T. "Public Historians and Oral History: Problems of Concept and Method." See no. *1341.*

Oral history is essential to the work of the public historian. It fills the gap in the archival record, recaptures the emotional tenor of the past, provides explanations about behavior, and adds information about groups and areas of life unrepresented in the documentary record. In designing an oral history project, the public historian must educate his patrons, perhaps in a one-day seminar, about the techniques of oral history research, its potential uses and importance to the sponsoring institution or organization, and the problems it necessarily involves (for example, transcribing, editing, and control of the memoir). (DAJ)

223. "Museum Studies." *Museum News*, Vol. LVII (November-December 1978), pp. 19-26.

In this special section of *Museum News*, the Museum Studies Committee of the American Association of Museums presents its report on "current museum training in relation to the professional needs of the museum community and to the public it serves" and its recommended "minimum standards for museum training programs." The section includes "Statement on Preparation for Professional Museum Careers," "Minimum Standards for Professional Museum Training Programs," and "Museum Positions, Duties, and Responsibilities." (DAJ)

224. "Museum Studies: A Second Report." *Museum News*, Vol. LIX (October 1980), pp. 26-40.

An update on the 1978 Report of the AAM Museum Studies Committee (see no. *223*), this report "suggests qualifications for [fifteen typical museum positions], describes the results of a survey of hiring practices, salaries, and fringe benefits, and a survey of museum training programs," and lists questions prospective students should ask as they consider museum training programs. (DAJ)

225. Quimby, George I., and James D. Nason. "New Staff for a New Museum." *Museum News*, Vol. LV (May-June 1977), pp. 50-52.

The authors, respectively the director and chair of the Division of Anthropology at the Burke Memorial Washington State Museum in Seattle, describe a museum training program developed cooperatively with the Makah tribe. The program was devised to train members of the Makah tribe who would be responsible for the development of a tribal museum related to archaeological work done in northwestern Washington. The article describes the program curriculum, including courses in museology, ethnography, cataloging and data retrieval, artifact reproduction, and exhibits, and reviews the actual evolution of the program over three years. (DAJ)

226. Winkler, Karen J. "Oral History." *Chronicle of Higher Education*, Vol. XXI (October 14, 1980), p. 3.

Winkler reports on papers delivered at the Oral History Association Meeting in Durango, Colorado, October 10, 1980. The author discusses oral history as it relates to the new field of "public" history, in which historians must meet demands associated with team-based, client-oriented research. Applications of oral history to this field are many, including historic preservation, entertainment, and gerontology. The author also notes the difficulties associated with contracted oral history work: invasion of privacy, conflict of interest, commercialization, selective editing, and piracy. (DAJ)

CHAPTER 3

PUBLIC HISTORY: BUSINESS MANAGEMENT

Robert W. Pomeroy III, editor

This chapter treats seven broad areas of business management that are of interest to practicing public historians. Latitude has been given to the terms "business" and "management" in order to provide a core of references that describe how activities are organized and directed for economic ends, keeping in mind at all times the special requirements of historians. The readings cover both theory and practice. Some deal with the philosophy of the covered areas, while others are guidebooks to procedure—how-to-do-it.

Most categories of the Standard Industrial Classification are represented, although a number of references consider management in relation to manufacturing. This form of industrial activity is most commonly singled out in the literature of business; more important, these writings offer information applicable to many other industries, whereas the reverse tends not to be true. Although manufacturing receives the lion's share of attention from students of business, historians should interest themselves in many other industries. No single industrial preserve should monopolize historical application or employment.

All sizes of business are treated in this chapter. Small business is essential; this category includes the consulting firm that the historians may manage as proprietor or partner. Big business represents another set of opportunities. A firm listed among the Fortune Five Hundred, fully capable of extensive specialization, can offer facilities that permit more concentration on writing and less on entrepreneurship.

The first section, "General Works," opens with citations of basic texts on economics and then narrows to the field of business, concluding with references on business mangement. Six separate sections follow in specific areas of management. Production management is not included because the subject is treated in other chapters. Distribution is treated as an aspect of marketing. The six specific topics should be approached stereographically. They may be viewed from the perspective of support, viewed as necessary for the economic well-being of the enterprise. They may be useful to the historian either as a manager or as an employee. They can also be regarded as career opportunities.

The section "Human Resources" concentrates on the ways a firm organizes, administers, and develops its staff. Historians, given their traditional concern for teaching, have a special interest in this matter.

The section "Financial Resources" describes the cycle of estimating, raising, applying, accounting for, and analyzing financing. No enterprise, public or private, can be maintained without due consideration of this subject. The historian's role in shaping the basis for managerial decision making remains to be exploited.

The subjects covered in the section "Information Management" should receive particular scrutiny. Archives and records management, library science, oral history, historical research and writing, and cliometric analysis are all expressions of information management. The historian is in the unique position of understanding the associated skills, of possessing the historical knowledge applicable to numerous business endeavors, of having the ability to manage information not as a relic or a bit of machine-readable data but as a vital resource. The implications for society are imposing; so are the opportunities for historians.

The section "Marketing" treats a subject that has received bad copy from humanists, especially the particulars of advertising and sales. Public historians deal significantly with intangibles, and the distribution of intangibles depends upon effective marketing. Public history, a rediscovered field that is unfamiliar to the public, requires a special effort on the part of its practitioners to market, advertise, and sell its products.

The subjects treated in the section "Internal and External Relations" range widely—from research, analysis, writing, and speaking to convincing third parties of the merits of one's enterprise. As such the area is closely linked to marketing and distribution. A number of historians are already employed in these activities. While they have often met with considerable success, many fear that they have lost their identities as historians. Reshaping of duties and enhanced professional confidence may alter this perception.

The section "Compliance and Responsibility" treats an area that involves close cooperation with another profession—the law. Corporate offices dealing with ethics and responsibility do exist; they might well benefit from the guidance of historians. The professional ethics of the practicing historical consultant remain quite unformulated, and require serious definition, for the protection of both client and historian.

Chapter 3 concludes with a section on reference works. Given the highly selective nature of this chapter, and the breadth of topics involved in business management, such aids take on special importance. Nevertheless, they should be approached with caution. Technological change, particularly in areas such as information management, speed the obsolescence of citations. Readers are urged to develop their own systems for monitoring current literature and seeking out fresh sources, whether by computerized bibliographic data bases or more conventional means.

A fundamental purpose of this chapter is to encourage its users to expand their knowledge of the material world. Little mention is made of this subject in traditional historical training, an omission that seems a shame. Just as a thorough understanding of history is a requirement for good management, so is a sound understanding of enlightened business theory and practice a requirement for good public history.

I. General Works

227. Baughn, William H., and Charles W. Walker, eds. *The Banker's Handbook*, Rev. ed. Homewood, Ill.: Dow Jones-Irwin, 1978.

The editors present a comprehensive review of current banking practices. Some 104 experts have contributed to the handbook's eighty-seven chapters. (RWP)

228. Boone, Louis E., and David L. Kurts. *Contemporary Business*. 2d ed. New York: Holt, Rinehart, and Winston, 1979.

This stimulating, inclusive text for the introductory business course integrates theory with actual business applications. Each chapter includes outlines of student behavioral objectives, profiles of interesting personalities, discussions of controversial issues, and real case studies. (ABA)

229. Brownlee, W. Elbert. *Dynamics of Ascent: A History of the American Economy*. New York: Knopf, 1974, 1979.

The author presents an economic analysis of the growth of the nation. (RJM)

230. Bruchey, Stuart. *Growth of the Modern American Economy*. New York: Dodd, Mead, 1975.

Bruchey provides an overview of the key economic components in the development of the nation. (RJM)

231. Chandler, Alfred D., Jr. *Strategy and Structure: Chapters in the History of the American Industrial Enterprise*. Cambridge, Mass.: M.I.T. Press, 1969.

This investigation of the changing strategy and structure of large American industrial enterprises was begun as an experiment in writing comparative business history. Following an introduction to the historical setting, four companies are examined: Du Pont, General Motors, Standard Oil (New Jersey), and Sears Roebuck. Further considerations on comparative analysis and multidivisional structure complete the study. (RWP)

232. Chandler, Alfred D., Jr., and Herman Daems, eds. *Managerial Hierarchies: Comparative Perspectives on the Rise of the Modern Industrial Enterprise*. Har-

vard Studies in Business History, 32. Cambridge, Mass.: Harvard University Press, 1980.

This collection includes seven essays by scholars that focus on the rise of modern managerial hierarchies in the four leading Western economies (U.S.A., U.K., Germany, France), with some of the broader implications of this development. (LMD-HBR)

233. Cochran, Thomas C. *American Business in the Twentieth Century*. Cambridge: Harvard University Press, 1972.

A leading business historian presents his perspective on American business and the relations of business to society in this century. This work appeared originally as *The American Business System* (1957). (RWP)

234. Cochran, Thomas C. *Business in American Life: A History*. New York: McGraw-Hill, 1972.

A distinguished historian offers this synthetic interpretation of business in America, a "history of the relation of business to its environment." It covers four periods from 1607 to 1970 and includes notes and an extensive bibliographical guide. (RWP)

235. Drucker, Peter F. *Management: Tasks, Responsibilities, Practices*. New York: Harper and Row, 1974.

A leading authority discusses the process of management, the characteristics of the manager, and the structure and role of the top management team. He provides a comprehensive bibliography. (RWP)

236. Drucker, Peter F. *The Age of Discontinuity: Guidelines to Our Changing Society*. New York: Harper and Row, 1968.

Age of Discontinuity is a book for managers. Drucker points out that the realities of the past would be far different than those of the future. He covers knowledge technologies, the shift from an international to a world economy, the society of organization, and the knowledge society. (MKP)

237. Gwartney, James D. *Economics: Private and Public Choice*. New York: Academic, 1976.

This college-level text concentrates on political economy. The history of economic thought is emphasized, and current and classical issues are subjected to economic analysis. It presents both microeconomics and macroeconomics. (RWP)

238. Harvard Business Review. *Business Policy: Part I*. Boston: Harvard Business Review, 1981.

Changing times call for new policies in managing a business. This collection of fifteen articles reprinted from the *Harvard Business Review* highlights critical areas in business policy and provides solutions to fit tomorrow's needs. Topics discussed include: the special skills of the general manager; the assessment of a company's strengths, weaknesses, and executive integrity; the involvement of top executives in corporate planning; and the challenge of managing for economic performance. Executive development, decision making, the management of change, and business leadership are also examined. (HBR)

239. Harvard Business Review. *International Business.* Boston: Harvard Business Review, 1981.

The thirteen articles reprinted from the *Harvard Business Review* that appear in this volume should provide reading for managers, business students, social scientists, and others who follow international business. The first section focuses on the social, cultural, and political problems of doing business in a foreign country. The second section describes various methods, approaches, and concepts that have proved helpful in making overseas operations more efficient and effective. (HBR)

240. Harvard Business Review. *Management of Nonprofit Organizations: Part I.* Boston: Harvard Business Review, 1981.

To meet the needs of all those interested in better management of hospitals, welfare agencies, community centers, and other nonprofit organizations, the *Harvard Business Review* has compiled this volume of nine reprint articles. Some of the varied problems and issues addressed in this collection are the need of hospitals for real management skills, the role of businessmen in the development of the modern hospital, government use of nonprofit companies, the nation's health care problems, and the future of federal contract research centers. (HBR)

241. Harvard Business Review. *Small Business: Part I.* Boston: Harvard Business Review, 1982.

This selection of sixteen articles reprinted from the *Harvard Business Review* probes a range of vital topics, from ownership and control to marketing management. The volume is of interest to small-business owners and those considering entrepreneurship. (HBR)

242. Harvard Business Review. *The Harvard Business Review Library.* Boston: Harvard Business Review, 1981.

This huge collection reprints more than sixteen thousand articles from the *Harvard Business Review* on the major issues of management. The 108-volume library is organized into eight major groupings: general management; organizational behavior; managerial economics; quantitative approaches to decision making; marketing; finance; international; planning and control; production and operations. A separate index, classified by author and subject, is available. Volumes are available separately or as a complete set. Certain volumes of particular interest to public historians are cited elsewhere in this chapter. (RWP)

243. Hawkes, G. R. *Economics for Historians*. Cambridge and New York: Cambridge Press, 1980.

This basic text places special emphasis on the elements of macroeconomic theory useful to historians who seek to explore national events and processes. (RJM)

244. Heilbroner, Robert L., and Lester C. Thurlow. *The Economic Problem*. Englewood Cliffs, N.J.: Prentice-Hall, 1968, 1981.

The authors provide a general introduction to economics as a social science for novices. Concepts are covered from the bird's and worm's eye perspectives— microeconomics, demand for output, growth and related questions, international economics, socioeconomic systems, statistics, and econometrics. (RJM)

245. Koontz, Harold, and Cyril O'Donnel. *Management*. 7th rev. ed. New York: McGraw-Hill, 1980.

The authors provide a conceptual framework for the nature of management. They discuss planning, organizing, staffing, directing, and controlling. The manager is presented in his social setting. References are listed at the end of each of the thirty-four chapters. (RWP)

246. Koontz, Harold, and Robert M. Fulmer. *A Practical Introduction to Business*. 3d. ed. Homewood, Ill.: Irwin, 1981.

The authors provide a basic introduction to business, stressing its nature, unity, and importance. They offer simple exposition, extensive illustrations, examples, and glossaries of terms. (RWP)

247. Krooss, Herman E., and Charles Gilbert. *American Business History*. Englewood Cliffs, N.J.: Prentice-Hall, 1972.

This business history, written by economic historians, emphasizes the contributions business has made to American life. It discusses the response of business to various problems. (RWP)

248. Mali, Paul, ed. *Management Handbook: Operating Guidelines, Techniques, and Practices*. New York: Wiley, 1981.

Some sixty authors, representing major corporations, consulting firms, and educational institutions, produced this extensive reference book. A large body of up-to-date management knowledge is covered, providing a useful reference tool when read in tandem with works on business theory. Tables, charts, references, and other resources accompany most of the sixty-seven articles. Each major section ends with a chapter of sample management forms and checklists. The work is organized to follow levels and areas of responsibility in an organization. (RWP)

249. Mescon, Michael H., Michael Albert, and Franklin Khedouri. *Management*. New York: Harper and Row, 1981.

Twenty chapters present a comprehensive view at an introductory level of management. After presenting an overview of the internal and external environments in organizations, the authors explain the linking processes—communication and decision making. Separate chapters explore management functions of planning, organizing, motivating, and controlling, followed by extensive coverage of power, leadership, conflict, change, and group dynamics. Management science and human resource management (personnel) are also introduced. Extensive illustrations and features are provided, the latter primarily excerpts from periodicals and books to aid in understanding concepts. (SAA)

250. Porter, Glenn, ed. *Encyclopedia of American Economic History: Studies of the Principal Movements and Ideas*. 3 vols. New York: Charles Scribner's Sons, 1980.

This work is a compilation of seventy-two commissioned articles by foremost scholars in their respective fields. It is arranged in five sections: historiography; chronology of economic history; the framework of economic growth (including economic indicators, business functions, and areas of business); the institutional framework (including labor, law, politics, and competition); and the social framework (including work, family, education, women, blacks, and poverty). (LMD-HBR)

251. Rachman, David J., and Michael H. Mescon. *Business Today*. 2d ed. New York: Random House, 1979.

This book offers broad coverage of nearly all business topics, including management, marketing, finance, quantitative tools, and the environments of business (legal, governmental, ethical, and technological). For example, chapter 2 offers a complete discussion of the forms of business organization: sole proprietorship, partnership, and corporation, along with a discussion of cooperatives and franchises. The section on finance, part 4 of the work, provides extensive coverage of basic concepts: short-term and long-term financing, the money and banking systems, the stock market, risk management, and insurance. An overview of business law is presented in chapter 14, which, among other things, introduces contract, agency, and tort law and bankruptcy. (SAA)

252. Reinecke, John A., and William F. Schoell. *Introduction to Business: A Contemporary View*. 2d ed. Boston: Allyn and Bacon, 1977.

Comprehensive contents include: economic ideas for business; business ownership, organization, and management; production; marketing; accounting; financial institutions; insurance and its use; personnel; labor relations; computer use; small businesses; international businesses; environment and human values; economy, law, and technology; and career choices. (ABA)

253. Rutenberg, David P. *Multinational Management*. Boston: Little, Brown, 1982.

This text provides a comprehensive analysis of multinational organizational structure, finance, manufacturing, marketing, and executive development. Case histories of actual firms introduce each of the eleven subsections. Emphasis is placed on decision making of the multinational enterprise at both headquarters and foreign-subsidiary levels. Long-term strategic policy as well as tactical planning and implementation are analyzed. Questions are posed for students. A companion manual may also be purchased, containing suggested case solutions and teaching notes for each chapter. (RWP)

254. Terry, George R. *Principles of Management*. Homewood, Ill.: Irwin, 1977.

This text was developed to reflect the dynamic changes occurring in the management field. However, the purpose of the book, to help students acquire management knowledge and management skills, remains the same. To achieve the purpose, the book is structured around the modified management process approach, a familiar central core around which current managerial concepts and activities are presented. (ABA)

255. Wiegand, G. Carl. *Economics: Its Nature and Importance*. Woodbury, N.Y.: Barron's Educational Series, 1976.

This introduction to economic principles contains a section on the history of selected economic institutions and two sections on economic theory along with a fifty-page glossary. (RWP)

II. Human Resources

256. ACME, Inc. *Common Body of Knowledge for Management Consultants*. Rev. ed. New York: Association of Management Consulting Firms, 1976.

This publication helps define the knowledge a management consultant must possess to be qualified to give professional counsel and to help clarify concepts of management, particularly the task of managing. (EDH)

257. ACME, Inc. *How to Get the Best Results from Management Consultants*. New York: Association of Management Consulting Firms, 1981.

This booklet is designed to provide managers with appropriate information so that they can make the best decisions on when, where, and how their organizations might use management consultants with the best results. (EDH)

258. ACME, Inc. *Personal Qualifications of Management Consultants*. Rev. ed. New York: Association of Management Consulting Firms, 1971.

This report identifies and defines certain capacities and attributes that are essential for management consulting work, and it summarizes various types and procedures of measurement for determining the presence of these characteristics. (EDH)

259. Argyris, Chris. *Intervention Theory and Method*. Reading, Mass.: Addison-Wesley, 1973.

This difficult book concentrates on intervention practice as an aspect of organization development (OD). This discussion is the closest thing to a definition of the professional values associated with OD. (AOM)

260. Blake, Robert R., and Jane S. Mouton. *Consultation*. Reading, Mass.: Addison-Wesley, 1976.

This work offers an overview of various consulting methods according to a structured model called the "Consulcube." This concept integrates three dimensions (units of change, kinds of interventions, and focal issues), providing a conceptual framework for the practitioner. (AOM)

261. Brown, Deaver. *The Entrepreneur's Guide*. New York: Macmillan, 1980.

For those who have thought about striking out on their own, this short book may give useful advice about starting and managing a new venture. Brown, a successful entrepreneur, gives practical information on marketing, sales, finance, and operations as well as an evaluation of an entrepreneurial career. (LMD-HBR)

262. Burack, Elmer H., and Nicholas J. Mathys. *Career Management in Organizations: A Practical Human Resource Planning Approach*. Lake Forest, Ill.: Brace-Park, 1980.

The authors, professors of management as well as human resource counselors and workshop leaders, have benefited from assistance from many practitioners and companies that provided documents and data on programs developed to respond to the need for better career planning. The book is in three parts: career management; careers and the individual; and applications and issues. (LMD-HBR)

263. Connors, Tracey Daniel, ed. *The Nonprofit Organization Handbook*. New York: McGraw-Hill, 1980.

Twenty-eight contributors from industry and nonprofit organizations provide advice on management and organization. Human resources, funding, public relations, and fiscal management are discussed as well as techniques such as management by objective. The handbook includes extensive examples, problems and solutions, checklists, and reading lists. (RWP)

264. Craig, Robert L., ed. *Training and Development Handbook: A Guide to Human Resource Development*, 2d ed. New York: McGraw-Hill, 1976.

Sponsored by the American Society for Training and Development, experts review the current body of knowledge in the field of human resource development. Beginning with a brief history of industrial training, organization theory, program development, media and methods are then discussed in forty-seven chapters. The utility of this compendium is pointed out in the foreword: no single academic base exists for the comprehensive set of skills and information required by human resource development professionals. (RWP)

265. Famularo, Joseph J. *Organization Planning Manual.* New York: AMA-COM, 1979.

This work is a reference manual for persons interested in (1) one hundred sample organization charts illustrating various aspects of corporate organization; (2) sample descriptions representing specific positions; and (3) sample policy statements for a variety of interests and subjects, from "accident prevention" to "working conditions." The data were collected from contacts with about two hundred companies representing various sizes and industries. Some examples of hospitals also appear. (LMD-HBR)

266. Fetridge, Clark, and Robert S. Minor, eds. *Office Administration Handbook.* 5th ed. Chicago: Dartnell Corporation, 1975.

The editors provide extensive information on office administration, including informative details on twenty-three thousand separate personnel and administrative matters. (RWP)

267. French, Wendell L., Cecil H. Bell, Jr., and Robert A. Zawacki. *Organization Development: Theory, Practice, and Research.* Dallas: Business Publications, 1978.

This book provides an overall description of organization development (OD). It traces the origins of OD, discusses methods and techniques, and provides critical evaluation along with a discussion of prospects for the future. (AOM)

268. Galbraith, Jay R. *Organization Design.* Reading, Mass.: Addison-Wesley, 1977.

This comprehensive work is of particular interest to practitioners involved in designing or diagnosing organizations. It provides an overview of current approaches to the field and provides a model that integrates various criteria for effective organization design. (AOM)

269. Genua, Robert L. *The Employer's Guide to Interviewing: Strategy and Tactics for Picking a Winner.* Englewood Cliffs, N.J.: Prentice-Hall, 1979.

This guide seeks to help those involved in hiring employees to "conduct an effective interview, evaluate and interpret the data gathered from the interview, make objective final decisions on candidates, and better understand strengths and weaknesses as an interviewer." (LMD-HBR)

270. Harvard Business Review. *Leadership: Part I*. Boston: Harvard Business Review, 1981.

Executives from all types of companies and organizations gain new insights into the complex issue of leadership through this collection. The problems of executive obsolescence, the fear of success, delegation, and executive time investment are examined. Other topics explored include the self-concept of the manager, the decision-making process, the unique role of the company president, managerial knowledge, and the management of change. (HBR)

271. Harvard Business Review. *Organizational Development: Part II*. Boston: Harvard Business Review, 1981.

What creates strong, flexible, growing organizations? For managers challenged by this complex question, HBR has selected seventeen articles on organizational development. Creativity, unhuman organizations, motivation, and organizational effectiveness under stress are among the topics handled in this collection. Specific recommendations for improving various aspects of the management function are included as well as methods for adapting the organization to new technology, measuring organizational performance, and helping engineers to achieve their career goals. (HBR)

272. Harvard Business Review. *Personnel Management: Part I*. Boston: Harvard Business Review, 1981.

How to manage people has become one of the most critical problems facing executives today. These articles treat personnel management. Problems related to motivating employees, handling the worrisome question of appraising workers' performance, establishing a fair set of pay differentials, and evaluating and applying the new supervisory tools provided by the social sciences are among the topics discussed in this volume. (HBR)

273. Harvard Business Review. *Training and Developing Executives*. Boston: Harvard Business Review, 1981.

Basic changes are going on in thinking related to executive training and development. These fourteen articles focus on these conceptual, technical, and philosophical changes. This collection also explores changes that reflect new elements and emphases in management training, such as increased attention to women and minority groups. The first section deals with new routes to the goal of improved management performance. Explanations for the disappointing results of many management programs and techniques are proposed in the second section. The final section analyzes equal opportunity, executive obsolescence, the success of General Motors, and Japanese industry. (HBR)

274. Irish, Richard K. *Go Hire Yourself an Employer*. Rev. enl. ed. Garden City, N.Y.: Anchor, Doubleday, 1978.

Richard Irish likes to shock the reader. "Parents, peers, and placement counselors stress career—professional development. To this day, I've developed a lively prejudice for the word 'career.' It strikes me as the phoniest word in the lexicon.'' For the author, top-jobs are not careers but "judgment jobs," those that demand the commitment of those motivated by "self-potency." Most people are not so motivated, he believes. The format of the book is question/answer; subjects range from the working woman to "le résumé." (JMC)

275. Jaques, Elliott. *A General Theory of Bureaucracy*. New York: Halsted Press, 1976; *Levels of Abstraction in Logic and Human Action*. London: Heinemann Educational Books, 1978.

These two books offer a theory of human development and intellectual capacity. (AOM)

276. Keeling, B. Lewis, Norman F. Kallaus, and John J. W. Neuner. *Administrative Office Management*. 7th ed. Cincinnati, Ohio: South-Western, 1978.

This work covers the theory and practice of office management and reviews both administrative and coordinating functions. Among the topics included are management thought, information systems, management science, cost control, office planning, equipment, cost reduction, and current office problems. (LMD-RWP)

277. Levinson, Harry. *Executive: The Guide to Responsive Management*. Cambridge, Mass.: Harvard University Press, 1981.

The author demonstrates how the executive can adopt the role of teacher, promote a cooperative atmosphere for work, and guide his organization to a responsible role in society—all without losing sight of his primary role of insuring the firm's survival. The key to success is generating and sustaining a positive spirit in employees. (RWP)

278. Levinson, Harry, with Janice Molinari and Andrew G. Spohn. *Organizational Diagnosis*. Cambridge, Mass.: Harvard University Press, 1979.

The author describes his method of diagnosing and analyzing organizations; the method has been applied, and it can be highly successful. It integrates psychoanalytic, sociological, and systems theories. It deals specifically with analyzing and assessing an organization's history, synthesizing data into a comprehensive description, conducting interviews, and presenting results. Details on implementation are included along with interviewing guides, sampling guides, and references. (RWP)

279. Lippitt, Gordon L. *Organization Renewal*. Englewood Cliffs, N.J.: Prentice-Hall, 1969.

This work treats the diagnosis of organizational problems and their cures. It discusses the interaction of organizations and their external environment and also the stages of organizational growth. (AOM)

280. McVicar, Marjorie, and Julia F. Craig. *Minding My Own Business: Entrepreneurial Women Share Their Secrets for Success.* New York: Richard Marek, 1981.

This book, based on the experiences of over one hundred female entrepreneurs, is a guide for women starting their own businesses. The elementary, and crucial, considerations of finding the right idea or purpose for a new business, forming a business plan, and initial steps in setting up a business begin the volume. Potential women entrepreneurs are advised on how to get financing, office space, and advertising as well as on engaging lawyers and accountants. Some types of businesses women might start—food services, retailing, and manufacturing— are briefly explored. The authors aim the book at readers with backgrounds like their own—both are former housewives who wanted to start their own businesses. The practical advice is interspersed with short vignettes about women entrepreneurs. Concerns such as day care and the pros and cons of operating in one's home are also examined. (NCB-HBR)

281. Medley, Anthony H. *Sweaty Palms: The Neglected Art of Being Interviewed.* Belmont, Calif.: Lifetime Learning Publications, Wadsworth, 1978.

This book reminds the reader that while many books and services teach one how to write a résumé and how to get an interview, it is knowing what to do in the interview itself that can ultimately lead to a job. Medley believes that people who make costly mistakes in the interview do so because they are unprepared. Among other things, he treats types of interviews, the significance of the choice of the color of one's dress, and the dynamics of silence and power. (JMC)

282. Merry, Uri, and Melvin E. Allerhand. *Developing Teams and Organizations.* Reading, Mass.: Addison-Wesley, 1977.

This book provides a general background on organizational development and gives step-by-step instructions on how to conduct interventions. (AOM)

283. Patten, Thomas H., Jr. *Manpower Planning and the Development of Human Resources.* New York: Wiley, 1971.

This primer offers a comprehensive overview of the entire spectrum of activity in the area of human relations. (AOM)

284. Pigors, Paul, and Charles A. Myers. *Personnel Administration: A Point of View and a Method.* 9th ed. New York: McGraw-Hill, 1981.

The authors maintain the point of view that people are the critical component of any organization. Moreover, they see the personnel function as increasingly significant. The first part of the book explores five key topics: management and personnel administration, the individual in the organization, diagnosing organizational health, the development of human resources and the personnel policy system, and pay and services. Illustrative case studies follow this discussion. (MVC-HBR)

285. Schein, Edgar H. *Career Dynamics: Matching Individual and Organizational Needs.* Reading, Mass.: Addison-Wesley, 1978.

This book describes the process of career evolution from the point of view of the organization trying to improve its human resource planning and from the point of view of the individual trying to develop a viable career throughout the entire life course. Part one deals with the individual and the life cycle, part two describes individual organization interactions, focusing on the development of career anchors, and part three describes the characteristics and dynamics of human resource planning and development systems. (LB)

286. Schein, Edgar H. *Organizational Psychology.* 3d ed. Englewood Cliffs, N.J.: Prentice-Hall, 1980.

This short textbook lays out the major issues of human behavior in organizations. Part one deals with the individual/organization interaction, and part two explores motivation and assumptions about human nature. Part three deals with leadership and participation. Part four describes the issue of groups in organization. Part five deals with organization structure and dynamics, focusing on an open-systems model of organization. The book reviews the major theories in the field but presents them in terms of an integrated open-systems model. (LB)

287. Walker, James W. *Human Resources Planning.* New York: McGraw-Hill, 1980.

This overview describes three major areas: needs forecasting, performance management, and career management. (AOM)

288. Warren, Malcolm W. *Training for Results: A Systems Approach to the Development of Human Resources in Industry.* 2d ed. Reading, Mass.: Addison-Wesley, 1979.

The seventeen chapters of this work describe various approaches to learning. The author covers the analysis of needs, training methods, costing, design, management, and organization. Charts, checklists for planning, evaluation guides, and a bibliography are also included. (RWP)

III. Financial Resources

289. Anthony, Robert N., and James S. Reese. *Management Accounting: Texts and Cases.* 6th ed. Homewood, Ill.: Irwin, 1979.

This work is aimed at management trainees or students with no accounting background. Following an introductory chapter on the way management uses accounting information, the text deals with four areas: accounting structure; use of information in financial statements; accounting in management control; accounting in business decisions. Numerous statements, illustrations, references, cases, and questions are given. (RWP)

290. Anthony, Robert N., John Dearden, and Richard F. Vancil. *Management Control Systems: Text, Cases, and Readings*. 3d ed. Homewood, Ill.: Irwin, 1976.

This text focuses on management control from traditional points of view, such as cost accounting and budgeting, and in new areas—multinationals and service and nonprofit organizations. It is designed for students with some familiarity with management accounting. Extensive use is made of cases; questions are given. (RWP)

291. Bickelhaupt, David L. *General Insurance*. 10th ed. Homewood, Ill.: Irwin, 1979.

This text introduces the concept of insurance risk and management. This work also deals with the structure of the insurance industry, taking up life, health, property, and liability insurance and also the industry's future. (RWP)

292. Brigham, Eugene F. *Fundamentals of Financial Management*. New York: Holt, Rinehart, and Winston, 1978.

Brigham offers an introduction to three traditional areas of finance: investments, capital markets, and business finance. After testing valuation concepts, the text demonstrates how financial management is employed to help maximize the value of a firm. (RWP-SBA)

293. Brigham, Eugene F., and Roy L. Crum. *Cases in Managerial Finance*. 4th ed. Hinsdale, Ill.: Dryden, 1980.

The authors cover analysis, planning and control; asset management, financial instruments and markets; financial structure; and other related topics. This standard work presents cases, two to three pages in length, keyed to each topic. Questions are then presented, designed to be solved by students in no more than approximately two hours. (RWP)

294. Cashin, James A., and Garland C. Owens. *Auditing*. 2d ed. New York: Ronald, 1963.

Cashin and Owens discuss auditing practices, professional responsibilities, evaluation, auditing itself, reporting, and special related activities. Chapters on electronic data processing and statistical sampling are included. (RWP)

295. Foulke, Roy A. *Practical Financial Statement Analysis*. 6th ed. New York: McGraw-Hill, 1968.

This seven-part volume summarizes the analysis of financial statements and provides a brief historical introduction to the field. Particular subjects are the analysis of small enterprises, ratio and financial statement analysis, the philosophy of financial statements, and the evolution of accounting principles and practices. (RWP)

296. Foundation Center. *The Foundation Directory*. 8th ed. New York: Foundation Center, 1981.

This directory describes 3,363 U.S. foundations, which in aggregate make 89 percent of all this country's grants. Details are presented on over six hundred corporate foundations. It includes statistical breakdowns, tabbed cross-indices, charts, and tables. (RWP)

297. Gross, Malvern J., Jr., and William Warshauer, Jr. *Financial and Accounting Guide for Nonprofit Organizations*. 3d ed. New York: Wiley, 1979.

This is a working guide to financial reporting, accounting, and control, as well as to federal and state reporting requirements for nonprofit organizations. It includes key financial concepts, financial statement presentation, and guidelines for accounting, control, and reporting. Examples of financial statements and a bibliography are given. (RWP)

298. Harvard Business Review. *Finance: Revised Parts 1 and 2*. Boston: Harvard Business Review, 1981.

This collection of fifteen articles considers in depth the crucial decision of investment choice, appropriate vehicle, and policy making. Concerning the investment decision, this volume explores the use of decision trees in capital investment, investment analysis, the problem of measuring the productivity of capital, new methods for evaluating debt capacity, and the use of risk analysis in capital investment. The second section discusses the special pitfalls of investing in special automatic equipment and the opportunities presented by investment financing. Captive finance companies and the problems of young entrepreneurs seeking financing for a new enterprise are also handled in this section. Section three, focusing on the task of policy making, considers: how a divergence of attitudes between management and stockholders toward corporate profits can lead to differences in major policy decisions; the advantages for small companies of selling stock to the public; repurchasing stock as a method of revitalizing equity; and the advantages of fitting the fiscal year to the business. (HBR)

299. Helfert, Erich A. *Techniques of Financial Analysis*. 5th ed. Homewood, Ill.: Irwin, 1982.

This volume provides the basic skills, concepts, and knowledge required for financial analysis. Cases, problems, and exercises are presented; references accompany each chapter. (RWP)

300. Jones, Ray G., and Dean Dudley. *Essentials of Finance*. 2d ed. Englewood Cliffs, N.J.: Prentice-Hall, 1981.

The authors cover three major areas of finance—financial management, investments, and financial institutions. Topics are the management and financing of current and fixed assets, including the cost of capital, financial structure, and valuation; investment alternatives such as U.S. government, municipal, and corporate bonds, preferred and common stocks, convertibles, and options; and fundamental technical and portfolio analysis. Additional topics include the time value of money, risk, small-business finance, and international finance. There is no treatment of real estate, insurance, and fund raising. (LJM)

301. Jones, Reginald L., and H. George Trentin. *Budgeting: Key to Planning and Control*. Rev. ed. New York: American Management Association, 1971.

This guide to corporate budgeting is written in nontechnical language for managers. It emphasizes manufacturing firms. The authors discuss the interaction between planning and budgeting systems. Extensive diagrams, exhibits, and explanations are given. (RWP)

302. Levine, Sumner N., ed. *Financial Analyst's Handbook*. Vol. I: *Methods, Theory, and Portfolio Management*. Vol. II: *Analysis by Industry*. Homewood, Ill.: Dow Jones-Irwin, 1975.

The contents of these volumes transcend their titles; seventy-eight authorities take up numerous aspects of financial analysis. Both volumes begin with identical sections on financial analysis, "inside" information, and the Securities and Exchange Commission. Volume I concentrates on analytic techniques—financial and economic analysis, mathematical and statistical aids, and portfolio analysis. Volume II provides an introduction to the analysis of twenty-seven industries from aerospace to utilities. (RWP)

303. Mautz, Robert K., and Hussein S. Sharaf. *The Philosophy of Auditing*. American Accounting Association Monograph No. 6. Menasha, Wis.: American Accounting Association, 1964.

This work covers in detail the philosophy, methodology, and practice of auditing. Of particular interest to historians is the chapter "Evidence," which describes and compares the nature of evidence in five fields, including history. Ethical conduct, professional independence, and fair presentation are also covered. (RWP)

304. Meigs, Walter B., Charles E. Johnson, and Robert F. Meigs. *Accounting: The Basis for Business Decisions*. 4th ed. New York: McGraw-Hill, 1977.

The authors present accounting "as an essential part of the decision-making process for the voter, the taxpayer, the government official, the business manager, and the investor." This is a comprehensive volume. Written as a beginning-college-level text, it has a glossary at the end of each of the twenty-eight chapters as well as review questions, exercises, and numerous tables. (RWP)

305. Midgett, Elwin W. *An Accounting Primer: The ABC's of Accounting for the Non-Accountant.* New York: Mentor, 1971.

Midgett offers a concise, thorough introduction to the basics of accounting. Many central concepts concerning the organization and operation of a business are discussed. Charts and tables supplement the written text. (RWP)

306. Myers, Margaret G. *A Financial History of the United States.* New York: Columbia University Press, 1970.

Myers provides a historical review of public and private finance in the United States from the colonial period until the 1960s, appending notes and an extensive bibliography. (RWP)

307. Pendleton, Neil. *Fund Raising: A Guide for Non-Profit Organizations.* Englewood Cliffs, N.J.: Prentice-Hall, 1981.

This guidebook outlines the steps required for preparing, writing, and presenting fund-raising campaigns. It includes sample proposals, examples of forms and letters, and checklists as well as a glossary and bibliography. (RWP)

308. Seldin, Maury, ed. *The Real Estate Handbook.* Homewood, Ill.: Dow Jones-Irwin, 1980.

This is not a book to be read from cover to cover but rather a reference work to consult when needing authoritative and brief information about a range of real estate subjects. It is organized according to transactions analyses (including appraisals, feasibility, and value), marketing, financing (including chapters on sources), and investment (ten different types in terms of use, plus chapters on condominiums and on joint ventures and syndicates). An appendix summarizes the requirements of forty-one real estate designations in the United States and Canada. (LMD-HBR)

309. Suchman, Edward A. *Evaluation Research: Principles and Practice in Public Service and Social Action Programs.* New York: Russell Sage Foundation, 1968.

This work deals with applied social science research. The historical development of evaluative research is introduced; the needs, concepts, and types of evaluations are discussed, as are effects, administrative aspects, and the future of the fields. (RWP)

310. Sweeney, Allen, and John Wisner, Jr. *Budgeting Fundamentals for Non-financial Executives and Managers.* New York: McGraw-Hill, 1977.

This is an introductory work which "explains what budgets are, how they work, and how to prepare, present and most importantly—defend them." Tables and questions appear at the end of each chapter. (RWP)

311. Vangermeersch, Richard. *Financial Reporting Techniques in Twenty In-dustrial Companies Since 1861*. University of Florida Accounting Series No. 9. Ann Arbor, Mich.: University Microfilms, 1979.

Vangermeersch offers a synopsis of the history of financial accounting in the United States. He introduces the philosophy and presentation of balance sheets, income statements, and supplementary financial statements. (RWP)

312. White, Virginia P. *Grants: How to Find Out about Them and What to Do Next*. 3d ed. New York and London: Plenum, 1976.

Sources of information on grants as well as sources of granting are described in this volume. Government agencies, foundations, and businesses are included. The reader is counselled on all phases of a grant application. White attaches appendices on types of grants and government acronyms. (RWP)

313. Wright, Wilmer. *Management Accounting Simplified*. New York: McGraw-Hill, 1980.

As the title implies, the author, a consultant, wrote this short book "to help take the mystery out of accounting for nonfinancial executives by making it simple for them to understand management accounting." He covers such topics as flexible budgeting made easy, zero-based budgeting streamlined, determining true product costs, and models for automation of management accounting. The book concludes with more than eighty pages of forms, including physical spec-ification and rate forms, as well as a short glossary. (LMD-HBR)

IV. Information Management

314. Albert, Kenneth J., ed. *Handbook of Business Problem Solving*. New York: McGraw-Hill, 1980.

This compendium examines methods used by professional, corporate problem solvers. The sixty-one short chapters, written by one or more senior members of consulting firms, follow a practical "how-to" format, with an easy style and frequent use of charts, checklists, guidelines, and case examples. They are arranged within nine sections: top management strategy, planning, and control; top management organization, staffing, and development; marketing; new prod-ucts; human resources; information systems and data processing; cost control and cost reduction; production; physical distribution; and materials management. (LMD-HBR)

315. Allio, Robert J., and Malcolm W. Pennington, eds. *Corporate Planning: Techniques and Applications*. New York: AMACOM, 1979.

This collection includes forty-seven articles from *Planning Review*, dealing with resource planning, social responsibility, and business strategy, as well as the process and future of planning. (RWP)

316. Alter, Steven L. *Decision Support Systems: Current Practice and Continuing Challenges.* Reading, Mass.: Addison-Wesley, 1980.

The third and latest in the Addision-Wesley series on decision support, this volume complements the earlier books in the series through its broad mapping of the use of computer systems in managerial tasks across a range of organizations, types of decision situations, and system architectures. (PMS)

317. Armstrong, J. Scott. *Long-Range Forecasting: From Crystal Ball to Computer.* New York: Wiley, 1978.

This review of forecasting methods, written in a relaxed style, includes the technique of evaluating forecasting models. It is aimed at students as well as managers lacking background in the subject. (RWP)

318. Ascher, William. *Forecasting: An Appraisal for Policy-Makers and Planners.* Baltimore: Johns Hopkins University Press, 1978.

As the title indicates, this book is for managers interested in learning about the accuracy of forecasts. Ascher has examined long- and short-term forecasting of population, economics, energy, transportation, and technology; and he evaluates these for both accuracy and methodology. One of his important conclusions is that the core assumptions underlying a forecast are more important for accuracy than is the choice of method. Charts are used throughout to illustrate the errors of specific forecasts. (LMD-HBR)

319. Ashley, Ruth, in cooperation with Nancy B. Stern. *Background Math for a Computer World.* New York: Wiley, 1973.

This is a book of programmed instruction for non-mathematicians. Twelve chapters present basic facts, techniques, and questions and answers on areas essential to computer users. The basis of computer logic and number systems, flow charting, computer arithmetic, probability, statistics, linear equations, matrix algebra, and game theory are all introduced. (RWP)

320. Bohl, Marilyn. *Information Processing.* 3d ed. Chicago: Science Research Associates, 1980.

This book presents an up-to-date survey of electronic data processing, of computer hardware and software systems in use today, and of current developments that are building a base for further advancements. Additional study helps are available in a companion workbook. (PMS)

321. Brooks, Frederick, Jr. *The Mythical Man-Month: Essays on Software Engineering.* Reading, Mass.: Addison-Wesley, 1975.

Brooks was the project manager for one of the major development efforts in the brief history of computers—OS/360, the operating system for IBM's "third generation" series of computers, introduced in 1964. The main reason for writing this book was to review what happened and answer a question the founder of

IBM asked him: "Why is programming so hard to manage?" It explains not only why things so often go wrong but also identifies certain, almost universal laws of large-scale software development. (PGWK)

322. Clark, Ignatius F. *The Pattern of Expectations, 1644-2001*. New York: Basic Books, 1979.

A professor of English wrote this survey of nonecclesiastical prediction; he is a specialist in studies of the future. He supports the process of forecasting but warns that accurate, literal prediction does not exist. (RWP)

323. Coleman, Emily R., ed. *Information and Society*. Basking Ridge, N.J.: American Telephone and Telegraph Co., 1981.

Experts analyze the "information age" from three points of view: "Communications: Commerce and Culture," "Information Technology and Decision-Making," and "The New Media." An interpretive essay on information and knowledge of AT&T's Corporate Planning/Emerging Issues by the Group Division Manager, a historian, completes the study. (RWP)

324. Condon, Robert. *Data Processing with Applications*. Englewood Cliffs, N.J.: Prentice-Hall, 1978.

Condon provides students with enough knowledge about the computer so that it can be used effectively as a business tool. Emphasis is on what the computer does and can do, not necessarily on how it does it. Contents include: what the computer does; hardware and software; storage systems; input and output; programming, logic, and COBOL; business applications and accounting functions; marketing functions; management information systems; and planning computer systems. (PMS)

325. Cornish, Edward. *The Study of the Future: An Introduction to the Art and Science of Understanding and Shaping Tomorrow's World*. Washington: World Future Society, 1977.

Here is a general purpose introduction written by the president of the World Future Society in collaboration with staff members. It not only covers the world today and the shape of things to come but offers a historical overview, a chapter on methods, a chapter on eleven leading futurists and their ideas, and case histories on futuristics in practice. There is an annotated bibliography, along with bibliographical notes and an appendix covering the names of future-oriented organizations and periodicals. (LMD-HBR)

Dollar, Charles, and Richard J. Jensen. *Historian's Guide to Statistics*. See no. *31*.

Written as a practical guide to the use of quantitative methods and computers in historical research, this work provides an introduction to quantitative analysis and basic statistics for numerous business applications. The sections on computer applications provide some historical background. (RWP)

326. Eliason, Alan L. *Business Information Processing*. Chicago: Science Research Associates, 1980.

This text provides a comprehensive examination of the equipment, design, and management alternatives typical in today's information-processing environment. By emphasizing the applied use of the computer in business, this text seeks to meet the need for material that integrates the technology of computing with the design of business computer applications and with the management of these applications. (PMS)

327. Floud, Roderick. *An Introduction to Quantitative Methods for Historians*. 2d ed. New York: Methuen, 1980.

Floud provides a practical introduction to quantification, including classification and arranging of historical data, mathematics, statistics, and an introduction to computers. The focus is by no means limited to purely historical studies; the subject matter is essential to quantitative decision making. (RWP)

328. Grant, Eugene, L., W. Grant Ireson, and Richard S. Leavenworth. *Principles of Engineering Economy*. New York: Wiley, 1982.

This book has introduced generations of engineering students to the concepts and methods of economic analysis. It contains an extensive treatment of interest and the time value of money. Formulas are developed and tables are included for handling compound-interest factors in economic analysis. A number of techniques are presented for preparing economic studies to compare the cost and benefits of alternative capital expenditures. (JFD)

329. Harvard Business Review. *Case Methods: Part I*. Boston: Harvard Business Review, 1981.

In dramatic-dialogue form, this volume of fifteen reprint articles covers a wide range of business problems that confront today's top-level executives. These exercises in analysis, logical thinking, and decision making are useful to businessmen who aim to refine their own decision making. (HBR)

330. Harvard Business Review. *Forecasting*. Boston: Harvard Business Review, 1981.

In keeping with the growing uses, sophistication, and potential value of forecasting methods to management, HBR has compiled a volume of twelve reprint articles. Among the varied topics covered in this collection are the accuracy of long-range planning, the future emergence of new types of employee benefits and their anticipated impact on industry, and businessmen's expectations of the economy in the 1970s. Methods for developing solid manpower forecasting, for choosing the right forecasting technique, and for evaluating the signals of technological change are outlined in this collection. This volume also includes discussions of new means of technological forecasting, the inevitability of technological change, and the use of regression analysis. (HBR)

331. Harvard Business Review. *Management Information: Part I.* Boston: Harvard Business Review, 1981.

This selection of fourteen articles focuses on the applications of management systems that provide decision-making information. Specific problems related to information technology and decentralization, improving estimates involving uncertainty, and methods of multiproject control are discussed, as well as the management information crises and the choice of who is to control information systems. Other topics include the use of operations research in marketing, the building of a marketing information system, and the necessity of monitoring the market continuously. (HBR)

332. Harvard Business Review. *Planning: Part I.* Boston: Harvard Business Review, 1981.

The sixteen articles in this volume address topics of both a broad and specific nature. The important topic of long-range planning receives extensive coverage. In addition to outlining the necessary steps for successful long-range planning of industrial research, mathematical approaches to long-range planning, and methods for evaluating corporate strategy. New techniques of use to executives are explored, including profit planning, industrial dynamics, game simulation, and PERT. Specific problems related to the business community's stake in regional planning, the development of strategies for diversification, and methods for setting realistic profit goals are also discussed. (HBR)

333. Hershey, Robert. "Commercial Intelligence on a Shoestring." *Harvard Business Review*, Vol. V (September-October 1980), pp. 22-30.

The author discusses techniques of market research for small companies. He demonstrates the means of conducting effective monitoring and business intelligence at minimum cost. (RWP)

334. Heyel, Carl, ed. *The VNR Concise Guide to Management Decision Making.* New York: Van Nostrand Reinhold, 1980.

Heyel's handy reference volume revises and updates only those sections of his more comprehensive *The Encyclopedia of Management* (2d ed., 1973) that relate to managerial decision making. Concise discussions of its fourteen concepts or practices are arranged in three divisions: advanced practice in the conventional techniques of financial projections, statistics as a tool of decision making, and the newer management sciences. (LMD-HBR)

335. Hillier, Frederick S., and Gerald S. Lieberman. *Introduction to Operations Research*, 3d ed. San Francisco: Holden-Day, 1980.

This book is written for the serious student of quantitative analysis and not for the casual reader interested in improving his general knowledge of operations research. It contains an extensive treatment of mathematical programming, including the theory and application of linear programming, dynamic programming, network analysis, and game theory. A presentation of the elements of probability theory precedes the section on probabilistic models that includes queuing theory and its application, inventory theory, Markovian decision processes, reliability, simulation, and decision analysis. Although clearly written with numerous examples, the book requires a background of college-level mathematics. (JFD)

336. International Business Machines Corporation. *IBM Systems Journal*, Vol. XII (1973).

This collection of six papers addresses the key aspects of financial planning—particularly the development and use of financial models in simulating business activities. Attention is also given to planning simulation and to forecasting techniques. Charts, brief case studies, equations, and references are included. (RWP)

337. Johnsen, Robert, Jacques Vallee, and Kathleen Spangler. *Electronic Meetings: Technical Alternatives and Social Choices*. Reading, Mass.: Addison-Wesley, 1979.

This book examines an aspect of decision making omitted in most discussions of computer use—how to make meetings more effective. The authors deal mainly with the uses of telecommunications in the complex and relatively unstructured context of group problem solving and cooperative information exchange among peers. Both electronic meetings and decision support systems require an approach that stresses *support* and *extension* rather than simply automation and efficiency. (PMS)

338. Keen, Peter G. W., and Michael S. Scott Morton. *Decision Support Systems: An Organizational Perspective*. Reading, Mass.: Addison-Wesley, 1978.

This book is the first of a series on one of the latest and most important developments in computer applications. It provides an overview of decision support thought, models for decision making, and a framework for analysis of decision support systems (DSS). Several specific examples of computer-based decision support systems are described, but the emphasis is on the organizational aspects of system design and on implementation rather than technical features. A strategy is presented for development of DSS in an organizational context. It has been recognized for some time that systems to assist managers in relatively complex and unstructured activities are different from the structured decision systems developed for the more operational tasks, such as payroll. DSS are management computer aids that penetrate to very high levels in an organization, often involving senior management directly with the computer terminal. (PMS-JFD)

339. Kidder, Tracy. *The Soul of a New Machine.* Boston: Little, Brown, 1981.

This introduction to the world of computers gives an account of a new computer at Data General Corporation. The complexity, chaos, exploitation, and loneliness as well as the strange, half-mad beauty of this field are drawn here. Management issues are discussed as well as many details of the actual process of conceptualizing and building the machine. (PMS)

340. Kesner, Richard. "Historians in the Information Age: Putting the New Technology to Work." *Public Historian,* Vol. IV (Summer 1982), pp. 31-48.

This article treats broad and significant aspects of information management as it concerns historians. The methodology and the technology involved is as applicable to business research as it is to historical inquiry. (RWP)

341. King, William R., and David I. Cleland. *Strategic Planning and Policy.* New York: Van Nostrand Reinhold, 1978.

The authors review planning methodology covering the process, its final products, and the four primary subsystems of corporate planning: planning decisions, strategic information, planning-organizational, and planning management. (RWP)

342. Linstone, Harold A., and W. H. Clive Simmonds, eds. *Futures Research: New Directions.* Reading, Mass.: Addison-Wesley, 1977.

This collection of twenty-one papers was written for researchers who may question the "why" of futures research. The essays are arranged under four headings: shifting foundations, managing complexity, questioning the methodology, and recent projects. The book also includes a prologue, epilogue, and bibliographical footnotes. (LMD-HBR)

343. Mader, Chris. *Information Systems: Technology, Economics, Applications, Management.* 2d ed. Chicago: Scientific Research Associates, 1979.

The five-part flow of this book answers the following questions: What are information systems? How do they work? How can we use them? How are they developed? How should they be managed? (PMS)

344. Nie, Norman H., C. Hadlai Hall, Jean G. Jenkins, Karin Steinbrenner, and Dale H. Bent. *SPSS: Statistical Package for the Social Sciences.* 2d ed. New York: McGraw-Hill, 1980.

This is the first of a three-book series dealing with the use of the Statistical Package for the Social Sciences (SPSS). SPSS is one of the most widely used computer applications in the area of statistics and research. The book, a reference manual for the batch version of SPSS, begins by introducing the computer. There follows a general view of data analysis, including techniques for coding, organizing, and managing data. Each method of analysis is discussed; information on obtaining results for SPSS is given. Two companion volumes are available. The first is *SPSS Update 7-9: New Procedures and Facilities for Releases 7-9,* which discusses three statistical procedures (MANOVA, a general linear models procedure; BOX JENKINS, for analysis of time series; NEW REGRESSION, for regression procedure). The second is *SPSS Primer*, providing general information on the capabilities of the SPSS system. (RWP)

345. Shorter, Edward. *The Historian and the Computer: A Practical Guide*. New York: Norton, 1975.

This elementary manual is designed to take historians through the principal steps of a quantitative study, from codebook design and processing to final analysis of results and data. A number of historians read the original manuscript and provided advice. (RWP)

346. Sprecher, David A. *Finite Mathematics*. New York: Harper and Row, 1976.

An introduction to finite mathematics, this text describes sets, symbolic logic, probability, linear relations, matrices, and markov chains. In addition to theory, numerous examples and exercises are provided. (RWP)

347. Steiner, George A. *Strategic Managerial Planning*. Oxford, Ohio: Planning Executives Institute, 1977.

This brief monograph discusses approaches to the identification and evaluation of planning strategies as well as the implementation and direction of planning processes in both profit making and not-for-profit firms. A revision of *Comprehensive Managerial Planning* (1971), it stresses managerial aspects. (RWP)

348. Stewart, Rosemary. *How Computers Affect Management*. Cambridge, Mass.: M.I.T. Press, 1971.

This volume is neither a how-to book for budding computer wizards nor a treatment of general management issues regarding computers in business. It is aimed at managers who want to learn how to employ the computer and computing specialists more effectively and at computer specialists whose interests are wider than the technical aspects of their work. (PMS)

349. Traenkle, Jeffery W., Edwin B. Cox, and John A. Bullard. "The Use of Financial Models in Business." *A Research Study and Report Prepared for the Financial Executives Research Foundation*. Cambridge, Mass.: Arthur D. Little, 1975.

The chief characteristics of computer-processed financial modeling are described in this book. Use, utility, and organization of modeling efforts are discussed (as opposed to how to model or what techniques to use). It provides a reasonable, explicit summary of why companies do or do not model. Experienced executives contributed to this work. (RWP)

350. Wexelblatt, Ronald L., ed. *History of Programming Languages*. New York: Academic, 1981.

The final proceedings of the Association for Computing Machines (ACM) History of Programming Conference (Los Angeles, 1978) are presented in this volume. Thirteen programming languages are discussed, including BASIC, FORTRAN, and APL. Transcripts of question-and-answer sessions, supplementary addresses, and miscellaneous material relevant to the conference are included. (RWP)

351. Wheelwright, Steven C., and Spyros Makridakis. *Forecasting Methods for Management*. 3d ed. New York: Wiley, 1980.

These two author-professors have written widely on forecasting methods. This introductory text gives managers an overview of a broad range of forecasting methods and an understanding of the strengths and weaknesses of each. They have presented it in terms easily understood without a substantial background in quantitative methods and without dwelling on theoretical questions. The material is organized in three parts: the first lays the groundwork; the second describes the different forecasting methods and how they are applied in business (with the most attention paid to quantitative forecasting techniques); the third deals with the forecasting function in organizations and with procedures for handling that function. Suggested references for further study are at the end of each chapter. (LMD-HBR)

V. Marketing

352. Barton, Roger, ed. *Handbook of Advertising Management*. New York: McGraw-Hill, 1970.

Experts in the field describe advertising management. (RWP)

353. Boyd, Harper W., Jr., Ralph Westfall, and Stanley F. Stasch. *Marketing Research: Text and Cases*. 4th ed. Homewood, Ill.: Irwin, 1977.

The authors describe the logical series of interrelated steps that make up the market research process, providing basic concepts and processes. New concepts of attitude-behavior measurement and data analysis have been incorporated into this work. (RWP)

354. Dirksen, Charles J., and Arthur Kroeger. *Advertising Principles and Problems*. 5th ed. Homewood, Ill.: Irwin, 1977.

This text introduces the nature of advertising and the character of the field. (RWP)

355. Ferber, Robert, ed. *Handbook of Market Research*. New York: McGraw-Hill, 1974.

This basic reference source of market research methods and applications is written for marketing research generalists. Sections are included on research, design, surveys, statistical techniques, computer, and behavioral science applications. New product design, sales analysis, advertising, and marketing are also included. (RWP)

356. Harvard Business Review. *Market Planning Strategy: Part I*. Boston: Harvard Business Review, 1981.

Thought and practice in the field of marketing planning change rapidly. Changes in marketing significantly affect consumers and exert an even greater impact on those who are pursuing careers in marketing management and general management. This collection of fifteen articles provides information regarding changes in marketing. The elusive problem of marketing orientation and the pressures on marketing exerted by consumer groups and government agencies are among the topics. The volume also focuses attention on the quest for a scientific method and for more reliable research techniques applicable to marketing. Finally, this collection explores future developments in the area of mathematical programming, advertising and persuasion, the role of the marketing manager, modes of competition, and do-it-yourself retailing. (HBR)

357. Kotler, Philip, and Keith K. Cox, eds. *Readings in Marketing Management*. Englewood Cliffs, N.J.: Prentice-Hall, 1972.

Leading authorities on marketing present the concept of marketing management and analyze the nature of market opportunities. They describe such aspects as optimum organization, planning, and control of marketing. A final section deals with broader social, legal, and ethical aspects of the field as well as international operations. (RWP)

358. Kotler, Philip, and Ravi Singh. "Marketing Warfare." *The Journal of Business Strategy*, Vol. VII (Winter 1981), pp. 30-41.

The authors offer an argument, by analogy, concerning the contributions of military strategy to marketing. Written by authorities in the field, this article provides an example of applied theory. (RWP)

359. Martineau, Pierre. *Motivation in Advertising: Motives That Make People Buy*. New York: McGraw-Hill, 1971.

Martineau discusses the use of motivation research techniques in advertising. (SBA)

360. Montana, Patrick J., ed. *Marketing in Nonprofit Organizations*. New ed. New York: AMACOM, 1978.

This compilation of articles by various knowledgeable authors provides information on developing marketing strategy, selecting a target market, and choosing an appropriate market mix, operations, and services. As the title states, it is written for nonprofit organizations. (RWP)

361. Pederson, Charles A., and Milburn D. Wright. *Selling: Principles and Methods*. 6th ed. Homewood, Ill.: Irwin, 1976.

The authors provide a general review of salesmanship, including characteristics of the field, knowledge and skills required, the sales process, salesmen's responsibilities, and sales management. (RWP)

362. Pope, Jeffery. *Practical Marketing Research*. New York: AMACOM, 1981.

This introduction to marketing research emphasizes experience in marketing consumer's goods but also considers wider applications. Interviewing methods, planning and executing a complete research project, problem solving, and research tools are all covered. (RWP)

363. Riso, Ovid. *Sales Manager's Handbook*. 13th ed. Chicago: Dartnell Corporation, 1980.

This reference book on sales management outlines the evolution of sales management, product (or service) development, market analysis, distribution, trade practices, sales policy and organization, and direction of sales force. It includes many examples from job descriptions to contracts and forms. (See also *Sales Promotion Handbook*, no. *364*.) (RWP)

364. Riso, Ovid. *Sales Promotion Handbook*. 7th ed. Chicago: Dartnell Corporation, 1979.

Sales promotion techniques are presented here with comments from experts in the field. The *Handbook* treats organization, budgeting, sales leads service, trade shows, motivation of salespeople, and related topics. Illustrations are included. (See also *Sales Manager's Handbook*, no. *363*.) (RWP)

365. Stansfield, Richard H. *The Advertising Manager's Handbook*. 2d ed. Chicago: Dartnell Corporation, 1977.

This comprehensive reference book on advertising includes information on the field from copy preparation and layout to media selection and budgeting. It presents hundreds of case histories and deals with over 2,600 subjects. (RWP)

366. Stanton, William J. *Fundamentals of Marketing*. 4th ed. New York: McGraw-Hill, 1975.

Stanton discusses the fundamental principles of marketing. (SBA)

VI. Internal and External Relations

367. Bernstein, Theodore M. *The Careful Writer: A Modern Guide to English Usage*. New York: Atheneum, 1968.

Bernstein, former assistant managing editor of the *New York Times*, issued many manuals on writing. This one provides an alphabetical listing of words and usages with brief and striking examples. (MKP)

368. Coleman, Emily R., ed. *Labor Issues of the 80's.* Basking Ridge, N.J.: American Telephone and Telegraph Co., 1980.

This work treats three broad concerns affecting all "labor": the future of pension funds, the rise of industrial democracy, and the impact of technological changes on the worker and the corporation. The AT&T division manager for the Corporate Planning/Emerging Issues Group, a historian, completes the study with a fine interpretive essay on "The New Industrial Revolution." (RWP)

369. Forestal, Dan, and Richard Darrow. *The Public Relations Handbook.* 2d ed. Chicago: Dartnell Corporation, 1979.

The authors, in collaboration with the Hill and Knowlton staff, have assembled a public relations handbook for all types of corporations. Planning, policy making, budgeting, staff recruiting, writing, and support services are all included along with case histories. (RWP)

370. Harvard Business Review. *Effective Communication.* Boston: Harvard Business Review, 1981.

This collection of seventeen articles includes studies of older episodes in communications and descriptions of recent experiments and experiences. The volume is directed toward managers and administrators who rely on the use of communication skills to obtain specific results. The opening section deals with basic communication processes and emphasizes the importance of both listening and speaking. The second section covers the writing of reports, memoranda, and letters. Formal and informal communication to large groups is discussed in the third section. The final section explores the many factors, other than information exchange, that influence effective meetings. (HBR)

371. Harvard Business Review. *Public Relations.* Boston: Harvard Business Review, 1981.

U.S. corporations frequently come under sharp criticism because of their large expenditures on public relations (PR). This volume of thirteen articles focuses on the role of executives in PR activities, corporate PR practices, ideology, and questions of organization. Though often critical, these articles take a sympathetic view toward business. An effort is made to point out why these programs fail and what might be done to improve them. The volume is divided into four main sections: "The Role of the Executive"; "Images and Mirages"; "The Corporate Posture"; and "Organizing for Improvement." (HBR)

372. Hill and Knowlton Executives. *Critical Issues in Public Relations.* Englewood Cliffs, N.J.: Prentice-Hall, 1975.

This collection of speeches by executives of an international public relations firm covers subjects ranging from public attitudes toward big business, financial public relations, government relations, public interest issues, management/employee relations, and advertising. The speeches are introduced by the late John

W. Hill, one of the pioneers of the profession and founder of the firm. He cautions that nothing escapes questioning today, that business must put its house in order to avoid a credibility gap. "A more sophisticated public is sick and tired of being fed pablum. Candor and straightforward talk" are needed. (MKP)

373. Hunsinger, Marjorie. *Modern Business Correspondence*. 4th ed. New York: McGraw-Hill, 1979.

This work offers instruction in both the basic and the advanced techniques of preparing business letters, memos, and reports. It also includes a concise review of the principles of grammar, punctuation, and style. Written in simple, easy-to-understand language, the text-workbook contains illustrations of written communications and provides students with opportunities to analyze samples of effective letters, memos, and reports before they apply the text principles. (ABA)

374. Kobrin, Stephen J. "Political Risk: A Review and Reconstruction." *Journal of International Business Studies*, Vol. X (Spring-Summer 1979), pp. 67-80.

This paper reviews the literature dealing with international managers' assessment and evaluation of political risk. It also defines the concept of political risk analysis, and it suggests directions for future research in the field. (RWP)

375. Leonard, Donald J. *Shurter's Communication in Business*, 4th ed. New York: McGraw-Hill, 1979.

This book includes a section devoted to nonwritten aspects of written communication that treats dictation, the oral presentation of reports, and communication reception. In addition, the book provides coverage of the legal aspects of business communication, including a discussion of government regulations that have affected the content and existence of certain types of report writing, and a contemporary treatment of application letters and data sheets is provided. (ABA)

376. Roodman, Herman, and Zelda Roodman. *Management by Communication*. Toronto: Methuen, 1973.

The Roodmans combine a nuts-and-bolts approach—how to conduct an interview—with case studies and a theory of communication. Subjects include the process of communication, the effect of motivation on productivity, managing communication by objectives, and how to make sound decisions from effective reporting. Examples dramatize the authors' points. (MKP)

377. Simms, Howard, and Joseph A. Califano, Jr., eds. *The Media and Business*. New York: Vintage, 1979.

Senior journalists and corporate executives with academicians as moderators gathered to discuss the basically antagonistic relationship between the press and business. The printed report gives the complaints—press inaccuracy, carelessness, negativism, and bias. Special barbs are reserved for television. The press countered with discussions of objectivity, fairness, and the perceived double standard concerning ethics. In three case studies, participants explore problems and principles, all useful to anyone new to business or journalism. (MKP)

378. Pool, Ithiel de Sola, Wilbur Schramm, Frederick W. Frey, Nathan Maccoby, and Edwin B. Parker, eds. *Handbook of Communication.* Chicago: Rand McNally, 1973.

Basically a handbook, this work covers a wide range of communications subjects—persuasion, attitudinal change, sociolinguistics, settings such as broadcasting or totalitarian societies, and research. Each is authored by an expert in the field. Extensive bibliographies conclude each chapter. (MKP)

Strunk, William, Jr., with revisions by Elwyn B. White. *The Elements of Style.* See no. *101.*

Elementary rules of usage, principles of composition, and comments on form and style are all covered in this short book. Examples of misused words and expressions are presented alphabetically, but there is no index. (RWP)

VII. Compliance and Responsibility

379. Ashcroft, John D., and Janet E. Ashcroft. *College Law for Business.* 9th ed. Cincinnati, Ohio: South-Western, 1981.

Designed for a short, intensive course in business law, this text covers law and its enforcements, contracts, sales, bailments, commercial paper, agency and employment partnerships, corporations, risk-bearing devices, and property. Each chapter contains cases and decisions. (RWP)

380. Babb, Hugh W., and Charles Martin. *Business Law.* 3d ed. New York: Harper and Row, 1981.

This volume provides an introductory overview of business law as well as the authors' interpretation of the rationale behind some of the law. It includes a discussion of contracts, partnerships, corporations, and sales, with illustrative examples to assist the reader. (WKK)

381. Donaldson, Thomas, and Patricia H. Werhane, eds. *Ethical Issues in Business: A Philosophical Approach.* Englewood Cliffs, N.J.: Prentice-Hall, 1979.

This anthology of readings and quite a few case studies contain both modern and traditional philosophical material on ethical issues in business. The collection, which grew out of the teaching experience of the editors at Loyola University of Chicago, is arranged in four parts: philosophical issues in business ethics; economics, values, and justice; rights, liability, and the state; and business in modern society. (LMD-HBR)

382. Drucker, Peter F. "Ethical Chic." *Forbes*, Vol. CXXVIII (September 14, 1981), pp. 160-173.

This essay treats ethics in business and the dangers of creating a special code of "business ethics." (RWP)

383. Groening, William A. *The Modern Corporate Manager: Responsibility and Regulation*. New York: McGraw-Hill, 1981.

This work is a guide to regulatory laws, written by an experienced corporate counsel. Current regulations are traced to their legislative origins, then analyzed. Both exposure to liability and compliance are clarified from the individual manager's point of view as well as that of the corporation. (RWP)

384. Harvard Business Review. *Ethics for Executives: Part I*. Boston: Harvard Business Review, 1981.

The problem and implications of increasing antibusiness sentiment are examined in this collection of fifteen articles. Among the issues explored are the relationship of business to society, the integrity of the marketing media, moral dilemmas faced by business executives, and the relationship between Christian concepts and the activities of business enterprise. This volume also includes a review of the literature concerning business responsibility, public control of business, "corporate conscience," and management ideology; an HBR case study; a survey of executives by HBR; and readers' reactions to several articles. (HBR)

385. Harvard Business Review. *Guides to Corporate Responsibility*. Boston: Harvard Business Review, 1981.

In this section of sixteen articles, business leaders appraise the American public's changing expectations of business. Section I examines the role of business leadership in a creative society, the emergence of a new business ideology, and some possible dangers of social responsibility. Section II focuses on social issues such as urban renewal, ecology, changing employee values, and relations with minority groups. Section III discusses action approaches. It describes corporate successes in meeting various public needs, analyzes a number of failures, and examines the prospects of developing a new industry devoted to environmental improvement. Section IV examines the various roles managers play—and can play—as community leaders. (HBR)

386. Harvard Business Review. *Philosophy of Business: Part I*. Boston: Harvard Business Review, 1981.

Issues related to the role of the manager and the role of management in society are discussed in this collection of sixteen articles reprinted from the *Harvard Business Review*. Articles reflect concern with the issues of the responsible use of power by business for the betterment of society, the responsibility incurred by a company to attend to the human needs of its employees, and establishing a balance between government and business responsibility for social change. Other topics explored in this volume include mangement as a profession, managerial philosophy, intellectuals and business, and business leadership. (HBR)

387. Hoffman, W. Michael, and Thomas J. Wyly, eds. *The Work Ethic in Business: Proceedings of the Third National Conference on Business Ethics.* Cambridge, Mass.: Oelgeschlager, Gunn and Hain, 1981.

The work ethic and the quality of working life are the major themes of these proceedings from the Bentley College conference. The volume contains twenty-five papers by representatives from industry, labor, and academia and recounts conference discussions in full. Viewpoints range from General Motors management to the United Auto Workers union. Topics include government regulation and the results of a Gallup poll on attitudes toward business and work. (NCB-HBR)

388. Howell, Rate A., John R. Allison, and Nathaniel T. Henley. *Business Law.* 2d ed. Hinsdale, Ill.: Dryden, 1981.

This is a voluminous discussion of the field of business law. Numerous cases are included to help illuminate the text. (WKK)

389. Lane, Marc J. *Legal Handbook for Nonprofit Organizations.* New York: AMACOM, 1980.

This volume is written by an attorney in nonlegal language. It is conceived as a guide to making legal decisions for nonprofit management, and it cites numerous examples of legal questions raised in the organization or operation of any type of nonprofit organization. An analysis of the tax-exemption process and tax techniques for fund raising are also presented. (RWP)

390. McCraw, Thomas K. "Regulation in America: A Review Article." *Business History Review*, Vol. XXXXIX (Summer 1975), pp. 159-183.

"Regulation is so broad a topic that its proper study compels the use of methods from many disciplines," especially history, economics, political science, and law, and more recently organization theory. The author surveys the various analytic approaches and conclusions contained in representative literature on state and national regulatory commissions. He evaluates the "public interest" and "capture" theses, competing views common to historical and political science writing. Whereas political scientists and lawyers have concentrated on "due process, legitimacy, and reform" economists have emphasized quantitative assessment of regulation's impact through "theory-oriented testing of market efficiency." (BCC)

391. Nash, Laura L. "Ethics without the Sermon." *Harvard Business Review*, Vol. LIX (November-December 1981), pp. 79-90.

This article addresses twelve key questions for examining the ethics of a business decision, written by an authority on business policy. It summarizes the shared conditions of some successful ethical inquiries. (RWP)

392. Parker, Donn B. *Ethical Conflicts in Computer Science and Technology.* Arlington, Va.: AFIPS, 1979.

Six major areas in which ethical conflicts may arise are covered: contracts, disputed rights to products, confidentiality, personal morality, responsibility for applications, and information. A separate workbook is available, presenting scenarios that the reader is invited to analyze. The author's responses are given to compare results. (RWP)

VIII. Reference

393. Association for School, College, and University Staffing (ASCUS). *Career Resource Directory.* Madison, Wis.: ASCUS, 1982.

This annotated bibliography is "designed to assist undergraduate and graduate students, beginning and experienced professionals, and career changers in locating various types of information related to career goals and objectives." Seven major categories are represented, including humanities and fine arts, career exploration, and job search. (CHS-RWP)

394. Bakewell, Kenneth G. B., ed. *Management Principles and Practice: A Guide to Information Sources.* Detroit: Gale, 1977.

This guide covers major reference works, books, and articles on virtually all aspects of management and provides citations for sources of information such as organizations, films, and other audiovisual materials. It has name, title, and subject indexes. (RWP)

395. Brannen, William H., ed. *Small Business Marketing: A Selected and Annotated Bibliography.* Series No. 31. Chicago: American Marketing Association, 1978.

Brannen lists over two hundred annotated references on small-business marketing. (RWP)

396. Carter, Robert M., ed. *Communications in Organizations.* Detroit: Gale, 1972.

This annotated sourcebook gives references on organizational communications. It has name, title, and subject indexes. (RWP)

397. Chonko, Lawrence B., and Ben M. Enis. *Selling and Sales Management: A Bibliography.* Series No. 36. Chicago: American Marketing Association, 1980.

The compilers include over three hundred annotated citations for categories including boundary relations, economic process, exchange, and organization. (RWP)

398. Christian, Portia, with Richard Hicks, eds. *Ethics in Business Conduct.* Detroit: Gale, 1970.

This annotated guide to the field includes author and subject indexes. (RWP)

399. Clarke, Bernice T., ed. *Basic Library Reference Sources.* Rev. ed. Small Business Bibliography SBB 18. Washington: Government Printing Office, 1978.

This book introduces basic reference sources, listing a few annotated citations for business-operating guides and handbooks, directories, economic and marketing information, general reference sources, and "where-to-find" publications. (RWP)

400. Damarest, Rosemary, ed. *Accounting Information Sources.* Detroit: Gale, 1970.

Damarest offers an annotated guide to the literature, associations, and federal agencies concerned with accounting. Author/editor, title, and subject indexes are included. (RWP)

401. Daniells, Lorna M., comp. *Business Forecasting for the 1980's—and Beyond: A Selected, Partially Annotated Bibliography.* Boston: Baker Library, Harvard Business School, 1980.

This work is divided into four sections: "General Forecasts"; "Forecasts of Industries or Subjects"; "Forecasting Methodology"; "Reference Sources." Over four hundred books, services, and articles on the subject, published since 1972, are included. (RWP)

402. Daniells, Lorna M. *Business Information Sources.* Berkeley, Calif.: University of California Press, 1976.

This comprehensive bibliographic guide includes twenty-one chapters on subjects ranging from methods of locating information sources to information sources themselves in a variety of management areas. Each chapter has a helpful introduction, and each reference is annotated. (RWP)

403. Daniells, Lorna M., comp. *Business Reference Sources: An Annotated Guide for Harvard Business School Students.* Rev. ed. Boston: Baker Library, Harvard Business School, 1979.

This selective, annotated guide to sources of information on business information, written as an aid for users of Harvard's Baker Library, has broad coverage of general utility. (RWP)

404. Ferber, Robert, Alain Cousineau, Millard Crask, and Hugh Wales. *A Basic Bibliography on Marketing Research.* 3d ed. Series No. 2. Chicago: American Marketing Association, 1974.

This work lists 2,500 publications and offers a brief description of each. Its thirty-one sections cover works on all principal aspects of marketing research written up to 1973. (SBA)

405. Franklin, Jerome L. *Human Resource Development in the Organization.* Detroit: Gale, 1978.

This annotated guide to information on organizational development includes author, title, and subject indexes. (RWP)

406. Gothie, Daniel L. *A Selected Bibliography of Applied Ethics in the Professions: A Working Sourcebook with Annotations and Indexes.* Charlottesville, Va.: University Press of Virginia, 1973.

This bibliography is organized by professions (business and management, engineering, general ethical philosophy, government and politics, health sciences, law science, social sciences). Some of the approximately 1,400 entries are annotated, and all are indexed by author and subject. (See also Jones, no. *410.* (RWP)

407. Hanson, Agnes O. *Executive and Management Development for Business and Government.* Detroit: Gale, 1976.

This annotated listing of information on executive and management development covers professional associations and accredited business schools and includes author, title, subject, and proper-name indexes. (RWP)

408. Hutchinsone, William K. *History of Economic Analysis.* Gail Information Guide Library (GIGL). Detroit: Gale, 1976.

The author "covers the period from 1600 to 1940, with chapters devoted to the forerunners of classical economics, the inductivists, the marginalists, U.S. economists, and Keynesian economists." This annotated bibliography is written for both specialist and nonspecialist. (RWP)

409. Jackson, Arlyne, A., comp. *Business Dictionaries.* Baker Library Mini-List No. 20. Boston: Baker Library, Harvard Business School, 1977.

This selection of over fifty dictionaries is compiled under thirteen subject headings: accounting, advertising, business and economics, computers, finance and investment, industrial relations, management, marketing, mathematics, real estate, statistics, transportation, and English/foreign language business dictionaries. (RWP)

410. Jones, Donald G. *Business Ethics Bibliography, 1971-1975.* Charlottesville: University Press of Virginia, 1977.

This annotated guide lists material on business ethics published primarily between 1971 and 1975. It covers a broad range of issues, from private ethics and personal integrity to business and social relations. (See also Gothie, no. *406.*) (RWP)

411. Kruzas, Anthony T., and John Schmittroth, Jr. *Encyclopedia of Information Systems and Services*. 4th ed. Detroit: Gale, 1981.

The compiler gives detailed descriptions of more than two thousand organizations that produce, process, store, and use bibliographic/nonbibliographic information. Data-base producers, publishers, on-line vendors, data banks, and time-sharing firms are included. (RWP)

412. Larson, Henrietta Melia. *Guide to Business History: Materials for the Study of American Business History and Suggestions for Their Use*. Boston: J. S. Canner, 1964.

This work, volume 12 of Harvard Studies in Business History, contains 4,904 annotated entries that treat subjects ranging from the historical background of American business to autobiographies of businessmen, company histories, and research and reference materials. (See also Lovett, no. *413*.) (RWP)

413. Lovett, Robert W., ed. *American Economic and Business History Information Sources*. Detroit: Gale, 1971.

This comprehensive, annotated bibliography treats works relating to economic, business, agricultural, transportation, and labor history as well as the history of science and technology in North America. It is intended in part as a supplement to Larson (see no. *412*). (RWP)

414. Marke, Julius J., and Edward J. Bander, eds. *Commercial Law Information Sources*. Detroit: Gale, 1970.

This annotated description of publications includes government works, bibliographies, and monographs dealing with various aspects of business law. (RWP)

415. Morrill, Chester, Jr., ed. *Computers and Data Processing Information Sources*. Detroit: Gale, 1969.

This annotated bibliographical data on literature and materials deals with various aspects of computers and data processing. It gives historical background as well as information on management of computer facilities, hardware, software, languages, and other references. Associations, societies, and other sources of information are appended as are author/editor, title, and subject indexes. (RWP)

416. Morrill, Chester, Jr., ed. *Systems and Procedures Including Office Management Information Sources*. Detroit: Gale, 1967.

This annotated guide lists the literature and institutions concerned with the systems and procedural aspects of organizations and management. It covers business, industry, and government, both small and large systems. (RWP)

417. National Coordinating Committee for the Promotion of History. *Career Alternative Bibliography*. Rev. ed. NCC Supplement No. 8. Washington: National Coordinating Committee for the Promotion of History, 1981.

This publication lists alphabetically by author over one hundred articles, reports, and books dealing with career development. Many deal with issues concerning Ph.D.s in the humanities; some specifically treat career development for historians. (RWP)

418. Norton, Alice, ed. *Public Relations Information Sources.* Detroit: Gale, 1970.

This annotated bibliography is divided into six main sections: general sources, special fields and special publications, public relations tools, public relations associations in the U.S., careers in public relations, and international public relations. (RWP)

419. Tega, Vasile G., ed. *Management and Economic Journals.* Detroit: Gale, 1977.

This analytic guide lists professional periodicals dealing with various aspects of economics and management. It includes tables and charts and indexes of subjects, special-issue subjects, and top business firms. (RWP)

420. The Future: A Guide to Information Sources. 2d ed., rev. Washington: World Future Society, 1979.

This is a revised and expanded edition of the most complete guide currently available. It covers: organizations engaged in futures research; individual futurists; futures books, reports, and periodicals; and educational courses and programs, films, audiotapes, games and simulations, and other media. The sections listing books and periodicals on the future and on forecasting techniques are partially annotated. (LMD-HBR)

421. Thomas, Roy E., ed. *Insurance Information Sources.* Detroit: Gale, 1971.

This annotated guide covers books, articles, libraries, schools, and associations concerned with many aspects of the insurance industry. It has eighteen sections covering subjects ranging from the history of insurance to career opportunities in addition to concentrations on specific areas of insurance. (RWP)

422. Uhr, Ernest B., and Lance P. Jarvis, eds. *Social Responsibility in Marketing: A Selected and Annotated Bibliography.* Series No. 27. Chicago: American Marketing Association, 1977.

This work centers on legal, ethical, and social aspects of marketing, covering literature that appeared from 1966 through 1976. (RWP)

423. Wasserman, Paul, and Janice McLean, eds. *Consultants and Consulting Organizations Directory.* 5th ed. Detroit: Gale, 1981.

The editors have compiled information on approximately seven thousand firms, individuals, and organizations active in some 135 fields of consulting. Names, addresses, phone numbers, and details on services offered are included. They are cross-tabbed by geographic location, subject area, names of firms and/or individual consultants. (RWP)

424. Wheeler, Lora Jeanne, ed. *International Business and Foreign Trade Information Sources*. Detroit: Gale, 1968.

This annotated guide to literature and organizations deals with procedures and policies of conducting business with other countries. Nineteen sections cover subjects such as the theory of international trade, statistical sources, and organizations dealing with international business. Specific fields receive coverage, for example, marketing, advertising, and finance. (RWP)

425. Woy, James B. *Business Trends and Forecasting Information Sources*. Detroit: Gale, 1965.

This annotated guide covers sources concerning business trends and forecasting. (RWP)

CHAPTER 4

ARCHIVES, RECORDS, AND INFORMATION MANAGEMENT

Richard M. Kesner, editor

As we approach the twenty-first century, efficient and economical management of information becomes an increasingly important aspect of our lives. Broadly conceived, information management encompasses both archival administration and records management. It entails collection, preservation, and dissemination of documents, ranging from clay tablets and incunabula to microform and computer tapes. The public historian has a vital role in all these activities but only if the individual historian develops those areas of technical expertise needed to complement scholarly tools. A blending of practical skills and the ability to analyze document contents and chart information flow undoubtedly affords interesting and satisfying opportunities for employment. The users of both "historical" and current information are bound to benefit from such a combination along with those historians who brave the technological and managerial challenges to take up these new occupations.

The field of information management is quite broad. No selective bibliography can accomplish more than to cite representative examples of readings from a rich and diverse body of literature. The readings in each of the following sections include a few of the standard reference works employed in the training of archivists, records managers, and information specialists. An effort is made to select recent publications. In most instances these books and articles refer to the older standard works in their footnotes and bibliographies. A number of bibliographies are included to assist those interested in pursuing a given subject beyond the capabilities of this work. By emphasizing current publications, this listing demonstrates the vitality and diversity of recent research and writing in these fields. It also suggests areas that require more work as well as those aspects of information management, for example, personal privacy and automated information indexing and retrieval systems, that are presently of intense concern to professionals.

Given their knowledge of documents and how they come into being, historians have the basic skills to deal with the information management needs of our society. They must add to their analytical and historical orientation a degree of technical training and experience in such areas as the conservation of historical objects, micrographics, and machine-readable records. One need master only those areas of personal and professional interest. From this base the public historian *cum* information manager may note any number of opportunities in a world increasingly dependent on the management of knowledge through the collection, preservation, and dissemination of documentary information. In the United States we are witnessing the emergence of a multibillion-dollar industry devoted to information processing. Educational institutions are slowly responding to the needs of these new enterprises. The time has come for historians to consider how they might best contribute to this development.

I. General Works

426. Bowman, Roland M., ed. *A Manual of Archival Techniques.* Harrisburg: Pennsylvania Historical and Museum Commission, 1979.

This manual is less a technical guide to archival operations than a collection of loosely related essays prepared by leading members of the profession. The volume includes a number of contributions dealing with day-to-day administration, such as collection processing and reference services, and there are also chapters on field work, survey techniques, and grantsmanship. This manual supplements other texts in the field, adding to the more traditional approaches of Duckett and Schellenberg (nos. *430* and *438*). (RMK)

427. Brooks, Philip C. *Research in Archives: The Use of Unpublished Sources.* Chicago: University of Chicago Press, 1969.

Both the nascent scholar and the nascent archivist can benefit from this thorough survey of the nature, services, and management problems of archival administration. In slightly more than one hundred pages, the author takes the reader through an archive, describing its general operating procedures, its primary functions, and its peculiar operating principles. The author's purpose is to expand the researcher's sensitivity toward the challenges faced by archivists in carrying out their mission to collect, preserve, and make more accessible documents of historical and research value. In so doing, the author assists his readers by making them more effective users of archives, and he assists archivists by creating greater empathy between scholars and the curators of research materials. (RMK)

428. Burnette, O. Lawrence, Jr. *Beneath the Footnote.* Madison: State Historical Society of Wisconsin, 1967.

This volume brings together a vast body of information about archival institutions in the United States. After a brief consideration of archives in the broadest sense, Burnette discusses governmental archives—federal, state, and local—university archives, business and corporate archives, religious archives, and a wide range of special institutional repositories. He provides descriptions of numerous archives and their holdings. The author also suggests where to go to seek historical documents relevant to specific research projects when an archive as such may not exist. These references are most useful to those in search of a new collecting focus or theme for an archive. (RMK)

429. Clark, Robert L., Jr., ed. *Archives-Library Relations*. New York: Bowker, 1976.

The uninitiated often confuse archivists with librarians. Many believe that the latter maintian current publications while the former preserve "old books." Actually, librarians are the keepers of published wisdom, and archivists are the custodians of unpublished, "original" documents. They have many of the same concerns, for example, paper conservation, collection security, and reference services. However, they do not always work cooperatively, and they do not always share resources effectively. This volume attempts to define the respective worlds of the librarian and the archivist in terms of commonality of interests. The editor argues that both groups would benefit from better understanding and more intra-institutional cooperation. He identifies specific strategies for a "team approach" to the management of books, documents, and related sources of information. (RMK)

430. Duckett, Kenneth W. *Modern Manuscripts*. Nashville: American Association for State and Local History, 1975.

Although archival administration is an ancient and noble profession, there are few general texts in the field. This book is an exception. The author has drawn upon his considerable experience as a curator of rare manuscripts and as a manager of corporate and personal papers to provide his readers with a comprehensive overview. He begins with a brief historical narrative but quickly moves on to general administrative considerations. He then covers collection development and professional ethics, collection processing and description, and finally expands his discussion to a review of special techniques required in the treatment of nontraditional archives, from photographs and film strips to computerized records and micrographics. (RMK)

431. Hefner, Loretta L., ed. *The WPA Historical Records Survey: A Guide to the Unpublished Directories, Indexes, and Transcripts*. Chicago: Society of American Archivists, 1980.

During the Great Depression of the 1930s, many scholars found work in the Historical Records Survey (HRS) of the Works Progress (Projects) Administration. Between the years of 1935 and 1942, survey teams produced thousands of cubic feet of unpublished inventories, indexes, transcripts, and other research tools pertaining to records held by governmental bodies, schools and universities, private businesses, and religious organizations. This publication consolidates information gathered by the Society of American Archivists on what has happened to the HRS materials since 1942. A four-page appendix summarizes these holdings by institution, showing at a glance the extent of surviving documentation. The publication also includes a microfiche supplement of ninety pages that reproduces more extensive finding aids to HRS materials where they exist. The survey remains of considerable value, and this *Guide* affords greater access to widely scattered materials. (RMK)

432. Jenkinson, Hilary. *A Manual of Archive Administration.* London: Perry Lund Humphries, 1966.

This volume, first published in 1922, rapidly became the standard work in English on archival administration. As deputy keeper of public records at the British Public Record Office, Jenkinson was in an ideal position to consider the various aspects of archives work in detail. His text deals with the origins and development of archives and archival practices, modern archival institutions, and the nature of document creation. Since many of the most basic operating tenets in this country were inherited from the British, Jenkinson's manual provides a full appreciation of the profession's evolution. (RMK)

433. McCoy, Donald R. *The National Archives: America's Ministry of Documents, 1934-1968.* Chapel Hill: University of North Carolina Press, 1978.

This award-winning volume represents the first comprehensive study of the United States National Archives and Records Service. The author traces the developments that finally resulted in the establishment of a centralized national program for the management of government records in this country. Britain, France, and Germany had established programs of their own well before the United States did so. McCoy concentrates his efforts on explaining how America's "Ministry of Documents" stands apart from these earlier precedents and the extent to which individuals and political circumstances affected the evolution of a national repository system. This volume traces the institutional history of the Archives and documents the influence exerted by the National Archives on other programs throughout the United States. (RMK)

434. Norton, Margaret Cross. *Norton on Archives.* Edited by Thornton W. Mitchell. Chicago: Society of American Archivists, 1975.

During her twenty-six years as state archivist of Illinois, Norton wrote several dozen professional articles. Mitchell's collection includes thirty examples of her prodigious work. The essays were selected because they deal with concepts, principles, and techniques of archival economy. Norton drew upon her own experience as the curator of a small program, and her advice therefore has particular relevance for many archivists today. The volume includes commentary on the scope, function, and purpose of archives; the organization and operation of archival facilities; conservation techniques; disaster preparedness; the treatment of photographic and micrographic collections; records disposal; and records management. Few anthologies provide a comparable body of information. (RMK)

435. Posner, Ernst. *American State Archives.* Chicago: University of Chicago Press, 1964.

This country did not develop a national archives program until after the Second World War. Prior to that time, the various state governments or state historical societies, operating in cooperation with state governments, provided the basis for a set of uncoordinated programs to collect and preserve the documentary heritage of this nation. Posner briefly surveys the development of state archival programs. He then examines each state program. The author tells his readers how each program began, when and how they were vested with the legal powers to collect and preserve documents, and how well they have done their job. Throughout this series of essays, Posner notes those elements that made each program distinct from its neighbors. (RMK)

436. Posner, Ernst. *Archives in the Ancient World.* Cambridge, Mass.: Harvard University Press, 1972.

Ernst Posner always referred to archival administration as the world's "second oldest profession." The justification for this observation is readily found in this piece of research. The author traces the history of archives from the Hittite and Babylonian periods through the early Roman Catholic Church archives of the Middle Ages. The oldest known archives employed labeled clay boxes to store documents, which were also made of clay. Papyrus (Egypt) and parchment (Greece and Rome) replaced clay as a recording medium. Unfortunately, the ravages of time were not kind to these latter types of records; few have survived. Archaeologists have, by contrast, unearthed complete Hittite archival repositories with their virtually indestructible clay tablets. The reader learns how these documents have allowed scholars to reconstruct civilizations long dead and to observe how ancient archivists plied their craft. (RMK)

437. Schellenberg, Theodore R. *Modern Archives Principles and Techniques.* Chicago: University of Chicago Press, 1956.

In 1945, Schellenberg received a Fulbright Lectureship to travel throughout Australia and present papers on the management and administration of public records. The University of Chicago Press issued these lectures in 1956. The volume includes an introductory section dealing with the nature of archives and their responsibilities in the area of information and records management. The author then discusses in detail the management of both current and historical records. Although Schellenberg emphasizes the files of the U.S. government, this work should interest anyone concerned with the development of archival theory in the United States. (RMK)

438. Schellenberg, Theodore R. *The Management of Archives.* New York: Columbia University Press, 1965.

For many years, Schellenberg and Ernst Posner served as the primary instructors of archivists in the United States. Schellenberg conducted training courses at the National Archives and Records Service (NARS) as well as summer sessions at the American University, the University of Texas, and the University of Washington. He wrote this volume to provide a clear statement of his views divided into two basic sections. The first, entitled "Development of Principles and Techniques," deals with his theory of archival administration; and the second, entitled "Application of Principles and Techniques," addresses practical problems and suggests solutions. The author bases his conclusions upon his experiences at the National Archives. Since most archives are very different from NARS, not all readers will find Schellenberg's suggestions applicable to their particular settings. (RMK)

II. Administration, Facility Development, and Security

439. Dearstyne, Bruce W. "Local Historical Records: Programs for Historical Agencies." American Association for State and Local History Technical Leaflet 121. *History News*, Vol. XXXIV (November 1979).

Many different types of historical agencies are called upon to serve as the repository for local historical records, but not all organizations are prepared to accept and manage them. This technical leaflet provides a body of basic operating procedures upon which small historical agencies may build an archives program. The author begins by encouraging the institution to carry out a self-evaluation, defining the objectives, support, budget, targeted researchers, and staff for the program. He next recommends the establishment of a historical records advisory service. Perhaps the most difficult aspect of this undertaking is the appraisal of local records for research value. Dearstyne also covers collecting and reference services, grantsmanship, and the search for outside assistance to the program. (RMK)

440. Flowers, Ann, and James Craven. *Disaster Plan for the Bentley Library*. Rev. ed. Ann Arbor: Bentley Library, University of Michigan, 1977.

Few historical agencies have disaster plans in place should a calamity befall their facility. Such a plan is essential, but, because it is needed only when an emergency actually occurs, most archivists procrastinate in developing a plan of their own. The Bentley Library has produced a disaster-preparedness strategy. Its step-by-step procedures are transferable to archives, library, and museum settings. One might also consider Hilda Boehm's *Disaster Prevention and Disaster Preparedness* (Berkeley: University of California Press, 1979) in this regard. (RMK)

441. Gondos, Victor, Jr., ed. *Reader for Archives and Research Center Buildings*. Chicago: Society of American Archivists, 1970.

Archives and records centers have special requirements that are not common to other buildings and facilities. They must, for example, protect the materials they house from the deteriorating effects of the environment. While they must allow for a degree of public access and easy document retrieval, they must also provide sufficient security to guard against theft, vandalism, and misuse. In this volume, the editor brings together a group of experts in the design and operation of archival and records management facilities. The essays include studies of archives in Illinois, New Jersey, Georgia, Pennsylvania, North Carolina, and a number of overseas repositories. Another group of authors discuss the latest developments in records center facilities (where noncurrent but not necessarily archival records are stored). The work's appendices include a note on record containers, a discussion of film records management, a consideration of records and fire protection, and a select bibliography. (RMK)

442. Holbert, Sue E. "Comments on Management Concepts and Archival Administration." *Midwestern Archivist*, Vol. IV (1979), pp. 89-94.

The author briefly examines the applications of popular management concepts such as "management of objectives" and "zero based budgeting" in terms of the peculiar administrative problems of archives. She points to the wealth of information available to archivists through the study of the literature pertaining to library administration but warns that methods and techniques in a library setting do not always apply to situations in an archival context. (RMK)

443. Hunter, John E. "Emergency Preparedness for Museums, Historic Sites, and Archives: An Annotated Bibliography." American Association for State and Local History Technical Leaflet 114. *History News*, Vol. XXXIV (April 1979).

The literature pertaining to disaster preparedness is so sparse that John Hunter has done his readers a considerable service in bringing together an annotated list of works on the subject. The works are arranged under broad headings, including: "Emergency Preparedness Planning"; "Emergency Preparedness Planning for Museums and Archives"; "Protection Against Bombings, Terrorism, and Civil Disturbances"; "Fire Protection"; "Fire Protection for Museums and Archives"; "Salvage and Recovery of Damaged Museum and Archival Collections"; and "Preservation of Collections during Energy Crises."(RMK)

444. Maher, William J. "The Importance of Financial Analysis of Archival Programs." *Midwestern Archivist*, Vol. III (1978), pp. 3-24.

Archivists often discuss the "efficiency" and "economical nature" of their program procedures without actually sitting down and computing costs. Maher demonstrates the usefulness of financial analysis as a dimension of program planning. He considers both regular institutional support and special grants for limited-term projects, discussing basic procedures for the management of typical archives situations. He comments on the measurement of staff activities in terms of the distribution of their work loads and presents his method for the computation of processing costs. He also discusses grants and their place within overall archives fiscal planning. (RMK)

445. Martin, Katherine F. "Security and the Administration of Manuscript Holdings at Southern Academic Libraries, Part I: Administrative, Staff, and Physical Security." *Georgia Archive*, Vol. VIII (Spring 1980), pp. 1-55. Also "Security and the Administration of Manuscript Holdings at Southern Academic Libraries, Part II: Security Procedures and the Patron." *Georgia Archive*, Vol. VIII (Fall 1980), pp. 61-76.

The tragic increase in the rate of theft and vandalism of archival materials has prompted great concern among archivists and has resulted in the development of a wide range of security procedures. However, many archival agencies still lack even the most rudimentary forms of protection against patron abuse. Martin presents a thorough consideration of the problem and possible solutions in this two-part article. She begins with a discussion of the problem and then moves on to present her study of some 210 libraries located in the southern United States. The author analyzes various approaches to archival and rare books collection security in light of the results of her survey. In the second portion of her study, she deals exclusively with repository/patron relations and the types of precautions that one must take before and during the time when researchers have access to manuscript materials. Her practical advice is supported by statistical and qualitative information gleaned from her survey. (RMK)

446. Mason, Philip P. "Archival Security: New Solutions to an Old Problem." *American Archivist*, Vol. XXXIV (October 1975), pp. 477-492.

Mason is a recognized authority on archival security and is regularly asked to advise on development of security systems for new archival facilities. He reviews a number of the most notorious thieves who specialized in stealing from archives. He then uses these illustrations as a base upon which to build a case for the systematic establishment of archival security systems. He concludes with a survey of security activities within the Society of American Archivists (SAA), including mention of the SAA "Security Newsletter" and its consulting service. (RMK)

447. Thompson, Enid T. *Local History Collections: A Manual for Librarians*. Nashville: American Association for State and Local History, 1978.

This manual provides an administrative overview of all aspects of local history collections administration. It serves the needs of librarians, curators, and local historical society directors who find themselves responsible for the maintenance of manuscript materials. The volume begins with a consideration of the nature of local history but quickly moves on to more practical problems, including: identification, collection, and preservation of historical materials; legal questions of ownership and copyright; collection processing; reference services; and staff and volunteer training. The author also briefly mentions how oral history projects and exhibitions might be integrated into a local history collections program. Thompson appends a list of organizations, sources of archival supplies, publication addresses, and a bibliography. (RMK)

448. Walch, Timothy. *Archives and Manuscripts: Security*. Chicago: Society of American Archivists, 1977.

As part of its educational and professional mission, the Society of American Archivists (SAA), with financial assistance from the National Historical Publications and Records Commission, has issued a series of basic manuals. This volume deals with archival security. The author covers the following topics: "Planning a Security Program"; "Security, Staffing, and Patrons"; "Security and Collections"; "Security Equipment"; "Security against Fire and Flood"; and "Archival Security and the Law." Like all of the volumes in the basic manual series, this work is illustrated with both photographs and diagrams. It also includes a statement concerning the SAA security program, a model law relating to library theft, a bibliography, and a repository security checklist. (RMK)

449. Worthy, James C. "Management Concepts and Archival Administration." *Midwestern Archivist*, Vol. IV (1979), pp. 51-88.

In this essay a management specialist shares some of his experiences with archivists. He discusses the need to develop personnel, pay scale, job description, and operating objectives policies as part of an overall administrative scheme. His approach is that of management by objectives; he suggests how this technique may be effectively integrated into planning and administrative procedures. (RMK)

III. Audiovisual Records

450. Averey, Harriet W. "Cataloging Motion Picture Film: A Descriptive Bibliography." *American Archivist*, Vol. XXXIX (April 1976), pp. 167-175.

Archivists and records managers are trained to handle paper records and files. However, modern society is turning away from these more traditional records and instead is generating machine-readable (computerized) and audiovisual documents. To meet today's information handling needs, archivists and records managers must become more familiar with these other record formats. This publication deals with the problems surrounding the management of motion picture film in an archives setting. Film, especially nitrate film, presents special preservation problems. Intellectual and physical control over film collections present their own challenges. For the uninitiated, Averey's annotated bibliography provides considerable guidance, especially in terms of the various options open to archivists in dealing with films and similar records. (RMK)

451. Harrison, Helen P. *Film Library Techniques: Principles of Administration*. New York: Hastings House, 1973.

This volume deals with the special problems involved in documenting, cataloging, and providing scholarly access to films and video tapes. The author outlines methods of analysis and practical steps to be employed in the management of audiovisual collections. Numerous examples and illustrations as well as the bibliography guide the inexperienced through the procedures recommended in the text. (RMK)

452. McWilliams, Jerry. *The Preservation and Restoration of Sound Recordings*. Nashville: American Association for State and Local History, 1979.

Archival sound recordings range widely, including phonograph records, reel-to-reel and cassette tapes, wire recordings, dictaphone disks, and even old Edison cylinders. Each of these materials is susceptible to the damaging effects of improper storage, extreme environmental conditions, and user abuse. Mc-Williams surveys the problems faced by archivists in the preservation of sound recordings and recommends a series of procedures designed to mitigate environmental and user damage. For those instances where damage has already occurred, he proposes a number of practical remedies. The author's advice may be employed in any number of archival settings. (RMK)

453. Noble, Richard. "Archival Preservation of Motion Pictures: A Summary of Current Readings." American Association for State and Local History Technical Leaflet 126. *History News*, Vol. XXXV (April 1980).

A recent disastrous explosion and fire at the National Archives film repository outside Washington, D.C., testifies to the fact that even professional keepers of historical materials may at times underestimate the natural forces operating against the survival of our documentary heritage. The cause of this disaster was the ignition of fumes released from deteriorating nitrate film. This technical leaflet examines the most recent research involving the preservation of motion picture film and makes some specific recommendations about how to treat volatile records of past human activity. (RMK)

454. Sargent, Ralph N. *Preserving the Moving Image*. Washington: Corporation for Public Broadcasting and the National Endowment for the Arts, 1974.

Nitrate film can be stored safely so that it does not endanger other archives collections, but the only way to preserve these records is to transfer them to safety film. Similarly, video tapes and other magnetic recordings have only a limited shelf life (perhaps twenty-five years). To preserve these materials, one must transfer them from a magnetic to an optical format. Sargent reviews the techniques and hardware required for these conversion processes. He also speculates about technological advances and what methods may be in use in the near future. The cost of these processes is considerable, but without them many valuable documents would be lost. Diagrams and illustrations help the author to communicate complex procedures. (RMK)

455. Vanderbilt, Paul. "Evaluating Historical Photographs: A Personal Perspective." American Association for State and Local History Technical Leaflet 120. *History News*, Vol. XXXIV (October 1979).

Archival appraisal is that complex and highly creative process by which archivists decide which documents have historical and research value and hence which records are preserved for posterity. The process as such is poorly documented at best and remains highly subjective. In only a few short pages, Vanderbilt presents a simple, rational approach to the evaluation of historical photographs. The presentation facilitates understanding of a rather difficult procedure. (RMK)

456. Weinstein, Robert A., and Larry Booth. *Collection, Use, and Care of Historical Photographs*. Nashville: American Association for State and Local History, 1977.

This volume serves a dual purpose. In its first section the authors present a thorough history of the photograph, touching on the cultural and social aspects of photography as well as the many technological breakthroughs in its evolution. The second section of the volume is more technical, detailing the steps required for management of photographic archives and restoration of historical photographs. The authors selected their illustrations to emphasize their advice. Both professionals and novices can benefit from the monograph. Summary tables, informational appendices, and a bibliography supplement the text. (RMK)

IV. Collecting, Processing, and Appraisal

457. Berner, Richard C. "Arrangement and Description: Some Historical Observations." *American Archivist*, Vol. XLI (April 1978), pp. 169-181.

Archivists have not arrived at a consensus on the proper approach to the arrangement and description of manuscript materials. Some programs establish guidelines from one collection to the next while others have standardized procedures so that all collections are treated in more or less the same fashion. Berner traces the historical precedents for a number of these approaches and discusses the costs and benefits of these developments in terms of the sharing of information both within the profession and between archivists and their user constituencies. (RMK)

458. Blouin, Francis X., Jr. "A New Perspective on the Appraisal of Business Records," *American Archivist*, Vol. LXXII (July 1979), pp. 312-329.

The author of this article reviews a number of publications dealing with United States business history and the records of private companies. He then moves beyond the consideration of these works to make a number of points about the importance of business records in the study of American history. In particular Blouin stresses the need to appraise the research trends and to solicit the papers of American companies and business leaders as aspects of broader collecting themes. (RMK)

459. Brichford, Maynard J. *Archives and Manuscripts: Appraisal and Accessioning*. Chicago: Society of American Archivists, 1977.

In archival administration, accessioning refers to bringing a collection into the archives and to establishing physical control over it. Appraisal, on the other hand, refers to that subtle and complex process whereby archivists choose what is kept for posterity and what is discarded. The author tackles both of these subjects in this volume of the Society of American Archivists' basic manual series. In actual fact, Brichford devotes only two pages to the mechanical and legal aspects of accessioning. The remainder of the manual concerns itself with the appraisal process. He discusses the quantitative and qualitative characteristics of records as well as their "administrative," "research," and "archival" values. He also considers the special qualities required of an appraiser and various appraisal techniques. The author includes an appendix of the functional categories of records grouped by relative importance. (RMK)

460. Boles, Frank. "Sampling in Archives." *American Archivist*, Vol. XLIV (April 1981), pp. 125-130.

Researchers would have archivists save everything. Costs of collection, processing, and storage, and the enormous volume of modern archival collections do not allow such an unselective approach to appraisal. Although archivists have never been in agreement either on how to employ sampling or when to employ it, the technique suggests a way out. The author proposes a statistical approach to sampling archives and offers a defense of it. (RMK)

461. Fishbein, Meyer H. "A Viewpoint on Appraisal of National Records." *American Archivist*, Vol. XXXIII (April 1970), pp. 175-187.

This essay provides insights into the appraisal process as seen from the perspective of a former distinguished staff member of the National Archives and Records Service. The author establishes an intellectual framework within which one may judge the "information" (research) value and evidential (administrative) value of United States federal records. Fishbein stresses the need for flexibility in the process so that the appraiser can deal with new types of records, such as machine-readable archives, and changes in user needs as these arise. (RMK)

462. Gracy, David B., II. *Archives and Manuscripts: Arrangement and Description.* Chicago: Society of American Archivists, 1977.

Few collections arrive at the archives ready for use by researchers; most require a certain degree of arrangement. These processing procedures are both mechanical—to insure the preservation of the collection—and intellectual—to assist in the use of the collection by the archives patrons. Once a collection is processed, it is described to enhance intellectual access to its contents. The description of archival materials ranges in format from three-by-five index cards to computer-generated indexes and abstracts. The archival profession has not as a whole standardized either arrangement or description, although the Society of American Archivists (SAA) has taken tentative steps toward the standardization of archival descriptive elements. The diverse nature of archival collections works against the development of rigid standards. Gracy therefore faces a difficult task in his attempt to discuss both processes in this SAA basic manual. In terms of arrangement, he analyzes the various "levels" of collection arrangement, starting with "record group" and working through "series," "file unit," and "document item." He then surveys the various methods of description currently used in U.S. repositories. The volume concludes with a consideration of the special problems created by records, such as still pictures, maps, sound recordings, and films. (RMK)

463. Kesner, Richard M. "Labor Union Grievance Records: An Appraisal Strategy." *Archivaria*, Vol. VIII (Summer 1979), pp. 102-114.

Appraisal of diverse but repetitive case files is an aspect of archival administration that requires more serious consideration. This study offers a systematic approach to appraisal of case files, using records of labor union grievances as an example. Although the record type in question is unique, the methodology presented has implications beyond those concerning the management of labor union records. The author advocates employment of both internal and external analysis of case files, that is, the study of file contents coupled with interviews with creators of the files as an essential procedure in dealing with this vexing problem. (RMK)

464. Lewellyn, Michael V. "The Yellow Square of Paper: The Archival Appraisal of Accounting Records." *Georgia Archive,* Vol. VII (Fall 1979), pp. 23-31.

This discussion of historical accounting records raises an extremely important point. Few archivists are experts on each type of documentation that crosses their desks. Financial records cause particular problems because their informational value is not always apparent to the untrained eye. It is therefore essential that archivists obtain experience with as wide a range of documentary evidence as possible and that when in doubt they seek expert advice. In this case, the author shares with his colleagues his considerable knowledge of accounting records and recommends procedures for their evaluation and appraisal. (RMK)

465. Vincent, Carl. "The Record Group: A Concept in Evolution." *Archivaria*, Vol. III (Winter 1976-1977), pp. 3-16.

This essay treats the concept of the "record group" as it applies to the arrangement of Canadian government records. The author considers the significance of the record group as a descriptive and organizational element in government archives and its implications during appraisal of these records for evidential and informational value. (RMK)

V. Conservation

466. Adelstein, P. Z. "Preservation of Microfilm." *Journal of Micrographics*, Vol. XI (July-August 1978), pp. 333-337.

Like any other type of record format, microfilm varies in quality and estimated shelf life. This brief technical note outlines essential steps for the proper storage and treatment of microfilm so as to insure its long-term survival. (RMK)

467. Baker, John P., and Marguerite C. Soroka. *Library Conservation: Preservation in Perspective*. Stroudsburg, Pa.: Dowden, Hutchinson and Ross, 1978.

This work serves as a companion to the Cunha study (no. *469*). It neither involves itself with the detailed mechanical procedures of book restoration nor concentrates in depth on the physical and chemical structure of books and papers. Instead, the authors update the Cunhas's findings and consider the latest technological developments, such as the research that has gone on in nonaqueous deacidification processes. Throughout, the authors emphasize the administrative implications of library conservation and how to implement procedures that protect books from the abuse of environmental conditions and careless users. (RMK)

468. Barrow Research Library. *Manuscripts and Documents: Their Deterioration and Restoration*. Charlottesville: University of Virginia Press, 1955.

Most modern papers contain ground wood and numerous impurities that result in their rapid deterioration. Barrow developed an aqueous process for the deacidification of paper. The so-called Barrow Process adds an alkaline buffer to paper, retarding and at times even eliminating acid deterioration. This study examines the causes of paper deterioration because of inherent fault (paper impurities) and the environment, such as heat, humidity, and ultraviolet radiation. The author then suggests ways of dealing with these problems. The Barrow Process remains a standard archival procedure for the restoration of paper objects. However, it may not be used with water-soluble materials. Researchers are currently at work on the development of a variety of effective and economical nonaqueous processes. (RMK)

469. Cunha, George, and Dorothy G. Cunha. *Conservation of Library Materials*. 2 vols. Metuchen, N.J.: Scarecrow, 1971.

This two-volume study by the Cunhas remains the single most comprehensive treatment of paper conservation available today. Volume I begins with an examination of the history of paper and printing. This is followed by a detailed analysis of all the components of a book, including skins, cloth covers, paper, inks, adhesives, book boards, and sewing materials. The authors then consider the "enemies of library materials"—preventive care, repair and restoration, and disaster preparedness. Procedures, chemical formulas, diagrams, illustrations, and case studies provide an important support element to the text. Though each chapter is fully documented with footnotes, the second volume is devoted entirely to bibliography. Each bibliographic section corresponds to an identically labeled section of text in Volume I. (RMK)

470. Library of Congress. *Preservation Leaflet Series*.

For many years now, the Library of Congress has maintained a chief preservation officer and a preservation department. As an aspect of this department's responsibilities, the Library of Congress has released a number of useful and practical "Preservation Leaflets." Topics covered in these leaflets include: *Selected References in the Literature of Conservation; Environmental Protection of Books and Related Materials; Preserving Leather Book Bindings; Protection by Polyester Encasement*. A number of leaflets are in press; the total should come to over fifteen. Individual copies are available, free of charge, from the Library of Congress. (RMK)

471. Morrow, Carolyn Clark, and Steven B. Schoenly. *A Conservation Bibliography for Librarians, Archivists, and Administrators*. Troy, N.Y.: Whitston, 1979.

The editors have divided this bibliography into two sections. The first section groups readings by subject categories, such as "environmental protection" or "conservation techniques," and then in reverse chronological order by publication date under these descriptive headings. Each citation is annotated; most of the works included in the bibliography were released between 1966 and 1977. The second section provides an expanded version of the list in the first section without annotations and arranged alphabetically by author. A subject index at the end of the volume directs the reader to specific citations in the second section. (RMK)

472. Rath, Frederick L., Jr., and Merrilyn Rogers O'Connel, eds. *Care and Conservation of Collections*. Nashville: American Association for State and Local History, 1977.

Prepared as a volume in the AASLH series on the "Conservation of Collections," this annotated bibliography brings together a rich and diverse body of literature. It differs from other bibliographies in the field because of its emphasis on the theory and education of conservators. The volume's subdivisions include: "Philosophy, History and Principles of Conservation"; "Conservation Laboratories and Instrumentation"; "Training of Conservators"; "Environmental Factors in Conservation"; "Conservation of Library Materials"; "Conservation of Paintings"; "Conservation of Works of Art on Paper"; "Conservation of Objects."

473. Trinkaus-Randall, Gregor. "Effects of the Environment on Paper: A Review of Recent Literature." American Assocation of State and Local History Technical Leaflet 128. *History News*, Vol. XXXV (July 1980).

This technical leaflet introduces the uninitiated to the environmental dangers faced by paper objects and to some of the rudimentary steps that can be taken to address these problems. A bibliography is included. (RMK)

474. Waters, Peter. *Procedures for Salvage of Water-Damaged Library Materials*. Washington: Library of Congress, 1975.

This book was prepared for the Preservation Department of the Library of Congress by Waters, who was then on their staff. It is a guide to library flood-damage preparedness. The author considers the effects of water on books and other unbound library materials, the use of freezing as a short-term solution to paper preservation after a flood, the establishment and management of a salvage team, and the various procedures for eliminating or reducing flood damage after a disaster. Waters provides a list of sources of assistance, primarily consulting services, and a list of sources of supplies and equipment for dealing with flood damage in libraries. (RMK)

VI. Machine-Readable Records and Automated Techniques

475. Bearman, David. "Automated Access to Archival Information: Accessing Systems." *American Archivist*, Vol. XLII (April 1979), pp. 179-190.

Like libraries, archives and record centers are now turning to the computer to assist them in the areas of information indexing and retrieval, word processing, and in-house administration. This essay recommends a strategy for evaluating automated retrieval systems for archival purposes based upon the author's experience in developing a system for the retrieval of information on the history of biochemistry and molecular biology. Among the topics covered are the comparative evaluation of systems performance and what archivists might do to structure archival requirements so that they are compatible with computer systems design. (RMK)

476. Dollar, Charles M. "Appraising Machine-Readable Records," *American Archivist*, Vol. XLI (October 1978), pp. 423-430.

Archival appraisal is a complex and difficult undertaking even in the best of circumstances. These problems are compounded when the records in question are machine-readable and hence unanalyzable to the naked eye. Dollar has served for many years as the director of the National Archives and Records Service (NARS) Machine-Readable Records Division. His article outlines the steps taken by NARS officials in appraising machine-readable records. Both the physical integrity of the medium (usually magnetic tape) and the intellectual integrity of the records themselves are considered. A flow chart of the process is provided as well as a survey of problem areas, such as cost. (RMK)

477. Dollar, Charles M. "Computers, the National Archives, and Researchers." *Prologue*, Vol. VIII (Spring 1976), pp. 29-34.

The computer has invaded most aspects of human activity. Information managers rely heavily on automated data bases and services, and it appears that this practice will become more prevalent in the future. This article offers a discussion of the growth of machine-readable data as a governmental information source and the growth of interest among researchers in the exploitation of these data bases when creating agencies are through with them. The author examines special problems, such as the technological obsolescence of hardware, in some detail. (RMK)

478. Geda, Carolyn L. "Social Science Data Archives." *American Archivist*, Vol. XLII (April 1979), pp. 158-166.

Universities and other research centers, like the federal government, have begun to amass machine-readable data archives. An official at the Inter-University Consortium for Political and Social Research, Geda presents a comprehensive survey of data archives operations in the United States with special emphasis on the history and development of data centers connected with universities. This article also addresses a number of important related issues, such as the appraisal of electronic data processing (EDP) records, reference services for data base archives, collection development, and the future applications of EDP archival materials in research. (RMK)

479. Geda, Carolyn L., Erik W. Austin, and Francis X. Blouin, Jr., eds. *Archivists and Machine-Readable Records: Proceedings of the Conference on Archival Management of Machine-Readable Records, February 7-10, 1979, Ann Arbor, Michigan*. Chicago: Society of American Archivists, 1980.

This set of proceedings brings together an international panel of specialists, primarily from the United States, Canada, and Great Britain, to discuss the field of machine-readable records and the management of data archives. The papers deal with a variety of topics, including research use of data archives, storage and other technical problems, user services, hardware and software innovations, and legal problems, such as the implications of U.S. privacy legislation. Although directed at the computer novice, this anthology contains many useful insights into the "state-of-the-art" of records and archives. (RMK)

480. Hickerson, H. Thomas. *Archives and Manuscripts: Automated Access*. Chicago: Society of American Archivists, 1981.

This long awaited addition to the Society of American Archivists' (SAA) basic manual series draws upon the considerable experience and knowledge of an expert in the area of archival automation and information management. The volume includes a brief description to computer applications in archives and currently operational automated indexing and retrieval systems employed by archivists. Machine-readable records are mentioned only in passing. The main body of the text provides practical information on how the computer might assist archival administrators. The work concludes with an essay concerning the direction of automation efforts in U.S. archives, the activities of the SAA National Information Systems Task Force, and the potential impact of these activities on the profession. (RMK)

481. Hickerson, H. Thomas. *SPINDEX II at Cornell and a Review of Archival Automation in the U.S*. Ithaca, N.Y.: Department of Manuscripts and University Archives, Cornell University Libraries, 1976.

SPINDEX is an information indexing and retrieval software package originally developed by the Library of Congress and rebuilt as SPINDEX II by the National Historical Publications and Records Commission (NHPRC) in conjunction with a number of large American universities and corporate and religious organizations. More recently, SPINDEX II has emerged, and many members of the SPINDEX Users Network have added their own enhancements to the system. This volume surveys the state of the art in automated archival systems as of 1976 and discusses in some detail the experiences of Cornell University archivists in their use of SPINDEX II. A cost-benefit comparison between manual and automated collection description as well as numerous examples and illustrations of the SPINDEX system in operation add to the coverage. (RMK)

482. Kesner, Richard M. *Automation, Machine-Readable Records, and Archival Administration: An Annotated Bibliography*. Chicago: Society of American Archivists, 1980.

Kesner compiled this annotated bibliography at the request of the Society of American Archivists Task Force on Automated Records and Techniques. It includes 293 citations arranged in alphabetical order by author. Author, journal title, and subject indexes may be found in the back of the volume. A revised version of this work will appear in 1983. The second edition will offer citations according to subject, with ''machine-readable records'' and ''automated techniques'' serving as the two overall chapter headings. (RMK)

483. Kesner, Richard M., and Don Hurst. ''Microcomputer Applications in Archives: A Report on a Study for Progress.'' *Archivaria*, Vol. XII (Summer 1981), pp. 3-19.

In the worlds of business, finance, government, and administration, information managers are turning to distributed processing in ever greater numbers. The microprocessor has made small, in-house computers inexpensive and yet powerful tools. This article reports on the efforts of an archivist and a systems analyst as they endeavor to develop administrative systems appropriate for an archival setting on a microcomputer. The essay provides an introduction to the microcomputer as well as a brief discussion of top-down software design and the objectives of the MARS (microcomputer archives and records management systems) project. The authors are currently preparing a final report for publication which will suggest how other archivists might involve their own institutions in the development of microcomputer systems. (RMK)

484. Lancaster, Frederick Wilfred. *Toward Paperless Information Systems*. New York: Academic, 1978.

A leading scholar in the fields of library and information science, Lancaster speaks with considerable knowledge of the latest advances in information management. This volume examines the prospects for a paperless office environment, the so-called office of the future, and its implications. The author argues that the replacement of paper communciations with electronic media is inevitable and that we must prepare for it technologically and psychologically. He employs the SAFE system of the U.S. Central Intelligence Agency as an example of the type of operating information system that he envisions even in small offices of the future. (RMK)

485. Lancaster, Frederick Wilfred, and Emily G. Foyen. *Information Retrieval On-Line*. Los Angeles: Melville, 1973.

Despite its age, this book is useful to archivists, records managers, and other information managers who come from more traditional training backgrounds and yet find themselves faced with demands for automated services. Lancaster and Foyen provide a thorough introduction to the nature of on-line (that is, interactive user-computer) information retrieval systems. They focus on bibliographic data bases, but what they say may apply equally to document retrieval systems. As researchers turn in greater numbers to these automated services, they will grow accustomed to the types of products generated by these demands with better and faster on-line systems. (RMK)

486. Machine-Readable Data Files Conference Secretariat, Data Used and Access Laboratories. *Report on the Conference on Cataloging and Information Services for Machine-Readable Data Files: Airlie House, Warrenton, Virginia, March 29-31, 1978*. Arlington, Va.: Data Use and Access Laboratories, 1978.

This report chronicles the proceedings of a conference held at Airlie House, Warrenton, Virginia, on March 29-31, 1978. It includes a series of papers on the state of the art in data base management, distributed processing hardware and software, and retrieval systems. Participants at the meeting also considered the status of federal (U.S.) government machine-readable resources and many important issues, such as access requirements and privacy, that machine-readable archives must face as they serve an ever-increasing group of users. (RMK)

VII. Professional, Ethical, and Legal Issues

487. Bazillion, Richard J. "Access to Departmental Records, Cabinet Documents, and Ministerial Papers in Canada." *American Archivist*, Vol. XLIII (April 1980), pp. 151-160.

This article provides useful insights into the problem of researcher access to Canadian federal government records. Although these papers are public documents, for "reasons of state" they are not always available to the public. Bazillion examines this complex problem in the Canadian context, focusing upon both the history and development of government policies in this area and current operating procedures. His essay also raises a number of issues that have broader ramifications for those working with government records elsewhere. (RMK)

488. Berkeley, Edmund, Jr. "Archives and Appraisals." *Georgia Archive*, Vol. V (Winter 1977), pp. 51-63.

Certain individuals view contributions to archives as a civic duty and as a way of insuring that historical records are preserved for posterity. Others view the opportunity to deposit their papers in an archives as an excellent tax deduction. The archivist may recognize the long-term research value of a collection but may have no idea of the gift's market value. In this article, Berkeley examines both aspects of appraisal. He is particularly helpful in his remarks on tax appraisal. The author provides sound advice but tempers his views with the recognition that at times only the lure of a healthy tax write-off attracts important collections into public repositories. (RMK)

489. Elston, Charles B. "University Student Records: Research Use, Privacy Rights, and the Buckley Law." *Midwestern Archivist*, Vol. I (1976), pp. 16-32.

In recent years, controversy has raged concerning the private rights of citizens to know what information concerning their personal and work lives is stored in government data banks and who has access to this information. Under the Freedom of Information Act, for example, individuals may request and obtain their own FBI files. This article explores the implications of this new legislation for the keepers and users of university student records. The status of those records and their confidentiality are not clearly defined, thus raising a number of problems for university archivists. The author proposes a number of approaches to dealing with this complex problem. (RMK)

490. Evans, Frank B. "Postappointment Archival Training: A Proposed Solution for a Basic Problem." *American Archivist*, Vol. XL (January 1977), pp. 57-74.

The archival profession in the United States as a definable group dates back only to the 1930s. It does not therefore enjoy the benefits of a long-standing educational tradition. Even the profession's umbrella organization, the Society of American Archivists, has until recently hesitated to set educational standards for those in the field. As a result, archives training programs tend to vary widely in both content and quality. Evans takes a studied approach to this problem and suggests a number of different ways by which U.S. archivists might be trained. Since the publication of this article, the Society has established basic criteria for the accreditation of archival training programs and practicums. As of yet, there is no accreditation mechanism *per se*, but this too is in the works. (RMK)

491. Hamby, Alonzo L., and Edward Weldon, eds. *Access to the Papers of Recent Public Figures: The New Harmony Conference*. Bloomington, Ind.:

American Historical Association, Organization of American Historians, and Society of American Archivists, 1977.

Within the archival profession, the New Harmony Conference is often referred to as the "Disharmony Conference" because of the heated discussions that took place at its sessions. The Conference brought together scholars and curators concerned with access to the papers of important twentieth-century political leaders. The question these people seek to address is the degree to which private papers of officials are to be made accessible to the public. The viewpoints range from a fifty- or a hundred-year rule to immediate open access. This volume brings together some of the sharpest barbs from the New Harmony gathering and is essential reading for anyone interested in this controversial subject. (RMK)

492. Knoppers, Jake V. Th. "Freedom of Information and Privacy, Part I." *Records Management Quarterly*, Vol. XIV (October 1980), pp. 28-34, 55-56. "Freedom of Information and Privacy, Part II." *Records Management Quarterly*, Vol. XV (April 1981), pp. 18-31.

These two articles represent the most comprehensive study yet of how the governments of western Europe, Canada, and the United States have attempted to deal with the issues of the rights of citizens to know about their government's activities and the rights of individuals to be protected from the intrusion of others into their private lives. In part one, the author carefully examines existing or planned legislation in each country under review. In the second section, he takes a look at what is happening in Canada, where he is the special advisor to the Public Archivist of Canada in the areas of information and privacy. Together these two articles indicate that we are a long way from dealing effectively with these problems. As we grow more dependent on computerized data bases, the situation will only become more difficult. (RMK)

493. Mason, Philip P. "The Ethics of Collecting." *Georgia Archive*, Vol. V (Winter 1977), pp. 36-50.

Collection development may at times pit one archive against another. In certain instances, a potential donor (person or organization) may find himself in a difficult position because of such competition. Until 1980, when the Society of American Archivists issued a series of ethical guidelines for the profession, most archivists received little training or guidance concerning the ethical aspects of their work. This article draws upon the extensive experience of one of the archival profession's leading educators. It served as both an impetus and a guide for the ethical standards now embraced by the profession as a whole. (RMK)

494. Miller, Jerome K. *U.S. Copyrights Documents: An Annotated Collection for Use by Educators and Librarians*. Littleton, Colo.: Libraries Unlimited, 1981.

The copyright law was originally passed in 1909 to protect the authors of books and magazine articles. Since that time, recordings (both audio and audiovisual), machine-readable records, and the photostatic copier have greatly augmented the difficulties involved in the enforcement of the 1909 law. Congress therefore revised the law in 1978. While these revisions protected phonographic record manufacturers and the like, they left the services provided by libraries and archives in a poorly defined state. This volume presents all of the vital copyright legislation, with both annotations and explanations. The book is useful to those concerned with the administration of information services in terms of their compliance with copyright legislation. (RMK)

495. O'Neill, James E. "Replevin: A Public Archivist's Perspective." *Prologue*, Vol. XI (Fall 1979), pp. 200-204.

In this article, the Deputy Archivist of the United States reviews the now-famous case of *North Carolina* v. *West* and its implications for the administration of archive programs. "Replevin" in this case refers to the return of previously alienated government records. The West case established a judicial precedent whereby a state or federal agency could sue an individual or organization for the return of government papers without demonstrating how the government agency in question lost possession of the documents. O'Neill takes a generous view of these proceedings, suggesting that in instances where the alienated materials are in another archives and accessible to the public, no replevin suits would result. (RMK)

496. Peterson, Trudy Huskamp. "After Five Years: An Assessment of the Amended U.S. Freedom of Information Act." *American Archivist*, Vol. XLIII (April 1980), pp. 161-168.

This brief essay provides an introduction to the U.S. Freedom of Information Act and considers its impact over the past five years on American archives, especially federal and state programs. (RMK)

497. Peterson, Trudy Huskamp. "The Gift and the Deed." *American Archivist*, Vol. XLII (January 1979), pp. 61-66.

Some archivists employ a "deed of gift" to transfer legally the physical and literary property rights of a collection to their organization. The practice is sound from both an administrative and ethical point of view. This article discusses appropriate formats for the deed-of-gift document and discusses when one ought to employ these simple legal tools. Peterson provides a number of examples. (RMK)

498. Price, William S., Jr. "N.C. vs. B. C. West, Jr." *American Archivist*, Vol. XLI (January 1978), pp. 21-24.

In this brief article Price reviews the now-historic West case, where the State of North Carolina sued a private collector for the return of colonial-period state records. The case went to the North Carolina Supreme Court, which ruled in the state's favor, thus establishing a precedent for writs of replevin. As a result of this ruling, government archives have obtained the return of long-alienated state papers through the threat of such a writ. The issue remains in the gray area of the law and will require a number of other high-court decisions before its significance is fully appreciated. (RMK)

499. Rapport, Leonard. "Fakes and Facsimiles: Problems of Identification." *American Archivist*, Vol. XLII (January 1979), pp. 13-58.

This essay discusses the very real problem of authenticating historical documents. The author reviews the problem and various techniques for dealing with it. He includes a number of case studies drawn in part from his many years of close association with the National Archives and Records Service. (RMK)

500. Rhoads, James B. "Who Should Own the Documents of Public Officials?" *Prologue*, Vol. VII (Spring 1975), pp. 32-35.

Until the Nixon years and "Watergate," all presidential papers were treated as private property. The papers of congressmen and senators remain the private property of their creators. The question naturally rises as to the propriety of this arrangement, given the fact that these elected officials generate records as part of their duties as public, tax-paid servants. All the papers of civil servants, by contrast, remain government property and are managed by the National Archives. In this brief essay, the former Archivist of the United States considers the need to revise laws and procedures so as to expand the definition of "public record" to include these materials. (RMK)

501. Rundell, Walter, Jr. "Historians, Archivists, and the Privacy Issue." *Georgia Archive*, Vol. III (Winter 1975), pp. 3-15.

Rundell has prepared a highly readable review of current privacy legislation and its implications for both archivists and their patrons. This essay is a starting point for anyone wishing to examine the issue of privacy versus accessibility as it relates to information management and historical research. (RMK)

502. Stewart, Virginia R. "Problems of Confidentiality in the Administration of Personal Case Records." *American Archivist*, Vol. XXXVII (July 1974), pp. 387-398.

Many organizations collect information, in the form of personnel files, student records, hospital reports, and the like, for a specific administrative purpose. When these files are no longer required for day-to-day operations, they are often retired to the institution's archives. However, they invariably contain information of a personal and confidential nature. This essay looks at the problems of research access to personnel files in the context of the archivist's need to protect the identity of those mentioned in the files. Confidentiality can be preserved while allowing researchers access to these types of files. Stewart explains how this can be done. (RMK)

503. Wallace, Carolyn A. "Archivists and the New Copyright Law." *Georgia Archive*, Vol. VI (Fall 1978), pp. 1-17.

In this essay, Wallace reviews the new copyright law (1978) and discusses its implications for the operation and administration of archives programs in the United States. This article is particularly useful to those concerned with the changes in copyright law but unable to fathom the complexities of the original legislation. The presentation by Wallace is directed at specific archival practices. (RMK)

VIII. Public Programs, Outreach, and Collection Development

504. Casterline, Gail Farr. *Archives and Manuscripts: Exhibits*. Chicago: Society of American Archivists, 1980.

This volume, in the second series of basic manuals prepared under the aegis of the Society of American Archivists, introduces archivists to the fundamental techniques of exhibiting documents. Casterline proceeds methodically through planning and development, conservation, design and display techniques, program coordination, and administrative considerations. By means of photographs, illustrations, and models, the author demonstrates the basic simplicity behind many approaches to exhibiting. The reader is introduced to all the elements of a successful exhibit program. The volume also includes a bibliography and appendices of human resources, suppliers of materials and equipment, a sample facilities report, and a sample loan form. (RMK)

505. Casterline, Gail Farr, and Ann E. Pederson. *Archives and Manuscripts: Public Programs*. Chicago: Society of American Archivists, 1981.

Yet another publication in the second series of basic manuals issued by the Society of American Archivists, this volume draws upon the experiences of two leading professionals in the area of public programs. While archives have traditionally served as centers for the collection and preservation of historical materials, many institutions are now working to expand their constituencies of users by bringing the archives to the general public. As Casterline and Pederson suggest, this process can involve simple display efforts or the creation of elaborate media events. The authors provide their readers with numerous examples of public programs in archives as well as practical advice on the planning and implementation of such programs where none hitherto exists. (RMK)

506. Fleckner, John A. *Archives and Manuscripts: Surveys*. Chicago: Society of American Archivists, 1977.

Many fine archives collections today came into the custody of responsible repositories because of the efforts of a survey staff. Even within a single organization, records surveys are essential before a records management program or archives comes into being. Surveys require organizational skill if they are to realize their objectives. Fleckner draws upon his extensive experience to discuss the planning, implementation, and completion of records surveys. The text is practical, carries a number of sample forms and procedures, and includes an index. For further information on record surveys, see the series of articles in the *American Archivist*, Vol. XLII (1979), introduced by Fleckner. (RMK)

507. Freivogel, Elsie Freeman. "Educational Programs: Outreach as an Administrative Function." *American Archivist,* Vol. XLI (April 1978), pp. 147-154.

As the director of educational programs for the National Archives and Records Service, Freivogel has produced numerous outreach programs for school children, scholars, and the general public. In this brief article, the author examines outreach programs in the context of archival administrative operations. She lobbies for the introduction of outreach programs as a formal aspect of all archives organizations and suggests approaches through which one may realize these ends. (RMK)

508. Hoover, David H. "Manuscript Collections: Initial Procedures and Policies." American Association for State and Local History Technical Leaflet 131. *History News*, Vol. XXXV (October 1980).

This primer deals with the steps required in the development of a collecting program for a manuscript repository. The author challenges the reader to begin with a careful consideration of the institution's collecting policy. He emphasizes the financial and ethical aspects of the process as well as the mechanical and intellectual ones. The leaflet also examines the steps that one ought to take in selecting a collection development director. In discussing collecting procedures, the text introduces a series of sample forms and legal documents used in the day-to-day operations of a collecting program as well as some useful advice on donor relations and fund raising. The pamphlet includes a brief bibliography. (RMK)

509. Jones, William K. "The Exhibit of Documents: Preparation, Matting, and Display Techniques." American Association for State and Local History Technical Leaflet 75. *History News*, Vol. XXIX (June 1974).

Most documents are rather fragile to begin with and are susceptible to the deteriorating influences of the natural environment and user abuse. It is therefore quite understandable that archivists hesitate to exhibit materials left in their care. While caution is advised, the proper display of documents can greatly enhance an archives' visibility and can share that archives' valued holdings with persons who might not otherwise venture into its facility. This technical leaflet explains the basic rules governing the safe display of archival documents. A bibliography, drawings, diagrams, and illustrations accompany the text. (RMK)

510. Kemp, Edward C. *Manuscript Solicitation for Libraries, Special Collections, Museums, and Archives.* Littleton, Colo.: Libraries Unlimited, 1978.

Every archivist must cultivate effective collecting techniques. However, it is nearly impossible, with the possible exception of ethical considerations, to generalize on the topic. Kemp's monograph, for example, focuses upon the collecting of rare (or valuable) manuscripts. He discusses the planning of a collecting program, specialized collecting, sources of donation, the sorting of manuscripts, and financial appraisal. He provides sample solicitation letters and deed-gift forms. (RMK)

511. Kesner, Richard M. "Archival Collection Development: Building a Successful Acquisitions Program." *Midwestern Archivist*, Vol. V (1981), pp. 101-112.

This article examines the various components of a successful archives collecting program. Kesner begins by discussing the necessity of defining and then exploiting a collecting focus or theme. He also stresses the importance of public relations in developing an archives image that makes donors confident enough to leave their records to the archives. He then discusses the more technical aspects of collecting lead files, case files, and lead/donor locater cards. Finally, the author suggests that collecting programs must be reviewed on a regular basis to insure that they accurately reflect the collecting focus and institutional goals of the archive. (RMK)

512. Pederson, Ann E. "Archival Outreach: SAA's 1976 Survey." *American Archivist*, Vol. XLI (April 1978), pp. 155-162.

This article presents the results of a 1976 survey conducted by the Society of American Archivists (SAA) of archival outreach programs in the United States and Canada. The study also served as an impetus for the SAA basic manual on public programs prepared by Pederson in conjunction with Casterline (see no. *505*). (RMK)

513. Stewart, Virginia R. "A Primer on Manuscript Field Work." *Midwestern Archivist*, Vol. I (1976), pp. 3-20.

In this article, Stewart brings together a body of advice and methods for the identification and location of manuscript materials in the field. The author also considers negotiating techniques and the processes for ultimately and legally securing manuscript materials for an institution. (RMK)

514. Taylor, Hugh A. "Clio in the Raw: Archival Materials and the Teaching of History." *American Archivist*, Vol. XXXV (July-October 1972), pp. 317-330.

As an established Canadian archivist, Taylor draws upon the experiences of his countrymen both in Canada and Great Britain and the example that they have established for bringing archival materials into the classroom. The author argues that in making history come alive for the student, original archival documents can play an important part in the educational process. He outlines how this can be done and cites a number of examples to illustrate his methods. (RMK)

IX. Records Management and Micrographics

515. Benedon, William. *Records Management.* Englewood Cliffs, N.J.: Prentice-Hall, 1969.

As one of the founders of the Association of Records Managers and Administrators and as the chief administrator of one of the United States' finest records management programs (Lockheed Corp.), Benedon is considered the "grand old man" of records management in this country. He covers most subjects thoroughly, including forms control, correspondence control, micrographics management, and work-flow analysis. The volume contains numerous illustrations and examples drawn from the author's personal experience at Lockheed and elsewhere. (RMK)

516. College and University Archives Committee, Society of American Archivists. *Forms Manual.* Chicago: Society of American Archivists, 1973.

It is a sign of the times that many university archivists are now being called upon to establish records management programs for their institutions. While one may argue that an archives serves the long-range educational objectives of the university, a proper records management program can save it money and enhance its efficiency on a day-to-day basis. This forms manual brings together hundreds of forms used by archives around the country. In addition to research registration forms and box labels, the manual includes samples of routing forms, survey sheets, retrieval and circulation forms, and call slips. This work is particularly helpful to those archivists in the process of establishing records management programs for the first time. (RMK)

517. Costigan, Daniel M. *Micrographic Systems.* Silver Spring, Md.: National Micrographics Association, 1975.

Facing increased costs for storage space, archivists, records managers, and other information handlers are obliged to find ways of converting paper records into a more condensed medium. Microfilm and microfiche afford such options. So does computer output microfilm (COM), which is no different than traditional microfilm except that it is generated by computers and is never rendered in paper form. The proliferation of micrographic formats and equipment poses a real problem for those unfamiliar with the technology. This survey provides considerable background information on a full range of micrographic hardware and software. The author also recommends additional sources of information for those interested in pursuing farther a particular aspect of micrographics. (RMK)

518. Dearstyne, Bruce W. "Microfilming Historical Records: An Introduction." American Association for State and Local History Technical Leaflet 96. *History News*, Vol. XXXII (June 1977).

This technical leaflet assumes no prior knowledge of micrographics. The author provides basic definitions and information dealing with microfilm stock, formats, reduction rations; the preparation of text for filming; targets; processing; inspection; and even storage and use. A bibliography accompanies the text. (RMK)

519. Dollar, Charles M. "Machine-Readable Archives: Records Managers Neglect Automation Files." *Records Management Journal*, Vol. XIII (Winter 1975), pp. 2-8.

As offices turn more and more to the computer, they cease to generate paper records and begin to accumulate machine-readable records. Unfortunately, records managers and archivists have given little thought to the retention and final disposition of these records. As the director of the Machine-Readable Records Division at the National Archives and Records Service, Dollar is very much aware of the problems that may accrue because of neglect. He therefore advocates a number of measures for dealing more effectively with the growing number of automated files and chides those who remain inactive. (RMK)

520. Fox, Michael J., and Kathleen A. McDonough. *Wisconsin Municipal Records Manual*. Madison: State Historical Society of Wisconsin and Wisconsin Department of Development, 1980.

Begun as a simple manual for municipal government workers in the state of Wisconsin, this volume has evolved into a records management tool. The authors establish the legal precedents in Wisconsin governing the preservation, access, and ultimate disposition of government records. The manual next considers municipal records management, justifying the adoption of such a program in terms of cost, space savings, and operating efficiency. Fox and McDonough also discuss document appraisal, retention and disposition schedules, and micrographics. The second and larger section of the book is devoted to a detailed description of the various types of municipal records, indicating state or federal standards for retention and final disposition. (RMK)

521. Gill, Suzanne L. *File Management and Information Retrieval Systems*. Littleton, Colo.: Libraries Unlimited, 1981.

This volume addresses the needs of those concerned with the establishment and maintenance of filing systems. It is directed at both the practitioner and the student working a library, small office, or corporate environment. The bulk of the book is devoted to a "procedures manual" for the development and operation of various filing systems. Automated as well as manual files are viewed in this context. (RMK)

522. Kuttner, Monroe S. *Managing the Paperwork Pipeline: Achieving Cost-effective Paperwork and Information Processing*. New York: Wiley, 1978.

In business, government, and even university settings, the cost and inefficiency of traditional information handling techniques have led administrators to consider technological solutions to the problems of information management. However, the most sophisticated technology cannot take the place of a well-conceived plan for the management of paper and information flow within the organization. This volume examines record generation within the office environment and how to restructure and reform these processes so as to enhance their responsiveness to institutional needs and to make them more cost-effective. (RMK)

523. Lybarger, Phyllis M. *Records Retention Scheduling*. Prairie Valley, Kans.: Association of Records Managers and Administrators, 1980.

This volume marks the beginning of a new series of educational publications issued by the Association of Records Managers and Administrators. Lybarger addresses the problems of records scheduling and the process by which documents are slated for temporary storage, long-term or permanent storage, or destruction. The author recommends analytical techniques as well as models of standard scheduling periods for a wide range of typical office documentation. The illustrations and examples assist the author in making her points. (RMK)

524. Rhoads, James B. "Records Management and the Archivist." *Record Management Journal*, Vol. IX (January 1974), pp. 4-8.

Rhoads, who served for many years as Archivist of the United States, discusses the role of records management within the context of archival administration. He points out the commonality of interests and responsibilities between archivists and records managers and suggests that they ought to cooperate closely to achieve their objectives. (RMK)

525. Ridge, Allan D. "Records Management for Tomorrow—New Opportunities and Critical Responsibilities." *Records Management Quarterly*, Vol. IX (April 1975), pp. 10-17.

Because of the paper explosion, offices have more records than they can handle or need. The infiltration of computers into the office place has added further to the need for a systematic approach to information management and paper (or record) flow. Ridge looks at the new technology and the increasing information demands placed on the modern office. He views the records manager as the person responsible for the efficiency and effectiveness of these operations. The author posits a series of approaches and techniques that the records manager must cultivate to meet the challenges of the future. (RMK)

526. State and Local Records Committee of the Society of American Archivists. *Records Retention and Disposition Schedule: A Survey Report*. Chicago: Society of American Archivists, 1977.

Information managers employ records retention and disposition schedules to plot the life spans of documents. They usually include information on where the document in question originated, how long it is to be stored, who is to have access to it, and the nature of its final disposition (for example, "send to archives" or "destroy"). This publication brings together a series of sample retention and disposition forms from both state and federal agencies (U.S.), as well as one from a Canadian provincial government. Each form is accompanied by a brief narrative and a key explaining form categories and entries. This reference tool is useful to anyone who must develop a retention and disposition schedule. (RMK)

527. Young, Daniel. "The Commission on Federal Paperwork and Micrographics." *Journal of Micrographics*, Vol. XI (May-June 1978), pp. 305-308.

In the late 1970s, the United States government began an evaluation of its paperwork problems. The findings of the Commission on Federal Paperwork stressed the need to reduce greatly document generation and duplication and to move the records themselves into more easily managed and stored formats, such as computer tapes and microfilm. This essay considers the implications of the commission's findings in the area of micrographics and the effect of the proposed changes on both the industry and the operation of the federal government. (RMK)

X. Reference Services and Information Retrieval

528. Committee on Finding Aids, Society of American Archivists. *Inventories and Registers: A Handbook of Techniques and Examples*. Chicago: Society of American Archivists, 1976.

In no other area of the archival profession is there the degree of disagreement found in the realm of collection description. Some archives calendar their collections, others list them in card catalogs, and still others employ computers in collection indexing and information retrieval. Indeed, it has gotten to the point where even within a single repository, different collections are described and cataloged differently. The Committee on Finding Aids therefore had a difficult task in attempting to provide a common basis for archival description. The manual includes numerous examples of forms and techniques used by a representative sampling of institutions in the Society of American Archivists. The volume also demonstrates the diversity of views in this area. (RMK)

529. Holbert, Sue E. *Archives and Manuscripts: Reference and Access*. Chicago: Society of American Archivists, 1977.

Archives and information centers do no good if potential users and information resources are not kept apart. The link between archives patrons and archives is reference services, and, indeed, a good reference staff reinforced by quality finding aids and reference tools is one of the keys to a successful archives program. Holbert takes a critical look at reference services. She makes recommendations concerning security, reading-room design, reference-staff screening, researcher orientation, collection access, and communications between staff and the user community. A bibliography supplements the text, with recommendations for specialized readings in specific areas of reference services. (RMK)

530. Lancaster, Frederick Wilfred. *Information Retrieval Systems*. New York: Wiley, 1968.

In this study, Lancaster examines the process of information retrieval. His approach is conceptual and not technological. The volume is therefore not as out of date as one might expect. The author develops a series of analytical models and uses these to evaluate information retrieval systems. This book argues for a systems approach to information handling and for the creation of integrated delivery systems in which archivists, records managers, and other information specialists join librarians in providing users with the information services they require. (RMK)

531. Lancaster, Frederick Wilfred. *Vocabulary Control for Information Retrieval*. Washington: Information Resources, 1972.

Indexing is one aspect of description. Through this process, the researcher is alerted to the location of desired information. The structuring of a vocabulary that accurately describes the item, volume, or collection in question is at the heart of this procedure. Lancaster, a recognized authority in the field of indexing, discusses both the theory of vocabulary control and the techniques of indexing for the purposes of information retrieval. This book provides assistance to those planning to create indexes to collections manually as to those who plan to turn to the computer for assistance. (RMK)

532. Lytle, Richard H. "Intellectual Access to Archives: I. Provenance and Context Indexing Methods of Subject Retrieval." *American Archivist*, Vol. XLIII (January 1980), pp. 64-75; "Intellectual Access to Archives: II. Report of an Experiment Comparing Provenance and Content Indexing Methods of Subject Retrieval." *American Archivist*, Vol. XLIII (April 1980), pp. 191-206.

Lytle, the director of the Smithsonian Institution Archives, also chairs the National Information Systems Task Force of the Society of American Archivists. In both of these capacities, he has concerned himself with intellectual access to documentary information. These two articles grew out of a Ph.D. dissertation completed for the University of Maryland's College of Library and Information Science. The author analyzes the traditional provenance approach to collection description in archives and then considers subject indexing and information retrieval. He argues that archivists need to integrate both techniques into their guides and reference tools. In addition, Lytle provides a quantitative approach to the evaluation of retrieval techniques and suggests a number of avenues for further investigation. (RMK)

533. Soergel, Dagobert. *Indexing Language and Thesauri: Construction and Maintenance*. Los Angeles: Melville, 1978.

As archivists and records managers turn to computers to assist in the indexing, abstracting, and administration of records, they need to become more familiar with the theory and process of indexing. In this volume, Soergel discusses the methodology of thesaurus construction. He also considers the indexing techniques necessary for an accurate reflection of document contents. Unlike more traditional finding aids, the author seeks to develop flexible descriptive structures that can grow and change over time to reflect shifts in user interest. He refers to this process as thesaurus maintenance. Through the use of automation and the methods he recommends, information managers can keep abreast of the changing demands and concerns of their patrons. (RMK)

534. "Theory and Foundations of Information Retrieval." *Drexel Library Quarterly*, Vol. XIV (April 1978).

The *Drexel Library Quarterly* often issues a volume based on a single theme. This particular issue examines the theory and foundations of information retrieval. Among the topics covered are: "Some Fundamental Concepts of Information Retrieval"; "Indexing Theory and Retrieval Effectiveness"; "Automatic Classification in Information Retrieval"; and "Data Retrieval and Rational Logic." (RMK)

XI. Repositories by Record Type

535. Anderson, R. Joseph. "Public Welfare Care Records: A Study of Archival Practice." *American Archivist*, Vol. XLIII (April 1980), pp. 169-179.

The last twenty years have witnessed a growing interest among both scholars and the lay public in local, regional, and what may be referred to as "grassroots" history. It is no longer acceptable to focus on the activities and accomplishments of society's elites; the common man and woman have come into their own. This research shift has had a tremendous impact on archives collecting themes. Labor-union records, the papers of working people, and the archives of welfare agencies are all in great demand. Anderson provides an overview of one such record type—welfare case files. He discusses their processing, their appraisal, and their problems within the context of a diverse archives program. He also considers their research value and their importance as documents of our age. (RMK)

536. Baker, Richard A. "Managing Congressional Papers: A View of the Senate." *American Archivist*, Vol. XLI (July 1978), pp. 291-296.

As historian of the United States Senate, Baker is in an excellent position to examine the problems of administering congressional archives from the user's as well as the archivist's point of view. In this brief essay, he shares his impressions of the environment in which senators' office files and personal papers are created, organized, and ultimately discharged. He reminds his readers that senators' papers are their own, and he traces the history of various collections and the problems of ensuring that they come to rest in a repository where scholars if not the general public will enjoy access to them. The author discusses the issues that arise between the creators of these records and the archivists who must weed out the vast majority of paper with only marginal research value. (RMK)

537. Bartlett, James, and Douglas Marshall. "Maps in the Small Historical Society." American Association for State and Local History Technical Leaflet 111. *History News*, Vol. XXXIV (January 1979).

For most archives, maps and other oversized documents raise special problems. They are difficult to store, and they require careful handling because of their vulnerability to the environment and to user abuse. In this technical leaflet, Bartlett and Marshall address the problems of map equipment and storage, arrangement and classification, and cataloging. Maps require descriptions that are quite different from those used in the description of other types of manuscript material, a topic treated in the last section of Bartlett and Marshall's work. The leaflet includes an annotated bibliography. (RMK)

538. Burckel, Nicholas C. "A Business Records Survey: Procedures and Results." *Georgia Archive*, Vol. VIII (Fall 1980), pp. 15-29.

The United States was built on private enterprise, and yet the Society of American Archivists has identified only 210 ongoing business archives. If we are able to preserve this central aspect of our national heritage, archivists must make an effort to seek out, collect, and preserve historical business records. Burckel has provided a model of how one goes about establishing the existence of corporate archives and how one establishes a program that either encourages companies to begin archives programs of their own or results in the donation of historical materials to appropriate repositories. The author argues for the need to act promptly; otherwise much will be lost. (RMK)

539. Burckel, Nicholas C. "The Expanding Role of a College or University Archives." *Midwestern Archivist*, Vol. I (1976), pp. 3-15.

Colleges and universities have been traditional resting places for archival materials. As complex organizations, these educational institutions generate considerable amounts of paper themselves; and as centers of learning and research, they also become the repositories for the private papers of their faculties and staffs. In addition, many college and university archives collect outside their own institutions, usually in accordance with a specific collecting theme, such as "social welfare archives," "labor archives," or "business archives." In this article, the author examines all aspects of college and university archives. He is particularly concerned with the development of solid, comprehensive programs. His recommendations provide the basis for the creation of both enlarged user and donor constituencies. (RMK)

540. College and University Archives: Selected Readings. Chicago: Society of American Archivists, 1979.

A subcommittee of the Society of American Archivists' Committee on College and University Archives, headed by Charles B. Elston, culled the professional literature in an effort to bring together the best readings on the subject of administering archives programs in institutions of higher education. The volume therefore includes a wide range of material pertaining to the history of college and university archives in the United States, their contribution to scholarly activities, the problems they face in terms of user access and donor privacy, minimum standards for their operation, and representative examples of their core missions and goals. Contributors to the volume include many of the university community's most prominent archivists. The work includes a brief bibliography of further readings and an index. (RMK)

541. "Core Mission and Minimum Standards for University Archives in the University of Wisconsin System." *Midwestern Archivist*, Vol. III (1978), pp. 39-58.

This selection is included here as a sample of the type of document that all archives—not just university archives—ought to have. A statement of core mission and minimum standards provides archives staff with a set of clearly defined objectives. It also alerts the parent funding agency and ostensibly guides oversight to archives operations. Through the creation of a document along the lines of this example from the University of Wisconsin system, archivists can demonstrably assist in the development of a coordinated collecting effort within their own institutions, and they can also move toward establishing minimum acceptable standards for the operation of their programs. (RMK)

542. Hedlin, Edie. *Business Archives: An Introduction.* Chicago: Society of American Archivists, 1978.

The author, who served for many years as corporate archivist for Wells Fargo Bank, systematically surveys the rationale behind the establishment of a business archives, methods for establishing a program where none had existed previously, staffing and physical requirements, appraisal techniques, the role of oral history, records management, arrangement, description, and conservation. As Hedlin explains in her concluding remarks, many corporate archivists have never received formal training but find themselves in the position of managing a business archives program. This work serves as an introductory text. There are, for example, recommendations on where to go to seek further help and a list of suggested readings. Finally, the work includes a microfiche of dozens of standardized forms that might serve as models for those establishing a new business archives. (RMK)

543. Henry, Linda J. "Collecting Policies of Special Subject Repositories." *American Archivist*, Vol. XLIII (January 1980), pp. 57-63.

This brief article comments on the growth of "special subject" archives throughout the United States. These repositories have emerged as a response to the growing interest and research demand in specific subject areas such as ethnic and working-class history. Many university programs, for example, have turned to collecting records along a specific theme in addition to their own institutional materials. The author examines these developments and suggests areas that are ripe for further attention by the archival profession. She also considers the administrative and collection development problems peculiar to these types of archives. (RMK)

544. Horn, David E. "A Church Archives: "The United Methodist Church in Indiana." *Georgia Archive*, Vol. VII (Fall 1980), pp. 41-53.

This case study sheds light on the intricacies of church organization and how one archival institution successfully negotiated a cooperative arrangement with the church leadership in that state. Horn is the archivist for DePauw University and more recently for the United Methodist Church of Indiana. His article takes a historical approach to the development of the church in Indiana, its archives, and its close relationship with the university. (RMK)

545. Jones, Houston G. *Local Government Records*. Nashville: American Association for State and Local History, 1980.

This volume is based upon a comprehensive survey of activities of statewide local government records programs in forty-two states and Puerto Rico as well as the first-hand knowledge of the author, who has worked with programs in the eight remaining states of the Union. He has created an introduction to the field of local government records and a training tool for those active as custodians of county and municipal public documents. Jones divides his volume into two parts. The first addresses subjects of interest to the managers of these records; the second speaks to the concerns of potential users. Thus the first five chapters discuss the establishment of a local records program, including inventory procedures and microfilming techniques. The last four chapters examine the various types of documents found among government records. (RMK)

546. Lathrop, Alan K. "The Archivist and Architectural Records." *Georgia Archive*, Vol. V (Fall 1977), pp. 25-32.

This article briefly introduces the reader to architectural records and their arrangement and description. Lathrop points out that these important records of the built environment have been neglected until very recently. He provides practical advice for those in the process of acquiring architectural records as part of their collecting focus. (RMK)

547. Lawton, James, ed. *Shop Talk: Papers on Historical Business and Commercial Records of New England*. Boston: Boston Public Library, 1975.

New Englanders have demonstrated a greater appreciation for the history and research value of their business and commercial records than inhabitants of other regions. This volume brings together the writings of a number of distinguished scholars and curators of New England's entrepreneurial heritage. The essays cover such subjects as preserving business records, the nature of the business archive, early New England medicine companies, business records and the history of technology, and nineteenth-century credit information. Among the contributors to this work are Ralph Hidy, Jerome Finster, Louise Sullivan, Eva Moseley, Peter Molloy, and Robert Lovett. (RMK)

548. Lucas, Lydia. "Managing Congressional Papers: A Repository View." *American Archivist,* Vol. XLI (July 1978), pp. 275-280.

Because of their sheer volume, congressional papers represent a real challenge for most archives. They tax the space they occupy within the facility and place pressures on staff resources for processing and servicing the collection. Furthermore, because congressional papers are the papers of a politically important personage, the archivist must often tread carefully when dealing with these types of collections. The author of this essay is head of Technical Services, Division of Archives and Manuscripts, the Minnesota Historical Society. She has drawn upon her experiences in working with a number of large congressional collections to provide readers with a series of recommendations concerning the processing of these materials. Lucas takes a practical view of these activities but does not lose sight of the special and often sensitive circumstances surrounding the accessioning of a congressional collection by an archive. (RMK)

549. Mackaman, Frank H. "Managing Case Files in Congressional Collections: The Hazards of Prophecy." *Midwestern Archivist,* Vol. IV (1979), pp. 95-103.

The size of congressional collections makes the weeding of these materials an absolute necessity. In many instances, the appraisal process takes care of much of the superfluous and repetitious material found among the archives of our elected officials. However, congressmen or their staffs maintain a wide range of case files dealing with everything from constituent mail to special development projects in their home states. Mackaman, as director of the Dirksen Center, faces this problem on a fairly regular basis. In this article he discusses the problems related to the appraisal of these case files and suggests various ways of dealing with the problem. He does not at this time see a way of sampling case files without sacrificing some of their informational value. The problem requires further research and deliberation. (RMK)

550. Sueflow, August R. *Religious Archives: An Introduction.* Chicago: Society of American Archivists, 1980.

Many religious organizations establish archives to manage the historical records created by their churches, schools, and affiliated organizations. Usually, a member of the church receives the responsibility for developing and maintaining such a program, but that person rarely has prior knowledge or training in archival administration. This volume provides a modicum of instruction for those working with records of religious bodies. The author includes sections on the history of church archives and their place within church organizations. He deals with the collections themselves, discussing basic program requirements, collecting focuses, processing, description, and reference services. In addition, he mentions archives exhibits and publications. The volume concludes with a bibliography and a series of informational appendices. (RMK)

551. Thompson, Enid Thornton. "Collecting and Preserving Architectural Records." American Association for State and Local History Technical Leaflet 132. *History News*, Vol. XXXV (November 1980).

The size and fragility of architectural drawings and blueprints causes special problems for the archivist charged with the collection, preservation, and servicing of these materials. This leaflet provides information on the basic care and handling of architectural records. Thompson begins with a consideration of appraisal and collecting policies and moves on to discuss cleaning, mending, storage, description, and cataloging. Thompson provides a bibliography, a list of architectural society organizations, and a list of conservation materials suppliers. (RMK)

XII. Periodicals

552. American Archivist. (Chicago, Ill.).

Established by the Society of American Archivists (SAA) in 1938 as the official journal of that organization, the *American Archivist* is published quarterly through SAA headquarters in Chicago, Illinois. Each volume includes scholarly articles relating to aspects of archival administration. The journal also carries briefer technically oriented essays, book reviews, letters to the editor, short notices pertaining to professional activities, and it reports on archival institutions located throughout the world. For many years, the U.S. National Archives and Records Service (NARS) dominated the editorial board of the journal, affecting its contents as well as the image of the profession that it sought to project. As of this date, the future editorial control of the journal is uncertain. NARS personnel no longer serve as the editorial staff; a special editor prepares each issue. The SAA also publishes a newsletter and an employment bulletin alternately on a monthly basis. (RMK)

553. Archivaria. (Ottawa, Canada).

Begun in 1975 as a semiannual publication, *Archivaria* marks a clear break from the *Canadian Archivist* and the earlier efforts of the Association of Canadian Archivists to model their publication on the *American Archivist* (see no. *552*). The editors have established a professional journal with a personality of its own. Many issues treat a particular theme, such as "Photography and Archives," "The Working Class Record," "International Archives Week," and "Archives and Medicine." The book review section tends to be more extensive than that of the *American Archivist*; it includes reviews of books on Canadian history and culture as well as works pertaining to archival administration. The Association of Canadian Archivists also publishes a newsletter that appears six times a year. (RMK)

554. Archivum.

The International Council on Archives produces this journal. It has appeared more or less on an annual basis since 1951. Each issue serves as an approximate set of proceedings for conferences of the Council; it is usually based on a particular theme, such as automation and archives. The articles and book reviews provide an interesting international perspective. In most instances, the host nation prepares and publishes the volume under the aegis of a Council editorial board. The majority of articles and bibliographies are published in either French or English. (RMK)

555. ADPA. (Liége, Belgium).

Published irregularly since 1977, *ADPA*, which stands for Automatic Data Processing in Archives, is the product of the International Council on Archives Working Party on ADP. This journal is unique in that it is the only publication of its kind devoted entirely to the uses and implications of the new technology for archival administration and information management. Articles appear in either French or English; brief summaries follow each essay. Book reviews and bibliographies occasionally appear in *ADPA*. The Working Party is developing an international bibliography dealing with automated records and techniques in an archival setting. (RMK)

556. Georgia Archive. (Atlanta, Ga.).

The Society of Georgia Archivists has published *Georgia Archive* on a semi-annual basis since 1973. The journal actually serves as a professional publication that draws upon a wide number of sources for its articles and book reviews. Most of its subscribers are located in the Southeast, but the editorial staff plans to rename the journal and develop a broader readership. Recent issues have focused on such subjects as the National Historical Publications and Records Commission and state archival programs and outreach activity planning in archives. (RMK)

557. History News. (Nashville, Tenn.).

The American Association for State and Local History is perhaps the largest and most active public history organization in the United States today. It produces many fine publications including *History News*, which, first issued in 1946, currently appears each month. While the primary focus of the journal is programming and techniques for the management of historical societies and small museums, archival administration and paper conservation are both subjects regularly covered in its pages. In addition, each issue contains a "Technical Leaflet.'' Many of these leaflets address information management issues in a concise, informative manner. Unlike other professional journals, the articles and technical leaflets in *History News* are usually the products of in-house staff research or are works solicited by the editor rather than referred submissions from the profession as a whole. (RMK)

558. *IRM*. (Hempstead, N.Y.).

IRM, which stands for Information and Records Management, is a typical trade journal publication produced by PTN Publishing Corporation and issued since 1966 on a monthly basis. The magazine carries very brief articles, no more than a page or two, dealing with the latest hardware and software developments in the area of information handling. The publication is useful to those interested in the latest news on micrographics and computer output microfilm technology and on modern office systems and equipment. (RMK)

559. *Journal of the Society of Archivists*. (Windsor, Berkshire, U.K.).

The Society of Archivists is the British equivalent of the Society of American Archivists. Its *Journal* is much like the *American Archivist* (see no. *552*), with scholarly articles, book reviews, technical notices, and announcements. Issued quarterly since 1967, it also contains a number of interesting differences from the American journal. First, given the nature of British as opposed to U.S. history, British documentary evidence tends to include incunabula and parchment scrolls as well as more modern records. The *Journal* carries articles in this area. The British also experimented with computers at an earlier stage than their colleagues in the United States and Canada. Thus, some of the first articles dealing with data processing applications in archives appear in the *Journal*. (RMK)

560. *Manuscripts*. (New York, N.Y.).

A quarterly publication of the Manuscript Society, *Manuscripts* began publication in 1948. The journal emphasizes manuscript collecting, the review of famous and interesting manuscripts, book reviews, and surveys of the current market price of ''collectable'' documents. This publication is primarily of use to professionals in this highly specialized and competitive field. (RMK)

561. *Prologue*. (Washington, D.C.).

Prologue is the quarterly journal of the National Archives and Records Service (NARS). Begun in 1969, the periodical carries articles about the National Archives and the use of federal records in scholarly research. Though the articles and reviews tend to come from NARS personnel, outside archivists and researchers also contribute to its contents. The journal occasionally serves as the forum for issues affecting the operation of federal archival repositories, such as the recent controversy over *North Carolina* v. *West* and replevin. *Prologue* is artfully packaged, with document reproductions, maps, and illustrations. (RMK)

562. Records Management Quarterly. (Bradford, R.I.).

The Association of Records Managers and Administrators (ARMA) has issued *Records Mangement Quarterly* since 1966. The journal includes articles, special features (longer essays), conference calendars, book reviews, and ARMA news and events. Individual contributions tend to be shorter and less scholarly than those found in the *American Archivist* (see no. *552*) and other archival journals. Emphasis is on the latest information in the fields of records management, forms and correspondence control, word processing, micrographics, and integrated information systems with its readers. Articles usually consider the activities within specific records management programs and at times present step-by-step approaches to program implementation. (RMK)

563. Technology and Conservation. (Boston, Mass.).

Published since 1975 on a quarterly basis by The Technology Organization, *Technology and Conservation* is sent without charge to qualified persons working in or managing programs involving analysis, preservation, restoration, protection, and documentation of art, buildings and monuments, historic sites, and antiquities. Its staff seeks the latest information concerning the high technology aspects of conservation work. As such the journal is unique. It regularly carries studies of paper and document conservation projects and has issued a number of articles on the planning of archival conservation laboratories and storage facilities. Like other trade magazines, it carries reports on the latest hardware used in conservation work. (RMK)

564. The Midwestern Archivist. (Minneapolis, Minn.).

The Midwestern Archivist, begun in 1976, is the semiannual publication of the Midwest Archives Conference. Certain issues emphasize a certain subject, such as collection development or security, but the readings tend to be eclectic, touching upon most subjects of interest to archivists and records managers. (RMK)

XIII. Bibliographies and Reference Works

565. Business Archives Affinity Group, Society of American Archivists. *Directory of Business Archives in the United States and Canada.* Chicago: Society of American Archivists, 1980.

This volume, one of the many reference tools prepared by a subgroup of the Society of American Archivists, lists 210 business and corporate archives operating in the United States and Canada as of the end of 1979. Citations are listed alphabetically by state or province and include company addresses, directors' names, collection span dates, establishment dates for archival programs, brief descriptions of archival holdings, finding aid descriptions, and guidelines for collection access. An index of corporate names follows the listings for easy access. Many major businesses in both countries operate without archives programs. This publication serves as a starting point for those seeking to enter this increasingly important aspect of the archival profession. (RMK)

566. College and University Archives Committee, Society of American Archivists. *Directory of College and University Archives in the United States and Canada.* Chicago: Society of American Archivists, 1980.

During the 1960s, the Society of American Archivists conducted a survey of college and university archives, resulting in a publication similar to no. *565.* However, this publication includes over fifteen hundred listings, testifying to dramatic growth in the number of college and university archives programs in the 1970s. The publication lists U.S. programs alphabetically by state. Canadian programs are listed in one alphabetical sequence. Each citation includes an institutional identification number, institutional name, nature of holdings (archives, manuscripts, or both), address, phone number, and staff names with responsibilities. An automated indexing and information retrieval system, SPIN-DEX, was employed in the preparation of the camera-ready copy as well as the name, institution, and subject indexes. (RMK)

567. Cox, Richard J. "An Annotated Bibliography of Basic Readings on Archives and Manuscripts." American Association for State and Local History Technical Leaflet 130. *History News,* Vol. XXXV (September 1980).

This bibliography brings together many of the standard readings recognized as essential for balanced archival education. The listings, with brief annotations, are arranged alphabetically by author within broad subject categories. While there is considerable overlap with the Evans bibliography (no. *568*), a number of citations are unique to each. Cox's effort constitutes a supplement to the items cited in this section. (RMK)

568. Evans, Frank B., ed. *Modern Archives and Manuscripts: A Select Bibliography.* Chicago: Society of American Archivists, 1975.

For most American archivists, this bibliography serves as a reference tool for works published prior to 1975. Since its publication, the *American Archivist* (see no. *552*) has issued a series of updates, usually on an annual basis. Although "select," this volume draws upon a wide range of U.S., Canadian, European, Soviet, and Indian publications—both articles and monographs. Evans has designed the work rigorously so that virtually every aspect of archival administration and records management is at least touched upon. The author moves from the general to the specific, covering methodology and techniques as well as institutional organization and services. The citations are not annotated, but the organization clearly indicates the primary concern of each entry. (RMK)

569. Evans, Frank B., ed. *The History of Archives Administration: A Select Bibliography.* Paris: United Nations Educational, Scientific, and Cultural Organization, 1979.

The author points out that this work "brings together many of these writings as they document the accomplishments and the needs of national communities throughout the world. It is intended to assist in the development of training courses and studies in which the past as recorded in archives is used to serve the needs of the present and the future." The first two sections of the bibliography deal with archival concepts, traditions, and procedures. From an American perspective, the most interesting section of the book is that dealing with the history and development of archival programs throughout the world. Evans includes chapters on various European countries, the Soviet Union, and Asian, Latin American, and African nations. The volume concludes with bibliographic information pertaining to international archival organizations. (RMK)

570. Evans, Frank B., Donald F. Harrison, and Edwin A. Thompson, comps., and William L. Rufes, ed. *A Basic Glossary for Archivists, Manuscript Curators, and Records Managers.* Chicago: Society of American Archivists, 1974.

Like most professions, information management is not without its specialized terminology, and it is not unusual to find major disagreements over the definition of even basic professional terms and concepts. In this pamphlet, reprinted from an article in the *American Archivist* (see no. *552*), a panel of distinguished archivists attempts to establish common ground in the area of archival and records management terminology. The glossary is useful to experienced as well as novice information managers, although the definitions are not universally accepted. These entries provide a useful starting point for further consideration and discussion of basic archival concepts. (RMK)

571. National Historical Publication and Records Commission. *Directory of Archives and Manuscript Repositories.* Washington: National Historical Publication and Records Commission, 1978.

Many years in the making, this work is the first comprehensive attempt to list and cross-index archival institutions since the Hamer Guide of nearly two decades ago. NHPRC employed both a mail survey and a phone survey to collect this information. The Commission entered all of this data into a computerized data base with the assistance of SPINDEX, an automated indexing and information retrieval system. Each entry includes basic information pertaining to individual programs, such as institutional names, addresses, phone numbers, collecting policies, availability of finding aids and photostatic copying, and restrictions on access. Entries are arranged alphabetically by state. Proposals are currently circulating concerning the use of this NHPRC data base as the foundation for a national network of archival information. In the meantime, the NHPRC plans to update the *Directory* regularly. (RMK)

572. Rath, Frederick L., Jr., and Merrilyn Rogers O'Connell. *Administration.* Nashville: American Association for State and Local History, 1980.

This volume is the fifth in a series of annotated bibliographies pertaining to the management and preservation of historical materials. Drawing upon both monograph and periodical sources published since 1945, the editors have brought together over twenty-four hundred citations. The bibliography is arranged by subject headings, including "Historical Organizations," "Resources for Administration," "Financial Management," "Fund Raising," and "Buildings." While most of these recommended readings are directed at the needs of historical societies and museums, section 13, entitled: "Library and Archival Administration," deals with concerns particularly germane to archival administrators. The work is indexed with brief annotations. (RMK)

573. Society of American Archivists. *Membership Directory, 1980-1981*. Chicago: Society of American Archivists, 1981.

From time to time the Society of American Archivists (SAA) issues a directory of its members. This publication includes the names, addresses, and telephone numbers of most, but not all, SAA members. In addition to its obvious uses, individuals interested in archival administration or records management as a career might employ the *Directory* to identify persons near their place of residence who might advise them in terms of employment opportunities and alternative career paths. The *Directory* also includes a listing of SAA Professional Affinity Groups, such as Business Archives, Religious Archives. (RMK)

CHAPTER 5

GENEALOGY AND FAMILY HISTORY

Glen M. Leonard, editor

In recent years the American public has taken an increased interest in tracing family roots. This popularization of genealogical research has broadened a widely practiced hobby and increased the demand for professional aid in genealogy. Numerous popular guides to research have appeared. The teaching of genealogy and family history has been added to the curriculum of many schools, and historians have looked into a field often neglected by them.

At the same time, the historical community has been delving into another interdisciplinary approach to the past, that of historic demography. The demographic approach to the history of the family is increasingly popular as a means of understanding communities as well as families in the past.

In this chapter, selected titles introduce the public historian to questions of interaction among historians, genealogists, and family historians. Other sections list works on basic, international, and special genealogical research methods. Methods and illustrative examples of studies in historical demography follow. The chapter concludes with a variety of helpful periodicals, guidebooks, indexes, directories, and bibliographies to assist in further research and reading.

I. The Historian and Genealogy

574. Anderson, Robert C. "The Genealogist and the Demographer." Series 209, in the Genealogical Society of Utah. *[Proceedings of the] World Conference on Records: Preserving Our Heritage, August 12-15, 1980*, Vol. XII, *Historical Changes in Population, Family, and Community*. Salt Lake City: Genealogical Society of Utah, 1981.

A professional genealogist invites historical demographers, who are using the same kinds of sources tapped by genealogists, to become acquainted with the methods of modern genealogical research. The professionalization of history in the late nineteenth century created a mistrust among historians for amateur genealogists. Higher standards in genealogy, pioneered by Donald Lines Jacobus between the two world wars, allow the genealogist to aid the historian in identifying reliable genealogical publications. Genealogists can help in historical studies of migration, family reconstitution, the family cycle or life course, and other political and economic questions. The author reports an example of his study of family communication networks created by migration prior to 1735 and the impact of these networks in spreading Jonathan Edwards's revival of 1734 from Northampton, Mass., to neighboring areas. (GML)

575. Crandall, Ralph J. "A Neglected Resource: The Value of Genealogy to the Study of the Nineteenth-Century Family in America." *Genealogical Journal*, Vol. IX (December 1980), pp. 165-181.

Students of the family should make use of the many compiled genealogies already in print. Crandall states that only by studying and comparing the actual experiences of many families over several generations will historians be able to write confidently of the life of the family in the nineteenth century. (KS)

576. Dismukes, Camillus J. "Aids for the Family Historian: Mechanics, Pitfalls, and Concepts of Genealogy." *National Genealogical Society Quarterly*, Vol. LVII (September 1969), pp. 163-178.

Dismukes reviews the mechanics of genealogical research, identifies common pitfalls in research, and offers a philosophy for family historians. (KS)

577. Hays, Samuel P. "History and Genealogy: Patterns of Change and Prospects for Cooperation." *Prologue*, Vol. VII (Spring 1975), pp. 39-43; Vol. VII (Summer 1975), pp. 81-84; Vol. VII (Fall 1975), pp. 187-191.

Hays examines the fields and sources of history and genealogy and shows that closer cooperation between these fields would be mutually advantageous. He argues for a closer relationship between social history and genealogy. (KS)

578. Lackey, Richard S. "The Value of Genealogy and Family History." *Genealogical Journal*, Vol. IX (December 1980), pp. 153-164.

Lackey attempts to answer the question of the value of genealogy and family history. He states that while individuals view genealogy and family history from vastly different perspectives, these areas of study contribute a great deal to society. (KS)

579. Sperry, Kip. "Professionalism Examined." *Genealogical Journal*, Vol. VI (June 1977), pp. 59-66.

Sperry demonstrates that a professional genealogist should have an active, ongoing program of professional development. He identifies ten attributes of a professional genealogist, such as continually seeking education and training in genealogy. (KS)

580. Sperry, Kip. "What Is a Professional Genealogist?" *American Genealogist*, Vol. LIII (July 1977) pp. 178-182.

Sperry defines and examines professionalism in American genealogy. He also identifies some of the opportunities for genealogical education in America. (KS)

581. Taylor, Robert M., Jr. "Genealogical Sources in American Social History Research: A Reappraisal." *New England Historical and Genealogical Register*, Vol. CXXXV (January 1981), pp. 3-15.

Taylor elaborates on the utility of compiled genealogies for social history and the value of published genealogies for studies of past family life and kinship. (KS)

II. The Historian and Family History

582. Anderson, Robert Charles. "The Genealogist and the Demographer." *Genealogical Journal*, Vol. IX (December 1980), pp. 182-197.

This article analyzes the fields of genealogy and demography from a genealogist's viewpoint. Anderson states that the practitioners of the new social history use the same records that genealogists have been using for over a century. Yet, as he notes, there has been little communication between genealogists and historians. The article looks at ways genealogy can aid the demographer. (KS)

583. Bitton, Davis. "Family History: Therapy or Scholarship?" *Genealogical Journal*, Vol. VII (March 1978), pp. 21-28.

Bitton analyzes some of the inherent problems in family history: whether or not family history can be used for therapy or scholarship. Bitton states that "the purpose of family history projects, of family history courses, and to some extent of the whole family enterprise in its various facets, is often less that of scholarship than that of therapy." Scholarship is at one end of the spectrum and personal therapy is at the other end. (KS)

584. Jeffrey, Kirk. "Varieties of Family History." *American Archivist*, Vol. XXXVIII (October 1975), pp. 521-532.

Jeffrey discusses trends in research and interpretation in American family history. This issue of *The American Archivist* includes two additional articles on family history. (KS)

585. Kyvig, David E., and Myron A. Marty. *Your Family History: A Handbook for Research and Writing*. Arlington, Ill.: AHM, 1978.

Many teachers have utilized family history, particularly oral history approaches, without knowing it or without proper guidance. As a subject, family history has begun to populate many collegiate curricula and is being used to heighten the individual's awareness of self. The authors of this handbook seek to assist teachers in bringing into proper focus a highly effective teaching technique as well as a most interesting historical approach. Although the handbook resulted from class-room efforts, it can be used by anyone interested in studying the family. (PJT)

586. Smith, Daniel Blake. "Perspectives in American Family History." In *Working Papers from the Regional Economic History Research Center*, Vol. III (1979), pp. 1-28.

Smith reviews recent findings on early American family structures and discusses the varied approaches to family history. (GML)

587. Spagnoli, Paul G. "Philippe Aries, Historian of the Family." *Journal of Family History*, Vol. VI (Winter 1981), pp. 434-441.

This review essay is essentially a biographical sketch of the author of *Centuries of Childhood* (Paris, 1960; New York, 1962), which created widespread interest in family history. Aries, born in Blois, France, in 1914, was a part-time demographic historian and political activist, journalist, iconographer, and bibliographer. He was also known for his work *Western Attitudes toward Death* (1974). (GML)

588. Stone, Lawrence. "Family History in the 1980s: Past Achievements and Future Trends." *Journal of Interdisciplinary History*, Vol. XII (Summer 1981), pp. 51-87.

This is one of nineteen articles published in two special theme issues on "The New History." Stone notes influences on the growth of family history since World War II and approaches used by historians. The major portion of the article discusses historiographical developments in these varied approaches: demography; household structure; economics; lineage, kin, and family; religion; values and emotions; and sexuality. He summarizes major themes and projects new methods and sources and unsolved problems awaiting research. (GML)

589. Tilly, Charles, and Louise A. Tilly. "Stalking the Bourgeois Family." *Social Science History*, Vol. IV (Spring 1980), pp. 251-260.

The Tillys criticize the work of Christopher Lasch and Lawrence Stone for their reaction against the social-science methods in family history. They argue that Lasch and Stone are idealists who fail to use methods of the new social history in their work on the modern bourgeois family. This article is useful as an example of the dialog over varying approaches to the study of the family. (GML)

590. Vann, Richard T. "History and Demography." *History and Theory*, Vol. I (Beiheft 9, 1969), pp. 64-78.

Vann argues that the eclecticism of historians prompts them to adopt new methods in their work. Historical demography answers questions not possible with traditional historical methods. But demography is not necessarily historical and history not necessarily demographic. (GML)

591. Watts, Eugene J. "Quantitative Methods in Historical Analysis: A Syllabus." *Historical Methods Newsletter,* Vol. V (March 1972), pp. 59-67.

This outline of a fifteen-week college course by an Indiana University historian identifies weekly discussion topics and reading assignments in three texts and other sources. (GML)

592. World Conference on Records (2nd, Salt Lake City, 1980). [Papers], Vols. 3-4. *North American Family and Local History.* Salt Lake City: Genealogical Department of the Church of Jesus Christ of Latter-day Saints, 1981.

These volumes, covering the second World Conference on Records at Salt Lake City in 1980, present fifty papers by fifty-three historians, genealogists, and archivists from throughout the United States and Canada. The topics range from broad to specific, but each is concerned with some aspect of gathering and writing local history, social history, biography or genealogy. Representative titles include "The Family Periodical and the Family Historian"; "Black Family History Resources in U.S. Military Records"; "Family History Resources: Sources for U.S. Local and Family History"; "The Families of Western Canada: Their Immigration and Multicultural Background"; "Personal Records of Pennsylvania Germans"; "In Search of Emma Smith: Techniques Used in Recovering Her Personal History"; "Family History Resources: U.S. Lineage Societies"; and "The Native American: Records That Establish Individual and Family Identity." The papers presented at this conference were published individually and also in thirteen bound volumes, the final one being an index. (RMS)

III. Basic Genealogical Research Methods

593. Adams, Golden V., Jr. "The Genealogical Research Process." *Genealogical Journal,* Vols. I and II (September 1972), pp. 59-65; (December 1972), pp. 95-98; (March 1973), pp. 10-14; (June 1973), pp. 59-61.

This four-part article covers the basics in genealogical research: defining genealogical objectives, evaluating evidence, note-keeping, and the research report. This series of articles is also of interest to professional genealogists. (KS)

594. American Society of Genealogists. *Genealogical Research: Methods and Sources.* 2 vols. Washington: The Society, 1971-1981.

Most genealogical textbooks begin by explaining basic genealogical research techniques but use the bulk of the text to discuss the location and use of specific types of genealogical source records. This work is a major exception; it covers those areas but then discusses the records of specific states and foreign countries, including a great deal of very specific detail not found in other texts. The more general chapters also provide information and analysis not found in other texts.

Each chapter is written by one or more genealogical experts, which makes for some difference in approach. Some chapters are largely narrative, while others are bibliographical essays. Volume I, issued in 1981, is a revision of the original first volume, which was published in 1960. (RMS)

595. Colket, Meredith B., Jr. "Creating a Worthwhile Family Genealogy." *National Genealogical Society Quarterly*, Vol. LVI (December 1968), pp. 243-262. Reprinted as a special NGS publication.

Colket describes types of compiled genealogies, shows how they should be prepared, and gives examples. He identifies several outstanding genealogies in a select list. (KS)

596. Helmbold, F. Wilbur. *Tracing Your Ancestry*. Birmingham, Ala.: Oxmoor House, 1976.

In a book of 210 pages, including bibliography and index, Helmbold presents some information not found in much more extensive texts. Pages 72-73 guide the reader through the complexities of the Campbell, Russel, and Cott indexing systems used in court record books. His explanation of mortgage records (pp. 75-77) points out ways in which these materials can be more useful genealogically than deeds. A brief discussion (pp. 84-85) of Baptist and Methodist church records summarizes the genealogical uses and limitations of these records. Pages 125-128 cover Confederate service and pension records in more detail than is found in other texts. Helmbold's discussion of public land records (pp. 134-140) not only explains the origin and nature of such records but compares their use to that of deeds found in county offices. Here and there Helmbold mentions regional differences in records, particularly in regard to the Gulf Coast states and the Confederacy. (RMS)

597. Kieffer, Elizabeth. "Some Common Genealogical Misconceptions." *National Genealogical Society Quarterly*, Vol. VIX (September 1971), pp. 190-195.

Kieffer briefly outlines common misunderstandings in genealogy, such as name changes, nicknames, and the limitations of printed works. (KS)

598. Lackey, Richard S. *Cite Your Sources*. New Orleans: Polyanthos, 1981.

Cite Your Sources shows how to format genealogical footnotes. In most aspects it is in harmony with better-known style guides, such as the University of Chicago's *A Manual of Style*, and it has the advantage of including many examples showing how to footnote information from manuscripts and microforms—an area in which the major style guides are not as complete. (RMS)

599. McLeod, Dean L. "Record Source Failure: Some Implications for Analysis." *Genealogical Journal*, Vol. VII (June 1978), pp. 98-105.

McLeod examines record source failure by genealogists, demonstrating the need for genealogists to look closer at record sources. McLeod states that sources are not what they seem. "Genealogical analysis can be separated into two fundamental problems: the first originates in our assumptions and the realities of record linkage, and the second comes from our notions about sources." (KS)

600. Markwell, Frederick C. "The Genealogist as Detective." *Genealogical Journal*, Vol. VII (December 1978), pp. 175-181.

There are many similarities between the way a detective sets out to solve a crime and the way a genealogist tries to unravel his ancestry. The examples cited in this article relate to English ancestry. (KS)

601. Parker, J. Carlyle. *Library Services for Genealogists*. Gale Genealogy and Local History Series, Vol. XV. Detroit: Gale, 1981.

This book is written as a how-to-do-it guide for librarians and covers all aspects of genealogical research. Most of the book can be utilized by the family historian. It contains a selected bibliography of how-to-do-it books for genealogical research in the United States in general, all of its states, and many foreign countries. Search strategies are included for all chapters that deal with sources: identifying the counties for cities, vital records, family histories, name indexes, county and city histories, periodicals, census schedules, and newspapers. One chapter covers the writing of family history and contains a bibliography of recommended examples of good family histories. Annotations are provided for all of the principal and supplemental reference tools that are recommended in the book. Besides the bibliographies mentioned above, it contains six additional select bibliographies for research materials. (JCP)

602. Parker, J. Carlyle. "Resources in the Field—Genealogy: Part I, Discrimination against Genealogists." *Wilson Library Bulletin*, Vol. XLVII (November 1972), pp. 254-256. "Resources in the Field—Genealogy: Part II, Basic Reference Tools for American Libraries." *Wilson Library Bulletin*, Vol. XLVII (November 1972), pp. 257-261.

This two-part survey article provides an overview of U.S. published sources. Writing for librarians, Parker defends the genealogical patron as a serious researcher. The sources cited are standard American genealogical reference books, although there are many others. (KS)

603. Vallentine, John F. "Pedigree Analysis and Research Planning." *Genealogical Journal*, Vol. III (September 1974), pp. 92-95.

Vallentine outlines the basic steps used in pedigree analysis, such as long-range objectives, the preliminary survey, setting individual objectives, research backgrounding, and the research plan. (KS)

IV. Special Problems and Techniques of Family History

604. Clark-Lewis, Elizabeth. "Oral History, Its Utilization in the Genealogical Research Process." *National Genealogical Society Quarterly*, Vol. LXVII (March 1979), pp. 25-33.

This overview of oral history is written for the genealogist. It outlines the various types of oral traditions and stresses the lack of reliability of oral sources. (KS)

605. Clifford, Richard A. "Tools Used in Analysis of a Century-Old Genealogical Research Problem." *Genealogical Journal,* Vol. IV (December 1975), pp. 155-167.

Clifford traces the solution of a genealogical research problem with the use of analytical tools. (KS)

606. Genealogical Department of the Church of Jesus Christ of Latter-day Saints. *Research Papers*. Salt Lake City: Genealogical Department of the Church of Jesus Christ of Latter-day Saints, 1966-.

Each paper is a report either on a country's genealogical research sources or on one specific type of source. Nearly all general country papers contain a summary table that lists the major genealogical sources of a country and their years of availability. Following this summary table, each source reported is described in a little more detail: period covered; type of information provided; and availability, including availability in microform. The availability report includes holdings of the Genealogical Department. Most of these papers are now out of print, but many are available on microfiche. Many of them are listed in Parker's *Library Services for Genealogists*, pp. 58-71 (see no. *601*). (JCP)

607. Kirkham, E. Kay. *The Handwriting of American Records for a Period of 300 Years*. Logan, Utah: Everton, 1973.

Of several books available on deciphering old American documents, this one is the most familiar to genealogists. It discusses and illustrates the manner in which each letter of the alphabet was commonly written—in upper and lower case—in seventeenth-, eighteenth-, and nineteenth-century America. The obsolete double *s* symbol, often misinterpreted as an *f* or *p*, is included, and the work contains a chapter each on numbers and abbreviations. Since the originators of many early American records were of Germanic origin, an appendix includes examples of the alphabet in German script and its forerunners, from the twelfth through nineteenth centuries. Photocopies of four seventeenth-century American documents (none with Germanic influences), and printed transcriptions, are included for study. (RMS)

608. Roderick, Thomas H. "Quantitative Genealogy: Methods Applied." *National Genealogical Society Quarterly,* Vol. LVIII (March 1970), pp. 3-9.

Roderick applies the use of mathematics and quantitative method to genealogical research problems. (KS)

609. Sheppard, Walter Lee, Jr. "Professional Ethics in Genealogical Research." *National Genealogical Society Quarterly*, Vol. LXVII (March 1979), pp. 3-11.

Sheppard considers professionalism in genealogy. He defines the terms *professional genealogist* and *ethics* in genealogy. This article is followed by a shorter article by Gary Boyd Roberts, "A Professional Guide for Genealogical Libraries and Librarians." (KS)

610. Stevenson, Noel C. *Genealogical Evidence*. Laguna Hills, Calif.: Aegean Park, 1979.

Stevenson is both a lawyer and a well-known genealogist. This book deals with the nature and use of genealogical evidence and is intended for use by genealogists and by lawyers involved in cases where family history or heirship is concerned. Among the topics covered are proving paternity and maternity; fabricated genealogies; abuse of heraldic claims; legal status of informal, irregular, and common law marriage in each of the fifty states; and the nature and reliability of the records commonly used in genealogical research. The types of records discussed are official vital records; probate and other court records; land and census records; and the major types of unofficial records, among them published and manuscript genealogies, church and family Bible records, data taken from genealogies, church and family Bible records, data taken from monuments and other memorials, and genealogical evidence in newspapers. The work concludes with chapters on the rules of evidence applied to genealogy and the admissibility of hearsay evidence. A brief glossary of legal terms pertinent to genealogy is included. (RMS)

611. Stevenson, Noel C., ed. *The Genealogical Reader*. Salt Lake City: Deseret Books, 1958; reprinted, New Orleans: Polyanthos, 1977.

Thirty-two timeless articles on various phases of genealogical research, originally appearing in various American genealogical periodicals, are reprinted here. Some of the titles are: "Pitfalls in Genealogical Research"; "Dates and the Calendar"; "Is Genealogy an Exact Science?"; "Tradition and Family History"; "Interpreting Genealogical Records"; "Commercialism in Genealogy"; "On the Marring of Research Sources"; "Public Officials and Professional Genealogists"; "Genealogical Research in the National Archives"; "Fraudulent Pedigrees"; and "Marital Rights in the Colonial Period." (RMS)

612. Yeandle, Laetitia. "The Evolution of Handwriting in the English-Speaking Colonies of America." *American Archivist*, Vol. XLIII (Summer 1980), pp. 294-311.

Yeandle describes the handwriting of early English colonists. The article is illustrated with good examples of early American handwriting, most of which are in the collections of the Folger Shakespeare Library. (KS)

613. Zabriskie, George Olin. "Personal Biases in Genealogical Research." *Genealogical Journal*, Vol. VI (December 1971), pp. 169-171.

Zabriskie identifies some of the pitfalls and personal biases in genealogical research, such as royalty in the family, the family coat of arms, and relationships to famous persons. (KS)

614. Zabriskie, George Olin. "Solving Major Genealogical Problems." *Genealogical Journal*, Vol. X (Fall 1981), pp. 141-146.

Zabriskie discusses finding solutions to major genealogical research problems. He emphasizes that all genealogical problem solving begins with a full, detailed understanding of the entire problem. A sample problem is presented. (KS)

V. Methods of Family History

615. Anderson, Robert Charles. "Genealogy and Record Linkage." *Genealogical Journal*, Vol. IX (March 1980) pp. 3-8.

Anderson defines nominal record linkage, family reconstruction, prosopography, genealogy, and family history. Each of these areas has its own uses, and they are discussed in this article, including their relationships. (KS)

616. Bean, Lee L., Dean L. May, and Mark H. Skolnick. "The Mormon Historical Demography Project." *Historical Methods*, Vol. XI (Winter 1978), pp. 45-53.

The authors outline one component of a major research effort, the Mormon Historical Demography Project, that involves physicians and others evaluating family group records in the Genealogical Library, Salt Lake City. (KS)

617. Dyke, Bennett, and Warren T. Morrill, eds. *Geneological Demography*. New York: Academic, 1980.

This volume contains sixteen papers presented as a symposium at the Forty-eighth Annual Meeting of the American Association of Physical Anthropologists, San Francisco, April 5, 1979. It is the third in an open-ended series edited by E. A. Hammel, "Population and Social Structure: Advances in Historical Demography." The papers generally describe the methods used and conclusions reached on specific questions about human population structure and include work in historiography, historical demography, and ethnology. Of particular interest to public historians are George A. Collier's description of KINPROGRAM, a package of computer programs for processing genealogical censuses; a study of name frequency patterns by Kenneth M. Weiss, et al.; Kenneth W. Wachter's discussion of procedures for determining the number of ancestors a person living in 1947 would have had at the Norman conquest; and a study of migration patterns at marriage in colonial New England based on genealogical records, by John W. Adams and Alice B. Kasakoff. (GML)

618. Hareven, Tamara K., ed. "Papers from Old Sturbridge." *Journal of Family History*, Vol. VI (Spring 1981), pp. 2-40.

The title refers to student papers produced in a cooperative program between Clark University and Old Sturbridge Village beginning in 1975. Hareven writes a brief foreword to the papers, which together form a special section on techniques of teaching family history using the sources of material culture. The papers include: Pamela Beall, et al., "Students and Family History: The View from Old Sturbridge Village," pp. 5-14. Warren Leon, "Picturing the Family: Photographs and Paintings in the Classroom," pp. 15-27; Peter S. O'Connell, "Putting the Historic House into the Course of History," pp. 41-46; and Ellen K. Rothman, "The Written Record," pp. 47-56. (GML)

619. May, Dean L. "Uses of Historical Demography in the Reconstruction of Family History." *Genealogical Journal*, Vol. VIII (March 1979), pp. 3-8.

May's overview clarifies the relationship between historical demography and family history and defines their uses, citing specific examples. (KS)

620. Skolnick, Mark H., Lee L. Bean, Sue M. Kintelman, and Geraldine Mineau. "Computers in Genealogy." Series 205 in Genealogical Society of Utah, *[Proceedings of the] World Conference on Records: Preserving Our Heritage, August 12-15, 1980,* Vol. XII, *Historical Changes in Population, Family, and Community.* Salt Lake City: Genealogical Society of Utah, 1981.

In a twelve-page report, the authors describe their development of a unique computer-based data management system for analyzing historical information. Earlier computerized systems for family history were designed for either simple data manipulation or the creation of families from individual records, such as parish reports, through automatic record linkage. The authors use a data base system with on-line access to two files containing individual records and marriage records, and auxiliary files for other information. The goal of the project was to develop a generalized system useful to other researchers, using a dedicated minicomputer and software written in FORTRAN. The test project is a genealogy of Utah Mormons from the 1840s to the present, comprising a computerized genealogy of 170,000 families (about one million individuals). (GML)

VI. Finding Ancestors Abroad

621. Falley, Margaret D. *Irish and Scotch-Irish Ancestral Research: A Guide to the Genealogical Records, Methods, and Sources in Ireland.* 2 vols. Evanston, Ill.: Author, 1976. Reprinted, Baltimore: Genealogical Publishing, 1981.

Volume I is a general guide to research in Ireland, including coverage of arms, heraldry, and nomenclature; records of the various churches; plantation and settlement records; directories and almanacs; government land surveys; and the standard research sources. Volume II contains many different bibliographies, indexes, and lists, including a list of manuscripts in the Public Record Office of Northern Ireland; and a bibliography of genealogical books concerning Irish-Americans. (JCP)

622. Gardner, David E., and Frank Smith. *Genealogical Research in England and Wales*. 4 vols. Salt Lake City: Bookcraft Publishers, 1956-1966.

This guide covers the use of the major genealogical records of England and Wales, including civil registration, parish registers of the Church of England and nonconformists, and bishops' transcripts, as well as how to read handwriting of old English and Latin records. (JCP)

623. Hamilton-Edwards, Gerald Kenneth Savery. *In Search of Scottish Ancestry*. Baltimore: Genealogical Publishing, 1972.

This work is for the family historian living or traveling in Scotland. Besides the coverage of standard research sources, it includes chapters on naming customs, testaments, sasines registers, service of heirs, clans and Scottish titles, the East India Company, and Scots heraldry. (JCP)

624. Jensen, Larry O. *A Genealogical Handbook of German Research*. Rev. ed. Pleasant Grove, Utah: Author, 1979.

This book provides detailed instruction in the reading of handwriting in German useful for genealogical research, with illustrations of sample documents and translations. Besides the general sources, it has chapters on the identification of old place names, naming practices, feast days, and determining places of origin. Appendices include a list of suffixes for place names and the use of Meyers, *Orts Und Verkehrs Lexikon*. (JCP)

625. Johansson, Carl-Erik. *Cradled in Sweden: A Practical Help to Genealogical Research in Swedish Records*. Logan, Utah: Everton, 1977.

This basic guide is designed to acquaint Americans of Swedish ancestry with the language, civil and ecclesiastical jurisdictions, place names, patronymics, feast days, old handwriting, and the standard genealogical research sources of Sweden. Appendices include a list of probate records by county and district or city, a list of parishes, and a list of Swedish and Latin words and expressions used in genealogical records. (JCP)

626. Jonasson, Eric. *The Canadian Genealogical Handbook: A Comprehensive Guide to Finding Your Ancestors in Canada*. 2d ed., rev. and enl. Winnipeg: Wheatfield, 1978.

In this general guide for the research of Canadian records, Jonasson provides a brief history of Canada with a selected bibliography of historical works concerning Canada and its provinces; all of the standard family history research sources for Canada, including coverage of French Canada and Acadia, United Empire Loyalists, and heraldry; the Public Archives of Canada; and brief summaries of the records of each province. (JCP)

627. Miller, Olga K. *Genealogical Research for Czech and Slovak Americans.* Gale Genealogy and Local History Series, Vol. II. Detroit: Gale, 1978.

Writing for her American countrymen, the Czech author includes chapters on history, geography, immigration, sources, archives, names, the calendar, language, and nobility and heraldry. An appendix contains a list of the branch libraries of the Genealogical Department of the Church of Jesus Christ of Latter-day Saints. (JCP)

628. Neagles, James C., and Lila Lee Neagles. *Locating Your Immigrant Ancestor: A Guide to Naturalization Records.* Logan, Utah: Everton, 1975.

Following several introductory chapters on the nature and content of naturalization and related records, this work outlines the availability of pre-1907 naturalization records in the United States. For each state the following information is given: repository (state or federal court, federal record center, or county name), dates for which naturalization records are available, and the types of records (naturalization petitions, declarations, certificates, and indexes). In most states, some counties did not respond to the authors' questionnaire; some of these counties may have naturalization records housed in difficult-to-reach locations. Other counties not listed were either created too late to have records prior to 1907 or reported no naturalization records for that time period. Where the records do exist, access to the originals is often difficult, but many of these records have been microfilmed by the Genealogical Society of Utah and can be examined at its main library or loaned for use at one of its branches. (RMS)

629. Platt, Lyman De. *Genealogical Historical Guide to Latin America.* Gale Genealogy and Local History Series, Vol. IV. Detroit: Gale, 1978.

This guide treats seventeen Central and South American countries, along with Cuba, the Dominican Republic, and Puerto Rico. Excluded are Belize, French Guiana, Guyana, and Surinam. General chapters cover research standards, civil registration, paleography, abbreviations used in older records, research aids, the colonial calendar, ecclesiastical divisions, population movements, and political divisions. Information concerning the countries includes a brief section on the country's history, its records, and archives. (JCP)

VII. Studies in Historical Demography

630. Glass, David V., and David E. C. Eversley, eds. *Population in History: Essays in Historical Demography.* London: Edward Arnold, 1965.

The twenty-seven essays in this volume are grouped under three headings: "General," "Great Britain," and "Europe and the United States." Only one essay deals with the United States. Two of the essays are "European Marriage Patterns in Perspective," by John Hajnal, and "A Demographic Study of British Ducal Families," by Thomas H. Hollingsworth. (JES)

631. Hareven, Tamara K., ed. *Transitions: The Family and the Life Course in Historical Perspective.* New York: Academic, 1978.

This work serves as a model of using data on a particular locale, Essex County, Massachusetts, to examine the changing nature of the family life course in historical time. Each contribution fleshes out the purely demographic definition of a life course turning point, for example, marriage, with sociohistorical analysis. (JES)

632. "Historical Population Studies." *Daedalus*, Vol. XCVII (Spring 1978).

This special issue of *Daedalus* contains seventeen contributions, ranging from general treatments of the topic of historical population studies to specific items on London in the seventeenth century, the plague in France, and Tokugawa, Japan. Wrigley's study, using family reconstitution for measuring mortality in Devon, is included. (JES)

633. Hollingsworth, Thomas H. *Historical Demography.* Ithaca, N.Y.: Cornell University Press, 1969.

This book treats the sources for historical demographic study. The introductory chapters on "Demography" and "History and Demography" present basic demographic concepts and their historical development. All of the sources mentioned in the book are discussed in the context of fundamental demographic questions. (JES)

634. Laslett, Peter. *Family Life and Illicit Love in Earlier Generations.* Cambridge: Cambridge University Press, 1977.

These broad-ranging essays summarize "Characteristics of the Western Family over Time" (chapter 1), review the important findings from the village of Clayworth and Cogenhoe (chapter 2), summarize "Long-Term Trends in Bastardy in England," and continue on the "Household and Family on the Slave Plantations of the U.S.A." (JES)

635. Laslett, Peter, and Richard Wall, eds. *Household and Family in Past Time.* Cambridge: Cambridge University Press, 1972.

This is a guide to household listings analysis. Laslett's introduction is a detailed explication of the method. Most of the essays use the method in one form or another to investigate household living arrangements and their meaning in the past. The widely used Hammel-Laslett scheme for classifying households according to their kinship composition as inferred from historical listings is presented in detail. (JES)

636. Lee, Ronald Demos, ed. *Population Patterns in the Past*. New York: Academic, 1977.

This volume consists of thirteen contributions ranging from reports on methodological developments to new data on historical populations. Of particular interest are Daniel Scott Smith's overview of thirty-eight family reconstitution studies (mostly French), E. A. Hammel and Kenneth Wachter's use of computer simulation to address issues of household kinship structure, and Ronald Lee's development of methods for analyzing historical time-series data on birth, marriage, and death. This volume gives the reader a firm sense of the variety of methods available, but it does not sacrifice interesting substantive questions. (JES)

637. Levine, David. *Family Formation in an Age of Nascent Capitalism*. New York: Academic, 1977.

Spanning several villages, this book uses simple demographic measures in an interpretive framework to "determine the role of different demographic elements in undermining the demographic equilibrium that existed before the onset of rural industrializations" (p. 5). The analysis emphasizes the role of the family and household to the changing economic structure of society during early industrialization. (JES)

638. Macfarlane, Alan. *Reconstructing Historical Communities*. Cambridge: Cambridge University Press, 1977.

Although not concerned with historical demography *per se*, this book emphasizes the practical methods needed for confronting rich collections of various types of data, including demographic data, on historical communities. The procedures recommended in the book are expressed entirely in the form of manual techniques for extracting, indexing, and analyzing data. These manual procedures are the foundation for more sophisticated, computerized methods with which the author has had experience but that are not directly reported in this book. The chapters on types of records found in English communities may be of particular interest to some readers. (JES)

639. Pressat, Roland. *Demographic Analysis*. Chicago: Aldine Atherton, 1972.

While principally concerned with the analysis of contemporary demographic data, this book is sensitive to historical applications. Throughout the book, the distinction between cohort analysis and period analysis is preserved. In cohort analysis, groups of people are followed through time, and the demographic events that they experience are recorded. In period analysis, a population is observed during a short period of time, and the demographic events are recorded for that period. Understanding the distinction between these two approaches is important to historical work. (JES)

640. Shryock, Henry S., Jacob S. Siegal, and associates. *The Methods and Materials of Demography*. 2 vols. Washington: Government Printing Office, 1974.

Volume I of this work is mostly concerned with concepts and procedures used by the U.S. Bureau of the Census in modern censuses and surveys. A summary of items included in the various censuses from 1790 to 1970 is included. Volume II emphasizes demographic methods in the more general sense of computing rates, proportions, and ratios from census data. Examples from U.S. and sometimes other national census reports are plentiful, as are step-by-step instructions for performing computations. Chapter 25, "Some Methods of Estimation for Statistically Underdeveloped Areas," is of use in historical studies, although the chapter is not written with that application in mind. A condensed, single-volume edition of this work is available from Academic Press under the authorship of Edward G. Stockwell. (JES)

641. Willigan, J. Dennis, and Katherine Lynch. *Sources and Methods of Historical Demography*. 2 vols. New York: Academic, 1982.

This work is divided into five major parts: the origins and early development of historical demography, major source materials in various countries, basic techniques for analyzing the data, interdisciplinary contributions to historical demography, and the explanation of demographic features of past societies. Historians interested in concise introductory statements on record linkage, demographic indices, log-linear modeling, and other quantitative techniques will find this work and its bibliography useful. (JES)

642. Wrigley, Edward A., ed. *An Introduction to Historical Demography*. New York: Basic Books, 1966.

This is a reference work on the use of the family-reconstitution method for English records. Some chapters deal with other types of historical demography, all primarily with reference to English records. The generality of the methods and their lucid presentation makes this book helpful to the historian who wishes to reconstruct simple demographic patterns from primary sources. (JES)

643. Wrigley, Edward A. *Population and History*. New York: McGraw-Hill, 1969.

This book treats the relationship between simple demographic observation and the substance of history. The book is self-contained in that the demographic measures used in it are explained clearly at the outset. Following the author's own background, the book emphasizes the relationship of population to the economy and concludes with some consideration of modern demographic and economic problems. (JES)

644. Wunsch, Guillaume, and Marc G. Termote. *Introduction to Demographic Analysis: Principles and Methods*. New York: Plenum, 1978.

This book is an intermediate treatment of demographic measurement and analysis. The relationship between cohort and period methods of analysis is emphasized. Of value to historians is the presentation of the Princeton Indices (called the Coale indices in the book) of fertility. These are widely used to identify the contributions of marriage, legitimate fertility, and illegitimate fertility to overall fertility rates of historical populations. Although this book uses mathematical notation, it requires only a background in college algebra. (JES)

VIII. Periodicals

645. APG Newsletter. P.O. Box 11601, Salt Lake City, Utah 84147.

Published by the Association of Professional Genealogists, this newsletter prints articles and news notes of interest to professional genealogists and others, brief items from other publications, notices of seminars and conferences, and some book reviews. Emphasis is on the profession in the United States, but the newsletter contains some foreign topics. (KS)

646. Genealogical Journal. P.O. Box 1144, Salt Lake City, Utah 84110.

The *Genealogical Journal*, published quarterly by the Utah Genealogical Association, serves as a medium for the publication of articles of international interest. Articles treat such topics as family and local history, genealogical research techniques and procedures, descriptions of record sources and collections, compiled genealogies, settlement patterns and migrations, historical studies, professionalism, and demography. Emphasis is on American sources, and most articles are scholarly and documented. Each issue includes critical and descriptive book reviews. Copies of source records, such as tombstone inscriptions, queries, and extracts, are not published. (KS)

647. Historical Methods. 4000 Albemarle Street, N.W., Washington, D.C. 20016.

This journal focuses on quantitative and interdisciplinary approaches to history, including articles and methodological reviews of works on family history (historical demography, household structure, family economic welfare, genealogical research). The publication began in 1967 as a newsletter designed to share information on the use of computers and cross-disciplinary methods in history, and the journal continues that interest under the sponsorship of the Department of History of the University of Illinois at Chicago Circle. (GML)

648. Journal of Family History. 1219 University Avenue Southeast, Minneapolis, Minn. 55415.

Founded in 1976 under the editorship of Tamara K. Hareven and published quarterly by the National Council on Family Relations, this interdisciplinary journal focuses on scholarly "studies in family, kinship, and demography." It is international in scope and publishes historical articles, review essays, selected dissertation abstracts, and bibliographies. It defines the family to include the study of internal structure and processes as well as the interaction of the family with the larger society. Family history thus defined suggests approaches combining history, historical demography, sociology, anthropology, psychology, economic theory, and literature. (GML)

649. National Genealogical Society Quarterly. 1921 Sunderland Place, N.W., Washington, D.C. 20036.

Although an emphasis is on American sources, and the Eastern states in particular, this journal includes some English source material. It publishes critical book reviews and covers documented genealogies, descriptions of collections, methodology, and record extracts such as Bible records and church records. (KS)

650. The American Genealogist. 1232 39th Street, Des Moines, Iowa 50311.

This journal emphasizes American sources, and New England in particular. Articles on families from the Middle Atlantic states are included, but few treat the southern states. It includes compiled genealogies, corrections to genealogies already in print, ancestor tables, queries, and some source material. In general the emphasis is on pre-1800 families and sources. Descriptive book reviews are written by the editor. (KS)

651. The Center for Historical Population Studies Newsletter. 211 Carlson Hall, University of Utah, Salt Lake City, Utah 84112.

This publication describes the microfilm collections of the Genealogical Society of Utah, Salt Lake City, including new microfilm acquisitions, and reports on studies and research in progress by researchers using the society. This newsletter is valuable in keeping researchers informed of the society's microfilming programs. The Genealogical Society of Utah has over one million rolls of microfilm and over 170,000 published volumes. These records include vital, church, census, probate, military, land, court, cemetery, and similar records. (KS)

652. The Genealogist. 380 Riverside Drive, No. 4-Q, New York, N.Y. 10025.

This semiannual journal publishes single-family studies and compiled genealogies that are international in scope. Articles may illustrate by actual examples specific methods and techniques of solving problems. Some critical book reviews are included, as are some illustrations. Excluded are articles on general methodology, queries, abstracts of records, and lists of names. (KS)

653. The Journal of Interdisciplinary History. 28 Carleton Street, Cambridge, Mass. 02142.

This scholarly quarterly, founded in 1970, is international in scope and interested in fields beyond family history but important to the historian of the family. Editors Robert I. Rotberg and Theodore K. Rabb seek interdisciplinary articles, research notes, comments, review articles, and book reviews in political, economic, family, and intellectual history; population history; anthropology and history; history of science; biography; and quantification. Three special issues devoted to family history appeared in 1975. (GML)

654. *The New England Historical and Genealogical Register.* 101 Newbury Street, Boston, Mass. 02116.

The *Register* is the oldest genealogical periodical published in America. It includes New England source material, such as town and church records, New England genealogies, and historical articles. Some articles show the origin of an immigrant. Queries are published, as are book reviews and short book notices. The *Register* has set the standard for numbering compiled genealogies, known as the "New England Register" system. (KS)

IX. Guidebooks, Handbooks, and Manuals

655. Babbel, June Andrew. *Lest We Forget: A Guide to Genealogical Research in the Nation's Capital.* 4th ed. Annandale, Va.: Annandale and Oakton, Virginia, Stakes of the Church of Jesus Christ of Latter-day Saints, 1976.

The National Archives, the Library of Congress, the Daughters of the American Revolution library, and the National Genealogical Society library are described in the first section of this work. The second section discusses their genealogically useful records: censuses, court records, directories (city and telephone), land records, maps, mortality census schedules, naturalization records, military pension and bounty land records, and military service records. This work is meant for on-the-spot use. It includes telephone numbers, hours of operation, access procedures, floor diagrams, self-orientation tours of the buildings, illustrated instruction for using the catalogs and some other guides that are encountered, and the procedures for requesting specific materials, photocopying, and obtaining staff services. Tips on locating in-house cafeterias, bus service, and other miscellaneous items are also included. (RMS)

656. Colket, Meredith B., Jr., and Frank E. Bridgers. *Guide to Genealogical Records in the National Archives.* Washington: National Archives and Records Service, General Services Administration, 1964.

The materials described in this guide are census records, ship passenger lists, military service records and pensions; land records, American Indian census and other records; naturalization records; and several miscellaneous types of materials. The information given for each type of record includes years covered, a citation to the statute authorizing the records, a physical description of the records, a summary of the information they contain, and a description of their indexes and pertinent research aids. The earliest records listed began in 1787, although some are based on military service rendered as early as 1775. Few of the records extend more than a decade or two into the twentieth century. Although much of the information in this work is summarized in several of the major genealogical textbooks, many of the details are not generally available elsewhere. A revised edition is in preparation. (RMS)

657. Cook, Michael L. *Genealogical Dictionary*. Evansville, Ind.: Cook Publications, 1979.

This work includes obsolete and current terms pertaining to probate and other legal matters, land measurement, kinship, and many other areas related to genealogical research. While it does not eliminate the need for more specialized works of greater depth, such as legal or historical dictionaries, it is more convenient to use. (RMS)

658. Evans, Barbara Jean. *A to Zax: A Glossary of Terminology for Genealogists and Social Historians*. Evansville, Ind.: Unigraphic, 1978.

Evans's work is similar in scope to Cook's *Genealogical Dictionary* (see no. *657*). The same comments apply. (RMS)

659. Greenwood, Val D. *The Researcher's Guide to American Genealogy*. Baltimore: Genealogical Publishing, 1973.

Although the first section of this work deals with the principles of genealogical research, the greater portion of the book is written for persons with some research experience. Greenwood's background in law is reflected in his extensive coverage of probate and other records, but his discussions of many other topics provide information not found in other textbooks. Among these subjects are: the mortality schedules of the U.S. census (pp. 185-187), the rectangular-grid survey system of land division (pp. 270-273), definitions of various types of land records (pp. 286-296), and many types of military service records and military pension records (chapters 21-22). Greenwood's discussion of the above-mentioned topics should be supplemented by the illustrations in Norman Edgar Wright's *Building an American Pedigree* (see no. *664*), which contains further data on various topics. (RMS)

660. Groene, Bertram H. *Tracing Your Civil War Ancestor*. Rev. ed. Winston-Salem, N.C.: John F. Blair, 1977.

This illustrated work is a comprehensive guide to obtaining military service information and other biographical data from Civil War service records, military pension records, and published Civil War histories. Confederate as well as Union service is included. The work contains information on Civil War memorabilia and an extensive list of published regimental histories. (RMS)

661. Kirkham, E. Kay. *A Handy Guide to Record-Searching in the Larger Cities of the United States*. Logan, Utah: Everton, 1974.

The 131 cities included in this work were chosen both by size and by historical importance; thus some large cities are omitted and some small towns included. Most of the smaller ones are in New England and in the Intermountain West, particularly Utah. Of the information given for each city, the following items are the most helpful: the years for which city directories are available in the Library of Congress and the Genealogical Society of Utah library, the title of the city official in charge of its vital records, and the year the records commence. Comparable information is usually given for divorce records. Maps are included for twenty-one cities; these are reprints of maps published in or near the years 1850, 1860, and 1880 and show ward boundaries. A gazetteer of street names, keyed to ward numbers, is included for each map. (RMS)

662. The Handy Book for Genealogists. 7th ed. Logan, Utah: Everton, 1981.

The *Handy Book* is probably the most widely used work in the history of American genealogy. The heart of the book is its state-by-state lists of counties, including the year each county was created, the federal censuses available for each, the names of the counties from which each was created, and the commencement dates of the vital, probate, land, and court records in each county. Additional information for each state includes, among other things, a county outline map, a list of published WPA inventories, and a list of major archives and genealogical collections. The U.S. material is followed by brief discussions of genealogical source records in Canada, South Africa, and the major European countries. This edition is essentially the same as the sixth edition, which is widely available in libraries serving genealogists. (RMS)

663. Utah Genealogical Association. ''Professional Genealogy Handbook.'' *Genealogical Journal,* Vol. V (March-June 1976), pp. 3-81.

Offering articles written for the professional genealogist, the handbook includes the Utah Genealogical Association's ''Professional Genealogist's Standard.'' Articles cover finding a professional genealogist, advertising, record keeping, and reporting to clients. (KS)

664. Wright, Norman Edgar. *Building an American Pedigree.* Provo, Utah: Brigham Young University Press, 1974. Reprinted as *Preserving Your American Heritage* (1981).

Wright provides comprehensive coverage of American genealogical research procedures and sources like that of Greenwood (see no. *659*), but one often provides details not given by the other. Particularly helpful are Wright's discussions of the mortuary records (pp. 121-122 and 371-381), the Soundex index to the 1880 and 1900 U.S. censuses (pp. 157-159), the mortality schedules of the 1850-1885 censuses (pp. 164-173), the probate process (pp. 204-216), and a list showing, for each state or territory, the name of the county probate court, the officer having custody of the probate records, and pertinent comments (pp. 599-627). Also of particular value are chapters on land and property records, military records, especially the treatment of records pertaining to the Civil War and World Wars I and II, and miscellaneous records. There is a chapter on settlement patterns and migration routes. The work includes photocopied illustrations of original records, located adjacent to appropriate pages of text. (RMS)

X. Indexes and Directories

665. Genealogical Periodical Annual Index. Vol. I (1962)-.

GPAI, as this work is usually called, now published by Heritage Books, Bowie, Maryland, indexes some 150 genealogical periodicals issued in the United States and Canada. This is less than one-third of those being published, but most of the periodicals not indexed are of local scope and limited circulation and are available in relatively few libraries. Over the years, *GPAI*'s indexing techniques have varied somewhat; but generally speaking, articles consisting of pedigrees or genealogies are indexed by the predominant surname(s) concerned, while articles consisting of transcribed genealogical sources records are indexed by indirect locality, that is, by state and by county or town thereunder. The remaining articles are indexed by subject. Family magazines—periodicals devoted entirely to the genealogy of specific surnames—are not indexed, but the titles of such periodicals are given under the surname(s) concerned. Volumes IX-XII (1970-1973) were never published, and thus far no multiyear cumulations have been issued. As of mid-1982, volume XIII, covering periodicals published during 1977, was the most recent volume available. (RMS)

666. Genealogical Society of Utah. *Microfilmed Card Catalog.* Salt Lake City: The Society, 1974-1980. 290 reels, 16 mm.
Genealogical Society of Utah. *International Genealogical Library Catalog.* Salt Lake City: The Society, 1981-. Microfiche.

The Genealogical Society of Utah has the world's largest genealogical library and possibly the largest local history collection, consisting of over one million reels of microfilm and nearly 200,000 bound volumes. The microfilmed card catalog is divided into two sections that include family histories and related items, and locality-oriented materials. Its microfiche successor, a computerized catalog, consists of four sections: surname, locality, author-title, and subject. At present both the microfilmed and microfiche catalogs must be used, but the older materials are being recataloged into the microfiche catalog, a process that is expected to be completed during the 1980s. An estimated twenty-three thousand family histories are listed in the microfilmed catalog alone; 23 percent are not known to be available in other libraries. No estimate is available for the much larger amount of locality-oriented materials. However, most such items are microfilmed copies of the original records that form the basis of local history and biography, that is, vital records; census and tax lists (including the complete 1900 U.S. census and its Soundex index); land records; probate and other court records; military records; immigration and naturalization records; church and cemetery records; indexes to genealogical materials in newspapers (the library also has the country's most extensive collection of microfilmed newspapers for

Georgia, Tennessee, and West Virginia); published histories and collective biographies for states, counties, and towns; some business records and diaries; and a wealth of other material. Extensive microfilming projects have been completed in the states east of the Mississippi River and are progressing in several states further west. Microfilming projects in foreign countries have thus far yielded several hundred thousand reels of film. This collection's enormous potential has yet to be tapped to any meaningful extent by historians, even though most of the microfilmed materials may be used either at the main library at Salt Lake City or loaned for use at any of its several hundred branch libraries located in Latter-day Saint meetinghouses throughout the United States and elsewhere. (RMS)

667. *International Genealogical Index*. Current edition. Salt Lake City: Genealogical Department of the Church of Jesus Christ of Latter-day Saints. Microfiche.

This index, often called the *I.G.I.*, is a list of deceased persons born from about A.D. 1500 onward. It provides the names of parent or spouse, the date and place of the person's birth/christening or marriage, and a reference to the source of the information. Several million names per year are added to this index, which in July 1982 contained some sixty-eight million entries on 5,463 microfiches. The possibility of confusing different persons of the same name, which would normally be a serious problem in a file of this size, is minimized by its arrangement. Each country is indexed separately except for the United States (indexed by state), Canada (by province) and England (by county). Within these geographical areas, entries are arranged alphabetically by surname and given name, and then by date of birth (or christening) or marriage. The *I.G.I.* is available at the Genealogical Society of Utah's main library and at many of its branches. It may also be consulted by mail for a small fee by using a form entitled "Temple Ordinance Indexes Request," available at the main library and its branches. (RMS)

668. Meyer, Mary Keysor. *Directory of Genealogical Societies in the U.S.A. and Canada*. Pasadena, Md.: Libra Publications, 1976-.

The current edition of Meyer's biennial directory lists nearly a thousand organizations. For each, most or all of the following information is given: address, year founded, number of members, yearly dues, description of its library, names of periodicals and newsletters published, descriptions of books and special projects completed or in progress, services offered, and sometimes other information. The directory is arranged alphabetically by state. It concludes with a list of independent genealogical periodicals and an index by name of genealogical society. (RMS)

669. Sperry, Kip. *An Index to Genealogical Periodical Literature, 1960-1977*. Detroit: Gale, 1979.

Eighty-eight journals, almost all of which are published in the United States and fairly widely available, are indexed in this work. Most are genealogical or historical; the rest are mostly devoted to archival or library science. Sperry's index is divided into two sections, subject and author/title. It includes articles on genealogical research techniques and genealogical and historical materials and collections. Articles dealing with research in specific libraries and archives are included; articles consisting of transcriptions of genealogical source records are excluded. Also omitted, for the most part, are articles concerning research techniques in specific cities and counties; most such articles appear in local genealogical periodicals of very limited circulation, available in few libraries. Sperry's work is the tool for locating journal literature dealing with genealogical research techniques and the use of genealogical collections. (RMS)

670. Stemmons, John "D", and E. Diane Stemmons. *The Cemetery Record Compendium.* Logan, Utah: Everton, 1979.

Arranged by state, then by county, and then by name of cemetery, this work lists the names of approximately twenty-five thousand cemeteries in the United States whose record books and/or tombstone records have been transcribed and published, or that are available on microfilm through the Genealogical Society of Utah and its network of branch genealogical libraries. For each entry the following citation is given: Genealogical Society of Utah library call number (usually), journal citation (sometimes), or name of repository (less often). (RMS)

671. Stemmons, John "D", and E. Diane Stemmons. *The Vital Record Compendium.* Logan, Utah: Everton, 1979.

The authors' definition of vital records includes records of birth or baptism, marriage, and death or burial, as found in official vital records, church records, newspapers, and the mortality schedules of the U.S. census for 1850-1880. Arranged by state, then by county, and then by city or town, this work lists more than thirty-four thousand published or microfilmed sources. For each source the following information is given: description (type of record and/or name of church, newspaper, and so forth), time period covered, and citation; Genealogical Society of Utah library call number (usually), journal citation (sometimes) or name of repository (less often). (RMS)

XI. Bibliographies and Catalogs

672. Filby, P. William. *American and British Genealogy and Heraldry: A Selected List of Books.* 2d ed. Chicago: American Library Association, 1975.

Filby has listed and annotated some five thousand titles of books and significant periodical articles pertaining to genealogy and heraldry not only in the United States and Great Britain, but in Canada, Latin America, the British West Indies, India, South Africa, Australia, and New Zealand. He has sought to include all important works dealing with these two subjects, aside from individual family histories and local histories. Items of archival, historical, or related interest are included when considered to be of genealogical importance. Published transcriptions of actual records are included when they cover an entire state or comparable area and often when they cover a smaller area. Although works limited to an individual town are seldom listed, the items of broader scope are often comprehensive enough to be of considerable value for a specific locality. (RMS)

673. Kaminkow, Marion J. *A Complement to Genealogies in the Library of Congress: A Bibliography: Twenty Thousand Additions from Forty-Five Libraries*. Baltimore: Magna Carta Book, 1981.

The genealogies here are listed alphabetically by surname, but no attempt is made to group together the variant spellings of a surname. This volume is a union list; that is, each item indicates those libraries that have copies. As noted by the author, some large and important holdings of certain libraries are not included because participation was not feasible. The omitted genealogical libraries include the nation's largest—the Genealogical Society of Utah library—as well as those of the New York Genealogical and Biographical Society and the various American lineage societies such as the Daughters of the American Revolution. (RMS)

674. Kaminkow, Marion J. *Genealogies in the Library of Congress: A Bibliography*. 2 vols. Baltimore: Magna Carta Book, 1972. Supplement, 1977.

Nearly 23,500 titles are included in this work and its supplement; most were published in the United States and Great Britain. Some unpublished manuscripts are included, as well as genealogical materials in books that are not primarily genealogical in nature. It is arranged alphabetically by surname (variant spellings are grouped together), with many references from the variant spellings and occasional references from other surnames included in a work. (RMS)

675. Miller, Olga K. *Migration, Emigration, Immigration: Principally to the United States and in the United States*. 2 vols. Logan, Utah: Everton, 1974-1981.

Miller's work is primarily a bibliography, including roughly 6,300 references to books, journal articles, and—in volume two—microfilmed records. Materials of general nature are listed first, grouped in broad subject classifications, followed by entries dealing with religious and refugee groups. The greater portion of each volume is arranged by state or foreign country, reflecting the fact that most literature in this field deals with migration to and from specific areas. Many of the works cited are lists of names. Miller's work concludes with an index of authors, localities, and subjects. (RMS)

676. New York Public Library, Local History and Genealogy Division. *Dictionary Catalog of the Local History and Genealogy Division*. 18 vols. Boston: G. K. Hall, 1974.

One estimate places the number of genealogies listed in this work at twenty-six thousand, of which some 25 percent are not known to be available in other libraries. The catalog is arranged alphabetically, with surnames and place names interfiled. It reproduces those catalog cards created through 1971 and is updated by *Dictionary Catalog of Research Libraries*, an automated catalog for the Local History and Genealogy Division and other divisions of the library. The genealogies cataloged in the New York Public Library as of April 1979, but not found in the Library of Congress—an estimated 6,100 titles—are also listed in Kaminkow's *A Complement to Genealogies in the Library of Congress* (see no. *673*). (RMS)

677. Powell, Ted F. "Saving the Past for the Future: Tales of International Search and Cooperation." *American Archivist*, Vol. XXXIX (July 1976), pp. 311-318.
Powell briefly describes the microfilm holdings and the microfilming program of the Genealogical Society of Utah, Salt Lake City. (KS)

678. Schreiner-Yantis, Netti. *Genealogical and Local History Books in Print.* 3d ed. Springfield, Va.: Genealogical Books in Print, 1981.
The scope of this catalog goes beyond its title, including periodicals, works on nonlocal history, heraldry, maps, atlases and gazetteers, description and travel, collective biography, the origin and meaning of names, and other pertinent subject areas. Works available in microfilm are included. Of the more than twelve thousand items listed, nearly 1,300 are individual family histories and similar works. Most of the rest are transcribed records of specific localities and tend to fall into various categories: official or church records of birth, baptism, marriage, death, or burial; newspaper records of birth, marriage, or obituaries; cemetery records; census, land, and probate records; county and local histories and collective biographies; and indexes to such materials. The other works listed are of broader scope and geographic coverage: state, regional, religious, and ethnic histories; genealogical textbooks, handbooks, and other guides. Prices, vendors' addresses, and some descriptive annotations are included. Since most genealogical publishers are individual persons, few of these items are found in the standard bibliographies of books in print. (RMS)

679. Soliday, Gerald L., ed., with Tamara K. Hareven, Richard T. Vann, and Robert Wheaton, assoc. eds. *History of the Family and Kinship: A Select International Bibliography.* Millwood, N.Y.: Kraus International Publications, 1980.
This bibliography grew out of a project initiated by the *Journal of Family History* and supported by the National Council on Family Relations and a grant to Clark University from the National Endowment for the Humanities. It contains a selected list of more than six thousand entries, organized by geographical area and appropriate subheads—such as general, country, and period—and indexed

by author. It is intended to serve persons interested in social, economic, cultural, and legal history, as well as demography, sociology of the family, anthropology, and psychology. The focus is on works of historical concern, with other disciplines included if they contribute to the history of family experience. Entries are included only if published or summarized in a western European language. Chapter headings are: "General Works"; "Europe"; "Great Britain and Ireland"; "France"; "Central Europe"; "The Netherlands and Belgium"; "Northern Europe"; "The Iberian Peninsula"; "Classical Antiquity"; "Italy"; "Greece"; "Eastern Europe, Russia, and the Balkans"; "The Middle East and North Africa"; "Africa South of the Sahara"; "South Asia"; "Southeast Asia"; "Australia and New Zealand"; "China"; "Japan"; "Korea"; "Canada"; "The United States"; and "Latin America." (GML)

CHAPTER 6

HISTORICAL EDITING

Suellen Hoy, editor

With the publication of the first volume of Julian P. Boyd's edition of *The Papers of Thomas Jefferson*, documentary editing entered a new age of prominence in American historical scholarship. The comprehensive listing below demonstrates the rapid development of this field in the years since 1950. When compared to the paucity of published material on the editing of historical monographs and journals, the literature on documentary editing is indeed extensive. It encompasses all facets of the field, including its history and place in the profession, priorities and policies, practices and practitioners, and financial and institutional support.

Although the editing of historical magazines and books continues to be an important undertaking within the profession, few publications discuss the general nature of the work or the special problems presented by periodicals or multi-volume monograph series. There is even less in print that reviews the evolution of this segment of the profession or records the experiences of distinguished editors. In spite of this dearth of material, students and practitioners of history will be richly rewarded by reading the views of many listed below, especially Martin Ridge, James H. Rodabaugh, Memory F. Mitchell, Stephen D. Zink, and C. L. Sonnichsen.

Editors of secondary works should be encouraged to reflect on their training, responsibilities, and craft and share their experiences and opinions in single articles or collected essays. The profession as a whole would benefit from such efforts. Students and their teachers would become more aware of ways in which history can be practiced and in the process would find new opportunities for developing satisfying careers. Historical editors who regularly and often anonymously transform sows' ears into silk purses would become more recognized in the profession and perhaps in time become as respected as historians who conduct original research and publish their discoveries.

Good editors, like good writers, are made; they learn their craft and become masters of it through instruction and practice. Yet in 1958, Lester J. Cappon, one of the profession's most accomplished historians and editors, observed that "our professional schools devote little time to editorial principles or problems, although every historian who engages in writing history gets involved in editing at one time or another" ("The Historian as Editor," in William B. Hesseltine and Donald R. McNeil, eds., *In Support of Clio: Essays in Memory of Herbert A. Kellar*, Madison: State Historical Society of Wisconsin, 1958, p. 176; see also no. *725*). Twenty-five years later—even with the completion of many fine letterpress and microfilm editions of documents, the proliferation and sophistication of historical journals and monographs, and the introduction of a smattering of courses in historical editing—Cappon's observation remains in large part true. Historians do not teach their students in any formal way to edit or to write.

Most departments of history give far greater attention to historiography and research than to editing. In a recent collection of essays (*Practicing History*, New York: Knopf, 1981), Barbara W. Tuchman compares "the problem of writing" to that of research: "People are always saying to me in awed tones, 'Think of all the *research* you must have done!' as if this were the hard part. It is not; writing, being a creative process, is much harder and takes twice as long" (p. 69). She also notes (p. 48) that "when it comes to language, nothing is more satisfying than to write a good sentence. . . . This does not just happen. It requires skill, hard work, a good ear, and continued practice."

Whether students of history choose to work in or out of the academy once they have completed their formal education, they must know how to conduct thorough research, analyze their findings, and present them in a format that will be read and understood by both professionals and nonprofessionals. Teachers of history are, therefore, urged to provide their students with opportunities to complement their understanding of the past with skills—in this particular case, editing and writing—that will enhance their value and that of the profession. The bibliography that follows seeks to provide a helpful tool with which to begin.

I. Documentary Editing

680. Adams, Charles Francis, Jr. "The Printing of Old Manuscripts." *Proceedings of the Massachusetts Historical Society*, Vol. XX (April 1882-1883), pp. 175-182.

In a paper read at a meeting of the Massachusetts Historical Society in April 1883, Adams sets forth "a few correct principles of antiquarian editing." Editors must first decide for whom their work is intended. If it is aimed at a popular audience, Adams believes that spelling, capitalization, punctuation, and typography need to be modernized; only the words themselves should be preserved. If, however, the work is intended for the scholarly few, spelling and capitalization should be kept as characteristics of the individual and the times, but shorthand abbreviations should not be retained. Preserving abbreviations is an "affectation" that causes extra work for the editor and difficulty for both compositor and reader. Adams asserts that if absolute reproduction is the goal, the manuscript should be photographed. (BEB)

681. Adams, Thomas Boylston, et al. "Proceedings of a Ceremony Held at the Massachusetts Historical Society, September 22, 1961, Commemorating the Publication of the *Diary and Autobiography of John Adams.*" *Proceedings of the Massachusetts Historical Society,* Vol. LXXIII (September 1961), pp. 119-150.

The Massachusetts Historical Society ceremony, celebrating publication of the first four volumes of *The Adams Papers,* featured Samuel Flagg Bemis as the major speaker. Bemis, professor of history at Yale University and biographer of John Quincy Adams, praises the project as one that does credit to John Adams's interest in history and the role he, his son, and his grandson played in the life of the nation. Bemis reviews the history of the Adams family manuscripts and explains why such a rich source of papers was so long unavailable to researchers other than family historians or those chosen by the family. The decision by the family trustees in 1950 that they could no longer handle the papers paved the way for their complete microfilming, their transfer to the Massachusetts Historical Society, and their subsequent publication. Other speakers at the ceremony included Thomas Boylston Adams, a trustee of the papers and president of the Massachusetts Historical Society; Lyman Butterfield, editor-in-chief of *The Adams Papers;* Thomas James Wilson, director of Howard University Press; Paul Herman Buck, professor at Harvard University; and Julian Boyd, editor of *The Thomas Jefferson Papers.* (BEB)

682. American Historical Association, Historical Manuscripts Commission. "Suggestions for the Printing of Documents Relating to American History." *Annual Report of the American Historical Association for the Year 1905.* Vol. I. Washington: Government Printing Office, 1906.

The "suggestions" adopted by the Historical Manuscripts Commission in 1905 are designed, as reported in the prefatory note, to help establish accepted editorial usage and a high standard of accuracy. Because they are meant to help a beginning editor, the suggestions are straightforward in presentation and specific in nature. They deal with the technical aspects of preparing a document for publication. There are suggestions for fourteen categories: heading, description, date, text, capitalization, paragraphing, conclusion and subscriptions, addresses, endorsements, order, list or contents, running heads, index, size of publication. Some of the dicta are brief, such as always to prepare an index. Others are more elaborate, as, for example, comments on the various exceptions that can or should be made to a literal text transcription. (BEB)

683. Angle, Paul M. "The Minor Collection: A Criticism." *Atlantic Monthly,* Vol. CXLIII (April 1929), pp. 516-525.

Angle establishes five tests that documents must pass before their genuineness can be accepted: physical criteria, pedigree, handwriting, content, and historical accuracy. He then applies these tests to documents from the Minor Collection that were published in serial form in *Atlantic Monthly* between December 1928 and February 1929. The authenticity of this series of supposedly documentary facsimiles by or about Lincoln had been called into question, and Angle responds with a "reasoned" evulation of the collection at the request of the magazine. The material from the Minor Collection passes only the physical test of appropriate paper, although even here the author surmises that the paper was originally endpapers in books. In all other areas, particularly that of historical fact, the documents fail Angle's test. He carefully establishes errors of fact and points out areas of doubtful probability and misplaced emphasis. He concludes that the Minor Collection is a fake, the work of a clever, skillful, but not historically trained forger. (BEB)

684. Anglo-American Historical Committee. "Report on Editing Historical Documents." *Bulletin of the Institute of Historical Research* (University of London), Vol. I (1923), pp. 6-25.

Prepared under the auspices of the Conference of Anglo-American Historians, this report is designed to suggest the "principles upon which historical documents should be edited." The report is divided into seven parts, each addressing problems that documentary editors encounter when working with material dating back to the Middle Ages, particularly British sources. The first section is designed for a transcriber and lists twenty rules to ensure the creation of a full and complete transcription. The second section provides twenty-six points of guidance for the editor working with the finished transcript; they range from the handling of abbreviations and spelling to the notation of changes in ink. Other sections of the report treat the subjects of calendar preparation, indexing, terms used in describing documents, methods of description, and explanation of English seals. (BEB)

685. Anglo-American Historical Committee. "Report on Editing Modern Historical Documents." *Bulletin of the Institute of Historical Research* (University of London), Vol. III (1925), pp. 13-26.

This report by the Anglo-American Historical Committee deals specifically with modern historical documents, meaning those of the post-medieval period. The committee endorses the basic principle that editors of documents of whatever era should add no subjective elements. They acknowledge that a major difference for editors in the latter period is the increased number of documents they face. Although they offer no advice on document selection (the subjective judgment of the editor plays too large a role), they suggest rules for the handling of material in forms other than full transcription. They also give guidance on preparing an introduction and notes, spelling and punctuation, dates, indexing, and general suggestions in presentation. (BEB)

686. Bailyn, Bernard. "Boyd's Jefferson: Notes for a Sketch." *New England Quarterly,* Vol. XXXIII (September 1960), pp. 380-400.

In this four-part review of volumes VII through XV of *The Papers of Thomas Jefferson,* Bailyn applauds the entire project and explains how these particular volumes (covering the period from 1760 to 1789) give new insight into the personality and style of Jefferson. Bailyn concludes that the fifteen published volumes introduce "a new era in the history of American documentary publications." (SH)

687. Bailyn, Bernard. "Butterfield's Adams: Notes for a Sketch." *William and Mary Quarterly*, 3d ser., Vol. XIX (April 1962), pp. 238-256.

Bailyn uses the first four volumes of *The Adams Papers* to explain the reason for all of the effort that has gone into the series of massive documentary projects begun after World War II. The full and exact reproduction of what Adams wrote, in its proper sequence and with supporting background information, allows readers to understand more fully both the man and the American Revolution. Bailyn lauds Lyman Butterfield's edition of John Adams's diary and autobiography for making clearer than ever the depth of Adams's fear of human passions and the direct link between his inner and outer life. (BEB)

688. Beale, Howard K. "Is the Printed Diary of Gideon Welles Reliable?" *American Historical Review,* Vol. XXX (April 1925), pp. 547-552.

Beale reports that his comparison of the manuscript and printed versions of the diary of Gideon Welles shows them to be substantially different. The manuscript diary contains numerous emendations of various lengths, written at different times by Welles himself. They reflect the additions, deletions, and alterations made by a man in retrospect. The printed diary contains all the entries without references, except in rare instances, to whether they are original or emended. In addition, Welles's son Edgar altered passages in the initial editing for supposed reasons of propriety. The version was passed on in typed form as a verbatim copy to John T. Morse to prepare for publication. The majority of the revisions are of slight importance in Beale's opinion and do not affect the printed diary's usefulness for the general reader. The differences do, however, make the printed version unreliable as source material for scholars. (BEB)

689. Beales, Ross W., Jr. "Documentary Editing: A Bibliography." *Newsletter of the Association for Documentary Editing,* Vol. II (December 1980), pp. 10-16.

The author has compiled a comprehensive listing of material "on all phases of editing, including its history and current state, practitioners, methods, funding, objectives, priorities, and role within the profession." This bibliography is reprinted with minor alterations from the *Maryland Historian,* Vol. X (1979), pp. 27-37. (BEB)

690. Bell, Whitfield J., Jr. "Editing a Scientist's Papers." *Isis*, Vol. LIII (March 1962), pp. 14-20.

Bell, associate editor of the papers of Benjamin Franklin, describes two basic decisions made by the editors of the project for handling Franklin's scientific letters and papers. First, they will not be separated from the rest of Franklin's writings but will be placed in chronological order with letters on all subjects. The editors believe that only in this way can Franklin's achievements and limitations be fully revealed, explained, and measured. Second, the editors will include the first version when faced with more than one authoritative text of a scientific paper because they wish to show "Franklin's knowledge *becoming*, not simply *achieved*." They will, however, use footnotes to indicate significant differences in subsequent versions. (BEB)

691. Bell, Whitfield J., Jr. "Franklin's Papers and *The Papers of Benjamin Franklin*." *Pennsylvania History*, Vol. XXII (January 1955), pp. 1-17.

Assistant Editor Bell reports on the Franklin Papers project after it had been under way for six months. Under the joint sponsorship of Yale University and the American Philosophical Society, the editors expect to collect, edit, and publish all the letters, papers, and writings by and to Benjamin Franklin, estimated to be twenty-five thousand to thirty thousand pieces, in twelve to fifteen years. They have adopted procedures and policies similar to those used on the Jefferson Papers project. They are microfilming or photostating all of the items, which are filed chronologically in large envelopes with editorial notes, and are using a subject index. The editors have decided to publish letters from Franklin in full while printing items to Franklin in full, abstract, or calendar form as the cases warrant. They are following a middle course in transcription between literal and modernized. (BEB)

692. Bentley, G. E., Jr. "William Blake's Protean Text." In D. I. B. Smith, ed. *Editing Eighteenth-Century Texts: Papers Given at the Editorial Conference, University of Toronto, October, 1967*. Toronto: University of Toronto Press, 1968.

As editor of the writings of the poet William Blake, Bentley has encountered unusual problems, which he describes in this article. Because Blake constantly made changes in his poems, Bentley finds it difficult if not impossible to establish a stable text. He believes the best he can do is to record the changes made in chronological order with some explanation of the reasons for each alteration and an indication of the poet's steady development. The relative scarcity of Blake's manuscripts and printed books makes the examination of every traceable copy a manageable project. He does not think that he will ever be able to answer all the questions relating to Blake's work but will be able to define the limits of uncertainty as narrowly as possible. (BEB)

693. Bergeron, Paul H. "True Valor Seen: Historical Editing." *American Archivist*, Vol. XXXIV (July 1971), pp. 259-264.

As a university historian and the editor of the James K. Polk papers, Bergeron has seen the "wall of prejudice" that exists between historians and editors. Although some historians believe editors are less able than themselves, the author argues that editing requires a high level of competence and fortitude. According to Bergeron, the tasks of editing demand that an individual function as both historian/editor and editor/historian. In the first role, the individual must conduct a full search for manuscripts, establish the nature and scope of the project, set the editorial rules, and undertake the difficult and time-consuming job of reading the gathered items fully. The second role, that of editor/historian, requires that an individual bring to bear his or her knowledge of history and full critical powers while reading the manuscripts and in producing useful annotations. (BEB)

694. Besterman, Theodore. "Twenty Thousand Voltaire Letters." In D. I. B. Smith, ed. *Editing Eighteenth-Century Texts: Papers Given at the Editorial Conference, University of Toronto, October, 1967*. Toronto: University of Toronto Press, 1968.

As editor of Voltaire's correspondence, Besterman sets forth his approach to directing a large-scale project. Unsupported by any outside organization or government agency, he is single-handedly publishing all correspondence by and to Voltaire as well as other supporting correspondence. The publication will run to 107 volumes and contain more than twenty thousand letters plus notes, appendices, index, and illustrations. Nearly all of the editorial problems with which he has grappled have been exacerbated by the size of the project. Most decisions were made before work began; with a project of such magnitude, there could be no second thoughts and subsequent changes. Besterman describes in some detail the selection process, layout, annotation, and other editorial decisions relating to the form of presentation. He also tells of his search for original manuscripts and the difficulties he has faced with both originals and various printed versions. (BEB)

695. Bestor, Arthur E., Jr. "The Transformation of American Scholarship, 1875-1917." *Library Quarterly*, Vol. XXIII (July 1953), pp. 164-179.

The author shows that the institutional arrangements supporting scholarly and scientific research changed dramatically in the quarter-century between 1875 and 1900. Before 1875 the organizational character of American intellectual life was unintegrated, and productive scholarship was neither directly nor closely associated with a career in college teaching. Scholars had to rely on their own libraries and dispersed specialized collections. With the rise of the "new" university, beginning in 1875, the structure of scholarly and scientific activity was altered fundamentally. Universities with their expanding facilities, such as research libraries, became the centers of study and research in America. Scholars and scientists became a part of an organized, institutionalized system. This organization of scholars and scholarship contributed to making manuscript records known and subsequently available and usable. Bestor cites particularly the calendaring of the papers of the founding fathers, begun by the Department of State in 1893 and transferred to the Library of Congress in 1903; the Historical Manuscripts Commission begun by the American Historical Association in 1895; and the guides to archives published by the Carnegie Institution beginning in 1904. (BEB)

696. Blegen, Theodore C. "Our Widening Province." *Mississippi Valley Historical Review*, Vol. XXXI (June 1944), pp. 3-20.

In his presidential address to the Mississippi Valley Historical Association in 1944, Blegen summarizes the history of the organization, offers his view of the current state of the profession, and makes suggestions for the future. He urges the historical profession to provide imaginative leadership for the study and writing of history. He calls upon manuscript repositories to organize their collections so they can be reported in a great central inventory of archives and manuscripts. Finally, to make source material more available, he urges the completion of the Territorial Papers project and the undertaking of a vast program of documentary publication to make "the past significant for the present," which is the challenge of the discipline. (BEB)

697. Bowers, Fredson. "The Education of Editors." *Newsletter of the Association for Documentary Editing*, Vol. II (December 1980), pp. 1-4.

The author would like to see the return of historical documentary editing to "the academic establishment where it can be at least partially subsidized by teaching salaries." He encourages history faculties to train their students to be editors as well as teachers and "to accept documentary research as a normal and valued area of specialization suitable for dissertation." He observes that Julian Boyd's *Susquehanna Company Papers* should have been his dissertation and that he should not have had to discontinue his graduate work to complete this undertaking. According to Bowers, the well-trained editor with a doctorate in history has "a special authority in the teaching of history as history, while at the same time his wider general background to that of the technician can make him of superior value within the editorial project." (SH)

698. Boyd, Julian P. "A Modest Proposal to Meet an Urgent Need." *American Historical Review*, Vol. LXX (January 1965), pp. 329-345.

The author recalls the beginnings of professional scientific history in the United States in the late nineteenth century under the leadership of Herbert Baxter Adams of The Johns Hopkins University. Boyd also reviews the career of J. Franklin Jameson, who followed Adams and devoted a great deal of effort toward developing historical societies and archival collections that could assist historians in their search for an understanding of the past. Boyd then calls upon his generation to take its work one step further by establishing a center for historical studies in Washington, D.C. The center, jointly supported by major universities, historical organizations, and the federal government, would be housed in a suitably imposing edifice. Modeled on the American School in Athens and the Institute of Historical Research in London, it would contain a major historical library and provide living quarters and fellowship aid for graduate students and other scholars. He suggests, too, the creation of a similar center in the capital of the United States for the study of the history of China. He recognizes that these undertakings would be costly, but he believes that America's aspirations toward becoming a major world civilization require the nation to undertake such a "modest proposal." (BEB)

699. Boyd, Julian P. "Editorial Method." In Julian P. Boyd, ed. *The Papers of Thomas Jefferson: Volume I, 1760-1776.* Princeton, N.J.: Princeton University Press, 1950.

Boyd describes the editorial method adopted by the editors of the writings of Thomas Jefferson. They made two major decisions: "to carry through the whole editorial process by the use of photofacsimiles" and "to gather for purposes of comparison and legibility every known copy of every Jefferson document." They also decided to preserve spelling and grammar "as they stand" in original manuscripts, to follow Jefferson's style of capitalization in the text, to expand contractions and abbreviations in ordinary documents but to retain as written all money designations and units of measure and weight. And Boyd explains how editorial insertions and corrections are indicated, the form of annotations, and the contents of editorial introductions. (SH)

700. Boyd, Julian P. " 'God's Altar Needs Not Our Polishings.' " *New York History,* Vol. XXXIX (January 1958), pp. 3-21.

The responsibilities of a historical editor are the same whether undertaking a small or a large project, according to Boyd. The editor must read each document carefully, transcribe it accurately, describe it precisely, and present it intelligently within its proper context. Through his review of historical editing from *The Whole Booke of Psalmes* in 1640 to the massive, multivolume series of the 1950s, Boyd shows how standards developed. The editors of the eighteenth and nineteenth centuries were independent men of letters who used original sources to create books with form, structure, and general integrity. The twentieth century witnessed a rise of concern from within the new historical profession that resulted in high standards of editorial scholarship and practice. He concludes by lamenting the fact that projects do not proceed from a general concern by members of the historical profession and, therefore, urges historical organizations to maintain and renew their support for the publication of documentary sources. (BEB)

701. Boyd, Julian P. "Historical Editing in the United States: The Next Stage?" *Proceedings of the American Antiquarian Society,* Vol. LXXII (October 1962), pp. 309-328.

With some pessimism, Boyd explores what he believes to be the problematic future of the scholar-editor in the United States. He sounds a warning that despite the fact that the decade of the 1950s has been a period of "flowering" for historical editing, the hardest years lie ahead. He indicts the historical profession, universities, and foundations for sharing attitudes that threaten the "roots" of scholarly editing. He is most critical of academic historians, who, he believes, accord inferior status to editors and who refuse to accept editing as "one of the oldest and most exacting forms of historical scholarship." Moreover, he finds that historians lack concern for the production of reliable, scholarly documentary series essential for good scholarship. And he faults institutions and foundations for allowing the spirit of competition to creep into the sponsorship of projects, weakening the financial base and systematic planning of the entire area. (BEB)

702. Boyd, Julian P. "Some Animadversions of Being Struck by Lightning." *Daedalus*, Vol. LXXXVI (May 1955), pp. 49-56.

Boyd summarizes his experiences as editor of the Jefferson Papers. He discusses the evolution of editorial standards and underscores several important changes: a greater fidelity to accuracy, more precision in descriptions, more freedom with editorial commentary, and greater service to scholars. He also responds to recent criticisms of the "great editorial enterprises." (SH)

703. Boyd, Steven R. "Form of Publication: A Key to the Widespread Availability of Documents." *AHA Newsletter*, Vol. X (September 1972), pp. 24-27.

Boyd argues against the expansion of letterpress editions of papers. Instead he urges a conversion of priorities by the National Historical Publications and Records Commission to microfilm editions. This form of publication is far less time consuming and much less expensive to produce. Not only would it yield more information on the "inarticulate" in America's past; but in one survey, professors, students, librarians, and archivists all preferred by substantial margins the microfilm publication of sources over letterpress editions. (JJC)

704. Brack, O. M., Jr. "The Ledgers of William Strahan." In D. I. B. Smith, ed. *Editing Eighteenth-Century Texts: Papers Given at the Editorial Conference, University of Toronto, October, 1967*. Toronto: University of Toronto Press, 1968.

Ten volumes of the ledgers of William Strahan, the great eighteenth-century printer of London, exist in the British Museum, and microfilm copies have been placed in a few libraries around the world. This distribution is not wide enough, argues Brack, for the most complete extant record of printing practices in the eighteenth century. He therefore proposes to undertake, with two associates, the annotation and book publication of these ledgers. Brack summarizes the contents of each of the ten volumes and outlines sample entries for the elaborate indexes that will accompany the ledgers. (BEB)

705. Brubaker, Robert L. "The Publication of Historical Sources: Recent Projects in the United States." *Library Quarterly*, Vol. XXXVII (April 1967), pp. 193-225.

In this article, Brubaker reviews the history of documentary source projects of the mid-twentieth century for librarians and those concerned with libraries' abilities to provide their clientele—faculty and students—with source material. He points out that the publication of sources for American history is not a new phenomenon but that the new series differ markedly from their predecessors in a number of ways, particularly comprehensiveness and accuracy. Brubaker places these projects within their historical context, describing in detail the role played by the National Historical Publications Commission. He summarizes the projects underway by 1966 and the sources of their funding. He makes clear the problems of cost but believes the outlook is good for the publication of primary source material for several decades. (BEB)

706. Bruner, Katherine Frost. "On Editing a Series of Letters." *Scholarly Publishing*, Vol. IX (October 1977), pp. 41-53.

Bruner describes in step-by-step fashion the work that went into producing *I. G. in Peking*, a two-volume series of 1,437 letters written between 1854 and 1908 by Sir Robert Hart, inspector general of the Imperial Chinese Maritime Customs Service and one of the most influential westerners in the Far East, to James D. Campbell in the London office of the Chinese Customs Service. Based on their plans to produce a definitive edition on a scholarly level, the editors established strict policies and procedures. Since they decided to let Hart speak as he did, the only editorial changes they made were in punctuation. Also, they chose not to add bracketed insertions in the text but to put all added material into notes. These notes, which contain several categories of explanation, are placed at the end of each letter. Finally, Bruner describes the seven steps of their annotation process, its rationale, and its benefits. (BEB)

707. Burke, Frank G. "The Historian as Editor: Progress and Problems." *Public Historian*, Vol. IV (Spring 1982), pp. 5-19.

The author, executive director of the National Historical Publications and Records Commission (NHPRC), describes the existing crisis in documentary editing. He also reflects on the history of the NHPRC, outlines basic problems (largely funding) in the field, and suggests the nature of the future of documentary editing and its editors. (SH)

708. Burnette, O. Lawrence, Jr. "Preservation and Dissemination of Historical Evidence." In *Beneath the Footnote: A Guide to the Use and Preservation of American Historical Sources*. Madison: State Historical Society of Wisconsin, 1969.

Burnette divides his comments on historical editing into three sections: editorial process, history, and forms and methods of reproduction. The author finds that while the editorial process depends on the nature and extent of the materials involved, contemporary projects display significant uniformity in both concept and application. He reviews the various plans commonly used for selection of materials and then mentions the sequence of steps that lead to publication. He also commends Clarence E. Carter for making explicit the editorial standards that "have been implicitly observed in American practice since the turn of the twentieth century." Burnette groups projects involving the dissemination of documents into four categories of sponsorship: proprietary, academic and scholarly, governmental, and special. He reviews at some length the history of publications within each of these groups, touching upon major impetuses for publication and particular problems. And in the final section, Burnette describes the various forms and methods of dissemination available, their costs, and their relative aesthetic and practical merits. He concludes with the observation that historical editing scholarship appears to lag twenty to thirty years in the utilization of modern technologies. (BEB)

709. Butterfield, Lyman H. "Archival and Editorial Enterprise in 1850 and 1950: Some Comparisons and Contrasts." *Proceedings of the American Philosophical Society,* Vol. XCVIII (June 1954), pp. 159-170.

Butterfield compares and contrasts 1950 with 1850 in three areas: control of manuscripts, editorial methods, and support for publication. He finds better control of manuscripts and wider public support in 1950 than in 1850. He also believes current editorial methods are better, "more scientific," than in 1850; editors have accepted the obligation to produce more literally faithful texts and to locate and describe all extant material. (BEB)

710. Butterfield, Lyman H. "Bostonians and Their Neighbors as Pack Rats." *American Archivist,* Vol. XXIV (April 1961), pp. 141-159.

According to Butterfield, the collecting and publishing of public documents and private papers began in the Boston area in the eighteenth century as a manifestation of filiopietism. He breaks the story of collecting and publishing in that region into seven periods grouped around the leading collector/editors of the time (Thomas Prince and Thomas Hutchinson; Jeremy Belknap and Isaiah Thomas; Jared Sparks; Justin Winsor; Worthington Ford; Clarence Brigham; and William Jackson, Stephen T. Riley, and Clifford K. Shipton) and contrasts these individuals and the private institutions they represented with the historical activities of the state of Massachusetts. He voices his concern over the current lack of contact between state officials and those professionally concerned with history. He observes that Massachusetts neither supports a historical publications program nor does it have an adequate archival program for the collection, preservation, and storage of records. He urges the state to remedy these deficiencies. (BEB)

711. Butterfield, Lyman H. "Editing American Historical Documents." *Proceedings of the Massachusetts Historical Society,* Vol. LXXVIII (January-December 1966), pp. 81-104.

The role of the historical editor, according to Butterfield, is to discover, organize, and present sources—to open vistas to the past. In America, historical editing has gone through distinct phases in terms of underlying motivation, support, and method, all of which he briefly touches upon. The standards of scholarly editing for both public and private documents, he assures the reader, have risen rather steadily, until they can now be characterized by the words "completeness" and "care." Such advances have come about as the result of editors assuming increased responsibility toward the documents with which they work and toward their intended audience. This increased care can be seen in the editor's four responsibilities: gathering, authenticating, rendering, and annotating. Butterfield makes use of examples to illustrate how various editors have approached their individual projects and the benefits resulting from their careful, thoughtful effort. (BEB)

712. Butterfield, Lyman H. "Historical Editing in the United States: The Recent Past." *Proceedings of the American Antiquarian Society,* Vol. LXXVII (October 1962), pp. 283-308.

Sharing speaking honors with Julian P. Boyd at the 150th meeting of the American Antiquarian Society, devoted to the subject of historical editing, Butterfield devotes his remarks to the history of historical editing in the twentieth century. He singles out J. Franklin Jameson, Worthington C. Ford, and Reuben Gold Thwaites as outstanding editors of the early part of the century and assesses their strengths and weaknesses. Max Farrand, Clarence E. Carter, John C. Fitzpatrick, and Edmund C. Burnett receive his attention as fine examples of the following generation of historical editors, each enlarging the sphere of editorial responsibility. The third generation is dominated by Julian Boyd and the Thomas Jefferson Papers project. It, he asserts, has had a double impact; its scholarly commitment to the presentation of "the whole man" ended the kind of editing that had lingered on from the nineteenth century; it also brought renewed government support to the publication of documentary sources. (BEB)

713. Butterfield, Lyman H. "The Adams Papers." *Daedalus,* Vol. LXXXVI (May 1955), pp. 62-71.

Butterfield, the newly appointed editor of the Adams Papers, gives an account of his plans for the project. He discusses the problems he faces and how he thinks he will overcome them. Most of his concerns relate to "the very long time-span and the great physical bulk of the records." Since the Adams Papers had never been out of the family's hands, Butterfield also reflects on the large curatorial task facing him and his staff. (BEB)

714. Butterfield, Lyman H. "The Papers of the Adams Family: Some Account of Their History." *Proceedings of the Massachusetts Historical Society*, Vol. LXXI (1953-1957), pp. 328-356.

Butterfield, editor of *The Adams Papers*, describes the collection with which he is working as without peer. He reviews the history of the papers' accumulation and preservation from the eighteenth century to their presentation to the Massachusetts Historical Society in the 1950s. The early users were family members, particularly Charles Francis Adams. Butterfield lauds Adams's editorial statement, which he finds to have been far in advance of its time in seeking to remain faithful to the record as written. Still, Butterfield finds that Adams chose through his selection process to portray more of the public than the private sides of his father and grandfather. The two major nonfamily members who used this collection while it remained in family hands were Worthington C. Ford and Samuel Flagg Bemis. Butterfield thinks highly of their work but agrees that only a comprehensive publication of the collection will make this rich treasure fully available to scholars. For a shortened, illustrated version of this article, see Lyman H. Butterfield, "The Adams Papers: 'Whatever you write preserve,' " *American Heritage*, Vol. X (April 1959), pp. 26-33, 88-93. (BEB)

715. Butterfield, Lyman H. "The Papers of Thomas Jefferson: Progress and Procedures in the Enterprise at Princeton." *American Archivist*, Vol. XII (April 1949), pp. 131-145.

In his report on the progress of and the procedures adopted by the editors of *The Jefferson Papers*, Butterfield concentrates on three major areas—gathering, processing, and turning into print. The editors are conducting a search for documents on a scale never previously undertaken because of their commitment to produce a comprehensive edition. They have also developed a sophisticated system for processing a huge quantity of paper, which Butterfield outlines in detail. In addition to the two file copies of every letter written by Jefferson, the editors maintain a subsidiary bibliographic file of all works written by or about Jefferson. Four-fifths of the gathered and processed material will be printed in chronological order. The remaining fifth will be published in a classified series. There will also be a biographical dictionary and a cumulative index. Until the latter is completed, a "throw away" index will be issued for every five volumes published. The scope of the project precludes exhaustive annotation. The editors have chosen instead to add only what is "essential to the understanding of each document." Notes will be placed in double columns following each item, and the note itself will be divided into descriptive, explanatory, and textual sections. (BEB)

716. Butterfield, Lyman H. "The Scholar's One World." *American Archivist*, Vol. XXIX (July 1966), pp. 343-361.

In this paper, first read in abridged form before the International Council on Archives in 1966, Butterfield describes the revolution that he believes has taken place in archives administration, historical scholarship, and relations between-archivists and historians in the United States between 1860 and 1960. He lauds J. Franklin Jameson for professionalizing both the archival and historical editing fields and applauds three projects—the National Archives microfilm project, begun in 1940; the microfilm publication of the presidential papers in the library of Congress, begun in the 1950s; and the National Historical Publications Commission-sponsored series, also begun in the 1950s—for advancing historical scholarship. Butterfield concludes by making four suggestions to help achieve full accessibility: separate the National Archives from the General Services Administration and return it to independent status within the executive branch; improve bibliographic control over photoduplicated materials; experiment with new technologies and means of disseminating materials; and place accessibility above ownership in international arrangements by copying entire series, not just parts. (BEB)

717. Butterfield, Lyman H. "The Tenth Anniversary of the Gift of the Adams Papers." *Proceedings of the Massachusetts Historical Society*, Vol. LXXVIII (January-December 1966), pp. 159-163.

Butterfield reports that in the decade since the trustees of the Adams Papers transferred ownership to the Massachusetts Historical Society, twelve volumes of the edited series have been published, an agreement for a paperback reprint has been reached, and the search for other Adams family material continues at home and abroad. He pays tribute to the various organizations and individuals that have cooperated to make this massive editing and publication project possible, including the Adams family, the Massachusetts Historical Society, Harvard University Presss, foundations, various libraries and archives, the federal government, and a dedicated staff. (BEB)

718. Butterfield, Lyman H. "Worthington Chauncey Ford, Editor." *Proceedings of the Massachusetts Historical Society*, Vol. LXXXIII (1971), pp. 46-82.

Butterfield provides a brief biography and critical assessment of Worthington Chauncey Ford (1858-1941), a man who has been called "the most prolific editor in American historiography." In his longtime roles as librarian and editor at the Boston Public Library, the Library of Congress, and the Massachusetts Historical Society, Ford consistently demonstrated his commitment to the principles of document accessibility and dissemination. Butterfield assesses Ford's work as an editor. He finds some weaknesses, particularly when Ford "lapses from his own exacting standards." Too little annotation and explanation of sources and methodology often mar Ford's work, as does some lack of textual accuracy. On balance, however, Butterfield lauds Ford as an editor. Indefatigable and totally dedicated, he brought forth newly discovered or neglected materials at a prodigious rate. In the final analysis, Ford provided an extraordinary service to historical scholarship. (BEB)

719. Callcott, George B. "Antiquarianism and Documents in the Age of Literary History." *American Archivist*, Vol. XXI (January 1958), pp. 17-29.

Callcott demonstrates that the period between 1800 and 1860 is characterized as much by the antiquarian collector and publisher of source material as by the great narrative writers like George Bancroft and Francis Parkman. During these years, magazines regularly published documents and "historical minutiae," and compilers and publishers of public and private papers encountered remarkable success. Callcott compares Jared Sparks's achievement in selling seven thousand sets of his writings of Washington (published in 1852) with Worthington Chauncey Ford's Washington series sale of only 750 copies some thirty years later. Callcott also found federal support of documentary publication projects to be at an all-time high. Between 1815 and 1860, the government supported eighteen major projects that resulted in the publication of 322 volumes at a cost of over seven million dollars—almost half the cost of the Louisiana Purchase. Callcott believes that three attitudes combined to create this interest in documentary history: a spirit of inquiry and a catholicity of interests, a growing demand for scientific history based on specific details, and a spirit of romanticism that manifested itself in a love of minutiae. (BEB)

720. Callcott, George H. "The Sacred Quotation Mark." *Historian*, Vol. XXI (August 1959), pp. 409-420.

Callcott defends early-nineteenth-century historians (1800-1860) against the charges of dishonesty and plagiarism leveled at them by later "scientific" historians. He points out that these earlier historians believed that they could make history more pleasing to the reader by making revisions that did not in any way damage essential truth. Such changes were always small and did not alter the original meaning or flavor. Nor, according to Callcott, is the charge of plagiarism fair. It was not considered wrong to use the words of another without employing quotation marks. (BEB)

721. Cappon, Lester J. "A Rationale for Historical Editing Past and Present." *William and Mary Quarterly*, 3d ser., Vol. XXIII (January 1966), pp. 56-75.

Cappon defines the historical editor as a historian whose responsibility consists of transmitting authentic and accurate texts of all extant documents within a rational frame of reference, of observing archival principles, and of making texts more intelligible. The editor is also obligated to search widely for documents and to discover new sources. Annotation beyond minimum identification, location, and description, in Cappon's judgment, is mandatory and offers the historical editor the opportunity for creative scholarship. He rejects the notion that the editor should in no way interpret materials; instead he agrees with Julian Boyd that "disciplined comment" must accompany accurately rendered texts. Cappon reviews the history of historical editing from Charles Francis Adams in the 1850s to the modern period, with special emphasis on the first generation of historical editors who flourished between 1885 and 1910 and issued the first spate of documentaries. In particular, he singles out J. Franklin Jameson as a pioneer and missionary in this field. For Cappon, 1950 marks a watershed in historical editing with the appearance of the first volume of *The Jefferson Papers*. Cappon defends the status of historical editors and calls for a more professional training of graduate students for work in the field. (JJC)

722. Cappon, Lester J. "American Historical Editors before Jared Sparks: 'they will plant a forest. . . .' " *William and Mary Quarterly*, 3d ser., Vol. XXX (July 1973), pp. 375-400.

Cappon cites Jared Sparks as a pivotal figure in the history of American historical editing. Before Sparks's *Writings of George Washington*, most documentary compilations were confined to laws and codes. A few of the more venturesome eighteenth-century editors included John Webbe, Benjamin Franklin, and Benjamin Vaughan, who assembled the first collection of papers by an American statesman, Benjamin Franklin, in 1780. Ebenezer Hazard was the first editor in the field of government archives. Thomas Jefferson strongly supported him and William W. Hening, who edited the *Statutes at Large* for Virginia and unlike other legal compilers included all of the laws and extensive annotation. By the early nineteenth century, four learned societies were involved in documentary projects: the Massachusetts Historical Society, the New-York Historical Society, the American Philosophical Society, and the American Antiquarian Society. But few of these early documentaries were financially successful. Cappon also notes the contributions of Hezekiah Niles, whose *Weekly Register* (Baltimore) began publishing public or state papers from the pre-Revolutionary period in 1811-1812 but quickly switched to contemporary diplomatic correspondence as the crisis with Great Britain grew. Cappon concludes that James Savage, along with Sparks, developed a consciousness of historical method through an empirical process. Savage was a prodigious scholar who used collateral sources and extensive annotation to edit the journal of John Winthrop. (JJC)

723. Cappon, Lester J. "Reference Works and Historical Texts." *Library Trends*, Vol. V (April 1957), pp. 369-379.

Cappon argues that while too many research aids in some areas might dull the curiosity and persistence of a scholar, this will never be the case with manuscript records—their uniqueness will always provide a challenge. He reviews the increase in the number of reference works in the archives and manuscripts field and applauds all that has been done. In terms of documentary texts, Cappon believes that many archivists and historians were misled in the 1930s into believing that microfilm technology would make the letterpress editions obsolete. He cites a number of reasons why this assumption proved false. In Cappon's opinion, a half-century of war and revolution produced a renewed interest in American history. One manifestation of the interest is the number of great statemen's papers being prepared for publication. Inspired by the high scholarly and editorial standards of Julian Boyd, promoted by President Harry S Truman through the National Historical Publications Commission, and sponsored by a variety of business, universities, historical societies, and university presses, the current generation, according to Cappon, is doing more than any previous generation in adding to its "inheritance of manuscript resources." (BEB)

724. Cappon, Lester J. "Tardy Scholars among the Archivists." *American Archvists,* Vol. XXI (January 1958), pp. 3-16.

According to Cappon, American archivists are scholars by virtue of their historical origins and the function they perform. To measure how well archivists are fulfilling their scholarly role, he compares the profession's recent contributions to scholarship with those during the period from 1899 to 1936—the years between the creation of the American Historical Association's Public Archives Committee and the founding of the Society of American Archivists. He points to the publication of state records surveys, guides to United States government and foreign archives, and series of documentary records as well as of personal and family papers during the earlier years. Since 1936, he observes, the National Archives and the National Historical Publications Commission have taken the lead, with too little done at the state level. Cappon acknowledges the difficulties inherent in handling an increasing volume of records but urges his colleagues to continue to fulfill their role as scholars as well as archivists. (BEB)

725. Cappon, Lester J. "The Historian as Editor." In William B. Hesseltine and Donald R. McNeil, eds. *In Support of Clio: Essays of Herbert A. Kellar.* Madison: State Historical Society of Wisconsin, 1958.

One of the profession's most accomplished editors demonstrates that "historical editing is as creative as historical writing" and that "they are also mutually dependent." He shows, too, that the editorial process requires more intellectual discipline than many authors apply to their monographs. However, Cappon regrets that so little effort is expended in graduate schools to train the promising young historian "as a potential editor, even though he might evidence capacity and interest in that field." He is also disappointed that "our professional schools devote little time to editorial principles or problems, although every historian who engages in writing history gets involved in editing at one time or another." Cappon identifies the earmarks of the successful historical editor—"his sense of form, his skill and artistry in presenting the material, and his consistency in maintaining unity throughout"—and shows the importance of exercising "scrupulous care at every stage." The author reviews the contributions of several prominent historical editors as well as the responsibilities and tasks of those who edit historical magazines, primary source materials, and multivolume history projects. (SH)

726. Carter, Clarence E. *Historical Editing*. Bulletins of the National Archives No. 7. Washington: Government Printing Office, 1952.

Carter's article on historical editing contains descriptions of common problems and the most widely approved methods of solving them. He explains to the novice the principles of historical editing as they have evolved in recent years. In so doing, he touches on practices and problems of the past and emphasizes the twentieth-century revolution in historical editing that has resulted in new, high standards of procedure and mechanics. Carter accepts Worthington C. Ford's dictum that the duty of the historical editor is "to furnish the material in its full and unaltered shape." Based on that belief, he explains in considerable detail the thirteen steps common to most documentary editions and the considerations that editors face within each. He discusses everything from the search for documents through the creation of printing specifications. Carter explains "textual criticism"; he makes it clear that he means external criticism—the establishment of textual authenticity, purity, and reconstruction—and not internal criticism, or interpretation. He offers numerous specific suggestions regarding transcription, arrangement, annotation, collation, preparation of copy for the printer, overall review, proofreading, processing of page proofs, indexing, book manufacture, and supplementary microfilm editions. Through all stages, Carter demonstrates a straightforward approach that provides practical guidelines for those undertaking historical editing work. (BEB)

727. Carter, Clarence E. "The Territorial Papers of the United States." *American Archivist*, Vol. VIII (April 1945), pp. 122-135.

Carter reviews how the Territorial Papers project came into being and its scope. He describes in detail the criteria established for the selection of documents as well as how and why those criteria have been modified. For Carter, who believes in Worthington Chauncey Ford's dictum that the editor's job is to furnish materials in their "full and unaltered state," a complete and exact copy is the most important goal. (BEB)

728. Carter, Clarence E. "The Territorial Papers of the United States: A Review and Commentary." *Mississippi Valley Historical Review*, Vol. XLII (December 1955), pp. 510-524.

As editor of the Territorial Papers project since 1931, Carter provides a summary of the history of the series, its editorial framework, and an assessment of its future. The genesis of the project was David W. Parker's *Calendar of Papers in Washington Archives Relating to the Territories of the United States (to 1873)*, published by the Carnegie Institution in 1911. The second step came in 1924 with the introduction into Congress of a bill authorizing the collection, copying, and publication of the *Territorial Papers* by the Department of State. The bill passed in 1925 without the publication provision. In 1929 the provision was enacted, and subsequent authorizations ensured the future of the project. In selecting the documents, the editors give preference to those relating to the project's unifying thread: territorial administration. In terms of presentation, the items selected are reproduced as literally as possible. "Editorial tampering with punctuation, spelling, paragraphing, and the like is anathema." Carter reports that in 1955 there are twenty published volumes. And because there is more material relating to the later territories, the project will experiment with a full microfilm copy to supplement the selective, annotated volume on the Wisconsin Territory. Carter states that despite the problems of size and money, the project (transferred to the National Archives in 1950) will ultimately be completed. (BEB)

729. Carter, Clarence E. "The United States and Documentary Historical Publication." *Mississippi Valley Historical Review,* Vol. XXV (December 1938), pp. 3-24.

Documentary history publications presuppose subsidies, either private or public. Because government aid is undoubtedly necessary for the reproduction of public papers, Carter limits his thoughts in this article to that subject. He reviews government support for documentary publications, beginning with Ebenezer Hazard's proposal in 1778. He finds that congressional patronage was greatest in the period after the War of 1812 to the years before the Civil War and that much of the work produced then remains indispensable, especially the *American State Papers* by Joseph Gales and William Seaton. Carter believes that the executive and congressional branches of government help support documentary publications when the historical interests of the nation make a concerted effort to express themselves. Responsibility rests, he argues, with those concerned with history rather than those in Congress. If the historical profession works with the newly created National Historical Publications Commission, the future should be bright—Congress should support a carefully planned program of documentary publication. (BEB)

730. Carter, Edward C., II. "The Papers of Benjamin Henry Latrobe and the Maryland Historical Society, 1885-1971: Nature, Structure, and Means of Acquisition." *Maryland Historical Magazine,* Vol. LXVI (Winter 1971), pp. 436-455.

The editor-in-chief of the Benjamin Henry Latrobe Papers describes the purpose, philosophy, background, and early work on this project. The purpose of the project is to prepare a comprehensive microfilm publication of the works of Benjamin Henry Latrobe and a selected eleven-volume series for publication. He expects that the project will last ten years. Although 70 percent of the known Latrobe materials are at the Maryland Historical Society (sponsor of project), the staff is conducting an extensive campaign to gather copies of the remaining material. Carter describes at some length the one aspect that is a complicating factor for this project—the amount of graphic material contained in the collection. (BEB)

731. Cook, Don L. "The Short Happy Thesis of G. Thomas Tanselle." *Newsletter of the Association for Documentary Editing*, Vol. III (February 1981), pp. 1-4.

Cook analyzes the arguments made by Tanselle in his influential article on the editing of historical documents and heartily endorses them. Cook rejects distinctions between historical and literary editors and stresses the responsibilities of *documentary* editors. As Tanselle has pointed out (see no. *813*), editors have too often assumed that scholarly editing begins when the "bibliographic complications of copy-text editing are encountered." Consequently, Cook says, massive erudition in the footnotes has obscured deficiencies in textual expertise, a situation reinforced by the indifference and uninformed nature of reviewers. Cook urges documentary editors to reflect on their principles as opposed to the methodologies of their discipline. (JJC)

732. Cox, Henry Bartholomew. "Private Letters and the Public Domain." *American Archivist*, Vol. XXVIII (July 1965), pp. 381-388.

Cox warns scholars against thinking that papers unrestricted for study in a repository are also unrestricted for publication. Common-law literary property rights might still be vested in heirs, either known or unknown, depending upon how the repository received the papers. Legal experts are beginning to question whether descendants should have rights over the publication of material in perpetuity. The author is concerned with the literary rights of historical manuscripts because the law does not recognize legitimate research needs. He suggests for consideration the enactment of a statute that would allow scholars after a certain waiting period (possibly twenty-five years) to publish historical materials without having to seek permission. (BEB)

733. Cox, Henry Bartholomew. "Publication of Manuscripts: Devaluation or Enhancement?" *American Archivist*, Vol. XXXII (January 1969), pp. 25-32.

Cox discovered in a series of interviews that lawyers, historians, editors, dealers, collectors, librarians, and curators do not share a common opinion on the value of manuscript publications. Historians, editors, and some collectors and curators believe that publication of a manuscript enhances its value. Dealers and other curators hold that publication decreases the worth of a manuscript and consequently forbid inclusion of such material in publications, whether monographic or documentary. The question of public versus private rights, therefore, appears a vexing one with no easy resolution in sight. The author makes a suggestion for resolving the question in certain situations: repositories taking public money should not be allowed to restrict the publication of historical manuscripts. (BEB)

733a. Cullen, Charles T. "20th-Century Technology and the Jefferson Papers." *Scholarly Publishing*, Vol. XIII (October 1981), pp. 45-53.

Cullen describes how computerization was introduced to prepare the text and cumulative index of the multivolume papers of Thomas Jefferson. (SH)

734. Daniel, Pete, and Stuart B. Kaufman. "The Booker T. Washington Papers and Historical Editing at Maryland." *Maryland Historian*, Vol. I (Spring 1970), pp. 23-29.

The authors describe the Booker T. Washington Papers project in general and show how it is "breaking the new ground of social history and black studies." Of particular significance is their explanation of the important role the project plays in the area of graduate study—for the individual student and for the history department's entire program. The authors urge that the kind of experience and training they have had "be accessible to a greater number of students." (SH)

735. Dunlap, Leslie W., and Fred Shelley, eds. *The Publication of American Historical Manuscripts*. Iowa City: University of Iowa Libraries, 1976.

This volume of papers results from a conference held at the University of Iowa in 1975. Cosponsored by the National Historical Publications and Records Commission (NHPRC) and the University of Iowa, the conference brought together nearly a hundred editors, historians, university press directors, archivists, librarians, curators, and others interested in various aspects of the publication of significant historical documents. According to Shelley, deputy executive director of NHPRC, the conference marked the first time that those sharing common interests could meet, talk, and learn together. The papers presented cover a wide range of topics: Eric H. Boehm's "Current Emphasis in the Dissemination of Information about Manuscripts"; Stanley J. Idzerda's "The Editor's Training and Status in the Historical Profession"; Donald Jackson's "The Editor's Other Functions"; Merrill Jensen's "The Bicentennial and Afterwards"; Albert T. Klyberg's "Memoirs of a Quarter-Master General's Quartermaster: The Role of the Sponsoring Institution in an Historical Publication Project"; Robert A. McGown's "Summary of the Proceedings of a Conference on the Publication of American Historical Manuscripts"; Daniel J. Reed's "The Private Property Claim in Presidential Papers"; E. Berkeley Tompkins's "The NHPRC in Perspective"; and Albert E. Van Dusen's "In Quest of That 'Arch Rebel' Jonathan Trumbull, Sr." (BEB)

736. East, Robert Abraham. "The Loyalist Program." *Proceedings of the American Antiquarian Society*, Vol. LXXXI (October 1971), pp. 239-242.

East reports on the Program for Loyalists Studies and Publications, which resulted from various meetings and conferences and has received support from the National Endowment for the Humanities. East and his colleagues envisage a giant project that will develop finding guides and publish highly selective material relating to those who returned to Britain during the American Revolution. He describes the procedures they have established for collecting information on relevant materials. (BEB)

737. Evans, Frank B. "Manuscripts on Microfilm: American Personal Papers." *Quarterly Journal of the Library of Congress,* Vol. XXIV (July 1967), pp. 147-151.

In 1963 the National Historical Publications Commission adopted a statement of policy for the encouragement of microfilming manuscript collections where publication in printed form is not justified. Evans reports on the status of this national program. The professional guidelines and technical standards adopted by the commission reflect the experience of older microfilming projects of the National Archives and the Library of Congress. The commission awards grants to assist in the arrangement, description, and publication of manuscript materials of national significance. The repository receiving the grant must agree to make the film available through interlibrary loan and the sale of copies. Because of insufficient funds, the grants do not allow for indexing. The commission will, however, periodically issue catalogs of all microfilm resulting from the program. (BEB)

738. Evans, Frank B., comp. *Modern Archives and Manuscripts: A Select Bibliography*. Chicago: Society of American Archivists, 1975.

This unannotated bibliography contains material that assists archivists "in discovering and selecting the most useful items for study and reading" related to archival administration. Of special interest is section twenty-one (pp. 97-101), "Publication Programs and Historical Editing." (SH)

739. Ford, Worthington Chauncey. "The Editorial Function in United States History." *American Historical Review*, Vol. XXIII (January 1918), pp. 273-286.

The author looks at the evolving role of the historical editor and finds that he "has been coming into his own, not rising in importance, but better recognized as a useful, albeit somewhat erratic adjunct to the writing of history." Ford discusses the factors that he believes contributed to this change. (SH)

740. Freidel, Frank, ed. "Editing and Printing." In *Harvard Guide to American History*, Vol. I. Rev. ed. Cambridge, Mass.: Belknap Press of Harvard University Press, 1974.

The *Harvard Guide*'s section on editing and printing is designed to help students of history who at some time in their career may confront the task of preparing manuscripts for print. In nine pages it "attempts to set forth the general principles of editing American documents." No two projects are exactly the same, so each individual must demonstrate flexibility and common sense. Consistency is most important; editors are urged to be consistent above all else. They should state their editorial method at the beginning of the work and then stick to it. The *Guide*'s dictum for historical editors is "Accuracy without pedantry. Consistency first, last, and always." The *Guide* outlines the three methods used in preparing documents for publication—literal, expanded, and modernized—

and sets down specific rules common to all and unique to each method. It also provides examples of material prepared according to each method. It is the *Guide*'s opinion that the choice of method to be used should depend partly on the material but mostly on practical considerations, particularly the purpose of the publication. (BEB)

741. Galloway, Patricia. "Dearth and Bias: Issues in the Editing of Ethnohistorical Materials." *Newsletter of the Association for Documentary Editing*, Vol. III (May 1981), pp. 1-6.

The author defines the major problems facing the ethnohistorian. The first is dearth, "made worse by the lack of an overall guide to existing materials." The documents that exist contain "the ethnohistorian's second nemesis: bias." Indian lifeways, for example, were described by Europeans whose feelings ranged "from fear and hatred to loving contempt." Galloway argues that a good editor can overcome these problems through proper selection and annotation of documents. She shows how this can be done by drawing upon her experience as editor on the Mississippi Provincial Archives: French Dominion project at the Mississippi Department of Archives and History. (SH)

742. Gehring, Charles. "New York's Dutch Records: A Historiographical Note." *New York History*, Vol. LVI (July 1975), pp. 347-354.

Gehring, who is translating and editing the New Netherland records under the direction of the Holland Society of New York, describes the project and gives a short history of the records. The author's goal is to see all the Dutch records in print. Historians will then "have in their hands the material needed to tell the true story of the Dutch in colonial America." (SH)

743. Gondos, Victor, Jr. *J. Franklin Jameson and the Birth of the National Archives, 1906-1926*. Philadephia: University of Pennsylvania Press, 1981.

The author details Jameson's crusade to persuade the American government to care for its records. In summarizing Jameson's early career, Gondos describes Jameson's editorship of the *American Historical Review* and his enduring commitment to the publication of significant public papers. (SH)

744. Graff, Henry F., and A. Simone Reagor. *Documentary Editing in Crisis: Some Reflections and Recommendations*. Washington, D.C.: National Historical Publications and Records Commission, 1981.

This report provides "an overview of the state of documentary editing as it has been encouraged, supported, and developed by the Commission during the past thirty years." It focuses "on the large, comprehensive projects, such as the Founding Fathers editions, with which the Commission has been so long involved." The report considers ways to complete long-term, comprehensive editions, accepted editorial principles, possibilities and problems that technological innovations pose for documentary editing, uses of these editions, and the future of documentary editing. One section summarizes the importance of documentary editing and presents a brief history. In conclusion, the report recommends that "the Commission encourage all long-term projects to strengthen their ties with sponsoring institutions; that it seek outside support for the projects under its aegis; that it encourage the adoption of new technological advances in the editing craft; that it require every project to establish and follow a coherent set of editorial principles; that it require long-term projects to undertake self-analysis to find methods of streamlining their work; that it increase the role of historians in the grant review process; and that it use its endorsement as a means of fostering growth of new projects." (SH)

745. Greene, Jack P. "The Publication of the Official Records of the Southern Colonies: A Review Article." *William and Mary Quarterly*, 3d ser., Vol. XIV (April 1957), pp. 268-280.

Greene reviews the colonial and revolutionary records published by five southern states: South Carolina, Maryland, North Carolina, Georgia, and Virginia. He evaluates each series of papers as to editorial standards and scholarship, provides a brief history of each of the five projects, and gives a general description of their contents and scope. Greene notes that among the southern states, North Carolina has performed the most complete job in publishing its early records. He concludes that the five southern states have made progress, but many more of their colonial and revolutionary documents need to be located and published. (JAM)

746. Grover, Wayne C. "Toward Equal Opportunities for Scholarship." *Journal of American History*, Vol. LII (March 1966), pp. 715-724.

This essay outlines the history of the National Archives Microfilm Publications program from 1936 to 1966. The program was begun to retard the deterioration of original federal records that received heavy use. The government increased microfilming during World War II as a security measure in case original records were destroyed by bombing. After the war, growing demand to purchase microfilm led to further expansion of the program. In the 1960s, the process was again accelerated. As the author points out, the National Archives has had some problems in microfilming federal records, and there are certain limitations to using microcopies. Nevertheless, the microfilm publications program has been a boon to scholars and such organizations as the National Historical Publications Commission. The availability of microfilm has particularly aided the "younger and poorer" graduate schools that award degrees in history. (JAM)

747. Hamer, Philip M. " '. . . authentic documents tending to elucidate our history.' " *American Archivist*, Vol. XXV (January 1962), pp. 3-13.

Hamer makes some general observations on various aspects of the publication of historical documents, but dwells particularly on the role of the National Historical Publications Commission. He presents a brief outline of the history of documentary editing in the United States, beginning with the works of Ebenezer Hazard during the American Revolution. Although Hamer discusses the merits of microfilm publications, he insists that microfilm will never replace well-edited printed volumes of historical documents. The author also ventures an opinion on what makes a good historical editor. (JAM)

748. Harlan, Louis R., and Raymond W. Smock. "The Booker T. Washington Papers." *Maryland Historian*, Vol. VI (Spring 1975), pp. 55-59.

The authors point out that when the Booker T. Washington papers project originated in 1967, it was the first to deal with the letters of a black individual. Thus it represents "an important step toward correcting an imbalance in historical editing." Harlan and Smock show that for the Washington papers the greatest rewards and problems stem from the same fact—the bulk (a million items in the main collection of the Library of Congress alone) and the richness of the papers. The authors discuss, in particular, the selection process, authentication of texts, and forms (letterpress versus microfilm) the publication may take. They conclude by demonstrating how the papers of black Americans can be used by students and teachers of history and the benefits of such use. (JAM)

749. Harlan, Louis R., and Raymond W. Smock. "What We Would Have Done Differently Now That It Is Too Late." *Newsletter of the Association for Documentary Editing*, Vol. II (May 1980), pp. 9-12.

These editors of the Booker T. Washington Papers share their experiences, "a catalog of particulars," of things done right and wrong. They note that many procedures are developed during the course of a specific project but observe that "the catch 22 is that many things an editor learns by doing are the sorts of things he cannot change once he has been locked in." (SH)

750. Hemphill, W. Edwin. "The Calhoun Papers Project: One Editor's Valedictory." *Proceedings of the South Carolina Historical Association* (1977), pp. 28-36.

Hemphill reviews the long history surrounding the compilation and publication of the Calhoun papers as well as the contributions of those (J. Franklin Jameson and Robert L. Meriwether) who preceded him. He also measures what has been accomplished against the goals set by the project's founders and given his general impressions of the "enigmatic" Calhoun. In conclusion, Hemphill reflects on his own career as an editor and enumerates the many roles he has had to play— "a grammarian and linguist, an essayist, an administrator and budget manager, a personnel officer, a public relations expert, an archivist, a librarian, a bibliographer, a correspondent, a proofreader, an indexer, a book designer and a typographer . . . , and a secondary sales and distribution manager." (SH)

751. Holmes, Oliver W. "Recent Writings Relevant to Documentary Publication Programs." *American Archivist*, Vol. XXVI (January 1963), pp. 137-142.

Holmes lists a number of writings that discuss various documentary publication programs. He admits that his selection is arbitrary but maintains that those works included in the list "indicate something of the attention that has been given documentary publication." Holmes deliberately concentrates on items that relate to the National Historical Publications Commission. His bibliography includes essays on editorial procedures but excludes the routine annual reports of the National Historical Publications Commission and book reviews of documentary publications. (JAM)

752. Hopkins, James F. "Editing the Henry Clay Papers." *American Archivist*, Vol. XX (July 1957), pp. 231-238.

Hopkins uses his experience as editor of the Henry Clay Papers to demonstrate the many problems that editors of documentary materials must overcome in publishing. Hopkins argues that the one greatest deterrent to successful editorial projects is a shortage of funds, and he warns prospective editors to be certain of sufficient financial backing before undertaking a project. Other problems are finding and duplicating material, authenticating sources, and transcribing difficult writing. Despite his unpleasant setbacks in editing the Clay papers, Hopkins found the job to be an enjoyable one. He also commends the unselfish assistance rendered by libraries, scholarly journals, and agencies such as the National Historical Publications Commission. (JAM)

753. Hornsby, Alton, Jr. "The Hope Papers Project: Problems and Prospects." *Maryland Historian*, Vol. VI (Spring 1975), pp. 51-54.

The editor of the John and Lugenia Burns Hope Papers project at Morehouse College reviews the contributions of the Hopes to American society. Hornsby explains in brief how the project was initiated and funded, and he summarizes some of the problems (while admitting that the Hope project is not typical) that may arise in editing and publishing the papers of black Americans. (SH)

754. Hunnisett, R. F. *Editing Records for Publication*. Archives and the User Series No. 4. London: British Records Association, 1977.

The author provides a booklet, the fourth in the Archives and the User Series, for documentary editors. Four chapters cover "Initial Decisions," "Transcripts," "Calendars," and "Introductions." Each reviews considerations in the normal sequence of editorial activities—from "choice of editor" to "what to transcribe" and "how to calendar" to the "contents and style" of introductions to record publications. (SH)

755. Irvine, Dallas D. "The Genesis of the *Official Records*." *Mississippi Valley Historical Review*, Vol. XXIV (September 1937), pp. 221-229.

Irvine explains the efforts that led to publication of the *Official Records* of the American Civil War. He gives credit for originating the project to Union General Henry W. Halleck, who had a scholarly appreciation for historical papers. Irvine also shows how government leaders of the Civil War and Reconstruction era assisted in the project. He emphasizes some of the editorial and financial problems that the *Official Records* faced before the first volume was published in 1881. The success of the *Official Records* is attributed largely to the editor, Captain Robert D. Scott. Irvine points out that the military documents were intended not only for professional historians but for the patriotic public in general. (JAM)

756. Jackson, Donald. "What I Did for Love—of Editing." *Western Historical Quarterly*, Vol. XIII (July 1982), pp. 291-297.

In a speech delivered at the annual banquet of the Western History Association in October 1981, the author-editor of the *Papers of George Washington*, the *Journals of Zebulon Montgomery Pike*, and the *Letters of the Lewis and Clark Expedition* reflects on his editorial career. Without ignoring the problems of documentary editors, he recounts many satisfactions. He also describes the positive relationship of editors with counterparts at university presses. (SH)

757. Jeffrey, Thomas E. "Microform Editions of Documentary Collections: Where Do We Stand? And Where Do We Go from Here?" *Newsletter of the Association for Documentary Editing*, Vol. IV (September 1982), pp. 1-5.

The author, associate editor of the Thomas A. Edison papers, has prepared a short introduction to the world of scholarly micropublishing. His essay includes a discussion of commercial micropublishers and "the contributions they can make toward the publication of a high-quality microform edition." It also alludes to recent developments in the micropublication of documentary collections, "such as comprehensive microfiche editions and microfiche supplements to printed books, computer-generated microfiche, and selected (rather than comprehensive) microform editions." Jeffrey does not discuss technical aspects of microforms or provide a step-by-step description of how to prepare a collection for filming. (SH)

758. Jensen, Merrill, Samuel Flagg Bemis, and David Donald. " 'The Life and Soul of History.' " *New England Quarterly*, Vol. XXXIV (March 1961), pp. 96-105.

These historians each reflect on what the microfilms of the Adams papers "contain of particular interest to students of the lives and times of three successive generations of Adams statesmen." The films cover a long period of time, 1639 to 1889. (SH)

759. Jones, H. G. *For History's Sake: The Preservation and Publication of North Carolina, 1663-1903*. Chapel Hill: University of North Carolina Press, 1966.

Jones's study is an account of North Carolina's concern for its documentary heritage from 1663 to 1903. The author is primarily interested in the creation, preservation, destruction, use, and publication of the public records of state and local government. A portion of the book details the difficulties associated with publishing the records relating to North Carolina's history through 1790 that, as the author notes, "marked the most significant achievement in almost a century of efforts on the part of many historians and state officials." Jones highlights the personalities and work of six individuals—Archibald D. Murphy, David L. Swain, William A. Graham, John H. Wheeler, William L. Saunders, and Walter Clark—who were largely responsible for uncovering and disseminating the documentary evidence of the state's history. (SH)

760. Jones, H. G. *The Records of a Nation: Their Management, Preservation, and Use.* New York: Atheneum, 1969.

The chapter "The Publication of Documentary Sources, 1934-1968" traces the history of the National Historical Publications Commission from 1934 to 1968. It demonstrates how the commission's responsibilities and contributions to the historical profession have increased over the years. Some federal laws that affect the commission and its publication projects are discussed. The report also deals with the topics of public and private funding, microfilm publication, and the commission's role as an advisory agency. (JAM)

761. Jordan, Philip D. "A Dedication to the Memory of Clarence Edwin Carter, 1881-1961." *Arizona and the West*, Vol. X (Winter 1968), pp. 309-312.

Jordan presents a biographical sketch of the longtime editor of *The Territorial Papers of the United States.* Jordan states that "Carter's devotion to textual accuracy, in a sense, was the very core of his editorial creed." He was a master craftsman and perfectionist whose biggest headache was "the matter of financing the project." Carter once admitted that nearly a fourth of his time was spent on budgetary matters. Between 1931 and 1955, he published twenty volumes, and all but the last (volume 26) were in preparation at his death. (SH)

762. Kammen, Michael. "Colonial Court Records and the Study of Early American History: A Bibliographical Review." *American Historical Review*, Vol. LXX (October 1964), pp. 732-739.

The author reviews some of the most recent publications (beginning in 1933) of colonial court records and shows how they have begun to alter historians' thinking about the "the origins of American legal institutions." He believes that they will assist historians in addressing critical issues concerning the history of colonial society: "the extensiveness of democracy, mobility, and opportunity." He also acknowledges the role of the American Historical Association's Committee on Legal History in inaugurating a series of volumes of unpublished sources in American legal history. (SH)

763. Kaufman, Stuart Bruce. "The Samuel Gompers Papers as Literature: Toward a Stream-of-Consciousness History." *Maryland Historian*, Vol. VIII (Fall 1977), pp. 54-59.

Focusing on the Gompers Papers, Kaufman explains how he treats documentary editions as literature. He argues that editors produce "multi-volume histories written in a form that allows experience to unfold continuously and kaleidoscopically in much the same way that the world must have actually unfolded. . . . " Kaufman justifies editorial projects for the usual reasons but states that "they are of major importance as creative enterprises" meant to be read as a part of the literature of the field and not used simply as a reference. He maintains too that "once the interpretive dimensions of historical editing become clearer" historians will learn "to appreciate the literary aspects of the edited work." (SH)

764. Kerr, Chester. "Publishing Historical Sources: A Prejudiced View of the Problem of Finance." *Proceedings of the American Philosophical Society*, Vol. XCVIII (August 1954), pp. 273-278.

This report deals with the problems that university presses face in financing the publication of historical books. It does not explore the difficulties of publishing periodicals. According to the essay, the tasks confronting university presses are different from those that commercial publishers must face—primarily because commercial firms are relinquishing the publishing of scholarly writing to the university presses. The report explains how the cost of publishing has risen and gives some advice on how to offset expenses. Techniques on selecting and marketing publishable material are briefly discussed. (JAM)

765. Koch, Adrienne. "The Historian as Scholar." *Nation* (November 24, 1962), pp. 357-361.

This essay briefly traces the progress of the National Historical Publications Commission between 1950 and 1962. It provides some general observations about the editors of the various documentary publications sponsored by the commission. The author of the article generally compares several of the commission's editorial projects in terms of size and number of projected volumes. Also included are some figures on the number of documents produced by the American republic's founding fathers. The author defends large-scale documentary publications against microfilming and argues that the volumes published by the commission will transform American history. (JAM)

766. Kohn, Richard H., and George M. Curtis III. "The Government, the Historical Profession, and Historical Editing: A Review." *Reviews in American History*, Vol. IX (June 1981), pp. 145-155.

The authors examine the effects of federal funding by the National Historical Publications and Records Commission and the National Endowment for the Humanities on historical editing. They ask: "What has this money accomplished, and what is being accomplished now, every year, by the expenditure of over three millon dollars in federal funds alone?" They direct their response to four critical issues confronting historical editing—what to edit, the form in which to publish documents, how they should be edited, and who should do the editing. Among their concluding observations, they urge that editing be better integrated into the profession by including editors on programs and in the leadership of historical associations, by supporting research leading to documentary publication, by offering courses at the undergraduate and graduate level, and by making hiring and advancement decisions that shape careers in academic and public history. (SH)

767. Labaree, Leonard W. "In Search of 'B. Franklin.'" *William and Mary Quarterly*, 3d ser., Vol. XVI (April 1959), pp. 188-197.

Labaree contends that historical editors usually have to spend long periods of time searching for the documents they plan to edit. For that reason, editors must be good hunters and detectives. Labaree recounts his efforts to locate and edit the papers of Benjamin Franklin. His experiences with the Franklin papers demonstrate the varied problems of finding, copying, and arranging documentary sources. The difficulties Labaree encountered in his search included exposing forgeries and dealing with elusive and uncooperative custodians and owners of manuscripts. His quest for Franklin materials went as far afield as Vienna and Moscow. (JAM)

768. Labaree, Leonard W. "The Papers of Benjamin Franklin." *Daedalus*, Vol. LXXXVI (May 1955), pp. 57-62.

Labaree maintains that editorial work today is a cooperative enterprise. In addition to a competent editorial staff, many other outside organizations and individuals are vital to successful historical editing. Labaree describes how his work with the Benjamin Franklin Papers project has been enhanced by the advice of editors from other projects and with the help of libraries and historical associations. He also gives an outline of his staff's methods in preparing the Franklin papers. (JAM)

769. Labaree, Leonard W., and Whitfield J. Bell, Jr. "The Papers of Benjamin Franklin: A Progress Report." *Proceedings of the American Philosophical Society*, Vol. CI (December 1957), pp. 532-534.

Labaree and Bell discuss a new and comprehensive edition of *The Benjamin Franklin Papers* to be published under the sponsorship of Yale University and the American Philosophical Society. The authors describe how some of the Franklin documents were found, duplicated, and edited for publication. They claim that the new edition will surpass, in quantity and completeness, previous editions of Franklin's writings. (JAM)

770. LaFantasie, Glenn. "Toward Better Reviewing of Local History Documentary Editions: A Nineteenth-Century Model." *Newsletter of the Association for Documentary Editing*, Vol. IV (February 1982), pp. 1-4.

The author finds instructive Samuel Gardner Drake's review of John Winthrop's journal (2d ed.) in the *New England Genealogical and Historical Register* for 1853. Because of the paucity of documentary editions that relate to local history, most reviewers of such works tend to be so pleased to have the publication that they do little more than "heap honors on the editor for a job well done." Reminding future reviewers that "no edition, no matter how valuable it might be as an historical source, should be above criticism," LaFantasie asks the reviewers to discuss editorial merits and shortcomings carefully. (SH)

771. Lee, Charles E. "Documentary Reproductions: Letterpress Publication—Why? What? How?" *American Archivist,* Vol. XXVIII (July 1965), pp. 351-365.

Lee, director of the South Carolina Archives Department, recounts the careers of two of South Carolina's state archivists, J. Harold Easterby and Easterby's predecessor, A. S. Salley. Lee analyzes the contribution both men made to the publication of documentary materials from the Palmetto state; he also gives some general rules on selecting documents to publish as well as when and how to publish them. Lee claims that for various reasons microfilming and other methods of copying are sometimes preferred over the letterpress publication of documents. He briefly discusses format, indexing, and general editorial practices. (JAM)

772. Leland, Waldo Gifford. "The Prehistory and Origins of the National Historical Publications Commission." *American Archivist*, Vol. XXVII (April 1964), pp. 187-194. Reprinted in slightly revised form as "J. Franklin Jameson and the Origins of the National Historical Publications Commission." In Ruth Anna Fisher and William Lloyd Fox, eds. *J. Franklin Jameson: A Tribute* (Washington: Catholic University of America Press, 1965).

Leland describes the role that the historian J. Franklin Jameson played in the creation of the National Historical Publications Commission. Besides being a teacher for a number of years, Jameson was director of the Department of Historical Research in the Carnegie Institute of Washington, D.C., and the chief of the Division of Manuscripts in the Library of Congress. Jameson also held the chair in American history at the Library of Congress and became editor of the *American Historical Review*. His concern for the publication of historical documents led to the establishment of the Historical Manuscripts Commission of the American Historical Association. As a result of Jameson's works in these organizations and his attempts to drive a bill through Congress, the National Historical Publications Commission was finally established in 1934, three years before his death. Although the Commission's initial success was "nominal," the organization was reactivated during the administration of President Harry S Truman. (JAM)

773. Lemisch, Jesse. "The American Revolution Bicentennial and the Papers of Great White Men: A Preliminary Critique of Current Documentary Publication

Programs and Some Alternative Proposals." *AHA Newsletter*, Vol. IX (November 1971), pp. 7-21.

The author calls for "a thorough review of officially sponsored publication programs" that "would draw upon the resources and conflicting perspectives of large numbers of people." This article is meant to provide a "preliminary outline" for such a review. Interested in history "from the bottom up," Lemisch above all criticizes "the tendency to skew the publications program in the direction of white male political leaders." In suggesting other directions, he underscores the need to look at nonelite groups such as blacks, women, and Indians. (SH)

774. Lemisch, Jesse. "The Papers of a Few Great Black Men and a Few Great White Women." *Maryland Historian*, Vol. VI (Spring 1975), pp. 60-65.

Lemisch expresses his regret that the focus of the National Historical Publications Commission changed only slightly since 1971. Instead of publishing solely the papers of "great white men," it now also publishes those of a "few great American black men and white women." He argues again that we need "the records of those who were not great, not 'notable,' not 'outstanding,' not 'distinguished.' " (SH)

775. Leopold, Richard W. "The *Foreign Relations* Series: A Centennial Estimate." *Mississippi Valley Historical Review*, Vol. XLIX (March 1963), pp. 595-612.

Leopold claims that the *Foreign Relations* series published by the U.S. Department of State is facing a crisis and discusses the various causes of it. He traces the history of *Foreign Relations*, beginning in 1861, and describes how its editors solved many difficulties in publishing caused by periods of diplomatic upheaval. In addition, Leopold notes that there are limits to the value of printed diplomatic papers and no easy solutions to the problems facing the *Foreign Relations* series in the present day. He insists, nevertheless, that historians have a responsibility to pressure the federal government to ensure that the *Foreign Relations* series maintains its quality and usefulness. (JAM)

776. Leopold, Richard W. "The *Foreign Relations* Series Revisited: One Hundred Plus Ten." *Journal of American History*, Vol. LIX (March 1973), pp. 935-957.

Leopold evaluates the progress of the *Foreign Relations* series published by the federal government. He reviews the last thirty-five volumes of the series, which cover the period 1943-1946. He concludes that these volumes are more complete and illuminating than those published ten years earlier. The recent loss of prestige of the series is attributed to lack of serious reviews, distrust of politicians, and a time lag in publication. He summarizes the contents of the new volumes and offers opinions about their contributions to American historiography. For updated information on the *Foreign Relations* series see articles in the *Newsletter* of the Society for Historians of American Foreign Relations:

David F. Trask and William Z. Slany, "What Lies Ahead for the *Foreign Relations* Series?" Vol. IX (March 1978), pp. 26-29; William Z. Slany, "Historians in the Department of State," Vol. IX (March 1979), pp. 18-22; William Z. Slany, "History of the *Foreign Relations* Series," Vol. XI (March 1981), pp. 10-19. (JAM)

777. Leopold, Richard W. "The Historian and the Federal Government." *Journal of American History*, Vol. LXIV (June 1977), pp. 5-23.

This article describes how federal policy toward historical research and documentary publication has changed in recent years. The author shows how political events such as the Viet Nam War and the presidency of Richard M. Nixon resulted in new concepts regarding archival custody of government papers and calls for historians to be alert to federal policies on access to and classification of government documents. (JAM)

778. Levy, Leonard W. "Book Review: *The Papers of James Madison*, Vols. 4-7." *Journal of American History*, Vol. LIX (June 1972), pp. 115-117.

Levy contends that "these four volumes covering twenty-six months of Madison's career as a member of the Continental Congress tell us nothing of consequence previously unknown." He also observes that the editors "never neglect trifles, whether documents or points for annotation, that do not deserve a moment's thought." Levy buttresses the latter statement with example after example and then points out the important biographies of prominent figures in American history prepared without the assistance of heavily annotated documents. He concludes the review by asking the critical question: "If such volumes as these on Madison's papers are not crucial to the major biographers, have they a purpose that can be justified by their inordinate cost, time, and labor?" (SH)

779. Lewis, Wilmarth S. "Editing Familiar Letters." *Daedalus*, Vol. LXXXVI (May 1955), pp. 71-77.

Lewis gives advice on how to edit private letters. He includes information on how to find, arrange, interpret, and index familiar correspondences. He cautions potential editors about common pitfalls and warns particularly against pedantry and efforts to be clever in writing. Lewis insists that the unattainable goal of every editor should be total familiarity with his material. (JAM)

780. Lingelbach, William E. "Benjamin Franklin's Papers and the American Philosophical Society." *Proceedings of the American Philosophical Society*, Vol. XCIV (December 1955), pp. 539-580.

Lingelbach recounts the long history that the American Philosophical Society has had in publishing *The Papers of Benjamin Franklin*. He describes how, for a century and a half, the society and other institutions have cooperated to ensure the survival and publication of the Franklin writings. Lingelbach mentions the contributions of a number of Franklin scholars and includes a description of the nature of the Franklin papers as well as an explanation of the efforts to locate, finance, and edit the documents. (JAM)

781. Link, Arthur S. "Where We Stand Now and Where We Might Go." *Newsletter of the Association for Documentary Editing,* Vol. II (February 1980), pp. 1-6.

The author makes six observations on the current status of historical editing and comments on each: (1) scholarly editors have failed "to formulate a methodology by which to go about their work"; (2) "documentary historical series are subjected to the least scholarly review before they are published"; (3) "there is no systematic program for training persons in the craft of editing"; (4) "our profession does not seem to be able to agree upon what constitutes appropriate annotation for general or special series, or even single volumes"; (5) there is a lack of consensus "concerning general principles or guidelines of selection that can be applied and used in all fields of documentary editing"; (6) the Association for Documentary Editing (ADE) is "too much of a group composed of persons who work with documents relating to the history or literature of the United States." Link concludes by encouraging ADE to address itself to "the problems of the absence of rigorous and critical reviews in scholarly journals" and to "the matter of provision for systematic training of documentary editors." (SH)

782. Malone, Dumas. "Tapping the Wisdom of the Founding Fathers." *New York Times Magazine* (May 27, 1956), p. 25.

Malone praises the editors who are preparing the published papers of the American founding fathers. He insists that the editors are justified in having a large number of volumes because men like George Washington, Thomas Jefferson, Alexander Hamilton, and John Adams were prolific writers. Their letters represent the records of a whole generation whose chief form of communication was writing. Malone theorizes that the general public will never embrace documentary publications with the same enthusiasm with which it flocks to Colonial Williamsburg. Nevertheless, he argues, the papers of the republic's founding fathers are for laymen as well as scholars because those documents are reminders of the past and provide guidance for the future. (JAM)

783. Middleton, Arthur Pierce, and Douglas Adair. "The Mystery of the Horn Papers." *William and Mary Quarterly,* 3d ser., Vol. IV (October 1974), pp. 409-445.

This article details the attempts of a committee of historians to determine if the Horn papers, a three-volume collection containing the papers of a family living in the Pennsylvania region from 1765 to 1795, were authentic or largely fabrication. Julian P. Boyd of Princeton claimed that many of the documents were forgeries; other authorities such as Paul Gates and Julian P. Bretz considered the materials authentic although badly edited. The committee unraveled the "mystery" and found that the Horn papers were forgeries. Uncovering the proof involved considerable research in voluminous papers and even examination of a large number of collateral artifacts such as lead plates, coins, Indian relics, tools, and other objects. This article describes the difficulties of verifying unauthenticity in a collection that is "popular" with local historians and genealogists. The report also reveals how complex historical forgeries can be. (JAM)

783a. Mitchell, Memory F. "Editing the Papers of a Contemporary Governor." *American Archivist*, Vol. XXXIII (January 1970), pp. 11-18.

The author, who bases this article on her experience as editor of the papers of North Carolina's Governor Terry Sanford, describes concerns that frequently arise in editing papers of a contemporary public official. Mitchell states that the "matter of selection" is of prime importance. Which speeches are most significant or representative? Which reflect on the administration or lead to later controversy? The author illustrates how elimination of repetitions can lead to difficulty and notes the importance of giving complete identifications of people named in documents and of providing complete headnotes. Misspellings and incorrect sentence structures require correction. The author describes the pleasures associated with work on the papers of a living person. (SH).

783b. Mitchell, Memory F. "Publication of Documentary Volumes by the [N.C.] Division of Archives and History." *Carolina Comments*, Vol. XXVIII (November 1980), pp. 164-171.

This article is a condensation of a report the author, administrator of the division's Historical Publications Section, prepared for an ad hoc committee to assess the documentary program of the Division of Archives and History. Mitchell takes a long look at past and present historiography, current market conditions, format, publishing costs, and the agency's enduring commitment to documentary publications. (SH)

784. Monroe, Haskell M., Jr. "Some Thoughts for an Aspiring Historical Editor." *American Archivist*, Vol. XXXII (April 1969), pp. 146-159.

Monroe sets forth guidelines for young scholars who aspire to be historical editors. He defines what he considers to be good documentary editing, and he gives a number of examples from the works of some of the leading editors in the field of American history. Monroe enumerates the prerequisites for a prospective historical editor and those steps necessary to plan and produce a useful documentary volume. (JAM)

785. Monroe, Haskell M., Jr. "The Grant Papers: A Review Article." *Journal of the Illinois State Historical Society,* Vol. LXI (Winter 1968), pp. 463-472.

Monroe, editor of the Jefferson Davis Papers, finds the first volume of *The Papers of Ulysses S. Grant* (John Y. Simon, ed.) "a tribute to the dreams of many persons who contributed manuscripts, money, influence, and goodwill to the project." It has made Grant "a thoroughly understandable figure." In presenting this conclusion, Monroe reviews the history of the project, the work of the editor and his staff, and the opinions of other reviewers of the volume. (SH)

786. Morgan, Edmund S. "John Adams and the Puritan Tradition." *New England Quarterly*, Vol. XXXIV (December 1961), pp. 518-529.

Morgan reviews four volumes of the *Diary and Autobiography of John Adams* edited by Lyman H. Butterfield. Morgan compliments Butterfield on his high standards and concludes that this new edition "gives us the full John Adams as we have never had him before." In a reassessment of Adams's character, Morgan states that "for all his worldly asceticism, for all his concern with vanity and self-improvement, John Adams was not quite a Puritan" and explains why. (SH)

787. Mugridge, Donald. "The Adams Papers." *American Archivist*, Vol. XXV (October 1962), pp. 449-454.

Mugridge maintains that there is an essential difference between *The Adams Papers* and other documentary publications sponsored by the National Historical Publications Commission. *The Adams Papers* encompasses the writings of an entire family; each of the other projects is concerned only with the papers of an individual. Mugridge mentions some of the problems in editing the documents of three or four generations of one family. He notes that most of the Adams material is provided by the family, and thus little assembly by editors is necessary. Mugridge also explains the projected format for the remaining volumes of the Adams Papers. (JAM)

788. Neiman, Stella Duff, and Lester J. Cappon. "Comprehensive Historical Indexing: The *Virginia Gazette* Index." *American Archivist*, Vol. XIV (October 1951), pp. 291-304.

Neiman and Cappon anticipate that their experience in preparing a two-volume index for the colonial newspaper *Virginia Gazette* will provide valuable guidelines for other editors who undertake similar projects. The editors of the *Virginia Gazette* index believe that four principal factors must be considered in indexing large amounts of historical material. These factors are finances, personnel, general policies, and specific procedures. Neiman and Cappon discuss each of these factors in depth as they relate to the *Virginia Gazette* project. They also give general criteria for a good index. (JAM)

789. Newcomer, Lee Nathaniel. "Manasseh Cutler's Writings: A Note on Editorial Practice." *Mississippi Valley Historical Review,* Vol. XLII (June 1960), pp. 88-101.

Newcomer insists that nineteenth-century editors employed standards and procedures that present-day historical editors would find unacceptable. To illuminate his point, Newcomer uses a nineteenth-century editorial example: the two-volume *Life, Journals, and Correspondence of Rev. Manasseh Cutler, L.L.D.*, published in 1888. Newcomer demonstrates how the editors of Cutler's writings (who were also Cutler's grandchildren) failed, in typical nineteenth-century fashion, to be objective. To reach this conclusion, Newcomer compared the published version of Cutler's papers to the original manuscripts. (JAM)

790. Nordloh, David J. "The 'Perfect' Text: The Editor Speaks for the Author." *Newsletter of the Association for Documentary Editing,* Vol. II (May 1980), pp. 1-3.

The author begins with some notion of the ideal: (1) consistent with external fact; (2) devoid of mechanical errors; (3) fully articulated; (4) chronologically and intellectually whole, with no internal revisions; (5) unique, existing in only one copy; and (6) unmediated. He then outlines general principles "to encourage the editor to restrict editing to what is editable—the text—but also to provide some directed flexibility in the face of uncertainty about and variety of intention." (SH)

791. Norton, David L. "The Elders of Our Tribe." *Nation* (February 18, 1961), pp. 148-150.

Norton describes the activities of the National Historical Publications Commission. Reconstituted in 1950 with the passage of the Federal Records Act, the commission encourages publication of crucial historical material and coordinates activities of the various agencies that might be involved. Comprehensiveness is its goal; Princeton University's work of collecting, editing, and publishing Jefferson's papers was its first model. Twenty-five other projects were fashioned after it and encouraged by the commission. Norton concludes with an assessment of the long-term meaning of commission projects for scholars and lay people. (NJS)

792. Oberg, Barbara. "Selection and Annotation: Deciding Alone." *Newsletter of the Association for Documentary Editing,* Vol. II (February 1980), pp. 6-9.

The author cites the main pitfall for the solo editor as "over-involvement with the subject." Although this article makes a strong argument for the place of the solo editor within the profession, Oberg details the additional problems that solo editors face with selection and annotation. (SH)

793. Owsley, Harriet Chappell. "Discoveries Made in Editing the Papers of Andrew Jackson." *Manuscripts,* Vol. XXVII (Fall 1975), pp. 275-279.

Owsley describes one of the benefits of an editorial project—uncovering new material leading to the discovery of important unknown information about the life of the person under study. The case examined here occurred in editing the Jackson papers. An associate editor of these papers, Owsley traced a long-overdue account owed by Jackson. Such a long-standing debt challenged Jackson's reputation of always carefully repaying his debts. In tracking down the information associated with the account, Owsley found that Jackson owned a plantation near Spanish Natchez and was involved in a number of lucrative and widespread business ventures. The documentary search also revealed a need to examine Spanish archival materials to elucidate more of Jackson's activities. (NJS)

794. Parton, James. "Popularizing History and Documentary Sources." *American Archivist*, Vol. XX (January-October 1957), pp. 99-109.

Parton, publisher of *American Heritage*, argues that history can be presented to and read by a wide range of educated people. He advocates "popularizing history" in a factual and scholarly fashion that includes three components: authenticity, good taste, and appeal to a nonscholarly audience. The key component, he contends, is the last, which gives the reader "a feeling of utility, a conviction that reading it was worthwhile." Parton began his career as an editor for *Time*. While serving in the United States Air Force in England in 1942, he became interested in British pamphlets describing the war effort. Carefully written, printed, and illustrated, each of these government-endorsed pamphlets sold over one million copies. Parton was assigned to adopt the British method—popularizing dreary documentary history—to convince the American public that daylight precision bombing was necessary. Later, as a historian for the Allied Air Force, he continued this practice and became convinced of its worth. In conclusion, Parton reviews Bruce Catton's statement of purpose for *American Heritage* and describes the magazine's interests and editorial standards. (NJS)

795. Reagor, Simone. "Historical Editing: The Federal Role." *Newsletter of the Association for Documentary Editing*, Vol. IV (May 1982), pp. 1-4.

The author believes that it would be unwise to continue funding for historical editions under past guidelines of the National Historical Publications and Records Commission. Reagor notes that the Commission has directed large sums of money to documentary editing in American history, has added funding to its advocacy role, and has gradually moved from supporting only the era of the founding fathers to the whole span of American experience. Contending that "no one originally intended that the commission should have such broad powers or influence," Reagor suggests that in the future the federal government should support documentary editions that "improve the function of or . . . serve the specific purposes of a branch of the federal government." Materials funded by the federal government should be "of use to a federal office, not to historians generally." John Y. Simon adds a comment "In Response. . . . " (SH)

796. Reingold, Nathan. "The Papers of Joseph Henry." *Smithsonian Journal of History*, Vol. II (Summer 1967), pp. 69-71.

Editing the papers of Joseph Henry posed an array of problems common to those working with successful and complex personalities. (Henry was a college professor, scientist, and first secretary of the Smithsonian Institution.) Reingold discusses many of these problems—from the diversity of Henry's works to translating many of his early laboratory notes and lecture notes. The comprehensive edition of the unpublished writings of Joseph Henry is a joint undertaking of the Smithsonian Institution, the National Academy of Sciences, and the American Philosophical Society. (NJS)

797. Rice, Howard C., Jr. "Jefferson in Europe a Century and a Half Later: Notes of a Roving Researcher." *Princeton University Library Chronicle*, Vol. XII (Autumn 1950), pp. 19-35.

Rice describes his European research work associated with gathering papers for the Jefferson documentary project. He demonstrates the value of tracking down these items to establish the most accurate and complete texts, to fill gaps in American records, or to find the recipient's copy replete with marginal comments and responses. Furthermore, he notes the importance of locating and identifying the principal buildings and residences where Jefferson entertained or conducted his business. Such work, he points out, can deepen understanding of the information contained in a collection and strengthen appreciation of the interests and activities of the personalities. (NJS)

798. Rundell, Walter, Jr. *In Pursuit of American History: Research and Training in the United States*. Norman: University of Oklahoma Press, 1970.

Documentary editing has always been a vital aspect of American history. Yet academic historians have too often acted as if editors were little more than "lesser" historians serving "greater" historians. Their main criticism seems to be that editors engage in less original writing and that a historian's full intellectual powers are not brought to bear as a "supervising technician." This view has generally spilled over into graduate schools, although several notable scholars have challenged the assumption and concluded that documentary editorial training has a place in graduate programs. Some have even argued that documentary editing projects are suitable dissertation topics. In "Documentary Editing," Rundell advocates these suggestions. He urges institutions engaged in major editing projects to hire graduate students as assistants. He also believes that the National Historical Publications Commission should assume greater responsibility for training editors. (NJS)

799. Rundell, Walter, Jr. "Uncle Sam the Historian: Federal Historical Activities." *Historian*, Vol. XXXII (November 1970), pp. 1-20.

Rundell surveys the work of public historians serving in the federal government and traces the emergence of various historical programs, especially those in the Department of Defense. (The largest program is that of the army.) Rundell notes that the government's commitment to recording the history of military operations far outweighs the interest and resources devoted to civil administrative history. The second most extensive area of historical activity is the work carried on in the Department of State. Here, as in the case of Defense, Rundell notes some of the problems in producing materials on a timely basis and discusses such issues as a parochial focus; the social utility of research; objectivity in research; and overall coordination, classifying, and access to documents. (NJS)

800. Runge, William H. "The Madison Papers." *American Archivist*, Vol. XX (January-October 1957), pp. 313-317.

Runge relates the history of the Madison papers. When James Madison died, he left to his wife Dolly his correspondence, essays, and proceedings and debates of the Constitutional Convention and of the Congresses in which he served. Unable to follow her husband's wishes that these be published immediately, Dolly sold portions of these papers to the government in 1837 and in 1848, but not until 1941 were all the manuscripts the government paid for finally collected in one place. In 1952 the director of the National Historical Publications Commission and a Virginia committee began the move for publication of the manuscripts. Two years later, the University of Chicago Press agreed to underwrite the cost of publication, while two University of Chicago professors, Leonard D. White and William T. Hutchinson, agreed to become editors. Grants from the Ford and Rockefeller foundations and an appropriation from the Virginia General Assembly began the project. (NJS)

801. Rutland, Robert A. "Recycling Early National History Through the Papers of the Founding Fathers." *American Quarterly*, Vol. XXVII (Summer 1976), pp. 250-261.

Rutland examines the post-World War II revival of documentary editing as a field in American history. He assesses the impact of the founding fathers projects and the remaining scholarly opportunities in editing. In particular, Rutland reviews the effect of the appearance of the first volume of the Jefferson papers. Julian Boyd's and Lyman Butterfield's work stimulated new projects. Thus, within a short time, the papers of Franklin, Madison, Hamilton, and the Adamses were initiated as editorial projects. Problems soon engulfed these projects. Rigorous editorial standards prevented project completion deadlines from being met, and the momentum of such endeavors waned in the early 1970s. In addition, new historical interests emerged. Criticism of such elitist work and a questioning of the narrow intellectual goals and aspects of the projects stemmed from the profession's concern for psychohistories and demographic and ethnic studies. But Rutland argues that the founding fathers projects are valid and worthwhile. They offer insight into the early American character as well as observations on local fauna and flora, climatic reports, and foreign manners and mores. (NJS)

802. Shaw, Peter. "The Adams Papers." *American Scholar,* Vol. XXXV (Autumn 1966), pp. 754-774.

Shaw reviews the deeding of the Adams family's papers to the Massachusetts Historical Society in 1952, the early sorting and cataloging of the collection, and the appearance of the first published volume in 1961. He also includes a brief description of the three series of Adams papers and the magnitude of the project. He argues that within the published volumes a reader finds the early political and social history of the emerging American nation. (NJS)

803. Shaw, Peter. "The American Heritage and Its Guardians." *American Scholar*, Vol. XXXV (Winter 1975-1976), pp. 733-751.

Shaw examines two different approaches to editing—one employed in editing literary texts and another in editing historical documents. He discusses in particular the harsh criticisms of Lewis Mumford and Edmund Wilson in their literary reviews and the work of the Center for Editions of American Authors. In contrast Shaw notes the more successful historical editing projects of Julian Boyd and Lyman Butterfield. Yet despite Shaw's favorable look at historical endeavors, he castigates all projects for their failure to produce editions readily available to a lay audience. He contends that expensive, slowly appearing, cumbersome editions generate poor sales and leave important writing unread by the general public. In conclusion Shaw calls for inexpensive and readable classics as well as the meticulously prepared scholarly versions. (NJS)

804. Sheldon, Richard N. "Editing a Historical Manuscript: Jared Sparks, Douglas Southall Freeman, and the Battle of Brandywine." *William and Mary Quarterly*, 3d ser., Vol. XXXVI (July 1979), pp. 255-263.

Sheldon, assistant to the executive director of the National Historical Publications and Records Commission, discusses the criticism by the historian Douglas Southall Freeman of the editing methods employed by the nineteenth-century historian Jared Sparks in publishing *The Writings of George Washington*. The example cited is the treatment of a dispatch—considered one of the most critical elements of the Battle of Brandywine—sent to Washington by General John Sullivan on September 11, 1777, the day of that battle. Providing evidence that Sparks had committed an act of "gross falsification in editing," Freeman postulates that Sparks published his form of the letter as a defense of Sullivan rather than of Washington. Although the Freeman version has been generally accepted by historians, Sheldon discredits it. He points out errors made by Freeman in editing and analyzing the documentary materials and concludes that Freeman's attack on Sparks was unjustified. (NJS)

805. Shelley, Fred. "The Choice of a Medium for Documentary Publication." *American Archivist*, Vol. XXXII (January 1969), pp. 363-368.

Shelley reports that the choice of a medium open to publishers is narrowing. Owing to the enormous printing costs and the shelf space required, letterpress editions of manuscript collections are under attack. Many former letterpress editors are, therefore, turning to microfilm. Although microfilm has decided drawbacks, these limitations are minor when considering the alternative of no manuscript publications. One of the benefits of using microfilm is the increased number of documents that can be included in a publication. Another alternative to letterpress editions outlined by the author is the use of photographic reproductions in volume form. The advantages of this method are that the reader gains a sense of viewing the original paper and that no microfilm reader is needed. (NJS)

806. Shelley, Fred. "The Interest of J. Franklin Jameson in the National Archives, 1908-1934." *American Archivist,* Vol. XII (January-October 1949), pp. 99-130.

Shelley discusses the problems associated with the construction of the National Archives, including a history of relevant legislation. The appeal for a "Hall of Records" began in 1890 when plans for a building were first drawn. In 1903, Congress enacted a law authorizing purchase of a site and construction of a building. A general lack of interest coupled with active opposition by the Librarian of Congress, Ainsworth R. Spofford, who wished to retain all records in the Library of Congress, delayed serious consideration of a national archives until 1907 when Spofford died. Jameson had long been aware of the problems of storing public documents. His primary interest was in publication, but he realized that documents had to be "physically safeguarded before they could be intellectually exploited." To this end Jameson labored for the next twenty-seven years. His work was hampered by a lack of funds for what many lawmakers considered nonessential public construction, confusion over the proper site, and the commencement of World War I. Constrution did not begin until 1933. Jameson's last efforts were directed toward creating an archival system that had the authority to publish and a director who would be a "capable scholar" in an agency independent of the Library of Congress. (NJS)

807. Shelley, Fred. "The Presidential Papers Program of the Library of Congress." *American Archivist,* Vol. XXV (January-October 1962), pp. 429-433.

In 1957, Congress passed a law allowing the Library of Congress to organize and publish in microfilm the manuscripts of the twenty-three presidents in its possession (George Washington to Calvin Coolidge). A year later, when funds were made available, the undertaking was begun. Owing to the difficulties of using microfilm, the law called for an index to each collection. Shelley describes the indexing process in some detail. He also explains other legislative requirements and the computer technology in use. (NJS)

808. Simon, John Y. "American Historical Editing Today." *AHA Perspectives: Newsletter of the American Historical Association,* Vol. XX (October 1982), pp. 5-7.

The author, executive director and a vice president of the Ulysses S. Grant Association, reviews developments since 1950 in the status of documentary editing in the United States and commentary on it. He discusses problems and possibilities that the computer has created and how recent reductions in federal funding have affected editorial projects in general. He notes that one consequence is that "the resourcefulness of editors has recently been demonstrated both in the corridors of Congress and in the manipulation of computers." (SH)

809. Simon, John Y. "Editorial Projects as Derivative Archives." *College and Research Libraries,* Vol. XXXV (July 1974), pp. 291-294.

Simon's major concern is the effect of photocopying on manuscript holders and documentary project editors and staff, who quickly come under pressure to copy and disseminate their holdings. Such pressures hinder staff work and radically diminish the uniqueness of editing projects and their collections. Simon reports on the actions taken by the Ulysses S. Grant Association to preserve the integrity of its project and guard its staff from becoming too absorbed in attending to research tasks of other scholars and with activities not associated with the Grant papers project. Simon's discussion raises many important questions associated with the ability to photocopy and disseminate documents so conveniently and easily and to amass valuable research collections in an instant. (NJS)

810. Simon, John Y. "The Collected Writings of Ulysses S. Grant." *Civil War History,* Vol. IX (September 1963), pp. 277-279.

In 1962 the Civil War centennial commissions of Ohio, Illinois, and New York agreed to sponsor a complete edition of the writings of Ulysses S. Grant. These states figured prominently in Grant's life: he was born and raised in Ohio, received his first command in Illinois, and retired to New York. Officers of the Grant Commission were drawn from all three states. At the time the article was written, the project was in the collecting stage. It used photoduplications of all documents received or written by Grant. The project expected to publish Grant's papers as completely as possible, excluding only routine papers that Grant signed but probably never read. The commission also planned to issue a new, annotated edition of Grant's *Personal Memoirs.* (NJS)

811. Syrett, Harold C., and Jacob E. Cooke. "The Papers of Alexander Hamilton." *Historian,* Vol. XIX (February 1957), pp. 168-181.

Syrett and Cooke discuss the difficulties that arose in preparing a new edition of Alexander Hamilton's writings. Originally scheduled to begin in the late 1930s, the project was delayed by financial shortfalls and World War II. In 1951 the National Historical Publications Commission recommended the publication of Hamilton's papers, but not until 1955, when generous grants were made to Columbia University Press, did the project become financially feasible. Hamilton's writings presented special problems. Originally collected by his widow, many papers critical of Hamilton were destroyed; others were lost in fires at the Treasury Department. The greatest problem, however, related to the diversity of Hamilton's experiences and interests and the wide dispersion of his writings throughout the United States and abroad. (NJS)

812. Tanselle, G. Thomas. "External Fact as an Editorial Problem." *Studies in Bibliography,* Vol. XXXII (1979), pp. 1-47.

Tanselle explores the editor's dilemma when confronted with textual references to external facts. Most of this discussion examines references to external facts as they appear in novels or other literary pieces. Tanselle attempts to distinguish errors calling for corrective action as opposed to those that must remain. Some attention is given to historical documents and the questions that arise in editing them. An examination of a handful of examples help illustrate this discussion and demonstrate the process of reaching critical emending decisions. (NJS)

813. Tanselle, G. Thomas. "The Editing of Historical Documents." *Studies in Bibliography,* Vol. XXXI (1978), pp. 1-56.

Tanselle notes that the twentieth century has become the age of editing and discusses several important editorial subjects, such as the validity of the text itself, the "critical edition," "modernization," the extent and kind of annotation, the contributions of Julian Boyd and other major editors, and the scholarly role of the editor. Tanselle reviews three statements of editorial policy that appeared in the 1950s: that of Julian Boyd, who espoused "scrupulous exactness" but practiced editorial latitude; that of Clarence Carter, whose editing of manuscript text was more conservative; and that of Samuel Eliot Morison, who prepared the manuscript section in the *Harvard Guide to American History* (no. *121*). In the final section, Tanselle asks important questions about textual points of view, and he comments on sound, praiseworthy practices found in a variety of editions. He calls for frank and open discussion among editors to produce better practices along with more consistent and intelligible policies to benefit the reader. (NJS)

814. Taylor, Robert J. "Editorial Practices—An Historian's View." *Newsletter of the Association for Documentary Editing,* Vol. III (February 1981), pp. 4-8.

Taylor sharply disagrees with the editorial precepts set forth by G. Thomas Tanselle (see no. *813*). Taylor prefers to make distinctions between historical editors and literary scholars and believes the former should have enough latitude to define and implement their own editorial methods to meet the needs of a particular project. Readability, in Taylor's opinion, is an overriding concern for historians or for a larger audience; "absolute fidelity to punctuation, deletions, and interlineations," as advocated by Tanselle, proves distracting. Partial modernization and regularization, Taylor contends, does not destroy the mood of a document. Readers are entitled to know the principles that an editor establishes, but the editor should have discretion to design those rules most applicable to the material with which he or she works. (JJC)

815. Tebbel, John. "Safeguarding U.S. History." *Saturday Review* (June 23, 1962), pp. 24-25, 52.

The author describes the role of the National Historical Publications Commission and university presses in caring for papers of famous Americans. He looks particularly at the Jefferson, Franklin, Clay, Calhoun, Adams, Hamilton, Madison, and Wilson projects and discusses their size and cost. Tebbel considers the publishing of these kinds of papers important but never ending. (SH)

816. Teute, Fredrika J. "Views in Review: A Historiographical Perspective on Historical Editing." *American Archivist*, Vol. XLIII (Winter 1980), pp. 43-56.

Teute argues that historical editing, especially since the appearance of the first volume of Julian Boyd's *Papers of Thomas Jefferson* in 1950, has been based on some faulty assumptions that the National Historical Publications and Records Commission has tended to accentuate. First, most long-term editorial projects have concentrated on prominent individuals, thereby giving only a partial history of the nation's past. Second, the historian-editors and their sponsors have insisted that the projects are free of value judgments and independent of the continuum of American historiography. In the past decade historians have started to question these assumptions, methods, and standards for historical editing inaugurated by Boyd, especially the extensive annotation and critical commentary that have become the norm in such projects. Historian-editors, she contends, are subject to the same biases, prejudices, and beliefs as others; the decisions they make in selecting documents and a framework can strongly shape a reader's image of the subject. Concealed in each editor are notions of historical significance and values. She warns that unwary historians in using such volumes may be lulled into a false sense of having all the materials before them or of not realizing textual problems such as sloppy and inconsistent transcriptions. Teute concludes that historian-editors should lower their claims and expectations for these projects and consider alternative approaches to documentaries, including microfilm editions. (JJC)

817. Vandiver, Frank E. "The Jefferson Davis Papers." *Civil War History*, Vol. IX (September 1963), pp. 279-280.

Jefferson Davis's writings were first compiled in 1923. New material has since been located and errors discovered in the 1923 edition. As a Civil War centennial project, these errors were to be corrected and new material added in a complete edition of the writings of Davis. In 1962 at Rice University, with a modest staff, a search for the Davis manuscripts was launched. Microfilm copies of all Davis documents were to be made as soon as funds were available. Final plans called for a complete edition of all the Davis papers. (NJS)

818. Vogt, George L., and John Bush Jones, eds. *Literary and Historical Editing*. Lawrence: University of Kansas Libraries, 1981.

This booklet is number 46 in the University of Kansas Publications Library Series. It contains introductions to the subject by the editors and five essays: James Thorpe, "Literary and Historical Editing: The Values and Limits of Diversity"; George C. Rogers, Jr., "The Sacred Text: An Improbable Dream"; G. Thomas Tanselle, "Literary Editing"; Martin C. Battestin, "A Rationale of

Literary Annotation: The Example of Fielding's Novels"; Charles T. Cullen, "Principles of Annotation in Editing Historical Documents; or, How to Avoid Breaking the Butterfly on the Wheel of Scholarship." (SH)

819. Williams, T. Harry. "Abraham Lincoln—Principle and Pragmatism in Politics: A Review Article." *Mississippi Valley Historical Review,* Vol. XL (June 1953), pp. 89-106.

Under the sponsorship of the Abraham Lincoln Association, a nine-volume edition of Lincoln's works was published in 1953. The edition replaced Nicolay and Hay's *Complete Works* (the Tandy Edition) published in 1905 and several other single-volume compilations. Five-eighths of the new edition deals with the presidential and war years. It also includes critical annotations not found in previous works as well as notes and supplementary documents. (NJS)

820. Wood, Gordon S. "Review Essay: Historians and Documentary Editing" (review of *The Papers of John Adams*, Vols. I-IV), *Journal of American History*, Vol. LXVII (March 1981), pp. 871-877.

Wood comments on the growing debate in historical editing circles on the criticisms of G. Thomas Tanselle, who has condemned the editorial methods and practices of the generation of historical editors since Julian Boyd. The partial modernization and silent alteration of texts adopted by Boyd and sanctioned by the *Harvard Guide to American History* (1954), (see no. *121*) have, in Tanselle's opinion, resulted in dozens of volumes of inaccurate and unreliable documents. Wood defends historical editors and cites the different needs and problems of literary editors and their audience versus historical editors and their audience. Historians are less concerned than literary scholars with textual matters and more interested in bits and scraps of information. Having editions in a highly readable form greatly assists historians in their research, and hence they prefer to allow editors to correct and modernize in a generally consistent fashion than to make "every historian his own editor." Wood goes on to raise serious questions about the editorial decisions made by the editors of the Adams papers, particularly in relation to selectivity, the omission of certain letters, and the lack of calendaring for those omissions. He also suggests that documents already printed elsewhere in modern scholarly editions need not be reprinted in each new series but merely calendared with appropriate references. (JJC)

821. Wright, Edmund. "Making History." *Listener* (November 15, 1962), pp. 803-804.

Wright praises American efforts to publish the manuscripts of revolutionary war heroes and others—the Boswell papers, the correspondence of Horace Walpole, and the papers of Benjamin Franklin and the Adams family. These expensive editions are a "treasure chest" to historians who study them. But Wright states that the sheer size of such projects can be a threat as well as an aid to historians. He outlines five areas of concern: (1) the role of the publisher, which is to reproduce the papers faithfully and not to reflect on the facts presented; (2) the fact that the manuscripts reflect the subject as he saw himself and not, in most cases, as his contemporaries viewed him; (3) often the correspondence of the articulate figure appears more important than that of a person who had difficulty with words; (4) correspondents were sometimes unreliable or too close to the events described; and (5) the historian's greatest task, which is to reduce a large, multivolume edition into one or two easily read monographs that present the real person. (NJS)

822. Wright, Edmund. "The Papers of Great Men." *History Today*, Vol. XII (March 1962), pp. 197-213.

In this review of *The Diary and Autobiography of John Adams*, Wright argues that—if the adoption of the German methods of historical research by Harvard and The Johns Hopkins universities was the first stage in the writing and publishing of U.S. history and the Andrews school of Imperial historians at Yale the second stage—U.S. historians are now entering a third stage. It is one dominated by the editor, a historian who lives with his subject and knows him inside out. The author also underscores the importance of President Harry S Truman's action in 1950, when he asked the National Historical Publications Commission to make available the manuscripts of prominent American figures who were "inadequately represented by their published works." The scholarly work arising from this mandate, Wright argues, is transforming the methodology and character of American history. (NJS)

823. Zall, Paul M. "The Manuscript and Early Texts of Franklin's *Autobiography*." *Huntington Library Quarterly,* Vol. XXXIX (August 1976), pp. 375-384.

Zall describes first the value of giving close scrutiny to Franklin's manuscript of his *Autobiography* and then the importance of tracing its course to publication. He reviews Franklin's manner of writing the manuscript and the difficulties encountered as its composition stretched over a lengthy time span and had to await Franklin's renewed attention after diversions to other tasks. Zall further treats the manuscript's transformation into print. The discussion of this complicated affair reveals a documentary editor's work and the attention required in properly studying a document. Zall concludes by noting that the various printed works fail to be faithful to Franklin's writing and have unfortunately diverted scholarly attention away from the original manuscript. (NJS)

II. Other Aspects of Editing

A Manual of Style. See no. *78.*
This work is a tool for editors, authors, and copywriters in their quest for "clarity and consistency within a publication." (SH)

824. Alderson, William T. "Marking and Correcting Copy for Your Printer." American Association for State and Local History, Technical Leaflet No. 51. *History News*, Vol. XXIV (June 1969).

In this twelve-page essay, the author describes and illustrates "the marking of manuscripts and proofs; the marking of photographs for the making of half-tones; and the estimating of copy to fit space to be filled in the finished publication." It is aimed at beginning editors and students of historical editing. (SH)

825. Cook, Ramsey. "Good-Bye to All That." *Canadian Historical Review,* Vol. XLIX (September 1968), pp. 275-277.

The editor of the *Canadian Historical Review* from 1963 to 1968 initially presented his views at a session entitled "Historians and Editors: The Changing Functions of Historical Journals" before the annual meeting of the American Historical Association in Toronto in December 1967. He observes that "now, as always, the historical journal's function is to provide a convenient vehicle for the publication of new research, fresh interpretations, and critical assessments of the new and old literature of the subject." He discusses the general problems of obtaining enough first-class material, satisfying authors who become impatient with the editorial process, and pleasing more specialized audiences, particularly as they affected management of the *Canadian Historical Review.* (SH)

826. Dempsey, Hugh A. *How to Prepare a Local History.* Calgary, Alberta, Canada: Glenbow-Alberta Institute, 1969.

This pamphlet of twenty-one pages contains practical suggestions on securing community sponsors and subscriptions. (SH)

827. Derby, Charlotte S. "Reaching Your Public: The Historical Society News-letter." American Association of State and Local History, Technical Leaflet No. 30. *History News,* Vol. XXII (January 1969).

This eight-page essay addresses the question: "How do we communicate with our own membership and with the public, so that our work can be better known and more readily appreciated?" The author discusses the purpose of a newsletter as well as its content; visual quality; "other considerations" related to frequency, mailings, extra copies, and so forth; and basic mimeographing supplies. (SH)

828. Ellsworth, S. George. "Ten Years: An Editor's Report." *Western Historical Quarterly,* Vol. X (October 1979), pp. 421-436.

As summarized by the author: "This, then, is a brief account of my stewardship of *WHQ*: its founding [1969], its relations, its operations, underlying guiding philosophies, and the state of western American history today as seen from my vantage point at *WHQ.*" Although Ellsworth discusses many of the particular problems and issues related to the *Western Historical Quarterly's* creation and development, his recollections will be useful to individuals and institutions considering publication of a scholarly journal. Several pages deal with selecting and editing manuscripts, writing letters to authors, and book reviewing. (SH)

829. Fahl, Ronald J. "Editing the *Journal of Forest History* (Part I)." *Forest History Cruiser: The Quarterly Newsletter of the Forest History Society*, Vol. I (October 1978). "Editing the *Journal of Forest History* (Part II)." *Forest History Cruiser: The Quarterly Newsletter of the Forest History Society*, Vol. II (March 1979).

"Steps Toward Production" is Part I of a two-part article in which the editor of the *Journal of Forest History* describes "physical and philosophical steps toward production of *JFH*." He discusses "long-range planning, keeping abreast of the field, cultivating and soliciting contributors, refereeing, copy editing, and other preparations for actual production." "Production and Delivery" is Part II, in which the author explains "the various production steps through to final printing of the magazine and its delivery by mail." (SH)

Felt, Thomas E. *Researching, Writing, and Publishing Local History*. See no. 52.

The author explains how to produce local history in printed form. In the foreword, William T. Alderson, director of the American Association for State and Local History, states that "there is scarcely a historical organization that has not produced, or will not some day undertake to prepare, a printed history of the community it serves." This book is intended "for the persons who will do the research and writing." There are brief sections on many important subjects for editors as well: quotations, documentation, constructing footnotes, the prepared manuscript, editing documents for publication, reprinting, design considerations, specifications, choosing a printer, proofreading, binding, packaging for shipping, promoting, pricing, and so on. (SH)

830. Ferguson, Rowena. *Editing the Small Magazine*. New York: Columbia University Press, 1958.

Although this book is limited to small history magazines, it is a how-to book that should be on the shelf of every editor of a small history journal. A paperback edition appeared in 1976. The author's advice is precise but flexible enough to address the needs and requirements of most small magazines. Ferguson believes that every good editor will know all the work that goes into publishing a small magazine, whether or not he personally is responsible for the details. She encourages editors to be aware of their audiences and the purposes of their publications; she also emphasizes the need for long-range planning that allows for last-minute changes. The author gives specific advice on layout and printing as well as on the table of contents and index. (SH)

831. Fiering, Norman S. "Editing the Historian's First Book." *Maryland Historian*, Vol. VII (Spring 1976), pp. 61-69.

The author, editor of publications at the Institute of Early American History and Culture in Williamsburg, presents "a few reflections on book publication by historians." He stresses the importance of good writing, reviews the differences between a dissertation and a finished book, explains how to choose a publisher, and describes the work of editors and their reliance on "outside" readers. Fiering concludes by reminding authors, especially beginners, of the large amount of "hard work that must go into a well-written book." (SH)

832. Gatewood, William B., Jr. " 'Rendering Striking Historical Service': North Carolina's Historical Publications Program, 1903-1978." In Jeffrey J. Crow, ed. *Public History in North Carolina, 1903-1978: The Proceedings of the Seventy-fifth Anniversary Celebration, March 7, 1978.* Raleigh: North Carolina Division of Archives and History, 1979.

The author, who reviews the work of those involved in North Carolina's historical program, is "impressed by their persistence in the quest for a comprehensive, professionally executed program of value to the broadest possible spectrum of the state's population." While maintaining "high quality and high standards" and avoiding complicity in the promotion of "official history," the state's historical commission and its Division of Archives and History are recognized for fulfilling statutory obligations to "stimulate historical investigation," to "diffuse knowledge in reference to the history and resources" of the state, and to encourage the study of history in North Carolina's schools. Gatewood presents a good deal of the background surrounding publication of numerous documentaries, the *North Carolina Historical Review,* the *Colonial Records* series, a roster of Civil War troops, county histories and inventories, bibliographical and genealogical guides, manuals, maps and facsimile editions, and dozens of pamphlets on aspects of the state's past. (SH)

833. Gore, Gary. "Spotting Mechanical Errors in Proof: A Guide for Linecasting Machine Proofreaders." American Association of State and Local History, Technical Leaflet No. 53. *History News,* Vol. XXIV (December 1969).

This four-page guide explains how and when to mark mechanical errors—a task not to be taken lightly. The author discusses and illustrates "points to remember." (SH)

834. Lawson, Steven F., and Robert P. Ingalls. "*Tampa Bay History*: An Experiment in Public History." *Public Historian,* Vol. III (Spring 1981), pp. 53-62.

The authors discuss the problems they faced in creating a new local history journal and point out ways it helped revitalize the University of South Florida's history department and increase its visibility within the university and community. They also show how the journal has assisted in the training of students. (SH)

835. Luey, Beth. "Book Editing Option Explored in New Program at Arizona State." *AHA Newsletter,* Vol. XVIII (June 1980), p. 11.

This article describes the Arizona State University program in book editing. Traditionally, most book editors learn their craft on the job, with supplementary training in summer seminars. The Arizona State program integrates professional training in book editing into the graduate program of the history department. (SH)

836. Luey, Beth. "Teaching for Nonteaching Careers." *Public Historian,* Vol. IV (Spring 1982), pp. 43-56.

The author, who directs historical editing and publishing at Arizona State University, describes ways to prepare history students for nonteaching careers, particularly in editing. She discusses teaching materials, class conduct and atmosphere, commonsense knowledge, and competence and confidence. (SH)

837. Madison, James H. " 'No Cheap Padding': State History Journals and American History." *Institute News* (of North Carolina Institute of Applied History), Vol. I (June 1982), pp. 6-8.

The editor of the *Indiana Magazine of History* examines the general operations and philosophies of state history journals. His conclusions are based on the results of two questionnaires: "one sent in 1980 to members of the Indiana Historical Society (with a 42% response), and a second . . . to forty-seven state journal editors early in 1982, receiving thirty-four responses." Madison urges the publication of "history with all the qualities of good scholarship, ranging from an awareness of the technical problem-solving literature to accurate footnotes, but . . . history that tells a story and tells it well to a public interested in that particular story." (SH)

838-840. Mitchell, Memory F. "Publishing in State Historical Journals." *Wisconsin Magazine of History,* Vol. LIX (Winter 1975-1976), pp. 135-142.

Mitchell focuses on the relationship between the editors and contributors to state journals. Using responses of thirty-five state history journal editors to a survey questionnaire, Mitchell describes the editorial operations of these publications and the nature of the authors and their submissions. She notes the different interests of scholarly and more popular contributors and readers as a major challenge of editing a state magazine. (SH)

841. Murray, Paul. "Thirty Years of the New History: A Study of the *North Carolina Historical Review 1924-1953.*" *North Carolina Historical Review,* Vol. XXXIII (April 1955), pp. 174-193.

Murray characterizes historical writings on North Carolina from 1886 to 1929, describes the founding of the *Review* (the first issue was published in January 1924), analyzes the *Review*'s content from 1924 to 1953, and evaluates its major effects on North Carolina history. The author shows the influence of Harry Elmer

Barnes's *The New History and the Social Studies* (1925) on the production of good state and local history, particularly in North Carolina. (SH)

842. Nodyne, Kenneth R. "The Community Life of Wheeling, West Virginia: The Challenge of the *Upper Ohio Valley Historical Review*." *Public Historian*, Vol. III (Spring 1981), pp. 63-70.

The author describes how a community history journal contributed to "a growing appreciation of local history in the Wheeling area." (SH)

843. Parramore, Thomas C. "Forging the Tremulous Link: The First Half-Century of the *North Carolina Historical Review*." *North Carolina Historical Review*, Vol. LI (October 1974), pp. 361-378.

The first issue of the *North Carolina Historical Review* was published in January 1924, the culmination of persistent efforts by "a small but earnest coterie of history teachers, publicists, and writers on North Carolina subjects" who had seen the establishment of historical quarterlies in South Carolina (1900), Maryland (1906), Tennessee (1915), and Louisiana and Georgia (1917). The *Review*, modeled in style and format after the *American Historical Review*, initially had difficulty in attracting acceptable manuscripts. When Albert Ray Newsome, a professional historian at the University of North Carolina, became editor, he was able "to fill the inevitable voids with articles of his own composition." Into the 1930s, Newsome was the leading contributor. Beginning in 1935, and for the next twenty-six years, the *Review* benefitted from the leadership of two professional historians—Christopher Crittenden, as editor, and David Leroy Corbitt, as managing editor. The 1950s represented "a watershed for the *Review* in defining its postwar character and strengthening its position as a leading periodical of its type." In 1961, with Corbitt's retirement, Memory F. Mitchell became editor and served in the position until mid-1982. (SH)

844. Reingold, Nathan. "What Is a Federal Historian? A Historical Editor." *Public Historian*, Vol. II (Summer 1980), pp. 89-91.

This short article was one of five papers presented at a session on "What Is a Federal Historian?" at the annual meeting of the American Historical Association in San Francisco on December 28, 1978. Other contributors discussed "an archivist, historic preservationist, military historian, and museum curator." Editor of the Joseph Henry Papers at the Smithsonian Institution, Reingold contends that his activities are "identical to those of a historical editor in a university or historical society." He describes his tasks and those of his staff: locating pertinent manuscript sources, preparing a transcript for editing and printing, conducting research for and writing annotations, and interpreting the contents of a letterpress edition. (SH)

845. Ridge, Martin. "An Editor's Report, 1966-1977." *Journal of American History,* Vol. LXIV (March 1978), pp. 1045-1061.

Ridge surveys the years of his editorship of the *Journal of American History,* during which time the profession and the journal changed significantly. He discusses each phase of editing the publication, giving special attention to handling manuscripts submitted for publication and dealing with book reviews and reviewers. He places special importance on fairness to contributors, the profession, and the cause of scholarship. He also considers the editor's dual role as servant to the profession and as advocate of changing scholarly interests. (JHM)

846. Rodabaugh, James H. "Historical Societies: Their Magazines and Their Editors." *Wisconsin Magazine of History,* Vol. XLV (Winter 1961-1962), pp. 115-123.

Rodabaugh provides data on the large number and variety of historical society publications. He explains the nature of the editor's responsibilities, the criticisms directed against editors by often uninformed contributors and readers, and the opportunities editors have to make contributions to historical scholarship and to expanding popular interest in history. (JHM)

847. Ryden, John G. "But What of It?" *Public Historian,* Vol. IV (Spring 1982), pp. 21-28.

The author, the director of the Yale University Press, describes the publishing activities of university presses. Within that context he reviews the role of the editor and touches on matters relating to training and developing a career in editing. (SH)

848. Scholarly Communication: The Report of the National Enquiry. Baltimore: Johns Hopkins University Press, 1979.

This publication reports the results and recommendations of a large study of the ways in which scholars communicate. Part two of the four-part book treats scholarly journals, described as "a troublesome link in the communications network" (p. 37). The discussion provides an overview of the issues and problems as perceived by editors and scholars, based on questionnaires sent to both. Authors were especially prone to complain about the slowness of the review process. Also discussed are practical matters such as copyrighting and finance for journals. (JHM)

849. Schroder, Alan M. *History, Analysis, and Recommendations Concerning the Public Programs of the Iowa State Historical Department, Division of the State Historical Society.* Iowa City: Division of the State Historical Society, 1981.

This report is the product of an institutional self-study project conducted at the Division of the State Historical Society between September 1, 1978, and October 31, 1979. Several sections in the report are devoted to descriptions of the society's publications program through its long history. Special attention is given to *Palimpsest,* the society's popular history magazine. (SH)

850. Sonnichsen, Charles L. *The Ambidextrous Historian: Historical Writers and Writing in the American West.* Norman: University of Oklahoma Press, 1981.

The author is editor of the *Journal of Arizona History* and a vigorous proponent of local and regional history. Chapter 10, "The Editor: A Necessary Evil," explains some of the challenges of editing a state or regional quarterly. Sonnichsen considers the different kinds of manuscript articles received by such publications and details some of the editor's trials in working with authors. (JHM)

851. Stainton, Elsie Myers. "A Bag for Editors." *Scholarly Publishing,* Vol. VIII (January 1977), pp. 111-119.

A veteran editor provides a potpourri of suggestions and encouragements for editors. Although her remarks are directed largely to book editors, many are applicable to journal editors also. Subjects range from selecting a title and sweet-talking an author to overburdened adverbs and the "false-windup" introduction. (JHM)

852. Steiner, Dale R. *Historical Journals: A Handbook for Writers and Reviewers.* Santa Barbara, Calif.: ABC-Clio, 1981.

The bulk of this publication consists of a directory of journals, covering all fields of history. For each journal listed there is included information on manuscript and book review policies, editor's name and address, and other information. Especially useful is Steiner's succinct advice on writing and submitting essays and reviews and his general explanation of the procedures followed by most scholarly journals in handling submissions. (JHM)

853. Stensvaag, James T. "Fifty Years of the *New Mexico Historical Review:* An Archival Record." *New Mexico Historical Review,* Vol. LI (October 1976), pp. 269-280.

This article was prepared in recognition of the *Review*'s fiftieth year of publication and the bicentennial anniversary of the United States. The author reviews the careers and contributions of the three editors who served the journal through 1964—Lansing Bartlett Bloom, Paul A. F. Walter, and Frank Driver Reeve. Stensvaag also observes that the *Review*'s professional growth "reflected the expansion of interest in and scholarly treatment of historical subjects in the Southwest." (SH)

854. Swint, Henry L. "William Campbell Binkley, 1889-1970: Historian, Editor, Teacher." *Journal of Southern History,* Vol. XXXVII (August 1971), pp. 353-366.

Binkley was a scholar whose "greatest contribution to his profession undoubtedly was in his work as an editor.'' He served as editor first of the *Tennessee Historical Quarterly,* then of the *Journal of Southern History,* and finally of the *Mississippi Valley Historical Review,* and, at all times, maintained ''rigorously high'' standards. Swint describes Binkley's work habits and explains how he viewed the role of the editor. He used words, as an artist, ''with surgical precision.'' In his work, as historian-editor, ''whether book, book review, article, departmental report, or letter, Binkley habitually revised sentence by sentence until his meaning was unmistakable.'' Regarding the historian's professional responsibility, Binkley stated that his ''duty is to establish and make known as complete and accurate a record of man's past as he can, and then to communicate a knowledge of this to the public—both lay and professional.'' Swint also reviews Binkley's involvement and commitment to historical associations. (SH)

855. Sylvester, Lorna Lutes, comp. *''No Cheap Padding'': Seventy-five Years of the Indiana Magazine of History, 1904-1979.* Indianapolis: Indiana Historical Bureau, 1980.

The introduction to this collection of reprinted articles from the *Indiana Magazine of History* consists of a brief history of this publication. Included is information about each editor and some assessment of the changing operations and contents of the magazine, as each editor struggled to avoid the publication of ''cheap padding.'' Their efforts produced one of the nation's more scholarly state journals. (JHM)

856. Tripp, Wendell. ''Fifty Years of *New York History.''* *New York History,* Vol. L (October 1969), pp. 355-396.

This article ''tells the story of the first fifty years of the New York State Historical Association's quarterly journal, including its antecedents, its creation, and a survey of the men and women who influenced it through the years.'' Tripp shows how the kinds of articles published in the magazine gradually changed from the single subject of wars to ''ethnic groups, historiography, education, industry, religion, journalism, and literature''; he notes their continuing value and explains how they advanced the field of local and community history. The author also describes the overriding and positive influence of Dixon Ryan Fox and Henry Allen Moe, first trustees and later presidents of the organization, on the association and its journal as well as the specific and enduring contributions of more recent editors—Louis C. Jones, Mary E. Cunningham, and Dorothy C. Barck. (SH)

857. Vitzthum, Richard C. ''The Historian as Editor: Francis Parkman's Reconstruction of Sources in Montcalm and Wolfe.'' *Journal of American History,* Vol. LIII (December 1966), pp. 471-486.

This article ''subjects *Montcalm and Wolfe,* the penultimate and probably finest work in the *France and England* series, to as systematic and thorough a comparison with its sources as Parkman's rather erratic bibliographic notes and the accessibility of the sources he used would permit.'' Vitzthum shows Park-man's ''blunders'' when he depends on secondary rather than primary material or ''when his sources lack the vividness and immediacy of manner which he believes the events they report demand.'' Parkman's editorial skills are also revealed. (SH)

858. Walklet, John J., Jr. ''Publishing in the Historical Society.'' American Association for State and Local History, Technical Leaflet No. 34. *History News*, Vol. XXI (April 1966).

The author discusses the general concerns of historical society publishing: ''types of publication, promotion, quality, preparation, design, manufacturing costs, personnel, publications program, publication funds, and distribution.'' (SH)

859. Zink, Stephen D. ''Journal Publishing in the Field of U.S. History.'' *Scholarly Publishing*, Vol. II (July 1980), pp. 343-359.

Based largely on a survey of editors of fifty-eight journals of United States national or regional history, this article concludes that poor communication between author and editor is the greatest problem facing these journals. The situation is largely the result of several factors: the pressure on historians to publish, the inability of many of them to write literate and lucid English, and their lack of concern about the manner in which their work is selected for dissemination. The article provides a good overview of the general processes as followed by most scholarly journals. (SH)

CHAPTER 7

HISTORICAL RESOURCE MANAGEMENT

Theodore J. Karamanski, editor

Historical resource management is an important part of public history, which also goes by the names historic preservation and cultural resource management. The term *historic preservation* is not used here because of its strong association with the built environment and because preservation of a historic resource is only one option reviewed by a historic resource manager. *Cultural resource management* is the term favored by archaeologists, but it is a misleading name. The historical resource manager is not concerned with protecting all facets of culture; opera, ballet, and literature, for example, are left to other experts. What the historical resource manager is concerned with is the careful exploitation of past material culture. Material culture encompasses the objects built by man to cope with his environment and express his individuality. It includes the shattered fragments of artifacts as well as whole buildings and entire landscapes. Concern for material culture unites the diverse work of the underwater archaeologist with the museum curator and the concerns of the industrial historian with the government official. Material culture represents the objects of the past, the artifacts of history. Historical resource management is the collection, utilization, protection, and interpretation of history's three-dimensional resources.

The practice of historic resource management takes place in several settings—federal agencies, historic preservation offices in the states, university research centers, museums, private consulting corporations, and community groups. Historic resource management is part of state and federal government policy. The reader would do well also to consult chapter 11, "Policy History," for more information on that aspect of the field. Oral history and archives and records management are also important tools to the historic resource manager. Current problems in historical resource management are discussed in *Historic Preservation* and *Preservation News*, published by the National Trust for Historic Preservation, and *History News*, published by the American Association for State and Local History.

I. History and Historical Resources

860. Dickens, Roy S., and Carole E. Hill, eds. *Cultural Resources: Planning and Management*. Boulder, Colo.: Westview, 1978.

This volume is a collection of sixteen papers on cultural resource management. It incorporates the perspectives of private contractors, agency officials, and academics. Agency-contractor relations are discussed. It advocates a broad view of historic resource management, incorporating the skills of sociologists, folklorists, and planners, as well as historians and anthropologists. (TJK)

861. Hosmer, Charles B. *Presence of the Past: A History of the Preservation Movement in the United States before Williamsburg*. New York: Putnam, 1965. Hosmer, Charles B. *Preservation Comes of Age: From Williamsburg to the National Trust*. Charlottesville: University of Virginia Press, 1981.

Historic preservation's roots in nineteenth-century America and the gradual emergence of a preservation movement are the themes of these two volumes. Hosmer focuses on important steps in the development of a national awareness for historic preservation, such as the fight to preserve Mount Vernon. Hosmer does not neglect many of the regional or local preservation campaigns whose role was equally important in maintaining America's historic properties. (TJK)

862. King, Thomas F., Patricia P. Hickman, and Gary Berg. *Anthropology in Historic Preservation: Caring for Culture's Clutter*. New York: Academic, 1977.

Written by archaeologists for archaeologists, this volume is a guide to the historic preservation system. The evolution of the federal government's involvement in cultural resource management is presented. The book emphasizes case studies that illustrate the application of preservation regulations and archaeological methods to development problems. Because federal policy has changed several times since the book was published, it should be used in tandem with updates from the *Federal Register*. (TJK)

863. Lynch, Kevin. *What Time Is This Place*. Cambridge, Mass.: M.I.T. Press, 1976.

Lynch reflects on the logical extension of historic preservation, that is, what is the human sense of time. Lynch maintains that "the quality of the personal image of time is crucial for individual well being." He stresses the importance of history and historic preservation in managing the physical environment that supports our image of time. (TJK)

864. Schlereth, Thomas J. *Artifacts and the American Past*. Nashville: American Association for State and Local History, 1980.

This collection of ten essays presents ways to utilize material historical sources for the study and teaching of American history. The essays range broadly, including a discussion of teaching strategies for student visits to historic house museums and classroom exercises on the use of maps in historical research. Perhaps most interesting is Schlereth's study of landscapes as historical artifacts and the use of vegetation as a historical clue. Through the implementation of the interdisciplinary approach outlined in the essays, the author believes that research on artifacts and the American past will "move beyond the merely descriptive stage of investigation into the more problematic area of historical analysis and interpretation." (TJK)

II. Historical Archaeology

865. Ferguson, Leland, ed. *Historical Archaeology and the Importance of Material Things.* Special Publication Series, No. 2. Society of Historical Archaeology, 1977.

This volume is a collection of papers given at a thematic symposium at the Eighth Annual Meeting of the Society for Historical Archaeology, Charleston, South Carolina, January 1975. The primary purpose of the volume is to stress the priority of artifactual remains or "material culture" in the analysis of historic sites. Each article demonstrates the importance of historic artifactual and structural remains from various research projects with subjects ranging from folklore to garbage. The volume is highly theoretical and interpretive in content and structure. (DJK)

866. Gould, Richard A., and Michael B. Schiffer, eds. *Modern Material Culture: The Archaeology of Us.* New York: Academic, 1981.

This collection of articles emphasizes the nature of archaeological reasoning in relationship to contemporary material culture. Articles focus on field work and observations of man and his material culture in American society. (DJK)

867. Historical Archaeology: Journal of the Society for Historical Archaeology. Ann Arbor, Mich.: The Society for Historical Archaeology.

This has been an annual journal until recently but is now distributed semiannually. The principal academic journal of The Society for Historical Archaeology contains both theoretical as well as substantive articles dealing with new developments in the field of historical archaeology and material culture. (DJK)

Noël Hume, Ivor. *Historical Archaeology.* See no. *40.*
Historical Archaeology is a "how-to" manual for the excavation of historic-era archaeology sites. Written by the longtime director of archaeology at Colonial Williamsburg, the book serves both the interested amateur and the serious student. In addition to discussing, step by step, the procedures followed to excavate and record a site, the author also addresses theoretical approaches to historical archaeology. Noël Hume is not an intellectual companion of Stanley South (see no. *869*). In the introduction to the 1975 edition of *Historical Archaeology* he maintained, "my damning of those who hide an ignorance of the relevant artifacts

and documents behind a screen of anthropological, sociological, and methodological, or any other crypto-academic jargon remains as unrepentantly strident as it was in 1967.'' This book is essential for the student interested in historical archaeology. (TJK)

868. Schuyler, Robert L., ed. *Historical Archaeology: A Guide to Substantive and Theoretical Contributions*. Farmingdale, N.Y.: Baywood, 1978.

Some thirty-five articles have been gathered together for this volume and grouped under the following topics: "The Emergence and Definition of a New Discipline"; "Subfields of Historical Archaeology, Substantive Contribution"; "Theoretical Positions"; and "Future Trends." The volume deals with every aspect of historical archaeology, from the interface between history and archaeology to the use of oral sources in archaeological research. (DJK)

869. South, Stanley. *Method and Theory in Historical Archaeology*. New York: Academic, 1977.

This book views historical archaeology as the scientific study of cultural processes. Using field-work examples largely from South Carolina, the author discusses the importance of quantitative studies to unlock the general facts of a site. Only through quantitative analysis will material culture-use patterns emerge. Because of the author's insistence that historical archaeology is a science and that humanistic approaches are "trivial, uninteresting and boring," the book is in many ways a polemic. South represents a considerable body of opinion in the archaeological community. His ideas must be addressed by any serious student of historical archaeology. *Method and Theory in Historical Archaeology* provides an entirely different perspective on archaeology than Noël Hume (see no. *40*). (TJK)

870. South, Stanley, ed. *The Conference on Historic Site Archaeology Papers*. Columbia: University of South Carolina.

This yearly publication presents select papers from the Annual Conference on Historic Sites. At present there are fourteen volumes. Articles cover a wide range of subjects pertinent to archaeological research on historic sites. (DJK)

871. State Historical Society of Wisconsin. *Wisconsin's Presentation Plan, 1971-1981*. Madison: State Historical Society of Wisconsin, 1970.

This is one of the earlier state historic preservation plans. It is essentially a compilation of state and federal statutes along with a historic site inventory. Problems and planning for the state are discussed in detail. (DJK)

872. *Technology and Conservation Magazine*. Boston: The Technology Organization.

This magazine is published quarterly; it contains articles dealing with the technical aspects of conservation and preservation. Articles are on subjects such as museum storage facilities, security systems, computer inventory programs, chemical treatment of historic documents, and building restoration. (DJK)

III. Preservation in Rural Areas

873. Coughlin, Robert E., John C. Keene, J. Dixon Esseks, William Toner, and Lisa Rosenberger. *The Protection of Agricultural Land: A Reference Guidebook for State and Local Governments*. Washington: Government Printing Office, 1981.

One of the products of a two-year study mandated by Congress, this guidebook represents one of the major conclusions of the National Agricultural Lands Study, that the protection of agricultural land will best be accomplished at the local and state levels. It summarizes land protection techniques, discussing and comparing tax incentives, purchase or transfer of development rights, agricultural zoning, and agricultural districts, among others. State and local farmland preservation programs are described and analyzed, and the legal issues of agricultural land protection programs are examined. (AEW)

874. Fraser, Elisabeth A., and Anne F. Morris. *Getting It All Together: The Application of Environmental Information to Land Use Planning*. Mendham: Association of New Jersey Environmental Commissions and New Jersey Conservation Foundation, 1980.

The environmental resources inventory (ERI) is the process of documenting environmental factors pertaining to geology, atmosphere, soils, surface water, watersheds, water quality, vegetation, and wildlife. Here, the ERI is described in lay terms for use by community groups in understanding and carrying out studies of their environmental resources, increasingly a process that in rural areas is performed together with a historic resources survey. Although the book is specific to New Jersey, it is useful anywhere. (AEW)

875. Hendler, Bruce. *Caring for the Land: Environmental Principles for Site Design and Review*. Chicago: American Society of Planning Officials, 1977.

Illustrations in this book accompany brief discussions of principles and techniques for land development. It treats the consequences of ignoring special environmental siting or design consideration. Among these are natural hazards, historic or scientific resources, recreational opportunities, topography, vegetation, visual impact, setback buffers, and open spaces. (AEW).

876. Hoose, Phillip M. *Building an Ark: Tools for the Preservation of Natural Diversity through Land Protection*. Covelo, Calif.: Island, 1981.

This "how-to" book was written by a staff member of the Nature Conservancy, the national organization dedicated to the protection of endangered species. It covers topics ranging from state natural heritage inventories to real estate and land management techniques. (AEW)

877. Kusler, Jon A. *Regulating Sensitive Lands*. Cambridge, Mass.: Ballinger, 1980.

State and local policies for resource conservation are examined in this comprehensive book, including methods of defining sensitive lands, performance standards, and regulatory programs aimed at area types, for example, wetlands and coastal areas. Some eight hundred ordinances are reviewed, interviews with program personnel in more than thirty states are reported, and legal considerations are discussed. Appendices annotate sixty-three court cases most often used as precedents and profile state or cooperative state/local programs in thirty-nine states. (AEW)

878. Lemire, Robert A. *Creative Land Development: Bridge to the Future*. Boston: Houghton Mifflin, 1979.

Natural resource protection can be integrated with land development to build balanced communities. The author brings home this message on the basis of his experience with a local land trust that went beyond tradition, not only acquiring land but developing it. The development was designed to protect natural and historic features of the sites, and to pay the costs of acquisition. Case studies of development projects in Lincoln, Massachusetts, are given, including one on an estate with an historic house and road that were preserved. (AEW)

879. Northeast Environmental Design, for Two Rivers Ottauquechee Regional Planning and Development Commission. *The Vermont Backroad: A Guide for the Protection, Conservation, and Enhancement of Its Scenic Quality*. Woodstock, Vt.: Northeast Environmental Design, 1974.

In the days before expensive gasoline, "driving for pleasure" was a well-known American pastime, ranked by recreation experts as high on the list of recreational activities. Even today, scenic roads are the way most Americans experience the pleasures of viewing the countryside. This book examines the methods for protecting and enhancing the scenic quality of Vermont backroads, emphasizing the mutual dependency of aesthetics and engineering standards that accept narrow winding roads, trees and shrubs in the right of way, and old bridges. (AEW)

880. Palmer, Arthur E. *Toward Eden*. Winterville, N.C.: Creative Resource Systems, 1981.

An active participant in the events he describes, the author chronicles the creation of an "Environmental Land Development regulatory system" in the township of Medford, New Jersey. The first half of the book is a blow-by-blow account, beginning in 1971 and ending in 1979, by which time Medford had revised its master plan and adopted a new zoning law. Such an account gives the reader a clear idea of the time it can take and the multiplicity of interests involved in getting (or not getting) good environmental planning and regulations in place in a rural or suburban municipality. The rest of the book consists of twenty documents that grew out of the process, including material produced by the Department of Landscape Architecture at the University of Pennsylvania. Technical publications in the planning field often neglect case studies and fail to go beyond the resource inventory to the process of implementing recommendations. This book is a rare in-depth account that should appeal to lay readers as well as professional land use planners and attorneys. (AEW)

881. Proudman, Robert D., and Reuben Rajala. *AMC Field Guide to Trail Building and Maintenance*. 2d ed. Boston: Appalachian Mountain Club, 1981.

In many parts of the country, the tradition of crossing others' land to hunt, fish, ski, or hike has afforded pleasure to rural residents and visitors. Groups seeking to promote and maintain this access may need more than tradition, however, as landowners begin to post their land in the face of increasing numbers of inconsiderate users. This how-to manual covers trail development, maintenance and protection, and working with private property owners. (AEW)

882. River Conservation Fund. *Flowing Free: A Citizen's Guide to Protecting Wild and Scenic Rivers*. Washington: River Conservation Fund, 1977.

When pioneers settled this country, they first sought fertile river valleys. Today, many of these rivers and streams winding through these agricultural valleys, dotted with old homes and barns, may qualify as "scenic" under the federal wild and scenic rivers program. Designation protects the rivers from damming and the surrounding lands from other detrimental federally-supported projects. Protection for rivers so designated is accomplished through cooperative easements bought from landowners by the U.S. Department of the Interior. A few state and local protection programs have also been designed. This book describes federal, state, and local programs, and outlines steps for citizen groups to take in implementing them. (AEW)

883. Shopsin, William C. *Saving Large Estates: Conservation, Historic Preservation, Adaptive Re-use*. Setauket: Society for the Preservation of Long Island Antiquities and the New York State Council on the Arts, 1977.

This book, a compendium of specially written articles, case studies, and reprints, examines preservation efforts on Long Island, in Westchester and Dutchess counties, and in the Adirondack and Catskill regions. Extensively illustrated with maps and site and building plans as well as photos, it profiles more than twenty adaptive-use projects and planning programs implementing farmland and open space preservation. (AEW)

884. Stipe, Robert E. *New Directions in Rural Preservation*. Washington: Government Printing Office, 1980.

This collection of articles by more than a dozen authors, a product of the U.S. Department of the Interior, Heritage Conservation and Recreation Service, examines the new awareness of the importance of rural cultural resources, generally at the national level. The focus is primarily on rural buildings, but several articles highlight rural recreation, social and economic issues, and folklife. (AEW)

885. Stokes, Samuel, and Joe Getty. *Rural Conservation.* Information Sheet No. 19, National Trust for Historic Preservation. Washington: Preservation Press, 1979. Bibliography revised, 1981.

"Rural Conservation," begin the authors, "is the protection of the countryside and includes the preservation of buildings and villages of cultural significance, the protection of the surrounding open space and the enhancement of the local economy and social institutions." Advocating an interdisciplinary approach to planning at the local level to preserve community assets, this monograph examines: cultural resources, surveys, landscape assessment, zoning, farmland retention techniques, local historic district ordinances, conservation commissions, regional planning, federal environmental controls, property acquisition and easements, greenline parks and greenbelts, and protection for scenic roads, trails, and rivers. An extensive annotated bibliography and lists of private non-profit organizations and federal agencies are included as appendices. (AEW)

886. Swaim, Doug, ed. *Carolina Dwelling: Towards Preservation of Place.* The Student Publication of the School of Design. Volume XXVI. Raleigh, N.C.: University Graphics, 1978.

This book celebrates North Carolina folk housing and the entire vernacular landscape, a task that takes its twenty-four contributors beyond traditional architectural history into analyses that make use of techniques of geographers and landscape architects. As an example of regional architecture studies, it conveys not only a sense of rural North Carolina but the rural South in general. A sample of titles makes clear an eclectic approach: "North Carolina Coastal Vernacular"; "The I-House as a Carrier of Style in Three Counties of the Northeastern Piedmont"; "Carolina Tobacco Barns"; "North Carolina Country Churches: Explorations in the Mountains and Tidewater"; "Site Selection of Pre-1940 Mountain Houses"; "Homeplace: Images and Impressions of an Appalachian Settlement." (AEW)

887. Watson, A. Elizabeth. *Establishing an Easement Program to Protect Historic, Scenic, and Natural Resources.* Information Sheet No. 25, National Trust for Historic Preservation. Rev. ed. Washington: Preservation Press, 1982.

An easement is a way for a concerned group or agency to protect private property without having to acquire it. In return for agreeing to preserve the property under the supervision of the group that receives the easement, the property owner receives certain tax benefits. This monograph explains the tax and legal aspects of creating easements and sets forth the steps an organization should follow in establishing an easement program. Criteria for accepting easements and review and enforcement procedures are among the points discussed, not generally found in other discussions of easements, which tend to focus on the benefits to the property owners rather than the responsibilities of the organization. The appendices include a sample easement and annotated bibliography. (AEW)

888. Watson, A. Elizabeth. *The Development of Rural Conservation Programs: A Case Study of Loudoun County, Va*. Information Sheet No. 29, National Trust for Historic Preservation. Washington: Preservation Press, 1981.

Loudoun County, Virginia, a highly productive farming community forty miles outside of Washington, D.C., exemplifies many rural regions that confront the pressures of growth from expanding urban areas. Loudoun is noteworthy because of the Goose Creek rural historic district, some ten thousand acres; preservation activities in the village of Waterford, a National Historic Landmark; county-wide agricultural preservation programs; and effective county planning and zoning. This case study documents and analyzes the efforts of grass-roots groups and county officials in pioneering multiple steps in managing growth while conserving the very qualities that attract that growth: "open spaces, clean air and streams, wildlife, fields and pastures, forests and a sense of place created by the farms and villages built in the past years." (AEW)

IV. Urban Preservation

889. Adaptive Use: Development Economics, Process, and Profiles. Washington: Urban Land Institute, 1978.

Adaptive use of historic buildings is an increasingly important form of development, particularly because of the generous tax incentives that have been offered over the past few years. This book describes the adaptive-use process in three parts. The first section discusses the real estate development process, relating it specifically to older buildings. The second part is a compilation of fifteen case studies of adaptive-use projects, illustrated by photographs, floor plans, and project data. The final portion of the book is comprised of 180 brief descriptions of adaptive-use projects with an introductory essay for each building type. (SS/HH)

890. Baumback, Richard O., Jr., and William E. Borah. *The Second Battle of New Orleans: A History of the Vieux Carré Riverfront-Expressway Controversy*. University: University of Alabama Press for the Preservation Press, National Trust for Historic Preservation in the United States, 1981.

One of the major threats to older neighborhoods and downtown districts has been the placement of a highway near or through a historic district. This book chronicles the twenty-five-year controversy over the siting of a highway in New Orleans, Louisiana, that ended in the defeat of the highway proposal. The discussion of each step of the campaign for and against the highway forms an analysis of the people and the process involved. (SS/HH)

891. Bowsher, Alice Meriwether. *Design Review in Historic Districts: A Handbook for Virginia Review Boards*. Washington: National Trust for Historic Preservation, 1978.

Effective design review is necessary in order to maintain and protect the physical character of a historic district. This handbook, written for members of design review boards in Virginia, discusses design review, how to develop effective design guidelines, and how to make design review work. Included in the text is a discussion of guidelines for rehabilitation, maintenance, demolition, and signs as well as chapters on how to publicize the guidelines. Also included is information on building public and governmental support, and administrative procedures and policies. The appendices include selected design review documents and legal aspects of design review. Although the book is about architectural review boards in Virginia, it is useful to people working in other states. (SS/HH)

892. College Hill: A Demonstration Study of Historic Area Renewal. Providence, R.I.: Providence City Plan Commission, 1967.

Completed in 1967, this study is an early example of a comprehensive historic preservation plan. The study follows the preservation planning process, describing the historical and architectural framework of the area. Specific subjects addressed are zoning and traffic problems, areas for new construction, neighborhood planning, and the institutional area of the city (site of Brown University). The study also includes a discussion of the method used to rank buildings on a comparative basis and the development of an interpretation area. (SS/HH)

893. Costonis, John J. *Space Adrift: Saving Urban Landmarks through the Chicago Plan*. Urbana: University of Illinois Press for the National Trust for Historic Preservation, 1974.

Many buildings in urban areas are demolished so that the site can be developed for a more intensive use. The transfer of development rights is a legal and planning technique designed to save threatened landmark buildings and to compensate the owner. The technique allows for the redistribution of development rights from the site of a landmark to another parcel of land. Although transfer of development rights has not been widely used to this date, this book provides the basic discussion of this very complex process that has been of considerable interest to preservationists. *Space Adrift* describes the conceptual basis of the method and provides an economic, legal, and design analysis of the process. The text is accompanied by photographs, tables, and illustrations that elucidate many of the concepts. (SS/HH)

Dennis, Stephen N. *Recommended Model Provisions for a Preservation Ordinance, with Annotations*. See no. *914*.

An ordinance provides the legal framework for a historic district. Therefore, it should be carefully written and, when necessary, modified to fit new circumstances. This handbook reviews the basic provisions that should be included in an ordinance and illustrates each point with an annotation and quotations from existing ordinances. A selection of models has been chosen to indicate the range of possible approaches to a particular issue and differing state enabling legislation as well as a variety of local factors such as community size and the history of local preservation efforts. (SS/HH)

894. Derry, Anne. *Guidelines for Local Surveys: A Basis for Preservation Planning*. Washington: National Register of Historic Places, Office of Archeology and Historic Preservation, National Park Service, U.S. Department of the Interior, 1977.

The cultural resource survey is the first step in any historic preservation effort. This publication describes, in detail, what constitutes a survey; how to plan and conduct a survey; and how to review, organize, and publish survey material. In addition, an appendix summarizes archaeological surveys, federal legislation, and legal and financial techniques for historic preservation. There is also an extensive, partially annotated bibliography of preservation publications. (SS/HH)

895. *Downtown Revitalization: A Compendium of State Activities*. Washington: International Downtown Executives Assocation, 1980.

Downtown revitalization efforts are an integral part of historic preservation in the city. This compendium describes the involvement of each state in downtown revitalization. In each case, the statewide organizations that have responsibility for downtown revitalization are described, along with programs, enabling legislation, and resources for program implementation. In addition, there are brief descriptions of revitalization programs in town and cities throughout each state. Also included are regional, local, and private programs that offer financial and technical assistance for downtown revitalization programs. (SS/HH)

896. *Historic Preservation Plans: An Annotated Bibliography*. Washington: Preservation Press, 1976.

The development of a comprehensive preservation plan is the key to incorporating preservation within the urban planning process. This bibliography lists ninety-one historic preservation plans and reports arranged in nine categories: districts, cities, regions, states, ethnic areas, historic areas affected by highways, plans for streets and roads, open space, and historic waterfront areas. These categories are subdivided geographically. Although issued a number of years ago, it contains citations for many plans that continue to serve as models for preservation planning today. (SS/HH)

897. How to Complete National Register Forms. Washington: National Register Division, Office of Archaeology and Historic Preservation, National Park Service, U.S. Department of the Interior, 1977.

This manual describes in detail how to complete a form for the nomination of a property to the National Register of Historic Places. The first portion of the handbook lists each question, with an explanation of the type and scope of information sought. In addition, many entries include suggestions of the type of information that should be included as well as short examples. There is also a guide to accompanying documentation. The appendices include directions for completing archaeological nominations, technical information for structures of engineering or industrial significance, and copies of relevant legislation. Also included in the appendices are samples of completed National Register forms for a variety of properties. (SS/HH)

898. Information: A Preservation Sourcebook. Washington: National Trust for Historic Preservation, 1980. Annual supplements.

Originally undertaken by the National Trust to provide concise information on basic and frequently used preservation techniques, this series of individual topics has recently been compiled in a binder that is available as a unit with annual supplements. The sourcebook is divided into six general areas: general preservation techniques, funding programs and techniques, building types and uses, legal considerations and techniques, preservation economics, and special subjects. Twenty-two titles are included in the sourcebook, five additional titles in the 1981 supplement. (SS/HH)

899. Jacobs, Jane. *The Death and Life of Great American Cities.* New York: Random House, 1961.

Jacobs provided the philosophical basis for much of today's urban preservation and urban planning in this study of the American city. By analyzing and evaluating how streets, parks, neighborhoods, and other elements of the city are used by people, she developed a theory of what makes a city healthy and safe that contradicted the thought behind much of the urban renewal of the 1950s and 1960s. (SS/HH)

900. Lynch, Kevin. *The Image of the City.* Cambridge, Mass.: M.I.T. Press, 1960.

Understanding the urban form and its components is essential to planning and preserving the urban environment. By looking at three American cities—Boston, Jersey City, and Los Angeles—Lynch developed a method that has come to be used by both city planners and urban preservationists to recognize and interpret the components of the urban landscape. A professor of Urban Planning at M.I.T., Lynch is also the author of *What Time Is This Place?* (1972), *Managing the Sense of a Region* (1980), and *A Theory of Good City Form* (1981). These works build upon the theories presented in this initial work. (SS/HH)

901. National Association of Housing and Redevelopment Officials. *Designing Rehab Programs: A Local Government Guidebook.* Washington: U.S. Department of Housing and Urban Development, Office of Policy Development and Research, 1979.

Community development programs are an increasingly important tool of the urban preservationist. This guidebook was prepared to assist local governments in designing housing rehabilitation programs appropriate to their situation. Using information collected from six programs, various elements in a rehabilitation are discussed. These include considerations when designing a program, providing financial assistance, and administering the program. Appendices provide a rehabilitation program model and case studies of programs in six cities. (SS/HH)

902. Old and New Architecture: Design Relationship. Washington: National Trust for Historic Preservation, 1980.

The appropriate design of new buildings within older neighborhoods and historic districts is a complex and often controversial issue. This publication, through a series of essays by designers, planners, and preservationists, discusses the history and theory of design relationships and regulating relationships between old and new architecture through the mechanism of design review. It includes four case studies that demonstrate a variety of approaches to relating old and new architecture. In addition, numerous photographs illustrate new designs in older areas. (SS/HH)

903. Plan and Program for the Preservation of the Vieux Carré: Historic District Demonstration Study. New Orleans, La.: Bureau of Governmental Research for the City of New Orleans, 1968.

This publication is a detailed and comprehensive preservation plan that summarizes a demonstration study of eight volumes prepared for the old French Quarter in New Orleans. The plan provides both an extensive description of all aspects of the Vieux Carré and a comprehensive plan for the preservation of the historic district. The study is illustrated with old photographs and engravings, tables, and maps to reinforce the text visually. The plan reflects an approach that considers not only the historic qualities of the Quarter but the social and economic aspects. Sections are included on such topics as housing, retail, industry, leadership attitudes within the district, and an analysis of the parameters of change within the district. (SS/HH)

904. Preservation and Rehabilitation of a Historic Commercial Area: A Demonstration of the Waterfront Historic District, New Bedford, Massachusetts. New Bedford, Mass.: New Bedford Redevelopment Authority in cooperation with the New Bedford City Planning Department and the Waterfront Historic Area League, 1972.

The preservation plan for the New Bedford waterfront was one of the first studies prepared for a historic commercial area and has continued to serve as a model. The study includes sections on how the study of New Bedford was carried out, a discussion of the objectives and features of the proposed plan, and recommendations for the revitalization of the waterfront area. The publication includes a question-and-answer technique to describe the findings and recommendations of the demonstration project; a discussion of how value ratings were assigned to each parcel of land; a system to evaluate the feasibility of the rehabilitation of individual structures; a description of design guidelines for street furniture; and a discussion of the benefit/cost analysis of rehabilitation in the waterfront districts. (SS/HH)

905. Preservation Case Studies. Washington: U.S. Department of Interior, Technical Preservation Services, 1979.

The preservation case studies series, prepared by the Technical Preservation Services, formerly part of the Heritage Conservation and Recreation Services and now a division of the National Park Service, offers in-depth information on a wide variety of types of rehabilitation projects. Studies in the series cover adaptive-use projects, conservation reports, landscape reports, and storefront rehabilitation. The reports are thirty to fifty pages long and contain detailed information on each project, including photographs, drawings, and tables. Not only do these reports contain useful technical information; they also provide sample formats for presenting similar reports. (SS/HH)

906. Survey of Architectural History in Cambridge. 5 vols. Cambridge, Mass.: Cambridge Historical Commission, 1965-1977.

This report on the survey work done in Cambridge, Massachusetts, has become a model of the comprehensive survey publication. Each volume deals with a separate section of the city, describing in detail the historical, architectural, topographical, and economic development of that area. The text is amply illustrated with current and historical photographs, maps, and plans. The last volume contains an index to the full survey. (SS/HH)

907. The Contribution of Historic Preservation to Urban Revitalization. Washington: Advisory Council on Historic Preservation, 1979.

Preservation is now recognized as a major factor in the process of urban revitalization. A series of conclusions about the effect preservation has had on urban revitalization are drawn, based on an analysis of four cities: Alexandria, Virginia; Galveston, Texas; Savannah, Georgia; and Seattle, Washington. The four detailed case studies that supplied the data are included. Both qualitative and quantitative data have been used to substantiate the claims that preservation has stimulated physical, social, and economic revitalization. (SS/HH)

908. Weinberg, Nathan. *Preservation in American Towns and Cities.* Boulder, Colo: Westview, 1979.

Historic preservation has changed radically in the 130 years since the movement began. The earlier emphasis on house museums has broadened to include historic districts and in recent years a concern for the overall fabric of the built environment. Following an overview of the history of the movement, Weinberg explores these changes, using specific case studies to illustrate contemporary practices and problems of historic districts and commissions, financing techniques, neighborhood preservation, small town preservation, and adaptive use of commercial and public buildings. (SS/HH)

909. Wright, Russell. *A Guide to Delineating Edges of Historic Districts*. Washington: Preservation Press, 1976.

The strength and effectiveness of a historic district is often determined by the establishment of appropriate and manageable borders. This guide describes briefly the factors to be considered in determining the boundaries of a successful district as well as the preliminary research of the area to be undertaken. The major portion of the *Guide* consists of twenty case studies that describe historic districts throughout the United States. For each district there is a discussion of its legal and historic framework, a detailed description of the boundaries with an explanation of why they were chosen, and the problems and successes encountered by each district as a result of the choice of boundaries. This *Guide* is helpful not only to those establishing a historic district but also for commissions wishing to revise the edges of their district. (SS/HH)

910. Ziegler, Arthur P., Jr. *Historic Preservation in Inner City Areas: A Manual of Practice*. Pittsburgh, Pa.: Allegheny, 1971.

The rehabilitation of the Mexican War Streets area of Pittsburgh, in the 1960s, was an early example of the successful revitalization of an inner-city neighborhood. This publication describes the process of organizing and carrying out a similar effort. The book discusses fundamental steps in organizing, use of revolving funds, creating community support, preserving a neighborhood without dislocating low-to-moderate income residents, attracting new residents, and involving residents in determining the future of their neighborhood. (SS/HH)

911. Ziegler, Arthur P., Jr., Leopold Adler, and Walter C. Kidney. *Revolving Funds for Historic Preservation: A Manual of Practice*. Pittsburgh, Pa.: Ober Park Associates, 1975.

The revolving fund is a basic preservation technique in which property is bought in order to save a structure or encourage revitalization of an area and then resold to sympathetic owners. This handbook describes how to administer a revolving fund, including a discussion of the purpose of revolving funds, basic real estate strategies, and a fund-raising campaign. Included in the handbook are a number of case studies of successful revolving fund activities, including programs in Charleston, Savannah, Pittsburgh, and Annapolis. (SS/HH)

V. Preservation Law

912. Andrews, Gregory E., ed. *Tax Incentives for Historic Preservation.* Washington: National Trust for Historic Preservation, 1980.

This compendium contains a discussion of federal, state, and local tax incentives for historic preservation. Contributors include Sally Oldham, Ward Jandl, Stanley Blend, Robert Stipe, Richard Almy, Russell Brenneman, and Peter Brink. Eight articles cover federal income tax incentives, including a dozen short case studies of projects around the country that have utilized the Tax Reform Act of 1976 incentives for the rehabilitation of certified historic structures. Another section explains those same incentives in a question-and-answer format. One article on the property tax incentives for owners of historic buildings in Oregon, Maryland, and the District of Columbia suggests ways to make property tax incentives more effective in stimulating rehabilitation of historic structures. The tax consequences of the donation of preservation easements are explained in two articles, and the tax treatment of nonprofit preservation organizations is also covered. The appendix contains the text of federal tax legislation and regulations as well as summaries of state legislation providing tax incentives to landmark owners. (RJR)

913. Connecticut Law Review Association. "Symposium: Perspectives on Historic Preservation." *Connecticut Law Review*, Vol. VIII (Winter 1975-1976).

This issue is totally devoted to historic preservation. Nine articles and comments cover the field but concentrate on historic preservation laws, ordinances, and techniques in the Northeast. Russell L. Brenneman summarizes the treatment of preservation restrictions such as conservation easements under state statutes in Massachusetts, Connecticut, New Hampshire, and Maryland. Another article by Professor Terry J. Tondro summarizes an effort to revitalize decayed historic neighborhoods in Hartford, compares it to efforts in Savannah, and explains the legal basis for various revitalization techniques. James Biddle, a past president of the National Trust for Historic Preservation, provides an overview of the historic development of preservation law and its widespread support across the United States. An article by Carol Galbreath summarizes the neighborhood-based preservation efforts in Norfolk, Pittsburgh, Seattle, San Francisco, Dallas, Detroit, St. Louis, Cincinnati, and Los Gatos, California. (RJR)

Costonis, John J. *Space Adrift: Saving Urban Landmarks Through the Chicago Plan.* See no. *893.*

914. Dennis, Stephen N. *Recommended Model Provisions for a Preservation Ordinance, with Annotations.* Washington: National Trust for Historic Preservation, 1980.

This analysis and commentary on typical provisions in local ordinances designed to protect historic buildings covers both designation of individual landmarks and historic districts. Everything from the creation and composition of a landmark commission, its statutory authority, and the operations of commissions to civil and criminal penalties for violation of landmark protection measures is discussed. Rather than give a true "model" ordinance, this publication provides examples of language from various ordinances around the country and then comments on the language of the particular section quoted. (RJR)

915. Gammage, Grady, Philip N. Jones, and Stephen L. Jones. *Historic Preservation in California: A Legal Handbook*. Stanford, Calif.: Stanford Environmental Law Society and the National Trust for Historic Preservation, 1975.

This book covers much the same ground as Morrison's *Historic Preservation Law*, (see no. *918*) but in a more readable format. It complements Morrison by covering the development of preservation law in the United States from 1965 to 1975. California law is featured, but it is placed in the context of the federal constitutional law and general principles of zoning and land-use law that underpin historic preservation law. The book summarizes a wide range of techniques for historic preservation, including acquisition by negotiation or eminent domain, acquisition or donation of less-than-fee interests, regulation through application of police power authority such as zoning and demolition controls, and tax incentives. The appendix has useful summaries of preservation ordinances in the twenty-seven California counties and cities as of 1975. (RJR)

916. Heritage Conservation and Recreation Services. *Federal Tax Provisions to Encourage Rehabilitation of Historic Buildings: An Assessment of Their Effect*. Washington: Government Printing Office, 1979.

This report summarizes the results of a survey to determine the impact and effect of the historic preservation incentives contained in the Tax Reform Act of 1976. The questionnaire form is included as well as a summary of the responses. Responses were solicited from owners of buildings taking advantage of the incentives; local landmark commissions; state and historic preservation offices; state and local planners; nonprofit preservation organizations; and professionals in tax law, real estate, lending, and architecture. Key issues and concerns are discussed. A statistical analysis of projects using the incentives is provided, and short summaries of eighteen certified projects are included. (RJR)

917. Kettler, Ellen, and Bernard Reams, eds. *Historic Preservation Law: An Annotated Bibliography*. Washington: National Trust for Historic Preservation, 1976.

About three hundred annotated entries are included in this comprehensive survey of the literature on historic preservation law. Reporting services as well as monographs and law review articles are covered. Chapter headings serve as an index to the materials and are divided as follows: "Background and Introduction"; "Historic Preservation Legislation"; "Historic Preservation Law Techniques"; "Case Studies in Historic Preservation Law"; "Urban Renewal";

"Archaeology"; and "Standing." The appendix includes a list of court cases and federal legislation affecting historic buildings. (RJR)

918. Morrison, Jacob H. *Historic Preservation Law*. Washington: National Trust for Historic Preservation, 1965.

This is the only comprehensive attempt to trace the origins and development of historic preservation law in the United States. It provides summaries of state enabling legislation for historic preservation and also of local ordinances. The case law, both state and federal, supporting historic preservation as a valid use of the police power is analyzed. It does not deal with historic preservation law since 1965. (RJR)

919. National Trust for Historic Preservation. *Preservation Law Reporter*. Washington: National Trust for Historic Preservation.

This is a bimonthly publication of the National Trust designed to keep attorneys and interested preservationists up to date on the latest developments in historic preservation law. The general format covers new developments and litigation, and it features articles on various aspects of historic preservation law. Every issue also has a bibliography and an index as well as permanent materials such as new state and local laws and regulations affecting historic preservation. A prepublication issue (Autumn 1981) describes the subject areas to be covered regularly as follows: real estate development, preservation tax incentives, local preservation ordinances, preservation covenants and easements, state preservation laws, federal regulations, estate and tax planning, zoning and land-use law, nonprofit organizations, and archaeological law. (RJR)

920. Practising Law Institute. *Historic Preservation Law*. New York City: Practising Law Institute, 1979.

This is a course handbook published by a continuing legal education organization. The handbook contains detailed outlines of a course presented in New York, Chicago, and San Francisco. The complete texts of many historic preservation ordinances are provided, including those of New York, District of Columbia, Loudoun County (Virginia), Nantucket, Crested Butte, and Galveston. The text of the landmark United States Supreme Court decision in *Penn Central Transportation Co.* v. *City of New York*, 438 U.S. 104, 98 S. Ct. 2646 (1978) is included, and articles by Frank B. Gilbert and Norman Marcus discuss the significance of the decision. Professor John Costonis provides a summary of the Chicago plan for historic preservation through transfer of development rights and analyzes the New York court of appeals decision in the *Penn Central* case. The volume contains the text of many federal laws and regulations affecting historic preservation and discusses the most recent cases involving federal protection of structures and areas listed in the National Register of Historic Places. (RJR)

921. Roddewig, Richard J., and Jared Shaeles. "Appraising the Best Tax Shelter in History." *Appraisal Journal*, Vol. L (January 1982), pp. 25-43.

This article summarizes the tax court decision delineating a method for the appraisal of conservation easements. Based upon that court decision, the authors suggest an appropriate method for determining what, if any, effect on value results from the donation of a conservation easement on a historic building. They critique the method for the evaluation of preservation restrictions set forth in *Space Adrift* (see no. *893*) by John Costonis and suggest that it is based on misleading appraisal techniques. The authors then set forth the tax-shelter benefits from the donation of conservation easements and provide examples of how such easements might be valued on three landmark buildings in Chicago's Loop. (RJR)

922. Section of Urban, State and Local Government Law. "Special Symposium: Preserving, Conserving, and Reusing Historic Properties." *Urban Lawyer*, Vol. XII (Winter 1980).

This entire issue is devoted to historic preservation law. An article by Sally G. Oldham, Chief, Tax Reform Act Unit of the National Park Service, summarizes the wide effect of the 1976 legislation providing federal income tax incentives for rehabilitation of historic buildings. Peter Brink, executive director of the Galveston Historical Foundation, sets out the wide array of legal tools (a revolving fund, matching federal grants, federal tax incentives, pooled bank financing, deed restrictions) used to prompt the rehabilitation of more than twenty buildings on The Strand in Galveston, Texas. Another article summarizes state and local legislation providing property tax incentives to owners of landmark structures, and yet another article descibes four cities' attempts to implement facade renovation ordinances and six cities' use of commercial-area management to encourage retail revival for historic shopping streets. Stephen N. Dennis of the National Trust for Historic Preservation provides a useful summary of historic preservation cases since the turn of the century. (RJR)

923. Weinberg, Steve. "Lobbying Congress—The Inside Story." *Historic Preservation*, Vol. XXXIV (January-February 1982), pp. 16-26.

This concise explanation of the two years of lobbying that led to the preservation incentives included in the Economic Recovery Tax Act of 1981 helps in understanding the purpose and intent of the new law. The article describes the roles of Preservation Action, the National Trust for Historic Preservation, local preservation organizations, and the Heritage Conservation and Recreation Service. The importance of the conversion of Congressman Dan Rostenkowski to the preservation cause is highlighted. As chairman of the House Ways and Means Committee, his support for historic preservation was crucial in enactment of a new 28 percent credit for certified rehabilitation of historic structures. (RJR)

VI. Underwater Archaeology

924. Arnold, J. Barto, III, ed. *Beneath the Waters of Time: The Proceedings of the Ninth Conference on Underwater Archaeology.* Austin: Texas Antiquities Committee, 1978.

Cockrell, Wilburn A., ed. *In the Realms of Gold: The Proceedings of the Tenth Conference on Underwater Archaeology.* San Marino, Calif.: Fathom Eight, 1981.

Watts, Gordon P., Jr., ed. *Underwater Archaeology: The Challenge Before Us: The Proceedings of the Twelfth Conference on Underwater Archaeology.* San Marino, Calif.: Fathom Eight, 1981.

Current information regarding underwater archaeology in the United States is contained in this series of publications compiled from the proceedings of the Conference on Underwater Archaeology. Each of the volumes contains contributions that describe current research projects. Conservation, ship reconstruction, and state-of-the-art methods, techniques, and equipment are also treated. Cultural resource management, which receives superficial attention in most treatments of underwater archaeology, is addressed by those currently involved in management activities. (GPW)

925. Arnold, J. Barto, III, and Robert Weddle. *The Nautical Archaeology of Padre Island.* New York, San Francisco, and London: Academic, 1978.

This work offers both an interpretation of the events that surrounded the loss of three ships from the Spanish fleet blown ashore off Padre Island, Texas, in 1554 and an examination of archaeological investigations associated with the remains of the wreck. In addition to providing insight into the interaction of history and underwater archaeology, the volume contains an illustrated catalog of materials recovered from the wreck sites, extensive bibliography of associated sources, and appendices associated with cargo registers, artifact inventories and measurements, vessel architecture, and conservation procedures. (GPW)

926. Bass, George F. *Archaeology under Water.* New York and Washington: Praeger, 1966.

This book was written to provide the reader with an understanding of the nature of underwater archaeology and how it has developed. While much of the text refers to research and investigation of Mediterranean sites, the methods, techniques, and equipment treated in the work have universal applications. Following an introductory discussion of the nature of underwater archaeology, the author systematically examines the complexities of conducting work in the subsurface environment. Search and survey, recovery, and salvage operations are illustrated with examples. Site mapping and documentation are given consideration, and tools and equipment are treated in detail. After drawing together the subject matter of the volume in a study of the first "complete excavation" at Cape Geledonya, Turkey, Bass concludes with a look into the future. (GPW)

927. Bass, George F., ed. *A History of Seafaring.* New York: Walker, 1972.

Not the traditional treatment of seafaring based on historical sources, *A History of Seafaring* examines that subject in light of the vessels that have shaped the history of Western civilization. Although the established context of maritime history is clearly in evidence, the threads of transition are developed in light of data generated by underwater archaeological research. In the twelve chapters that trace seafaring from its earliest documented origins in the eastern Mediterranean to the development of steam navigation, contributing authors furnish the reader with insight derived from their extensive research experience. From antiquity, ship development is traced through Greece and Rome and into the vessels of Byzantium and the Italian maritime republics. Northern traditions from Scandinavia and northwest Europe have been drawn together with those of the Mediterranean to provide the background for post medieval developments that shifted the emphasis of seafaring history from the coast of western Europe to the Iberian Peninsula, the British Isles, and subsequently into and across the Atlantic. (GPW)

928. Blackman, David J., ed. *Marine Archaeology: Proceedings of the Twenty-third Symposium of the Colston Research Society.* London: Butterworth, 1973.

While primarily oriented toward research in Mediterranean and British waters, presentations in the *Proceedings of the Twenty-third Symposium of the Colston Research Society* have reference beyond their immediate geographical environment. Considerable attention is devoted to sea-level and coastline studies, and the examination of harbor facilities is treated in eight individual studies. Three contributions address methods, techniques, and problems encountered in search and survey operations. Only one presentation addresses problems of conservation, but ten are devoted to investigations of diverse aspects of "shipping" in Mediterranean and British waters. The volume closes with an examination of the archaeology of ships that explores frequently overlooked aspects of conservation and preservation. (GPW)

929. Burgess, Robert F. *Man: 12,000 Years under the Sea.* New York: Dodd, Mead, 1980.

This work offers an introduction to underwater archaeology that blends the excitement and romance that often characterize underwater work with the science that rarely escapes technical publications. It examines the origins of archaeological interest in underwater sites identified and first worked by explorers and salvors and traces the development of scientific research spawned by this interest. Examination of research activities in the Mediterranean, Europe, and the United States includes both prehistoric and historic sites spanning more than twelve thousand years. An examination of the present state of the art concludes the volume with an indication of future development. (GPW)

930. Hamilton, Donny Leon. *Conservation of Metal Objects from Underwater: A Study in Methods.* Austin: Texas Antiquities Committee, 1976.

Conservation is an indispensable element of underwater archaeology. Cultural material from the marine environment requires sophisticated and complex procedures to prevent deterioration when excavation and recovery have disturbed its stable environmental equilibrium. Using the conservation of material recovered from a Spanish ship wrecked off Padre Island on the Texas coast in 1554 to illustrate the text, the author systematically examines those steps in the conservation that take both ferrous and nonferrous material from the seabed to the museum. The mechanics of corrosion, preliminary documentation, evaluation, storage, and detailed treatments in the conservation of ferrous and nonferrous artifacts are accorded major consideration, although the role and tenets of conservation and its application as an archaeological technique are addressed in both int. oduction and summary. (GPW)

931. Lenihan, Daniel J., Toni Carrel, Stephen Fosberg, Sondra Rayl, John Ware, and Lawrence Murphy. *The Final Report of the National Reservoir Inundation Study*. 2 vols. Santa Fe, N. Mex.: U.S. Department of the Interior, 1981.

The impact of inundation on archaeological resources has been the subject of considerable attention and speculation. In 1976 the National Park Service in cooperation with the United States Bureau of Reclamation, United States Soil Conservation Service, and the United States Army Corps of Engineers initiated a comprehensive study designed to generate scientific data that would provide a reliable data base for formulating management decisions. Volume I of the study identifies the project research design and addresses reservoir processes, the impact of inundation, and the problem of mitigation. Volume II contains a series of related technical reports that present the various field and laboratory studies, operational guidelines, and an annotated bibliography. While the study is oriented toward reservoir inundation, information in the report has considerably broader application in terms of both research and management of submerged cultural resources. (GPW)

932. McGrath, Tom, and Doug Ashley. *Historic Structure Report: USS Cairo, Vicksburg National Military Park, Vicksburg, Mississippi*. Denver, Colo.: Denver Service Center, National Park Service, U.S. Department of the Interior, March 1981.

While recovery and conservation of the remains of the U.S.S. *Cairo* perhaps best serve to illustrate the pitfalls that can turn the well-preserved remains of a historic ship into an embarrassing liability, this report illustrates how surviving vessel structure and associated artifacts are being prepared for an impressive public exhibition by the National Park Service. Although not dealing specifically with underwater archaeology, the text addresses many of the complex considerations facing those working with submerged cultural resources. The study provides excellent insight into conservation problems and their relationship to restoration and display criteria. A discussion of eight restoration options provides a diverse spectrum of possibilities to be considered when recovery is the end result of excavation and provides an extremely valuable reference source. In light of the catastrophic nature of the *Cairo*'s recovery and treatment, this volume indicates that the "Hardluck Ironclad" may well become an example of innovative restoration and interpretation. (GPW)

933. Marx, Robert F. *The Underwater Dig: An Introduction to Underwater Archaeology.* New York: Henry Z. Walck, 1975.

Written to serve as an introduction to underwater archaeology, *The Underwater Dig* treats the spectrum of associated activities that begins with historical research and terminates in preservation and publication. Marx explores the origins of underwater archaeology and its definition. Methods and techniques of research, site location, investigation, identification, and dating are developed in a manner suitable for both amateur and student. The conclusion examines the future of underwater archaeology and the direction that development of the discipline is taking. A selected bibliography organized by topic provides reference for those interested in additional information on related subject matter. (GPW)

934. Morrison, Ian A., ed. *International Journal of Nautical Archaeology and Underwater Exploration.*

The most up-to-date source of international information on underwater archaeology, the *International Journal of Nautical Archaeology (IJNA)* offers articles on current research activities, conservation, legislation, management, and other facets of the broad spectrum of associated activities. In addition to contributions from eminent authorities, the *INJA* contains abbreviated sections for notes and news and reviews of current volumes related to underwater archaeology. (GPW)

935. Muckelroy, Keith. *Maritime Archaeology.* Cambridge: Cambridge University Press, 1978.

Maritime Archaeology represents one of the more recent and comprehensive efforts to provide insight into the scope and potential of the discipline. The author attempts to identify those problems that represent valid considerations, examines the extent to which research has addressed such problems, and explores potentially productive avenues for future investigation. The first of two sections in the volume provides a definition of maritime archaeology as reflected primarily in Mediterranean and European research activities. In developing this description, the first section is organized to introduce and define the subject, examine the problems and advantages to be anticipated in conducting research on underwater sites, describe the broad spectrum of current research, and explore the unrealized potential of future research. The second section defines theoretical concepts that apply to maritime archaeology. In addition to considering the processes and elements that combine to influence the archaeological record preserved at a site, Muckelroy examines the ship and its various functions and the archaeological site in a broader social, cultural, and historical context. Theory and practice are interfaced in drawing the work to a close. (GPW)

936. Peterson, Mendel. *History under the Sea: A Handbook for Underwater Exploration*. Washington: Smithsonian Institution, 1965.

Although published at a time when the investigation of submerged cultural resources was only beginning to attract the interest and attention of archaeologists and historians, *History under the Sea* contains information useful to those engaged in both research and management. An introductory reference, the volume provides treatments of methods and techniques employed in the conduct of underwater archaeological investigations. Following a brief analysis of the distribution of underwater sites in the Caribbean, Gulf of Mexico, and along the Atlantic coast of North America during the period of exploration and colonization, the author examines several early research expeditions associated with those previously identified areas. While much attention is directed toward the mechanics of locating, surveying, and excavating underwater sites, considerable emphasis is also placed on a description of conservation materials recovered from the marine environment. The work is drawn to conclusion with a chapter referencing diagnostic materials, a selected bibliography that identifies additional sources, and an appendix of maritime museums and archival repositories. (GPW)

937. *Protection of the Underwater Heritage*. UNESCO, Technical Handbooks for Museums and Monuments #4. Paris: UNESCO, 1981.

Four individually authored sections separate *Protection of the Underwater Heritage* into examinations of underwater archaeology, conservation, museology, and legislation. "Archaeology in an Underwater Environment," prepared by Colin Martin, covers that spectrum of activities involved in defining planning, organizing, conducting, documenting, and reporting on the investigation of underwater sites. Colin Pearson's "Conservation of the Underwater Heritage" presents both on-site and laboratory conservation methods, techniques, and procedures in an examination of activities associated with underwater archaeological research. "Museology Problems Associated with the Underwater Heritage," authored by Richard F. Harrison, examines the problems associated with museum curation of collections assembled as a result of underwater archaeological investigations. In the final section, "Law and the Underwater Heritage," Lyndel V. Pratt and Patrick J. O'Keefe examine current legislation enacted to protect or that is relevant to the protection of underwater archaeological sites, interpretation of those laws, and suggestions for the drafting of protective legislation. Each section includes a selected bibliography and/or appendices containing associated materials. (GPW)

938-939. *Underwater Archaeology: A Nascent Discipline*. Paris: UNESCO, 1972.

Twenty-six contributions were selected to provide those interested in the discipline with a concept of developments that shaped the first decade of investigating underwater archaeological sites. Articles by both eminent archaeologists and explorers whose activities shaped this early development are organized into two sections. The first covers activities such as the discovery, investigation, and preservation of major shipwreck and inundated archaeological sites. The second section examines problems that face archaeologists working on underwater sites and methods, techniques, and equipment developed to facilitate the conduct of that research. Contributions treat the spectrum of activities involved in site location, documentation, excavation, recovery, and conservation. Acoustic and magnetic remote sensing, a wide variety of photographic applications, and conservation techniques are covered in detail. The volume concludes with an appendix containing details of how underwater archaeology is regulated in France. (GPW)

VII. Industrial Archaeology

940. Comp, T. Allan. "The Best Arena: Industrial History at the Local Level." *History News*, Vol. XXXVII (May 1982), pp. 8-11.
Mullin, Marsha, and Geoffrey Huys. "Industrial History on Exhibit." *History News*, Vol. XXXVII (May 1982), pp. 12-16.
Craig, Tracey Linton. "Delicate Balance." *History News*, Vol. XXXVII (May 1982), pp. 17-21.

America's industrial heritage is the theme of the May 1982 issue of *History News*. Three articles examine the industrial past from the perspective of local history. T. Allan Comp offers a definition of industrial history and stresses the importance of local or regional studies. Mullin and Huys review the research sources—documentary, oral, and material—for industrial history and how they may be used to create an exhibit. Linton discusses the role of the industrial museum as the interpreter of technology's effect on our lives. (TJK)

941. Hudson, Kenneth. *World Industrial Archaeology*. London: Cambridge University Press, 1979.

Industrial archaeology is the study and preservation of the relics of past industry. Hudson marks out ambitious goals for industrial archaeology. While the physical remains of industry are central to the work of the industrial archaeologist, the goal must always be to place those remains in the context of social, economic, and political history. Hudson demonstrates how this can be done through an extensive review of current work throughout the world. Extractive industries, food, construction, metal processing, transportation, textiles and clothing, power, and chemical industries are all discussed in detail. (TJK)

942. *IA: The Journal of the Society for Industrial Archaeology*. Washington: Society for Industrial Archaeology.

IA is the annual journal of the North American chapter of the international Committee for the Conservation of the Industrial Heritage. The journal publishes current research in the field. Articles represent the work of engineers, architects, and hobbyists as well as professional historians. (TJK)

943. Kemp, Emory L., and Theodore Anton Sande, eds. *Historic Preservation of Engineering Works*. New York: American Society of Civil Engineers, 1981.

The volume is a collection of papers given at an Engineering Foundation Conference in 1978. A total of nineteen papers are presented on the theme of industrial archaeology. The four principal subjects covered are: (1) technology and historical interpretation; (2) how to record endangered industrial structures; (3) case studies of the preservation of engineering works; (4) legal and financial elements of industrial preservation. (TJK)

944. Sande, Theodore Anton. *Industrial Archaeology: A New Look at the American Heritage*. West Hanover, Mass.: Penguin, 1976.

This is a visually impressive volume that documents the range and richness of America's industrial past. The brief text with extensive photographs provides an introduction for students. (TJK)

VIII. Historical Resources and Education

945. Alderson, William T., and Shirley Payne Low. *Interpretation of Historic Sites*. Nashville: American Association for State and Local History, 1976.

This guidebook describes the way to develop effective interpretive programs at historic sites. The authors consider many aspects of developing and conducting interpretive programs—from defining objectives and presenting the site to selecting, training, and costuming interpreters. Two appendices offer concrete, step-by-step examples of how to organize a model interpretation program at a historic site. (PA)

946. Benedict, Paul L. *Historic Site Interpretation: The Student Field Trip*. Technical Leaflet Number 19. Nashville: American Association for State and Local History, March 1971.

This technical leaflet suggests guidelines for museum or historic site educators to consider when planning and preparing field trips for students. The author discusses methods of defining a field trip's educational objectives, techniques to help prepare students for a field trip, steps to take to encourage student involvement in the trip, and possible follow-up programs. Several case studies offer useful ideas on how to accomplish field trip objectives successfully. (PA)

947. Collins, Zipporah W., ed. *Museums, Adults, and the Humanities: A Guide for Educational Programming*. Washington: American Association of Museums, 1981.

As part of the growing interest in adult education, the museum community over the past decade has been turning its attention to the specific educational needs and interests of adult audiences. This collection of essays by noted humanists, educators, and museum professionals offers a view of museums as unique resources for lifelong learning, especially when programming is designed to explore the basic human concerns that museum collections reflect. Based on a series of seminars sponsored by the American Association of Museums, this volume combines theory and practical advice. Essays are organized into sections that discuss humanities themes and museum education, adults as learners, and the most effective ways to develop and fund adult humanities programs. Eight case studies offer detailed descriptions of successful programs for museum audiences as diverse as teachers' groups, volunteers, and senior citizens. (CK)

948. Cook, Peter W. "The Craft of Demonstrations." *Museum News*, Vol. LIII (November 1974), p. 10.
Ronsheim, Robert D. "Is the Past Dead?" *Museum News*, Vol. LIII (November 1974), p. 16.
Sidford, Holly. "Stepping into History." *Museum News,* Vol. LIII (November 1974), p. 28.

The November 1974 cover of *Museum News* exclaims that "History Lives!" Three articles examine that premise, raising questions that need to be asked when planning or evaluating the craft demonstrations, role playing, and visitor participation so popular today in museum interpretation programs. Cook considers such practical matters as use of museum objects, visitor traffic patterns, acoustics, and storage. Ronsheim suggests that selective knowledge imparted to visitors along with appeals to touch, smell, and taste can not only be misleading but can actually serve to discourage inquiry about larger historical issues. Sidford points out that successful visitor participation must be preceded by an orientation to the nature and goals of the experience being offered. All three authors stress the role of interpreters who conduct living-history programs. To show a skill or play a part is not enough. If visitors are to gain a better understanding of the past, interpreters must encourage them to explore the broader historical spectrum. (NL)

949. Elder, Betty Doak. "Drama for Interpretation." *History News,* (June 1981), pp. 8-12.
Floyd, Candace. "Drama for Training." *History News*, (June 1981), pp. 17-20.
Hubner, Mary. "Drama Based on Oral Tradition." *History News,* (June 1981), pp. 12-17.

This issue of *History News* explores how theater techniques aid in the interpretation of local history. The first article discusses how theater has been used as a vehicle for interpretation in three diverse museums. At the Hermann-Grima House in New Orleans, theater professionals developed a play that takes visitors through a day in the life of a nineteenth-century household. Tryon Palace in North Carolina offers interpretive performances produced by a theater repertory company, while street theater is featured at Old Cowton Museum in Wichita, Kansas. Descriptions of all these programs provide examples of theater articulating history. Hubner's article discusses theater based on oral tradition and describes several programs, including the "Voices of Baltimore" project which presents ethnic histories of that city's neighborhoods. Floyd's article examines theatrical approaches designed to assist museum personnel in their interpretive work. (JJ)

950. Lehman, Susan Nichols, and Kathryn Igoe, eds. *Museum School Partnerships: Plans and Programs.* Washington: Center for Museum Education, George Washington University, 1981.

The focus of this book is on museums and educational institutions working together to create programs for students from primary grades to the college level. Section headings such as "Early Planning," "Reaching Teachers," and "Seeking Financial Support" underline the practical approach in the book's more than fifty program descriptions. Contributors of these descriptions represent a variety of museum disciplines, but their experiences provide a wealth of ideas that rises above the specific subject matter of the programs. The reader can find additional information through an annotated bibliography. (NL)

951. Newson, Barbara Y., and Adele Z. Silver, eds. *The Art Museum as Educator.* Berkeley: University of California Press, 1978.

This resource book of 830 pages from the Council on Museums and Education in the Visual Arts describes the state of visual arts education in the 1970s as it is practiced in art museums and, to the degree that art museums are affected, as it is practiced in schools and community arts organizations. It gives schools and museum educators a sense of the ideas behind these programs and pitfalls encountered as the program authors tried to carry out each project. Seventy-one institutions and 105 programs were surveyed and reported on by the project's participants. The programs are diverse in concept, content, staffing, and technique. Information about each program includes title, audience, objective, funding, staff, location, time, and other information and documentation available from the institution. Although the projects described are in art museums, the thought and planning behind them are of interest to educators of all kinds. (JW)

952. Rath, Frederick L., Jr., and Merrilyn Rogers O'Connell, eds. *Interpretation.* Vol. III: *A Bibliography on Historical Organization Practices.* Nashville: American Association for State and Local History, 1978.

This bibliography, part of a comprehensive series on museum work, directs its attention to the educational activities of museums and historical agencies. Listings cover such topics as interpretation, program planning and evaluation, and collaborative efforts between museums and schools. A short section suggests readings on exhibit planning and design. References include the most significant books, pamphlets, and articles published through 1976. A separate listing of nineteen thoroughly annotated sources is recommended as a basic reference shelf. (CK)

953. Reque, Barbara. "From Object to Idea." *Museum News*, Vol. V (January-February 1978), pp. 45-47.

"Reading Museum Exhibits," a study in teacher education conducted at the Field Museum of Natural History, was designed to help teachers plan and execute their own field trips. This article, which describes the study, presents ways to develop the relationship between museums and schools and to help students improve their reading skills. It also notes basic principles on museum interpretation and education materials. (CK)

954. Schroeder, Fred. *Designing Your Exhibits: Seven Ways to Look at an Artifact.* Technical Leaflet 91. Nashville: Association for State and Local History, November 1976.

Schroeder outlines an approach for exhibit design and educational programming aimed at enhancing the museum patron's ability to "read" an artifact. He emphasizes that artifacts exist within an environment and offers seven avenues of inquiry that encourage visitors to consider how an artifact was used, its former environment, its development through time, cross-cultural comparison, influences in design and decoration, and finally its functional meaning and value. The author encourages the individual to seek something concrete and familiar when approaching unfamiliar museum objects, a means of promoting a healthy approach to material culture and history. (JJ)

955. Tilden, Freeman. *Interpreting Our Heritage.* Rev. ed. Chapel Hill: University of North Carolina Press, 1967.

In this work, first published in 1957 and revised ten years later, the author develops a philosophy of historic site interpretation that is based on his many years of experience with the National Park Service. Tilden stresses the need to make historic objects, events, and sites personally meaningful to visitors. He fills his text with examples of ways to do just that for visitors of every age, interest, and background. (CK)

956. Vanderway, Richard. *Planning Museum Tours for School Groups.* Technical Leaflet Number 93. Nashville: American Association for State and Local History, March 1977.

The author provides a practical discussion on planning and conducting museum tours for school groups, covering such issues as the development of subject matter pertinent to school audiences, the need for adequate research on tour subjects, and the effective use of objects and exhibits during a tour. Also included are examples of techniques to help students learn through active participation in the tour. (PA)

IX. Historical Resources and Historical Research

957. Deetz, James. *In Small Things Forgotten*. New York: Anchor/Doubleday, 1977.

Deetz presents the archaeology of early American life. The "small things forgotten" are the material items of everyday life—ceramics, furniture, houses, even cuts of meat and garbage pits. To Deetz, one of the deans of historical archaeology, these artifacts of the past are eloquent sources that reveal the lifeways of the first three generations of Americans. He integrates his material culture evidence with documentary sources to offer a new interpretation of culture change in colonial America. The book is an example of the potentialities of archaeological perspectives on American history. (TJK)

Hareven, Tamara K., and Randolph Langenbach. *Amoskeag: Life and Work in an American Factory City*. See no. *1461*.

When the giant New England textile concern, the Amoskeag Manufacturing Company, was liquidated in 1936, it left behind a hundred years of American industrial history. Hareven and Langenbach took up the task of recording the impressive physical presence of Amoskeag. Photographic essays document the massive cotton mills and iron foundries that stretch for miles along the Merrimack River. The text is dominated by excerpts from oral history tapes made with former Amoskeag employees. Industrial archaeology and oral history are blended into a comprehensive chronicle of workers, industrialists, and machines. (TJK)

958. Kvyig, David E., and Myron A. Marty. *Nearby History: Exploring the Past around You*. Nashville: American Assocation for State and Local History, 1982.

Nearby history is the study of the broad range of persons, places, and things that make up the environment of the individual. Through this approach, the authors incorporate what is traditionally called local history, family history, and material culture studies. The authors outline procedures for locating and integrating written resources, artifacts, oral informants, photographs, and historic landscapes. The book serves as a guide for the avocational historian and an example of a holistic approach to the study of historical resources for the cultural resource specialist. (TJK)

959. McDaniel, George W. *Hearth and Home: Preserving a People's Culture*. Philadelphia: Temple University Press, 1982.

This book examines tenant farming in southern Maryland. McDaniel advocates an integrative approach in historical resource management, which incorporates preserving the material remains of the past, utilizing oral history to understand that resource and the role of that information in site interpretation and further study. This is an example of how to blend material culture studies with social history. (TJK)

960. Quimby, Ian M., ed. *Material Culture and the Study of American Life.* New York: Norton, 1978.

The volume is composed of eleven papers originally presented at a 1975 conference at the Winterthur Museum. The authors discuss problems of collecting, analyzing, and presenting American material culture. The authors represent the disciplines of archaeology, architecture, history, and museology. The original purpose of the authors was to address the question "How has our study of artifacts altered our perception of American history?" The nascent state of material culture studies forced them to offer only preliminary observations and suggestions for future research. The book serves as an introduction to the study of historical resources. (TJK)

961. Schlereth, Thomas J., ed. *Material Culture Studies in America.* Nashville: American Association for State and Local History, 1982.

This anthology is composed of twenty-five broad-ranging essays that demonstrate the utility of three-dimensional objects to the study of the American past. The work of major figures in the study of material culture, such as Henry Glassie, James Deetz, and Wilcomb Washburn, is presented. Unconventional approaches are included, such as the archaeological study of modern garbage as well as more traditional discussions of folk art and vernacular architecture. Schlereth himself contributes a bibliographic essay on material culture studies in America. The volume is designed as a reader for educational programs that embrace the study of artifacts. (TJK)

CHAPTER 8

LIBRARY SCIENCE

Richard Hume Werking
and Boyd Keith Swigger, editors

The amount of literature about libraries is vast, which is hardly surprising for a learned occupation several millenia old. Hence any attempt to include in a chapter such as this even a majority of the important works is bound to be futile. What we have sought to do instead is to *introduce* historians to the literature of librarianship, especially the recent literature.

Two principles guided selection of entries for this bibliography. First, we sought works that represent librarians' views of their profession, of the missions of libraries in terms of collecting materials and providing services, of the place of libraries within institutions they serve and society at large, and of the ways that libraries ought to function. We have tried to select works supporting major positions taken on important issues rather than those that agree with the editors' ideas.

Second, we have included pieces that explain the rationale and procedures of library administration; technical processes such as cataloging, classification, and acquisitions; and public services such as reference and circulation. Understanding how libraries work as information systems is very helpful for understanding them as public institutions and for using them effectively as research resources.

We begin with a section that includes textbooks commonly used in library schools, texts that provide introductions to libraries as functional systems and that also discuss the principles and professional ideology of librarianship. Entries in the categories that follow are also selected to serve this same dual purpose. The headings under which the articles are arranged are obviously not watertight; there is unavoidable overlapping.

Included among the citations in sections I and XXV are introductory reference works, major indexes, and some of the most important journals, all of which should be especially useful for readers who wish to go beyond what they encounter here.

A number of these abstracts have been reprinted or adapted from abstracts in two publications: *The Library Quarterly* (with the permission of the University of Chicago Press) and *College and Research Libraries* (with the permission of the American Library Association). The cooperation of these organizations and journals is gratefully acknowledged.

I. General Works

962. Ash, Lee, comp. *Subject Collections, A Guide to Special Book Collections and Subject Emphases as Reported by University, College, Public, and Special Libraries and Museums in the United States and Canada.* 5th ed. New York: Bowker, 1978.

The subtitle of the work describes its content. Data are collected from questionnaires sent to libraries listed in the *American Library Directory*. The arrangement is alphabetical by subject heading, following the headings list of Library of Congress Subject Headings. Entries contain names of libraries holding materials on a subject, size of collection of relevant materials, and notes describing collections in terms of emphasis, dates of coverage, available finding aids, and access. Materials of all types, including books, are reported. (BKS)

963. Bonk, Wallace John, and Rose Mary Magrill. *Building Library Collections.* 5th ed. Metuchen, N.J.: Scarecrow, 1979.

The objective of this text is to introduce "common principles, accepted procedures, unresolved questions, and current selection and acquisition tools." Through a combined presentation of principles and practice, the authors state the ideology underlying the profession's collection building and also describe its implementation in various types of libraries. A useful appendix contains policy statements of the American Library Association related to intellectual freedom. (BKS)

964. Busha, Charles H., and Stephen P. Harter. *Research Methods in Librarianship.* New York: Academic 1980.

The authors describe a set of research techniques used in librarianship, detailing the rationale of each and illustrating with examples from published studies in librarianship. Major topics included are experimentation, survey research, historical research, and operations research. There are six chapters introducing descriptive and inferential statistics, as well as chapters on computer aids to research, writing research proposals, and writing reports. (BKS)

965. Gates, Jean Key. *Introduction to Librarianship.* 2d ed. New York: McGraw-Hill, 1976.

The stated purposes of this text are "to set forth some of the fundamental elements of librarianship," including historical background; to describe "library objectives, services, and needs"; and to introduce librarianship as a profession and a career. Written for students entering the field, this textbook gives a sense of the attitudes and issues that students confront in preparation for the profession. There are major sections on library history, librarianship as a profession, and kinds of libraries and library services. (BKS)

966. Katz, William Armstrong. *Introduction to Reference Work,* Vol. I: *Basic Information Sources;* Vol. II: *Reference Services and Reference Processes.* 2d ed. New York: McGraw-Hill, 1974.

Katz's two volumes are reference textbooks. Volume I describes the nature and uses of basic reference sources and includes detailed descriptions of specific works. Volume II is concerned with the actual nature of reference work: types of reference services provided by libraries and instruction in ways to implement reference services. (BKS)

967. Kent, Allen, and Harold Lancour, eds. *Encyclopedia of Library and Information Science.* 33 vols. New York: M. Dekker, 1968-1982.

This set has entries ranging from "Abbreviations" to "Zoological Research." Like many specialized encyclopedias, it is an excellent place to begin gathering information about a topic because it provides an overview and, frequently, references to other sources. (RHW)

968. Lancaster, Frederick Wilfred. "Whither Libraries? or, Wither Libraries?" *College and Research Libraries,* Vol. XXXIX (September 1978), pp. 345-347.

The claim is made that society is evolving from one whose formal communication patterns have, for centuries, been based primarily on print on paper to one in which communication channels will be largely paperless (electronic). Some reasons why this transition seems inevitable are discussed. A scenario for a paperless communication system is presented, and some technological achievements that lend credibility to this scenario are described. The profession is urged to give immediate and serious consideration to the role of the library in an electronic society. (RHW)

969. "Library." In *The Encyclopedia Americana,* Vol. XVII (1978 ed.), pp. 307-394.

Apparently written in the early 1970s, the short articles comprising this section provide an introduction to the variety of librarianship. The articles are authored by leaders in the profession, and they conclude with brief bibliographies. (RHW)

Sheehy, Eugene Paul. *Guide to Reference Books.* See no. *139.*

Sheehy's guide is a handbook for reference librarians, a massive compilation annotating reference works of all types. Arrangement is by subject, with major headings for general reference works, the humanities, social sciences, history and area studies, and pure and applied sciences. Within each major category, works are arranged by discipline. A two-hundred-page author/title/subject index makes the volume easy to use. The chapter on "Librarianship and Library Resources" provides a more exhaustive and detailed set of annotations than could possibly be provided here. (BKS)

970. Shera, Jesse H. *The Foundations of Education for Librarianship*. New York: Wiley-Becker and Hayes, 1972.

Shera was one of the most respected and prolific commentators on libraries and librarianship. This book is a comprehensive study of the history and requirements for professional education. Because Shera insists on seeing librarianship in its cultural context, the work is also a commentary on the nature of communication, the history of libraries, the role of libraries in societies generally and in the dissemination of information, and the place of librarianship among the professions. Education for librarianship is compared to education for other professions. (BKS)

971. Wynar, Bohdan S. *Introduction to Cataloging and Classification*. 6th ed. Littleton, Colo: Libraries Unlimited, 1980.

Wynar's work is a textbook in introductory cataloging and classification courses. It provides an overview of classification, descriptions of the purposes and applications of cataloging rules for all types of materials, explanations of the major classification systems used for subject analysis, descriptions of library cooperative cataloging networks, and discussions of the routine work of maintaining catalogs. (BKS)

II. Bibliographic Control

972. Comaromi, John P. "Knowledge Organization Is Knowledge Kept: The Dewey Decimal Classification, 1873-1976." *Quarterly Journal of the Library of Congress*, Vol. XXXIII (October 1976), pp. 311-331.

Melville Dewey's decimal notation scheme, copyrighted in 1876, provides a means of numbering books so that the location notation on the work and in the catalog does not have to be changed as the collection grows. The system of knowledge adapted to the notation was drawn from T. Harris's catalog system for the St. Louis Public School Library, which was influenced by Hegel's notion of the faculties of Memory, Imagination, and Reason. Following discussions of the origins of the system, Comaromi traces its development through the eighteenth edition, 1971, and describes the administrative bodies responsible for maintenance of the classification. (BKS)

973. Dix, William S. "Of the Arrangement of Books." *College and Research Libraries*, Vol. XXV (March 1964), pp. 85-90.

It is a library axiom that no one arrangement of books will please everyone. This fact is understandable since a library is a collection of books arranged for use and different people use books in different ways. Dix reviews the "surprising variety of ways in which books can be arranged," and he suggests that "any reasonably logical and complete classification, applied consistently, will work." The basic question regarding classification is how the books should be arranged to get into the reader's hands the book he wants when he wants it; indeed, this criterion "is the first principle, and . . . from it stem nearly all the things we do or ought to do in libraries." Like the great majority of librarians who consider the benefits and costs of centralization versus decentralization of library resources on a campus, Dix favors the former, although he is willing to compromise. "In the long run, is it not better for everyone, increasing his chances of finding the book he wants when he wants it, to keep as many books as possible together?" (RHW)

974. Hickey, Doralyn Joanne. "The American Librarian's Dream: Full Bibliographic Control with Complete Freedom of Access." *Library Lectures*, nos. 28-30 (1978), pp. 15-31.

Hickey reviews American bibliographic history in terms of the tension between librarians' conflicting goals, complete freedom of access to information, and full bibliographic control of materials. The tension is seen in terms of the effect of American social systems on the development of bibliography. Full bibliographic control demands carefully planned and administered bibliographic structures while free access calls for diverse approaches to bibliographic records and the material they represent. Hickey offers a synthesis of demands for control and demands for access, featuring layering or nesting of collections to serve a variety of user needs; a better understood bibliographic system; increased access paths to information and materials; and development of a cadre of bibliographic experts who would perform in combination many of the functions now separately performed by catalogers and reference librarians. (BKS)

975. Lucker, Jay K. "Library Resources and Bibliographic Control." *College and Research Libraries*, Vol. XL (March 1979), pp. 141-153.

The future of academic libraries is discussed from the perspective of their resources and bibliographic control. Emphasis is focused on collection philosophy, book selection, the collection itself, resource sharing, adequacy of library space, preservation, new cataloging rules, a national bibliographic data base, and subject access. To provide a better forum for discussion of these matters and to assist in the solution of related problems, the author sees the need for a national library agency. (RHW)

976. Rubanowice, Robert J. "Intellectual History and the Organization of Knowledge." *Journal of Library History*, Vol. X (July 1975), pp. 264-271.

The author complains that hierarchical classification schemes such as the Dewey system and the Library of Congress classification, along with the drawing of disciplinary boundaries in scholarship, have led to debilitating administrative systems and to distortion of the knowledge they purport to map. Knowledge is truly transdisciplinary. Classification principles that librarians ought to follow will involve exhaustive, analytical, pre-coordinate, facet subject cataloging. Rubanowice argues that new electronic technologies give librarians an opportunity to experiment with new classification schemes that transcend limitations of the past, such as restrictions on the number of subject terms assigned to each document. (BKS)

977. Simonton, Wesley. "AACR 2: Antecedents, Assumptions, Implementation." In Michael H. Harris, ed. *Advances in Librarianship*, Vol. X. New York: Academic, 1980.

Simonton discusses the major theoretical principles and substantive provisions of the second edition of the *Anglo-American Cataloguing Rules*, published in 1978. These rules are the prescribed standard for cataloging practice. He relates AACR 2 to the Anglo-American cataloging tradition and to major theoretical work on cataloging. The content of the new rules and their underlying assumptions are treated, as well as the influences of technology and the current bibliographic milieu on their formulation. The article concludes with a discussion of implementation of the revised code. (BKS)

978. *Statement of Principles Adopted at the International Conference on Cataloguing Principles, Paris, October 1961*. London: International Federation of Library Associations Committee on Cataloguing, 1971.

Representatives of fifty-three nations met in Paris in 1961 to consider steps leading to international bibliographical standardization. The statement of principles approved at that meeting became the basis for the *Anglo-American Cataloguing Rules* published by the Catalog Code Revision Committee of the American Library Association in 1967 and the revision, AACR-2, published in 1978. The "Paris Principles" of 1961 state the purposes that the cataloging rules intended to accomplish. (BKS)

979. Swanson, Don R., ed. "The Role of Libraries in the Growth of Knowledge: Proceedings of the Fortieth Conference of the Graduate Library School." *Library Quarterly*, Vol. L (January 1980).

Swanson, organizer and editor of the proceedings of this annual conference held by the Graduate Library School of the University of Chicago, introduces the collection of papers: "This conference was conceived in the context of what at first seemed a straightforward question: What kinds of problems are libraries intended to solve? I soon found that I had opened Pandora's box and set free a swarm of mischievous questions. If libraries are intended to do anything at all, who is it that does the intending? What kinds of problems are people who use libraries trying to solve? In particular, what is the nature of the problems faced by scientists and scholars in trying to contribute to the edifice of knowledge? How should we describe the process by which knowledge grows? And how can research libraries best facilitate that growth? Are these questions to be answered differently for the sciences than for the social sciences or humanities? What is the process by which libraries themselves adapt to new problems? Are the issues raised peculiar to the institution of libraries, or do they apply as well to information services within the commercial sector?" (RHW)

980. Walker, Donald E. "The Organization and Use of Information: Contributions of Information Science, Computational Linguistics, and Artificial Intelligence." *Journal of the American Society for Information Science,* Vol. XXXII (September 1981), pp. 347-363.

Through a review of recent developments in information science, computational linguistics, and artificial intelligence, Walker shows how these three fields share concerns with the concepts of information, language, and knowledge. In all three fields, efforts have been made to resolve the problem of representation of knowledge by developing techniques for characterizing the content of data and the content of queries and for relating data and queries to each other. Following a review of these efforts and explanation of the importance of the issue in each field, Walker describes a research program for understanding the organization and use of information among communities of scholars and scientists. The bibliography is particularly useful. (BKS)

III. Public Libraries

981. Berelson, Bernard. *The Library's Public.* New York: Columbia University Press, 1949.

This book is a product of the Public Library Inquiry, a research project funded by the Carnegie Corporation from 1946 to 1949. It reports results of two studies of the use of public libraries, one based on a national survey of adults, the other based on a review and synthesis of published studies of library and book use. The report analyzes the characteristics of library users and their reasons for using the library, with discussion of the social situations that produce demand for library services. The report's major finding, that a small group of relatively well educated people account for a large proportion of library use, led to considerable discussion among librarians about the proper mission of public libraries and the proper nature of library services. (BKS)

982. Blake, Fay M., and Jane Irby. "The Selling of the Public Library." *Drexel Library Quarterly,* Vol. XII (January-April 1976), pp. 149-158.

The authors articulate the differences between public libraries, which provide information at no direct cost to patrons, and the information industry, which produces and sells access to machine-readable data bases. Public libraries and the information industry have different motives, different goals, different clientele, and different relationships with the poor. Rather than attempting to work in partnership with the industry, selling its services for a fee through libraries, libraries should be community information resources, developing their own data bases and search systems through library cooperatives. Libraries ought to regard the information industry as another kind of publisher, selecting among its products and providing them to the public without charge to individuals. (BKS)

983. Haynes, C. Goddard. "An Economic Analysis of Library Benefits." *Library Quarterly*, Vol. XLI (July 1971), pp. 244-255.

Goddard, an economist, uses a welfare economics perspective to suggest which groups of library users provide the greatest return to society. An evaluation of the traditional library functions of education, information, and leisure suggests that libraries should direct their resources toward educational activities and not toward recreation when public monies are involved. A case can be made for subsidizing the library activities of school-age children, others explicitly involved in education, disadvantaged minority groups, and government officials and staff. (RHW)

984. Ladenson, Alex D. "Is the Library an Educational Institution?" *Wilson Library Bulletin,* Vol. LI (March 1977), pp. 576-581.

Ladenson argues that in a strictly legal sense the public library is an educational institution and therefore ought to be funded in the same ways as public schools are funded, through property taxes, states' general revenue funds, and federal aid. Opinions of supreme courts of nine states, in cases dating from 1877 to 1971, are reviewed, in which the courts determined that public libraries are educational institutions. (BKS)

985. Monroe, Margaret E. "A Conceptual Framework for the Public Library as a Community Learning Center for Independent Study." *Library Quarterly,* Vol. XLVI (January 1976), pp. 54-61.

Public libraries, in responding to growing interest in adult independent study, are beginning to reexamine their role as community learning centers. Different kinds of learning centers emphasize: priority on provision of materials; collaboration with academic institutions and agencies through an independent-study information and referral service; a multimedia center supported by educational counselling and study guidance; and a community task force approach, which provides learning-center services in the midst of community problem solving. Differences among learners, learning situations, and learning styles as well as in library resources and community programs affect the evolution of any particular library community learning center. (RHW)

986. Rayward, W. Boyd, ed. "The Public Library: Circumstances and Prospects: Proceedings of the Thirty-Ninth Conference of the Graduate Library School." *Library Quarterly*, Vol. XLVIII (October 1978).

A product of the annual conferences of the Graduate Library School, University of Chicago, this volume includes papers dealing with various aspects of the public library: its place in the communications setting; its financial and technological settings; its role in cooperation and networking; the future of reference and information service in the public library; services for adults, young adults, and children; recent developments in the United Kingdom; and prospects for change. (RHW)

IV. Special Libraries

987. Jackson, Eugene B., ed. *Special Librarianship: A New Reader.* Metuchen, N.J.: Scarecrow, 1980.

Special libraries, those libraries with collections and services tailored to the information needs of a particular clientele, are usually thought of as units within institutions in the private sector. This collection of articles, most of which were written expressly for this anthology, comprises sections on the nature of special libraries, special librarians, management of special libraries, public relations, and tools and formats for materials, as well as a section on host-organization related matters. In the latter are articles on the nature of special libraries in the federal civil service, academic departmental libraries, human services institutions, and hospitals. These articles detail the nature of library work in publicly supported special libraries. (BKS)

988. Myers, Mildred S., and William C. Frederick. "Business Libraries: Role and Function in Industrial America." *Journal of Education for Librarianship,* Vol. XV (Summer 1974), pp. 41-52.

The authors trace the development of business literature from the eighteenth to the twentieth century, noting a shift from focus on business to focus on management in the early twentieth century. Types of information needed by business are described and types of business libraries are reviewed, with comments on the functions of each type. (BKS)

989. Robbin, Alice. "The Pre-acquisition Process: A Strategy for Locating and Acquiring Machine-readable Data." *Drexel Library Quarterly,* Vol. XIII (January 1977), pp. 21-42.

The scope of this article is broader than the title suggests. Robbin begins with a concise explanation of the nature of the special library, differentiated from other types of libraries in its mission, the staff's specialized training in subject matter of the collection, and its philosophy of user services, which focuses on delivery of information rather than reference to bibliography. Special library collections are designed to serve the immediate information needs of clientele. Robbin discusses in detail the factors that influence collection development and acquisition policies and procedures. Specific examples refer to a social science data library, but the processes described are relevant to many kinds of library materials and to special libraries generally. (BKS)

V. School Libraries

990. Coughlin, Caroline M. "Children's Librarians: Managing in the Midst of Myth." *School Library Journal,* Vol. XXIV (January 1978), pp. 15-18.

Library administrators' commitments to children's services have deteriorated in recent years because children's librarians, according to Coughlin, have persisted in clinging to a Victorian view of their role, "obligating themselves to nurture their charges into a mode of behavior that places primary value on general goodness and beauty as found in literature." While children's librarians have continued trying to dispense goodness, all other groups in librarianship have become concerned with dispensing ideas. The nurturing image of themselves held by children's librarians is dysfunctional in a modern library environment, wherein managerial ideas now dominate. If children's librarians want places in library decision making, they must learn management skills and adopt managerial perspectives. Their own careers would then prosper, and library service to children would improve as it shifted from moral education to helping children acquire information and knowledge. (BKS)

991. Dane, Chase. "The Changing School Library: An Instructional Media Center." In Melvin J. Voigt, ed. *Advances in Librarianship,* Vol. I. New York: Academic, 1970.

The instructional media center (IMC) as an alternative resource to replace the traditional school library is described. The purpose of the IMC is to make available to students the best way of acquiring information, recognizing that not all information is best represented in print and that not all students learn best from reading. Facilities, materials and equipment, and services in IMCs are discussed. (BKS)

992. Hodson, Yvonne D. "The School Media Center: A Conceptual Model." *Journal of Education for Librarianship,* Vol. XX (Summer 1979), pp. 36-43.

A model and rationale for the school media center as a strategic learning facility are described. The model is based upon research in media and education dealing with behavioristic psychology, cognitive psychology, personality theory, and theories of learning as information processing. Hodson argues that there can be no distinct demarcation between the overlapping functions of information service and instruction. She concludes with a discussion of the evolution of the concept of the integrated media center from the 1930s to the present. (BKS)

993. Shields, Gerald R., and John Robotham. "At What Age Freedom?" *Collection Building,* Vol. I (1979), pp. 18-33.

The authors make an argument for free and open collections of materials for children and young adults. The young should be allowed to develop the ability to make important decisions about themselves and to profit from their mistakes, and libraries should help them in that process. Libraries should be part of the process of learning from experience. Examples of materials that are controversial because they relate to sex and/or violence are discussed. The authors conclude that it is the librarian's professional responsibility to protect the information rights of children. (BKS)

994. Wilson, Pauline. "Children's Services in a Time of Change." *School Library Journal*, Vol. XXV (February 1979), pp. 23-26.

Noting that children's services have been denigrated or diminished within library systems in recent years, Wilson assesses the situation and distinguishes between contributing factors over which children's librarians have control and those they do not. Among the latter, she says, are social problems such as the decline of educational standards in the public schools, deleterious effects of television viewing, divorce rates, the breakdown of the traditional family structure, growth in institutional child care, and the declining birth rate. Library eductors are faulted for making their courses too easy, for not making potential children's librarians take a wide variety of courses that would prepare them for management, and for not producing research that would solve the problems facing children's librarians. Children's librarians have failed to clarify their role, which is "to help form or shape children in desirable ways." Children's librarians have not articulated well the merits of their programs to library managers. (BKS)

VI. Junior College Libraries

995. Giles, Louise. "On the Cutting Edge of Change: The Community College Library." In E. J. Josey, ed. *New Dimensions of Academic Library Service*. Metuchen, N.J.: Scarecrow, 1975.

Giles notes that all librarians have been challenged to change traditional practices in response to diversification in the formats for presentation of information. The challenge has been especially felt by community college librarians, who, unlike research librarians, must manage collections of materials in a wide variety of formats used by new instructional technologies and in new, individualized instruction modes. Administration, services, and physical facilities of learning resource centers are described. (BKS)

996. Gleazer, Edmund J., Jr. "The State of the Junior College in Its Library." *College and Research Libraries*, Vol. XXVII (July 1966), 263-317.

As in any other institution, a library in a junior college must be determined by the function of its parent organization. Junior colleges have characteristics distinct from those of the four-year college or university. Gleazer, executive director of the American Association of Junior Colleges, discusses some of these unique characteristics, relating them to the library. Recent developments are outlined. (RHW)

997. Veit, Fritz. "The Community College Library in the United States." *Journal of Library and Information Science,* Vol. I (April 1975), pp. 36-48.

The mission, collections, and administration of community college libraries, or learning resource centers, are described in the context of the functions of the institutions they serve. Veit describes professional standards and guidelines for community college library service and briefly reviews the major functions of these and other academic libraries. (BKS)

VII. College and Research Libraries: General

998. Biggs, Mary. "Sources of Tension and Conflict between Librarians and Faculty." *Journal of Higher Education,* Vol. LII (March-April 1981), pp. 182-201.

Until this century, Biggs contends, libraries were administered by individuals who considered themselves scholars, not administrators or even necessarily librarians, and they were expected to have very broad knowledge. "Once creatures of the same order," librarians and faculty have since "evolved into quite different creatures, each insistent upon professional autonomy, stubbornly holding sometimes disparate visions of the library's mission, and communicating very little with each other." The author notes that there are no easy answers to this very important problem. (RHW)

999. Blackburn, Robert T. "College Libraries—Indicted Failures: Some Reasons—and a Possible Remedy." *College and Research Libraries,* Vol. XXIX (May 1968), pp. 171-177.

Blackburn, a professor of higher education at the University of Michigan, finds the performance of liberal arts college libraries wanting when compared with their purported aims, and he identifies as the principal cause conflicts between librarians and teaching faculty. Although "some kinds of contention are rather easily removed," others range in seriousness to such a depth that "realistically a solution is most likely not possible." The author proposes that some of the deeper-seated conflicts result from fundamental differences in competing ends held by faculty members and librarians, some result from "characterological" differences between them, and others inhere in the sometimes opposing roles the two groups are called upon to play. Examples are given. (RHW)

1000. Gore, Daniel. "The Mismanagement of College Libraries: A View from the Inside." *AAUP Bulletin,* Vol. LII (Spring 1966), pp. 46-51.

The author, who has since served as library director at Macalester and Lewis and Clark colleges, paraphrases Georges Clemenceau to the effect that academic libraries "are much too important to be left to the librarians." Most tasks performed by professional librarians could be handled by clerical staffs, if the librarians would allow it. Moreover, library schools cannot prepare students adequately for genuinely professional performance. "Until they demand that college libraries serve readers first, and librarians second," Gore concludes, "college faculties and students will continue to be plagued by the substandard book collections that are the inescapable consequence of spending the lion's share of library funds on librarians rather than books." (RHW)

1001. Holley, Edward G. "What Lies Ahead for Academic Libraries." In Herbert Poole, ed. *Academic Libraries by the Year 2000*. New York: Bowker, 1977.

This paper addresses the climate in which higher education has operated since the 1960s and will continue to operate until the year 2000. Holley discusses the health of academic libraries and identifies various changes that they and their staffs will face. All librarians will have to accept unpleasant realities—both general and those peculiar to their type of institution and library. Private academic schools might have to decide between allocating funds for library materials or salaries for faculty positions, while university libraries will continue to deal with the concept of multiple subscriptions/copies of heavy-demand items versus that of obtaining as great a number of unique titles as possible. (CMG)

1002. Johnson, Pyke, Jr. "A Day with a College Librarian." *Publisher's Weekly*, Vol. CCXIII (January 9, 1978), pp. 41-44.

Johnson, managing editor of Doubleday, visited Earlham College and its highly regarded librarian, Evan Farber. In an article of interest to anyone concerned with higher education, the author provides a detailed account of his visit. (RHW)

1003. Moody, Robert E. "Our Academic Leadership: From the Faculty?" *College and Research Libraries*, Vol. XXI (September 1960), pp. 362-368.

"My argument is simply this: that academic libraries are an integral part of the scholarly process, that their leadership ought to be in the hands of scholars, that technical knowledge of librarianship as such should be subordinated to scholarly knowledge of what libraries are and what they are for, and that the practical education of scholars who intend to teach is not incompatible with the practical education of scholars who intend to become librarians. Let us not create barriers by refusing to recognize that the guild of scholars embraces all who love learning. I want academic librarians to be members of the group *in every respect*, not merely technicians who serve it." (RHW)

1004. Munn, Robert F. "The Bottomless Pit of the Academic Library as Viewed from the Administration Building." *College and Research Libraries*, Vol. XXIX (January 1968), pp. 51-54.

Library administrators could better assess their likely fortunes in the academic tug of war for funds if they understood more clearly the attitudes of institutional administrators toward libraries, contends the author, acting provost and dean of the graduate school in West Virginia University. Some administrators view the library as "a bottomless pit"; all recognize that the library is unlikely to generate much political pressure for its own aggrandizement. Many young institutional administrators are coming to apply more sophisticated measures to their funding formulas than have been utilized in the past. Librarians therefore would be well advised to become more proficient in modern mangagement techniques and program budgeting concepts. (RHW)

1005. "The President Views the Campus Library." *Journal of Academic Librarianship*, Vol. III (September 1977), pp. 192-199.

The editors asked the presidents of several colleges and universities: "In light of the current economic outlook and potential technological breakthroughs, what kind of future do you, as President, predict for your campus library? What courses of actions [*sic*] do you recommend?" The eight responses given here come from seven presidents and one vice-president at the University of Pittsburgh, Earlham College, Indiana University, Northern Virginia Community College, Oregon State University, the University of Alabama, the University of Arizona, and Rosary College. (RHW)

VIII. Collections and Collection Development

1006. Clapp, Verner W., and Robert T. Jordan. "Quantitative Criteria for Adequacy of Academic Library Collections." *College and Research Libraries*, Vol. XXVI (September 1965), pp. 371-380.

The authors challenge accepted doctrine, which asserts that the adequacy of an academic library cannot be measured by the number of books it contains. Out of their feeling that the Standards for College Libraries and the Standards for Junior College Libraries are inadequate for estimating the sizes (in volumes) required for minimum adequacy by libraries of institutions of higher education of widely differing characteristics, they develop new formulas for this purpose. These formulas attempt to identify the principal factors affecting academic needs for books and to ascribe suitable weights to each factor. The authors then illustrate the application of the formulas to specific institutions and conclude that while the results are useful, further research is needed. They end by suggesting specific topics for such research. (RHW)

1007. DeGennaro, Richard. "Escalating Journal Prices: Time to Fight Back." *American Libraries*, Vol. VIII (February 1977), pp. 69-74.

Academic librarians and faculty members have a collector's instinct that makes them addicts to journals: they want all journals, and each in a complete set. Publishers, aware of the addiction, have raised prices, using library subscriptions to support their publications. Librarians must now fight back by weeding low-use journals from their collections. Techniques for ranking journals by use are briefly reviewed. (BKS)

1008. Downs, Robert B., and Robert F. Delzell. "Price Tag on a University Library." *College and Research Libraries,* Vol. XXI (September 1980), pp. 359-361, 404.

Published estimates and guesses on the cost of developing a university library and its resources are, by and large, at such wide variance that one can only conclude the figures have little actual basis. No major research collection could today be duplicated for the total amount the collection had cost over the years, if one were to attempt to assemble original materials. Important intangible factors are the contributions to a research library, over many years, of scholars in guiding the development of resources and also of private book collectors who have frequently given or sold to the library their lifetime accumulations. (RHW)

1009. Edelman, Hendrik, and G. Marvin Tatum, Jr. "The Development of Collections in American University Libraries." *College and Research Libraries,* Vol. XXXVII (May 1976), pp. 222-245.

Good scholars need good libraries, and good libraries attract good scholars. This interaction is the dominant theme in the story of American university libraries. With very few exceptions, the prominent graduate programs at the turn of the century created the outstanding library collections of that time. Twenty-five years later, a review of perceived quality in graduate education closely correlated with the numerical ranking of the library collections. In 1965 it was again found that the top twenty-five humanities and social science programs are located at the universities that have the largest book collections, although the relative ranking in individual subject fields does not necessarily match the overall strength of the respective libraries. In building the collections of American university libraries, it has been the scholar who provided the impetus; the librarian has made it possible. The article concludes with a useful table showing library holdings of, and Ph.D. degrees awarded by, major American public and private universities, 1876-1975. (RHW)

1010. Gore, Daniel. "Thinking the Unthinkable about Libraries: A Theory of the No-Growth Collection." In William Katz and R. Burgess, eds. *Library Lit 5: The Best of 1974.* Metuchen, N.J.: Scarecrow, 1975.

Gore suggests that the answer to the question, how large should a library be, should be determined by recognizing that the main function of an academic library is to provide books for readers who want to read them now. If libraries pursue that function instead of trying to collect everything, either to preserve materials for posterity or to anticipate the future demand, they can limit the size of collections by regular, sharp weeding of unused titles. Money saved by not maintaining unused works can be used to speed up document delivery and to provide larger selection of material in current demand. Three measures of library performance are explained, which can be used to relate collection size to the level of service. (BKS)

1011. Schad, Jasper G., and Ruth L. Adams. "Book Selection in Academic Libraries: A New Approach." *College and Research Libraries,* Vol. XXX (September 1969), pp. 437-442.

Traditional modes of book selection by instructional faculty working on a part-time basis with limited coordination often result in the growth of imbalanced collections. In an attempt to solve this problem, libraries have begun to utilize bibliographers, who are often assigned responsibility for subjects they cannot adequately cover. By employing systematic methods similar to those developed by bibliographers for surveying and building collections, members of the instructional faculty, by virtue of the added factor of their specialized knowledge, can often be effectively utilized in building collections. (RHW)

1012. Stewart, Blair. "Periodicals and the Liberal Arts College Library." *College and Research Libraries,* Vol. XXXVI (September 1975), pp. 371-378.

College libraries are encountering increasing difficulties in meeting their readers' needs for access to periodical literature. Analysis of the periodical holdings of the ten liberal arts college libraries that created the ACM (Associated Colleges of the Midwest) Periodical Bank shows that the "basic list" of periodicals every such library holds is very short and that these titles are the ones from which the member libraries most frequently requested photocopies. The study also suggests that little or no use is being made of most of the periodicals on college library holdings lists. (RHW)

1013. White, Herbert S. "Publishers, Libraries, and Costs of Journal Subscriptions in Times of Funding Retrenchment." *Library Quarterly,* Vol. XLVI (October 1976), pp. 359-377.

A study funded by the National Science Foundation examined the economic interaction between libraries and publishers of scholarly and research journals for the period 1969-1973. Drawing from the findings of the study, the validity of the fears of librarians of growth in the number of journals published and publishers' profits and the fears of publishers of unlimited photocopying in libraries are examined. The complex price structure of journal subscriptions, their increasing cost, and the problems these pose both to publishers and librarians are discussed. How libraries allocate their budgets is also examined. (RHW)

IX. Preservation

1014. Grove, Lee E. "Paper Deterioration—An Old Story." *College and Research Libraries,* Vol. XXV (September 1964), pp. 365-374.

Grove traces the problem of paper deterioration from the fifteenth century to the last third of the twentieth. Particularly in the last century, librarians, publishers, and others have sought solutions, with limited success. It is too expensive to deacidify and laminate every book printed during nearly almost all of the past hundred years, and "the cost of microfilming everything is both financially and bibliographically appalling,'' while "the problem is daily being aggravated as materials printed on weak papers continue to pour from the presses in increasing number.'' (RHW)

1015. Hendrick, Clyde, and Marjorie E. Murfin. ''Project Library Ripoff: A Study of Periodical Mutilation in a University Library.'' *College and Research Libraries,* Vol. XXXV (November 1974), pp. 402-411.

A questionnaire assessed 168 students on their knowledge and opinion about periodical mutilation in the Kent State University Library. Three mutilators were also interviewed in detail. Fourteen students (8.3 percent) admitted to mutilation of journals. Statistical tests revealed few differences between mutilators and nonmutilators, although mutilators had generally less favorable attitudes toward the library. The data suggested certain preventive measures; the most important were a publicity campaign to educate students about the costs of mutilation and specific penalty warning signs strategically located in the library. (RHW)

1016. Stange, Eric. ''From Rags to Ruin.'' *Atlantic Monthly*, Vol. CCXLIII (June 1979), pp. 90-93.

The history of the chemistry of paper making is examined here. The use of sulphuric acid in the manufacture of paper is responsible for the deterioration of many library materials since the mid-nineteenth century. The acid eventually destroys the paper. The prohibitively expensive process of deacidification is described. Although techniques are readily available and in use for alternative ways of making paper, publishers have not demanded acid-free papers, and most seem unconcerned about the problem. Stange offers libraries little hope for preservation of their collections, except through the microfilming of material. (BKS)

1017. Winger, Howard W., ed. ''Deterioration and Preservation of Library Materials: Proceedings of the Thirty-fourth Annual Conference of the Graduate Library School.'' *Library Quarterly*, Vol. XL (January 1970).

The deterioration of library materials, constant since libraries began, has accelerated to alarming proportions in 1969. Researchers have predicted that all paper-based records of this century, as well as those of earlier years, face imminent ruin. Without new and effective efforts for their preservation, most will not be usable in their present form in the next century. Collectively, these articles discuss the scholarly needs for preservation, the physical nature of the materials to be preserved, the means and care required in manufacture and storage and handling to achieve the greatest possible permanence, the effects of different manufacturing techniques, programs for conservation and restoration, and personnel needs and requirements. (RHW)

X. Library Buildings

1018. Ellsworth, Ralph E. "Consultants for College and University Library Building Planning." *College and Research Libraries,* Vol. XXI (July 1960), pp. 263-268.

During the years just before World War II, there was no college or university librarian alive who could, today, qualify as a consultant in the college and university field. Within the American Library Association, it was not until 1940 that anyone realized the need for specialized planning for college and university libraries. This article outlines what a building consultant is supposed to do, how he works, how he should be selected and paid, and how his work should be evaluated. When something has been done properly at another library, the idea should be borrowed if it is relevant. "We need not worry about monotony for the simple reason that there are too few good examples to follow." Ellsworth is widely recognized as one of the foremost authorities on academic library buildings. (RHW)

1019. Metcalf, Keyes D. *Planning Academic and Research Library Buildings.* New York: McGraw-Hill, 1965.

Metcalf wrote numerous articles on special aspects of library architecture and planning and served as consultant to many building projects. He presents detailed chapters on matters to consider in designing buildings and a set of chapters to guide library administrators through the planning process step by step. (BKS)

1020. Orne, Jerrold. "Academic Library Buildings: A Century in Review." *College and Research Libraries,* Vol. XXXVII (July 1976), pp. 316-331.

Any thoughtful review of a century-long experience with building academic libraries and even casual awareness of current library planning must lead to the rueful conviction that though we have a large body of experience and considerable professional awareness, we may not have learned very much. We find libraries built tall, deep, or broad for reasons that are hard to comprehend. Even worse, we see new libraries planned for numbers, purposes, or goals not clearly established. "Architects and architecture have reached a new low in matching good functional design with the architect's imagination. Many of our new libraries are now monuments again, but not in the sense of a hundred years ago. These are monuments to some architect's ego . . . This is not to say that all are bad. Some excellent libraries can now be found in any state of our country. Some can also be found whose planning is little short of hopeless." (RHW)

1021. Schell, Hal B. "Buildings, Library." In *Encyclopedia of Library and Information Science,* Vol. III. New York: Marcel Dekker, 1970.

The ways in which the nature of materials stored in libraries have determined the forms of library buildings are recounted. The article is profusely illustrated with photographs and floor plans of various types of libraries in the United States and Europe. Schell emphasizes ways in which the shift from stress on the storage function of libraries to stress on the retrieval and service functions of libraries is affecting library design. (BKS)

XI. Library Management

1022. DeGennaro, Richard. "Library Administration and New Management Systems." *Library Journal,* Vol. CIII (December 15, 1978), pp. 2477-2482.

Scientific management systems, such as management by objectives, cost-benefit analysis, and program budgeting, are not designed for academic libraries, contends DeGennaro, one of the most respected library directors in the country. Library managers benefit much more from knowledge of how their respective systems function, how the library fits into the whole academic operation, and from skills developed by dealing with day-to-day activities. The faddish new management systems are too complex, too theoretical, and confusing for advantageous application to library operations. In the business world, management and decision making often do not result from extensive planning, organizing, and coordinating. Management and decision making are arts, not sciences, that require practical thinking and common sense for success. (CMG)

1023. Dickinson, Dennis W. "Some Reflections on Participative Management in Libraries." *College and Research Libraries,* Vol. XXXIX (July 1978), pp. 253-262.

Participative management is highly touted as a panacea for the ills—real and imagined—afflicting libraries. Apologists for this managerial strategy often fail to define it adequately, proceed from a number of unwarranted assumptions and suppressed premises in their arguments for it, and overlook some of the consequences that would follow from its implementation. This article examines these assumptions, draws out the premises, and considers some of the possible ramifications of participative management in its various forms in order to arrive at a clear and workable, albeit restrained, understanding of the concept. (RHW)

1024. Dix, William S. "Leadership in Academic Libraries." *College and Research Libraries*, Vol. XXI (September 1960), pp. 373-380, 388.

Dix, a library director at Rice and Princeton universities, was himself a leader in academic librarianship. In this article he describes a dual role of the library director: as an educator (talking and working with faculty, individually and collectively) and as a builder and organizer of collections. Twenty percent of the director's time is spent finding money ("Never ask for anything which you don't sincerely believe is important") and another twenty percent finding important collections of books and manuscripts. Of the remainder of his time, thirty percent is for internal operation of the library, twenty percent for public relations with the library's many publics, and ten percent for miscellaneous activities. Ideally, the library director will be "a born teacher," a scholar in almost any field, and will possess "a thorough knowledge of library theory and procedures, from acquisitions to weeding. And he must know these operations in human terms, for they will be carried out by people under his direction." (RHW)

1025. Drucker, Peter F. "Managing the Public Service Institution." *College and Research Libraries,* Vol. XXXVII (January 1976), pp. 4-14.

In this essay a respected outsider questions some of the profession's basic assumptions. Important factors involved in the management of public service institutions, of which the library is one example, are discussed. Included are the requirement to know the publics and their expectations and service needs; the problems related to the introduction of new programs; the roles of the administrator and the professional; the mission of the institution; and the need to communicate effectively to society the institution's unique contribution in order to merit and to receive continuing support. (RHW)

1026. Fussler, Herman H., John E. Jueck, and Don R. Swanson. "Management Education: Implications for Libraries and Library Schools: Proceedings of the Thirty-sixth Annual Conference of the Graduate Library School." *Library Quarterly,* Vol. XLIII (October 1973).

In recent years there have been extensive changes and developments of the concepts and theories of management and management processes. During this same period many individual libraries have grown in size and complexity to the point where inherently difficult management problems have emerged. These problems, in turn, have been made even more difficult by the growing recognition that many libraries must analyze more critically the effectiveness of their own internal operations and must, at the same time, engage in the planning and development of new and very complex interdependent systems of various kinds that can provide improved access to a rapidly growing worldwide corpus of literature and information. Papers at this conference reflect a heavy reliance upon experts from the field of graduate education in business. (RHW)

1027. Haas, Warren V. "Managing Our Academic Libraries: Ways and Means." *College and Research Libraries,* Vol. XL (March 1979), pp. 109-119.

There is a new library ecology in which interdependence is the dominant force, and the establishment of new operating mechanisms (such as a national periodicals center and a national library agency) is discussed. Funds in the amounts required to meet libraries' traditional needs will not be forthcoming, and thus libraries must transform themselves and make substantial changes in their operations. There is also the need for better ways to set basic policies that determine a library's capabilities, costs, and services. In their self-management, academic libraries have not done as well as their parent institutions in developing reliable data and in putting them to use. But while libraries need the attributes of scientific management, they must not make the mistake of thinking library management is *only* a science. (RHW)

1028. McAnally, Arthur M., and Robert B. Downs. "The Changing Role of Directors of University Libraries." *College and Research Libraries*, Vol. XXXIV (March 1973), pp. 103-125.

This article, written by men who were former library directors at the University of Oklahoma and University of Illinois, respectively, is an introduction to the world of a library director in a large library. The role of the university director has changed markedly during the previous decade, the authors contend. The position of library director has become a difficult role to serve. Directors have been subjected to pressures from different quarters. Five sources are identified by the authors, including pressures from the president's office, library staff, faculty, and students. These difficulties, coupled with a declining ability to meet user needs, the lack of cohesive library planning, and an institutional inability to accommodate change, have all contributed to the declining status of the library director. Recommendations as to ways to ameliorate the problem are offered. Among the suggestions included are better planning, improved budgeting techniques, and the introduction of new organizational patterns. The article concludes with the section "Qualities of a Model Director." (RHW)

XII. Staffing Patterns and Organizational Aspects

1029. "Centralization and Decentralization in Academic Libraries: A Symposium." *College and Research Libraries,* Vol. XXII (September 1961), pp. 327-340, 398.

Three library administrators address the topic from the perspective of their own campuses. Douglas W. Bryant, associate librarian of Harvard University, discusses Harvard's system of "coordinated decentralization" as it applies to the library system, concluding that, like walking a tightrope, it requires alertness. At the time, that system contained more than ninety libraries, about half of them a part of the Harvard College Library. Library Director Stephen McArthy, summarizing his situation at Cornell, contends that while "a simple, unified library administration may not be possible in a complex institution, a more flexible approach to centralize administration may offer real opportunities in such situations." Finally, Donald T. Smith of Boston University, describing a library system that is more in flux than most, aptly emphasizes that "the determining factor in whether a library organization shall be centralized or decentralized should be the extent of *service* that is feasible." Since resources are limited at Boston University (as at most places), the university has had to choose between "decentralized mediocrity and centralized excellence," opting for the latter course. (RHW)

1030. Dunlap, Connie R. "Organizational Patterns in Academic Libraries." *College and Research Libraries,* Vol. XXXVII (September 1976), pp. 395-407.

Covering organizational developments in academic libraries during the past century, Dunlap provides an overview for a wide range of important issues.

These include: departmental libraries; centralization versus decentralization; undergraduate libraries; special collections; staff organization; management planning; automation and networks; organizational conflict; and future organization. (RHW)

1031. Gration, Selby U., and Arthur P. Young. "Reference-Bibliographers in the College Library." *College and Research Libraries,* Vol. XXXV (March 1974), p. 133.

The authors contend persuasively that one approach to making a college library more relevant, dynamic, and intelligible is to employ specialists with broad subject competence, thoroughly familiar with the terminology, bibliographic tools, and major writings of several related disciplines. These subject specialists or reference-bibliographers provide reference and instructional services and serve as coordinators between academic departments and the library. A significant increase in the quality of library service is attained with reference-bibliographers both building and interpreting the collection. The reference-bibliographer concept is examined from several perspectives: historical antecedents; relationship to the academic setting; and the authors' experience with a staff of subject specialists at a predominantly undergraduate college library during 1969-1972. (RHW)

1032. Kilpela, Raymond. "The Administrative Structure of the University Library." *College and Research Libraries,* Vol. XXIX (November 1968), pp. 511-516.

The typical large university library is a highly decentralized structure composed of numerous divisions and/or departments and departmental libraries. The popularly accepted notion that the university library usually comprises the two divisions of technical and public services, each administered by a division head who is responsible for the coordination of all such services, is more apparent than real. There is an average of seven librarians with line authority reporting to the library director. There appears to be a need to reduce this number and to place this responsibility in two or three officers on a secondary level. (RHW)

1033. Moffett, William A. "The Academic Job Crisis: A Unique Opportunity, or Business as Usual?" *College and Research Libraries,* Vol. XXXIV (May 1973), pp. 191-194.

Moffett not only reiterates the familiar dimensions of the academic job crisis, and the resulting opportunity for library recruitment, but calls attention to the danger of permitting the librarians' own job market to be overrun by candidates who may not have a genuine commitment to library service. As a "think-piece," Moffett's article is deliberately general and suggestive, with footnotes and statistics kept to a minimum. "Librarians have always drawn new colleagues from the classroom," Moffett observes. "The novelty lies in the unprecedented numbers of prospective recruits of outstanding caliber, and the urgency of taking prompt and deliberate action to turn the crisis to the maximum benefit of the profession.'' At the time, Moffett, a Ph.D. in English history from Duke, was assistant professor of history at the University of Massachusetts, Boston, and a student in the School of Library Science at Simmons College. He is presently library director at Oberlin College. (RHW)

XIII. Library Staff

1034. Bergen, Daniel Patrick. "Librarians and the Bipolarization of the Academic Enterprise.'' *College and Research Libraries*, Vol. XXIV (November 1963), pp. 467-480.

Drawing on Talcott Parsons's definition of a social system and applying that definition to the college and university, Bergen contends persuasively that librarians and teaching faculty belong to different, often mutually exclusive, subcultures within academe. Library administrators, especially but not exclusively those drawn from the technical services side of the library, often are "obsessed with the intralibrary ends of efficiency and production.'' Another important difference is that teaching faculty, especially at the more prestigious universities, have a strong orientation to their disciplines and a relatively weak orientation to the institution that employs them; academic librarians, in contrast, have a strong institutional orientation, in part because they are sensitive to the demands of an all-campus constituency. (RHW)

1035. Bundy, Mary Lee. "Conflict in Libraries.'' *College and Research Libraries*, Vol. XXVII (September 1966), pp. 253-262.

Bundy explores intergroup conflict in libraries, including conflict between departments, between professionals and bureaucracy, and between older and newer staff members. Other special interests such as informal powerholders and the subprofessional are identified. This analysis shows that existing organizational relationships in libraries let means become ends, while strong forces toward conformity hamper desirable growth and change. (RHW)

1036. Bundy, Mary Lee, and Paul Wasserman. "Professionalism Reconsidered.'' *College and Research Libraries*, Vol. XXIX (January 1968), pp. 5-26.

Like many people in other maturing professions, librarians often spend considerable time agonizing about whether their work is truly "professional.'' The authors here consider the question of librarianship as a profession in terms of the three key relationships of a professional—client, organizational, and professional. Professional practice in this field is thus cast against accepted norms and standards of professional behavior. This critical assessment suggests that librarianship falls far short of the professional model. Major shifts in the nature of the services performed by librarians and in their bureaucratic relationships will be required if librarianship is to advance. The contribution of the professional associations and of library schools to the advancement of the process of professionalization is also analyzed. Progress in the field is viewed to be inextricably tied to the success or failure that librarianship achieves in its quest for true professional attainment. (RHW)

1037. Dawson, John M. "Not Too Academic." *College and Research Libraries,* Vol. XXVII (January 1966), pp. 37-39, 55.

Nonprofessional staff who have been properly selected, trained, and supervised are capable of a wide range of tasks often considered professional, including cataloging and classifying, bibliographic verification, reference and interlibrary loan work, and of course, circulation. The role of the librarian lies in planning; in the selection of materials and courses of action; and in the training, supervision, revision, and inspiration of nonprofessional and student assistants. Because the academic librarian is usually in an uneasy limbo between the teaching and the clerical staffs, the necessity of distinguishing between professional and non-professional activities is even more critical in academic libraries than in the "real world." The basic problem is that we have not clearly defined the professional work of librarians. (RHW)

1038. Michener, Roger E. "Unions and Libraries: The Spheres of Intellect and Politics." *Southeastern Librarian,* Vol. XXIII (Winter 1974), pp. 15-25.

Five hypotheses explain the growth in unionism among librarians since 1965; economic retrenchment, dissatisfaction with increased bureaucratization in the postwar era, legislation enabling public employees to organize, status-defensive responses to egalitarian movements of the later 1960s and early 1970s, and librarians' discontent with a perceived imbalance between their roles as professionals and their lack of influence in making library policy. The first and last hypotheses are the most important. Michener reviews labor legislation and union policies and concludes that unions are inimical to the best interests of libraries because libraries do not fit the industrial model that shaped unionism. Unions are political devices, but libraries are intellectual institutions; political activities of unions subvert the intellectual traditions and freedom of inquiry that libraries serve. (BKS)

1039. Trumpeter, Margo. "Non-Librarians in the Academic Library." *College and Research Libraries,* Vol. XXIX (November 1968), pp. 461-465.

This article explores some differences between a group of people working professionally in academic libraries who do not regard themselves as librarians and an individually matched group of librarians who do identify with the profession. The differences explored are: salaries, education, nonlibrary associational affiliations, fulfillment of career expectations, and position classification. Significant differences were found with regard to library training, nonlibrary associational affiliations, and level of education as measured by highest nonlibrary subject degree held, while there appeared to be little difference between the two groups with regard to salary, position level, and career satisfaction. (RHW)

XIV. Library Technology

1040. Boss, Richard W. "Automated Acquisitions Systems." *Journal of Library Automation,* Vol. XIII (September 1980), pp. 156-164.

Boss traces the history of automated acquisitions systems since the early 1960s and finds that while the specifications for a system in terms of the tasks it will accomplish have changed little, the ways of accomplishing those tasks have. Some of those shifts are responses to developing technology—automated systems should now operate in on-line, interactive modes. Others reflect changes in library practice, particularly strong emphasis in recent years on collection development, the emergence of subject-specialist bibliographers, and new financial pressures demanding that what is acquired be demonstrably useful. These changes lead Boss to believe that any acquisitions system ought to be adopted with the goal in mind of eventually integrating that system with other automated systems, such as circulation. (BKS)

1041. DeGennaro, Richard. "Library Automation: Changing Patterns and New Directions." *Library Journal,* Vol. CI (January 1976), pp. 175-183.

Libraries' approaches to automation have changed since the early work in the 1960s. First steps toward automation were taken by individual libraries whose goal was to build integrated systems that would automate all technical processes. The prohibitive costs and technical demands of such systems led to new approaches by the mid-1970s that focused on development of computer-based networks and in-house development of systems to automate specific library functions. In the 1980s, DeGennaro expects to see in-house systems developed that will interface with national library networks for sharing bibliographic data and resources. (BKS)

1042. Malinconico, S. Michael. "The Library Catalog in a Computerized Environment." *Wilson Library Bulletin,* Vol. LI (September 1976), pp. 53-64.

Computerized library catalogs do not change or negate traditional cataloging principles; but the computer, if properly used, can help librarians realize the objectives of the catalog. The catalog defines a library collection by collocating entries under subject headings, so users can determine what works on a particular subject are available, or under author-name entries, so that users can find all the works by a particular author. While it is true, says Malinconico, that computers enhance searching by increasing the number of available access points to a work, the machine cannot impose an order on the collection that is not present in the data. Computerized catalogs should be used to store networks of linkages among subject headings, so that headings can be related and if necessary changed in time, and to store authority files to normalize authors' names. By interacting with these subject networks and authority files, the cataloger insures the integrity of the catalog data base. (BKS)

1043. Mason, Ellsworth Goodwin. "The Great Gas Bubble Prick't; or, Computers Revealed—by a Gentleman of Quality." *College and Research Libraries*, Vol. XXXII (May 1971), pp. 183-196.

Mason argues that librarians' enchantment with computer technology is foolish. High costs of automation make it unfeasible for library operations. Automation is irresponsible and irrational, deriving from American society's deluded belief that technology will solve all problems. The author claims that facts contradict claims for automation, such as that it will increase the speed of processing, develop shared systems, and promote efficiency. In addition, automated systems are virtually irreversible, making the computer an agent against change. In an era of shrinking financial support, automation for libraries is foolish. (BKS)

1044. Montague, Eleanor. "Automation and the Library Administrator." *Journal of Library Automation*, Vol. XI (December 1978), pp. 313-323.

Montague describes three phases in the development of library automation: the development phase during the early 1960s to early 1970s, in which a small number of libraries experimented with systems; an operational phase, from the late 1970s, in which shared systems and networks, vendor-supplied systems, and broad library participation evolved; and a new integrative phase now beginning, in which systems will be integrated across functional lines, national networks will be implemented, and automation will have more impact on technical processes and services. Management reactions to these phases are characterized, and problems and prospects for library service in the future are discussed. (BKS)

1045. Veneziano, Velma. "Library Automation: Data for Processing and Processing for Data." In Martha E. Williams, ed. *Annual Review of Information Science and Technology*, Vol. XV (White Plains, N.Y.: American Society for Information Science, 1980), pp. 109-145.

Automation is creating a political maelstrom among librarians, according to Veneziano, because networking to achieve automation has become a political and economic necessity for libraries. Her discussion of issues and problems includes sections on: the utilities that provide access to bibliographic data for processing, such as Online Catalog Library Center and Research Libraries Information Center; ownership and other economic issues related to the production of bibliographic data for network participants to access; techniques for creating data bases, particularly for older titles acquired before automation; bibliographic standards for content of data bases and data base integrity in terms of record structures and format; and protocols for computer-to-computer communication of data. (BKS)

1046. Webster, James K., and Carolyn L. Warden. "Comparing the Bibliographic Utilities for Special Librarians." *Special Libraries*, Vol. LXXI (December 1980), pp. 519-522.

A bibliographic utility is a computer-based telecommunications network that provides individual libraries access to bibliographic records created in machine-readable form by the network's member libraries. This article is aimed at special librarians, but the comparison of utilities is useful to a wider audience. Webster compares the Online Catalog Library Center, Washington Library Network, Research Libraries Information Network, and the University of Toronto Library Automation System in terms of their membership policies; hardware characteristics and required equipment; and software supporting library processes, such as cataloging, circulation, acquisitions, interlibrary loan, and on-line subject searching. (BKS)

1047. Williams, Martha E. "The Impact of Machine-readable Data Bases on Library and Information Services." *Information Processing and Management*, Vol. XIII, no. 2 (1977), pp. 95-107.

A machine-readable data base is defined as an organized collection of information in machine-readable form, that is, in a format and medium manipulated by computers. The information may be natural language text, numeric data, or bibliographic data. The rapid increase in the number and availability of these data bases in the 1970s affects the acquisitions and loan policies, the staffing and training practices, and the types of services provided by libraries. Following a technical explanation of these data bases, Williams discusses implications for service, including selective dissemination of information, the role of intermediaries who will actually search these data bases for patrons, the training of intermediaries, and the need for resource sharing and networking. (BKS)

XV. Services to Patrons

1048. Blake, Fay, and Edith Perlmutter. "The Rush to User Fees: Alternative Proposals." *Library Journal*, Vol. CII (October 1, 1977), pp. 2005-2008.

Support for publicly funded libraries is being reduced at the same time that new information technologies, such as cable television and on-line searching of machine-readable data bases, make provision of expanded reference services more expensive. In response, many libraries are charging direct fees for service. The authors argue that such fees impose inequities on library users and hamper the efficiency of libraries as educational institutions by limiting them to provision of information resources that are rationed through a pricing mechanism. They encourage librarians to lobby politically for increased public funding, arguing that the whole society will benefit from continued development of knowledge "which we must assume expanded access to information makes possible." (BKS)

1049. Dervin, Brenda. "Useful Theory for Librarianship: Communication Not Information." *Drexel Library Quarterly*, Vol. XIII (July 1977), pp. 16-32.

This article examines library services and activities concerned with information and information delivery to clients. Because each user is unique, there is no all-serving reference strategy. Rather, librarians must identify and practice alternative communications strategies. Library research should focus more on questions related to interactive services and how library services and resources can be made more beneficial, through improved communication, for the user and the potential user. (CMG)

1050. Hock, Randolph E. "Providing Access to Externally Available Bibliographic Data Bases in an Academic Library." *College and Research Libraries,* Vol. XXXVI (May 1975), pp. 208-215.

The ready availability of externally processed bibliographic data bases has made it possible for an academic library to provide computerized searches on a large number of data bases with a very small initial investment and utilizing its own personnel. The experience of the University of Pennsylvania Libraries has confirmed, contends the author, that such an approach is indeed feasible. This article discusses the approach, questions and problems encountered, and the factors considered in their resolution. Also discussed are the role of the data services librarian, the costs incurred, and some observations about the philosophy of the approach. (RHW)

1051. McElderry, Stanley. "Readers and Resources: Public Services in Academic and Research Libraries, 1876-1976." *College and Research Libraries,* Vol. XXXVII (September 1976), pp. 408-420.

Expansion of the curriculum, the steady increase in enrollments, particularly at the graduate level, changes in instructional methods, and emphasis on research profoundly influenced academic library development during the past century. The initial response to these new responsibilities was an emphasis on collection development and the development of bibliographic tools. In the late 1930s and early 1940s, the increasing information about reader behavior began to affect service policies and procedures. Academic librarians were more successful in developing congenial study environments than in discovering appropriate service patterns. (RHW)

1052. Neill, Samuel Desmond. "The Contact Factor." *Canadian Library Journal,* Vol. XXX (January-February 1973), pp. 48-54.

Neill accuses librarians of being too passive and impersonal in their relations with library users. The proper role of the librarian is to communicate with users about the ideas in works in the collection and their relationship to the user's questions. Communication requires personal contact, dialog with the user about his/her question, human feedback, and attention to individuals. This model for librarianship is contrasted to the information-science model that seeks to deliver information to patrons in standardized ways, minimizing insofar as possible subjective, individually unique interpretations of index terms and questions. (BKS)

1053. Rothstein, Samuel. "Reference Service: The New Dimension in Librarianship." *College and Research Libraries,* Vol. XXII (January 1961), pp. 11-18.

Traditionally the role of the librarian has been that of custodian, collector, and cataloger. The provision of direct services to readers in the United States and some other parts of the world is a fairly recent phenomenon; it is by no means an inevitable part of the library order. Rothstein identifies three kinds of reference work: instruction in the use of books and libraries; guidance in the choice of books; and information service, whereby the librarian supplies the information itself and not just the books in which that information may be found. He also finds three levels of reference service, which he labels "minimum, middling, and maximum," to describe the lengths to which the reference librarian will go to provide the desired information. (RHW)

1054. Rothstein, Samuel. *The Development of Reference Services through Academic Traditions, Public Library Practice, and Special Librarianship.* Chicago Association of College and Reference Libraries, 1955.

Rothstein traces the development of reference services in American research libraries from the 1850s to the 1950s and records the transformation of occasional and casual courtesy into a complex and highly specialized service of steadily increasing scope and importance. He notes that reference service is almost a peculiarly American development. It is not merely the product of a simple and logical unfolding of tendencies inherent in the very structure of research libraries everywhere, but the result of a collocation of particular historical factors distinctive to the American library scene. (RHW)

1055. Rowe, Judith S., and Mary Ryan. "Library Service from Numerical Data Bases: The 1970 Census as a Paradigm." *College and Research Libraries,* Vol. XXXV (January 1974), pp. 7-15.

This article discusses some of the problems of introducing machine-readable data bases into the library service environment. The authors, a social scientist at a computer center and a government documents librarian, describe the diverse approaches used in making tapes of the *1970 Census of Population and Housing* available to users through the library. (RHW)

1056. Schiller, Anita. "Reference Service: Instruction or Information." *Library Quarterly,* Vol. XXXV (January 1965), pp. 52-60.

This article is concerned with two antithetical principles underlying the provision of reference service in libraries—one aiming to show the patron how to go about finding the sources of information, the other aiming to provide him or her with the desired information. These principles are antithetical because in the latter case direct information is offered freely, and in the former it frequently is not. The real future of library reference service lies in the direct provision of comprehensive and accurate information to satisfy user demands; instructing the user in the techniques of information searching is an important, but secondary, goal and is not necessarily a reference function. (RHW)

1057. Smith, Eldred R., Connie R. Dunlap, Anne Grodzins Lipow, and Thomas J. Michalak. "Library Services to the Graduate Community." *College and Research Libraries,* Vol. XXXVII (May 1976), pp. 246-265.

In this product of a symposium at an American Library Association convention, three university librarians bring to the topic a wealth of experience and insights. Dunlap discusses the unique problems and special needs of graduate students, and she describes how the graduate library at the University of Michigan attempts to provide specialized programs to meet their needs. Lipow describes how services offered at Berkeley are evaluated in terms of their relevance to graduate students. Michalak details how the program of information service provided at the Indiana University Library relies upon direct contact between the user and the subject-specialist librarian. In his introduction, Smith cautions that the articles are not necessarily intended as models for other institutions to follow. Rather, they indicate ways that have been found or are being found to meet a basic issue that confronts all university librarians. (RHW)

XVI. Library Use

1058. "A Reference Encounter." *Library Journal,* Vol. XC (April 15, 1965), pp. 1818-1824.

This taped discussion features two prominent library educators, interviewed at a library conference by editors of *Library Journal*. Wallace J. Bonk of the University of Michigan and Thomas J. Galvin of Simmons College, and since president of the American Library Association, expound their very different views about educating students in reference services and also about the proper character of library reference service itself. (RHW)

1059. Kent, Allen, Jacob Cohen, K. Leon Montgomery, James G. Williams, Stephen Bulick, Roger R. Flynn, William N. Sabor, and Una Mansfield. *Use of Library Materials: The University of Pittsburgh Study*. New York: Marcel Dekker, 1979.

This study, which has received a great deal of attention in library circles, was undertaken in order to determine the extent to which library patrons use library materials and also the costs of that use. Findings corroborated the already well-established point that a small fraction of a library's collection accounts for the major portion of its circulation. They also indicated that, at least for the University of Pittsburgh library during a seven-year period, forty percent of the books added in the first year of the study had not circulated by the end of the seventh year.

In-house use was also examined and found by the investigators to parallel external use. In an era of shrinking resources for higher education, the Kent study seemed to many librarians to raise some basic questions about collection building in university libraries. (RHW)

1060. Madden, Michael. *Lifestyles of Library Users and Nonusers.* Occasional Papers No. 137. Urbana, Ill.: University of Illinois Graduate School of Library Science, February 1979.

Using data collected in 1973 as part of a national study of household lifestyles, Madden investigated attributes of persons that relate positively and negatively to use of libraries. In addition to studying use in relation to demographic variables such as age, sex, and income, Madden looks at types of activities in which respondents were engaged and their attitudes on social and economic issues. (BKS)

1061. "Pittsburgh University Studies of Collection Usage: A Symposium." *Journal of Academic Librarianship,* Vol. V (May 1979), pp. 60-70.

Seven critics and supporters of the Kent study (see no. *1059*), including Professor Kent, discuss the study and the issues they believe it raises or fails to raise. (RHW)

1062. Trueswell, Richard W. "User Circulation Satisfaction vs. Size of Holdings at Three Academic Libraries." *College and Research Libraries,* Vol. XXX (May 1969), pp. 204-213, and (July 1969), p. 361.

Among the most influential research on library circulation and its implications has been the work of Trueswell. This article, written when the author was head of the department of industrial engineering in the University of Massachusetts, reports an effort to determine certain facts concerning the relation of circulation satisfaction to collection size, in which the author sampled the "last circulation date" of stack books and of circulation books in three considerably different kinds of academic libraries. The experience of these three libraries proved to be surprisingly similar. Trueswell speculates concerning potential uses to which such data might be profitably applied; for identifying those books requiring mutiple copies; for predicting conversion work loads for changes in classification systems or circulation systems; in studies of high-use and low-use books; for stack thinning; and as a guide in the selection of titles for new libraries. (RHW)

XVII. Educating Library Users

1063. Clark, Virginia. "Teaching Students to Use the Library: Whose Responsibility?" *College and Research Libraries,* Vol. XXI (September 1960), pp. 369-372, 402.

In a relatively early article addressing the issue summarized in her title, Clark concludes that it is the faculty's responsibility. Drawing heavily on Harvie Branscomb's study, *Teaching with Books*, she emphasizes that student library habits result from faculty requirements. Consequently, in addition to providing both personal and printed guidance to patrons who present themselves for library assistance, librarians should systematically inform faculty about what the library has to offer their particular courses. Not only are there fewer faculty than students, but the evidence also indicates that this is the only way to reach the student body as a whole. Moreover, there are already enough "volunteer" library users to keep the faculty and librarians too busy to worry about the others. (RHW)

1064. Kennedy, James R., Jr. "Integrated Library Instruction." *Library Journal*, Vol. VC (April 15, 1970), pp. 1450-1453.

For several years, Earlham College in Richmond, Indiana, has been widely recognized for its programs of bibliographic instruction. In this article, a reference librarian at Earlham provides a detailed description of the program. Kennedy observes that "the greatest benefit of an effective program of library instruction is that it can bring the library into its rightful position as an essential element in a college education." (RHW)

1065. Lubans, John, Jr., ed. *Educating the Library User*. New York: Bowker, 1974.

This is an embarkation point for those wishing to gain an introduction to the scope of bibliographic instruction. Thirty-nine chapters are arranged under broad headings like "Rationale," "Faculty Involvement," and "Implementation and Evaluation of Programs." (RHW)

1066. Marshall, A. P., ed. "Current Library Use Instruction." *Library Trends*, Vol. XXIX (Summer 1980).

This compilation of articles describes the state of the art in various aspects of bibliographic instruction. The topics covered include: historical perspective, current trends, research strategies, preparation in library schools, and evaluation. (RHW)

1067. Werking, Richard Hume. *The Library and the College*. Document #ED 127917. Appleton, Wis.: Educational Resources Information Center, 1976.

The author describes and analyzes the development of three well-known programs for educating students about library use: Louis Shores's "Library College" movement during the 1960s; Patricia Knapp's experiment at Montieth College of Wayne State University in the late 1950s; and Evan Farber's work at Earlham College since the early 1960s. (RHW)

XVIII. Historical Research in Libraries

1068. Bogue, Allan G. "The Historian and Social Science Data Archives in the United States." *Library Trends*, Vol. XXV (April 1977), pp. 847-866.

During the last thirty-five years or so, social scientists have recognized the desirability of converting quantitative research data into machine-readable form and making it widely available to other researchers. In this article the historian Allan Bogue describes the work of various data archives, especially the Inter-university Consortium for Political and Social Research, and how historians have increasingly worked with these centers and their data. He also urges greater attention to computer capabilities for historical research. (RHW)

1069. Clarke, Jack A. "Popular Culture in Libraries." *College and Research Libraries*, Vol. XXXIV (May 1973), pp. 215-218.

The study and teaching of popular culture is one of the most rapidly developing disciplines on American university campuses. Pop-culture scholars require a wide range of subliterary materials, including dime novels, comic books, phonograph recordings, and even three-dimensional objects. No single library can hope to acquire and organize for use more than a fraction of the primary sources of popular culture. Interinstitutional cooperation in identifying and preserving these fragile records of American culture is underway, but many unsolved problems remain for librarians and scholars. (RHW)

1070. McFeely, William S. "The Civility of Scholars." *College and Research Libraries*, Vol. XXXV (July 1974), pp. 286-290.

The author makes a case for open access to historians of the files in the editorial offices of the projects for the publication of the papers of major historical figures. Historians should lend support to the research activities in the libraries on their campuses and in the public archives. They should follow the lead of research librarians and help in the collection of documents for the letterpress projects. When it comes to using the product of this searching once it is in the files of "The Collected Works of . . . " civility is the key to the question of access. In sum, historians, research librarians, archivists, and editors can sit down and work out ways to work so that each can get his work done. (RHW)

1071. Rundell, Walter, Jr. "Relations between Historical Researchers and Custodians of Source Materials." *College and Research Libraries*, Vol. XXIX (November 1968), pp. 466-476.

Rundell, then professor of history in the University of Oklahoma, reports a survey dealing with various problems encountered by history scholars while doing research. Among them are lack of accommodations for visiting researchers, use of microforms, intramural friction between librarians and history professors, and admission policies of private libraries. The survey found that researchers generally enjoy good relations with librarians. By identifying areas where friction remains and where relations can be improved, the article aims at constructive criticism. Rundell concludes: "While relationships between custodians and researchers are predominantly satisfactory, both parties can take steps to improve them. Historians and librarians on university campuses can recognize each other's needs and work to meet them. And both historians and custodians involved in extramural research should realize that problems always seem heightened to travelers. Nonetheless, the problems are real, and custodians should operate on the premise that their basic function is to serve scholarship, not impede it.'' (RHW)

1072. Simon, John Y. "Editorial Projects as Derivative Archives." *College and Research Libraries,* Vol. XXXV (July 1974), pp. 291-294.

A paper delivered at the same American Library Association conference as McFeely's (see no. *1070*), Simon's piece serves as a rebuttal to it. The author discusses the difficulties inherent in such open access, most notably the restriction placed upon photocopies supplied to the editorial project by many other libraries, "which would be most distressed to find them in wider use." As the editor of the multivolume *Papers of Ulysses S. Grant,* Simon examines the policy that his organization adopted as it attempted to provide the greatest aid to all other scholars in the field without harming the project itself. (RHW)

XIX. Library History

1073. Bach, Harry. "The Snows of Yesteryear." *College and Research Libraries,* Vol. XXX (July 1969), pp. 301-306.

Based on information found in institutional histories, this paper calls attention to rules, regulations, and general conditions prevailing in American academic libraries of the late eighteenth and nineteenth centuries and attempts to examine these rules, regulations, and general conditions in terms of how they affected students, faculty, and librarians. Some examples: At Brown University in 1783, freshmen were not allowed to use the library. As late as 1853, students at the City College of New York had to fill out a detailed form and have it countersigned by at least three faculty members. At the University of Wisconsin in 1871, the library was open only from 2:00 to 2:30 p.m. on Monday, Tuesday, Thursday, and Friday, with gentlemen only allowed on two of the days and ladies only on the other two. Bach concludes: "Librarians . . . may be rightly proud of how far they have come in so little time. Yet, somehow the question must occur whether or not in their present glory they may be as blind to the ludicrous aspects of some of their policies and procedures, rules and regulations as colleagues of the last century were to theirs." (RHW)

1074. Bestor, Arthur E., Jr. "The Transformation of American Scholarship, 1875-1917." *Library Quarterly,* Vol. XXIII (July 1953), pp. 164-179.

Bestor analyzes the framework of organized scholarly activity in the United States and how it got that way. Both the scholar and the scholarly library have undergone great transformation, "swept along in an intellectual revolution greater than either." (RHW)

1075. Casey, Marion. "Charles McCarthy's 'Idea': A Library to Change Government." *Library Quarterly,* Vol. XLIV (January 1974), pp. 29-41.

A powerful force in Wisconsin progressivism early in the twentieth century was the Legislative Reference Library, brain child of the historian-librarian Charles McCarthy. From its inception in 1901 until his death in 1921, his unique library in the Madison capitol furnished legislators with up-to-date syntheses of thought on current topics and also drew up requested bills in uniform fashion in the "bill factory" division. McCarthy's "idea" was to have efficient government result from the expertise channeled through his library. His brainchild was imitated in many states, in municipal centers, and in other countries. In 1914 the reference library for congressmen established at the Library of Congress was formed on the Wisconsin model. (RHW)

1076. Clarke, Jack A. "Gabriel Naudé and the Foundation of the Scholarly Library." *Library Quarterly,* Vol. XXXIX (October 1969), pp. 331-343.

Personal librarian to Cardinals Richelieu and Mazarin, Naudé has been remembered by history chiefly as a pioneering librarian. He wrote the first treatise on library economy that consistently treated libraries as "instruments for the dissemination of scholarship rather than as the playthings of rich men." Keenly alive to the needs of scholars, he won much praise for the readiness with which he placed his knowledge at their disposal. He believed that libraries should be opened to men of all classes, not just the friends of rich men, and the books should be loaned without restrictions to those who needed them. (RHW)

1077. Dain, Phyllis. "Ambivalence and Paradox: The Social Bonds of the Public Library." *Library Journal,* Vol. C (February 1, 1975), pp. 261-266.

Dain writes in response to Harris's revisionist view of public library history (see no. *1081*), which sees public library development as a means used by the governing classes to preserve social order in a time of change, rather than as a movement toward popular democracy. Dain argues the past is more complex, that the motives of librarians and library supporters must be seen in a richer cultural context. She argues, for example, that simply because library founders and trustees tended to be from elite classes does not imply that ordinary people could not and did not want to use libraries. She lists a number of research questions in public library history that remain unanswered: What were the socioeconomic traits of librarians? What were the viable alternatives to the tax-supported, free public library? Did the lower classes use libraries? How did libraries allocate resources? Dain claims that research on such issues is required before public library history can be evaluated fairly. (BKS)

1078. Davis, Donald G., Jr. "Problems in the Life of a University Librarian: Thomas James, 1600-1620." *College and Research Libraries*, Vol. XXXI (January 1970), pp. 43-49.

The founder of the reconstituted library at Oxford University, Sir Thomas

Bodley (1545-1613), has enjoyed the praise of historians and librarians. The achievements of his librarian, Thomas James (1573-1629), have been less celebrated but are possibly equal in importance to those of Bodley. Evidences of the conflict between these two personalities reveal differences in objectives and approaches to librarianship. After examining four episodes at Oxford between 1600 and 1620, the author concludes that James represented a progressive position in academic library services. (RHW)

1079. Dictionary of American Library Biography. Littleton, Colo.: Libraries Unlimited, 1978.

This reference work contains biographies of more than three hundred American librarians deceased before 1976. The format and length of entries are similar to entries in the *Dictionary of American Biography.* For each biographical essay there is a bibliography, and all essays are signed. Contributors include professional librarians and faculty of library schools. (BKS)

1080. Goldschmidt, Eva. "Archibald MacLeish, Librarian of Congress." *College and Research Libraries,* Vol. XXX (January 1969), pp. 12-24.

When Archibald MacLeish became librarian of Congress in 1939, the library profession objected to the appointment of an untrained librarian. Yet, within five short years MacLeish infused new life and spirit into the library. He introduced modern fiscal and administrative concepts, arranged for systematic surveys of the collections, defined goals and priorities for acquisitions and services, and initiated progressive personnel policies. But his most enduring contribution to American librarianship is his dynamic philosophy and his insistence that librarians be not mere keepers of books but active participants in the education of the people in the values of their democratic heritage and the defense of intellectual freedom. (RHW)

1081. Harris, Michael H. "The Purpose of the American Public Library in Historical Perspective: A Revisionist Interpretation." ED 071 668; LI 004 063. Washington: ERIC Clearinghouse on Library and Information Sciences, 1972.

Harris claims that librarians have mistakenly described their antecedents by believing in "the myth of public library origins" in the mid-nineteenth century. The elements of that myth are that humanitarian, liberal reformers began the public library movement because they believed in human perfectibility, saw books as a means to that end, and so sought to make books available to the common man through libraries. Harris uses study of the thought of the founders of public libraries to argue that the purpose of the public library was to control the average man by helping him to learn and accept the social doctrines of the controlling classes. Library directors and library boards use libraries for social control rather than to promote intellectual growth. Libraries are not democratic and humanitarian, but are an elitist tool. (BKS)

1082. Harris, Neil. "Cultural Institutions and American Modernization." *Journal of Library History,* Vol. XVI (Winter 1981), pp. 28-47.

This article discusses changing cultural institutions in late nineteenth- and early twentieth-century America and how scholars have perceived the roles of these institutions. It uses libraries to demonstrate the patterns of thought, action, and reaction during this period of "modernization" in the United States. (CMG)

1083. Hilgert, Earle. "Calvin Ellis Stowe: Pioneer Librarian of the Old West." *Library Quarterly,* Vol. L (July 1980), pp. 324-351.

Calvin E. Stowe, professor and librarian at Lane Seminary in Cincinnati from 1833 to 1850, was chiefly responsible for the development there of what apparently was the largest academic library in the West. Stowe's contributions extended not only to collection building but also to a heightened sense of the importance of student use of library resources. This article, based largely on manuscript materials, identifies factors that contributed to Stowe's understanding of librarianship, traces the development of the Lane library, and seeks to evaluate his contributions. (RHW)

1084. Holley, Edward G. "Academic Libraries in 1876." *College and Research Libraries,* Vol. XXXVII (January 1976), pp. 15-47.

Academic libraries in 1876 were small but expanding. They were not yet a significant part of the educational process but were striving toward that goal. Housed often in inadequate quarters, their library reading rooms and stacks would grow increasingly crowded before relief came in the form of massive, if not quite handsome, buildings. Within these buildings a faculty member served as part-time librarian, frequently with some student assistance and occasionally with a full-time assistant librarian. Since their primary duties did not involve librarianship but classwork in several disciplines, the libraries probably received less attention than they needed, but the evidence clearly indicates that students and faculty also often received better service than they deserved. The advance guard of the full-time librarians shared the general optimism of the age, and they expected libraries to become a vital part of college experience. If they were often confused about the place of the library in the curriculum, their confusion was no more unnatural than that of their parent institutions, which often were confused about their role and mission. This heavily illustrated article also contains several tables of useful statistics of higher education and academic libraries in 1876. (RHW)

1085. Jackson, Sidney L. "Bodley and the Bodleian: Collections, Use, and Administration." *Library Quarterly,* Vol. XXXIX (July 1969), pp. 253-270.

The outset of the seventeenth century was marked in library history by the rebirth of the noted library tradition at Oxford University. Thomas Bodley's four prerequisites (1609) for founding a library were: knowledge of ancient and modern languages and "sundry other sorts of scholastic Literature"; "Purse-ability"; "Honorable Friends"; and time. (RHW)

1086. Otness, Harold M. "Baedeker's One-Star American Libraries." *Journal of Library History*, Vol. XII (Summer 1977), pp. 224-234.

Otness summarizes comments on American libraries in the first (1903) and fourth (1909) editions of Baedeker's *The United States, with an Excursion into Mexico: A Handbook for Travelers*, written by James F. Muirhead. The guide-books cited more big-city public libraries as institutions worth visiting than any other type of library, commenting favorably on these libraries' architecture, large collections, public and philanthropic support, and public access. The guidebooks provide a European perspective on American librarianship. (RHW)

XX. Cooperative Efforts and Networks

1087. DeGennaro, Richard. "Austerity, Technology, and Resource Sharing: Research Libraries Face the Future." *Library Journal*, Vol. C (May 15, 1975), pp. 917-923.

Research libraries must abandon the goal of self-sufficiency in materials and the notion that library quality is measured by size and the growth rate. A more realistic goal is designing selective acquisitions policies that will meet the actual needs of particular libraries and their users. To make that goal politically and practically feasible, research libraries need to lobby for a national library re-sources center, to which libraries could go directly for needed materials; the hierarchical access model used in most existing American library networks does not work well because in practice libraries go directly to the largest library in the network. For its support, the national center requires a computer-based national bibliographical and communications system. (BKS)

1088. Gore, Daniel. "The View from the Tower of Babel." *Library Journal*, Vol. C (September 15, 1975), pp. 1599-1605.

Academic libraries face a dilemma: they have more books than they can shelve, yet they are unable to deliver books they do have to patrons who want them. Gore reviews studies showing that substantial portions of collections are unused, yet their maintenance drains resources needed for the titles in demand. The solution proposed is establishment of a national cooperative warehouse for little-used titles, from which any library could borrow. (BKS)

1089. Information for the 1980's: Final Report of the White House Conference on Library and Information Services, 1979. Washington: Government Printing Office, 1980.

The report includes proceedings of the conference, transcripts of open hearings and the joint congressional hearing, conference resolutions, and outlines for proposed legislation. The conference proposed a National Library and Information Services Program that calls for substantial increases in national support for libraries through such steps as creation of the position of "Assistant Secretary for Library and Information Services" in the Department of Education; a strengthened role for the Library of Congress as a national library; federal support for resource-sharing systems; and increased assistance to community library services, state libraries, and educational programs for library and information services. (BKS)

1090. Kaser, David Edwin. "Toward a Conceptual Foundation for a National Information Policy." *Wilson Library Bulletin*, Vol. CII (March 1978), pp. 545-549.

Kaser asserts that "full actualization of democracy" depends upon adequate access to information. Rejecting the notion that information can be viewed as a commodity in the marketplace, he asserts the proposition that *"all information must be available to all people in all formats* purveyed through *all communication channels* and delivered at *all levels of comprehension."* Consequently, a unit of the federal government must implement and administer a national information program; federal funds should be appropriated for libraries; the responsibilities to library service of federal, state, and local governments should be clarified; a national information program should be built that will be compatible with other nations' programs; laws concerning confidential information should be clarified; and equal access to information resources should be guaranteed by legislation. (BKS)

1091. Markuson, Barbara Evans. "Cooperation and Library Network Development." *College and Research Libraries,* Vol. XL (March 1979), pp. 125-135.

Networks function as change agents for libraries because they provide three critical services—research and development, capital acquisition, and technology-transfer mechanisms. Areas in which network participation has an impact on the academic library include the management of change, economic and attitudinal change, and cost accountability. Because of their early successes, networks have given rise to increased expectations for solutions to many critical library problems and for the equally rapid development of a national library network. (RHW)

1092. Palmour, Vernon E., Marcia C. Bellassai, and Nancy K. Roderer. *Resources and Bibliographic Support for a Nationwide Library Program: Final Report to the National Commission for Libraries and Information Science.* Washington: Government Printing Office, 1974.

This report considers the role of resource centers and bibliographic centers as components of a national network of libraries and information services. The report contains extensive data on the current bibliographic systems and systems for resource sharing. The study makes a set of recommendations that have become the basis of discussion and policy development in the creation of a national library network. (BKS)

1093. Sager, Donald J. "A National Periodicals Center: Too Limited a Goal." *American Libraries,* Vol. X (September 1979), pp. 465-466.

The call for a national periodicals center (NPC), which has wide support among librarians, is criticized because such a center would not solve the problems libraries face. The NPC would be a federally funded national repository for complete runs of periodicals. Sager argues that librarians should seek funding for a national information utility that would serve a larger clientele. The NPC proposal is criticized because it would serve only a small scholarly elite; most libraries have little demand for periodicals backfiles but need more subscriptions to multiple copies of current periodicals; if the NPC permitted libraries to cancel their own subscriptions to periodicals, publishers would respond by raising prices; an NPC would undermine local and regional networks; and an NPC might serve as a model to centralized collection of other types of materials, tempting legislators to cut local network funding. (BKS)

1094. *Towards a National Program for Library and Information Services: Goals for Action.* Washington: National Commission on Libraries and Information Science, 1975.

The NCLIS program document states goals for national information service. The statement has been a source of controversy in the profession since preliminary drafts first appeared in 1974. The document is often cited in support of federal aid to libraries, as in the program suggested by the 1979 White House Conference on Library and Information Services (see no. *1089*). The broad goal stated is the creation of a national network that will provide to every individual "equal opportunity of access to that part of the total information resource which will satisfy the individual's educational, working, cultural, and leisure-time needs and interests, regardless of the individual's location, social or physical conditions, or level of intellectual achievement." (BKS)

1095. Trezza, Alphonse F. "The NCLIS View—a Full Service Network." *Journal of Library Automation,* Vol. X (June 1977), pp. 170-176.

Trezza, then executive director of the National Commission on Libraries and Information Science, describes the Commission's view of the nature and services of a national information network. The National Library and Information Service Network envisioned by NCLIS would provide a full range of information services to all individuals and corporate units. The network would rationalize the pattern of services of information suppliers and the procedures of information seekers. The network would utilize all means of communication, from mail, delivery truck, and teletype to cable, satellite, computer, and videodisc. The role of NCLIS is to provide access to information, wherever located and in whatever form. A full-service network would, through integrated and cooperative activity, encompass all of the services that lead to the provision of information to those who seek it. Trezza describes NCLIS projects leading toward that goal. (BKS)

1096. Weber, David C. "A Century of Cooperative Programs among Academic Libraries." *College and Research Libraries,* Vol. XXXVII (May 1975), pp. 205-221.

A review of cooperative programs among colleges and universities over the last century leads to the conclusion that a few very significant developments and changes have taken place during the previous decade after ninety years of laborious and diverse effort toward cooperative programs dominated by the effects of national policy and economic conditions. The first part of the article chronologically presents selected examples of cooperative programs. The latter section includes details on a few programs of current special significance, comments on some strengths and weaknesses, and arrives at a few conclusions: American academic libraries have reached a watershed that is almost as significant as the change from block printing to printing with movable type. This conclusion is based on the presumption that on-line computer-based operational programs constitute a radical and permanent change in cooperative style. When one is freed from most of the constraints of the card catalog, of the U.S. mail, and of locally prepared cataloging data, this adoption of sophisticated on-line computer-based programs "may well be by far the most significant change ever achieved in library operations. It is a permanent change in the mode of library operations which should be accomplished during the period 1965 to 1990." (RHW)

XXI. Research on Libraries

1097. Bookstein, Abraham. "Models for Shelf Reading." *Library Quarterly,* Vol. XLIII (April 1973), pp. 126-137.

Though unshelved books are a problem in every library, little systematic effort has been made to design an optimal solution. The author presents a mathematical model, which seeks to minimize user frustration consistent with restrictions on the number of hours available for shelf reading. Resulting from this model is a schedule on which each section of the collection is assigned its own shelf-reading frequency. The method is to find a point where the cost of reading shelves is balanced by the costs resulting from misshelved books. (RHW)

1098. Bookstein, Abraham, and Don R. Swanson, eds. "Operations Research: Implications for Libraries: Proceedings of the Thirty-fifth Annual Conference of the Graduate Library School." *Library Quarterly,* Vol. XLII (January 1972).

Library operations in recent times have been characterized by a great increase in complexity. In this setting, managerial decision making in the library has become an unenviably difficult task. It is reasonable to ask whether techniques such as operations research that have proved valuable in similar situations for business and government might not also be of service in libraries. Recently, a number of operations researchers have turned their attention to library and information systems and have produced significant research. The purpose of the conference was to introduce the library audience to some of these accomplishments. (RHW)

1099. Morse, Philip M., and Ching-chih Chen. "Using Circulation Desk Data to Obtain Unbiased Estimates of Book Use." *Library Quarterly*, Vol. XLV (April 1975), pp. 179-194.

Data on book circulation can be obtained most easily from the books cards left at the circulation desk when books are withdrawn or returned. But these data by themselves are biased with respect to the library collection as a whole, being more representative of the high-circulation books and completely unrepresentative of the books that did not happen to circulate within the time interval of data gathering. This paper shows how simple probability theory can serve to remove this bias so that estimates of total yearly circulation and circulation distribution for each book class, and predictions of future circulation, can be calculated from the biased circulation desk data. (RHW)

1100. Shearer, Kenneth. "The Impact of Research on Librarianship." *Journal of Education for Librarianship*, Vol. XX (Fall 1979), pp. 114-128.

The article examines the impact of two research publications on the knowledge base of librarianship, as ascertained by citation counts, and on the practice of librarianship in real libraries. More evidence is found of impact of research on the former than the latter. Librarianship fails in two basic ways: it often fails to teach the ramifications of sound research in library education, and it fails to implement carefully researched recommendations. (BKS)

XXII. The Library Profession

1101. Butler, Pierce. "Librarianship as a Profession." *Library Quarterly*, Vol. XXI (October 1951), pp. 235-247.

Butler describes American librarians' self-conscious concern with recognition as professionals and agrees that librarianship ought to be a profession. He chastises librarians, however, for trying to assert their professionalism merely by adopting the trappings of other professions: professional schools, a professional association, certification procedures, and obeisance to scientism. A true profession, he argues, is one in which a science, a technology, and a humanistic study of motivation are integrated by their relevance to a cultural activity. Librarianship is a profession only in the degree that library scholarship achieves that organic completion. (BKS)

1102. Ellsworth, Ralph E. "Critique of Library Associations in America." *Library Quarterly*, Vol. XXXI (October 1961), pp. 382-395; and David H. Clift, "Discussion." Ibid., pp. 395-400.

The relationship between a practicing professional and a national association is not always easy to understand, nor does it remain constant from decade to decade, nor can it be divorced from the factor of size, nor can it escape the consequences of the impact of personalities or specific events. To illustrate these points, Ellsworth draws upon his thirty years of experience with the American Library Association (ALA), including a couple of stints as president of its academic arm, the Association of College and Research Libraries. He concludes that the ALA "can only become more complex and more bureaucratic and further removed from reality if it is allowed to go on as is. Radical surgery is called for. . . . Much of the sound and fury which is mistakenly thought of as the American Library Association would dry up and never be heard from again, because it is nothing more than the clanking of the machinery of the association." David H. Clift, executive director of the ALA, provides a rejoinder. (RHW)

1103. Elman, Stanley A. "The Humanization of Information Science." *Special Libraries,* Vol. LXIX (September 1976), pp. 421-427.

This article reviews the conflict between the emerging discipline of information science and traditional librarianship. Definitions of information science are reviewed, and criticisms of its paradigm are summarized. Information scientists are characterized as concerned with the manipulation of information by machines while librarians are described as those who deal with the human aspects of information and those who seek it. Elman proposes several types of dialog to help humanize information science and prevent the dehumanization of libraries. (BKS)

1104. Emery, Richard. "Philosophy, Purpose, and Function in Librarianship." *Library Association Record,* Vol. LXXIII (July 1971), pp. 127-129.

Emery argues that there can be no basic philosophy of librarianship because librarianship is a secondary activity, concerned with utilization rather than creation of human resources. Those who talk about "a philosophy of librarianship" are confused; they are really talking about purpose, sets of professional ideals and guides for conduct, or function. Failure to distinguish between purpose and function indicates lack of clarity in theoretical discussions of librarianship. This confusion interferes with precise formulation of library goals and their implementation by means of realistic functional activities. The purpose of libraries is to assist in best utilization of existing resources and development of individuals. Libraries' function is a set of activities by which purposes are fulfilled. (BKS)

1105. Newmyer, Jody. "The Image Problem of the Librarian: Femininity and Social Control." *Journal of Library History,* Vol. XI (January 1976), pp. 44-67.

Newmyer investigates the origins, maintenance, and reality of the image of the librarian as dependent, conservative, nonintellectual, and feminine. Librarianship was one of the few occupations open to women in the nineteenth century, and by 1910 women occupied most positions in library work. The mission of the library as guardian of culture corresponded to the popular conception of the role of women. In the first half of the twentieth century, libraries had two goals, efficiency and humanitarianism, both of which were perceived in American culture as best pursued by women. Research on librarians since the 1950s using personality profile tests have supported the notion that librarians are feminine, but Newmyer argues that these tests themselves use sexist definitions of masculinity and femininity. (BKS)

XXIII. Educating and Training Librarians

1106. Boaz, Martha. "The Future of Library and Information Science Education." *Journal of Education for Librarianship,* Vol. XVIII (Spring 1978), pp. 315-323.

A Delphi survey of a sample of members of the Association of American Library Schools conducted in 1977 elicited educators' opinions about the events of the next twenty years that most likely will influence libraries and library education. Respondents were asked to characterize the list of events in the final Delphi round in terms of both probability of occurrence and desirability of occurrence. The three most likely events, which were also described as desirable by most respondents, were: the development of a network of communication links encompassing a variety of types of private and public institutions, development of central data storage facilities with wide public access, and devotion of an increased share of the nation's resources to the production and distribution of information. Implications of findings of the study for library education are discussed. (BKS)

1107. Boll, John J. "Basis for Library Education." *Library Quarterly,* Vol. XLII (April 1972), pp. 195-211.

This article describes the pressures that beset library education at the present time and the five commonly considered, but apparently irreconcilable, views regarding suitable solutions to these pressures. It suggests that optimum solutions can be reached only by a coordinated, nationwide, factual study of professional trends and needs, that is, by a taxonomy of librarianship's educational objectives, which takes into account the immediate as well as the more distant future. (RHW)

1108. Galvin, Thomas J. "The Profession's Response to a Crisis-based Society." *Journal of Education for Librarianship,* Vol. XVIII (Spring 1978), pp. 269-277.

Galvin examines implications of rapid social change for libraries and library education. As information becomes a more prized resource and as communications technology changes the ways information is transferred, libraries will receive less public support and may see their traditional role taken on by other institutions. Galvin encourages librarians to lobby for a national information policy, to align themselves with business and education, and to use technology to shift from a materials-centered mode of operation to a client-centered mode. Library schools should train people for high-level positions in a variety of information professions rather than continuing to produce vocationally trained, entry-level librarians. (BKS)

1109. Hughes, Everett C. "Education for a Profession." *Library Quarterly,* Vol. XXXI (October 1961), pp. 336-343.

In law, medicine, and nursing, the students invariably want the teaching done in a shorter perspective than the teachers. They want to know something specific and immediately practical. If one were to leave it to the vote of the people entering an occupation, they would vote for less general education and more vocational training. What kinds of general knowledge—human knowledge, scientific knowledge—and wisdom are essential for the profession are difficult to ascertain. But it does seem that if library educators are not in a continual state of strain with their students over this point, they are probably not doing their job very well. (RHW)

1110. "Papers Presented at a Workshop on the Integrated Core Curriculum." *Journal of Education for Librarianship,* Vol. XIX (Fall 1978), pp. 151-173.

Here are five papers presented at a workshop of the University of North Carolina in 1977. Two papers make arguments in favor of a core set of courses that provides both the common knowledge all students should acquire and the foundation upon which other courses can build. Three papers describe library schools' experiences with a core curriculum. (BKS)

1111. White, Herbert S. "The Library Education Accreditation Process: A Retreat from Insistence on Excellence." *Library Journal,* Vol. CV (November 15, 1980), pp. 2377-2382.

White, dean of the Library School at Indiana University, roundly condemns the process by which library schools are accredited and reaccredited by the American Library Association. He argues that the accreditation process does not work in denying accreditation or reaccreditation to programs which do not meet minimum standards for library education, and that schools can probably gain accreditation ultimately through a process of attrition and exhaustion. (RHW)

1112. Wilson, Pauline. "Impending Change in Library Education: Implications for Planning." *Journal of Education for Librarianship*, Vol. XVIII (Winter 1978), pp. 159-174.

Three factors, says Wilson, indicate that education for librarianship is at a turning point: the reduced market for new librarians, the dissatisfaction with library schools expressed by workers in the field of information science, and the widespread dissatisfaction with the American Library Association as a suitable accrediting agency for library schools. She proposes that library education's goals for the future ought to be production of professionals with managerial skills and skills in use of new electronic information technologies, more exacting admissions and performance requirements, and expansion of the knowledge base of librarianship. Some ways library schools might implement these goals are suggested. (BKS)

XXIV. The Library and Society

1113. Boorstin, Daniel J. "Knowledge and Information." *Texas Libraries*, Vol. LVI (Winter 1979), pp. 147-151.

The historian Daniel Boorstin, who is Librarian of Congress, observes that against humankind's growing appetite for keeping informed with the latest developments by obtaining facts and figures, libraries move dangerously close to tragic neglect. The cumulative body of knowledge represented by libraries is being obscured by the more glamorous, though random and miscellaneous, information industry. Consequently, a precarious imbalance is in the offing. A citizenry must be knowledgable as well as informed, and it must be realized that knowledge is a product that is acquired by each individual—not a service that is provided by others. Libraries and librarians are challenged with providing a variety of resources and services for their users. The implementation of computer technology and the inclusion of information services are necessary and valuable if the "main and proper mission of our libraries" is not forgotten. Library collections and services are more important than ever for perspective, pleasure, and knowledge. (CMG)

1114. Busha, Charles H. "Intellectual Freedom and Censorship: The Climate of Opinion in Mid-western Public Libraries." *Library Quarterly*, Vol. XLII (July 1972), pp. 283-301.

An attempt to quantify the attitudes of more than 3,200 public librarians toward intellectual freedom, censorship, and certain antidemocratic ideas is reported in this article. It was found that sixty-four percent of these public librarians were neither highly favorable nor unfavorable toward censorship practices. (RHW)

1115. Castagna, Edwin. "Censorship, Intellectual Freedom, and Libraries." In Melvin J. Voigt, ed. *Advances in Librarianship*, Vol. II. New York: Seminar Press, 1971.

Following a brief summary of Western philosophers' statements concerning censorship and intellectual freedom, Castagna recounts trends in American librarians' attitudes towards censorship. The profession's official concern with censorship and intellectual freedom is traced from the adoption of the library Bill of Rights by the American Library Association (ALA) in 1939. ALA organizations such as the Committee on Intellectual Freedom, the Office for Intellectual Freedom, and the Freedom to Read Foundation are described. (BKS)

1116. Clapp, Verner W. "The Copyright Dilemma: A Librarian's View." *Library Quarterly,* Vol. XXXVIII (October 1968), pp. 352-387.

Where his own official activities are concerned, a librarian must now increasingly view copyright as a form of exterior control that threatens serious limitations of his library's freedom to put its collections to work in the service of its users. These threatened limitations include those prompted by technological developments, most notably photocopying, as well as by a natural desire to take advantage of a source of profit. The options among which librarians fear that they may have to choose in response to such limitations are: (a) to abandon completely the affected services; (b) to dispense with the use of modern technology and to revert to archaic and inefficient methods for providing such services; or (c) to pay in burdensome and discriminatory fees and red tape in order to be permitted to use the more effective methods. Out of this situation arises the "copyright dilemma." Is it possible to write a law that will reconcile the claims of copyright proprietors with the needs of the public to make use of the copyrighted materials which have been acquired in the public's name and for its benefit by libraries? If not, how is the conflict to be resolved? (RHW)

1117. Curley, Arthur. "Information from the People to the People." *American Libraries,* Vol. X (June 1979), pp. 316-320.

Curley describes the 1969 annual meeting of the American Library Association as a watershed event in which young activitists within the profession initiated a shift in public librarians' views of the social responsibility of libraries. In the following decade, the focal point in definition of public library service and determination of service objectives shifted from maintenance of collections to services to people. The primary example of the shift in emphasis is the development of "information and referral services" in which libraries work cooperatively with other community agencies to gather and distribute information about public services available, job information, crisis hotlines, and so on. Information is no longer perceived as information in traditional publications but any information necessary for "life-support needs of all people in a complex multicultural society." Since 1969, says Curley, libraries have begun to see themselves as both participants and agents in social change. (BKS)

1118. Flanagan, Leo N. "Defending the Indefensible: The Literature of Intellectual Freedom." *Library Journal*, Vol. C (October 15, 1975), pp. 1887-1891.

Flanagan reviews the *Intellectual Freedom Manual* published by the Office for Intellectual Freedom of the American Library Association (ALA) in 1974, which comprises forty years of ALA papers on intellectual freedom, including the library Bill of Rights and the Freedom to Read statement. While Flanagan finds many of the papers useful contributions to discussion of the subject, he attacks the introduction, which he finds representative of much current thought in librarianship, as manifesting impracticality, oversimplification, legal difficulties, anti-intellectualism, and want of professionalism. (BKS)

XXV. Important Series, Journals, and Indexes

1119. Advances in Librarianship. New York: Academic, 1970-.

Volumes in this annual contain from six to twelve review articles on major issues in librarianship. The review articles include both analysis of issues and discussion of major relevant research and publications. Contents of volumes vary from year to year. (BKS)

1120. ALA Yearbook: A Review of Library Events. Chicago: American Library Association, 1976-.

Volumes in this annual series comprise feature articles addressing major issues of concern to professional librarians; reviews of major events of the past year related to particular libraries, agencies, or topics affecting librarians; and state-by-state reports on library activities. The series serves as a periodic review of the state of the profession. (BKS)

1121. American Libraries. Chicago: American Library Association, 1907-.

The official journal of the American Library Assocation covers the wide range of libraries and library issues in a newsy style designed to appeal to a heterogeneous membership. (RHW)

1122. American Library Directory. New York: Bowker, 1908-.

The *Directory*, published biennially from 1908 to 1978, has been updated annually since 1978. It contains a listing of public, academic, and special libraries in the United States and Canada, using for each entry data supplied by the library described. Entries include the name and address of the library, names of administrative staff, quantitative data on library holdings, and titles of special subject collections. (BKS)

1123. Annual Review of Information Science and Technology. White Plains, N.Y.: American Society for Information Science, 1966-.

The purpose of the series is "to describe and appraise activities and trends in the field of information science and technology." Bibliographic review essays are organized under four general headings in each volume: planning information systems and services, basic techniques and tools, applications, and the profession. The number and topics of chapters under these broad headings vary from volume to volume. The reviews are excellent general introductions to the literature of specific subjects. The series is particularly useful for current information on information technology, information services that complement traditional libraries, and national and international information policy. (BKS)

1124. Berman, Sanford. "Alternative Library Lit." In William Katz, ed. *Library Lit. 9—The Best of 1978.* Metuchen, N.J.: Scarecrow, 1979.

This is an annotated list of bibliographies, newsletters, magazines, bulletins, and directories devoted to social change and reform in library practices. The compilation also features guides to materials relating to such issues as racism, sexism, and censorship. (BKS)

1125. Bowker Annual of Library and Book Trade Information. New York: Bowker, 1955/56.

The *Bowker Annual,* sponsored by the Council of National Library and Information Associations, Inc., is librarianship's almanac. It contains summaries of developments in librarianship, including activities of federal agencies and professional associations; reports on legislation and funding; data on library education, placement, and salaries; research statistics on libraries and the book trade; bibliographies; and a directory of library and book trade organizations from the state to the international levels. (BKS)

1126. College and Research Libraries. Chicago: Assocation of College and Research Libraries, 1939-.

This is the official journal of the Association of College and Research Libraries, a division of the American Library Association. (RHW)

1127. Journal of Academic Librarianship. Ann Arbor, Mich.: Mountainside, 1975-.

Independent of any association, this journal uses a magazine format. (RHW)

1128. Journal of Library History, Philosophy, and Comparative Librarianship. Austin, Tex.: University of Texas Press, 1966-.

The scope of this quarterly is broad, covering library history without geographic or period limitations. Each issue contains major articles, research notes, and a useful book review section. A biennial review essay (annual until 1978) on the literature of American library history gives a useful summary of issues and accomplishments in the field. (BKS)

1129. Lee, Joel M. "Library Periodicals in Review." *Serials Review,* Vol. V (July-September 1979), pp. 7-49.

This article provides in-depth descriptions of journals briefly described in this section, and other important titles as well. The author is headquarters librarian at the American Library Association. (RHW)

1130. Library Journal. New York: Bowker, 1876-.

This is a magazine full of news and commentary, and a self-styled iconoclast. Together with *American Libraries,* it provides an overall view of library developments in the United States. (RHW)

1131. Library Lit. Metuchen, N.J.: Scarecrow, 1970-.

Library Lit. is an annual anthology of approximately thirty articles per year selected by the editor and a panel of judges comprised of librarians, publishers, and library educators. The aim of the series is to present articles that "reflect the best in current thinking about libraries and related matters." Each volume contains sections on libraries and librarians, technical services, readers' services, communication and education, and "the social prerogative." Articles selected are more often essays and opinion pieces than research reports. The series is representative of positions on current issues in librarianship. (BKS)

1132. Library Literature. New York: Wilson, 1921-.

This is the most basic author and subject index to materials about librarianship and information science. In addition to periodical articles, its coverage includes books, pamphlets, research papers, and other formats. (RHW)

1133. Library Quarterly. Chicago: University of Chicago Press, 1931-.

For over half a century this has been a publication of the Graduate Library School. (RHW)

1134. Library Resources and Technical Services. Chicago: Resources and Technical Services Division, American Library Association, 1957-.

The official journal of the Resources and Technical Services Division, American Library Association, deals chiefly with articles about such topics as cataloging, acquisitions, collection development, and serials. (RHW)

1135. Resources in Education. Washington: National Institute of Education, 1966-.

RIE is a monthly abstract journal announcing recent report literature related to the field of education. It is sponsored by the Educational Resources Information Center (ERIC), National Institute of Education. Studies of libraries and library-related topics frequently are published as ERIC documents, available both in microfiche and typescript, and accessed by means of *RIE*. (RHW)

1136. RQ. Chicago: Reference and Adult Services Division, American Library Association, 1960-.

The official journal of the Reference and Adult Services Division, American Library Association, deals chiefly with various aspects of user services. (RHW)

1137. Special Libraries. Special Libraries Association, 1910-.

Articles in this monthly are usually directed to particular concerns of practicing special librarians. The journal is of interest to a wider audience because articles often treat issues related to information technology that pertain to libraries of all types. Problems in building and maintaining collections of special types of materials are discussed also. (BKS)

1138. School Library Journal. New York: Bowker, 1954-.

This magazine is devoted to working with children and teenagers in libraries. (RHW)

1139. Wilson Library Bulletin. New York: Wilson, 1914-.

This monthly *Bulletin* has the format of a news magazine and is useful as a source of information on current publications and events in librarianship. Each issue also contains opinion and research articles. The *Bulletin* is aimed at a broad audience, thus providing a general view of the nature of the profession. (BKS)

CHAPTER 9

MEDIA AND HISTORY

Gerald H. Herman, editor

During most of the twentieth century, film and electronic media have thoroughly permeated almost every aspect of our lives. Most information comes via radio and television, and critics warn that literacy may be declining in consequence. Up until 1970, historians largely ignored this development in favor of more traditional modes of activity. Historians occasionally worked as advisors on film or electronically transmitted projects and even created some of them for secondary school use, but they rarely executed their own historically valid projects. Such endeavors required comparatively large resources; they also required a cooperative approach that is alien to the individual training of most scholars. At the same time, training limitations and the slipshod nature of many commercial documentaries convinced historians that little was to be gained from studying film or other nonprint materials as useful scholarly sources. In consequence the historical film/electronic media business flourished largely without historians. Commercial producers and distributors with varying degrees of sensitivity, antiquarians, "buffs," and purveyors of nostalgia provided leadership.

Since 1970, a growing number of historians, both abroad and in the United States, have become interested in the range of source materials and dissemination mechanisms such nonprint media can provide. This chapter offers a bibliographic introduction to this rapidly expanding, even explosive, field. The chapter is organized into two basic parts. The first one, sections I-IV, comprises a selected list of sources—largely bibliographical—useful to historians in the three ways such media are used by them: as archival materials, as production materials and mechanisms, and as programming subjects for audiences. The second part, sections V-XI, explores each of the major types of media, giving sources that describe their usefulness to historians in general and providing examples of their successful employment. It concludes with a look at future technological possibilities, although not specifically through the eyes of the historian.

The reader should bear several things in mind when referring to this chapter.

First, two basic sources should be consulted as one begins to read about any of these subjects. In the archives, productions, and "uses" sections, the Society of American Archivists' *Modern Archives and Manuscripts* (edited by Frank B. Evans) cited in section I below is recommended. In the production, audience attraction, and "uses" section, the various indices of the National Information Center for Educational Media cited in section I should be checked as appropriate.

Secondly, because history in the media is a diverse and rapidly developing field, formal texts and guides have not yet appeared for some subjects. For these subjects, the only information exchanges yet available are the networks and organizations that practitioners themselves have formed, especially in the archival area. A sampling of such organizations is included. The film/tape distribution business is subject to such rapid turnover that reference directories often have trouble keeping abreast of developments. The catalogs of distributors, although not always to be counted on for dispassionate evaluations of the materials, are often the only reliable source of information available at any given time. Such catalogs are not listed in this bibliography. It is well worth the small charge for some catalogs to have a few major ones available for easy reference. Also valuable for their unusually specific subject indices are the catalogs of the Library of Congress, published in quarterly, annual, and quinquennial compilations. A selection of media journals that specialize in historical approaches has been cited throughout the bibliography, and these should be consulted for expert evaluations. It should be remembered, however, that a wide variety of nonspecialized journals, magazines, and newspapers also review historical films, and these may be accessed through the *Reader's Guide to Periodical Literature* under "Moving Picture Plays" at the time of release, or in the various indices for specific newspapers.

I. General Guides to Nonprint Media

1140. Allen, Nancy. *Film Study Collections: A Guide to Their Development and Use*. New York: Frederick Unger, 1979.

This book gives general advice on the development and assessing of such collections and presents a guide to the major American collections. (GHH)

1141. American Association for State and Local History. *History News* Technical Leaflets series.

The Technical Leaflets series, begun in *History News* in 1962, provides brief, practical suggestions and guides on specific issues or techniques for public historians. Among the nearly 150 titles available, the following are of particular interest: (GHH)

"Tape Recording Local History" (no. 35)
"Filing Our Photographs: Some Basic Procedures" (36)
"Producing the Slide Show for Your Historical Society" (42)

"Cataloging Photographs: A Procedure for Small Museums" (57)
"Photographing Historical Collections: Equipment, Methods, and Bibliography" (63)
"Data Retrieval without a Computer" (85)
"Organizing Your 2 x 2 Slides: A Storage and Retrieval System" (88)
"Photographing Tombstones: Equipment and Techniques" (92)
"Microfilming Historical Records: An Introduction" (96)
"Old Movies: A Source of Local History Programs" (100)
"The Evaluation of Historical Photographs: Local History Perspective by Paul Vanderbilt" (120)
"Archival Preservation of Motion Pictures: A Summary of Current Findings" (126)
"Copying Historical Photographs: Equipment and Methods" (139)

1142. Bowser, Eileen, and John Kuiper. *A Handbook for Film Archives.* Brussels: Fédération Internationale des Archives du Film, 1981.

This is the only source book that details the film archival process, including acquisitions and criteria for selection, preservation techniques, cataloging documentation, and related technological aspects. (FCS)

1143. Davies, Brenda, ed. *International Directory of Film and TV Documentation Sources.* 2d ed. Brussels: Fédération Internationale des Archives du Film, 1980.

This directory presents a list, by country, of the most important archives in these fields and a brief description of the major holdings of each. It also contains an "Index to Special Collections," listing notable individuals and organizations and where collections relating to them may be found. (FSC)

Evans, Frank B. *Modern Archives and Manuscripts: A Select Bibliography.* See no. *568.*

This basic reference book lists the essential pre-1975 sources; it should be consulted as a starting point for each of the categories listed in this chapter. Of special relevance are the following chapters: 16, "Still Pictures and Other Pictoral Records and Archives"; 17, "Motion Pictures and Film Records and Archives"; 18, "Sound Records and Archives"; 19, "Machine Readable Records and Archives"; and 20, "Microphotography and Other Copying Methods." In addition to the archival functions of cataloging, preservation, storage, and accessing such materials, each chapter is broken down into such categories as basic readings, value and use, select reference works, and bibliographic aids. Books and articles describing major collections are also cited. (GHH)

1144. Pickett, Andrew G., and Meyer M. Lemcoe. *Preservation and Storage of Sound Recordings.* Washington: Library of Congress, 1959.

Although this report was written twenty-three years ago, the information on problems and needs of sound-recording preservation is quite current. (FCS)

1145. Poe, William. "Preservation of Research Sources: Film and Videotape." *Humanities Report* (October 1981), pp. 13-17.

Poe identifies major film and television archives in the United States and reviews the current problems facing the moving of large archive collections. (FCS)

1146. Poe, William. "Preservation of Research Sources: Sound Recordings." *Humanities Report*, Vol. IV (May 1982), pp. 4-8.

This brief article contains a survey of some of the major sound archives and of the state of preservation technology. A boxed section at the end gives the reader a directory of the leading American archivists in this field. (GHH)

1147. "Report of Education and Standards Committee on Acquisition Standards for Sound Recordings, Unique Materials to Be Preserved, Making Recordings Available for Use." *ARSC Journal*, Vol. I, no. 213 (1968).

This is one of the few articles discussing archival process for sound recordings. The title fully describes its contents. ARSC stands for the Association for Recorded Sound Collections. (FCS)

1148. Schreibman, Fay. "Searching for Television's History: A Step by Step Approach in Locating Past Television Programs." In James Fletcher and Joseph Domineck, eds. *Broadcasting Research Methods: A Reader*. Boston: Allyn and Bacon, forthcoming.

Because there is no publication for television similar to the Bowser and Kuiper *Handbook* for film (see no. *1142*), this article serves as a procedural format on locating past television programs, reviews all the literature that assists in identifying programs, and describes all major television collections throughout the United States. Fletcher has also written *Handbook of Radio and Television Broadcasting: Research Procedures in Audience, Program, and Review*. New York: Van Nostrand-Reinhold, 1981. (FCS)

II. Guides to Preservation, Cataloging, Copyright, and Availability of Nonprint Media

1149. FIAF Cataloging Commission. *Film Cataloging*. New York: Burt Franklin, 1979.

This manual on the cataloging of films for archives compares several systems used around the world. FIAF stands for Fédération Internationale des Archives du Film (see no. *1308*).

1150. Gartenberg, Jon. *Film Cataloguing Manual: A Computer System*. New York: Museum of Modern Art, 1981.

The Museum's assistant curator presents a guide to the computer-based cataloging system now in use. It describes the entry rules and display categories of the system, describes its history, and provides an evaluation of its strengths and weaknesses. (GHH)

1151. Guidelines for Off-Air Taping of Copyrighted Programs for Education Use: Thirty Questions Librarians Ask. Chicago: American Library Association, 1982.

This publication discusses the responsibility a library takes on when taping programs off the air. It includes the fair-use guidelines approved by Congress. (FSC)

1152. Hart, William M. *The Fair Use of Televised News Broadcasts: A Guide to the Copyright Act for Patrons of Television News Archives*. Washington: George Washington University, forthcoming.

Hart provides a detailed accounting of the fair-use implications within the Copyright Revision Act of 1976 regarding the use of television news broadcasts and other such material for educational and other nonprofit purposes. It is geared for the scholar and researcher in use of the materials as well as for the librarian and archivist who collects the programs. Examples of the major lawsuits and decisions are cited to assist in defining fair uses in this most complicated subject area. (FCS)

1153. Laurence, John Shelton, and Bernard Timberg, eds. *Fair Use and Free Inquiry: Copyright Law and the New Media*. Norwood, N.J.: Ablex, 1980.

At this writing, the authors provide the only book that concentrates on the newly revised copyright law in terms of access to mass media. They discuss the implications of the law for archival collections. (FCS)

1154. McWilliams, Jerry. *The Preservation and Restoration of Sound Recordings*. Nashville: American Association for State and Local History, 1979.

This manual describes the means of preserving the variety of sound recordings, which includes disc, cylinder, wire, and audiotape media. It contains directories of manufacturers, suppliers, and sound archives in North America, and also a bibliography. (FCS)

1155. Rules for Archival Cataloguing of Sound Recordings. Manassas, Va.: Associated Audio Archives-ARSC, 1980.

This work adopts and expands Anglo-American Cataloging Rules 2 (AACR2) explicitly for archival collections of sound recordings. (FCS)

1156. Sargent, Ralph N. *Preserving the Moving Image*. Washington: Corporation for Public Broadcasting, 1974.

Sargent updates and expands the information found in *Film Preservation* (see no. *1158*) and includes information on the preservation of videotape. (UNESCO plans to combine all the moving-image preservation information into one publication for worldwide distribution.) (FCS)

1157. Utterback, W. H., Jr. "The Suitland, Maryland, Nitrate Film Fire: An Opinion." *Journal of the University Film Association* (Summer 1980).

This article recounts the cautionary tale of the National Archive storage vault fire in December 1978 that destroyed 12.5 million feet of nitrate film and forty thousand feet of safety film. Utterback gives an opinion of the reasons for the fire. A summary version appears in *Film and History*, Vol. X (September 1980), pp. 55-60. (GHH)

1158. Volkmann, Herbert, ed. *Film Preservation*. Brussels: Fédération Internationale des Archives du Film, 1965.

This basic technical manual, used for black-and-white and nitrate film preservation, was developed by the FIAF Preservation Commission. (FSC)

1159. Volkmann, Herbert, ed. *The Preservation and Restoration of Colour and Sound in Films*. Brussels: Fédération Internationale des Archives du Film, 1978.

A companion volume to Volkmann's *Film Preservation* (see no. *1158*), this book concentrates on the development and techniques of archiving color film. It also includes a discussion of preserving kinescopes or "television films" as so identified in the work. (FCS)

Weinstein, Robert A., and Larry Booth. *Collection, Use, and Care of Historical Photographs*. See no. *456*.

This practical guide to the maintenance of photographic resources also contains resource lists and a bibliography. (GHH)

1160. Weston, Murray. "Videotape Handling and Storage Guidelines." British Universities Film Council Ltd. *Newsletter*, no. 43 (May 1981), pp. 15-16.

Weston offers a brief overview of the storage requirements for videotapes. (GHH)

1161. Wheeler, Jim. "The Long Term Storage of Video Tape." *SMPTE Journal* (Society of Motion Picture and Television Engineers), forthcoming.

Wheeler's article is the only technical document based on scientific testing that offers recommendations for the proper handling and storage for videotape. It contains a technical bibliography. (FCS)

III. Production of Nonprint Media

1162. American Film Institute, Educational Services Program. *Profiles*, 202 North Western Avenue, Los Angeles, California 90027 (available in photocopy).

The Educational Services Program of the AFI has published Institutional Profiles of numerous organizations. Among them are: "Anthology Film Archives"; "Walt Disney Archives"; "Vanderbilt Television New Archives"; "The Library of Congress Motion Picture, Broadcasting, and Recorded Sound Division"; "Museum of Modern Art"; "Rocky Mountain Film Center"; "George Eastman House"; "The Museum of Broadcasting"; "The Academy of Motion Picture Arts and Sciences"; "Wisconsin Center for Film and Theater Research"; "U.C.L.A. Theater Arts Library"; "U.C.L.A. Film, Television, and Radio Archives"; "Educational Film Library Association"; "Center for Southern Folklore"; "Pacific Film Archive"; "The National Center of Jewish Film"; and "National Federation of Local Cable Programmers."

The same unit publishes another series entitled *Factfile*. It contains such titles as: *Film and Television Periodicals in English; Women and Film/Television; Independent Film and Video; Film/Television Research Guide; Film/Television: Grants, Scholarships, Special Programs.* (GHH)

1163. *Audio Visual Market Place: A Multi Media Guide*. New York, Bowker, annual.

This advertisement list of production resources also includes a reference section on awards, funding sources, and bibliographies. A state-of-the-art preface is also often included. (GHH)

1164. Baddeley, W. Hugh. *The Techniques of Documentary Film Production*. 3d rev. ed. London: Focal, 1975; New York: Hastings House, 1975.

This is part of a comprehensive series in volumes in the Focal Press/Hastings House Library of Communication Techniques. Each volume in the series introduces a particular technique—such as film animation, film editing, film music, make-up, the motion picture camera, special effects, television production—in a step-by-step manner and presents the practical problems and solutions that are likely to come up as production goes forward. This volume contains chapters on script preparation, budgeting, gathering resources, equipment, shooting in a studio and on location, at home and abroad, sound recording, artwork and animation, postproduction editing, duplication, and distribution. It constitutes a general introduction to the field of documentary production. (GHH)

1165. British Universities Film Council. *Researcher's Guide to British Film and Television Collections*. London: BUFC, 1981.

In addition to an annotated and comprehensive guide to British film and television archives, the *Researcher's Guide* also contains chapters on the process of film research, on methods used by historians for research on films and for a

Thames Television series, and on applicable British copyright law. It includes a bibliography of books, periodicals, parliamentary acts, government and other relevant reports and surveys, and organizations and festivals. (GHH)

1166. CBS News. "Making a Documentary." (1973).

Using a CBS television documentary by Luigi Barzini on the Catholic Church, this film shows, step by step, how a news and public affairs documentary is made. (GHH)

1167. Costner, Tom. *Motion Picture Market Place.* Boston: Little, Brown, annual.

This book is described as "the directory of United States production, professional talent, services and equipment for theatrical and television film." (GHH)

1168. Dean, Jeff. *Architectural Photography: Techniques for Architects, Preservationists, Historians, Photographers, and Urban Planners.* Nashville: American Association for State and Local History, 1981.

This is a basic manual for making architectural photographs with a 35-mm single-lens-reflex camera. Its chapters include directions on perspective control, equipment, formating composition, compensating for interior and exterior settings, developing the results, and "special considerations." (GHH)

1169. Eastman Kodak Corporation. *Your Programs from Kodak.* 1981.

This is a catalog of print materials, slide shows, and film available from Kodak to aid in improving photographic techniques. Kodak also publishes technical leaflets on virtually every aspect of photography and projection. (GHH)

1170. Gardner, Joel. "Equipment Review." *International Journal of Oral History,* Vol. II (June 1981), pp. 139-142.

Oral historians have been reluctant to incorporate the visual media in their work, but the quality and quantity of video equipment now available defies them to ignore it. The basic components of a video system are described and specific models are assessed in terms of performance and cost. The maintenance of a video archive is covered, including duplication, cassettes, discs, and hardware. (PMH)

1171. Haney, John B., and Eldon Ullmer. *Educational Communications and Technology: An Introduction for Teachers.* Dubuque, Ia.: Willliam C. Brown, 1975.

Designed primarily for teachers, this book presents brief, illustrated, and simple descriptions of the various audiovisual media available for the display of historical and other information. It is an introduction for the novice in the field. (GHH)

1172. International Film Bureau, Inc. *Facts about Film.* 3d edition. (1975).

This collection of short films, available either in 16 mm or on video cassettes, provides an audiovisual introduction to the field of film making. The titles are *A Film about Filmmaking, Making a Sound Film, A Film about Editing*, and *A Film about Cinematography.* (GHH)

1173. Josephson, Larry, et al. *Making Radio: News and Public Affairs.* Forthcoming.

Experienced radio "hands," mostly from National Public Radio's (NPR) "All Things Considered" but also from other NPR divisions and programs, from CBS, independents, and the Pacifica Foundation, present articles on radio production for public radio stations. Its chapters include: "Planning Stories and Interviews"; "The Art of the Interview"; "Editing"; "Writing News for Radio"; "Feature Writing"; "Putting It All Together"; "Field Recording"; "Studio Production"; "Funding, Distributing, and Marketing"; and "Legal Concepts." (GHH)

1174. Lee, Robert, and Robert Misiorowski. *Script Models: A Handbook for the Media Writer.* New York: Hastings House, 1978.

The authors/compilers present general information about the demands of writing for filmstrips, multimedia, radio, television, and theatrical and nontheatrical motion pictures. Each section contains notes, a sample of an actual script, and other useful information and development hints. A final section presents "Writers' Aids" about such matters as storyboards, timing tips, copyrights, and a bibliography. (GHH)

1175. Leff, Leonard J. "I Hear America Typing." *Quarterly Review of Film Studies*, Vol. VI (Summer 1981), pp. 279-294.

This review covers eight of the script-writing manuals now available. (GHH)

1176. Legge, Nancy E., comp. *Access.* Los Angeles: American Film Institute Educational Services, 1978.

"Developed under a contract from the Media Arts Program of the National Endowment for the Arts, *Access* is a comprehensive review of publicly available film and video equipment facilities in the United States." It "includes extensive listings of where to find production and post-production equipment. The facilities described range from small community centers to large media complexes offering extensive resources for training, equipment access and distribution." (GHH)

1177. McDarrah, Fred W., ed. *Stock Photo and Assignment Source Book.* New York: Bowker, 1977.

Subtitled "Where to find photographs instantly," this guide lists some four thousand names, addresses, and telephone numbers of those holding collections of still photos available for use by historians and others producing media. It is divided into twenty-seven sections by topic. Of special interest is the section entitled "Historical Sources," subdivided into institutions and societies in the United States and abroad, and historic sites at home and abroad. The guide also lists reference sources, researchers and consultants, photographic associations, and film libraries. A technical section at the end deals with such matters as copyright and releases. McDarrah is also the editor of Bowker's *Photography Marketplace*, a basic reference tool for accessing equipment, raw materials, reference works, skilled personnel, educational resources, exhibition space, review and other specialized periodicals, and funding sources in this field. (GHH)

1178. Mehr, Linda Harris. *Motion Pictures, Television, and Radio: A Union Catalogue of Manuscripts and Special Collections in the Western United States.* New York: Hall, 1977.

This guide, sponsored by the Film and Television Study Center, Inc., presents an annotated directory of the resources available in the western United States. (GHH)

1179. Mercer, John. *Glossary of Film Terms*. Carbondale, Ill.: University Film Association, 1978.

This spiral-bound volume of ninety-six pages is UFA monograph #2. It provides a basic set of film definitions. (GHH)

1180. North American Film and Video Directory: A Guide to Media Collections and Services. New York: Bowker, 1976.

This annotated guide to film and video resources in the United States and Canada was compiled in cooperation with the AV/Public Library Association of the American Library Association, the Film Library Information Council, and the Educational Film Library Association. Some 1,300 institutions are listed, along with their major collections, facilities, equipment, and policies. (GHH)

1181. Pyramid Films. *Basic Film Terms: A Visual Dictionary*. This film illustrates the basic vocabulary of motion picture photography and the steps involved in film production. (GHH)

1182. Rose, Ernest D. *World Film and Television Study Resources: A Reference Guide to Major Training Centers and Archives*. Bonn-Bad Godesberg, German Federal Republic: Friedrich Ebert Stiftung, 1978.

The guide, available from the University Film Association, provides an annotated listing of programs, holdings, and activities in these fields (GHH)

1183. Rowan, Bonnie G. *Film and Video Collections*. Scholars' Guide to Washington, D.C. Washington: Smithsonian Institution Press, 1980.

The sixth in a series of scholars' guides to scholarly resources in the nation's capital, this volume provides access to visual media repositories. Entries are arranged alphabetically by name of organization and are designated a collection, referral service, or academic program. Information provided includes name of organization, address, telephone, hours open for research, staff contact, eligibility for use, description of the collection, referral aids, policies for access, and notes on related materials. Extensive appendices provide data on related organizations and a bibliography. Six indexes offer access by organization; name of collection; foreign productions; production date, type, and content. The series is under the editorship of Zdeněk V. David for the Woodrow Wilson International Center for Scholars. (PMH)

1184. Schoenherr, Steven E. *Multimedia and History: A Guide to Slide-Tape Production and Technique.* Newark, Del.: University of Delaware, History Media Center, 1973.

This work is a step-by-step production guide developed for students in the media and history program at the University of Delaware. It contains detailed and illustrated instructions on all aspects of slide-tape production, including advice on topic selection, research sources, costs, and other matters. (GHH)

1185. Sietsema, Robert. *Hart Picture Archives.* New York: Hart, 1978.

The several volumes in this series contain pictures "of many periods culled from 64 known sources subdivided into 22 categories in the public domain, and may be used for any purpose without fee or permission." (GHH)

1186. Strong, William S. *The Copyright Book: A Practical Guide.* Cambridge, Mass.: M.I.T. Press, 1981.

This guide to the 1976 Copyright Law contains chapters on infringement and fair use, noncommercial broadcast use, and programs and database protection. It is a complement to the *General Guide to the Copyright Act of 1976*, published by the Copyright Office of the Library of Congress in September 1977. (GHH)

IV. Programming of Historically Valid Presentations

1187. *Americana Film Institute Catalog: Feature Films, 1921-1930.* 2 vols. New York: Bowker, 1979. *American Film Institute Catalog: Feature Films, 1961-1970.* 2 vols. New York: Bowker, 1976.

Both of these two-volume sets on feature films provide detailed subject indexes to films of these two decades. Volume I contains the listings and descriptions of films made in the identified years by title; volume II contains credit and subject indexes. A pair of volumes on the 1911-1920 period is being prepared. (JEO/FCS)

1188. "American Labor Films." *Film Library Quarterly*, Vol. XII, no. 2/3 (1979).

The articles in this combined issue deal with the depiction of work and workers in American film and the manner in which films have been used to regulate the workplace by labor, by management, and by the government. It contains 250 entries and twenty illustrations, forty individual film reviews, and five essay-reviews. (GHH)

1189. Blackaby, Linda, Dan Georgakas, and Barbara Margolis. *In Focus: A Guide to Using Films.* New York: Zoetrope, 1980.

This is a basic guide to the "nuts and bolts" of planning a film screening or series. Fourteen chapters offer thoughtful publicity and specific problems such as "what to do when the film breaks." (JEO)

1190. Ferris, Bill, and Judy Peiser, eds. *American Folklore Films and Video-tapes—An Index.* Memphis, Tenn.: Center for Southern Folklore, 1976.

This work includes a detailed subject index to 1,800 titles on social, cultural, and anthropological themes. Among topic areas are "occupational lore" for circus people, farmers, fire fighters, and fishermen. A new volume on material produced since 1976 is forthcoming from R. R. Bowker.(JEO)

1191. Film Evaluation Guide. New York: Educational Film Library Association, 1965.

This basic guide provides capsule evaluations of educational films. There have been two supplements (1965-1967, 1967-1971), and the evaluations are updated bimonthly for libraries. In addition to film descriptions and distribution infor-mation, these guides provide evaluative comments and suggestions for use. (JEO)

1192. Goldstein, Ruth M., and Elizabeth Zarnow. *Movies for Kids: A Guide for Parents and Teachers on the Entertainment Film for Children.* New York: Frederick Unger, 1980.

In addition to distribution information, this guide includes evaluations of 430 features, "featurettes," and documentaries suitable for public programs. There is also a selected bibliography and a list of television and film periodicals. (JEO)

1193. International Film Bureau, Inc. *Facts about Projection.* 3d ed. (1975).

This fourteen-minute film introduces the subject of using and maintaining 16-mm projectors and provides hints for programs under various lighting conditions in various physical environments. (GHH)

1194. International Index to Film Periodicals: An Annotated Guide. Washington: The American Film Institute Archives Publications, annual.

This reference book had been published since 1972 by the International Fed-eration of Film Archives (Brussels). The American Film Institute began distri-bution with the 1979 edition, published in 1981. The index contains eleven major categories: general references; institutions, festivals, and conferences; the film industry—economics, production; distribution and exhibition; cinema and society; film education; aesthetics, theory, and criticism; history of the cinema; individual films; biography; and miscellaneous. Indices by director, article authors, and by subject are also included. The volume indexes articles from film journals worldwide. The 1972 and 1973 volumes were published by St. Martin's and those for 1974 through 1978 by R. R. Bowker. Another periodical, *Film Literature: Current* (Filmdex, Part II, Inc.) began monthly publication in 1979, containing reproductions of the tables of contents of journals that contain articles on film. (GHH)

1195. Klotman, Phillis Rauch. *Frame by Frame: A Black Filmography*. Bloomington, Ind., and London: Indiana University Press, 1979.

This detailed guide to films and sources is indexed by black performers, authors, screenplay writers, producers, and directors. (JEO)

1196. Landers Film Reviews. Escondido, Calif.: Landers Associates, 1956-.

This service has published reviews up to several hundred words in length for educational and informational films as they appear. There are no cumulative issues, but an index is published annually. (JEO)

1197. Landrum, Larry. "Sources for the Study of Popular Film." *Journal of Popular Film and Television*. Part I: "Reference Works," Vol. VII, no. 1 (1978), pp. 108-119; Part II: "History and Analysis," Vol. VII, no. 2 (1979), pp. 222-230; Part III: "Themes and Genres," Vol. VII, no. 3 (1979), pp. 339-350.

These articles provide a bibliographical survey of the field. (GHH)

1198. Limbacher, James L., comp. and ed. *Feature Film on 8mm, 16mm, and Videotape*. 7th ed. New York: Bowker, 1982.

This source for the programmer lists alphabetically the titles of feature-length theatrical films available for lease or rental in film or video in the United States. Information provided for each film includes production company, date of production, length in minutes, whether sound or color, and the names of the director and featured players. A code identifies the distributor who handles each title. Limbacher maintains currency through regular updating and supplements published in *Sightlines* from the Educational Film Library Association. (GHH)

1199. Loy, Jane M. *Latin American Sights and Sounds*. Gainesville, Fla.: Latin American Studies Association, 1973.

This guide to motion pictures and music, intended for those planning college courses, includes both detailed summaries and critical appraisals. (JEO)

1200. Medialog. New York: National Endowment for the Humanities and the Film Fund, 1982.

This catalog lists over three hundred films and radio and television programs produced over the last ten years with NEH funds and available to schools, libraries, museums, and community groups. (GHH)

1201. Media Review Digest. Volume X. Ann Arbor, Mich.: Pierian, 1980.

This work is a guide to reviews of both feature and educational films as well as videotapes, filmstrips, records and sound tapes, and "miscellaneous media." In addition to identifying the issues of publications where reviews can be found, this volume provides digests or quotes from some reviews. (JEO)

1202. Minas, Johnny, and William Storm Hale. *The Film Superlist: 26,000 Pictures in the Public Domain.* 2 vols. Hollywood, Calif.: Seven Arts, 1973.

This annotated list covers movies of all kinds that appear to be free of copyright restrictions. The films were made in the period 1894-1939. A second *Superlist* exists for films produced in the period 1940-1949. (GHH)

1203. Moses, Kathlyn J., and Lois B. Watt. *Aids to Media Selection for Students and Teachers.* Washington: U.S. Department of Education, 1976.

Designed primarily for teachers, the second half of this guide is an annotated bibliography of audiovisual directories, periodicals, and review sources. A special section deals with "sources of multiethnic materials." (GHH)

1204. National Center for Audio Tapes. *Catalog.* Boulder, Colo.: University of Colorado, biennial.

Sponsored by the University of Colorado and the National Association of Broadcasters, the National Center stores, duplicates, and disseminates audiotapes on all manner of educational topics. The *Catalog* lists almost fifteen thousand titles, and provides for each a Library of Congress number, grade level for which use is appropriate, series title, production information, running time, and brief description. (GHH)

1205. National Information Center for Educational Media. *Index to 16mm Educational Films.* 4 vols. 7th ed. Los Angeles: National Information Center for Educational Media (NICEM), University of California, 1980.

The first volume consists of a subject index and directory of producers and distributors. Volumes II, III, and IV include alphabetical listings of films with very brief descriptions. NICEM also publishes the following media indices: *Index to Educational Audio Tapes,* 5th ed., 1980; *Index to Educational Overhead Transparencies,* 6th ed., 1980; *Index to Educational Records,* 5th ed., 1980; *Index to Educational Video Tapes,* 5th ed., 1980; *Index to 8mm Motion Cartridges,* 6th ed., 1980; *Index to 35mm Filmstrips,* 3 vols., 7th ed., 1980; *Index to Educational Slides,* 4th ed., 1980; *Index to Producers and Distributors,* 5th ed., 1980. There are also some specialized indices by field. Though the number of volumes in each varies, their organization is similar. New editions of these indices are generally prepared every two years. In addition, the Center publishes *The NICEM Update of Nonbook Media* on a quarterly basis. (JEO)

1206. Pettit, Arthur G. *Images of the Mexican American in Fiction and Film.* College Station: Texas A & M University, 1980.

This study, published posthumously, supplements George H. Roeder, Jr.'s unpublished "Mexicans in the Movies: The Image of Mexicans in American Films, 1894-1947," and makes at least some of this work more accessible to users. (GHH)

1207. Peyton, Patricia, ed. *Reel Change: A Guide to Social Issue Films.* San Francisco: The Film Fund, 1979.

This filmography and guide to distributors has sections on such social concerns as aging, energy, gay issues, race relations, and urban issues. A separate section lists international cinema classics on political movements, work and labor movements, urban and rural issues, and more. Film descriptions vary in depth and are sometimes evaluative. (JEO)

1208. Reed, Maxine K., ed. *The Video Source Book.* Syosset, N.Y.: National Video Clearing House, 1979-1982.

This index lists alphabetically entertainment, educational, and all other video programs available to home audiences. The listings include an indication of format, title and production information, release date, a subject category, brief content description, intended audience level, awards list, distributor, and availability guide. Other publications, including *The Video Program Index* and *The Video Newsletter*, are available from Clearing House. A telephone hotline, based upon its computerized data base, is also available to subscribers. (GHH)

1209. Samples, Gordon. *How to Locate Reviews of Plays and Films: A Bibliography of Criticism from the Beginning to the Present.* Metuchen, N.J.: Scarecrow, 1976.

This concise work, organized by topic and time period with annotated bibliography, treats plays and films in separate sections. (JEO)

1210. Sullivan, Kaye. *Fims for, by, and about Women.* Metuchen, N.J.: Scarecrow, 1980.

This filmography includes information and educational films as well as selected features, with brief descriptions and distribution information on each. There is a subject index and an index on women film makers. (JEO)

1211. The New York Times Film Reviews, 1913-1968. 6 vols. New York: New York Times, 1970.

This basic collection and the supplements for 1969-1970, 1971-1972, 1973-1974, 1975-1976, and 1977-1978 lack subject indexes, but the production information and critical judgments of the *Times*'s reviewers provide guides in choosing feature films. (JEO)

1212. Thompson, Lawrence, Richard Welch, and Philip Stephens. "A Vietnam Filmography." *Journal of Popular Film and Television*, Vol. IX (Spring 1981), pp. 61-67.

This article provides two filmographies. One lists the sixty or so American films dealing with the Vietnam War; the second lists the films that have Southeast Asia as a backdrop. Two studies of the ways in which the Vietnam War has been dealt with on film also exist. They are Julian Smith's *Looking Away, Hollywood and Vietnam* (New York: Scribner's, 1975); Gilbert Adair, *Vietnam on Film from "The Green Berets" to "Apocalypse Now"* (New York: Proteus/Scribner, 1981). (GHH)

1213. Tippman, Don, comp. *Film Etc.: Historic Preservation and Related Subjects*. Washington: Preservation Press, 1979.

This catalog of 16mm film and videotapes on historic preservation and related subjects was compiled by the National Trust for Historic Preservation (NTHP). The volume lists films from a variety of sources in addition to NTHP productions—museums, universities, construction companies, public television. Entries are arranged by subject categories, such as archaeology, architecture, folklore, and urban planning, and are supplemented by a title index. The title is followed by the date of production, a brief description, length, format, rental fee, name and address of owner. Productions range from public T.V. programs focusing on development issues to interviews of craftsworkers. *Film Etc.* is available free of charge from the NTHP, 1785 Massachusetts Avenue, N.W., Washington, D.C. 20036. (PMH)

1214. Weatherford, Elizabeth. *Native Americans on Film and Video*. New York: The Museum of the American Indian, 1981.

Focusing on documentation and issue-oriented works produced since 1970, this guide also includes ethnographic films and documentary classics. The approximately four hundred films and videotapes surveyed here were all viewed by the staff of the museum's ongoing film and video project. (JEO)

1215. Weaver, Kathleen, ed. *Film Programmer's Guide to 16mm Rentals*. 3d ed. Albany, Calif.: Reel Research, 1980.

Like Limbacher's work (see no. *1198*), this reference lists feature film titles alphabetically. Many popular short films are also included. It lists the cost of rental from various distributors. No such guide can indicate to what extent a less expensive rental may reflect a low quality, an overused, or an otherwise damaged print. (JEO).

V. Radio and Television: Guides, Evaluations, Applications

1216. Breitbart, Eric. "From the Panorama to the Docudrama: Notes on the Visualization of History." *Radical History Review*, no. 25 (October 1981), pp. 115-125.

This article by a radical film maker is part of a special issue called "Presenting the Past: History and the Public." It offers a perspective on the ways in which media use history. (GHH)

1217. Brown, Les. *The New York Times Encyclopedia of Television*. New York: New York Times Books, 1977.

This work contains material on technology, history, regulations, foreign systems, personalities. The entries are cross-indexed, and a bibliography is included. (GHH)

1218. Goodchild, Peter. *J. Robert Oppenheimer, Shatterer of Worlds*. Boston: Houghton Mifflin, 1981.
Kee, Robert. *Ireland: A History*. Boston: Little, Brown, 1980.

Both of these books owe their origins, like many before them, to television series. Goodchild, who had previously produced a television biography of Madame Curie, produced and wrote the BBC/WGBH dramatic reconstruction *Oppenheimer*, with Sam Watterson in the title part. The series appeared on the Public Broadcasting System "American Playhouse" during the 1981-1982 television season. Kee, the former anchor of the BBC's "Panorama," presented a thirteen-part documentary history of Ireland for the BBC, with dramatic inserts. It appeared on public television in the United States during the 1981-1982 season. Together they illustrate the historical potential of the medium. (GHH)

1219. National Public Radio. "A Question of Place: Sound Portraits of the Twentieth Century." 1980.

This thirteen-part radio series, partly documentary and partly dramatic recreation, examines the work of twelve seminal figures in modern intellectual history in order to uncover our contemporary concept of humanity and our place in the scheme of things. The humanists explored in these one-hour programs are Sigmund Freud, James Joyce, Robert Frost, Igor Stravinsky, Bertrand Russell, Noam Chomsky, Simone de Beauvoir, William Faulkner, Claude Levi Strauss, W. E. B. Du Bois, Bertolt Brecht, and Michael Foucault. The thirteenth hour is devoted to synthesis and summary. (GHH)

1220. O'Connor, John J. "Historical Dramas—Fact or Fancy." *New York Times*, Sunday, May 25, 1975.
"Blowing the Whistle on Dramatic License." *New York Times*, Sunday, October 24, 1976.
"When Dramatic License Leads to Reckless Storytelling." *New York Times*, Sunday, September 25, 1977.

"Playing Fast and Loose with Recent History." *New York Times*, Sunday, October 9, 1977.

These articles from the pen of the *New York Times* television critic exemplify critiques of televised docudramas supposed to be historically accurate. (GHH)

1221. Sane Education Fund. "Shadows of the Nuclear Age." 1980.

This series of thirteen half-hour radio documentaries produced by WGBH, Boston, for the Sane Education Fund and the National Endowment for the Humanities, traces the history of nuclear arms and the threat of nuclear annihilation. The series combines historic sound, historical narrative, and contemporary interviews to present and examine a pressing current issue. (GHH)

1222. Television Factbook. Washington: Television Digest, annual.

Beginning around 1960, this annual publishes information concerning the range of subjects related to television worldwide. The entries are updated by the bimonthly periodical, *Television Digest.* (GHH)

1223. Thames Television. "The World at War, 1939-1945." n.d.

Extensive oral history interviews of participants in World War II were utilized for this television series. Edited excerpts of the interviews were integrated with newsreel footage and narratives to provide an unusual and personal perspective on the war. The collection of interviews was deposited at the Imperial War Museum in London. A catalog of the collection, " 'The World at War, 1939-1945': Thames Television Recorded Interviews," has been published as part of the museum's Department of Sound Records, *Oral History Recordings* series. (GHH)

1224. Wilhoit, Frances Goins. "The Network News as History: Using Television Archives." A paper presented to a joint session of the History Division of the Association for Education in Journalism and the American Historical Association, Washington, D.C., December 29, 1980.

Wilhoit, the head of the Journalism Library at Indiana University, provides an introduction to his subject. (GHH)

1225. WRFG. "Living Atlanta." Atlanta, Ga., 1981.

"Living Atlanta" is a documentary radio series of fifty half-hour programs on life in a segregated southern city between the two world wars. The programs emphasize race relations while covering a wide spectrum of topics, such as entertainment, politics, the Atlanta fire of 1917, strikes, bootlegging, occupational studies, and the etiquette of race relations. Interviews with over two hundred Atlantans are interpreted by narration based on documentary research. Period and topical music provide background. The programs can be grouped topically in subseries or used alone. Cassettes are available from the producer, Harlon Joye, Living Atlanta Project, c/o WRFG, P.O. Box 5332, Atlanta, Georgia 30307. (PMH)

1226. Zito, Stephen. "Out of Africa: Alex Haley's Roots." *American Film*, Vol. II (October 1976), pp. 8-17.
Bruce Cook. "Public Television's Big Splash: The Adams Family Saga." *American Film*, Vol. I (December 1975), pp. 6-13.
These two articles represent accounts of two attempts by television—one commercial network and one public television station—to recreate history. (GHH)

VI. Theatrical Movies: Guides, Evaluations, Applications

1227. Burns, E. Bradford. "Conceptualizing the Use of Film to Study History: A Biblio-Filmography." *Film and History*, Vol. IV (December 1974), pp. 1-11.
Burns offers an introduction and basic source list. (GHH)

1228. "Symposium on the Methodology of Film History." *Cinema Journal*, Vol. XIV (Winter 1974-1975).
This special issue recounts the conference held as part of the Thirtieth Annual Congress of the International Federation of Film Archives. Articles by leading film archivists and historians are supplemented by an appendix on "Reference Works for Film Study." (GHH)

1229. Historians' Film Committee. *Film and History*. Newark, N.J., 1970-.
The quarterly journal *Film and History* has been a focal point for the study of film as a reflection of society's values, as a propaganda/education mechanism for society, and as reconstructer of the historical past. The journal publishes scholarly articles on individual films and genres as well as book and film reviews. (GHH)

1230. International Association for Audio-Visual Media in Historical Research and Education. *Historical Journal of Film, Radio and Television*. Oxford, U.K., 1981-.
This quarterly journal describes itself as "an interdisciplinary journal concerned with the evidence provided by the mass media and with the impact of mass communications on the political and social history of the twentieth century. The needs of those engaged in research and teaching are served by scholarly articles, book reviews, and by archival reports concerned with the availability of records. The journal also reviews films, television, and radio programmes of historical importance." The "IAMHIST" also publishes a quarterly newsletter. (GHH)

1231. O'Connor, John E., ed. *Film and the Humanities*. New York: Rockefeller Foundation, 1977.
This working paper resulted from a Humanities Program Conference held in 1976. It surveys the uses of film in history, literature, philosophy, and anthro-

pology. A bibliographical guide to books, journals, organizations, and other sources is also included. O'Connor is the author of "Historians and Film: Some Problems and Prospects," *History Teacher*, Vol. VI (August 1973), pp. 543-552. (GHH)

1232. O'Connor, John E., and Martin Jackson, eds. *American History/American Film: Interpreting the Hollywood Image*. New York: Frederick Unger, 1977.

This book brings together American film historians who study the ways in which feature-film makers have defined and portrayed portions of America's past. O'Connor and Jackson are the founders of the Historians Film Committee and editors of its journal, *Film and History*. (GHH)

1233. Popular Culture Center, Bowling Green State University. *Journal of Popular Film and Television*, Bowling Green, Ohio, 1971-.

This quarterly journal "is dedicated to popular film and television in the broadcast sense. Concentration is on commercial cinema and television: stars, directors, producers, studios, networks, genres, series, the audience, etc. Articles on film and television theory/criticism appear as well as interviews, filmographies and bibliographies." (GHH)

1234. Roads, Christopher H. *Film and the Historian*. London: Imperial War Museum, 1969.

This book is pioneering investigation by the author of "Film as Historical Evidence," *Journal* of the Society of American Archivists, Vol. III (October 1966), pp. 183-191. (GHH)

1235. Short, Kenneth R. M., ed. *Feature Films as History*. Knoxville: University of Tennessee Press, 1981.

Short brings together British and American film historians to write on their areas of specialization in order to illustrate the scope of methodological approaches to the subject of historical film and society. The book has its origins in 1977 and 1979 international conferences on "Film and History" sponsored by the Zentrum für interdisziplinäre Forschung of the University of Bielefeld. (GHH)

1236. Smith, Paul, ed. *The Historian and Film*. Cambridge: Cambridge University Press, 1976.

Basing itself on the proceedings of the groundbreaking conference in April 1968 at University College, published as *University Vision*, no. 1 (British Universities Film Council), this book presents a comprehensive guide to the interrelationship between history and film. It contains articles on film resources and preservation, on the evaluation of historical evidence, newsreels and fact, and on the making and use of historical film by the producer of the "World at War" television series, among others. The book concludes with a select bibliography and a list of film-and-history organizations. (GHH)

1237. Sorlin, Pierre. *The Film in History: Restaging the Past.* Totowa, N.J.: Barnes and Noble, 1981.

In this series of lectures initially delivered in England, Sorlin argues that historical films—he calls them "fictional documentaries"—deserve careful study as a "living archive for the social historian." After a "principles and methods" introduction in which he traces the making and analysis of the historical film, Sorlin selects seven "reference periods" ranging from the French Revolution to the Italian resistance in the Second World War and suggests methods for "reading" their historical content. (GHH)

VII. Nonbroadcast Film and Video: Guides, Evaluations, Applications

1238. Aldgate, Tony. "The Production of *Spanish Civil War.*" Part I: "The Archives and the Newsreels," *University Vision*, no. 11 (April 1974), pp. 16-23; Part II: "A Film in the Making," *University Vision*, no. 12 (December 1974), pp. 42-52.

This step-by-step account reports the research and making of the compilation film made by the Department of History at the University of Edinburgh for the Inter-University Film Consortium. It was the third production made for the British Consortium, the earlier two being *The Munich Crisis* and *The End of Illusions: From Munich to Dunkirk.* Aldgate directed and edited the film that is the subject of these articles. (GHH)

1239. American Issues Forum. New York: Educational Film Library Association, 1975.

In connection with the bicentennial of the American Revolution a series of public programs addressed nine issues of concern to Americans. This annotated list of films was the contribution of the Educational Film Library Association. The topics include (among others) immigration, the westward-ho movement, civil rights, government, and business. The films include classic documentary films as well as films made for T.V. and relevant features. (JEO)

1240. Barnouw, Erik. "The Hiroshima-Nagasaki Footage: A Report." *Historical Journal of Film, Radio, and Television*, Vol. II (March 1982), pp. 91-100.

Barnouw provides an account of the "liberation," analysis, compilation, and release of the newsreel footage shot by Japanese cameramen after the atomic bombings of the two Japanese cities and the films' subsequent seizure by the U.S. occupation authorities. (GHH)

1241. Bohlen, Anne, Lynn Goldfarb, and Lorraine Gray, producers. *With Babies and Banners: Story of the Women's Emergency Brigade*. The Women's Labor History Film Project, 1979.

On December 30, 1937, the auto workers at the General Motors plant in Flint, Michigan, began a forty-four-day strike and occupation of the factories. Their subsequent victory was pivotal in the rise of the United Auto Workers and the CIO. The Women's Emergency Brigade was organized by women workers and the wives, mothers, and sisters of the strikers to provide support from outside the plant, and played a vital role in the success of the sit-down strike. This forty-five-minute, 16 mm, color documentary interweaves oral history interviews of nine women who were in the brigade with archival films of the strike to portray the central role the Women's Emergency Brigade played in the confrontation. Prints are available from New Day Films, P.O. Box 315, Franklin Lakes, New Jersey 07417. (PMH)

1242. Bush, Greg. "Mission Hill and the Miracle of Boston: A Review." *History and Film*, Vol. IX (September 1979), pp. 64-66.

Mission Hill is a superb "neighborhood preservation" film funded in part by the people about whom it was made. As such, it bears the faults and virtues of its origins. This review calls attention to public historians engaged in this kind of project. (GHH)

1243. *Educational Film Locator*. 2d ed. New York: Bowker, 1980.

This is essentially a master catalog to the University Film Libraries, which includes a subject index. Film descriptions are more complete than those in the NICEM index (see no. *1205*). This is particularly important as a source for films that no longer are available from the commercial distributors. (JEO)

1244. Ferro, Marc. "1917: History and the Cinema." *Journal of Contemporary History*, Vol. III, (October 1968), pp. 45-61.

This article gives a detailed account of how film research and detailed, shot-by-shot analysis by the French pioneer in this field can add to our historical knowledge of the period of the First World War and Russian Revolution. (GHH)

1245. Field, Connie, producer. *The Life and Times of Rosie the Riveter*. Franklin Lakes, N.J.: Clarity Educational Productions, 1980.

This one-hour, 16 mm, color documentary combines oral history interviews of five women with recruitment films, stills, posters, ads, and music of the war era to document the role American women played during World War II. As the existing labor force was called to active service, black males and then white and black females were recruited for heavy manufacturing of boats, planes, and munitions. Production levels rose as did women's incomes. Feminine self-perceptions changed through competence in new skills, pride in their work, and union involvement. As the war ended, however, the traditional image of "women's work" was reasserted, and women were forced from their new workplace.

The role of propaganda in drawing women to industrial plants and in returning to "traditional" women's jobs is revealed. The film is available on 3/4" video-cassettes as well from Clarity Educational Productions, Inc., P.O. Box 315, Franklin Lakes, New Jersey 07417. (PMH)

1246. "Gallaudet Completed Oral History Video Series." Oral History Association *Newsletter*, Vol. XIV (Summer 1980), p. 4.

Oral history interviews of the executive committee of the World Federation of the Deaf, videotaped in international sign language, were recently completed at Gallaudet College. (See also no. *1265.*) (PMH)

1247. Griffin, Patrick. "The Making of a Documentary Film—*1900: A Montage.*" *University Vision*, no. 9 (November 1972), pp. 25-38.
Griffin, Patrick. "The Making of *Goodbye Billy.*" *Film and History*, Vol. II (1972), pp. 6-10.
Rollins, Peter C. "The Making of *Will Rogers' 1920's.*" *Film and History*, Vol. VII (1977), pp. 1-5.

These three articles describe efforts by American historians to produce scholarly documentaries under the banner of Cadre films. Unpublished accounts of these and other Cadre films have also been written for various conferences. (GHH)

1248. Elder, Harris. "The First Cadre Film: *Goodbye Billy: America Goes to War, 1917-1918*: Historian Filmmakers Tackle the Compilation Genre" (1971).
Rollins, Peter C. "The Second Cadre Film: *The Frozen War: America Intervenes in Russia, 1918-1920*" (1973).
Raack, Richard C. "The Fourth Cadre Film: *Storm of Fire: World War II and the Destruction of Dresden*" (1978).

These three papers are available from their authors: Elder at North Adams State College, Massachusetts; Rollins at Oklahoma State University, Stillwater; and Raack at California State University, Hayward. *A Film Resource Materials Guide* was produced by Arthur Peterson of the San Francisco Unified Schools District for *Will Rogers' 1920's: A Cowboy's Guide to the Times* and is available from the Audio-Visual Center at Oklahoma State University, Stillwater, Oklahoma, 74074. (GHH)

1249. Handfield, Gerald F., Jr. "The Importance of Video History in Libraries." *Drexel Library Quarterly*, Vol. XV (October 1979), pp. 29-34.

Video history is defined as an interview that is preserved by recording an audio and a video signal. Video interviews provide more raw data than audio oral-history interviews and allow for insertion of supplementary visual items, such as photographs. Modern Americans are more attentive to an audio recording when it is accompanied by visual images. Libraries should collect and/or create video history. Video technology is now an important component of contemporary society, but preservation of video programming has not become a priority. To avoid irretrievable losses like those of early films, television programs, and recordings, immediate steps should be taken to preserve video materials. (PMH)

1250. Jolly, Brad. *Videotaping Local History*. Nashville: American Association for State and Local History, 1982.

Video technology can document and interpret historical data in innovative ways. This volume provides a technical overview of videotaping, equipment evaluations, and instructions for operating video apparatus. Ideas are presented on how video can augment traditional museum and historical agency exhibits and programs for the disabled. The use of video in oral history interviewing as well as training and information programs is discussed. A glossary and guidelines for maintaining a video archives are provided. (PMH)

1251. Marwick, Arthur, ed. *Archive Film Compilation Booklet*. British Open University, Arts: A Third Level Course, War and Society, 1973.

This booklet contains several essays. Marwick writes on using archive film as source material, and Lisa Pontecorvo comments on newsreel and documentary research. Edward Hayward discusses production problems. An additional pamphlet, *Supplementary Material A301*, contains a film and audio source list for the War and Society course. Marwick's book, derived from the course, *War and Social Change in the Twentieth Century* (London: MacMillan, 1974), contains a chapter called "Notes on the Use of Archive Film Material" (pp. 226-234). An Open University film entitled *Archive Film and the Study of War and Society* is also available. (GHH)

1252. Page, Don. "A Visual Dimension to Oral History." Canadian Oral History Association *Journal*, Vol. II (1976-1977), pp. 20-23.

The oral history program of the Historical Division of the Department of External Affairs aims to uncover the characters of the actors and circumstances surrounding events in Canadian diplomatic history. Since 55 percent of communication is through facial exression, gestures, and postures, a videotape reveals much about the personality and emotional state of the interviewee. The External Affairs program uses video selectivity—ten- to thirty-minute segments—to reveal this added dimension and complement the oral history interview series conducted on audiotape alone. Video is not used for the entire series because of the artificiality of studio settinngs, lack of spontaneity before the camera, high cost of videotaping, and the use of the end product for historical research, not public presentation. Video is flashy but should be used discriminately. A project must balance cost-effectiveness, loss of spontaneity, and the added dimension of visual images. (PMH)

1253. Public Broadcasting System. "The New American Neighborhood Road Show." Owings Mill: Maryland Center for Public Broadcasting, 1981.

This videotaped program is the end-product in a series of interpretations of community history materials. The Baltimore Neighborhood Heritage Project, conducted by the Baltimore Region Institutional Studies Center of the University of Baltimore, sought to preserve the ethnic history of many communities within the city through traditional research, oral history, and artifacts. Exhibits on neighborhood history were displayed throughout the city. Transcripts of the oral history interviews were adapted for a play, *Baltimore Voices*, which portrays the diversity and common concerns of daily life of Baltimore's residents. The play was then adapted and videotaped for television by the Maryland Center for Public Broadcasting and named "The New American Neighborhood Road Show." The program, in ninety- and sixty-minute versions with a study guide for public school classes, is available from MCPB, Owings Mills, Maryland 21117. (PMH)

1254. Research Center for the Federal Theatre Project. "List of Videotapes." Fairfax, Va.: George Mason University, n.d.

The Federal Theatre Project collection consists of manuscripts from this Works Project Administration project, supplemented by over two hundred oral history interviews of project participants. Some twenty-five hours of interviews have been filmed with designers, writers, performers, and directors. The collection is growing and is available for research use. The manuscript collection includes production designs and some 2,500 radio scripts. (PMH)

1255. Rollins, Peter C. "Television's Vietnam: The Visual Language of Television News." *Journal of American Culture*, Vol. IV (Summer 1981), pp. 114-135.

This article constitutes a study of the television evening news coverage of three events of the Vietnam War in 1968, and their effects on U.S. domestic politics based on historical accounts of the events and on Peter Braestrup's *Big Story: How the American Press and Television Reported and Interpreted the Crisis of Tet 1968 in Vietnam and Washington* (Boulder, Colo.: Westview, 1976). A ninety-minute documentary film called *Television's Vietnam*, produced by Rollins, David Culbert, and Townsend Ludington and funded in part by the Rockefeller Foundation, resulted from this research. (GHH)

1256. Schuursma, Rolf. "Film and History in The Netherlands." *Film and History*, Vol. II (December 1972), pp. 10-16.

This brief historical and sociological account of historians working as film makers in the Netherlands is by their best-known member, Rolf Schuursma, of the Foundation for Film and Science, Utrecht, producer of *Anton Mussert*. The Foundation is described in *University Vision*, no. 9 (November 1972), pp. 44-47. (GHH)

1257. Seegal, David. "Videotaped Autobiographical Interviews, An Adjunct for Medical Education." *Journal of the American Medical Association*, Vol. CLXXXXV (February 21, 1966), pp. 650-652.

Scholarship is enlivened by the presence of the scholar, but his influence usually is directly personal. Traditional printed and manuscript sources cannot reveal to the medical student the full nature of important medical researchers. Videotaped autobiographical interviews can convey the intellectually charismatic nature of doctors who have made important and varied contributions to the world of medicine. "Hero worship" can provide stimulus for learning and develop an appreciation for the individual as a person and a scientist by providing models for excellence. (PMH)

1258. Smith, Arthur L. "Filming the Past at Colonial Williamsburg." *History and Film*, Vol. II (December 1972), pp. 1-9.

This article is a brief account of the use of media in historical restoration and exhibition work by the Audio-Visual Department director at Colonial Williamsburg. (GHH)

1259. Whitaker, W. Richard. "Why Not Try Videotaping Oral History?" *Oral History Review*, Vol. IX (1981), pp. 115-124.

Oral history adds a new dimension to traditional historical research. Videotaping can further this expansion by capturing the visual element. Video technology is rapidly developing and becoming affordable for many projects. Currently available equipment is evaluated by the author in terms of quality and price. A director is needed to control the session and guide the participants. Tips are provided on making a production visually interesting and on editing a final product. A bibliography is included. (PMH)

1260. Wilson, David L. "Governors Past: A Video History Project." *International Journal of Instructional Media*, Vol. VI (1978-1979), pp. 253-264.

A proposal for "Governors Past: A Video History Project" is outlined. Florida has seven living ex-governors, whose terms spanned over thirty years of growth and change. Videotaped historical interviews of these ex-governors will provide humanistic and personal perspectives on the state's history. Videotaping reveals more about the individual than printed or audio resources and allows for incorporation of other media, such as film clips and photographs. The literature on Florida's history is reviewed, and a brief biography of each governor is provided. The proposed project would research print and nonprint resources to produce videotaped histories of each ex-governor's term. (GHH)

VIII. Nonbroadcast Audio: Books, Articles, Evaluations

1261. Espinola, Judith, producer. "Voices of Washington State." Seattle: Metrocenter YMCA, n.d.

Produced through a Washington Commission for the Humanities grant, this radio series is based on a Bicentennial oral history project in six counties. These 350 interviews focused on biographical and occupational studies of common men, women, and ethnic minorities, and were supplemented by six thousand photographs. From this oral history and photograph collection, thirty-five radio programs of thirteen minutes' duration were produced on the lives of common men and women; ethnic, racial, and religious minorities; blue-collar workers; union members; farmers; fishermen; immigrants; and migrants. Eight of the programs are accompanied by slides and have been transferred to videotape as well. "Voices" is available from the producer, Metrocenter YMCA, 909 4th Avenue, Seattle, Washington 98104. (PMH)

1262. Godfrey, Donald. "History Held a Microphone." *Film and History*, Vol. III (February 1973), pp. 13-16.
    This article describes the luck and acumen that combined to create the Milo Ryan Phono Archives at the University of Washington. (GHH)

1263. Lance, David. "Dissemination of Audio Resource Materials." *Phonographic Bulletin* (December 1978), pp. 29-33.
    Archives must be used in order to justify their existence. The sound archive of the Imperial War Museum disseminates its collection through use and access. Recordings are used as background for exhibits, as integral parts of exhibits, for educational programs, and in radio broadcasting. Oral history interviews have been collected for these purposes. Access is provided to researchers through a reference collection and by sales of duplicate tapes. A lending collection was too costly to maintain. (PMH)

1264. *One Man's Alaska*. National Park Service, n.d.
    This twenty-eight-minute, 16mm, color film portrays one man's needs for wilderness. A profile of Dick Proenneke is provided through narrative discussions of his philosophy of wilderness and wildlife and through an account of the events leading to his decision to settle in Alaska. Contemporary film is combined with footage shot by Proenneke when he built his cabin years earlier. Prints are available from the National AV Center, GSA, Washington, D.C. 20409. (PMH)

1265. "Oral History of and for the Deaf Begins at Gallaudet." Oral History Association *Newsletter*, Vol. XI (Fall 1977), p. 3.
    Gallaudet College, a center for learning by the deaf, has begun a series of videotaped oral history interviews conducted in sign language. The project will document campus life and history as well as provide a study of signed communication. (See also no. *1246*.)

1266. "Southwest Library Association Public Programming Completed." Oral History Association *Newsletter*, Vol. XV (Summer 1981), pp. 1, 6-7.
    The Southwestern Library Association sponsored a model project on oral

history in public programming through the National Endowment for the Humanities grants to sixteen libraries in six states. Projects produced videotapes, exhibits, slide-tape shows, dramatic sketches, tour cassettes, and radio scripts, as well as transcript collections. These varied projects are described briefly. (PMH)

1267. Terkel, Louis (Studs). "Hard Times: The Story of the Depression in the Voices of Those Who Lived It." Caedmon Records (2) TC 2048.

These phonograph records consist of the original audiotaped interviews made by Terkel in preparation for his book, *Hard Times*. (GHH)

1268. *The Fishermen of Isle Royale*. National Park Service, n.d.

The last remaining commercial fishermen on this island in Lake Superior are profiled in this eighteen-minute, 16mm, color film. Footage of daily work scenes is combined with individual statements. The audio consists entirely of edited interviews of the fishermen explaining what they do and how fishing has changed. Produced by the AV Center of the National Park Service, the film is available for rent or sale from the Harper's Ferry Historical Association Bookstore, Harper's Ferry, West Virginia 25425. (PMH)

1269. WGBH. "Voices of the Thirties." (1980).

Largely based on interviews made in the 1930s with Americans from all walks of life by personnel of the Works Progress Administration, this six-part radio series dramatizes these written accounts in order to convey to the listener what it was like to live and work in the 1930s. The episode titles are: "Troupers and Pitchmen"; "A Vanishing World"; "When You First Come to This Land, Making Ends Meet"; "Smoke and Steel"; and "Harlem Stories." A book compiled by Ann Banks called *First-Person America* (see no. *1458*) also resulted from the project. (GHH)

1270. Wheeler, Anne, and Lorna Rasmussen. *Great Grandmother: A History and Celebration of Prairie Women*. New York: National Film Board of Canada, 1978.

The stories of frontier women who settled the western plains are told in this twenty-nine-minute, 16mm, color film. The production weaves oral history interviews of surviving frontier women with still photographs and dramatic reenactments from old diaries to document the struggle to survive and establish new homes on the prairie. A companion study guide for high school and college classes uses photographs and narrative excerpts to deepen understanding of the lives of pioneer women in the West. The film is available from New Day Films, P.O. Box 315, Franklin Lakes, New Jersey 07417. (PMH)

1271. WNYC. "New Yorkers at Work: Oral Histories of Life, Labor and Industry." New York, 1981.

The New York City work experience is the subject of this radio series based on three hundred years of oral history interviews. The programs were co-produced by WNYC and the Robert F. Wagner Labor Archives, which houses the oral history collection. Memories of the work experiences of secretaries, painters, teachers, tunnel workers, electricians, department store workers, garment workers, longshoremen, municipal workers, jewelry workers, and others were edited into eight half-hour segments. Program focuses are craft workers, immigrants, the CIO in the thirties, the postwar labor movement, discrimination, public servants, clerical workers, and current unemployment. The programs, which are narrated by Martha Greenhouse and Frederick O'Neal, contain interview segments interspersed with music composed by Oscar Brand and others. The series is available from the producer, Debra Bernhardt, Robert F. Wagner Labor Archives, Elmer Holmes Bobst Library, 70 Washington Square South, New York, New York 10012. (PMH)

IX. Multi-Image/Multi-Media, Pictorial, and Graphic Presentations: Guides and Applications

1272. Boni, Albert. *Photographic Literature: An International Bibliographic Guide to General and Specialized Literature on Photographic Processes; Techniques; Theory; Chemistry; Physics; Apparatus; Materials and Applications; Industry; History; Biography; Aesthetics; Etc.* Hastings-on-Hudson, N.Y.: Morgan and Morgan, 1962.

This reference book indexes over twelve thousand English and foreign language printed materials on all the photographic arts from the fifteenth century to 1960. A second volume, covering the period from 1960 to 1970, was published in 1972 and covers more than twenty thousand entries. (GHH)

1273. Educational Sound Filmstrip Directory. Dukane Corporation, Audio Visual Division.

This equipment manufacturer publishes an unannotated list, by topic, of the distributors of software in this field. Addresses are included. (GHH)

1274. Flanders, Robert. *Sassafras, An Ozarks Odyssey.* South West Missouri State University, Center for Ozark Studies, 1979.

This is a complete, multi-image exploration of Ozarks lifestyles and folklore, using stereophonic sound and over nine hundred slides. It includes dramatizations of historic accounts of Ozarks life, Sassafras recorded stories and reflections of native, and scholarly interpretation to spread Ozarks life before the audience. It uses the same multi-image technologies that various cities—such as Boston; Newport, Rhode Island; and New York City—have successfully and profitably used to introduce tourists to the history and diversity of interest that they offer. In this case, twelve slide projectors are computer-synchronized on a three-hundred-square-foot screen. Flanders is also at work on a filmed record of the fast-disappearing culture of this region. (GHH)

1275. Herman, Gerald. "Making Multi-Media Lectures for Classroom Use: A Case Study." *Film and History*, Vol. II (December 1972), pp. 17-23.

This article offers a "nuts and bolts" approach to creating simple slide-tapes on historical subjects. (GHH)

1276. Jensen, Oliver. *America's Yesterdays: Images of Our Lost Past Discovered in the Photographic Archives of the Library of Congress*. New York: American Heritage, 1978.
Fern, Alan, Milton Kaplan, and the Staff of the Prints and Photographs Division. *Viewpoints: The Library of Congress Selection of Pictorial Treasures*. New York: Arno, 1972.
Goodrum, Charles A. *Treasures of the Library of Congress*. New York: Harry N. Abrams, 1981.

These three picture books survey the pictorial resources available through the Library of Congress. (GHH)

1277. Markel, Helen. "The Bettmann behind the Archives." *New York Times Magazine*, October 18, 1981.

This brief article recounts the story of the Bettmann Archives and its founder. (GHH)

1278. Niver, Kemp. *Motion Pictures from the Library of Congress Print Collection, 1894-1912*. Berkeley: University of California Press, 1967.

For copyright purposes, paper contact prints were made of each scene of movies produced before the "ephemeral" film itself was allowed to be copyrighted. These constitute an important source for the study of the films of this period. Some of the print files are so complete that they have been used to reconstruct missing parts of the films themselves. Niver has constructed an annotated index to the collection. (GHH)

1279. Riley, Glenda. "History Goes Public." Washington: National Council on Public History, 1981.

Produced by the University of Iowa with funds from the National Endowment for the Humanities, this slide-tape introduction to the broad field of public history is designed for undergraduate students and the public at large. (GHH)

X. Computer-Based Data Access and Transmission: Overviews, Directories, Examples

1280. A Guide to DIALOG Searching and *Guide to DIALOG Databases*. Palo Alto, Calif.: Lockheed DIALOG Information Retrieval Service, 1979. Monthly updates.

The DIALOG Information Retrieval Service offers the largest number of databases of interest to the historian and public affairs researcher. Its *Guide* to searching gives a comprehensive explanation of the essential elements and special features of this information retrieval system. The guide to databases has detailed chapters on each of the more than 150 databases in science, technology, business, social sciences, humanities, and general interest information available for public access. Information on using DIALOG's private file service is available separately from the company at 3460 Hillview Avenue, Palo Alto, California 94304. (JDF)

1281. Annual Review of Information Science and Technology. American Society for Information Science, 1966-. (ASIS was formerly the American Documentation Institute.)

Compiled by leaders in the field of information science (the earliest volumes were edited by Carlos Cuadra and those since 1976 by Martha E. Williams), these annual collections of articles by specialists offer state-of-the-art reviews and extensive bibliographies on various aspects of information work and topics of high current interest. Examples of topics covered in one or more volumes are: database management systems, computers in publishing, information systems for research in progress, evaluation and design of bibliographic databases, numeric databases and systems, information systems in Latin America, databases in the humanities, information marketing, and several on new technology. (JDF)

1282. Brown, Jessica S., comp. *ABC-Clio Online User Manual*. Santa Barbara, Calif.: ABC-Clio, 1982.

America: History and Life (AHL) and *Historical Abstracts* (HA), the databases specifically in the field of history, also include much material in the other social sciences and humanities. This guide to searching the files on DIALOG Information Services system updates and expands the original user aid written by Joyce Duncan Falk (*AHL and HA on Lockheed DIALOG*, 1981). It supplements the DIALOG guides (see no. *1280*) by providing more specific details, search hints, and examples. User manuals for other files, such as *Psychological Abstracts, Sociological Abstracts*, and *Social Science Citation Index*, are published by the respective database producers. (JDF)

1283. BRS System Reference Manual and Database Search Guides. Scotia, N.Y.: Bibliographic Retrieval Services, 1981. Monthly updates.

How to use the BRS search system is explained in the basic reference manual with detailed chapters on each database in the search guides section. Some databases are available only through BRS; some are available on BRS and on one or more other information retrieval systems such as DIALOG or System Development Corporation's ORBIT. BRS's pricing structure has been especially attractive to academic library subscribers. In addition to the databases available to all subscribers, BRS offers a private service to organizations wishing to use the BRS search software for their own private files. Information is available directly from Bibliographic Retrieval Services, 1200 Route 7, Latham, New York 12110. (JDF)

1284. Cuadra, Ruth N., David M. Abels, and Judith Wagner, comps. and eds. *Directory of Online Databases.* Santa Monica, Calif.: Cuadra Associates, 1981.

This directory, updated quarterly, lists current information about databases and distinctly named files within database families available both through international telecommunications networks and through on-line retrieval services limited to one or a few countries. Each brief database entry gives name, type (for example, textual, bibliographic, source), subject, producer, on-line service, content, coverage, and updating. There are indexes to the databases by subject, producer, on-line service, and name, and an index to telecommunications networks by on-line service. (JDF)

1285. Database: The Magazine of Database Reference and Review. 1978-.

This quarterly journal concentrates on reviews and explanations of databases and news of current developments. Articles, written by practicing searchers, usually bring another viewpoint to the literature provided by database producers and search systems. The review of *United States Political Science Documents,* for example, gives a brief description of the database accompanied by sample citations, a sample search, a list of pluses and minuses, and a chart summarizing the features of the file. Other articles compare the content and retrieval features of databases, covering the same or similar subjects or databases for particular uses, such as for the legal profession. (JDF)

1286. Falk, Joyce Duncan. "In Search of History: The Bibliographic Databases." *History Teacher,* Vol. XV (May 1982), pp. 523-540.

This paper, written specifically to help historians understand what computer-searchable bibliographies offer, gives a brief introduction to the terminology, describes the bibliographic databases available for on-line searching, and outlines the characteristics of a search. Sample searches illustrate the searching process. (JDF)

1287. Falk, Joyce Duncan. "Searching by Historical Period in the History Databases." In Martha E. Williams and Thomas H. Hogan, comps. *National Online Meeting Proceedings—1981.* Proceedings of the Second National Online Meeting, New York, 1981. Medford, N.J.: Learned Information, Inc., 1981.

In addition to explaining how to search by dates or historical period specifically in the bibliographic databases in history, this article offers general observations on the use of the humanities databases (history, art, literature, philosophy, and music) and the problem of historical period searching in them. (JDF)

1288. Falk, Joyce Duncan. "The Historian Enters the Electronic Age: Bibliographical and Database Publishing." *Public Historian*, Vol. IV (Spring 1982), pp. 35-42.

Besides information on working in a particular type of publishing, this article emphasizes that historians must learn enough about the use of computers in research and records management that they can function effectively in today's society, and that they need to understand the intellectual implications of such use in order to put their particular training in history to its best use. Skills and experience in database publishing are transferable to nonpublishing jobs in public history. (JDF)

Geda, Carolyn L., Erik W. Austin, and Francis X. Blouin, Jr., eds. *Archivists and Machine-Readable Records: Proceedings of the Conference on Archival Management of Machine-Readable Records, February 7-10, 1979, Ann Arbor, Michigan*. See no. *479*.

This collection includes papers both on machine-readable archives in the usual sense of records and documents and on data archives. There are articles on research in state archival data, college and university records, and the use of business records in research in economic history. There are two articles on machine-readable data for social research, one in the Inter-University Consortium for Political and Social Research and one on the Roper Center archive of sample survey data. Other articles address techniques used, examples of archival programs for machine-readable records, and developments in computer technology. (JDF)

1289. Gerhan, David, and Loretta Walker. "A Subject Approach to Social Science Data Archives." *RQ*, Vol. XV (Winter 1975), pp. 132-149.

This brief introduction to social science data archives provides a directory of forty archives, giving name and address, subject scope, fee structure, restrictions on data or users, guides available, and output format and hardware. There is also a subject index to the directory. (JDF)

1290. Hoover, Ryan E., ed. *The Library and Information Manager's Guide to Online Services*. White Plains, N.Y.: Knowledge Industry Publications, 1980.

Although written primarily for librarians, this work serves the historian as an introduction to on-line information retrieval, types of databases, producers and distributors of on-line services, and the mechanics of on-line searching. It includes a glossary of terms, and each chapter has a substantial list of references. A selected bibliography covers the general subject and is especially helpful for its inclusion of serial publications from search services, professional organizations, and independent commercial publishers or individuals. (JDF)

1291. *Information Industry Marketplace 1982: An International Directory of Information Products and Services*. New York: Bowker, 1982.

Formerly titled *Information Market Place* and now published annually, this directory lists and briefy describes database publishers, databases, and print products, and gives a subject index to the databases. It includes information distributors (vendors, telecommunication networks), retailers of information, support services and suppliers, associations, government agencies, conferences, courses, reference books, and periodicals. (JDF)

1292. International Computer Programs, Inc. *ICP Software Directory*. (Previous title, *ICP Directory*.)

This semiannual directory, a comprehensive source of software product and service information, is published in six volumes, each appearing twice a year: (1) *Data Processing Management*, including software for medium to large computers ranging from basic utility to comprehensive data management systems; (2) *Business Management: Cross Industry Applications*, for example, financial planning; project control; accounting; personnel; text editing, processing, indexing, and publication; (3) *Business Management: Industry Specific Applications*, including education and government; (4) *Mini-Small Business Systems: Industry Specific*; (5) *Mini-Small Business Systems: Cross Industry*; and (6) *Software Product & Service Suppliers*. Together they list more than nine thousand products and services and information on about two thousand suppliers. The 1981 and 1982 volumes include brief articles on evaluating a software products vendor, guidelines on evaluating software and services, and negotiating contracts with vendors. Each volume has detailed tables of contents and explanations of how to use the publication. (JDF)

1293. Inter-University Consortium for Political and Social Research. *Guide to Resources and Services, 1981-1982*.

This annual publication is a thorough guide to the services and holdings of a major social science data archives collection located at the University of Michigan, the Inter-University Consortium for Political and Social Research. Access to the data is through institutional memberships; most members are colleges and universities. (JDF)

1294. McCrank, Lawrence J., ed. *Automating the Archives: Issues and Problems in Computer Applications*. White Plains, N.Y.: Knowledge Industry Publications, 1981.

This volume consists of the proceedings of the symposium on Automation: Future Access to the Past, held at the University of Maryland, College Park, April 1980. Among the discussions relevant to the work of the public historian are the ones on the administrator (with samples from three publications) and on the profession (a review of basic expectations to be met by archival automation). Descriptions of the Philadelphia Social History Project, the Baltimore Region Institutional Studies Center (BRISC), the Midwest State Archives Project, the National Historical Publications and Records Commission with its related SPIN-DEX programs for archives and records management applications, all accompanied by samples and bibliographies, are useful for their specific techniques and as examples from which broader generalizations can be made. (JDF)

1295. Mogren, Paul, et al. "A Sampler of Databases for Searches in History." *RQ*, Vol. XXI (Summer 1982).

Brief reviews of eight databases highlight their relevance to topics in history research, including contemporary history of public affairs such as U.S. government land use. A list of seven additional databases for searches in history is appended. This review article supplements the discussions in three papers presented on the program, "Computer-assisted Reference Service in History," at the 1981 annual conference of the American Library Association and published in the same issue of *RQ*. (JDF)

1296. Online Review: The International Journal of Online Videotex Information Systems. 1977-.

The subtitle indicates the scope of this journal, published every other month in England, which is slightly broader than *Online* (see no. *1297*). *Online Review* tends to have more technical articles and a more international content. It covers general issues in the on-line and videotext industry as well as specific databases, search strategies, training, indexing vocabularies, the profession, and bibliography. An example of a particularly pertinent article is one on the accessibility and availability of U.S. government publications in volume 4 (March 1980). (JDF)

1297. Online: The Magazine of Online Information Systems. 1977-.

One of the major sources of current information, this quarterly journal covers all aspects of on-line information systems, such as comparisons of search systems, management of a searching service, training, reviews of new technology and equipment, and discussions of specific databases or applications for particular fields. Examples of the latter are articles on the use of on-line databases for legal research or the courtroom and review articles on the *American Statistical Index*, the *CIS Index* (publications of the U.S. Congress), and the *Congressional Record Abstract* file. (JDF)

1298. Raben, Joseph, and Gregory Marks, eds. *Data Bases in the Humanities and Social Sciences*. Proceedings of the IFIP Working Conference on Data Bases in the Humanities and Social Sciences, Dartmouth College, Hanover, N.H., 1979. Amsterdam: North Holland Publishing Company, 1980.

The short articles in this collection range from relatively simple descriptions of databases to highly technical papers on systems and technology. Unfortunately, the brevity of the papers precludes detailed presentations on most topics; nevertheless, the number and variety of subjects included make this book an important source of information on projects and methodologies relevant to public historians' work. There are articles on the Criminal Justice Archive; the National

Longitudinal Surveys of Labor Market Behavior; the Knights of Labor Data Bank; the University of California, Berkeley, Survey Research Center's retrieval system for survey data; the development and potential of public use samples; immigration and family history; the 1980 census; and databases in political science, history, and the social sciences; and more. (JDF)

1299. SDC Search Service ORBIT User Manual. Santa Monica, Calif.: System Development Corporation, 1979. (Updates.)

ORBIT has fewer databases than the other two major on-line information retrieval systems (DIALOG, BRS) of interest to the historian, but some are unique. The system is explained in this basic manual. ORBIT user manuals for particular files are also available. (JDF)

1300. The Information Bank Thesaurus. 8th ed. Parsippany, N.J.: Information Bank, 1981.

Many databases have a thesaurus to show the indexing vocabulary used and thus facilitate effective use of the database. This thesaurus serves as an example of one of the standard types of tools used in computerized information retrieval. The title page notes that it is "a guide for searching the *Information Bank* and for organizing, cataloguing, indexing and searching collections of information on current events." (JDF)

Williams, Martha E., and Sandra H. Rouse. *Computer-Readable Bibliographic Data Bases: A Directory and Data Sourcebook.* (See no. *154.*)

Updated at two-year intervals, this comprehensive directory of publicly available databases used for information retrieval purposes lists databases and has producer, processor, name-acronym-synonym, and subject indexes. The entry for each database includes basic information (name, frequency, time span), producer, availability and charges, subject matter and scope, indexing, data elements present, services offered, and user aids available. (JDF)

XI. State of the Art and Future Directions

1301. Brown, Velma, and James Von Schilling. "A Selected Annotated Bibliography of Literature on the Community and Personal-Service Usage of Cable Television." *Journal of Popular Film and Television*, Vol. VII, no. 4 (1980), pp. 471-480.

This article represents a unique attempt to bring together the scattered literature on cable access and programming. (GHH)

1302. "Gallery." *Video Systems*, Vol. XIII (July 1982).

This issue of *Video Systems* is largely devoted to the new video technologies and digital effects and computer graphics, and it serves as a visual introduction to the usage possibilities of such video developments. A series of articles on special aspects of this field also appears in this issue. (GHH)

1303. Martin, James. *Telematic Society*. Englewood Cliffs, N.J.: Prentice-Hall, 1981.

This is the second edition of Martin's much-acclaimed *The Wired Society*, published in 1978. It presents an updated survey of the new information technologies and predicts ways in which they will alter society. (GHH)

1304. "Windows on the Future: Planning for Public Television in the Telecommunications Era." *Public Telecommunications Review*, Vol. VI (July/August 1978).

This special issue provides an overview of the myriad telecommunications technologies becoming available in the 1980s as well as a proposed program for incorporating these technologies in noncommercial broadcasting. (GHH)

XII. Organizations and Networks

1305. Association for Recorded Sound Collections (ARSC). C/o Les Waffen, Executive Secretary, P.O. Box 1643, Manassas, Virginia 22110.

This association includes private collectors, archivists, and librarians who are responsible for all types of sound recording materials and genres, including radio. It distributes several publications on a regular basis: *ARSC Journal, ARSC Bulletin,* and *ARSC Newsletter*. (FCS)

1306. Committee for the Preservation of Sound Recordings. C/o Mary Hoos, Executive Director, 4317 Barrington Road, Baltimore, Maryland 21229.

This relatively new group is comprised of audio archivists, engineers, and individuals from magnetic tape production companies who are concerned with the exploration of an archival-quality recording medium. It plans to update the Pickett and Lemcoe report of 1959 (see no. *1144*). Joint meetings are held with professional engineering groups such as the InterMag-MMM Conference, Magnetics Society, IEEE, and the American Institute of Physics. (FSC)

1307. Fédération Internationale des Archives de Télévision (FIAT). C/o Monsieur C. Castellani, Secrétaire Général FIAT, 1, place des Mercuriales, 93170 Bagnolet, France.

The Fédération is primarily an international representation of television network production archivists for exchange of information. Associate membership is permitted for nonproduction archives. The FIAT also produces several publications relating to management of production archives. (FCS)

1308. Fédération Internationale des Archives du Film (FIAF). Secrétariat, Gallerie Ravenstien 74, 1000 Brussels, Belgium.

This international organization includes film archivists of public collections (film-industry representatives are excluded). It publishes the *FIAF Bulletin* on a regular basis and distributes various publications on the preservation of film and other archival-related works. (FSC)

1309. Film Archive Advisory Committee (FAAC). C/o Lawrence Karr, Administrator of Preservation, American Film Institute, John F. Kennedy Center for the Performing Arts, Washington, D.C.

This group is an informal association of North American film archivists whose institutions hold collections accessible for research. The group meets twice a year to exchange information. (FSC)

1310. International Association of Sound Archives. Secretariat, c/o David G. Lance, Keeper of Sound Records, Imperial War Museum, Lambeth Road, London SE1 GHZ, Great Britain. (FCS)

1311. Television Archives Advisory Committee (TAAC). C/o Lawrence Karr, Administrator of Preservation, American Film Institute, John F. Kennedy Center for the Performing Arts, Washington, D.C.

Similar to the FAAC (see no. *1309*), this committee includes representatives from the television networks' archives. (FCS)

CHAPTER **10**

ORAL HISTORY

Enid H. Douglass, editor

Oral history is a technique or tool used to obtain and retain information otherwise untapped or lost. It is the deliberate conducting of tape-recorded interviews to collect raw material for present and future researchers to use as sources of historical information and insight. But it has developed in such a manner that it is almost considered a separate field of endeavor. As Louis M. Starr, the first president of the National Oral History Association, stated in 1977, it is "more than a tool and less than a discipline." Oral history has been widely incorporated into the curriculum of public history programs, and public history professionals frequently use it in their work.

This chapter cites the significant and representative statements that have been made about oral history. The hundreds of oral history programs and projects in the United States and elsewhere are not addressed. This information can be found through other sources (see the "Reference" section of this chapter).

The first four sections deal with broad topics central to the oral history movement and are arranged in a sequence designed to lead the reader from fundamental considerations and understanding to more specific discussions of interviewing and evaluation problems. The first section, "General," is a listing of well-known basic statements about oral history and comprehensive overviews of the field. It also identifies pertinent standing and special oral history publications. The "Theory and Methods" and "Evaluation, Standards, and Criticism" sections are drawn from a wide variety of types of sources. The materials cited deal with problems inherent in the oral history process, the need for and use of evaluation standards, and criticisms of oral history.

Sections V-XVII deal with topics more specific in nature. The "Technique: Manuals and Guides" section is a representative listing of the many aids available. Because there is an increasing interest in and use of oral history in the classroom, the "Oral History and Teaching" section deals with oral history as a tool in teaching elementary school, high school, and college students. The

"Oral History: Biography" section is a partial listing of many biographies that make extensive use of oral history, including some that are entirely oral history biographies. Because of the interdisciplinary nature of oral history, there are several sections that address academic subjects, ranging from the arts to women's studies. Section XVIII, "Oral History: International," cites particular articles of interest and lists international periodicals. The last section provides reference information.

The intent of this chapter is to provide a master, select bibliography on oral history both for the neophyte and the experienced oral historian, exemplifying the wide spectrum of available readings. The editor has attempted to arrange the listings in a manner that makes it easy to identify needed information and that leads to an overall understanding of oral history. The authors of these annotations are nationally known oral historians who have been leaders in the movement.

I. General

1312. Benison, Saul. "Oral History and Manuscript Collecting." *Isis*, Vol. LIII (March 1962), pp. 113-117.

Documents necessary for historical research are often destroyed or lost, are sterile, or are not generated because of technological communications. Oral history fills this growing gap by collecting autobiography, the steps in which are four: (1) researching the background for context; (2) conducting the interview; (3) verification of the data; and (4) final editing. The resulting detailed autobiographies are documents that must be evaluated. While memory is tenuous, arising contradictions stimulate further research. The person who lies is giving valuable information about himself. The main responsibility for valid oral history is the interviewer's, however. Future historians may use this as a tool to train students to deal critically with both primary and secondary material. (TLC/RSJ)

1313. Benison, Saul. "Reflections on Oral History." *American Archivist*, Vol. XXVIII (January 1965), pp. 71-77.

Benison speaks of the purposes of oral history and its role in augmenting autobiography. A "superabundance of records" awaits those who research contemporary history, Benison asserts, as he disagrees with those who believe that modern communication methods have all but eliminated confidential documents. The historian-interviewer's operation is fourfold: (1) he prepares in all existing sources to see historical relationships and problems; (2) armed with the tape recorder, he spurs the interviewee's memory of the past; (3) he gathers supporting documentation to check and supplement the oral memoir; and (4) he aids the subject through the editing of the oral memoir. The resulting autobiography is a new kind of historical document—a joint creation of the memoirist and the historian-interviewer. The obligation of the historian-interviewer is to explain his research, include the questions in the oral memoir, and append bibliographies of primary sources and secondary works used in the work. Preferring long and intensive interviews, Benison agrees that shorter interviews can be useful in examining particular historical problems, but he urges oral historians to ask themselves whether they want to work for themselves or the historians of the future. Interviews are needed with those who, until recently, were studied mainly by anthropologists. Less-known persons—recent immigrants, farm and industrial people, and Negroes—can add much to the understanding of recent American history. The study of recorded voices in interviews and the "envelope of sound" that surrounds and is a factor in history are stressed by Benison, who also urges the study of undergraduate and graduate instruction in oral history. (TLC/RSJ)

1314. Douglass, Enid H. "Oral History and Public History." *Oral History Review*, Vol. VIII (1980), pp. 1-5.

Public history is defined as the employment of historians and the historical method outside of academia. Oral history is one of the most important tools for a public historian in retrieving the history of public and private organizations. Decision making in such institutions is seldom documented in a manner conducive to understanding the reasoning behind conclusions. The inclusion of oral history as a public history technique is indicative that oral history is becoming a part of the mainstream of the social sciences. (TLC/RSJ)

1315. Eustis, Truman W., III. "Getting It in Writing: Oral History and the Law." *Oral History Review*, Vol. IV (1976), pp. 6-18.

The *Estate of Hemmingway* v. *Random House, 23 N.Y. 2d 341, 244 N.E. 2d 250 (1968)* is the only known court case to have ever considered the copyright status of oral history materials. Although the decision of the New York Appeals Court offered no definitive ruling, the case at least provides a fact pattern for oral historians to consider in relation to the work they carry on. Eustis also provides a number of capsule summaries of leading U.S. Supreme Court cases dealing with libel and privacy. Although none of these cases relates directly to oral history, they lay out the major tests that courts use to determine whether someone has been libeled or their privacy rights invaded. (JAN)

1316. Grele, Ronald J., ed. *Envelopes of Sound: Six Practitioners Discusss the Method, Theory and Practice of Oral History and Testimony*. Chicago: Precedent, 1975.

The book centers on a session at the April 1973 annual meeting of the Organization of American Historians held in Chicago. Theoretical papers by the historian Ronald J. Grele and the anthropologist Dennis Tedlock, accompanied by the immigration historian Alice Kessler-Harris's introduction, form the core of the book. Also presented are Grele's recorded interview with Studs Terkel on his interviewing and editing methods and a transcript of the latter's WFMT radio interview in Chicago with the former and four other academics: Saul Benison, a historian of medicine; Jan Vansina, an anthropologist of oral tradition; Kessler-Harris; and Tedlock, a scholar of the Zuni Indian tribe. In the two-hour radio interview, the oral historians explain their personal introductions to the field and raise numerous methodological problems. (TLC/RSJ)

1317. Hand, Samuel B. "Some Words on Oral Histories." *Scholarly Publishing*, Vol. IX (January 1978), pp. 171-185.

Oral history, as a research tool, exists to collect and preserve human memories. The interview method, dating back to the ancient Greeks and forward to Allan Nevins and his successors throughout the world, has led to a movement of great magnitude and diversity. Regrettably, most oral historians, whether they interview prominent persons or ordinary people, are print-oriented. The nature of their product as source material is in need of study, but serious discussions of oral history are scarce. Criticial analyses transcending the ongoing work on oral history practitioners are needed. Consumers of oral history tapes and transcripts may profit from knowing about an interviewer's (or an interviewee's) preparations and the circumstances of a research interview. A sizable audience awaits analyses that attempt to fill this "vacuum in the literature about oral history." (TLC/RSJ)

1318. Hoffman, Alice M. "Who Are the Elite, and What Is a Non-Elitist?" *Oral History Review*, Vol. IV (1976), pp. 1-5.

Hoffman states that she is considered a nonelitist oral historian because she interviews steelworkers. She defines the elite as either the choice part or a minority group that exerts decisive power over others. Union leadership fits into both definitions. Oral history is not limited to captains and kings but may be extended to privates and lieutenants. Ronald Blythe's *Akenfield* (see no. *1476*) is cited as a good example of nonelitist oral history. The great events of this century involved many besides the leaders. Oral history makes possible the concept expressed by Carl Becker in the title of his book, *Everyman His Own Historian*. (TLC/RSJ)

1319. Hoover, Herbert T. "Oral History in the United States." In Michael Kammen, ed. *The Past before Us: Contemporary Historical Writing in the United States*. Ithaca, N.Y.: Cornell University Press, 1980.

Despite his relegation of the oral history movement to semiprofessional status, Hoover recognizes the impact it has had on historiography in the United States. By focusing on individuals and works that have contributed mightily to the field, the author highlights the growth of oral history in the post-World War II period. Hoover offers criteria by which to judge oral history collections: project design, adequate funding, selection of interviewers, interviewer preparation and professionalism, processing, and use rights. This article is the most current overview of oral history in the United States. (EHD)

1320. Meckler, Alan M., and Ruth McMullin, comps. and eds. *Oral History Collections*. New York and London: Bowker, 1975.

A comprehensive international directory of oral history projects and holdings in libraries, oral history centers, and archives, this work updates the Oral History Association's 1971 *Directory*. The Meckler-McMullin work is the result of a questionnaire sent in 1973 and 1974 to over five thousand libraries and institutions. Contrary to the book's own explanation, it is arranged in three parts: (1) an index of interviewees' names and subjects (content, length, date); (2) a section, alphabetized by state, listing and describing U.S. oral history centers (general information, accessibility, program purpose, publications based on collection research, and major collections); and (3) a section listing and describing foreign oral history centers (general information and program purposes). (TLC/RSJ)

1321. Morrissey, Charles T. "Why Call It 'Oral History'? Searching for Early Usage of a Generic Term." *Oral History Review*, Vol. VIII (1980), pp. 20-48.

Morrissey discovered the term "oral history" as early as Winslow C. Watson's 1863 usage in his prefatory remarks to a paper read before the Vermont Historical Society. "Oral history" has frequently been attributed to Allan Nevins, the founder of the Columbia University oral history program; his first use of the term was in 1948. Many believe he borrowed the words from Joe Gould, a Greenwich Villager who in 1917 began compiling "An Oral History of Our Time," a 7.3-million-word tome that was never published. Oral history as a concept had been practiced by many from the fifth century B.C. to the New Deal, but no one used the name. Nevins made the practice a fixture so that his nomenclature became generic; early members of the Oral History Association were unable to develop a substitute. Morrissey has found no source from which Watson could have borrowed "oral history" but leaves his research open to revision. (TLC/RSJ)

1322. Neuenschwander, John A. "The Oral History Book: A Review Essay." *Journal of the Richmond Oral History Association*, Vol. II (Fall 1979), pp. 1-14.

This essay assesses the methodology and content of the oral history book, a new genre that emerged in the 1970s and continues to flourish. Most oral history books are social histories presented by interviewer-editors who are social science academicians or journalists, but few are historians. The authors of these books are not to be confused with oral historians, who are active in the oral history movement founded by Allan Nevins and see their goal as developing historical materials for use by researchers. Neuenschwander surveys recent popular books by subject-matter category. This new genre of book is appealing because of its literary quality and focus on experiences of common folk, whose accounts can now readily be captured by tape recorder. But the author points out the problems of having nonhistorians, who do not follow strict codes of gathering and interpreting data, creating oral history. (EHD)

1323. Nevins, Allan. *The Gateway to History*. Boston: Heath, 1938.

In a statement urging the launching of an oral history movement in the United States, the preface to Nevins's volume of essays contains a clarion call for "a systematic attempt to obtain, from the lips and papers of living Americans who have led significant lives, a fuller record of their participation in the political, economic, and cultural life of the last sixty years." Chapter seven, "Pilate on Evidence," bemoans the shortage of useful evidence available to the historian and analyzes the problem of bias in historical materials. Favoring personal sources over many others, Nevins urges historians to test and cross-examine personal evidence for biases; to adopt a scientific attitude; and to summon "all witnesses available" in order to understand the complexity of the past. (TLC/RSJ)

1324. Nevins, Allan. "Oral History: How and Why It Was Born." *Wilson Library Bulletin*, Vol. XL (March 1966), pp. 600-601.

A precaution for those who realize that they will not be able to speak from the grave, oral history "was born of modern invention and technology." The telephone, the telegraph, and other communications devices have robbed the historian of the rich, priceless documents of earlier generations. Great letter writers still exist, but their numbers are fewer and they face great difficulties. The planners of oral history at Columbia University, inspired by both the early spirit of H. H. Bancroft and a zeal to slow the loss of knowledge, began work in New York City and "at every turn they met a new experience, a fresh view of history. . . ." Beginning with modest recording ventures, the Columbia researchers undertook national projects, such as the Henry Wallace, Frances Perkins, and Henry Stimson series. In time, as the memoirs mounted in number, better equipment, better interviewing, and better typing and editing were added at Columbia. Increased funding—from the university, an endowment bequest from Frederic Bancroft, and grants—made possible the growth of the work begun after World War II. Hopefully, the spread of the research movement will continue. (TLC/RSJ)

1325. Roddy, Joseph. "Oral History: Soundings from the Sony Age." *RF Illustrated* (The Rockefeller Foundation), Vol. III (May 1977), pp. 9-11.

This article is a summary of the oral history projects that the Rockefeller Foundation (RF) has helped fund. Columbia University's Oral History Research Office (OHRO) contributed material to eight Pulitzer Prize-winning books from 1970 to 1977. OHRO has documented many topics at great length. No transcripts are tampered with, as compared to the heavily edited work of Studs Terkel. Duke University covers specific subjects instead of autobiographies. Students cover all traditional research first, then do a "problem-centered" oral investigation. They pride themselves on being nonelitist and praise Terkel's work. The University of North Carolina's Southern Oral History Program interviews key Southern political figures. The North Carolinians contend that oral sources are at least as reliable as written ones. The Appalachian Oral History Project at Alice

Lloyd College conducts interviews with miners and other mountain people. RF has also funded work at the universities of California, Michigan, Texas, Florida State, Yale, and Princeton. (TLC/RSJ)

1326. Romney, Joseph. "Legal Considerations in Oral History." *Oral History Review*, Vol. I (1973), pp. 66-76.

Nearly every history handbook and workshop devotes some attention to potential legal problems. Since there is virtually no case law on the collection, use, and publication of oral history materials, Romney stresses how programs and interviewers can both anticipate legal difficulties and take appropriate steps to avoid such. The relevant arguments of contract, copyright, libel, and privacy law are covered in this comprehensive article as well as such important issues as criminal liability and source disclosure. (JAN)

1327. Rundell, Walter, Jr. "Main Trends in U.S. Historiography Since the New Deal." *Oral History Review*, Vol. IV (1976), pp. 35-47.

The government's increased role since the New Deal is generally too new for measured historical treatment, and oral history can provide valuable data. Political biography and Cold War diplomacy have also emerged as leading topics. A bibliographical essay provides titles of scholarly works on this period. Societal needs should also receive increased historical treatment. Historians must not lose their perspective and should not ignore their milieu. Historians may answer questions from the past that speak to present problems. A bibliographic essay on current problems is included. History must employ the tools of the social and behavioral sciences as well as orthodox historical training. Oral history has many research prospects. (TLC/RSJ)

1328. Schlesinger, Arthur, M., Jr. "On the Writing of Contemporary History." *Atlantic Monthly*, Vol. CCXIX (March 1967), pp. 69-74.

Serious questions about the method and ethics of contemporary history have been exemplified by the controversies over the historical literature on John F. Kennedy, climaxing in the legal contest over William Manchester's *Death of a President*. History students have a need for and right to knowledge about contemporary events. Manuscript collections tend to be open to scholars sooner than ever before. Yet developments in communications technology have eroded the value of documents, and the insistence for opening papers to scholars has led to dilution and distortion of the written record. A person's oral history becomes a part of his papers and as such should have conditions of access. The difficulty for Manchester came through a contractual error that did not provide for family review of the use of materials. Jacqueline Kennedy assumed that she was speaking for the future in her interviews, while Manchester took the information for immediate use. The invasion of privacy of a public figure is not necessary for public history. Yet contemporary history is increasingly necessary, for it involves writing in the face of whose who can contradict the record. (TLC/RSJ)

1329. Starr, Louis M. "History, Warm." *Columbia University Forum*, Vol. V (Fall 1962), pp. 27-30.

The director of the Oral History Research Office at Columbia Unversity interviews himself. Most of the source material in this age lacks the "intimate, candid quality of inner revelation." Oral histories, though not as immediate as letters or diaries, can be much more detailed and just as candid. Subjects seldom turn down the opportunity; rather, they put it off in fear of concluding their lives. Oral histories record autobiographies and subject areas. Frequently, interviewees are those who were in a position to observe rather than act in a situation. Tapes are erased because interviewees edit their transcripts. Scholars who use oral histories must be wary; memory is treacherous and some interviewees cannot recall anything essential, while others hold minute details. (TLC/RSJ)

1330. Starr, Louis M. "Oral History." In *Encyclopedia of Library and Information Science*, Vol. XX (1977), pp. 440-463.

Oral history is defined as "primary source material obtained by recording spoken words—generally by means of planned, tape-recorded interviews—of persons deemed to harbor hitherto unavailable information worth preserving." Research is not for immediate use but for the edification of future scholars. Oral history must be used cautiously but no more than other primary sources. As a replacement for letters and other written communications, oral histories run the gamut of topics. An ongoing debate of tape versus transcript is subsiding because transcript use is much more convenient. Guides to oral history collections and microfilm distribution help disseminate the information throughout the country. Most programs are funded by the parent institution and by grants. The movement is active outside the United States, especially in Britain, Canada, Australia, and Mexico, and is found on every continent. Oral history, still a new idea to many, will eventually win acceptance by all scholars. (TLC/RSJ)

1331. Thompson, Paul. *The Voice of the Past: Oral History*. Oxford, London, and New York: Oxford University Press, 1978.

With considerable attention to English and other European examples of oral history activity and publications, the author, a social historian and cofounder of the Oral History Society of the United Kingdom, offers both theoretical and practical approaches to the use of oral sources. In asking, "*whose* is the voice of the past?" Thompson argues that oral history can have a transforming impact on communities and families. Chapter 2, "Historians and Oral History," reviews the historical profession's research methodologies, concluding that, as the *first* kind of history, "oral history gives back to historians the oldest skill of their own craft." The achievements of the movement; the nature of oral evidence (oral, memory, and perception); field-work enterprise, such as school-oriented projects; interviewing methodology ("most people can learn to interview well"); the myriad of problems related to "storing and sifting" oral memories; and how to interpret oral history as an accessible source comprise the remaining parts of the book. Oral history, carefully evaluated and used, will have great effect on both the teaching and writing of history, the author argues. (TLC/RSJ)

1332. Van Dyne, Harry. "Oral History: Sharecroppers and Presidents, Jazz and Texas Oil." *Chronicle of Higher Education* (December 24, 1973), pp. 9-10.

Oral history has overcome the skepticism that greeted Allan Nevin's early advocacy; Columbia University's collection has been a source for biographies, histories, and other books, including best sellers and prize winners. Projects are increasing all over the United States on a multitude of topics. Access rules are crucial for maintaining the credibility of oral history; one breach could endanger a whole collection of candid interviews. While official papers proliferate, they contain little real information; oral history can fill the gap left by diaries, letters, and other materials that are no longer generated. A poor interview may be just as informative as a good one. To Barbara Tuchman's complaint that oral history is the "artificial survival of trivia" (see no. *1372*), Louis Starr replies (see no. *1330*), "What is trash to one researcher is gold to another." Finding aids are essential to ease of use. The Boston University historian, Howard Zinn, has accused Columbia of ignoring the poor, the obscure, the radical, and the outcast. Starr responded by pointing out titles of books on poverty and dissent, based on the Columbia collection, and mentions the book that Zinn wrote with the use of the collection. (TLC/RSJ)

II. Theory and Methods

1333. Benison, Saul. "Reflections on Oral History." *American Archivist*, Vol. XXVIII (January 1965), pp. 71-77.

This short essay, by one of the most insightful historians working in the field of oral history, discusses the relationship of oral history to the recent revolution in communications, the nature of an autobiographical narrative, oral tradition, nonelite interviewing, and oral history as a teaching tool. It is an introduction to some of the deeper historiographical problems raised by oral history. (RJG)

1334. Benison, Saul. "Oral History: A Personal View." In Edwin Clarke, ed. *Modern Methods in the History of Medicine*. New York: Oxford University Press, 1971.

The most comprehensive statement of Benison's views on oral history as a first interpretation and joint creation by historian and respondent, this essay is a call for the highest research standards possible in the conduct of an interview. While directed primarily to the professional historian, Benison's strictures are applicable to beginners and nonprofessional practitioners as well. (RJG)

Benison, Saul. Introduction to *Tom Rivers: Reflections on a Life in Medicine and Science*. See no. *1389*.

In his brief introduction, Benison sets forth the goals of oral history that guided the research and production of his oral biography of Tom Rivers. He notes the close relationship between the use of the oral and written record, the new kind of documentation offered by oral history, and the unique role of the historian/interviewer. He then describes his research techniques. He notes that while the end result looks neat and logical, the process itself was not because of the use of memory and the nature and course of conversation. He also discusses his editing procedures. (RJG)

1335. Clark, E. Culpepper, Michael J. Hyde, and Eva N. McMahan. "Communication in the Oral History Interview: Investigating Problems of Interpreting Oral Data." *International Journal of Oral History*, Vol. I (February 1980), pp. 28-40.

Using general paradigms devised by phenomenologists, the authors set forth a series of structures that allow users to examine oral history narratives as "speech acts" and conversations. (RJG)

1336. Finnegan, Ruth. "A Note on Oral Tradition and Historical Evidence." *History and Theory*, Vol. IX, no. 2 (1970), pp. 195-201.
Oral Literature in Africa. Oxford, Clarendon, 1970.

In both her article and book, Finnegan contributes to understanding of an oral narrative as not only a historical statement but also a performance. She discusses such narratives as not only evidence but as social occasions. (RJG)

1337. Friedlander, Peter. "Introduction: Theory, Method, and Oral History." In Peter Friedlander, *The Emergence of a UAW Local, 1936-1939*. Pittsburgh: University of Pittsburgh Press, 1975.

In this essay the author sets forth the theoretical model derived from linguistics and the method of interviewing upon which he constructed his examination of the shop-floor origins of the UAW in one automotive plant. He also speculates on the way in which oral historians can discover the language of the past. (RJG)

1338. Frisch, Michael. "Oral History and Hard Times, A Review Essay." *Red Buffalo*, Vol. I, nos. 2-3 (1972), pp. 217-231.

Frisch examines the assumptions and method of Studs Terkel. In this essay Frisch notes the close connection between historical memory and consciousness and the way present concerns influence how we see the past. This article is reprinted in *Oral History Review*, Vol. VII (1979), pp. 71-79. (RJG)

1339. Grele, Ronald J. "Movement without Aim: Methodological and Theoretical Problems in Oral History." In Ronald J. Grele, ed. *Envelopes of Sound: Six Practitioners Discuss the Method, Theory and Practice of Oral History and Oral Testimony*. Chicago: Precedent, 1975.

This is Ronald Grele's final chapter in a book based on oral presentations by six leading oral historians (Studs Terkel, Jan Vansina, Dennis Tedlock, Saul Benison, Alice Kessler-Harris, Ronald J. Grele). Grele's article is an attempt to discover and analyze the underlying linguistic, social, and ideological structure of oral history interviews. The entire book is recommended reading for those who wish to understand the nature and use of oral testimony. (RJG/EHD)

1340. Hareven, Tamara K. "The Search for Generational Memory: Tribal Rites in Industrial Society." *Daedalus*, Vol. CVII (Fall 1978), pp. 137-149.

This article covers a wide spectrum of theoretical and methodological problems. Among other points, Hareven notes the lack of serious attention paid to the questions of the nature of the interview process and the function of oral traditions in a "modern, literate society." Arguing that generational memory and real traditions do exist and noting the value of oral history as a tool to understand the subjective aspect of human experiences, the author also notes that the new surge of familial and ethnic consciousness can lead to ethnocentric isolation. There is also discussion of the claims for a new democratic history in oral history. (RJG)

Montell, William Lynwood. Preface to *The Saga of Coe Ridge*. See no. *1480*.

A classic statement of the relation of folk traditions and oral history, the preface to this work is also a discussion of the author's use of those traditions in the re-creation of the history of Coe Ridge. The essay explores new ground for oral historians and points to the usefulness of a broader understanding of oral testimony. (RJG)

1341. Morrissey, Charles T. "Public Historians and Oral History: Problems of Concept and Methods." *Public Historian*, Vol. II (Winter 1980), pp. 22-29.

This article is a starting point for those interested in oral history and public history. Morrissey, one of the founders of the Oral History Association, discusses his view of interviewing those who are primarily leaders, but his strictures apply more broadly. Pointing out the necessity for a clinical but cordial understanding between interviewer and interviewee, he notes that we must remain "professional" rather than "court historians" and have the obligation to disclose the unarticulated premises that institutions very often wish to ignore. The essay raises in bold form the tensions inherent in public history. (RJG)

1342. Morrissey, Charles T. "Rhetoric and Role in Philanthropy: Oral History and the Grant-Making Foundations." *Oral History Review*, Vol. VI (1978), pp. 5-19.

Based upon the author's experience as director of the Ford Foundation Oral History Project, this essay is an early attempt to discuss the usefulness of oral history in particular, and history in general, to an institution. Morrissey argues that within philanthropy the oral histories can make the institution more historically conscious, aid in evaluation and programming, build a needed monographic literature, contribute to public understanding of philanthropy, and help build a body of concepts to define the field. (RJG)

1343. Moss, William W. "Oral History: An Appreciation." *American Archivist*, Vol. XL (October 1977), pp. 429-439.

This article is an attempt by an articulate spokesman for oral history to set forth a theory of evidentiary value within which to understand oral history. Intrigued by the impressive promise and untested product of oral history, Moss sketches the steps whereby one can judge the value of oral histories based upon their authenticity and their content. These standards of evaluation are based upon the soundness of the evidence, the thoroughnesss of the interview, and the need of the information. Moss also offers standards for evaluating the conduct of an interview and the soundness of an oral history project. (RJG)

1344. Neuenschwander, John. "Remembrance of Things Past: Oral Historians and Long-Term Memory." *Oral History Review*, Vol. VI (1978), pp. 45-53.

One of the few examinations of the relations of oral history and memory, this essay summarizes much of the current psychological literature on memory. Behavioral in accent, this article should be read in conjunction with William W. Cutler III, "Accuracy in Oral Interviewing," *Historical Methods Newsletter*, Vol. III (June 1970), pp. 1-7. (See no. *1357*.) (RJG)

1345. Rosenthal, Robert. "The Interview and Beyond: Some Methodological Questions for Oral Historians." *Public Historian*, Vol. I (Spring 1978), pp. 58-67.

Rosenthal opens this essay with a discussion of "the problems of disposal"— how are oral histories to be used. Because use determines methodology, the author, basing his comments on his own work in the Seattle general strike of 1919, attempts to assess both use and method from a variety of social science techniques. In general favorable to some form of quantifiable product, Rosenthal is also aware of the usefulness of nonquantifiable data engendered in the interviewing situation. (RJG)

1346. Tamke, Susan S. "Oral History and Popular Culture: A Method for the Study of the Experience of Culture." *Journal of Popular Culture*, Vol. XI (Summer 1977), pp. 267-279.

This essay is one of the very few attempts to explore the use of oral history in documenting the history of popular culture. While Tamke does not discuss the intrusion of popular culture upon memory, she recognizes the value of interviews in discerning individual and popular consciousness. Noting the scientific, elitist, and literary biases against oral history, she discusses method whereby idiosyncratic evidence can be used for cultural analysis. (RJG)

1347. Vansina, Jan. *Oral Tradition: A Study in Historical Methodology.* Chicago: Aldine, 1965.

Vansina's book treats the analysis of oral testimony and oral tradition for historical purposes. It is a statement of the problems of historical field work, offering guidelines for the interpretation of oral evidence. (See also no. *1438.*) (RJG)

III. Interviewing

1348. Benison, Saul. "Reflections on Oral History." *American Archivist*, Vol. XXVIII (January 1965), pp. 71-77.

At the risk, self-admittedly, of offering "a counsel of perfection," Benison suggests a fourfold procedure for the "historian-interviewer"—a term he prefers to oral historian: "(1) he must prepare himself in extant primary and secondary sources so as to be able to see relevant historical relationships and define historical problems; (2) armed with a tape recorder, he must so handle himself and his preparation as to spur the chosen subject's memory of past events; (3) he must gather from the subject supporting contemporary documents as a check on memory's tenuousness and to supplement the account gathered; and (4) he must aid the subject in the final preparation of the memoir so that it says what the subject wants it to say." The fourth step obligates the historian-interviewer to specify the materials he researched to prepare his interview and to disclose his philosophical and historical preconceptions. This meticulous commitment should result in interviews that are deep and comprehensive. An autobiography gathered by oral history methods is "an attempt at a first interpretation of a series of given events" and "the first reduction and ordering of a mass of primary and secondary material germane to a particular man's life." (CTM)

1349. Douglass, Enid H. "Oral History: Interviewing the Elderly." *History News*, Vol. XXVIII (November 1973), p. 264.

Older respondents may not reflect the stereotype assigned to the elderly; they may be alert and possess excellent recall. But initial contacts with elder respondents should be made in a considerate manner—first an explanatory letter, then a phone call—and interviews with them should be situated in familiar settings. The value of recollections should be emphasized, and informants should be alerted beforehand about topics to discuss, but specific questions should not be submitted. Interviews launched with questions about parents and childhood often induce rapport. A slow pace, gentle demeanor, and simple questions avoiding "yes" or "no" answers are effective. "Trust in the interviewer and what he represents is crucial." Interviewers should react intuitively and try to spark specific recollections, bearing in mind that older people often recall the distant past more ably than the recent past. "Elderly people are not alike any more than other persons in our society. Personalities vary enormously." (CTM)

1350. Fry, Amelia R. "The Nine Commandments of Oral History." *Journal of Library History*, Vol. III (January 1968), pp. 63-73.

Don't be fooled: this is a spoof. Some Texans took it seriously at an oral history workshop in 1972. Presented as a transcript of an interview with Ora W. Laudsworthy, "the grand dame of oral history" and the author of a non-existent handbook entitled *The Nine Commandments of Oral History*, it illustrates that oral history is an art, not a science. Ms. Laudsworthy's interviewer is Sheila Edgeworth Tufswallow, who mistakenly believes that oral history interviewing can be reduced to an unbending set of do's and don'ts. Ms. Laudsworthy makes these points about the art of interviewing: avoid abstract language; don't assume you already know your subject thoroughly; thorough research is worthwhile, but knowing your interviewee's role in past events is more valuable and practicable; don't become a prisoner of pre-interview questions; use tape-recording equipment that is sufficient for the occasion and not so technologically sophisticated that it becomes too difficult to control; use documents in an interview without allowing an excessive number of documents to swallow the interview; edit transcripts to correct errors and invite elaborations; and in projects with limited budgets be sure to interview sufficient individuals first and defer "common man" interviews until funding permits them. The Tenth Commandment is stated this way: "The important thing is to get the interview. Be flexible." (CTM)

1351. Gebhard, Paul H. "Securing Sensitive Personal Information by Interviews." In Peter D. Olch and Forrest C. Pogue, eds. *Selections from the Fifth and Sixth National Colloquia on Oral History* (1970, 1971). New York: Oral History Association, 1972.

Speaking as director of the Institute for Sex Research at Indiana University, Gebhard outlined for oral historians attending the 1971 Colloquium of the Oral History Association how he interviewed people about private sexual behavior. His advice: cite "parallel experience" regarding education, home towns, and so forth at the outset to build rapport; invite factual data to buttress opinions from moralists about reversing the permissive sexual behavior of young people; be solicitous of first-person narratives; be objective and neutral; protect confidential disclosures; be sensitive and supportive, avoid euphemisms; phrase questions without judgmental overtones; use a checklist of fixed questions; also use a "range reduction" technique to ascertain dates and frequencies of sexual practices; derive internal consistencies. (CTM)

1352. Hoffman, Alice. "Reliability and Validity in Oral History." *Today's Speech*, Vol. XXII (Winter 1974), pp. 23-27.

Reliability is the consistency with which an interviewee tells the same story about the same event on different occasions; validity is the degree of conformity between a recalled event and independent evidence of it in diaries, letters, photographs, and other documents. While a reminiscence can be reliable, it may not be valid, and unreliable versions of the past are clearly invalid. Oral historians seek valid reports about the past, but an interviewer's demeanor and other characteristics will affect the responsiveness of interviewees. Professionals in speech communications can aid oral historians in their quest for reliable and valid collections. (CTM)

1353. Menninger, Robert. "Some Psychological Factors Involved in Oral History Interviewing." *Oral History Review*, Vol. III (1975), pp. 68-75.

Little is known about memory, and our ignorance is compounded by our inability to study memory in its pure form. But we do know that almost any emotion will influence what we remember or don't recall, varying individually at different times under different conditions. Accuracy is warped as all of us mold, bend, subtract, or add facts and observations to memories, depending on emotions. Forgetting is not always illogical or pathological; sometimes it is very therapeutic. But in general, "Talking about themselves does most people good and on that basis alone it qualifies as one of the most noticeable therapeutic benefits of an oral history." (CTM)

1354. Morrissey, Charles T. "On Oral History Interviewing." In Lewis Anthony Dexter, ed. *Elite and Specialized Interviewing*. Evanston, Ill.: Northwestern University Press, 1970.

Drawing on his experiences interviewing people close to Presidents Harry S. Truman and John F. Kennedy, Morrissey itemizes the skills that induce worthwhile oral history interviews. He suggests using a two-sentence format to phrase questions in open-ended and jargon-free language; letting respondents volunteer their own reminiscences through careful listening; pursuing intimations and generalized statements by requesting details; spacing sensitive questions; ascertaining how close respondents were to events recounted; searching for accuracy through choice of questions; identifying other sources illuminating the events discussed; using documents as memory prods; returning to discussed topics in order to induce fresh recollections prompted by new angles of vision on them; focusing on the dynamics of events as they evolve as distinct from subsequent conclusions extracted from the unfolding events. (CTM)

1355. Morrissey, Charles T. *Oral History and the Mythmakers*. Washington: National Trust for Historic Preservation, 1964.

In this pamphlet the author argues that oral history becomes mythmaking if respondents are allowed to contrive spoken memories that are incomplete, knowingly distorted, or deliberately falsified, even if they sound plausible. Oral historians can counter these dangers by employing various strategies—being skeptical of the "instant mythology" that often colors media reports of emerging events; asking a respondent to defend a reminiscence against a hypothetical detractor; measuring oral accounts against independent written documents concerning the same events; seeking multiple witnesses of the same events; inducing a respondent's willingness to cooperate fully with an interviewer; and safeguarding sensitive passages through legal restrictions governing access and dissemination. The limitations of memory are also mentioned, together with the hazards of asking respondents to venture beyond what their memories actually encompass. (CTM)

1356. Stewart, John F., and staff. "Oral History Interviewing in Recent Sensitive Political Subjects." In Peter D. Olch and Forrest C. Pogue, eds. *Selections from the Fifth and Sixth National Colloquia on Oral History* (1970, 1971). New York: Oral History Association, 1972.

Stewart and staff members of the John F. Kennedy Library identify prominent types of respondents encountered in interviews recorded between 1966 and 1971: the reticent interviewee who distrusts frankness and/or questions the propriety of candor in interviews; the reserved interviewee who doubts his personal objectivity; the reluctant interviewee who minimizes his role in past events; the overenthusiastic interviewee who exaggerates his role; the biased interviewee; the forgetful interviewee; the "rehearsed" interviewee who trots out predictable and familiar rhetoric; and various crossbreeds of all these types. They contend that "a conservative policy in opening materials for research" is necessary to prevent damage to an ongoing oral history program "or to oral history in general." They conclude that "the only way to maintain the essential trust between ourselves and our interviewees that is necessary to acquire a good collection is for there to be an acute sensitivity on the part of interviewers, staff and users in protecting the confidence of the interviewee and the integrity of the program." (CTM)

IV. Evaluation, Standards, and Criticism

1357. Cutler, William W., III. "Accuracy in Oral History Interviewing." *Historical Methods Newsletter: Quantitative Analysis of Social, Economic, and Political Development*, Vol. III (June 1970), pp. 1-7.

Practitioners of oral history seek ways of maximizing accuracy in the face of human failings of the people interviewed (memory, bias, cultural value intrusions), the influence of the interviewer's bias and the unnatural synthetic interview situation on the respondent's "natural" responses, uncritical rapport, interviewee fears and embarrassments. There are techniques for dealing with these through offering security and confidentiality, diversification of questioning, repetitive questioning, generalized questions to bring out unanticipated areas of testimony or attitude, and the like. There are also external sources of error in the selection of interviewers and interviewees, project goals and foci, amount of research (by both parties), transcription and editing errors, and distortions. These can all contribute to inaccuracy or a skew in the product. Inaccuracies are common, but oral historians will not cease to refine their craft. (WWM)

1358. Fry, Amelia R. "Reflections on Ethics." *Oral History Review*, Vol. III (1975), pp. 16-29.

The ethical dilemma of whether an oral historian should advocate the preservation of taped evidence collected by means contrary to the *Goals and Guidelines* of the Oral History Association (OHA), occasioned by the discovery of Richard Nixon's taping system in the White House, is used as an opportunity to review and explicate the association's statement. Oral historians are both users and producers of historical evidence. The OHA ethics document focuses on a "Trinity"—the researcher, the interviewee, and the sponsoring institution—with goals and guidelines for each, implying reciprocal obligations and prohibitions. The adequacy of each guideline is examined against practice, and for each a series of perplexities, dilemmas, or contradictions is raised. Ethical relations among projects, the commercial use of oral history, and the question of value exchanged ("consideration" or *quid pro quo*) between interviewer and interviewee are raised. Should the definition of oral history be broad or narrow, and with what ethical implications? (WWM)

1359. Grele, Ronald J. "Can Anyone over Thirty Be Trusted: A Friendly Critique of Oral History." *Oral History Review*, Vol. VI (1978), pp. 36-44.

With age, experience, and growing acceptability, oral history must face the responsibility of candidly assessing the work to date. Catalogs are incomplete and ineffective. The usefulness of oral history needs to be examined. Reviewers of works based on oral sources seldom question them as they would written sources. Clearly oral history has produced both significant data and trivia, powerful documentary vision and sentimental trash. It has excited historians, but with excitement come dangers: to see oral history as a panacea for revitalizing the profession; to distort evidence by the very enthusiasm of the activity. Rather than using sophisticated theory to ask mundane questions, oral history uses naive theory to ask profound questions. Problems need to be addressed: Given a historical question, how do we determine that oral history can produce the answer? And how? What contributions lie in the linguistic and cognitive structure of historical memory and dialog? In the role of history in the culture? Three prominent aspects of oral history influence discussion of a theoretical base: oral history documents are not products of the past investigated, but rather of the present time of investigation; oral history forces people into unnatural historical self-justification; and oral history encourages personalization of events and experience. (WWM)

1359a. Handlin, Oscar. *Truth in History*. Cambridge, Mass.: Harvard University Press, 1979.

This *tour de force* collection of essays on the state of the history profession in the United States catalogs Handlin's grievances with the discontinuity and degeneration of historical standards, particularly in the post-World War II period. Of particular pertinence to oral history is the chapter on historical criticism, especially the section dealing with testimony of witnesses in which specific reference is made to oral history. Tape-recorded oral history lacks the continual contemporary critique of oral traditions, and much of the field lacks documentary verification. The techniques of verification require evaluation of provenance, knowledge of the stake of the witness in the testimony, and concordance of the testimony with other evidence. Throughout, Handlin reminds readers of the underlying universal of the search for truth, expressed not so much as an absolute empirical objective but rather as fidelity to evidence. Two sentences describing nineteenth-century historians who tried to write of the life of the people, rather than of statesmen and events, echo much of a failing of oral history noted elsewhere in this section: "Unable to formulate the appropriate problem, they found themselves in the position of Tolstoy's deaf man answering questions no one had asked. Useful as their work was, it lacked consistency of theme or of interpretation in the absence of a definition of the subject that supplied a guide to what was worth studying and why." (WWM)

1360. Hoyle, Norman. "Oral History." *Library Trends*, Vol. XXI (July 1972), pp. 60-82.

Oral history is dedicated to production of new documentation for the future through interviews with those who have something to say of lasting value. This article describes the state of affairs in the field of oral history. Definitions and terminology are unsettled; despite problems the field has grown impressively. There are three basic approaches: autobiographical interviews with a primary subject; biographical interviews with others about a primary subject; and interviews centered on a specific topic or event. Programs may use one of these approaches or combinations of them. Oral history work tends to be based on shared experience rather than a theory of interviewing, and the interviewing tends to be elite instead of survey in nature. The contrary pulls between directive and nondirective, precise and exploratory, and closure and expansiveness in interviewing make for a difficult conceptual problem that has not been explored in depth. It is still unclear what oral history does best and to what ends it can most effectively be employed. Preoccupied with techniques, practitioners have ignored these larger questions. Content analysis has not been done, comparisons for accuracy have not been performed, and studies have not been made of actual and potential users. Measures of quality and usefulness need to be developed before achievement can be assessed. (WWM)

1361. Morrissey, Charles T. "Oral History and the California Wine Industry: An Essay Review." *Agricultural History*, Vol. LI (July 1971), pp. 590-596.

Twenty-four manuscripts of figures in the California wine industry, developed by the Regional Oral History Office of the University of California, Berkeley, are evaluated. The project was funded by the Wine Advisory Board and focuses on key figures. Interviewing is not inhibited by its funding source. No survey of wine industry records (disrupted during Prohibition) was done, but research in published sources seems to have been thorough. Some editing rearranges testimony, and some relies on written exchanges to supplement transcribed interviews but usually retains the spoken character of the original interviews. (WWM)

1362. Moss, William W. "In Search of Values." *Oral History Review*, Vol. VII (1979), pp. 1-5.

Success in oral history, if measured by specialization, uncritical acceptance, glib facility, freedom from ideological bias, or degree of nonabstract practical application, does not lead to development of a high state of the art. The Oral History Association wishes for values by which to assure both recognition and reliability but finds rubrics difficult to frame, in part because the technique does not belong to that small group but rather to the whole community of scholars and beyond them to the amateur history buffs. But some evaluation of the product will occur, no matter what the Association does. In the long run, reliability and durability of oral history products will depend on (1) the veracity of the testimony; (2) the rigor of the research and inquiry and care and deliberateness of the processing; (3) the applicability of the product for all scholarly disciplines; (4) the honesty with which the product is used in analysis; (5) the degree to which the product is made available; and (6) the degree to which the privacy, rights, and interests of narrators are respected. Success should be measured as achievement rather than self-satisfaction. (WWM)

1363. Moss, William W. "The Future of Oral History." *Oral History Review*, Vol. III (1975), pp. 5-15.

Three trends in oral history are likely to grow but also to develop discriminating factors: books based on the oral testimony of the "common man," local and institutional history, and oral history interviewing as an adjunct of graduate research projects. There is a need for critical examination and evaluation of oral history practice and product. Technological gimmicks will likely invade the field of oral history: videotapes and cinematic film, magnetic tagging and indexing of tapes and film, electronic analysis of voices and tape authenticity, and oral history as a teaching tool. Oral historians will face some ethical problems: surreptitious taping of conversations for publication, invasion of privacy, the memory as individual property, the psychiatric implications of interviewing, the candor of communicating interviewer motives and purposes to interviewees, and the question of exploitation of sources. The question of the confidentiality of sources is omitted. (WWM)

1364. Olch, Peter D. "A Dirty Mind Never Sleeps and Other Comments on the Oral History Movement." *Bulletin of the Medical Library Association*, Vol. LIX (July 1971), pp. 438-443.

The desire of historians for candid, raw history is evoked by quotations from *A Dirty Mind Never Sleeps* by Max Wilk. Surreptitious recording is *not* a practice of the oral historian but candid commentary is. It is a worthy goal if coupled with standards to honor the desires of respondents for restrictions on access. The term "oral history" is misleading because the product is often a written transcript and it is one person's view rather than a "history." Oral history is here to stay, more because of the simplicity and ease of operating a tape recorder than its proven value to scholars. The limited time that can be devoted to oral history would probably be better spent if each interview were a basis for the next interview. The oral history movement is characterized by enthusiasm tempered by awareness of pitfalls. As a technique it is gaining modest respectability, but the burden of proof falls on its practitioners; and the product must stand on the merit of its content, not on the unique qualities of the technique. (WWM)

1365. Olch, Peter D. "Oral History and the Medical Librarians." *Bulletin of the Medical Library Association*, Vol. LVII (January 1969), pp. 1-4.

The growth, popularity, process, and products of oral history are briefly described. The oral history memoir is a record of the recollections of an individual in response to thoroughly prepared questions. Though the audiotape and transcript suffer the same weaknesses as written autobiography, compounded by interviewer influences, they are a valuable addition to source materials if readers are made aware of limitations. If reasonable standards are followed and concentration is applied to quality rather than quantity, the future of oral history is bright. The National Library of Medicine closely integrates its oral history collecting with its manuscripts acquisition program, and its collection consists of in-depth autobiographical memoirs and a series of subject-area investigations, plus selected taped lectures and speeches. (WWM)

1366. "Oral History Evaluation Guidelines." *Oral History Review*, Vol. VIII (1980), pp. 6-19. Also printed separately as a pamphlet by the Oral History Association, 1980.

The report of the Oral History Association's 1979 Wingspread Conference, approved by the Association's annual business meeting in October 1979, presents consensus guidelines for evaluating oral history projects and product in the form of outlines of questions to be used by reviewers and evaluators. Major headings for each series of guiding questions include: "Program/Project Guidelines," "Ethical/Legal Guidelines," "Tape/Transcript Processing Guidelines," "Interview Content Guidelines," and "Interview Conduct Guidelines." Notes on the background of the conference, task forces, and a bibliography are included. The declared purpose of the evaluation guidelines is for the use of those called upon to evaluate existing or proposed programs and projects as well as for the use of individuals to test their own procedures and funding agencies to appraise proposals. (WWM)

1367. Rapport, Leonard. "How Valid Are the Federal Writers' Project Life Stories: An Iconoclast among the True Believers." *Oral History Review*, Vol. VII (1979), pp. 6-17.

Researchers working on the Federal Writers' Project life stories seem uninterested in tests for validity. In fact, from the author's experience, the stories are wanting in evidence to substantiate authenticity as first-person accounts, except in rare instances. The employment of writers, who are tempted to be creative, instead of less intrusive "court reporters" is seen as detrimental to validation of the evidence. As literary truth, capturing spirit instead of literal fact, most of the work falls below the quality of writers such as James Agee, but the stories will probably endure and become part of the stuff of American history. See the response to this article by Tom E. Terrill and Jerrold Hirsch, no. *1371*. (WWM)

1368. Reingold, Nathan. "A Critic Looks at Oral History." *The Fourth National Colloquium on Oral History*. New York: The Oral History Association, 1970.

A verbatim transcript of the concluding session records Reingold's impressions from consulting the existing literature and attending the Colloquium in November 1969. He notes there are many different things called oral history and no experience or standards to differentiate one from another. Oral historians must decide whether they are "doing history," taking a step in the writing of history, or producing documentation. They need to know just what it is one does or does not get from oral histories and whether they are worth the expense. If oral history is aimed at reproducing a hypothetical "total body of information," it may be unrealistic. Contrary to claims of oral historians, twentieth-century paper records are richer and more plentiful than those of earlier times. Where much documentation exists, money might be better spent in organizing and describing the written records. Neither anthropological nor sociological interviewing is recommended as a model. So much oral history is sponsored that critical analysis may be inhibited. There is a call for sampling in the research design. There were several responses and comments: oral historians "document" the interview, not the past (which is the subject of the interview); oral histories should be submitted to be reviewed; oral history may be able to supply *why* things happened since the written record tends to record only *what* happened. (WWM)

1369. Schruben, Francis W. "An Even Stranger Death of President Harding." *Southern California Quarterly*, Vol. XLVIII (March 1966), pp. 57-84.

Opening with the question "How valid is oral history?" the article examines an oral memoir (compiled) of Ralph Palmer Merritt concerning the death of President Warren G. Harding and does so against such facts as may be established from other contemporary and memoir sources. Specific points in the Merritt narrative are tested against specific evidence from other sources, and the conclusion is that the Merritt story "as a whole must be discounted." Oral evidence should be collected, but it should be regarded as a raw stuff of history, not a refined product. (WWM)

1370. Soapes, Thomas F. "The Federal Writers' Project Slave Interviews: Useful Data or Misleading Source?" *Oral History Review*, Vol. V (1977), pp. 33-38.

The scope, content, and process of the interviews are briefly described. The instructions of the project directors, designed to retain authenticity and avoid creative writing by the editors, were not always followed, and a question of accuracy is raised. Scholars have disagreed on the historical value of the Federal Writers' Project oral histories of slavery. The comments of John W. Blassingame, Norman R. Yetman, and George P. Rawick are noted. The resolution of these conflicting estimates lies in how historians use the interviews (the uses by Eugene D. Genovese are noted). The important point is that a pattern of similar evidence was obtained through a number of separate interviews and that this evidence was confirmed by other sources, making it an important complement to sources on the history of American slavery. (WWM)

1371. Terrill, Tom E., and Jerrold Hirsch. "Replies to Leonard Rapport's 'How Valid Are the Federal Writers' Project Life Stories: An Iconoclast among the True Believers.' " *Oral History Review*, Vol. VIII (1980), pp. 81-92.

Rapport's critique of the Federal Writers' Project life histories and of the historians using them is seen as excessive (see no *1367*.) The users do, in fact, compare and collate with other documentary evidence. Rapport's equation of verbal accuracy with authenticity is wrongheaded and ignores the value of the feelings expressed and the uniqueness of the evidence. Rapport generalizes from a very narrow base to condemn a whole body of material. Posing the question of authenticity in either/or terms leads to a simplistic use of the materials. If scholars take into account their limitations, these life stories provide useful material. Rapport, who replies, challenges the authors to prove the authenticity of one story, "Tech 'Er Off, Charlie," by using internal evidence and available documentation for corroboration. If they can do that, he promises to "eat crow."(WWM)

1372. Tuchman, Barbara W. "Distinguishing the Significant from the Insignificant." *Radcliffe Quarterly*, Vol. LVI (March 1972), pp. 9-10.

The difference between research in past history and that in contemporary history is the stance and intent of the historian. In the latter, personal involvement and apologia are much more likely than a more detached perspective common to the former. The chief difficulty in contemporary history is overdocumentation. The tape recorder and acolytes of oral history are producing a few veins of gold but also "an artificial survival of trivia of appalling proportions" and "a vast mass of trash." Verbal interviews are useful, and the tape recorder is useful "in skilled hands and in needful circumstances"; but the long-run effect will be a downgrading of source material and what is made from it. The quantitative contributions of the computer are likewise mixed, clearly valuable in quantifiable fields such as economics and demography but often producing conclusions that "the unassisted human would have no difficulty in arriving at by ordinary deduction or intuition." Films and diaries are valuable for contemporary history, but diaries bring events down to too small a scale, making the broader generalizations difficult. (WWM)

1372a. Vansina, Jan. "The Evaluation of Testimonies."In Jan Vansina. *Oral Tradition: A Study in Historical Methodology.* Chicago: Aldine, 1965.

Despite varying points of view on the reliability of oral traditions as historical sources, there has been no theoretical study of the problem. Oral traditions are chains of testimony transmitted in different ways with varying effects and subject to distortions of memory and explanatory interpretations. Understanding testimony requires knowledge of language and society. Testimony is a mirage of reality affected by its function in the society and affected by the society's cultural values. Evaluating historical information from traditions varies according to the type of tradition. (A typology is offered.) Oral tradition as a whole has limitations and bias influenced by the political system, and the historian must use data supplied by other sources and disciplines in order to deal with it. The historian using oral sources applies the same sorts of tests as would be applied to other sources, and, although he arrives at a lower degree of probability, he is still doing valid history. To search for oral traditions one must study language and culture, survey extent of traditions in the society, classify them as to types, and then embark on systematic collection or sampling. (WWM)

V. Technique: Manuals and Guides

Allen, Barbara, and William Lynwood Montell. *From Memory to History: Using Oral Sources in Local Historical Research.* See no. *1473.*

This essay on using and evaluating oral testimony fills a gap in the technical literature. Its focus is local history, and its perspective is the predominantly folklore background of both authors. There is conceptual material on the distinctive nature of oral evidence. Another chapter offers internal and external validity tests. The folklorist's bent is evident in another section on discovering the hidden truths in testimony. Nearly one quarter of the texts consists of a case study based on a celebrated murder case in Tennessee. This book's message is both sobering and reassuring as to oral history's credibility and value. (CD)

1373. Baum, Willa K. *Oral History for the Local Historical Society.* Nashville: American Association for State and Local History, 1974.

The author has considerable experience in the profession as director of the Regional Oral History Office at the University of California, Berkeley. This primer, first published in 1969, offers advice on launching a program, selecting equipment and tapes, observing legal and ethical standards, conducting an interview, and preserving the product. There are brief sections on processing tapes and encouraging their use. (CD)

1374. Baum, Willa K. *Transcribing and Editing Oral History*. Nashville: American Association for State and Local History, 1977.

A knowledgable and experienced oral historian delivers systematic and practical advice in this 127-page booklet, which includes an annotated bibliography. Willa Baum explores the ways of transcribing and then explains each processing step: transcription, auditing, editing, narrator's review, indexing, final steps, and depository arrangements. A unique feature is the enclosed phonograph disc, which enables the beginner to practice transcribing and then test the results against a definitive version. (CD)

1375. Charlton, Thomas L. *Oral History for Texans*. Austin: Texas Historical Commission, 1981.

This volume is one of a growing collection of state-centered oral history textbooks. The author is a veteran practitioner and director of the oral history program at Baylor University. He synthesizes information and advice from many sources. While both the focus and the examples are limited to Texas, the advice applies universally, e.g., the section on interviewing. Nearly half of the book consists of appendices, several of which offer information of general interest. A bibliography, footnotes, and an index are included. (CD)

1376. Davis, Cullom, Kathryn Back, and Kay MacLean. *Oral History: From Tape to Type*. Chicago: American Library Association, 1977.

A textbook, this 141-page volume stems from its authors' experience at Sangamon State University's Oral History Office. It divides the craft into three basic activities: collecting, processing, and disseminating, within which it elaborates on eight oral history steps from "Getting Ready" to "Reaching the Public." The emphasis is not conceptual or analytical but practical, with ample illustration, a glossary of terms, an editor's style manual, and various exercises designed for readers to test their skills. Detailed processing instructions are included. (CD)

1377. Hoopes, James. *Oral History: An Introduction for Students*. Chapel Hill: University of North Carolina Press, 1979.

Tagged and subtitled as the only oral history manual designed pointedly for students, this volume explains how to collect and employ interviews for course assignments. After a brief historiographical introduction there follow remarks on the interaction of personality, culture, and society in shaping human behavior. Another section offers advice on arranging and conducting interviews. Concluding chapters deal with using the materials in term papers, observing legal strictures, and locating oral sources collected by others. (See also no. *1382*.) (CD)

1378. Ives, Edward D. *The Tape-Recorded Interview: A Manual for Field Workers in Folklore and Oral History*. Knoxville: University of Tennessee Press, 1980.

A folklore perspective and a bent for explaining recorder technology are the distinctive features of this manual. The author bases most of his advice and examples on years of experience collecting folklore and oral history in New England. Over one-quarter of the text is devoted to explaining the mechanics and electronics of tape recorders. This section is a full analysis in simple language of how a recording instrument actually works. A section on interviewing offers advice and several conceptual points. (CD)

1379. Lance, David. *An Archive Approach to Oral History*. London: Imperial War Museum, 1978.

From England comes a sixty-four-page manual for the archivist and librarian faced with producing, preserving, and servicing oral history materials. The author's work with sound archives at the Imperial War Museum is evident in his approach to the specialized housekeeping problems associated with oral history. Drawing examples from a project on sailors in the Royal Navy, Lance briefly covers basic steps in the oral history process, devoting greater attention to the important questions of library cataloging and indexing. There is also information on the preservation of sound recordings. A feature of the section on use is its primary attention to performance opportunities such as radio broadcasts and exhibits. (CD)

1380. Moss, William W. *Oral History Program Manual*. New York: Praeger, 1974.

Considerable thought and experience underlie the instructions and advice in this book. The author's association with the massive oral history program of the John F. Kennedy Library is evident in the examples offered and the standards established. The book is more a guide for mature programs than a text for beginners. It features chapters on starting a program, conducting interviews, processing tapes, record keeping, and operating a major oral history program. An appendix offers additional information, including specific instructions on transcribing. (CD)

1381-1382. Oblinger, Carl. *Interviewing the People of Pennsylvania: A Conceptual Guide to Oral History*. Harrisburg, Pennsylvania: Historical and Museum Commission, 1978.

The subject matter is limited to one state, but the perspective and information are of general interest. Drawing on the experiences of an extensive working people's project in Pennsylvania, the author offers an emphatic "grass roots" or people's history approach. Analysis of industrialization's impact on family, ethnic, and community history is coupled with straightforward advice on technique. Among the appendices is an interview for family and work topics. The emphasis in this book is conceptual, with frequent references to other manuals for detailed technical assistance. (CD)

VI. Oral History and Teaching

Hoopes, James. *Oral History: An Introduction for Students*. See no. *1377*.

This comprehensive guidebook is intended for the college student. The introductory chapters on "Personality," "Culture," and "Society" show how oral history is intimately related to the disciplines of psychology, anthropology, and social science. Hoopes also explores the similarities and differences between traditional historical methodology and oral history. The last half of the book provides a step-by-step, how-to-do-it guide for students and considers some legal and ethical issues. (See also no. *1377*.) (JAN)

1383. Humez, Jean M., and Laurie Crumpacker. "Oral History in Teaching Women's Studies." *Oral History Review*, Vol. VII (1979), pp. 53-69.

The widespread emergence of women's studies courses and programs in the 1970s has helped to expand the use of oral history in teaching. Since the lives of twentieth-century women were much less likely to be documented by traditional sources, oral history serves to enrich understanding of both the public and private lives of women in America. Humez explains how she has used oral history at the University of Massachusetts (Boston) to help students develop their research and writing skills as well as to facilitate deeper personal awareness of feminism. Crumpacker provides an overview of her use of oral history in teaching women's history at Boston University and particularly the use of an Erik Erikson life-cycle schemata. (JAN)

1384. "Oral History as a Teaching Tool: Panel Discussion." *Oral History Review*, Vol. I (1973), pp. 29-47.

This work presents proceedings of a panel presented on November 11, 1972, at the Seventh Annual Colloquium on Oral History, Austin, Texas. Three of the panelists—Eliot Wigginton (Rabun Gap-Nachoohie School, Georgia), Barbara Gallant (Gainesville High School, Florida), and Edward Ives (the University of Maine)—were pioneers in the development of oral history as a teaching tool. All three provide candid commentary about how to set up a successful oral history project for students. Wigginton explains how the *Foxfire* series came into being, while Gallant discusses the more conventional high school classroom, and Ives comments on the intensive college-level folklore and oral history experience for students. (JAN)

1385. Neuenschwander, John A. *Oral History as a Teaching Approach*. Washington: National Education Association, 1976.

The successful use of oral history in teaching usually requires both a willingnesss to set reasonable goals and some firsthand experience with interviewing. Teachers who are unwilling to roll up their sleeves and devote substantial amounts of time to training students to interview and then going over the results should avoid large-scale oral history projects. The thesis of this primer is that experience in historical research should be the goal of most student-based projects rather than trying to create oral history research collections. By means of their own "discovery," students learn that all history is not fact and that multiple viewpoints exist on even the most common historical incidents and events. (JAN)

1386. Sullivan, Margaret. "Into Community Classrooms: Another Use for Oral History." *Oral History Review*, Vol. II (1974), pp. 53-58.

Most publications on oral history as a teaching approach focus on the students as interviewers. Sullivan views oral history in teaching from the librarian's perspective and suggests a number of ways in which oral history collections can be utilized to enrich classroom materials. Skillful use of interview materials can make national events like the Great Depression or World War II seem more real, while contemporary controversies like teachers' strikes can be used to illustrate the multiplicity of views and positions that often exist. (JAN)

VII. Oral History: Biography

1387. Albertson, Dean. *Roosevelt's Farmer: Claude R. Wickard and the New Deal*. New York: Columbia University Press, 1961.

Purporting to be a biography of Claude Wickard, secretary of agriculture, 1940-1945, this book is in reality a study of New Deal agriculture. It describes the shifts in policy, the conflicting personalities, and the struggles for power in wartime Washington. The text is based in large measure on extensive oral history interviews with Wickard, Henry A. Wallace, M. L. Wilson, and many other agricultural and political leaders of the New Deal preserved in the Columbia Oral History Collection. The verbatim excerpts from the oral history interviews are set off in italics and carefully footnoted in each case. (EBM)

1388. Baum, Willa K. "Oral History, the Library, and the Genealogical Researchers." *Journal of Library History*, Vol. V (October 1970), pp. 359-371.

This article considers the usefulness of existing oral history materials to the genealogist, with a definition and brief account of the development of oral history up to 1970. The author describes research aids for locating pertinent oral history material, with some indication of major centers at that time. In another section, she suggests ways in which the genealogist can use oral history techniques to gather information not only for his own purposes but for wider historical research, and she urges libraries to welcome and preserve such tape-recorded accounts. (EBM)

1389. Benison, Saul. *Tom Rivers: Reflections on a Life in Medicine and Science*. Cambridge, Mass.: M.I.T. Press, 1967.

The introduction to this volume explains in detail the circumstances under which this oral history memoir was created and offers an exegesis of oral history itself—its values and drawbacks. The book consists of the transcribed oral history interviews that took place over fifteen months with an American pioneer of research on viruses. The transcripts have been minimally edited by Dr. Benison; he tells us he arranged the material in chronological and chapter order, eliminated repetitions, and inserted missing names and dates. (EBM)

1390. Dunaway, David King. *How Can I Keep from Singing: Pete Seeger.* New York: McGraw-Hill, 1981.

This biography of Pete Seeger, America's political activist-folksinger, makes heavy use of 110 interviews conducted by Dunaway with Seeger, his contemporaries, relatives, and friends. A musician of considerable achievement in the area of folksongs and folk music-making techniques, Seeger's musical career has been overshadowed by political controversy. The book covers his clash with the House Committee on Un-American Activities during the McCarthy period, court battles, blacklisting in the music industry, and Seeger's lifelong support of trade unions and political movements. The author researched Seeger's own files and 1,600 F.B.I. documents released under a Freedom of Information Act suit. Direct quotations from the interviews are woven into the text, and there are footnotes, a detailed bibliography, and a complete discography of Seeger's commercial discs. (WKB)

1391. Martin, George. *Madam Secretary: A Biography of Frances Perkins.* Boston: Houghton Mifflin, 1976.

In his introduction, the author explains his decision to write a biography rather than a history and discusses his extensive use of dialog, most of it taken from Miss Perkins's taped and transcribed interviews in the Columbia Oral History collection. He makes a case for her leadership in social legislation from 1925 to 1945, though he admits that his reliance on her account of events means that to some extent reality is perceived through her eyes. He conducted many interviews of his own as well as using Miss Perkins's voluminous papers and oral history, and the sources for each chapter are noted and described. The book is a contribution to women's history and labor history as well as to accounts of the New Deal years. (EBM)

1392. Meltzer, Milton. "Using Oral History: A Biographer's Point of View." *Oral History Review,* Vol. VII (1979), pp. 42-46.

Meltzer provides a perceptive analysis of the importance of an oral history transcript to a biography. He describes the contribution of the oral history interviews conducted with his subject, Dorothea Lange, by the Regional Oral History Office at the University of California, Berkeley, and then considers the ways in which his own interviews (over a hundred) supplemented those done by others. His understanding of the oral history product is laid out in brief terms: the omissions and distortions, the essential cross-checking, the personal bias of some speakers, the need to guard against uncritical acceptance. Suzanne Riess, the interviewer/editor who conducted the Berkeley oral history of Dorothea Lange, responds to Meltzer from her special point of view. (EBM)

1393. Miller, Merle. *Lyndon: An Oral Biography.* New York: G. P. Putnam's Sons, 1980.

Page after page of this biography interweaves quotations from one speaker after another on the topic under discussion. The author himself conducted 180 interviews, and associates added several more; 276 interviews were consulted at the Lyndon Baines Johnson Library, eighty-nine at the John F. Kennedy Library, and various at other libraries and collections. The difficulty lies in the attribution of the material; it is not always clear where precise quotations come from. Some are identified in the notes; others are covered in occasional general statements ("Unless otherwise specified, quotes of Lyndon's that appear in this book come from various radio and television interviews throughout his political career.") (EBM)

1394. Miller, Merle. *Plain Speaking: An Oral Biography of Harry S. Truman.* New York: Berkley; distributed by G. P. Putnam's Sons, 1973.

This biography of President Truman derives from a series of conversations, some taped, in 1961 and 1962, plus other material. The purpose of the conversations was to gather material for a television series, but when that did not materialize, the author organized the questions and answers into this book. Words are attributed to Truman without the possible corroboration of tapes and transcripts in a recognized repository. The kind and degree of editing of the President's words is not clear. (EBM)

1395. Mintz, Sidney W. "The Anthropological Interview and the Life History." *Oral History Review,* Vol. VII (1979), pp. 18-26.

The article examines the ethnographic interview as used in collecting life histories and argues the need for broader study of the community within which the principal informant lives and works. The author describes the relationship between culture and personality, and he points out that the ethnographer and the informant are in essence interrogating each other. The ethnographer's role in helping the reader see the informant within the culture and society is made plain. The insights into interviewing in this article are of interest to others besides anthropologists. (EBM)

1396. Parmet, Herbert S. *Jack: The Struggles of John F. Kennedy.* New York: Dial, 1980.

This first part of a comprehensive two-volume biography deals with the pre-presidential years of John F. Kennedy, drawing heavily from oral history interviews at the Kennedy Library and in other collections as well as on much additional published and unpublished material. Vivid personal glimpses from interviews with intimates provide highlights in the background tapestry of the political and social currents of the period. The author conducted many interviews of his own to resolve inconsistencies and fill gaps. The book adds new information and objectivity to a figure about whom one would think little new could be said. (EBM)

1397. Perlis, Vivian. *Charles Ives Remembered: An Oral History*. New Haven: Yale University Press, 1974.

Perlis has properly subtitled her book on Charles Ives; it is indeed an oral history, or rather a mosaic of fifty-eight transcribed oral history interviews, about an extraordinary man. The transcripts have been edited, we are told, to eliminate repetition and to correct factual error. (EBM)

1398. Phillips, Harlan B. *Felix Frankfurter Reminisces: Recorded in Talks with Dr. Harlan B. Phillips*. New York: Reynal, 1960.

This is perhaps the earliest publication of close-to-verbatim oral history transcripts. The inclusion of the questions is of particular importance; we are told in the foreword that Dr. Phillips had access to the justice's files, and the questions reflect the use he made of that privilege. The extent and kind of editing employed may be judged by comparison with the transcripts of some of the earlier interviews, available at the Columbia Oral History Collection. Phillips tells us that this experience, done without thought of publication at the time, was for the justice "just talk," not an autobiography. (EBM)

1399. Pogue, Forrest C. *George C. Marshall: Education of a General, 1880-1939; Ordeal and Hope, 1939-1942; Organizer of Victory, 1943-1945*. New York: Viking, 1963, 1966, 1973.

This multivolume biography of General Marshall provides a distillation of information from many sources, of which oral history is an important one. The author stresses his extensive use of General Marshall's papers and of official documents, but these are leavened by material from the interviews with the general and with more than three hundred of his associates. In addition to the overall bibliographic note, the chapters carry general summaries of sources used, and each quotation is meticulously attributed. The reader can, therefore, trace the contributions of the oral history and the other material and thereby note the way in which the variety of sources is used to present a full-length portrait. (EBM)

1400. Rosengarten, Theodore. *All God's Dangers: The Life of Nate Shaw*. New York: Knopf, 1974.

This account of the life of a black sharecropper and tenant farmer in Alabama, told in his own words, has been carved out of 120 hours of recorded tape. The editing, we are told, consisted of condensation and elimination of repetition. Nate Shaw was a natural storyteller who knew how to combine his individual story with those of his people and region. Oral history here preserves a story that could have been known in no other way. (EBM)

1401. Stursberg, Peter. *Diefenbaker: Leadership Gained, 1956-62.* Toronto: University of Toronto Press, 1975.

This first volume of a two-volume history of the Diefenbaker era in recent Canadian history is an example of oral history from many associates of the central figure. The respondents are identified in each case and allowed to speak for themselves, with linking text from the author. Varying views of the same event, different assessments, and contradictory statements are drawn from some forty participants in interviews that ranged from one to four hours and totaled more than a million words. Diefenbaker himself was interviewed for nineteen hours by Peter Stursberg, only to sign a contract to write his own memoirs and enjoin Stursberg's use of the interviews. The author characterized the book as "the recorded table talk of cabinet ministers and other insiders and, as such, . . . the raw material of history."(EBM)

1402. Toland, John. *Adolf Hitler.* New York: Doubleday, 1976.

This detailed and comprehensive biography is based in significant part, the author tells us, on his more than 250 interviews with Hitler's surviving adjutants. While many previously unpublished documentary sources were also used, the notes illustrate how frequently the interviews provided humanizing touches and the kind of detail that comes from personal observation. The tapes have been preserved and made available for later scholarly use. (EBM)

1403. Williams, T. Harry. *Huey Long.* New York: Knopf, 1969.

The author interviewed nearly three hundred of Long's intimates, including most of the key men in his political machine. The interviews are candid and detailed in their recollection of events. The sources are carefully identified (although not the dates of the interviews), and the author has used available documentary material. The biography is a blueprint of how a political machine was built, an account of the use and corruption of power. (EBM)

VIII. Oral History: The Arts

1404. Cook, John W., and Heinrich Klotz. *Conversations with Architects.* New York: Praeger, 1973.

The authors have interviewed eight architects (Philip Johnson, Kevin Roche, Paul Randolph, Betrand Goldberg, Morris Lapidus, Louis Kahn, Charles Moore, and Robert Venturi) who represent the contemporary American architectual tradition. The two prompt the architects to talk freely about their ideas and theories. Selected examples of an architect's work are critiqued in an effort to understand how each attempts to accomplish his design goals. The book contains abundant illustrations of both the subjects' buildings and those of other architects referred to in the interviews. (BG)

1405. Cummings, Paul. *Artists in Their Own Words.* New York: St. Martin's, 1979.

The author conducted lengthy interviews for over a dozen years for the Archives of American Art. Interviews with Rockwell Kent, Thomas Hart Benton, Ivan Albright, Katherine Schmidt, Walker Evans, Isamu Noguchi, Fairfield Porter, Kenneth Noland, Philip Pearlstein, Carl Andre, Lucas Samaras, and Robert Smithson have been edited for this book. Half of the subjects had died by the time of publication. The introduction offers suggestions on how to conduct an "unstructured" interview and how to elicit the artist's story. Cummings favors the long interview: "The more hours taped, the more rewarding the interview." The interviews are organized by birthdate, and a short introductory statement provides some basic biographical information, describes the circumstances of the interview, and delineates the artist's unique style and place in history. Photographs of the artists and of their works accompany the interviews. (BG)

1406. Cunningham, Kitty, and Michael Ballard. *Conversations with a Dancer.* New York: St. Martin's, 1980.

Kitty Cunningham is a writer on the dance, and Michael Ballard is a soloist and dance captain of the Murray Louis Dance Company. The course of their conversations takes them from a motel room in Moscow, Idaho ("What is a nice boy like you doing in a town like this?"), to a cemetery in Saratoga Springs, a psychiatrist's office in New York, under a tree at the Jacob's Pillow Dance Festival, and finally to the Ben Franklin Hotel in Philadelphia. The interviews range over a period of several years, beginning March 1975. The book is about performing and about the work and pleasure that Ballard has experienced in his chosen profession. They discuss his background, the teaching and choreography of Alwin Nikolais and Murray Louis, and the difficulties of touring. The book is a spirited exchange between two people who enjoy talking about dance. (BG)

1407. Mitchell, Loften. *Voices of the Black Theatre.* Clifton, N.J.: James T. White, 1975.

Through individual recollections, the book captures the long tradition of black theatre in America. The publisher approached Mitchell to tape-record key figures in the black theatre movement: Eddie Hunter, Dick Campbell, Abram Hill, Frederick O'Neal, Regina Andrews, Ruby Dee, and Vinnette Carroll. In an introductory essay, the author offers his view of the history of the black experience in America and how it found theatrical expression and form with Harlem as its creative center. This select group of black artists discusses their involvement with the Harlem Experimental Theatre, American Negro Theatre, and Urban Arts Corps, plus their own personal pursuits as actors, playwrights, directors, and managers. The writer acknowledges the other pioneers and other movements not represented in the volume. (BG)

Perlis, Vivian. *Charles Ives Remembered*. See no. *1397*.
There is a recording of segments of the oral histories used in this book. It is a disc, playing time 48 minutes 53 seconds, entitled *Charles Ives Remembered*, included in the album, *Charles Ives: The 100th Anniversary* (Columbia M4 32504 c CBS, Inc.).

1408. Powers, James. "The Film History Program of the Center for Advanced Film Studies of the American Film Institute." *Performing Arts Resources*, Vol. I (1974), pp. 79-87.
Powers gives the background of the establishment of the American Film Institute (AFI) and, particularly, the Film History Program administered by the Center for Advanced Film Studies. He describes the Film History Advisory Committee and its role in the selection of oral history subjects. "Oral Historians" are directly funded through an Institute grant and have at their disposal AFI's full supportive program of screening rooms and film research material. Special problems in interviewing the famous elderly are noted—for example, the pros and cons of screening films for the subject as a stimulus to memory. Powers stresses the importance of the interviewer as alert listener and discusses how the interview material is processed and made availablle. (BG)

1409. Previn, Andre, ed. *Orchestra*. Garden City: Doubleday, 1979.
Interviews with thirty-one musicians from the ranks of the great orchestras of Britain and America have been organized into a full narrative of orchestra life. The result is an intriguing look at the orchestra as seen from the players' platform. The book is divided into thirteen sections comprised of the musicians' views on a solo theme—training, work, instruments, playing, and so forth. All individual responses are identified except in the chapters on the players' beginnings and their opinions of famous conductors. Michael Foss's role as interviewer and his methodology in the production of the book receives no elaboration. The work is handsomely illustrated. (BG)

1410. Rosenberg, Bernard, and Harry Silverstein. *The Real Tinsel*. New York: Macmillan, 1970.
The authors acknowledge that as social scientists they are more interested in the "life history" than in history. Through taped, informal, three-way conversations they have collected the oral life histories of twenty-four veteran Hollywood film executives, directors, players, and technicians, many of whom were involved with picture making from its early beginning—Hal Roach, Sr., Adolph Zukor, Conrad Nagel, Edward Everett Horton, Max Steiner. Taken together, these recollections of their life and work give human dimension to a business dedicated to larger-than-life productions. Each describes what it was like to be

part of this ever-changing industry over a span of decades. The writers express faith in the reliability of these oldsters' memories and the authenticity of their stories: "Time liberates the chronological survivor from opportunism." In presenting the material they strive to retain style, tone, and mannerism. The tapes have been deposited in historical archives for future use. (BG)

1411. Rosenberg, Deena, and Bernard Rosenberg. *The Music Makers.* New York: Columbia University Press, 1979.

This book of thirty-two interviews by a father/daughter (sociologist/musicologist) team attempts to document the broad range of endeavors and interaction of thirty-two composers, conductors, performers, critics, managers, impresarios, and scholars—Aaron Copeland, Michael Tilson Thomas, Claudio Arrau, Rudolph Bing, among others—in the classical-music world. The volume is the first published product of the Project for the Oral History of Music in America (POHMA) at the City University of New York, directed by Barry S. Brook, who wrote the foreword. Brook builds a case for the use of oral history documentation, especially in music, and speaks of other projects under POHMA sponsorship. The Rosenbergs conducted the interviews in tandem, but for publication they have incorporated their questions within the subjects' responses. In the overview the authors explain their strategem and defend the sociological approach of their inquiry. The book covers a range of themes: socialization and estrangement of the musician, European-American cross-fertilization, horizontal and vertical mobility, and the resistence to contemporary music. (BG)

1412. Schafer, William J., and Richard B. Allen. *Brass Bands and New Orleans Jazz.* Baton Rouge: Louisiana State University Press, 1977.

The book draws on oral histories and other research material in the Hogan Jazz Archive in the Tulane University Library to produce this study of New Orleans brass bands and their influence on jazz music. The bands were part of a greater American musical tradition in the post-Civil War era, when municipal bands of amateur players, some with military-band experience, were formed throughout the country. Although brass-band music contributed incalculably to jazz, street bands and jazz groups are seen as having separate histories and traditions. The book traces the development and mingling of these two notable American musical inventions. (BG)

1413. Schipper, Merle. "Los Angeles Art Community: Group Portrait (A Year-End Report)." *LAICA Journal*, no. 12 (October-November 1976), pp. 6-7. Los Angeles Institute of Contemporary Art.

In 1975 the UCLA Oral History Program, through a grant from the National Endowment for the Humanities, undertook an interview project, "Los Angeles Art Community: Group Portrait." This article describes the genesis of the project and how it was implemented. Schipper, a project member, relates how the interviewers were recruited and trained. The project staff interviewed thirty people prominent in the Los Angeles art scene—dealers, curators, artists—to document the local development of contemporary art and the emergence of Los Angeles as an international art center. The writer evaluates the effectiveness of the project's use of videotaping for documentation. (BG)

1414. Shaw, Arnold. *Honkers and Shouters: The Golden Years of Rhythm and Blues*. New York: Collier Books/Macmillan, 1978.

Working in the pop music field from 1944 to 1966, the author-musicologist-composer brings an insider's view to this comprehensive study of rhythm and blues (R&B). To document the development of R & B from its roots in country blues, he has included twenty-five taped interviews ("grooves") with artists, songwriters, record producers, and others who pioneered this "indigenous black art form and style." Shaw focuses on the period 1945-1960, from the post-swing era to the pre-Beatles invasion when R & B became absorbed into the mainstream of pop music. Interviews with major figures associated with the R&B scene— Jimmy Witherspoon, B. B. King, T-Bone Walker, Johnny Otis, Louis Jordan, Jerry Wexler, and others—have been edited to read as continuous narratives. The volume contains a discography and select bibliography. (BG)

1415. Steen, Mike. *Hollywood Speaks: An Oral History*. New York: G. P. Putnam's Sons, 1974.

The twenty-five chapters of the book correspond to the various categories in movie credits. Each category is represented by an interview with an outstanding practitioner in that particular field (that is, leading man, Henry Fonda; director, William Wellman; costume design, Edith Head; director of musical numbers, Busby Berkeley). The interviews follow a similar pattern: the subjects offer biographical details, tell how they broke into the motion-picture business, describe their jobs, reminisce about their films and colleagues, and sometimes express opinions of the industry. In the introduction, Steen offers his concept of oral history and tells how he edited the transcripts for publication. His questions remain in the text. The complete interviews are in the oral history collection of the American Film Institute. (BG)

1416. Suid, Lawrence H. *Guts and Glory: Great American War Movies*. Reading, Mass.: Addison-Wesley, 1978.

More than three hundred interviews with people in the motion-picture industry, the media, and the military comprise the primary source for this book, which examines selected war movies from World War I to the 1970s. The author describes how the changing presentation of the American military image in the Hollywood feature film has influenced the nation's attitude toward war and its perception of the military establishment. Production problems and film makers' efforts, not always successful, to secure the assistance and cooperation of the Department of Defense for movie projects receive special attention. (BG)

IX. Oral History: Ethnic and Minority History

1417. Bullock, Paul. *Watts, the Aftermath: An Inside View of the Ghetto by the People of Watts.* New York: Grove, 1969.

The 1965 riot in this Los Angeles Negro ghetto had both conventional and ideological significance; however, the book is designed to explore more than the community's reaction to the riot. The problems it faces every day are continually significant. The author opted not to follow rigid conventional research techniques but rather to probe deeply into the feelings of people with whom he had a long-established personal tie and rapport. Questions of validity, representativeness, and others are examined in the light of this approach. About thirty people were interviewed between 1966 and 1969, often several times. All interview passages are presented with little editing, but pseudonyms are used throughout to protect the narrators, who often discuss illegal behavior. Each chapter begins with an introduction to its subject, and bridging material appears between interview excerpts. After chapters focused on the riot, employment, the police, schools, drugs, welfare, and so on, the book closes with the author's very subjective observations. (BMK)

1418. Epstein, Helen. *Children of the Holocaust: Conversations with the Sons and Daughters of the Survivors.* New York: G. P. Putnam's Sons, 1979.

The daughter of survivors of the concentration camps of Auschwitz and Terezin, in order to come to terms with her parents' past and her own confusions and fears, expands her quest to interviews with "hundreds" of other such children, most of whom are approaching thirty years of age. The book is deeply personal and yet succeeds in generalizing the traumatic effects of the camp experience on the survivors and their children. Several synthesizing chapters, deeply introspective, are spaced among a selected few interviews. One chapter and the bibliography detail the professional literature on the subject, which by 1978 amounted to only twenty-five items. Only two of these are considered to be substantive. (BMK)

1419. Fontana, Bernard. "American Indian Oral History." *History and Theory,* Vol. VIII, no. 3 (1969), pp. 366-370.

Ethnohistory is defined as the history of nonliterate people. In the case of Indians, it is the history of Indians based on evidence written by someone other than Indians themselves. Fortunately, there are many other forms of data available to piece together the history of nonliterate societies. The questions of oral tradition as historical fact and the validity of oral testimony are examined. The anthropologist collecting oral history from American Indians is most likely to collect culture history, descriptions of the way people live from day to day. The truth or untruth of oral traditions is irrelevant; the aim is to retrieve the Indians' point of view. Navajos today wish to correct the history that has been written for them by the white man. (BMK)

1420. Fry, Gladys-Marie. *Night Riders in Black Folk History*. Knoxville: University of Tennessee Press, 1975.

Oral testimony, recent and of earlier periods, is used to describe efforts to intimidate southern blacks by exploiting any fear of the supernatural they might have, during slavery, the post-Civil War decades, and in the District of Columbia up to about 1915. The prologue is a critical analysis of what is available as historical source material for the early periods: several publications before 1900 and twentieth-century efforts including the "Slave Narratives" of the Works Projects Administration, which had gathered two thousand narratives by 1939. The last chapters include interview excerpts from well-identified D.C. natives who were children about 1900-1910. The question of the validity of all this material is addressed throughout. (BMK)

1421. Haley, Alex. "Black History, Oral History, and Genealogy." *Oral History Review*, Vol. I (1973), pp. 1-3.

The author of *Roots* describes, three years before publication, his exciting search for his ancestors, beginning with boyhood evenings spent listening to older relatives recall family stories and on to later searches in Africa and England, numerous libraries, naval and other government archives, and with linguistic specialists and historians both here and abroad. All of his earlier experiences have worked together to provide him with the necessary inspiration, contact, or expertise to result in a successful conclusion. His cooperation with Malcolm X in writing *The Autobiography of Malcolm X* is described. *Roots* will offer evidence that the study of black genealogy and black history is feasible and worthwhile. (BMK)

1422. Krech, Shepard, III. *Praise the Bridge That Carries You Over: The Life of Joseph L. Sutton*. Cambridge, Mass.: Schenkman, 1981.

This intensive biography deals with a black farm laborer who lived quietly for ninety-four years in an out-of-the-way rural area in Maryland. The author, an anthropologist, painstakingly follows that methodology in his interviewing technique, his search for corroborative evidence, the inclusion of helpful graphic material, and a history of the county involved. A second appendix explains the rationale and options in preparing eighty hours of interview transcript for publication, both as to editing down and as to making Sutton's vocabulary and speech patterns easy reading. The book displays professional awareness of problems to be faced in both biographical interviewing and the preparation of local history. (BMK)

1423. Mitson, Betty E. "Looking Back in Anguish: Oral History and Japanese-American Evacuation." *Oral History Review*, Vol. II (1974), pp. 24-51.

Over 110,000 West Coast Japanese, 60 percent of whom were American-born, were sent inland to relocation camps at the outset of World War II, and most remained there until the war ended, never fully recovering their personal property, homes, or businesses. It is necessary to collect oral evidence for this huge evacuation from both administrators of the program and the Japanese because the moves were made so swiftly, leaving few contemporary documents. Quotes from the interviews now held at the University of California, Berkeley, and at California State College, Fullerton, supply material on the Japanese failure to organize resistance efforts, the roundup of key leaders and elders first, unsuccessful efforts to help the Japanese by Herbert V. Nicholson, and the treatment accorded a loyal Japanese-American and his Caucasian wife. (BMK)

Montell, William Lynwood. *The Saga of Coe Ridge*. See no. *1480*.

1424. Morrison, Joan, and Charlotte Fox Zabusky. *American Mosaic*. New York: Dutton, 1980.

The intention of the authors is to supplement studies of American immigration with the stories of people who actually experienced it. The book is not a who's who of American immigration, although a few prominent people were interviewed, but a cross-section of interviewees representing a wide variety of immigrants. With the tape recorder as their only research tool, the authors focused on three main questions: Why did the immigrant come? How did he come? What did he find when he got here? The book presents responses only in monologue form. The researchers ascertained that many of the reasons for immigration matched those of empirical studies but also that each individual was humanly unique. This uniqueness supports the main premise of the book: that the "melting pot" idea of conforming to an American life-style is being slowly eroded, but with the surge in ethnic pride, people see themselves as being an individual piece that contributes to the American mosaic. (EHD)

1425. Motley, Mary Penick. *The Invisible Soldier: The Experience of the Black Soldier, World War II*. Detroit: Wayne State University Press, 1975.

The Invisible Soldier is a compilation of oral histories pertaining to the experience of the black soldier in World War II. Having overcome the difficulties of tracking down black ex-servicemen and then gaining their confidence to speak to a woman about their experiences, the author relates the problems of a black man in a white man's army. The interviewees are grouped together by fighting units, and each chapter describes the unit, where it fought, and its accomplishments. The author acknowledges that accounts conflict because of the thirty-year lapse in retrieving the information, but these are noted within the work, and sometimes the recollections of one man's story fills the gaps of another man's story. In addition to stories dealing with heroism, cameraderie within black units, and racism, the author demonstrates that blacks did not shun their duty in defending America during wartime. (EHD)

1426. National Council of Jewish Women Pittsburgh Section. *By Myself I'm a Book! An Oral History of the Immigrant Jewish Experience in Pittsburgh*. Waltham, Mass.: American Jewish Historical Society, 1972.

A large-scale, professionally done oral history project can be designed and carried out by an all-volunteer women's group, in this case the Pittsburgh Section of the National Council of Jewish Women, working under the supervision of a university professor of anthropology. Over two hundred Jewish immigrants who came to Pittsburgh between 1909 and 1924 were queried about their lives before emigration, the trip and arrival here, and Pittsburgh experiences in working, education, recreation, health, religiosity, social and political activities, and Americanization. Chapters present interview excerpts focusing on each of these areas, with considerable bridging material. The full history of the Jewish population of Pittsburgh is found in a lengthy appendix. The introduction details how three sets of volunteers were organized to execute the project. (BMK)

1427. Painter, Nell Irvin. *The Narrative of Hosea Hudson: His Life as a Negro Communist in the South*. Cambridge, Mass.: Harvard University Press, 1979.

Described by Painter as a "collaborative oral biography," the book gives, in first person, a chronicle of Hudson's activities as a Communist Party organizer and as organizer and official of other radical and labor groups there between 1917 and 1948. There was a widespread feeling among southern blacks that the National Association for the Advancement of Colored People (NAACP) was only for the "better class of Negroes" and recruitment by the Communists therefore profited. There is an introduction by Hudson and another by Painter. The latter explains at length Painter's role in the long interview period and in preparing the material for publication. Labor history in the South of this period is dealt with in detail. (BMK)

1428. Patrick, Mary. "Indian Urbanization in Dallas: A Second Trail of Tears." *Oral History Review*, Vol. I (1973), pp. 48-65.

Indians who had testified at the Dallas hearings for the National Council on Indian Opportunity in 1968 were interviewed to determine what progress had been made in the subsequent three years in their social and economic conditions and the psychological adjustments required of Indians moving from the reservations to Dallas. The Indians' cooperation was good, after initial frustrations on the interviewer's part. Besides the above points, interviews covered education, housing, employment, recreation, health, legal problems, orientation of human life, and communication problems. Individual interviews are cited in a discussion of the project findings. The entire collection of interviews, along with notes on the records of the Bureau of Indian Affairs Relocation Program, can be found in the Texas Collection, Baylor University, Waco, Texas. (BMK)

1429. Raines, Howell. *My Soul Is Rested: Movement Days in the Deep South Remembered*. New York: G. P. Putnam's Sons, 1977.

The author, a political reporter, feels that there is a New South and that the civil rights movement created it. His goal was to assemble the story of its activists for the years between 1955 (Rosa Parks's arrest) to 1968 (Dr. Martin Luther King's assassination) as they themselves recalled it. About a hundred interviews are used, some from well-known names but many not. They were organizers, Freedom Riders, marchers, leaders of SNCC (Student Nonviolent Coordinating Committee) and SCLC (Southern Christian Leadership Conference), politicians, opponents, and reporters. Besides the historical record developed, the interviews reveal long-held aspirations, the deep religious faith of many, stoic courage, and the exaltation found in the struggle. The choice of interviewees and transcribing and editing steps are explained, and a chronology is given; Raines's questions often become part of the text. (BMK)

1430. Shockley, Ann Allen. "Oral History: A Research Tool for Black History." *Negro History Bulletin,* Vol. XLI (January-February 1978), pp. 787-789.

Shockley, librarian at Fisk University, describes sources of black history to be found in black narratives before the advent of the tape recorder and the place of black folk historians (griots) and musicians in preserving the laws, customs, and history of Africans. Black oral history is particularly necessary at this time because of the long neglect and racist attitudes of some historical societies, libraries, colleges, and universities in failing to collect archival and manuscript materials relating to blacks. Six current programs are described and examples given of the kinds of material being accumulated at Fisk. All black institutions should have an oral history program, even if only on a limited basis. Six guidelines are given for judging the quality and resourcefulness of interviews; oral history evidence should receive the same critical textual examination as written records and its value placed in the same context. (BMK)

1431. Stands in Timber, John, and Margot Liberty. *Cheyenne Memories.* New Haven, Conn.: Yale University Press, 1979.

John Stands in Timber had spent much of his life listening to the last members of his tribe who could relate the Cheyenne legends, religious ceremonies, and early history. Many hours were spent in his old age recording the information for this book since publication of this material was exceedingly important to him. Most of the book is given over to this handed-down narrative, particularly the conflicts with the westward movement of the whites. The Custer battle of Little Big Horn is described from the Indian point of view. Only the last chapters are autobiographical. A lengthy bibliography and full index are included. (BMK)

X. Oral History: Folklore and Anthropology

Allen, Barbara, and William Lynwood Montell. *From Memory to History.* See no. *1473.*

1432. Danielson, Larry. "The Folklorist, the Oral Historian, and Local History." *Oral History Review*, Vol. VIII (1980), pp. 62-72.

While researchers in folklore and oral history have often speculated on the boundaries between these fields, few of their informants understand (or worry about) the differences. Thus the folklorist has much to offer the local historian despite his lack of training in historiography. He understands the traditional motifs of oral narratives in ways the historian may overlook; he understands how local legends, folk beliefs, and customs interrelate; and he is able to "personalize" local history through specialized methods of collecting and interpreting oral testimony. The author concludes with an example of how a folklorist successfully worked on a local history project in Homer, Illinois. (DKD)

1433. Dorson, Richard N. "The Oral Historian and the Folklorist." In *Selections from the Fifth and Sixth National Colloquia on Oral History*. New York: Oral History Association, 1972.

Oral historians and folklorists differ both in methodology and orientation. The oral historian interviews, based on prior research; the folklorist in the field collects, often from chance encounters. The historian researches primarily national political structures: laws, politicians, battles, social and economic trends; the folklorist seeks out "people's history." The author suggests broadening the term *oral history* to *oral folk history*, which includes oral personal history (first-person folk narratives) and oral tradition history (sagas and legends). Those interested in folk history ("the versions of past events that have remained in folk memory and folk tradition") are often as interested in the legendary growth that surround century-old events as in the solid kernel of fact. (DKD)

Finnegan, Ruth. "A Note on Oral Tradition and Historical Evidence." See no. *1336*.

Based on anthropological fieldwork in Africa, the author suggests that oral tradition can be divided into three distinct categories: oral literature, generalized historical knowledge, and recollections. Each of these forms holds different challenges for those constructing history out of oral testimony. Oral literature is best suited for studies of intellectual and cultural history; generalized historical knowledge can fill in genealogies; and recollections serve a broad variety of historical ends, although verification is made difficult by factors such as personal prejudices and special interests. All forms of oral tradition must be scrutinized by historians for the contextual and performance elements that shape historical meaning: individual artistry, audience participation, style, and structure of local performance traditions. (DKD)

Ives, Edward D. *The Tape-Recorded Interview*. See no. *1378*.

1434. Joyner, Charles. "Folklore and History: The Tangled Relationship." Paper No. 78-2. *The Newberry Papers in Family and Community History*. Chicago: Newberry Library, 1978.

This brief essay provides a bibliographical survey of folk and ethnohistory while discussing chronicling efforts to separate historical verity from oral tradition and ritual. "Few historians," the author points out, "are trained in the analysis and critical use of oral interviews"; oral history may be a meeting ground between the disciplines of history and folkore. (DKD)

1435. Joyner, Charles. "Oral History as a Communicative Event: A Folkloristic Perspective." *Oral History Review*, Vol. VII (1979), pp. 47-52.

One often-neglected dimension in the interpretation of oral history is the performance and sociolinguistic elements of the interview situation. The author asserts that oral history is the most important single method of historical research but asks its practitioners to publish "a full description of the context in which the testimony was taken, including mannerisms and gestures of the informant and the reactions of the audience . . . [and] meaningful interpretation of what those testimonies mean to the people who transmitted them." (DKD)

1436. Lewis, Oscar. *The Children of Sanchez: An Autobiography of a Mexican Family*. New York: Random House, 1961.

The anthropological life history differs from oral biography by its emphasis on daily-life activities and popular or folk culture. This study portrays a "culture of poverty" through edited personal narratives replete with details of income, migration, education, and housing. The author offers these narratives as the "beginning of a new kind of literature of social realism" made possible by the tape-recorded reflections of the "unskilled, uneducated, and even illiterate." While the book's external structure concerns one family's history, its inner core is the self-description of a life-style on the economic margin. (DKD)

1437. Mintz, Sidney W. "The Anthropological Interview and the Life History." *Oral History Review*, Vol. VII (1979), pp. 18-26.

Anthropologists and ethnographers share with their colleagues in history a number of techniques for eliciting and interpreting oral testimony. In the anthropological life history, however, "the biographer-ethnographer must have a conception of how people are at once products and makers of the social and cultural systems within which they are lodged." Seeking direct observation of customary behavior in particular societies, the anthropologist turns to the life history for insights into these cultural systems. (DKD)

1438. Vansina, Jan. *Oral Tradition: A Study in Historical Methodology*. Chicago: Aldine, 1965.

A distinction between oral history and oral tradition may be useful to serious researchers. The first is recorded based on observations, thoughts, and recollections of an individual. Oral tradition, according to the author, is based on "verbal testimonies that are reported statements concerning the past''—the work of a community process, over time. The interpretation, transmission, and function of oral tradition are extensively analyzed. (See also no. *1347*.)

XI: Oral History: Gerontology and Life Review

1439. Achenbaum, W. Andrew. *Old Age in the New Land: The American Experience Since 1790*. Baltimore: John Hopkins University Press, 1978.

Since oral historians customarily deal with persons in the elderly life stage, it is important to understand the history and demography of this population. The principal contribution of this book is its historical perspective on the subject. Noting both the continuities and changes in public perceptions of age, the author identifies pre- and post-Civil War eras, followed by the emergence of old age as a national problem in the twentieth century. For another study of similar scope, see David Hackett Fisher, *Growing Old in America* (New York: Oxford University Press, 1977). (CD)

1440. Barnhart, Jacqueline B. "Doing Oral History: The Yountville Project." *AHA Newsletter*, Vol. XVIII (December 1980), pp. 5-6.

The author, an instructor at California State University, Chico, describes an oral history project carried out with the residents of the Veteran's Home in Yountville, California. Barnhart reviews the preparations that need to be made prior to interviewing, the problem of fatigue encountered in interviewing elderly subjects, and ways of dealing with interviewees older than seventy years, who tend to see their autobiographies as "historical." (DAJ)

1441. Baum, Willa K. "Therapeutic Value of Oral History." *International Journal of Aging and Human Development*, Vol. XII (1980-1981), pp. 49-53.

Most of the information on oral history's therapeutic nature must be inferred from what gerontologists have written about life-review therapy. An exception is this brief essay by an oral historian. Adapted from a 1977 paper, it is addressed to gerontologists and accordingly raises important conceptual and methodological questions. The author effectively asserts that the convergence of gerontologists and oral historians on reminiscing must not mask their fundamental differences in purpose and technique. She identifies and comments perceptively on important points of departure. (CD)

1442. Blythe, Ronald. *The View in Winter: Reflections on Old Age*. New York: Harcourt, Brace, Jovanovich, 1979.

The author is a British historian who in this sensitive portrait has captured the feelings and outlooks of elderly persons through interviews. Several dozen people talk about their past and their present, their war and work experiences, as well as their family and community associations. Blythe artfully merges their vignettes with his commentary, creating a poignant tale of human feelings. This book says a great deal about old age, and by example it also reveals the rich potential of oral history. (CD)

1443. Butler, Robert N. "The Life Review: An Interpretation of Reminiscences in the Aged." *Psychiatry*, Vol. XXVI (February 1963), pp. 65-76.

This is an early and definitive statement of the life-review concept. The author explains the reminiscing tendencies of older people as a universal mental process inherent in that stage of human development. He further describes its manifestations and its relationship to certain late-life disorders. Life review can also encourage certain positive developments, such as candor, serenity, and wisdom. The essay includes literary allusions as well as references to the relevant psychiatric literature. The implications for oral history are obvious but not explicit. (CD)

1444. Butler, Robert N. *Why Survive? Being Old in America.* New York: Harper and Row, 1975.

Being old in America's youth-centered culture is to experience entrenched and demeaning myths about age and to suffer from a form of prejudice or "ageism." This book offers statistical and descriptive information about our aged population. Angry in places, it portrays neglect, abuse, and exploitation. Among the remedies suggested is an important section on life review. The author characterizes reminiscing as a natural and healthy process that enables older persons to reconcile their life experiences and face their circumstances positively. Briefly noting the parallel work of oral historians, he adds an appeal for "relatively untrained persons" to volunteer as listener therapists. This book is a synthesis of what gerontology has to offer oral historians. (CD)

1445. Jenkins, Sara. *Past Present: Recording Life Stories of Older People.* Washington: St. Alban's Parish, 1978.

This unusual volume combines one hundred pages of oral history samples with half the amount for instruction and advice. It is based on a successful oral history project at a senior citizens center, and it features the gerontological perspective of life-review therapists like Robert Butler. With relatively limited attention to technical instruction, the coverage is necessarily slight, though there are valuable sections on training interviewers and administrating a program. Of more enduring interest are the oral history excerpts, which are edited and illustrated. (CD)

1446. Lewis, Myrna I., and Robert N. Butler. "Life-Review Therapy: Putting Memories to Work in Individual and Group Psychotherapy." *Geriatrics*, Vol. XXIX (November 1974), pp. 165-169, 172-173.

In a brief essay the authors develop a thesis about the therapeutic value of reminiscing by older people. The discussion is based on extensive clinical experience in both individual and group psychotherapy. Prominent among seven techniques they employed for evoking memory were "written or taped autobiographies." Several other techniques, for example, genealogy and memorabilia, also relate to interviewing technique. Oral historians will find in this essay an early statement of gerontology's relationship to their craft. (CD)

Menninger, Robert. "Some Psychological Factors Involved in Oral History Interviewing." See no. *1353*.

1447. Myerhoff, Barbara. *Number Our Days*. New York: Dutton, 1978.

This book offers revealing insights by an anthropologist into the values and problems of older people. It is based on extensive interviews with members of a Jewish senior citizens center in Venice, California. As Holocaust survivors and European emigrants, these individuals now feel the compounded estrangement of being elderly outcasts in a youth-oriented community. Myerhoff explores their lives, demonstrating how older people cope with neglect and abuse by banding together and reminiscing about the past. In describing her subjects and their lives, she by example reveals the power of eyewitness testimony. (CD)

XII: Oral History: Science, Technology, and Medicine

1448. Bennett, William, and Joel Gurin. "Science That Frightens Scientists: The Great Debate Over DNA." *Atlantic* (February 1977), pp. 43-62.

This prize-winning article examines the debate over recombinant DNA, "the first innovation submitted to public judgment before the technology had been put into widespread use and before heavy investment had given it a momentum that was hard to oppose." The authors focus on the question of who should make decisions governing or limiting the scope of scientific study. Drawing heavily upon M.I.T.'s Recombinant DNA Oral History Collection, the authors acknowledge the collection's usefulness in their acceptance of the 1977 AAAS-Westinghouse Science Writing Award, magazine division. Material from the collection was used to trace the debate within the scientific community, and eventually the public, over the potential hazards of recombinant DNA research. The M.I.T. collection includes interviews with scientists and public figures, as well as tapes and videotapes of various government deliberations. In some cases follow-up interviews were conducted to record unfolding events and changing attitudes. The Recombinant DNA Collection is housed in M.I.T.'s Institute Archives. (RJG)

1449. Benson, Charles D., and William Barnaby Faherty. *Moonport: A History of the Apollo Launch Facilities and Operations*. NASA History Series. Washington: Scientific and Technical Information Office, National Aeronautics and Space Administration, 1978.

True to its title, *Moonport* is the story of Apollo launch facilities from the beginning of design through astronauts Eugene Cernan and Harrison Schmitt's explorations on the moon. Not all NASA history volumes employ oral history, but Benson and Faherty found interviews with participants to be "among the most valuable sources of information. Whenever possible they evaluated the objectiveness and accuracy of an interview against other accounts of the same events." The authors included a list of their approximately 150 interviews in their bibliography. The transcripts are available in the Kennedy Space Center archives. (SBH)

1450. Brooks, Courtney G., James M. Grimwood, and Lloyd S. Swenson, Jr. *Chariots for Apollo: A History of Manned Lunar Spacecraft*. NASA History Series. Washington: Scientific and Technical Information Office, National Aeronautics and Space Administration, 1979.

Chariots for Apollo is one of over a dozen titles in the National Aeronautics and Space Administration (NASA) history series on space projects. *Chariots* begins with the creation of NASA and the definition of a manned space flight program to follow Mercury, and it concludes with Apollo 11 and the moon landing. The authors, who began their research before a moon landing had been completed, drew heavily upon the Apollo archives, supplemented by the desk archives and reminiscences of participants. More than three hundred of the latter agreed to taped oral history interviews. About two-thirds of these were transcribed and deposited with the Johnson Space Center Archives in Houston, Texas. (SBH)

1451. Courtwright, David T., Herman Joseph, and Don C. Des Jarlais. "Memories from the Street: Oral Histories of Elderly Methadone Patients." *Oral History Review*, Vol. IX (1981), pp. 47-64.

The authors, who participated in a project sponsored by the New York State Division of Substance Abuse Services (DSAS), maintain that "if the history of narcotics use in the United States is ever to be told from the addict's point of view, oral history will play an indispensable role." Their interviews with older clients of the New York City methadone maintenance programs, "many of whom had been addicted for more than fifty years," elicited information "about a period when the social, legal and pharmaceutical circumstances of addiction were different from today." The authors also provide a discussion of the veracity and reliability of their interviews and contend that their project has methodological implications "for anyone interested in interviewing members of a deviant subculture." (SBH)

1452. Evans, Christopher. *The Making of the Micro: A History of the Computer*. New York: Von Nostrand Reinhold, 1981.

In this short, popular history of the computer (113 pages), approximately half the text is devoted to developments since 1940. The work is not annotated, but the author interviewed "pioneers of computing" in the course of preparing the volume. At the time of publication, ten of these sixty-minute interviews had been deposited with the Science Museum in London and ten more were in production. The interviews appear to have become an ongoing project; the bibliography also identifies individuals scheduled for postpublication taping. (RJG)

1453. Hewlett, Richard G. "A Pilot Study in Contemporary Scientific History." *Isis*, Vol. LIII (March 1962), pp. 31-38.

Hewlett, whose service began on the staff of the Atomic Energy Commission in 1953, describes the use of interviews in compiling historical records on the Experimental Breeder Reactor for the Atomic Energy Commission history project. The study "forcefully demonstrated the limitations of the interview as an historical source." (RJG)

1454. "Science and Technology: Roundtable Discussion." In *The Fourth National Colloquium on Oral History*. New York: Oral History Association, 1970.

This discussion by oral history practitioners places some emphasis upon the relationship of oral history to manuscript collections. Psychiatry, biology, physics, medicine, and the Public Health Service are among the areas covered. (RJG)

1455. Smith, Alice K., and Charles Weiner, eds. *Robert Oppenheimer: Letters and Recollections*. Cambridge, Mass.: Harvard University Press, 1980.

The editors used oral history interviews in preparing their commentaries, and some interviews conducted for the volume "were intended as a permanent oral history archive which will be useful to scholars working on related topics." The final-typed copies of these transcripts have been deposited in the oral history collection of the Massachusetts Institute of Technology Libraries. The editors also utilized the oral history collections of the Archive for the History of Quantum Physics and the Center for the History of Physics of the American Institute of Physics. Included among the History of Quantum Physics interviews were those Thomas Kuhn conducted with Robert Oppenheimer during November 1963. (RJG)

1456. Szilard, Leo. "Reminiscences." In Donald Fleming and Bernard Bailyn, eds. *The Intellectual Migration: Europe and America, 1930-1960*. Perspectives in American History, Vol. II. Cambridge, Mass.: Belknap Press of Harvard University Press, 1969.

Szilard, an eminent physicist whose experiments with chain reactions involved him intimately in the science and politics of the atomic bomb, considered writing his autobiography but never did. "However, at times he enjoyed giving interviews to interested visitors. On a few such occasions his wife switched on the tape recorder." An editorial note states that the "reminiscences" are "an exact transcription of parts of these tapes, with editing [by Gertrud Weiss Szilard and Kathleen R. Windsor] limited to the minimum necessary to change spoken to written English." (SBH)

1457. Weiner, Charles, ed. *Exploring the History of Nuclear Physics*. American Institute of Physics Conference Proceedings No. 7. New York: American Institute of Physics, 1972.

These are transcripts of discussions at two conferences in which the participants probed into the recent history of a field of physics to identify needs and opportunities for documentation and study of its development. The participants included physicists who had played roles in the development of nuclear physics during the 1930s and 1940s. Joining them in these discussions were historians, philosophers, and sociologists who were either undertaking studies of the history of nuclear physics or were involved in related aspects of the development of the twentieth-century science. Together, they attempted to identify questions of historical interest, offered recollections or interpretations of specific events or processes, and suggested sources and methods of historical documentation so that serious study of these developments would be possible in the future. (SBH)

XIII. Oral History: Labor History

1458. Banks, Ann, ed. *First-Person America*. New York: Knopf, 1980.

Eighty interviews by writers from the New Deal Federal Writers' Project are collected in this volume and published with notes based on oral interviews conducted by the editor. The interviews are grouped by particular industries, for instance, meat packing and granite. The narratives were culled, for the most part, from the Folk Song Archives at the Library of Congress, which became the repository for a large part of the narratives collected by the Federal Writers' Project. Some of the narratives presented here have been dramatized and presented in a six-part series by WGBH (Boston) for National Public Radio. The interviewers did not use tape recorders but wrote the narratives from notes made during the interview; therefore, questions remain as to how authoritative they are as oral history. See discussion of this matter published in two issues of the *Oral History Review*: Rapport, "How Valid Are the Federal Writers' Project Life Stories: An Iconoclast among the True Believers," no. *1367*; Terrill and Hirsch, "Replies to Leonard Rapport's 'How Valid Are the Federal Writers' Project Life Stories: An Iconoclast among the True Believers,' " no. *1371*.

1459. Brooks, Thomas R. *Communication Workers of America: The Story of a Union*. New York: Mason/Charter, 1977.

Much of the personal documentation in this book derives from considerable reliance on the Communication Workers of America (CWA) Oral Archives at Iowa University. The author acknowledges his debt in a bibliographical note at the conclusion of the book; "the oral history interviews conducted by John S. Schacht . . . were invaluable." This is not a scholarly analysis of the use of oral documentation in the study of oral history but a short readable history of the union that achieves its immediacy by reliance upon transcribed tape-recorded interviews. (AMH)

1460. Friedlander, Peter. *The Emergence of UAW Local 1936-1939: A Study of Class and Culture*. Pittsburgh: University of Pittsburgh Press, 1975.

An analysis of the social dynamics of a United Auto Workers (UAW) local of Polish immigrants in suburban Detroit is provided by presenting a detailed oral reminiscence of an early organizer and president of the local, Edmund Kord. Friedlander's theoretical discussion of the uses of oral history in the study of working-class culture sets the framework for this reminiscence about the formation and early development of Local 229, which was a local likely to challenge orthodoxy both from within the UAW and in the community. (AMH)

1461. Hareven, Tamara K., and Randolph Langenbach. *Amoskeag: Life and Work in an American Factory City*. New York: Pantheon, 1978.

The techniques of social history and oral history are brought together to provide an authentic view of a New England textile mill town from the early twentieth century until the closing of the mill. We see the world through the eyes of workers, managers, and those who lived in the community. The dislocation experienced by all those whose lives were influenced by the Amoskeag mill is rendered in their own words. The understandings this book attempts to convey are enhanced by a series of photographs—both archival photographs collected from informants and the contemporary photographs of the empty mill taken by Randolph Langenbach. (AMH)

1462. "Here Comes a Wind: Labor on the Move." *Southern Exposure*, Vol. IV, no. 1-2 (1976).

This issue is devoted to oral histories of industrialization in the South. The narrators are workers in the J. P. Stevens campaign, Farah strikes, and in the coal mine struggles in Harlan County. (AMH)

1463. Hoffman, Alice M. "Using Oral History in the Classroom." In Barbara M. Wertheimer, ed. *Labor Education for Women Workers*. Philadelphia: Temple University Press, 1981.

Oral history as a teaching methodology for workers' education is described. An outline for a labor history course using oral histories is provided as well as the content to be included in an oral history workshop. There is also a bibliography on oral history resources for the classroom. (AMH)

1464. Keeran, Roger. *The Communist Party and the Auto Workers' Union*. Bloomington: Indiana University Press, 1980.

Making use of previously collected oral interviews and supplementing them with his own interviews, the author attempts to prove that communist trade unionists were as devoted to the welfare of their unions as to the advancement of their ideology. The book documents the activities of communists during the period 1923-1949. (AMH)

1465. Lynd, Alice, and Staughton Lynd. *Rank and File: Personal Histories by Working Class Organizers*. Boston: Beacon, 1973.

While the Lynds define the rank and file as workers on the job, not paid union leadership, this book provides the personal histories of eighteen radical labor organizers and officials who attempted to gain or extend influence within their unions. For the most part, the Lynds conducted the interviews, edited them, and compiled them with an introduction. However, two of the narratives are edited versions of written personal histories, and seven others are based upon edited speeches. Most of the narratives were from the Midwest, and many were from the steel industry in Chicago, where the Lynds lived while compiling the book. The interviews with the women informants provided the basis for a film entitled *Union Maids*. (AMH)

1466. Maurer, Harry. *Not Working: An Oral History of the Unemployed*. New York: Holt, Rinehart, and Winston, 1979.

This is a companion volume to Studs Terkel's *Working* (see no. *1469*). *Not Working* is about the unemployed; their words fill its pages. The book is about struggle and about feelings of winning and losing. It contains role models who are triumphing over economic distress and details about how they are doing it. (AMH)

1467. "No More Moanin'." *Southern Exposure*, Vol. I, no. 3 (1973).

Southern organizers, coal miners' wars, participants in bitter strikes, and survivors of the depression all describe their experiences in this issue, entirely devoted to stories of southern workers' attempts to organize. (AMH)

1468. Robinson, Archie. *George Meany and His Times: A Biography*. New York: Simon and Schuster, 1981.

George Meany was president of the AFL-CIO for twenty-seven years (1952-1979). This book is very largely George Meany's own story from transcribed interviews conducted with him between late 1975 and July 1979. Excerpts from the transcribed tapes are set off from the connecting material written by Archie Robinson. The result is an oral history biography in that it is very largely a book to present George Meany as he saw himself. (AMH)

1469. Terkel, Louis (Studs). *Working: People Talk about What They Do and How They Feel about What They Do*. New York: Pantheon, 1974.

Terkel asked over one hundred individuals to tell him and the tape recorder how they felt about their work. He edited their narrations into the excerpts that are presented here. Most have been selected to reinforce Terkel's theme of daily humiliation, powerlessness, and lack of opportunity for individual expression, which is characteristic of much of the work experience in industrial America. Those narrators who find satisfaction in their work describe vocations or jobs that reward and reinforce individuality. Some workers describe creative avenues that they had found to adjust the job itself so as to permit individual expression. (AMH)

1470. Terrill, Tom E., and Jerrold Hirsch, eds. *Such as Us: Southern Voices of the Thirties.* Chapel Hill: University of North Carolina Press, 1978.

This is a book about southern mill workers as told by southerners. It is in some ways a sequel to William T. Couch, ed., *These Are Our Lives* (Chapel Hill, N.C.: University of North Carolina Press, 1939). Like the earlier book, this one also presents edited interviews from the Federal Writers' Project files. This anthology is selected from interviews stored in the Southern Historical Collection at the University of North Carolina. (AMH)

1471-1472. Wolley, Bryan. *We Be Here When the Morning Comes.* Photographs by Ford Reid. Lexington: University of Kentucky Press, 1975.

This book makes use of oral history interviews to document the strike of Brookside miners agains the Duke Power Company who owned the mines. The accounts are intensely dramatic; the miners and their wives describe in their own words a violent struggle deeply felt by its narrators. (AMH)

XIV. Oral History: Local and Regional History

1473. Allen, Barbara, and William Lynwood Montell. *From Memory to History: Using Oral Sources in Local Historical Research.* Nashville: American Association for State and Local History, 1981.

Oral history is not only a method of acquiring information but a body of knowledge about the past that is uniquely different from the information contained in written records. Folklore materials with historical content are collected in the same way as oral history; therefore, traditional folklore methodology can be profitably put to use by the oral historian to locate oral sources, apply tests for historical validity, recognize submerged truths in oral testimony, separate out folklore themes, and make use of anecdotes and legends that cannot pass tests for validity. Understanding the characteristics and settings of orally communicated information enables the historian to deal more effectively with this material. The final chapter advises on incorporating this sort of information into a written manuscript. A long appendix examines oral testimonies gathered to complete the story of a triple murder in Tennessee, as contrasted with the court record, newspaper stories, and the legends that grew up around the event. (BMK)

1474. Baskin, John. *New Burlington: The Life and Death of an American Village.* New York: Norton, 1976.

The author lived in this Ohio village during the year before it was flooded to become a water reservoir. He states his goal to be a book of "stories and voices in which the characters ponder some of their time on earth." The resulting "oral history" recalls small-town America, reminiscent of Ronald Blythe's *Akenfield* (see no. *1476*). The book lacks the conventional documentation—concise historic background, discussion of the interview methodology, maps, more than occupational information about the narrators, and a bibliography. (BMK).

1475. Baum, Willa K. "Building Community Identity through Oral History—A New Role for the Local Library." *California Librarian*, Vol. XXXI (October 1970), pp. 271-284.

The local library is the most suitable site for headquartering a volunteer community oral history program and housing its resulting tapes and transcripts. The library can provide the necessary institutional sponsorship; one staff member can give part-time leadership, and there will be no question about the final custodianship of the collection. In this way continuity and status can be assured. Steps in setting up a program are outlined, suggestions made for types of information to record, six library projects in California described, and a list of resource books and organizations given. (BMK)

1476. Blythe, Ronald. *Akenfield: Portrait of an English Village*. New York: Dell, 1969.

This is an early example of an assembly of interviews to illuminate the life of a very small village that is suffering from changing agricultural patterns. The editor may have done considerable editing. There is no discussion of preparation of the interviews and very little supporting documentation. The historic background and personal reminiscences of the difficult relations between Suffolk farmers and farm laborers and the formation of the National Union of Agricultural Workers are dealt with at length; in fact they are used to explain, at least in part, the villagers' characteristic dour, unimaginative view of life. (BMK).

1477. Bragg, Melvyn. *Speak for England: An Oral History of England, 1900-1975*. New York: Knopf, 1977.

The author, a successful novelist and BBC interviewer, has chosen his hometown, Wigton in Cumberland in northern England, as a microcosm of what happened in England in this period of seventy-five years. In presenting the story by way of oral history interviews, all quotations are as direct and accurate as possible with no lines added by the author. The interviews show that the townspeople wanted to record and remember not national history but human history, the common body of daily life during wars and depressions. "Theme" chapters by the author alternate with "portrait" chapters devoted to a single person speaking at some length about his or her own life. Social, educational, and economic changes have improved everyone's lot, and yet the old days are recalled as happy days. The appendix contains area maps, descriptions of the town layout, employment data in the two boundary years, and a listing of the narrators that gives information for each one: date and place of birth, number of brothers and sisters, places of residence, all employment, schools and the highest level reached, religion, political affiliation, married or single, and number of children. Perhaps this much data is not necessary, but it allows the reader to become well acquainted with the informants. (BMK)

1478. Hall, Jacquelyn Dowd. "Documenting Diversity: The Southern Experience." *Oral History Review*, Vol. IV (1976), pp. 19-28.

Arguments are stated for the particular suitability of the use of oral sources in writing southern history, and their utilization in the South up to 1976 is reviewed with special attention to the Federal Writers' Project and the Slave Narratives of the 1930s. The Southern Oral History Program at the University of North Carolina, Chapel Hill, is described in detail: its origin and goals; the functions it fulfills for the history department, the university, and the state; and its several specific areas of inquiry, which include biographies of outstanding North Carolinians, southern women before World War II, southern labor history, and the transition of the southern Piedmont from an agrarian to an industrial society. (BMK)

1479. Kahn, Kenneth. "Reconstructing the History of a Community." *International Journal of Oral History*, Vol. II (February 1981), pp. 4-13.

The author discusses his experiences and problems in writing the history of the Petaluma Jewish Community in California. In dealing with three generations of informants—the original settlers, their children and his contemporaries, their grandchildren—there was a progressive weakening of the community members' appreciation for their own historical significance. The author's own qualities of credibility and perspective were tested. In the search for the best way to make sense of his historical data, various other local history publications were examined for ways to organize and interpret the interviews without objectifying the narrators, remaining aware always of the ethical dimensions of this effort to accommodate both their interpretations and the author's interpretation of the community's history. History is literature as well as social science. Ultimately the decision was made to speak as author only in a long introduction, with the text entirely in the words of the narrators "speaking to each other" in chapters arranged chronologically and topically. Some newspaper and historical accounts are interspersed. (BMK)

Krech, Shepard, III. *Praise the Bridge That Carries You Over*. See no. *1422*.

1480. Montell, William Lynwood. *The Saga of Coe Ridge: A Study in Oral History*. New York: Harper and Row, 1972. Torchbooks reprint from the University of Tennessee Press original, 1970.

This book is a methodological model of local history in areas where practically the only available source is the spoken word. It is equally useful for those who are working with an ample supply of documentation to provide structure and corroboration for their interviewing programs. Coe Ridge was an isolated black colony in the Cumberland hills of southern Kentucky that developed and disappeared between the Civil War and about 1958. The story of the early years is drawn from family legends and history of both blacks and the dominant white family of the area; later periods are more likely to be described by eyewitnesses. References to the few available documentary sources appear frequently in foot-notes. Techniques for using oral information are given in prologue and epilogue, along with sketches of the informants, genealogical charts, maps, a table of common folk motifs, a bibliography, and an index. (BMK)

1481. Morrissey, Charles T. "Evoking the Vermont Experience: Oral History and the Forms of Remembrance." *Vermont History* (Spring 1981), pp. 85-91.

There is a need for Vermonters to become more aware of spoken reminiscences as historical documents and to collect them in tape-recorded interviews. Examples of pre-recorder reminiscences, many published in *Vermont History*, suggest the likelihood of undiscovered oral history respondents of genuine talent who can open up the story of Vermont during the radical and far-reaching changes of the twentieth century. Historians who intend to engage in oral history should become acquainted with these and similar articles and books. Several cited are specifically recommended, not only for content but for guidance in handling problems that may arise during an interview session. Comparing orally received information with traditional manuscript sources serves as a check for the validity of each. (BMK)

1482. Shackleford, Laurel, and Bill Weinberg, eds. *Our Appalachia: An Oral History*. New York: Hill and Wang, 1972.

Students and staff interviewers from a four-school consortium (Alice Lloyd College, Pippa Passes, Kentucky; Lees Junior College, Jackson, Kentucky; Appalachian State University, Boone, North Carolina; and Emory and Henry College, Emory, Virginia) began the Appalachian Oral History Project in 1971. The project is fully described, including the fact that the full collection is available at Alice Lloyd College. *Our Appalachia* is drawn from the words of forty-seven narrators from all walks of life, discussing the earlier, simpler years and the present pressures by stripmining interests. Narrators are identified, biographies are included, and pictures are provided for most of them. Their names appear in boldface in the index. Each quotation is lengthy and selected from one to six hours of interviews extending over years in some cases. Historical data are integrated with the reminiscences. (BMK)

1483. Wolcott, Reed. *Rose Hill: A Documentary of Shared Experience*. New York: G. P. Putnam and Sons, 1976.

After a one-page explanatory note, composed of condensed demographic statistics for this southeastern North Carolina small town and the author's preface describing the townspeople and some past events recalled in the interviews, the text is presented entirely as long interview passages, organized by categories of people. About one hundred narrators are included; of these, forty-six remain anonymous. Scanty biographical information and several themes slowly emerge.

A seemingly unsponsored Ku Klux Klan meeting in town, a dismissed liberal minister, petty political corruption rarely challenged, integration problems, and union resistence are dealt with quite indirectly in the words of the interviewees. The local accent is consistently indicated, mostly by dropped final *g*'s and *d*'s, regardless of the speaker's educational or social level. The interview material is skillfully handled by a journalist who spent several months in Rose Hill. The result is a demonstration of professional acumen, although it is not conventional local history. (BMK)

XV. Oral History: Military History

1484. Buell, Thomas B. *Master of Sea Power: A Biography of Fleet Admiral Ernest J. King*. Boston: Little, Brown, 1980.

This biography of Fleet Admiral Ernest King is a combination of military and strategic considerations with national and international developments during World War II. Always a controversial personality, Admiral King is portrayed here as a grand strategist of the Allied war effort as well as the wartime commander-in-chief, United States Fleet. The author has used many manuscript sources, both official and unofficial, and extensive collections of correspondence. He conducted many interviews, and he drew heavily on oral history interviews from the Naval Institute Collection and the Columbia Collection; there is a note to each chapter detailing the sources used, but it is not possible to distinguish oral history quotations from other source material. (EBM)

1485. Buell, Thomas B. *The Quiet Warrior: A Biography of Admiral Raymond A. Spruance*. Boston: Little, Brown, 1974.

An excellent biography of a legendary naval officer of whom little is known, the book uses many unpublished primary sources, including oral histories. There is a short section on Spruance's education and preparation and another on his service after World War II as president of the Naval War College and ambassador to the Philippines, but the meat of the book is a graphic account of Spruance's commands in the Pacific after Pearl Harbor, beginning with the battle of Midway. There are source notes for each chapter and a detailed bibliography; an annotated manuscript is available at the Naval War College for those interested in specific sources. Since Spruance was notably taciturn and refused to do an oral history, much material has come from others. (EBM)

1486. Frank, Benis M. *Okinawa: The Great Island Battle*. New York: Elsevier-Dutton, 1978.

This is a careful and detailed account of a major amphibious landing and the subsequent battle for the island of Okinawa during World War II. Although there is much here for the military historian, the book is written so that lay persons can appreciate the preparation, tactics, and operations described and can share the feelings of both opponents. Clearly the material has been drawn from many of the oral histories in the Marine Corps Collection, but there is no mention of oral history as a source or a listing of the Marines interviewed. The author acknowledges use of interviews conducted by John Toland, although these are not identified. (EBM)

1487. Frank, Benis M. "Oral History: Columbia and USMC." *Fortitudine*, Vol. III, No. 2 (Fall 1973), pp. 19-20.

In a brief article, the director of the Marine Corps Oral History Program describes its history, purposes, and accomplishments to date. Frank stresses the different groups then being interviewed: Marines returned from Vietnam; those being interviewed on the scene by Fleet Marine Units; and retired distinguished Marines, who were contributing in-depth interviews of their entire careers. This combination of very recent operational reporting with longer-range, more detailed retrospective accounts has characterized the program from the beginning. Used in conjunction with documentary sources, the oral history interviews are designed to be "a valuable institutional memory of experiences and lessons learned to be used by generations of Marines to come." (EBM)

1488. Leutze, James. *A Different Kind of Victory: A Biography of Admiral Thomas C. Hart*. Annapolis, Md.: Naval Institute Press, 1981.

Admiral Hart had an outstanding naval career, including a difficult relationship with General MacArthur in the Philippines and a controversial Allied command (ABDA) in the Southwest Pacific. This story of his life is based on his diary, his papers, and his oral history, and the contribution from each source is clearly apparent. The naval, political, and personal elements in his life are examined in this survey of an influential career. (EBM)

1489. Marshall, S. L. A. Foreword to *The Fatal Decisions*, ed. Seymour Freiden and William Richardson. New York: William Sloane, 1956.

In his foreword the military historian S. L. A. Marshall calls this book "an informed critique of failure in the boldest aggression of our times." He describes the concept of having seven German generals analyze the strategy and tactics of the great Axis defeats in the battles of Britain, El Alamein, Stalingrad, Moscow, Normandy, and the Ardennes. The discussions of memory and the effect of misconceptions on the part of the commanding officers are particularly valuable to oral historians. (EBM)

1490. Pogue, Forrest C. *The Supreme Command*. Washington: Office of the Chief of Military History, Department of the Army, 1954.

This volume, which forms part of the official U.S. Army history of World War II as one in the series dealing with the European Theater of Operations, is a study of coalition warfare. The focus is on the supreme commander of the Allied Forces and his staff; the decisions they reached, the actions they took, and the reasons for them. The author has integrated documentary material from many official sources with private papers and interviews conducted with nearly a hundred British, U.S., and French officers and civilians. The sources of statements are attributed in the footnotes, and the attentive reader can trace the contributions from written as well as oral sources. Pogue uses material from German sources. (EBM)

1491. Ryan, Cornelius. *The Last Battle.* New York: Simon and Schuster, 1966.
The story of the assault and capture of Berlin in April and May of 1945 is recreated from the point of view of the participants, military and civilian. The author tells us that some seven hundred men and women provided written accounts and/or interviews, and he lists their names. This personal information supplements the outline of military action prepared from official sources. The stories are told in dramatic terms with a good deal of dialog; the reader has no way of knowing how much is drawn from oral or written sources and how much is supplied by the author. (EBM)

1492. Stillwell, Paul, ed. *Air Raid: Pearl Harbor! Recollections of a Day of Infamy.* Annapolis, Md.: Naval Institute Press, 1981.
The editor tells us that this collection of personal narratives of the attack on Pearl Harbor seeks to provide a sampling of diverse experiences and viewpoints of a single event. Of the forty-seven firsthand accounts, twenty are taken from oral history memoirs. There is some editing, and the questions are deleted, but the flavor of speech is unmistakable. The contributions from three Japanese officers—including Captain Mitsuo Fuchida, who led the attack on Pearl Harbor—offer an unusual counterpoint. Numerous photographs illustrate the accounts. (EBM)

XVI. Oral History: Political and Social History

1493. Aaron, Daniel. "The Treachery of Recollection: The Inner and Outer History." In Robert H. Bremner, ed. *Essays on History and Literature.* Columbus: Ohio State University Press, 1966.
If the historian of the past may be likened to the naturalist who deals with specimens, then the historian of the present "resembles rather a hunter stalking his unpredictable quarry in a jungle." The contemporary historian is confronted with an abundance of facts that do not reveal as much as they obscure. When he comes to know his subjects, they cease to be merely historical figures or literary abstractions. The profusion of evidence compounds the possibility of error, but newspaper accounts are equally unworthy of trust. "The history of the sixteenth and seventeenth centuries was once contemporary history for the witnesses on whose evidence" the historian of the past relies. Though the contemporary historian can construct only a facsimile of the present, his "clumsy

probings . . . may ultimately prove to be of greater usefulness than he suspects.''
(JG)

1494. Broadfoot, Barry. *Ten Lost Years, 1929-1939: Memories of Canadians Who Survived the Depression*. Garden City, N.Y.: Doubleday, 1973.

Despite the profound effects of the Great Depression on the population of Canada, the era is largely unknown by today's Canadians, and it is not taught in the nation's schools. Hundreds of anonymous speakers describe their reaction to the events of the years 1929-1939 in this work, which was compiled with tape-recorded interviews. The reactions are varied, but nearly all portray a nation in distress, its citizens forced to cope with situations beyond their knowledge, control, or comprehension. (JG)

1495. Coles, Robert. *Children of Crisis: A Study of Courage and Fear*. Boston: Little, Brown, 1967.

The perspective of a child psychiatrist is brought to bear on a generation of children living through a critical era of social and political change. The southern experience from the 1950s to the present is the background, and the author's clinical eye is cast upon the children of the South. These "children of crisis" recount "the way [their] lives have come to terms with the political and social changes . . . in a particular region of this country." The method is "direct and sustained observation": talking with people, listening to them, watching them, and "taking a long time." Other works by Coles are *Migrants, Sharecroppers, Mountaineers* (Boston: Little, Brown, 1971) and *The South Goes North* (Boston: Little, Brown, 1971). (JG)

1496. Crowl, Philip A. "The Dulles Oral History Project: Mission Accomplished." *AHA Newsletter*, Vol. V (February 1967), pp. 6-10.

Oral history is a species of archive and not really history at all. Oral history programs fall into three categories: autobiographical reminiscences, biographical series, and topical projects. The biographical John Foster Dulles project was launched in February 1964 under the auspices of Princeton University, financed by the Rockefeller Foundation. By the project's conclusion in 1967, 280 interviews had been placed in the university library. The value of the project is evident in its ability to fill in gaps, to enlighten the historian as to the everyday decision-making process in the Department of State in the 1950s, and to offer clues and guidelines as to the study of the vast documentation on the era by identifying documents of signal importance. The oral history interviews are "not a substitute for but a supplement to the record." (JG)

1497. Frisch, Michael, and Dorothy L. Watts. "Oral History and the Presentation of Class Consciousness: The *New York Times* Versus the Buffalo Unemployed." *International Journal of Oral History*, Vol. I, No. 2 (June 1980), pp. 88-110.

The authors examine the way in which oral histories become public documents, with special reference to the authors' experiences publishing interviews conducted with unemployed workers in Buffalo in the magazine section of the *New York Times*. The article details changes required by *Times* editors and speculates on the reasons for those changes. (RJG)

1498. Jensen, Richard. "Oral History, Quantification, and the New Social History." *Oral History Review*, Vol. IX (1981), pp. 13-25.

The current trend in historical research that seeks to encompass more of the human experience brings together the new fields of oral history and quantification. A principal failing of oral history as applied to social history projects has been selection of a valid sample. One striking exception is Paul Thompson's *The Edwardians* (see no. *1503*), which matched respondents to a British census. The Americanist, too, can use census information as well as poll samples. Considerations in choosing respondents should include age, sex, race, education or class, and the size of the place where the respondent lives. A greater number of respondents will provide a more accurate sampling. The historian can benefit, too, from tapes made in sociological projects, which are likely to have been drawn from carefully selected samples of the population. (RJG)

1499. Joseph, Peter. *Good Times: An Oral History of America in the Nineteen-Sixties*. New York: Charterhouse, 1973.

If the depression years were hard times (as perceived by respondents in Studs Terkel's book of that name [see no. *1502*]), the sixties were good times to many who recall the era. This "impressionistic collage" is in the style of Terkel; the author set out "not to report comprehensively every facet of the decade, but to direct the focus in order best to convey the sense of the times." Respondents recall the heady optimism of the Kennedy years, the struggles of the civil rights and antiwar movements, the turmoils of the Johnson and Nixon administrations: from riots to rock festivals, from murders to the moon shot. Many Americas come to life in these 125 vignettes, and each is accompanied by the author's notes establishing the respondent in time and place. The author admits that he concentrates on "certain events, certain trends and ideas, certain people." (RJG)

1500. Sargent, James E. "Oral History, Franklin D. Roosevelt, and the New Deal: Some Recollections of Adolf A. Berle, Jr., Lewis W. Douglas, and Raymond Moley." *Oral History Review*, Vol. I (1973), pp. 92-110.

This article uses extensive excerpts and quotations from the author's interviews with Berle, Douglas, and Moley on a variety of questions concerning the personality of Franklin D. Roosevelt and the politics of the New Deal to point out the usefulness of oral history as a complement to the manuscript sources in recent political history. (RJG)

1501. Schulte, Renee K., ed. *The Young Nixon: An Oral Inquiry*. Fullerton: California State University at Fullerton Oral History Program, 1978.

This work presents a representative sampling of the 199 interviews conducted by the California State University at Fullerton Oral History Program on the childhood and early career of Richard M. Nixon. Most of those interviewed were either neighbors of the Nixon family or their friends. (RJG)

1502. Terkel, Louis (Studs). *Hard Times: An Oral History of the Great Depression*. New York: Pantheon, 1970.

The Great Depression, which for a decade had an impact on every American, is retold here by ''an improvised batallion of survivors.'' Though impoverishment is portrayed from myriad perspectives, those who made fortunes during this era recount a different tale. Economic displacement led to social unrest, which is described by followers of organizations both left and right, acolytes of Trotsky alongside worshippers of Father Coughlin. The tellers range from the commonest of men and women to power brokers from New York and Washington; their arenas are the streets, the speakeasies, and the seats of stock exchanges. Among the youngest respondents, though, the Great Depression has all but been forgotten, so well have they been shielded from its memory. (RJG)

1503. Thompson, Paul. *The Edwardians: The Remaking of British Society*. Bloomington: Indiana University Press, 1975.

Most historical studies on the Edwardian era have been offered from the perspectives of elites; therefore, a look from the bottom up offers a different point of view. The methods of the sociologist and the historian join to draw information from five hundred men and women, selected as participants because they represent the social class and geographical differences of Great Britain as reflected in that nation's 1911 census. At the dawn of the twentieth century, great inequalities existed as a result of distribution of wealth, a rigid class structure, and a social structure that limited mobility for most Britons. Social change was spurred by changes in the economy, by such movements as the trade unions and feminism, and, ultimately, by World War I. (RJG)

1504. ''Twenty-Fifth Anniversary Issue.'' *Forest History*, Vol. XVI, no. 3 (October 1972).

The Forest History Society, which publishes *Forest History*, originated in 1947 at the University of Minnesota. Elwood Maunder became director in 1952, and the project moved to Santa Cruz, California, in 1969. The first interview was tape recorded in 1953, and experience and training have contributed since then to lifting the program's level of professionalism. At this writing, 170 interviews representing six hundred hours of tape have been collected. This issue contains an editorial, ''Why Oral History,'' and eleven samples of interviews offering different perspectives on forest history. (JG)

1505. Van Voris, William H. *Violence in Ulster: An Oral Documentary*. Amherst: University of Massachusetts Press, 1975.

The atmosphere of Northern Ireland today was poisoned by conflicts hundreds of years old, and yet the increasingly desperate straits in which Catholics and Protestants find themselves are the result of a continuing series of minor events that grew to enormous proportions. The work offers "statements of people from opposing sides, particularly those who took some part in the events immediately before and during the years 1968-72." The author adds historical commentary before, after, and within each statement. Most of all, the myopia of these participants in many cases "shows the contradictions of human experience." (RJG)

XVII. Oral History: Women's Studies

1506. *Frontiers: A Journal of Women's Studies*, Vol. II, no. 2 (Summer 1977).

This issue is entirely devoted to oral history as it relates to women's history. The lead article by guest editor Sherna Gluck ("What's So Special about Women?") sets the tone as she explains that women's lives, private and public, are governed by a special rhythm and require special kinds of questions. "Women's oral history is a feminist encounter...it is the validation of women's experiences; it is the communication among women of different generations; ...it is the development of continuity which has been denied us in traditional historical accounts." The steps of doing women's oral history are detailed, down to how to summarize and index the tapes. Other articles describe the how-tos, the problems, and the content of projects such as: Italian, Jewish, and Slavic grandmothers in Pittsburgh; mothers and daughters on the Alberta frontier; black women in Colorado; Chinese women immigrants; a Navajo weaver; southern women writers; a woman moralist and a woman trade organizer; what one can or cannot learn from oral history, illustrated by the life of suffragist leader Alice Paul; and the value of life review as a therapeutic tool with the aged. The issue ends with a list of interview questions for women, a bibliography of books in women's oral history, and a directory of women's history projects and collections, which make the issue a reference work. (WKB)

1507. Gluck, Sherna, ed. *From Parlor to Prison: Five American Suffragists Talk about Their Lives, An Oral History*. New York: Vintage, 1976.

Gluck, director of the Feminist History Research Project in Los Angeles, has presented the oral histories of five rank-and-file suffragists. From Sylvie Thygeson, age 104, a one-time midwestern housewife and activist for birth control, to Ernestine Kettler, age seventy-nine, a one-time Greenwich Village radical and labor union organizer, the women talk about the motivations behind their commitment to suffrage, strategies of the movement, and the effect of suffrage and other reform activity on their lives and those of their fellow suffragists. The many hours of taped interviews have been edited in five narratives unbroken by questions; the full interviews are available at the Feminist History Research

Project. There is a brief introduction and afterword for each narrator; a long introduction on the history of the suffrage movement and where these five women fitted in; and a detailed chronology of the movement. Supplemental to the book, which has been adopted by women's history classes as a text, is a slide-tape show using the women's voices. (WKB)

1508. Kahn, Kathy, ed. *Hillbilly Women*. Garden City, N.Y.: Doubleday, 1973.

These selections are from interviews with nineteen poor, white women from the Southern Appalachians, recorded by Kahn, an organizer of poor and working people. The women talk about life as a miner's wife, daughter, or widow; of work in factories and cotton mills; of fighting the coal companies' agents and mill bosses; of trying to organize into unions; of illegitimacy, widowhood, courtship, sex, childbirth, and childdeath; and anger and pride in their roles. Kahn has written a brief narrative to set the scene for each selection, and occasionally she cuts in on the speaker to add information or compress the account of events and then lets the speaker go on in her own voice. This is an action book. "I did not write this book to be read and then set up on a shelf to gather dust. I wrote it with the hope it will generate some action from the people who read it." The last section is a list of grass-roots organizations and publications and what the reader can do to help them. (WKB)

XVIII: Oral History: International

1509. "Archives Orales: Une Autre Histoire." *Annales Economies, Societés, Civilisations*, Vol. XXXV (January-February 1980).

The growing importance of oral history in France is recognized in this special oral history issue of the prestigious journal *Annales*. Because much French work combines historical, sociological, and anthropological concerns, several themes unite the essays: the use of memory in historical reconstruction; epistemological concerns, the use of life histories, and the subjectivity of memory. Several of the essays make a contribution to any theoretical discussion of oral testimony. (RJG)

1510. Berg, Maclyn. "An Oral Historian in Moscow: Some First-Hand Observations." *Oral History Review*, Vol. II (1974), pp. 10-23.

Although most of the article recounts the author's experience in the Soviet Union, there are some interesting comments on the views of oral history held by Soviet scholars and some mention of projects. (RJG)

1511. Bertaux, Daniel. "L'Histoire Orale en France: Fin de la Prehistoire." *International Journal of Oral History*, Vol. II (June 1981), pp. 121-127.

Bertaux, one of France's leading sociologists and a motive force in the movement to revive the life-history method, reviews several programs in France and assesses their relation to French scholarly and intellectual life in general. (RJG)

1512. Brown, Kenneth, and Michael Roberts, eds. "Using Oral Sources: Vansina and Beyond." *Social Analysis: Journal of Cultural and Social Practice*, Vol. IV (September 1980).

This special issue of the Australian journal *Social Analysis* is directed primarily to anthropologists and secondarily to historians and sociologists; Brown and Roberts have assembled eight articles by a number of leading scholars working with oral testimony. The articles reflect the current state of the art and current debates among those collecting oral data; they deal with both field work and theoretical practice. (RJG)

1513. Brown, Lyle. "Methods and Approaches in Oral History: Interviewing Latin American Elites." *Oral History Review*, Vol. I (1973), pp. 77-86.

This article discusses the author's planned project to interview American historians and political scientists whose field is Mexican history and government, and it provides a longer description of the work of James W. Wilkie. It has information on the development of oral history in Mexico and some areas of Latin America as well as some speculation about the different traditions informing those efforts. (RJG)

1514. *Bulletin de l'Institut d'Histoire du Temps Present*. Published by the Institut d'Histoire du Temps Present, 806 Rue Lecourbe, 75015 Paris.

The first issue of the *Bulletin* (June 1980) contains a basic bibliography on oral history in France. (RJG)

1515. *Cahiers Internationaux de Sociologie*, Vol. LXIX (1980).

This special issue is devoted to life-history methodology. It carries a number of articles of interest to oral historians. The articles also reveal the close connection in Europe between using oral testimony as an approach to reformulate the problems of the social sciences and as a method for understanding social reality. (RJG)

1516. *Canadian Oral History Association Journal*. Published annually by the Canadian Oral History Association, P.O. Box 301, Station A, Ottawa, Ontario K1A ON, Canada.

1517. Foronda, Marcelino A., Jr. "Oral History in the Philippines: Trends and Prospects." *International Journal of Oral History*, Vol. II, no. 1 (February 1981), pp. 13-25.

During the past two decades a number of oral history projects have been started in the Philippines. Foronda reviews them, assessing their strengths and weaknesses. All but one are housed in universities and closely connected to research. All face common problems of funding and staff. As the author notes, there are "a few bright spots in an otherwise gloomy picture." (RJG)

1518. Il Fonti Orali. Turin: Instituto Gramsci Piedmontese.

This work provides the proceedings of the first Italian conference on oral history. The Institute has also published a list of projects in Italy represented at the conference. Turin is heavily represented, but some articles deal with the south of Italy. A yearly journal is being planned. (RJG)

1519. International Journal of Oral History. Meckler Books, 520 Riverside Avenue, Westport, Conn. 06880.

This American journal, which appears three times each year, includes articles, news and notes, bibliographic section, book reviews, and equipment reviews. It publishes a wide variety of materials on oral history throughout the world, placing emphasis on theoretical and methodological issues as well as interdisciplinary and cross-cultural approaches to oral testimony. (RJG)

1520. "International Reports: Australia, Brazil, Mexico, Latin America and the United Kingdom." *Oral History Review*, Vol. IV (1976), pp. 48-64.

This article provides brief historical descriptions and discussions of problems and prospects by Juan Campbell, George P. Browne, Eugenia Meyer, and David Lance. Read in conjunction, these reports show the variety of traditions within which oral history has developed. The Browne and Meyer reports reflect a difference in direction and tone. (RJG)

1521. Lance, David. "Oral History in Britain." *Oral History Review*, Vol. II (1974), pp. 64-77.

David Lance of the Imperial War Museum has not only been a leading oral historian in Great Britain but an active participant in the International Association of Sound Archivists. This article reflects the dual interest as well as some of the tension within British oral history between social historians and those doing elite interviews. Lance, formerly on the side of the elite interviewing on the American (archival) model, describes his own project and some of the efforts of the BBC. The article also lists oral history centers in Great Britain and Ireland. A more up-to-date list is available from the Oral History Society in Essex. (RJG)

1522. Miller, Joseph C., ed. *The African Past Speaks: Essays on Oral Tradition and History*. London: William Dawson, 1980.

The most current update of the debates over Jan Vansina's monumental work, *Oral Tradition* (see nos. *1347* and *1438*), these essays present a synthesis that, while accepting many of the criticisms of Vansina, reasserts the historical value of oral traditions. Nine case studies, an introduction, and a general essay by Vansina, "Memory and Oral Tradition," comprise the volume. These essays provde an introduction to the current state of research in African oral traditions. (RJG)

1523. Neithammer, Lutz, ed. *Lebenserfährung und Kollektives Gedachtnis: Die Praxis Der "Oral History."* Frankfurt am Main: F. R. G. Syndikat, 1980.

Many of these articles by British, American, and continental oral historians have been published elsewhere, but taken together with the previously unpublished German essays in this volume, they indicate the concerns and thrust of oral historical work in Germany. Neithammer's introductory essay assesses the role of oral history and historical memory in the context of post-World War II Germany and its potential for a "democratic history." (RJG)

1524. *Oral History: The Journal of the Oral History Society*.

This journal publishes issues twice a year from the Department of Sociology, University of Essex, Colchester, CO4 35Q. It includes articles, news events, conferences, and reports on projects. In addition to articles and reports of oral history in Great Britain, the journal carries extensive coverage of oral history elsewhere in Europe. (RJG)

1525. Page, Melvin. "Malawians and the Great War: Oral History in Reconstructing Africa's Recent Past." *Oral History Review*, Vol. VIII (1980), pp. 49-61.

While devoted to a close examination of one historic episode in one African nation, this article is an example of how oral traditions and oral history complement each other in African historiography. Page's evaluation of African and European sources reveals how useful native testimony is in reconstructing the history of the colonial period in Africa. (RJG)

1526. Passerini, Luisa. "Italian Working Class Culture Between the Wars: Consensus to Fascism and Work Ideology." *International Journal of Oral History*, Vol. I, no. 1 (February 1980), pp. 4-27.

Italian work in oral history has shown a synthesis of theory and practice. This article reflects much of this type of work: the interest in subjective aspects of experience, the role of language in historical memory, the interest in the theories of Antonio Gramsci, and the close interaction of consciousness and politics. More than an empirical report on working-class life, this article is a historical reconstruction of the past through oral histories. (RJG)

1527. *Proceedings*. Regina: Saskatchewan Archives Board, 1981.

These proceedings of the Saskatchewan Oral History Conference held at the University of Regina, May 1-2, 1981, contain a number of articles on oral history in Canada. Of note are the presentations by Richard Lockhead, "The Character of the Oral History Movement in Canada," pp. 1-8, which notes the differences between developments in Canada, the United States, and Great Britain; Derek Reimer, "Oral History in an Archives Setting," pp. 8-15, which describes work in British Columbia. (RJG)

1528. Sound Heritage.

This journal is published quarterly by the Aural History Society, Province of British Columbia Provincial Archives, Victoria, British Columbia. It carries a number of articles, usually organized around a theme for each issue, dealing with the history of British Columbia. Reflecting the Society's concerns with sound history, many of the articles give excellent advice and insights into these problems. (RJG)

1529. The Oral History Association of Australia Journal.

This journal presents articles, reviews, workshop and seminar reports, news of projects, correspondence, guides, and bibliographies. The publisher is the Oral History Association of Australia, Secretary, 2 Ivey Street, Lindfield, New South Wales, 2070. The Association also publishes a newsletter.

1530. Thompson, Paul. "The New Oral History in France." *Oral History*, Vol. VIII (Spring 1980), pp. 14-21.

Thompson discusses current French efforts in oral history set against the backdrop of French intellectual traditions. He mentions and categorizes most of the projects being developed in France. He describes projects outside Paris that reflect strong local and regional roots. (RJG)

XIX: Reference

1530a. American Association for State and Local History. *History News*. Vols. XVIII-XXX (May 1973-September 1975).

Each issue in these volumes has a column on oral history. The contributors were members of the Oral History Association. Each one deals with a specific issue, e.g., interview preparation, equipment, and interviewing the elderly. (EHD)

1530b. Directory of Oral History Programs in the United States. Sanford, N.C.: Microfilming Corporation of America, 1982.

This guide presents information concerning all aspects of professional oral history. (EHD)

1530c. Oral History Association: standing publications.

Published *Proceedings* of the early annual meetings of the Oral History Association (OHA), 1966-1971, were almost verbatim transcripts of the programs. In 1973 OHA began publishing an annual journal, *The Oral History Review*, which contains articles, special reports, book reviews, and minutes of OHA council meetings. OHA also publishes a quarterly *Newsletter*, providing current information about oral history projects, personalities, grants, regional organizations, and book notices. For information write the Executive Secretary, Oral History Association, P.O. Box 13734, North Texas State University, Denton, Texas 76203. (EHD)

1530d. Oral History Association: special publications.

The Oral History Association has published Manfred J. Waserman, comp., *Bibliography on Oral History*, rev. ed. (1975); *Goals and Guidelines*, rev. ed. (1980), a one-page sheet that addresses the rights and obligations of interviewee, interviewer, and sponsoring institution; and *Oral History Evaluation Guidelines* (1980), a set of guidelines developed for use in evaluating existing or proposed programs and projects. (EHD)

CHAPTER 11

POLICY HISTORY

Peter N. Stearns, editor

A great deal of history is relevant to policy. Any political history, even a good biography, can contribute to a sense of how the policy process functions and can provide examples of impulses to emulate and impulses to avoid. Much social history conveys a grasp of the dynamics of policy problem areas; indeed, a list of lively topics in social history considerably overlaps a list of domestic policy issues—family, crime, mental illness, and work, among others. The more contemporary the history, the more probable that it bears on policy. Certainly one hopes that those involved in current policy research and formation possess a general understanding of the forces that have shaped contemporary society. No limited list of works in policy history should discourage a sense of the wide policy relevance associated with diverse kinds of historical study.

The list below emphasizes kinds of history that have been written with some explicit intention of contributing to the policy process. It thus avoids stress on the history of policy *per se*, which typically is a part of contemporary political history or written in the fashion of a celebratory memorial of an agency or business. Histories of policy or of policy-making institutions have clear utility, and they may have more than a factual bearing on actual policy formulation. Some examples of the genre are included in the present list, particularly in some of the less familiar policy areas such as policing. There is also some focused social history that sets context for a policy problem, much as analytical political history does for the policy process. But the newer surge in policy or applied history strives for more direct bearing on the policy process than is usually possible through a descriptive background narrative, and the present listing concentrates on this more assertive approach.

The first section, on theory, deals directly with statements of how historical research fits policy research, not just in developing some sense of how the world works or even in providing a general perspective on a policy issue, but as an integral part of the policy-study process. Subsequent sections include examples of this kind of applied history, plus other work that essentially fits this mode. Emphasis is on subject areas where historical participation in policy research has been carried farthest, beginning with foreign and strategic policy, where a historical component has long been held valuable. Even here there is no pretense at being comprehensive. Much policy-relevant history has been excluded on various grounds: some work because the principal focus was a history of policy or a policy-making institution rather than a contribution to policy research, although the boundary line is not always easy to draw; some others because, although the contribution to the policy process is real, the result was unintended by the historian; and some others simply in the interest of producing a list of manageable size.

From the diplomatic and military areas the list moves to sections on domestic policy, where the historical mode is less accepted in the policy community but where much of the newly explicit applied history is being developed. The most elaborate listings relate to technology, welfare, and urban policy. Again, there is no pretense at thorough coverage, which would dictate inclusion of a vast body of contemporary political history and recent social history; the emphasis is on work that is illustrative of methods and concepts. The list, in sum, is intended to provide grounding in the characteristic approaches and problems of this distinctive branch of public history.

Where possible, in pursuance of this interest in methods of approach, works in the substantive policy areas are identified in terms of one or more possible history-policy linkages: background or perspective; policy evaluation; analogy; contribution to theory; trend assessment; comparative assessment; analysis in terms of larger context. These approaches, discussed explicitly in various of the works detailed in the opening section, gain reality through their use in a number of current policy areas.

I. Definitions and Case Studies

1531. Benson, Lee. "Changing Social Science to Change the World." *Social Science History*, Vol. II (Summer 1978), pp. 427-441.

Benson attempts to diagnose the ills of American social science, using Marx's rejection of impractical, abstract philosophy as a starting point. He contends that American social science suffers from an ill-advised intellectual orientation that marries French positivist scientism and German idealist historicism. This marriage, he argues, has led to alienation of social scientists from their work and to an ahistorical approach to the study of human behavior. Benson urges that history be restored to the social scientific study of human behavior. In addition to his comments on the relation of history to social science, Benson also makes two other suggestions of interest to applied historians. First, he notes the need to distinguish between social science theories of different levels of generality. Second, he observes that historical periodization is a crucial factor in formulating social science theory. (PNS)

1532. Campbell, Ballard C. *Representative Democracy: Public Policy and Mid-western Legislatures in the Late Nineteenth Century*. Cambridge, Mass.: Harvard University Press, 1980.

This book provides a multivariate analysis of policy making in the legislatures of Illinois, Iowa, and Wisconsin, 1886-1895. Focused on "contested issue" roll calls (in number, one thousand), Campbell describes the policy context of controversial legislation and identifies the lines of cleavage on these issues. The study illustrates how the application of a systematic research design that integrates quantitative and conventional evidence illuminates institutional and behavioral phenomena. The varied patterns of partisan, cultural, urban, and other influences on decision making documented in this case study contradict customary portraits of state law making. An appendix describes techniques of analyses. (BCC)

1533. Fischoff, Baruch. "For Those Condemned to Study the Past: Reflections on Historical Judgment." In R. A. Shweder and D. W. Fiske, eds. *New Directions for Methodology of Behavioral Science: Fallible Judgment in Behavioral Research*. San Francisco: Jossey-Bass, 1980.

After the author makes a rather reluctant admission of the necessity of historical research for social science, he renders a comment on the difficulties of generalization and uncertainty. He notes common errors of social scientists in using historical method. (PNS)

1534. Fogelson, Robert M. "The Morass: An Essay on the Public Employee Pension Problem." In David J. Rothman and Stanton Wheeler, eds. *Social History and Social Policy*. New York: Academic, 1981.

In 1976, Los Angeles spent $103 million for its police and fire pension system, an amount equal to a third of the city's property tax, and had an unfunded liability of $1.5 billion, which equalled a sixth of the city's assessed value. The creation of this fiscal time bomb is found in the way that the system evolved since 1899. A series of incremental program liberalizations over the years, vigorously promoted by unions and approved by voters, left Los Angeles with a scheme that was primarily noncontributory and unfunded, tied to the consumer price index, increasingly expensive, and difficult to change. This case study illustrates how analytically oriented history can explain modern political dilemmas. (BCC)

1535. George, Alexander L. "Case Studies and Theory Development: The Method of Structured, Focused Comparison." In Paul G. Lauren, ed. *Diplomacy: New Approaches in History, Theory, and Policy*. New York: Free Press, 1979.

George attempts to synthesize the political scientist's quantitative methods and the historian's qualitative approach to analysis. Drawing on the work of Eckstein and Lyphart, George offers one approach to translating the "lessons of history" into predictive theory. He suggests that focused comparison of case studies can lead to theory development through accumulation of data from individual cases. These data may then be used to test existing theories and to discern new areas for investigation. This approach is germane because it blends social science and historical perspectives. Noting the tension between case-study analysts and statistical-correlative analysts, George suggests that the two methodologies need not conflict and may complement each other: statistically generated theories can provide a general framework for case studies, and in turn case studies can test and expand upon general theories in controlled, focused settings. (PNS)

1536. Graham, Patricia A. "Historians as Policy Makers." *Educational Researcher*, Vol. IX (December 1980), pp. 21-24.

This is a reprint of a paper delivered to the American Educational Research Association. The author, director of the National Institute for Education and professor of the history of education at Harvard University, argues that history is invaluable to the policy-making process. Only through a knowledge of the policy process can administrators and policy makers, past and present, learn how intention and actual practice are associated. The major area in which historically trained policy makers can make a contribution, she notes, is at the state and local level. In the field of education, particularly, policy is by and large created in state and local, not federal, agencies. (DAJ)

1537. Hofferbert, Richard I. *The Study of Public Policy.* Indianapolis: Bobbs-Merrill, 1974.

The work reviews methodological approaches to the study of policy making and proposes, through theoretical and empirical presentations, the utility of comparative multivariate research designs. The author's model places quantitative observations within wider dynamic and historical contexts. Sections on the behavior of policy makers, evaluations of representative case studies, the role of political elites, and typologies of policy content complement this comprehensive treatment of the field. (BCC)

1538. Hofstetter, C. Richard. "Malapportionment and Roll-Call Voting in Indiana, 1923-1963: A Computer Simulation." *Journal of Politics*, Vol. XXXIII (Fall 1971), pp. 92-111.

Malapportionment of state legislatures did not skew policy very much according to this study of 6,895 roll calls from the Indiana House, when a single apportionment prevailed. Despite various weightings, only 1.5 percent of the voting results changed. Separate longitudinal analysis produced similar results. Malapportionment affected regulatory measures the most, and yet the experiment suggests that greater equity in apportionment would not have increased the scope of Indiana government. (BCC)

1539. Holsti, Ole R. "Historians, Social Scientists, and Crisis Management: An Alternative View." *Journal of Conflict Resolution*, Vol. XXIV (December 1980), pp. 665-682.

Communication and collaboration between diplomatic historians and social scientists are necessary and essential in the development of an empirical, policy-relevant set of theories of crises and their resolution. (RPC)

1540. Kousser, J. Morgan. "Progressivism—For Middle-Class Whites Only: North Carolina Education, 1880-1910." *Journal of Southern History*, Vol. XXXXVI (May 1980), pp. 169-194.

Progressivism in education policy in North Carolina reduced the equality of school expenditures between the races and to a lesser degree between rich and poor whites, a development attributed to the effect of disfranchisement on black political influence. This conclusion emerges from spatial and longitudinal analyses of school tax and expenditure data at the county level, apportioned through regression estimates by race. Findings elevate the importance of political factors as compared with socioeconomic structure as a determinant of policy. (BCC)

1541. Mandelbaum, Seymour J. "The Past in Service to the Future." *Journal of Social History*, Vol. XI (Fall 1977), pp. 193-205.

Mandelbaum examines the methods by which historians can become more active in making policy. He suggests that their specific tasks include accurate tracing of current policy issues to determine opportunities and adjustments as well as utilizing valid comparative analogical statements. Also, the historian should address the evolution of values relevant to policy decisions while considering potential obstacles and possible trade-offs to be expected under various courses of action. The expansion of the historical approach into the realm of policy analysis certainly presents an alternative method of inquiry to the decision maker, but this affiliation raises difficult ethical questions. Mandelbaum addresses optimistically the issue of the further professionalization of historical scholarship. He concludes that the relationship between policy maker and historian can be mutually beneficial if both move beyond their biases to develop "a more wisely imagined future and a more richly conceived past." (PNS)

1542. May, Ernest R. *"Lessons" of the Past*. New York: Oxford University Press, 1981.

This work deals mainly with foreign policy, but it also provides a general set of guidelines for the use of analogy. May examines recent events (World War II, the Cold War, Korea, and Vietnam), focusing on the making of decisions. He explains how policy makers have misinterpreted and misused historical analogies and shows how to break down analogies into constituent ingredients in order to apply them more accurately. If history can be properly used, the historian's contribution to policy will prove to be an "enormously rich resource for people who govern." (PNS)

1543. McClelland, Peter D., and Alan L. Magdovitz. *Crisis in the Making: The Political Economy of New York State since 1945*. New York: Cambridge University Press, 1981.

The authors explain fiscal crises in New York during the mid-1970s by means of reconstructing economic, fiscal, demographic, and political trends over several decades. Various causes of difficulty emerge. Detailed analyses of public spending and budgeting appear in the text and in appendices. (BCC)

1544. McCurley, James. "The Historian's Role in the Making of Public Policy." *Social Science History*, Vol. III (Winter 1979), pp. 202-207.

The author notes the traditional exclusion of historians from the policy process and suggests some approaches that historians can use to make their work more attractive and useful to policy makers. Historians must be willing to use new tools to make their work policy-relevant. Historians possess certain skills unavailable to most analysts. McCurley believes that the historian's role can include assessment of change over time, the use of historical analogs to illuminate current issues, and evaluation of the role that values play in policy issues and in society. The rigor of historical inquiry, when combined with the diversity of evidence that historians examine, can provide a more holistic view of the issues than can other analysts. (PNS)

1545. Read, Conyers. "Report of the Ad Hoc Committee on Historians in the Federal Government." In AHA *Annual Report for 1951*, Vol. I: *Proceedings and Lists of Members*. Washington: Government Printing Office, pp. 55-60.

This report reviewed some professional issues of concern to federal historians in 1951. The committee recommended that criteria for appraising historical products of federal historians be established and advocated a role for historians in policy formation and appraisal as well as in recording actions. (RPC)

1546. Rein, Martin. *Social Science and Public Policy*. New York: Penguin, 1976.

Among the formal works on public policy, Rein's book is unusually sensitive to the historical dimension. His empirical work on welfare demonstrates similar historical intelligence. (PNS)

1547. Rothman, David J., and Stanton Wheeler, eds. *Social History and Social Policy*. New York: Academic, 1981.

This collection illustrates the contributions of a sociohistorical approach to a grasp of current policy issues. Many social historians choose topics in areas where current policies are losing legitimacy and so automatically contribute to policy-relevant analysis. Early essays detail the paradigmatic approach to education, mental health, and hospitals in discussing the origins of assumptions presumed still to dominate the field. A second section offers more direct histories of current social problems in the areas of public employee pensions, preventive health, and criminal justice. A final section, using illustrations from urban policy,

policy toward black families, and policy toward children, traces more generally the actual and potential uses of history in the sphere of policy. (PNS)

1548. Scheiber, Harry N. "Federalism and the American Economic Order, 1789-1910." *Law and Society Review*, Vol. X (Fall 1975), pp. 57-118.

This analysis demonstrates that attention to the effects of the federal system advances understanding of policy evolution during the nineteenth century. The distinction between "formal authority" and "real power" provides a conceptual framework for integrating judicial evidence and information about the political economy. "American federalism before 1861 was decentralized," which stimulated "rivalistic state mercantilism." Thereafter a trend toward centralization emerged. The author's survey in *Law and Society Review*, Vol. XIV (1980), provides a comprehensive bibliography on the interaction of federalism and policy since 1789. (BCC)

1549. Shambaugh, Benjamin F., ed. *Iowa Applied History Series*. 6 vols. Iowa City: State Historical Society of Iowa, 1912-1925.

This series deals with the government of Iowa on the state, county, and municipal levels. The editor's introduction in volume I provides an example of what the writers in the series saw as the definition of applied history. Subsequent volumes combine this definition with practical knowledge and experiences in an attempt to provide a scientific interpretation of past issues to solve present-day problems. The reader is shown that systematic use of case studies can explain the failure of past policies. These failures can then be redressed in order to correct the problems and increase the chances of gaining a more positive outcome. Despite its age, the Iowa series does more than serve as an example of a forerunner of modern applied history; it provides detailed illustration of an evaluative use of history for policy purposes. (PNS)

1550. "Special Issue on Applied History." *Journal of Social History*, Vol. XIV (June 1981).

This collection offers various approaches to applied history in different policy fields by means of case studies. Policy areas include educational testing, nutrition, pollution control, police, retirement, women's employment, and environment. Explicitly applied history approaches include narrative background, trend assessment, historical and comparative context toward improving problem definition, and analogy. The collection is one of the few casebooks available in this field, designed to contribute substantively in the various areas but collectively intended to flesh out a definition of the applied-history concept. (PNS)

1551. Stearns, Peter N. "History and Policy Analysis: Toward Maturity." *Public Historian*, Vol. IV (Summer 1982), pp. 5-29.

This article addresses the question of identity currently being explored by applied historians. They are neither conventional historians looking for new places to display their wares nor social scientists operating with some historical data. The applied historian must choose research topics that fill the needs of public and private clients, not those that follow academic tastes. The article assesses the main analytical approaches of the new policy discipline. (PNS)

1552. Stearns, Peter N., and Joel A. Tarr. "Applied History: A New-Old Departure." *History Teacher*, Vol. XIV (Summer 1981), pp. 517-532.
The authors describe the teaching implications of training in policy-relevant history, including the outline of a suitable introductory course in the genre. (PNS)

1553. Trask, David F. "A Reflection on Historians and Policymakers." *History Teacher*, Vol. XI (February 1978), pp. 219-266.
The author, chief historian of the U.S. Army Center of Military History, advocates greater participation of historians in policy analysis. Statesmen concerned with future processes draw from historical experience. The historian is trained to analyze past processes, concentrating on change and continuity in past trends. Trask proposes two ways that historians can contribute to policy analysis: recent history and prophecy. First, the policy maker's interest in processes requires reference to past experience, and historians are best qualified to interpret recent history. Second, the experience of a historian at identifying factors that influenced the direction of events in the past may well enhance an ability to suggest possible consequences of different policy proposals. (PNS)

1554. Woodward, C. Vann. "The Age of Reinterpretation." *American Historical Review*, Vol. LXVI (1960), pp. 1-20.
The author urges reinterpretation of American history in the light of the nation's new world power position and its related loss of innocence. Woodward sees historical reassessment as vital to an ability to handle new situations. Historical meaning is essential to the ability to act; if historians do not provide it, others will. (PNS)

1555. Yarwood, Dean L., and Thomas B. Alexander. "History and Policy Studies." *Policy Studies Journal*, Vol. VII (Summer 1979), pp. 803-811.
The authors discuss several ways in which history bears on policy studies. They discuss the concept of the past as a laboratory for policy, the perspective that history offers on current policies, and the fact that history can serve as a source for rare or unique occurrences as well as a source for values useful to justify current and suggested policies. (RPC)

II. Foreign Policy: Analogies and Contemporary History

1556. Allison, Graham T. *Essence of Decision: Explaining the Cuban Missile Crisis*. Boston: Little, Brown, 1971.

This work demonstrates how policy analysis, through three conceptual frames of reference, can produce different explanations of and answers to the same question. He suggests that the classical or rational-actor model, which views decision making as the result of purposeful, rational, and value-maximizing acts of unified national governments, may not adequately address the scope of a policy problem. Other models focus on intragovernmental systems and person-alities involved in the policy process. The organizational-process model assumes that decisions result from standardized "outputs" of semiautonomous, loosely allied organizations within the governmental infrastructure. The bureaucratic-politics model describes decisions as the result of competition, compromises, and the political infighting of intranational actors within the government hier-archy. For applied historians, a working synthesis of the three frameworks aids in evaluation of policy problems and fosters concentration on the intragovern-mental factors that help determine policy decisions. (PNS)

1557. Benson, Sumner. "The Historian as Foreign Policy Analyst: The Chal-lenge of the CIA." *Public Historian*, Vol. II (Winter 1981), pp. 15-25.
Historical skills are applied in an intelligence agency in several ways. In one setting the individual analyzed a critical issue, the strategic arms limitations talks. In another effort, part of an institutional research program, the product described an aspect of the Organization of Petroleum Exporting Countries. (RPC)

1558. DePorte, Anton W. *Europe between the Superpowers: The Enduring Balance*. New Haven, Conn.: Yale University Press, 1979.
DePorte examines the European state system from the First World War to the late 1970s. He investigates the system's changes in response to the two World Wars, the Cold War, and Europe's continuing military, economic, and political dependence on the United States and the Soviet Union. The author contends that the two-bloc system emerging from the Cold War is better suited to promoting political stability and deterring aggression than was the post-World War I set-tlement. DePorte points out the historical context of the role of ideology in shaping U.S. and Soviet perceptions of Europe and each other. Although DePorte makes no specific policy recommendations, he furnishes an example of how history may be used to inform policy analysis and reevaluate assumptions about international relations. (PNS)

1559. George, Alexander L. *Presidential Decisionmaking in Foreign Policy: The Effective Use of Information and Advice*. Boulder, Colo.: Westview, 1980.
This study addresses a major policy issue in terms of historical data, building toward general theory. He relegates historians proper to the testing of analogies while assigning to political scientists the task of integrating a variety of historical cases into a comprehensive, policy-usable theoretical statement. The result chal-lenges applied historians, even if they aspire to a somewhat more ambitious role than tester of analogies. George examines the misuse and nonuse of foreign-

policy information by American presidents and their advisors, showing how complex issues, constraints of time, and the advisory system can distort the policy maker's perception of policy information. He distinguishes between three models of presidential advisory systems: competitive, formalistic, and collegial models. He favors the latter. This work provides concrete examples of the strengths and flaws of past decision making and demonstrates how misuse of information can shape policy choices. (PNS)

1560. Janis, Irving. *Victims of Groupthink: A Psychological Study of Foreign-Policy Decisions and Fiascoes.* Boston: Houghton Mifflin, 1972.

The author makes use of a variety of historical cases to explore the bases of faulty decision making. (PNS)

1561. Kahler, Miles. "Rumors of War: The 1914 Analogy." *Foreign Affairs,* (Winter 1979-1980), pp. 374-396.

Recently many have argued that China's emergence as a superpower will reduce world tensions. The author uses his "1914 analogy" to identify several similarities between the current structure of world power and the one that existed before the First World War. The multipolar system at that time increased insecurity. The principal contemporary danger is that superpowers may expand their alliance systems in order to gain certainty in their international relationships. This might result in being drawn into war over a local quarrel, as in 1914. Analogy leads Kahler to recommend that policy makers view the actions of opponents as responses to particular situations rather than as calculating steps toward an evil design. Alliances should be viewed as collections of individual states rather than as monoliths. Kahler advises caution against the presumption that every gain by "them" is an intolerable loss for "us." This fear dominated Europe before the First World War. (PNS)

1562. Karklekas, Anne. "History of the Central Intelligence Agency." In U.S. Senate, Select Committee to Study Governmental Operations with Respect to Intelligence Activities. *Book III, Final Report.* Washington: Government Printing Office, 1978.

This article reports the findings of a historian called upon to do research that was immediately relevant to policy. The report played a significant role in legislation regulating the Central Intelligence Agency. (PNS)

1563. Kissinger, Henry. *The White House Years.* Boston: Little, Brown, 1979.

This memoir centers on the conflict in Vietnam and its ultimate resolution, although it also provides extensive treatment of the Middle East and Soviet-American negotiations. Grist for the contemporary historian's mill, this book offers larger interpretive insights that derive from the author's sense of history. (PNS)

1564. Kissinger, Henry. *Years of Upheaval*. Boston: Little, Brown, 1982.

This second volume of memoirs covers the period from the author's appointment as secretary of state until the end of President Nixon's administration in 1974. It concentrates on the onset of serious problems in the Middle East and the failure of "the year of Europe." It is preoccupied with adverse effects of the Watergate scandal on foreign policy. (PNS)

1565. Lowenthal, Abraham. *The Dominican Intervention*. Cambridge, Mass.: Harvard University Press, 1972.

Lowenthal offers a critical analysis of the U.S. intervention in Santa Domingo that took place in 1965. Concentrating on policy assumptions and decision-making procedures, he concludes that officials erred in accepting an inadequate conceptual framework while making "seemingly rational" decisions. (PNS)

1566. Mastny, Vojtech. *Russia's Road to the Cold War: Diplomacy, Warfare, and the Politics of Communism, 1941-1945*. New York: Columbia University Press, 1979.

This book traces both events and basic assumptions that led Russia to its characteristic Cold War stance. The approach, although narrative in large part, maintains analysis, and a concluding section relates the historical coverage to longer-range issues of foreign policy. (PNS)

1567. Neustadt, Richard E. *Alliance Politics*. New York: Columbia University Press, 1970.

Neustadt believes that relations with peacetime allies are no different than wartime associations. This circumstance results from the fact that governments in both situations are controlled by an innergovernmental process and that each nation attempts to maximize benefits from the alliance to its best advantage. Neustadt attempts to prove his thesis by means of case studies, citing American and British examples (the Suez crisis and the Skybolt affair). He contends that crisis behavior remains similar throughout both episodes, even if they differ in outcome, intensity, symbolism, and timing. (PNS)

1568. Paige, Glenn D. *The Korean Decision, June 24-30, 1950*. New York: Free Press, 1966.

Paige provides a theoretical framework on decision making and a thorough historical background. He goes through the critical days of decision, evaluating events in terms of implications for crisis management. (PNS)

1569. Quandt, William B. *Decade of Decisions: American Policy toward the Arab-Israeli Conflict, 1967-1976*. Berkeley: University of California Press, 1977.

Beginning with the Arab-Israeli War of 1967 and culminating with the Lebanon crisis in 1976, Quandt examines case studies that illustrate the importance of crisis situations in the reassessment and formulation of Middle East policy. He criticizes the recent practice of presidents of participating in Middle Eastern affairs only during emergencies. He claims that policies developed during crises continued in periods of relative stability and became ineffective with the passage of time. The study indicates how historical analysis can produce policy proposals. Quandt presents guidelines to help minimize the chance of repeating past misconceptions. For example, he argues that a realistic policy must avoid overemphasis of U.S.-Soviet conflict and concentrate on understanding the complicated relationships between countries of the region. (PNS)

1570. Radosh, Ronald. "Historian in the Service of Power." *Nation*, Vol. CCXXV (August 6, 1977), pp. 104-109.

This article examines the role of the historian Arthur M. Schlesinger, Jr., in the Kennedy administration, centering on the CIA activity against Castro and the coverup of American involvement. (RPC)

1571. Safran, Nadav. *Israel, the Embattled Ally.* Cambridge, Mass.: Belknap, 1978.

Safran traces the history of Israel and its "special relationship" with the United States, using a four-stage periodization. The two nations have developed steadily closer connections over the years, although the United States has improved its rapport with the Arabs. The author predicts that an American-Israeli mutual defense agreement and increased U.S. aid to the Arabs will guarantee a peace agreement in the Middle East. This conclusion represents an extrapolation of existing trends in American relations with these nations. (PNS)

1572. Talbott, Strove. *Endgame: The Story of SALT II.* New York: Harper and Row, 1979.

This effort at contemporary history is based on exhaustive coverage of journalistic sources. The study illustrates the strengths and the limitations of the contemporary history/narrative approach and contributes background to an ongoing policy issue. (PNS)

1573. Ulam, Adam B. *The Rivals: America and Russia since World War II.* New York: Viking, 1971.

This study approaches American-Russian policy issues explicitly as an outgrowth of historical developments. Ulam examines the main causes and manifestations of the interaction between the two superpowers. He assails U.S. policy makers for lack of realism and unwillingness to compromise. Too often they have acted on a conception of the United States as the moral guardian of the world. This trend has led to overcommitment and to continued misconception of Soviet actions and intentions. In addition, the moralistic tone of U.S. policy has contributed little toward achieving world stability and peace. (PNS)

1574. Wohlstetter, Roberta. *Pearl Harbor: Warning and Decision*. Stanford, Calif.: Stanford University Press, 1962.

Wohlstetter provides a narrative and analysis of the diplomacy surrounding Pearl Harbor, including strategic and intelligence factors on both sides. The author does not draw detailed lessons but is concerned with what this incident suggests about future intelligence reliability and strategic planning, including the ability to cope with the unexpected. (PNS)

1575. York, Herbert. *Race to Oblivion: A Participant's View of the Arms Race*. New York: Simon and Schuster, 1970.

Race to Oblivion offers a subjective evaluation of the arms race, drawing upon the author's experience as a physicist, as director of defense research and engineering under Eisenhower, and an analyst for the Department of Defense. He notes two absurdities resulting from the arms race. First, U.S. military power increased since World War II, but security diminished; second, the need for sophisticated early-warning systems caused a shift in the decision to use nuclear weapons from high government officials to the lower echelons and to machines. This book demonstrates how Cold War ideology fostered overreaction to Soviet scientific and military advances and caused the United States to accelerate the arms race. It is of interest to applied historians because of its policy analysis and recommendations, its examination of the arms race in its ideological and administrative contexts, and its assessment of the role of technology in weapons development. (PNS)

III. Military and Strategic Policy

1576. Albion, Robert G. *Introduction to Military History*. New York: Appleton-Century, 1929.

Chapter 6 sets forth the standard argument of old-line military historians that policy makers should learn their craft by studying the careers of the "great captains." The work is essentially a textbook for military officers. (PNS)

1577. Beard, Edmund. *Developing the ICBM*. New York: Columbia University Press, 1976.

This book deals mainly with the process leading to the American Inter-Continental Ballistic Missile (ICBM) system. Beard contends that the ICBM could have been developed earlier but that organizational structure and belief hindered development. He contends that the military is not the best judge of which weapons are feasible or most useful. Technological exploration and development are much too important to be caught up in the rigidity of bureaucratic routine. Beard provides a working example of the organizational structure and decision-making process, in much the same manner as Allison (see no. *1556*). (PNS)

1578. Brown, Richard C. *The Teaching of Military History in Colleges and Universities in the United States.* U.S.A.F. Historical Study, Vol. 124. Montgomery, Ala.: Air University, 1955.

The author concludes that "one justification for the study of the history [in academic programs] is that it helps to throw light on current problems and to suggest avenues of solution for these problems." (PNS)

1579. Clausewitz, Karl von. *On War.* Edited and translated by Michael Howard and Peter Paret. Princeton, N.J.: Princeton University Press, 1976.

This modern translation has introductory essays by Paret and Howard. Bernard Brodie contributes both an introductory essay and a commentary on the text. Clausewitz insists that historical examples are the best means of confirming the truth of generalizations about war. (DFT)

1580. Conn, Stetson. "The Pursuit of Military History." *Military Affairs*, Vol. XXX (Spring 1966), pp. 1-8.

This article describes the renewal of interest in military history during the 1960s and the historical programs in the Department of Defense. (PNS)

1581. Craven, Frank. *Why Military History?* Vol. I: *Harmon Memorial Lectures in Military History.* Montgomery, Ala.: U.S. Air Force Academy, 1959.

Craven takes it for granted that military policy makers must read and understand history, although he cautions that "the lessons of history are rarely, if ever, so exact as to permit their adoption as unfailing principles for the guidance of future action." (PNS)

1582. Critchley, Julian. *Warning and Response: A Study of Surprise Attack in the Twentieth Century and an Analysis of Its Lessons for the Future.* New York: Crane, Russak, 1978.

This book, a recent example of historical writing on military affairs, is designed to educate policy makers in the dynamics of sudden aggression. (PNS)

1583. Greenfield, Kent Roberts. *The Historian and the Army.* New Brunswick, N.J.: Rutgers University Press, 1954.

The author discusses the Army's historical program during and after World War II in which he was a participant. Greenfield believes that official histories are valuable. He states: "We enjoyed a basic advantage in the fact that in World War II the Army wanted a history of its experience for its own guidance, and for this it needed full and frank history." (PNS)

1584. Historical Evaluation and Research Organization. *A Survey of "Quick Wins" in Modern War: A Report Prepared for the Director of Net Assessment, Office of the Secretary of Defense.* Dunn Loring, Va.: HERO, 1975.

The author notes "some factors of particular importance in attempting to gain a quick victory." (PNS)

1585. Huntington, Samuel P. *The Common Defense: Strategic Programs in National Politics*. New York: Columbia University Press, 1961.

Huntington makes use of contemporary history (World War II to 1960) to provide the basis for generalizations about the relationship between military planning and politics in the executive and legislative branches. He concentrates on the alternation between equilibrium and change. (PNS)

1586. Huntington, Samuel P. *The Soldier and the State: The Theory and Politics of Civil-Military Relations*. Cambridge, Mass.: Harvard University Press, 1957.

Huntington offers a historical sketch from the American Revolution onward, enhanced by theoretical and comparative perspectives. Huntington sees the period 1940-1945 as a major departure from the past. He proceeds from this characterization of contemporary history to a set of policy recommendations. (PNS)

1587. Jessup, John E., Jr. and Robert W. Coakley, eds. *A Guide to the Study and Use of Military History*. Washington: Government Printing Office, n.d.

The U.S. Army Center of Military History developed this guide for the use of "the young officer just entering upon a military career," but it is helpful to all interested in the study of military history. The *Guide* has four basic parts. Part I treats military history in general—its nature and use. Part II provides bibliographical guidance to the sources and authorities for the field in general, for military history, and for the American experience. Part III examines "U.S. Army historical programs and activities and how the Army uses or has used military history." Part IV deals with "military history outside the Army—in other elements of the Department of Defense, in foreign military establishments, and the academic world." The editors note that "the volume is. . .not a guide to research and writing, although certainly parts of it should be useful to the researcher." (DFT)

1588. Karsten, Peter. "Demilitarizing Military History: Servants of Power or Agents of Understanding?" *Military Affairs*, Vol. XXXVI (October 1972), pp. 88-92.

Karsten believes that applied military historians "militarize minds." He severely criticizes "policy-oriented 'servants of power' who regard as their mission the reconstruction of tactical, strategic or leadership 'lessons of the past' for those training military leaders of tomorrow." (PNS)

1589. Kennedy, Paul M., ed. *The War Plans of the Great Powers, 1900-1914*. London and Boston: George Allen and Unwin, 1978.

Although the contributions do not attempt to draw policy lessons directly, their approach to strategic planning before the First World War treats technical as well as more conventional military factors of interest to students of policy. (PNS)

1590. Koistinen, Paul A. C. "The 'Industrial-Military Complex' in Historical Perspective: The Interwar Years." *Journal of American History*, Vol. LVI (Spring 1970), pp. 819-839.

The author continues the theme stated in another article (see no. *1591*) for the next period of American history, maintaining that interwar developments, established during the interwar years, held at least through the Cold War. (PNS)

1591. Koistinen, Paul A. C. "The 'Industrial-Military Complex' in Historical Perspective: World War I." *Business History Review*, Vol. XLI (December 1967), pp. 378-403.

Koistinen emphasizes military procurement and by this device clarifies the war's legacy for government-business relationships. He sees the experience as formative for the business-military links that created the fabled complex. (PNS)

1592. Liddell-Hart, Basil H. *Strategy*. 2d. ed. New York: Praeger Books, 1967.

This work uses historical cases to study the development of modern strategy. Liddell-Hart argues that new military ideas gain acceptance when they can be presented "not as something radically new, but as the revival in modern terms of a time-honoured principle that had been forgotten." The tank revived the armored horseman, and strategic histories even from the classical and medieval period have their utility as studies of policy. (PNS)

1593. Lyons, Gene M., and Louis Morton. "History and the Social Sciences." In Gene M. Lyons and Louis Morton, eds. *Schools for Strategy*. New York: Praeger, 1965.

The authors argue that "professional training in history develops qualities that are most valuable in the study of national security and policy planning." They express regret that few historians undertake careers in public service. (PNS)

1594. MacGregor, Morris J., Jr. *Integration of the Armed Forces, 1940-1965*. Washington: Government Printing Office, 1981.

This volume traces the process by which the armed forces broke down the pattern of racial segregation that had existed through World War II. It discusses the development of policy as well as its application. (DFT)

1595. Millett, Allan R. "American Military History: Over the Top." In Herbert J. Bass, ed. *The State of American History*. Chicago: Quadrangle, 1970.

Millett asserts that military history has gained academic respectability because "most of us have abandoned the military's definition of military history as 'lessons' of command and strategy." (PNS)

1596. Millis, Walter. *Arms and the State*. New York: Twentieth Century Fund, 1958.

In the introduction to this work on military affairs, Millis says: "Until the unlikely day when social scientists so far reduce human behavior to laws as to eliminate from practical calculations the effects of chance and purpose, the data of history—and analogies and inferences based upon them—will supply the main guides to policy choices." (PNS)

1597. Morton, Louis. "Historia Mentem Armet: Lessons of the Past." *World Politics*, Vol. XXII (January 1960), pp. 155-164.

Morton pleads for a return to the analysis of history as a means of understanding the present and planning for the future. Most of the article is devoted to pointing out specific historical circumstances where an understanding of the past should have informed policy choices. (PNS)

1598. Morton, Louis. "The Historian and the Study of War." *Mississippi Valley Historical Review*, Vol. XLVIII (March 1962), pp. 599-613.

Morton offers a defense of military history as an academic discipline with a plea for recognition of "public service as a legitimate aim of graduate teaching." This article anticipates views set forth in another article (see no. *1593*).

1599. Quester, George H. *Deterrence before Hiroshima.* New York: Wiley, 1966.

Studying the strategic significance of aerial bombing from 1900 to 1945, Quester contends that the concerns of strategists before the advent of atomic weapons were quite similar to those of their counterparts in the postwar world. He observes that the logic of deterrence, based on each nation's ability to inflict unacceptable destruction in retaliation for a preemptive aerial strike, has remained much the same since the inception of aerial bombing. Quester's study is relevant to applied history because of its use of historical analogies to inform discussion of policy questions. (PNS)

1600. Ropp, Theodore. "Military History and the Social Sciences." *Military Affairs*, Vol. XXX (Spring 1966), pp. 8-13.

Ropp argues that historians could make their analyses more useful to military policy makers by employing methodologies from other disciplines, particularly computer modelling. (PNS)

1601. Ropp, Theodore. *War in the Modern World.* New York: Collier, 1962.

In the introduction to this study of discontinuities in modern military history, Ropp says: "When soldiers speak of the 'principles of war' they are referring to those principles of action which can be illustrated by the military events of any historical period, the maxims of the soldier's trade." (PNS)

1602. Scheips, Paul J. "Military History and Peace Research." *Military Affairs*, Vol. XXXII (April 1972), pp. 72-76.

Scheips suggests that the study of military history, by elucidating the causes and nature of war, contributes to the attainment of peace. (PNS)

1603. Showalter, Dennis. "A Modest Plea for Drums and Trumpets." *Military Affairs*, Vol. XXXIX (April 1975), pp. 71-74.

Similar to Millett (no. *1595*), Showalter believes that military history is a legitimate academic field only if it is not applied. He refers to a "growing conviction that the study of war must move away from policy-oriented analyses which favor the status quo by purporting to show students how to perform more effectively in given situations." (PNS)

1604. Shy, John. "The American Military Experience: History and Learning." *Journal of Interdisciplinary History*, Vol. I (Winter 1971), pp. 205-228.

Shy deals with a theoretical approach to the historical study of war; showing concern for periodization in the American experience, he argues that war is tightly bound up in American national identity and that historians must make use of theories of personality to understand the present and to anticipate the future. Shy is especially concerned with the post-Vietnam revulsion against things military, which produced a severe and protracted national impact. "American society is in some sense a living organism whose behavior reveals coherence and consistency, and which can be said to learn from and remember its military past." (PNS)

1605. Van Creveld, Martin L. *Supplying War: Logistics from Wallenstein to Patton*. Cambridge: Cambridge University Press, 1977.

The author provides historical summaries of most major modern wars. Seventeenth- and eighteenth-century procedures are characterized in an initial chapter. The author does not offer specific policy recommendations save to note the immense difficulties endemic in the logistics areas; these problems recur in different guise when solved in an earlier form. In addition to recurrence, the book notes fairly consistent inattentiveness to logistics compared with other aspects of military planning. (PNS)

1606. Weigley, Russell F. *The American Way of War: A History of U.S. Military Strategy and Policy*. New York: Macmillan, 1973.

From a policy standpoint, Weigley offers an extensive background study, dealing with basic assumptions and policy continuities. (PNS)

1607. Wells, Samuel F., Jr. "Sounding the Tocsin: NSC 68 and the Soviet Threat." *International Security*, Vol. IV (Fall 1979), pp. 116-158.

This article examines the factors motivating the Truman administration to implement the proposals for increased military expenditures contained in a recommendation of the National Security Council in 1950. Wells contends that economic, political, and technological developments rather than careful consideration of U.S. defense needs and capabilities were primary influences. In particular, Wells notes the importance of the Korean War in fueling the administration's fear of Soviet and communist aggression. Wells's approach dovetails with that of applied history in his attempt to take a historical view of his subject, his use of analogy, and his consideration of the implications of past events on present policy. While noting the similarities between the Committees of the Present Danger of 1950 and 1976, for example, Wells warns against predicting behavior by using analogies that minimize social and historical change. (PNS)

1608. Wells, Samuel F., Jr. "The Origins of Massive Retaliation." *Political Science Quarterly*, Vol. XCVI (Spring 1981), pp. 31-52.

Wells examines the historical context in which the Eisenhower administration enunciated the doctrine of massive retaliation. The Truman administration laid the foundation for massive retaliation by expanding the U.S. nuclear arsenal during the Korean War. Eisenhower, in turn, relied on this arsenal to deter Soviet aggression. Wells contends that Eisenhower agreed, in part, with the doctrine, although he did not contemplate a preemptive strike on the Soviet Union. Massive retaliation served Eisenhower's political as well as military objectives by allowing him to reduce conventional forces (and thus, the defense budget) and to appear to break significantly with Truman's policies. This approach is instructive for applied historians because it traces the historical evolution of massive retaliation. Wells discerns a trend toward massive retaliation that began during the Truman administration rather than the abrupt policy change attributed to Eisenhower and Dulles. (PNS)

1609. Wright, Quincy. *A Study of War*. Chicago: University of Chicago Press, 1965.

In his introduction, Wright lists four uses of the past. Professional practitioners and decision makers select events that "contribute to current utility." Scientists choose those that "contribute to verifiable generalizations." Orators and literary writers emphasize events that "concern the public they address." Historians select those that best illustrate "what the public of the time and place written about deemed important." (PNS)

IV. Technology and Related Issues

1610. Anderson, Alan D. *The Origin and Resolution of an Urban Crisis: Baltimore, 1890-1930*. Baltimore: Johns Hopkins University Press, 1977.

From the standpoint of an economic historian, Anderson analyzes changes in city services as a function of changes in factor prices as mediated by changes in transportation systems—the introduction of the streetcar and the automobile. He urges the relevance of this analysis for current changes in factor costs, given pollution and congestion, in showing that urban innovation is possible but also that a comprehensive view of the urban system is essential. Anderson sees an analogy between Baltimore's crisis of congestion and pollution and contemporary concerns, in part because of their mutual relationship to transportation. He suggests the "systems analytic approach," which urges examination of urbanization as a whole system of economics, politics, technology, and spatial patterns. (PNS)

Brooks, Courtney G., James M. Grimwood, and Lloyd S. Swenson, Jr. *Chariots for Apollo: A History of Manned Lunar Spacecraft*. See no. *1450*.
This book is of interest from the standpoint of technological as well as political development. (PNS)

1611. Cain, Louis P. *Sanitation Strategy for the Lakefront Metropolis: The Case of Chicago*. DeKalb: Northern Illinois University Press, 1978.
Cain offers a detailed policy history of an important urban example, intermingling technical and political factors. (PNS)

1612. Cain, Louis P. "The Search for an Optimum Sanitation Jurisdiction: The Metropolitan Sanitary District of Greater Chicago, A Case Study." *Essays in Public Works History*, Vol. X (1980), pp. 20-23.
Cain traces the interaction between political and technological concerns germane to issues of pollution. (PNS)

1613. Cheape, Charles W. *Moving the Masses: Urban Public Transit in New York, Boston, and Philadelphia, 1880-1912*. Cambridge, Mass.: Harvard University Press, 1980.
Concentrating on the period 1880-1912, Cheape probes a volatile era of rapid growth and technological advancement in the mass transit systems of New York, Boston, and Philadelphia. He sees changing technology as the primary stimulus behind the developments in policy. By 1890 private monopolies emerged to coordinate and standardize the operation and cost of the complicated transit networks. The public nature of the service and expense of new technology eventually resulted in government ownership of the transit facilities, which were leased to private operators. (PNS)

1614. Hays, Samuel P. *Conservation and the Gospel of Efficiency, the Progressive Conservation Movement, 1890-1910*. Cambridge, Mass.: Harvard University Press, 1959.
Hays pinpoints the origins of today's main environmental actors and disputes. His analysis ends around 1920. Conservation is not simply a two-sided struggle between corporate exploitation and preservation of natural beauty, but a complex political struggle containing a series of overlapping disputes. Levels of government compete among themselves and with diverse private interests for control of policy. The book cautions decision makers against oversimplifying the issues. (PNS)

1615. Mazlish, Bruce, ed. *The Railroad and the Space Program: An Exercise in Historical Analogy.* Cambridge, Mass.: M.I.T. Press, 1965.

The avowed purpose of this book is "to see whether the study of the past could serve as a device of anticipation for the future." The editor's introduction comments on the construction, usage, and limitations of historical analogy. This methodological chapter provides a set of objectives for applied historical research. Mazlish points out that we cannot use analogy without fully examining its structural and functional position in the surrounding patterns of change. (PNS)

1616. Mazmanian, Daniel A., and Jeanne Nienaber. *Can Organizations Change? Environmental Protection, Citizen Participation, and the Corps of Engineers.* Washington: Brookings, 1979.

Mazmanian and Nienaber trace the Army Corps of Engineers' response to the National Environmental Policy Act of 1969 (NEPA). They identify setting new goals, modification of output, reorganization, and new decision-making processes as criteria by which to measure organizational change. By these standards the Corps showed a significant degree of change as a result of NEPA. Although the authors are political scientists, *Can Organizations Change?* exhibits several features of applied history. The Corps of Engineers' policy problems are set in historical perspective, with emphasis placed upon the forces of change that operated during the last decade. Structures and goals of the Corps' system that were inherently resistent to change are identified. (PNS)

1617. Melosi, Martin J., ed. *Pollution and Reform in American Cities, 1870-1930.* Austin: University of Texas Press, 1980.

This book introduces policy precedents in this area. While not directed explicitly at present concerns, the collection takes up a number of important analogies and also some underlying assumptions that still affect the policy process and the perception of pollution problems. Various aspects of urban technology are treated in the bibliography. (PNS)

1618. Nass, David L. "Public Policy and Public Works: Niagara Falls Redevelopment as a Case Study." *Essays in Public Works History*, Vol. VII (1979), pp. 81-94.

Nass shows how the policy history of technology can suggest underlying policy assumptions valid for understanding current options and constraints. (PNS)

1619. Pushkarev, Boris, and Jeffrey M. Zupan. *Urban Rail in America: An Exploration of Criteria for Fixed Guideway Transit.* Chicago: University of Chicago Press, 1981.

The authors use historical criteria and cases as part of a complex assessment of future policy options in this area. (PNS)

1620. Rose, Mark N. *Interstate: Express Highway Politics, 1941-1956*. Lawrence: Regents Press of Kansas, 1979.

Beginning with a chapter on highway policy and advocacy from 1890, Rose develops a clear historical periodization to trace the emergence of the current highway system. A final chapter provocatively assesses ''highways and the values of Americans.'' (PNS)

1621. Roshold, Robert. *An Administrative History of NASA, 1958-63*. Washington: NASA, 1966.

Roshold offers a narrative account of a key period in technological-political development. (PNS)

1622. Swenson, Lloyd S., Jr., James M. Grimwood, and Charles C. Alexander. *This New Ocean: A History of Project Mercury*. Washington: NASA SP 4201, 1966.

The authors provide a policy account in the narrative vein. See also Alex Roland, *A Guide to Research in NASA History* (History Office, NASA Headquarters, Washington, D.C. 20546), for further references, including some forthcoming work. (PNS)

1623. Tarr, Joel A., ed. ''The City and Technology.'' *Journal of Urban History*, Vol. V (1979), pp. 275-407.

These essays deal with urban transportation, energy choices, street paving, and sewage. Focus is on the early twentieth century, although as several essays note, decisions taken and technologies installed in this period continue to affect the urban environment, constraining and influencing current technological and budgetary choice. (PNS)

1624. Tarr, Joel A. ''Transportation Innovation and Changing Spatial Patterns in Pittsburgh, 1859-1934.'' *Essays in Public Works History*, Vol. VI (1978).

This case study treats general characteristics of the relationship between transportation and the use of urban space. In broad terms Tarr offers a kind of retrospective technology assessment from which to draw analogies or constituent factors relevant to current policy concerns. (PNS)

1625. Tarr, Joel A. ''Urban Transportation: History and Planning.'' *American Public Works Association Reporter* (December 1977), pp. 14-16.

Tarr demonstrates that ''problem-oriented'' historical inquiry can contribute to understanding the impact on society of current and future technological advances. He stresses two types of analysis employed by applied historians. Directing his argument to transportation planners, Tarr emphasizes the predictive potential of carefully drawn historical analogies. For instance, he notes that knowledge of the social upheaval caused by railroad construction in American cities could have forewarned planners of the disruptive impact on residences and businesses that followed construction of urban freeways. Through retrospective analysis, the second approach, an applied historian might further help planners by explaining the evolution of present conditions. Such an approach can identify past shifts in policy and analyze the positive and negative aspects of the rejected plans. (PNS)

V. Welfare Policy and Related Social Groupings

1626. Achenbaum, W. Andrew. *Old Age in the New Land: The Experience since 1790.* Baltimore: Johns Hopkins University Press, 1978.

Achenbaum's study of old age in America demonstrates the utility of a historical perspective on contemporary policy analysis. Juxtaposing past trends in people's popular conceptions of persons over sixty to that group's demographic and socioeconomic realities since 1790, Achenbaum reveals that changes in the way people perceive the elderly tend to be unrelated to the actual circumstances of older Americans. He emphasizes that this discontinuity persisted in the 1970s, when most Americans saw the elderly as an inactive and unhappy group despite recent reports to the contrary. Studies showed considerable variations in the energy level and physical and mental state of the older generation. While denying the ability of historians or anyone else to predict the future, Achenbaum explains that the conditions of aged persons have undergone much change in the past; therefore he warns policy makers against constructing long-range policies that presume the continuation of present circumstances. (PNS)

1627. Berkowitz, Edward D. "The Historian as Policy Analyst: The Challenge of HEW." *Public Historian*, Vol. I (Spring 1979), pp. 17-25.

Public historians attempt to answer questions posed by people outside academe and the history profession. By definition, the history profession finds it easier to answer its own questions than those posed by current policy makers and administrators. Using evidence from an investigation conducted in the Department of Health, Education, and Welfare (HEW), the author suggests the sorts of contributions that historians can make to public administration. (RPC)

1628. Berkowitz, Edward, and Kim McQuade, eds. *Creating the Welfare State: The Political Economy of Twentieth Century Reform.* New York: Praeger, 1980.

These essays trace the development of American welfare from 1900 through the 1950s. In each section, generalizations are drawn that stress key continuities in the American approach to welfare. The concluding essay eschews formal recommendations but shows that American traditions make some welfare approaches unfeasible and others particularly promising, an illustration of the way that history can contribute to realistic policy discussions in the future. (PNS)

1629. Bremner, Robert Hamlett. *From the Depths: The Discovery of Poverty in the United States*. New York: New York University Press, 1956.

Bremner inquires into the emergence of modern attitudes and levels of information concerning poverty. The book does not directly contribute to current policy debates. As policy history it is distinctly in the category of background material, but it thoroughly explores a major change in outlook that still defines important policy parameters. (PNS)

1630. Derthick, Martha. *Policymaking for Social Security*. Washington: Brookings, 1979.

Derthick provides a historical study of Social Security from the standpoint of institutional development and political conflict. Derthick clearly defines the contemporary problem setting in relation to the political past. (PNS)

1631. Fischer, David Hackett. *Growing Old in America*. New York: Oxford University Press, 1977.

This book provides a sweeping history of the position of the elderly in American society. Emphasis falls on a distinct deterioration of attitudes toward the elderly around 1800; in this sense the book is a paradigmatic approach to current policy problems, seen as flowing inevitably from a much earlier change in outlook. Twentieth-century problems are also treated, particularly in the retirement area, and Fischer offers a set of recommendations for future policy, tied to the history itself. (PNS)

1632. Flora, Peter, and Arnold Heidenheimer, eds. *Development of Welfare States in Europe and America*. New Brunswick, N.J.: Transaction, 1980.

This collection of essays treats modern welfare history in a variety of "Atlantic" countries, building on earlier comparative insights (see no. *1639*). Along with the analysis by Hugh Heclo (see no. *1638*), these essays edited by Flora and Heidenheimer contribute historical data and concepts vital to the understanding of modern welfare policies. (PNS)

1633. Gaylin, Willard, ed. *Doing Good: The Limits of Benevolence*. New York: Pantheon, 1978.

This collection of essays treats the intentions behind American approaches to welfare and their characteristic constraints, dealing with historical patterns in relation to contemporary problems. (PNS)

1634. Graebner, William. *A History of Retirement: The Meaning and Function of an American Institution*. New Haven, Conn.: Yale University Press, 1980.

This detailed and challenging history relies on institutional development rather than social experience. Richest in the treatment of the onset of retirement systems prior to World War II, it links this analysis to the new attacks on retirement that arose during the 1970s. (PNS)

1635. Graebner, William. *Coal Mining Safety in the Progressive Era: The Political Economy of Reform.* Lexington: University of Kentucky Press, 1976.

At the turn of the century increasing competition, low profits, cheap immigrant labor, deep mines, and increased use of machinery and explosives characterized coal mining. Hundreds of miners were killed each year in accidents. Each disaster caused a public cry for new safety measures. Yet, the creation of the U.S. Bureau of Mines in 1910 resulted from the coal industry's advocacy. Graebner notes that national regulatory legislation was not passed until the mine owners decided that safety was in their best interest. This explanation runs counter to the motivation conventionally assigned to the Progressive Era, the desire to achieve social reform for humanitarian purposes. The author deals briefly with the difficulty of reforming the highly competitive coal business in comparison with the relative ease of such reform in monopolistic industries such as steel. (PNS)

1636. Graham, Otis, L., Jr. *An Encore for Reform: The Old Progressives and the New Deal.* New York: Oxford University Press, 1967.

Graham provides background on continuities in basic American reform assumptions. (PNS)

1637. Grongjerg, Kirsten A. *Mass Society and the Extension of Welfare, 1960-1970.* Chicago: University of Chicago Press, 1977.

This analytical history of the extension of welfare in the 1960s relates developments to sociological theories of the mass society. A host of variables are tested, a great deal of information is conveyed, and a statement of periodization is developed to challenge the historian of modern welfare. (PNS)

1638. Heclo, Hugh. *Modern Social Politics in Britain and Sweden: From Relief to Income Maintenance.* New Haven, Conn.: Yale University Press, 1974.

This account of two major cases of welfare development isolates different descriptive patterns and a factor mix that produced them. It makes a case for the use of history in understanding contemporary policy settings and for the comparative method in policy analysis. (PNS)

1639. Heidenheimer, Arnold J. *Comparative Public Policy: Policies of Social Choice in Europe and America.* New York: St. Martin's, 1975.

The contributions provide an example of comparative analysis in identifying differing basic assumptions in the formation of modern welfare policies. Heidenheimer suggests that the key differential between American and European approaches lies in the American emphasis on equality of opportunity, which logically led to primary attention to education rather than welfare. This situation contrasts with the European assumptions of a social hierarchy cushioned by welfare. Analysis of this sort depends on a highly conceptual historical approach, while contributing directly to an understanding of current policy settings. (PNS)

1640. Janowitz, Morris. *The Last Half Century: Societal Change and Politics in America.* Chicago: University of Chicago Press, 1978.

This book offers a sweeping interpretation of leading trends in recent American history, viewed through a social control model. Considerable amounts of data support a somewhat pessimistic interpretation of advanced industrial society, particularly its American version. Because of changes in occupational and residential structure and the rise of the welfare state, Janowitz discerns a decided shift away from agreed-upon political values and a corresponding decrease in the governability of American society. While not directly policy history, the book's sweep and consistent analytical rather than descriptive focus provide important background for applied history *per se.* (PNS)

1641. Lubove, Roy. *The Struggle for Social Security.* Cambridge, Mass.: Harvard University Press, 1968.

Lubove offers analytical background history, stressing distinctively American factors in the process of developing security policy. (PNS)

1642. Marmor, Theodore. *The Politics of Medicare.* Chicago: Aldine, 1973.

In this work Marmor uses historical factors and some comparative analysis as integral parts of his policy assessment. Marmor traces the historical shaping of key positions on the Medicare issue, and he uses history as one of his points for evaluation and recommendation. (PNS)

1643. New Designs for Youth Develoment. Association for Youth Development, P.O. Box 36748, Tucson, Ariz. 85740.

The historical articles included in this quarterly journal, which began publication in 1979, are directed at a policy and social-work audience, providing policy-relevant analysis in the youth and youth services area. The historical essays generally provide background statements on key aspects of youth history rather than directly policy-relevant analysis, but they point toward the concept that historical generalization can provide a guide to current policy approaches concerning youth. (PNS)

1644. Piven, Frances Fox, and Richard A. Cloward, eds. *Regulating the Poor: The Functions of Public Welfare.* New York: Pantheon, 1971.

The authors trace the jerky progression of welfare legislation in the United States, with particular emphasis on the New Deal and Great Society. They hold that American officialdom responds with welfare to pressure from below, but that it pulls back when pressure is reduced. Extensive welfare is assumed to be a desirable goal. (PNS)

1645. Piven, Frances Fox, and Richard A. Cloward. *Poor Peoples Movements: Why They Succeed, How They Fail.* New York: Pantheon, 1977.

Piven and Cloward compare case studies of protest movements of the unemployed and industrial workers during the Great Depression with those of southern blacks and welfare recipients in the decades following World War II. The authors define their purpose as offering "historical wisdom" to enhance future political struggles of lower-class groups. They charge that past organizers undermined the potential of the movements because of their preoccupation with building organizations that became dependent upon the support of society's elites. This dependency stifled their most effective weapon, the power of disruption. The authors downplay some of the accomplishments of civil rights groups. The study applies historical research to policy analysis. (PNS)

1646. Platt, Anthony M. *The Child Savers: The Invention of Delinquency*. Chicago: University of Chicago Press, 1969.

Arguing that most research on children and crime has focused on the juvenile and the environment, Platt studies the child savers and the institutions that they helped to create between 1870 and 1900. Platt highlights the reform movement in Chicago and Illinois, where the first juvenile court was enacted in 1899. He emphasizes how the upper-class and middle-class backgrounds of the reformers influenced their perception of acceptable behavior and their definition of delinquency. The ideals of the "child saver's ethic" were institutionalized in the new penology and juvenile courts. This study shows how history can benefit policy analysis. Platt demonstrates the folly of the child savers, whose definition of delinquency was based on rural values but was applied to the youth of the urban poor. He shows that the nineteenth-century child saver's ethic survived in policy thinking of the 1960s. He feels that present standards used for judging delinquency need reconsideration. Platt provides an example of the paradigmatic approach to policy history, in which an initial paradigm is evaluated and the continued relevance of both paradigm and evaluation asserted without detailed examination of the intervening period. (PNS)

1647. Rimlinger, Gaston V. *Welfare Policy and Industrialization in Europe, America, and Russia*. New York: Wiley, 1971.

Rimlinger treats the evolution of basic welfare policies in the context of social and economic development, deriving both historical and comparative perspective from this approach. This book does not treat current policy problems directly, but it demonstrates the use of diverse cultural contexts in explaining durable policy orientations. (PNS)

1648. Seifer, Nancy. *Absent from the Majority: Working Class Women in America*. New York: National Project on Ethnic America, 1973.

This study examines the problems of life style and change for the working-class women of America, but implicitly it is the story of a labor problem. Working-class women are followed from their narrow, insecure world of the 1950s through nearly two decades of change and social upheaval. Like other women, their roles were changing, but unlike many women they felt victimized. At the bottom of the educational and occupational ladder, these women worked out of economic necessity rather than self-actualization. Routine jobs and day-care problems added to their frustration. The problems working-class women faced when entering the work force become apparent under historical analysis. In addition to being female, these poor, uneducated, laboring women faced real psychological obstacles because of their traditional view of female roles. Social history contributes to the definition of a policy issue. Although Seifer sees some sign of change in younger women, she recommends a range of programs from day-care to supportive services to further needed change. (PNS)

1649. Stearns, Peter N. "Political Perspective on Social Security Financing." In Felicity Skidmore, ed. *Social Security Financing*. Cambridge, Mass.: M.I.T. Press, 1981.

Stearns analyzes current and prospective political reactions to possible changes in social security financing in terms of origins, causes, and continuities in interest group positions. He notes perceivable or possible changes in position according to shifts away from the causes of the historic stance; he urges the importance of the political context, historically interpreted, as a factor in social security policy, and he offers some tactical warnings and recommendations. (PNS)

1650. Tishler, Hall S. *Self-Reliance and Social Security*. Port Washington, N.Y.: Kennikat, 1971.

Definitely in the history of policy rather than the policy-history mode, this book provides important background to the development of modern American welfare patterns during the crucial period when the purely charitable approach was under intense challenge. The author details early proposals in areas such as health insurance and identifies the factors involved in such proposals, by dint of treating still-unresolved policy issues. (PNS)

1651. Titmuss, Richard M. *The Gift Relationship: From Human Blood to Social Policy*. New York: Pantheon, 1971.

Titmuss uses historical data as part of a sweeping comparative inquiry into different patterns of blood donation, particularly in the United States and Britain, and makes additional comments on countries such as South Africa and the Soviet Union. The overall approach is more cross-sectional than historical, but a comparative pattern is developed that yields insight into different national characteristics and treats an important aspect of contemporary medical policy. (PNS)

1652. Trattner, Walter I. *From Poor Law to Welfare State: A History of Social Welfare in America*. New York: Free Press, 1974.

Trattner traces the development of select areas of private and public welfare services from the colonial period to the 1970s, with stress on the social and intellectual factors that shaped welfare practices during different periods of history. Emphasizing the preference for private over public aid, the study describes the traditional characteristics of American welfare and relates the increase of welfare services to hardships caused by war, economic depression, immigration, and industrialization. Trattner treats most thoroughly child welfare, health, and the settlement house movement. Increased federal involvement dominates the narrative of the twentieth century. The work provides historical perspective on varying welfare policies through a clear periodization; it characterizes the perception of welfare at different periods of history. Trattner gives only cursory coverage to the 1960s and 1970s. (PNS)

VI. Urban Policy: Crime and Police

1653. Berry, Brian J. L. *The Human Consequences of Urbanization: Divergent Paths in the Urban Experience of the Twentieth Century*. New York: St. Martin's, 1973.

The relationship between divergent social and political factors and effective urban planning is the subject of Berry's book. The author presents a comparative historical analysis of twentieth-century urbanization in order to challenge the notion that modernization and its consequential effects on society have developed a universal model of urban planning. By contrasting the maturation of urban environments in the United States, Europe, Japan, and the Third World, Berry focuses on the fundamentally different processes of urbanization that have arisen out of differences in time and culture to meet human needs. His study emphasizes that paths of deliberate urbanization can be enriched by an accurate assessment of what has not worked in the past and why. (PNS)

1654. Blumenfeld, Hans. "Continuity and Change in Urban Form: The City's Identity Problem." *Journal of Urban History*, Vol. I (February 1975), pp. 131-148.

Blumenfeld is concerned with the ways in which continuity and change interact to form a city's "identity." He makes use of the applied historical approach in order to dispel the popular feeling that new construction and growth will destroy the character of our existing cities. A historical analysis is made of several new- and old-world cities to assess the impact of change upon their identity. Although his survey is not exhaustive, Blumenfeld concludes that a city's identity evolves and improves as a result of physical alterations. As generations remake the city to suit their needs, historic elements tend to be reinforced rather than obscured or destroyed. Current policy makers should not fight to restrict new developments in cities. Instead they must channel change so that historic constants such as street patterns, topography, and architectural landmarks are articulated. This work does not make specific suggestions about ways that preservationists might distinguish between "expendable" and irreplaceable urban elements. Blumenfeld's approach represents an application of history to show that a current problem is also an opportunity for the improvement of cities' identities. (PNS)

1655. Condit, Carl W. *Chicago, 1930-1970: Building, Planning, and Urban Technology*. Chicago: University of Chicago Press, 1974.

Condit offers a thorough descriptive history, with emphasis on key technological and planning factors. He is extremely critical of uncontrolled consumer technology and poor design, the latter including the failure of Chicago's Model Cities Program. He urges a radical program of physical and moral reconstruction initiated by the people themselves. Here is an interesting case of using history to urge its reversal: "By the mid-twentieth century it seemed clear that the American system in its traditional form could no longer produce a livable urban environment." (PNS)

1656. Conley, John A. "Prisons, Production, and Profit: Reconsidering the Importance of Prison Industries."*Journal of Social History*, Vol. XIV (Winter 1980), pp. 257-275;
"Beyond Legislative Acts: Penal Reform, Public Policy, and Symbolic Justice." *Public Historian*, Vol. III (Winter 1981), pp. 26-39.

Despite the perceived belief that prison reform is for the good of the incarcerated, Conley argues that the real reason for this reform movement in the past has been the political and financial aspirations of individuals and interest groups. He specifically points to the problems that the legislature encounters as it battles the governor and the interest groups; how the interest groups keep certain actions from occurring; and how the governors seek change, only to be turned down. Throughout all these conflicts runs an underlying message: as long as reform movements took place, regardless of their impact, the public was reassured and supportive of the prison system. Although Conley does not act as a problem solver, he demonstrates through the use of case studies that the prison system is becoming a "custodial service" for the courts. (PNS)

1657. Fisher, Robert, and Peter Romanofsky, eds. *Community Organizations for Urban Social Change: A Historical Perspective*. Westport, Conn.: Greenwood, 1981.

This work contains short narrative histories of various community action programs, from the community center movement of the early twentieth century to comments on the "seeds of democratic revolt" of the 1970s. Several essays, including an introductory one by Zane Miller on the historical concept of neighborhood in American history, are more wide ranging; the case studies are drawn from various regions, although with focus on big-city types. In terms of scope and of policy use of history in this area, this is a pioneering volume. (PNS)

1658. Fogelson, Robert M. *Big City People*. Cambridge, Mass.: Harvard University Press, 1977.

This book traces the history of urban policing from the late nineteenth century to the 1970s, with the explicit goal of providing historical data and perspectives on current policy problems, notably in the area of police-civilian relations.

Previous currents of police reform and professionalization are traced with an eye to contributing to the understanding of what the author terms a contemporary standstill in further progress. The book draws both on original research and on the considerable body of case-study police histories that have been generated over the past two decades. (PNS)

1659. Fogelson, Robert W. *Violence as Protest: A Study of Riots and Ghettos*. Garden City, N.Y.: Doubleday, 1971.

This book stemmed from two experiences, the author's work as an urban historian of Los Angeles and his role as consultant to the President's Crime Commission and the Riot Commission. This study blends historical perspective and sociological data, dealing directly with the policy dilemmas that confront those seeking to deal with violence in the ghetto. Fogelson provides a scholarly assessment of the Kerner Commission's report. The book demonstrates how a historian makes use of policy-relevant theories of social action. (PNS)

1660. Graham, Hugh Davis, and Ted Robert Gurr, eds. *Violence in America*. Beverly Hills, Calif.: Sage Publications, 1979.

A call on historians to contribute to public policy, this volume updates the original collection for the Kerner Commission on the causes and prevention of violence. (See the Commission's final report, *To Establish Justice, To Insure Domestic Tranquility*, December 1969.) The present volume offers a number of interesting studies on the history of American violence, although some of the original essays have been deleted and a larger social science section has been added. The essays also raise important questions about how historians can contribute, when called upon rather suddenly, in an acute but rather amorphous policy area. (PNS)

1661. Greenberg, Stephanie W. "Neighborhood Change, Racial Transition, and Work Location: A Case Study in an Industrial City, Philadelphia, 1880-1930." *Journal of Urban History*, Vol. VII (May 1981), pp. 267-314.

Greenberg asserts that the economic and social dynamics that currently favor the suburbs over urban centers operated *within* the cities during the period 1880-1930. This study serves as an example of applied history for several reasons. Trends of suburbanization, new technology, improved transportation, and decentralization of industry dictated growth throughout the period. The author offers a general model of neighborhood change; failure to retain industrial employment encourages neighborhood decline and an influx of minorities. Decisions on factory location made at a nonlocal level are identified as being the ultimate cause of neighborhood change. (PNS)

1662. Johnson, David A. *American Law Enforcement: A History*. St. Louis: Forum, 1981.

While not a policy study, this book provides useful general background in the flourishing research area of crime and police history. Along with Walker (see no. *1669*), it provides a survey of these subjects, communicating a sense of stages of police policy development and a context for current policy concerns. (PNS)

1663. Lapping, Mark B. ''The Emergence of Federal Public Housing: Atlanta's Techwood Project.'' *American Journal of Economics and Sociology*, Vol. XXXII (Summer 1973), pp. 379-385.

Lapping deals with a pioneering project under New Deal legislation, which introduced many legal elements and other innovations that became part of the United States Housing Act of 1937. (PNS)

1664. Lujn, Frederick. ''Policy Perception of Program Failure: The Politics of Public Housing in Chicago and New York City.'' *Urbanism Past and Present*, No. IX (Winter 1979-1980), pp. 1-12.

Lujn deals with the influence of government policies on public perception of an institution, in this case public housing ''having to look like'' it was built for poor people, and with the influence of this perception on changing policy. Case studies are drawn from Daley's Chicago and Lindsay's New York, with emphasis on constraints on site selection and legal issues. (PNS)

1665. Miller, Roberta Balstad. *City and Hinterland: A Case Study of Urban Growth and Regional Development*. Westport, Conn.: Greenwood, 1979.

Miller examines the regional economic development and interrelationship of Onandaga County, New York, to the nation as a whole from 1790 to 1869—a period of rapid urban growth and technological change. Her case study focuses on the impact of transportation innovations and other socioeconomic reformations that transformed the individual market system of the frontier settlement into an urban, regional economy centered in the city of Syracuse. She concludes that county development patterns were determined not by industrialization but by the interplay of local conditions and the impact of state and federal initiatives. The installation of the Erie Canal and later the railroads in particular reorganized local and regional migration patterns as well as traditional economic relationships. While her investigation is limited in scope to a particular urban growth configuration during the nineteenth century, her retrospective analysis has present-day policy implications. (PNS)

1666. Monkkonen, Eric. *Police in Urban America, 1660-1920*. Cambridge: Cambridge University Press, 1981.

While not directed explicitly at current policy analysis, this work advances both methodology and concepts of vital importance to a historical contribution to policy issues in the police area. The author's efforts to categorize trends in police functions and their correlation with crime patterns provide historical insights that are directly relevant to applied historical work on the subject. (PNS)

1667. Mumford, Lewis. *The Urban Prospect.* New York: Harcourt, Brace & World, 1956. Rev. ed., 1968.

In a collection of articles, essays, and addresses presented over a twenty-year period, Mumford examines the characteristics and components of the modern American city and concludes that their deterioration and decline are the results of misplanned growth and the pursuit of maximum financial profits. He notes that urban planners have failed miserably in their attempts to utilize land intelligently, relate industry and technology to the community, and halt urban sprawl. Their bureaucratic pursuit of standardization, regimentation, and centralized control have given birth to the "Megalopolis," which ignores the central task of the city—to provide communities with opportunities for interaction, the exchange of human faculties as well as economic goods and services, and to encourage frequent participation in a biologically and socially satisfying environment. Mumford calls for an evaluation of the methods and objectives from a historical and sociological perspective in order to understand the social, political, and economic roots of urban problems. Policy makers in this field need a multidimensional, historical analysis of previous attempts to right urban wrongs before new programs are adopted. (PNS)

1668. Teaford, Jon C. *City and Suburb: The Political Fragmentation of Metropolitan America, 1850-1970.* Baltimore: Johns Hopkins University Press, 1979.

Teaford describes the obstacles faced by reformers who have tried to bind divisions between city and suburbs with schemes of metropolitan federations. He reviews somewhat critically the permissive practices of suburban incorporation that accompanied rapid urban growth between 1850 and 1910 and produced complex local political fragmentation. Despite central city growth through annexations, Teaford shows that support for self-rule among local units continues to complicate the present administration of metropolitan services. To the fragmented American system he compares the more efficient form of British municipal government, which evolved subject to greater controls by the central government, and he notes that urban elites in America used as a model for their reform proposals the federal formula that integrates London with its surrounding boroughs. (PNS)

1669. Walker, Samuel. *Popular Justice: A History of American Criminal Justice.* New York and Oxford: Oxford University Press, 1980.

This book, although a survey approach to the history of crime, police, and particularly the penal system, offers direct lessons for policy makers in the field. It critiques lingering liberal ideas that the American penal system has ever functioned well, but it does not adopt a simple social-control perspective. Rather, the book shows that the penal system has not been caught up in a single "modern paradigm." The author believes that changes of the past fifteen years, "many of them suggestive of a new sensitivity as well as of lowered expectations," have been quite dramatic. (PNS)

1670. Warner, Sam Bass, Jr. *The Urban Wilderness: A History of the American City*. New York: Harper and Row, 1972.

Critical of the failure to develop "humane" cities in the United States, Warner presents his urban history as an aid to understanding the problems that planners and others active in urban affairs must confront. He describes segregation and discrimination as the predominant social problems and bemoans these inequities. They exemplify an elite hegemony that has emphasized the goals of guarded competition and innovation above those of total community benefit. To implement a more egalitarian community development, Warner argues for the establishment of democratic national and regional planning. (PNS)

1671. Yates, Douglas. *The Ungovernable City: The Politics of Urban Problems and Policy Making*. Cambridge, Mass.: M.I.T. Press, 1977.

Yates presents a sobering historical assessment and structural analysis of the urban policy-making dilemma. Drawing on the recent experiences of New York City and New Haven, Connecticut, he examines the bureaucratic character of city government and its function in urban service delivery. He concludes that the inherently pluralistic structure of local administrations and their decentralized distribution of services have given rise to a fragmented policy-making process, exacerbating the routine yet persistent problems facing city government. Yates introduces a reactionary model of urban problem generation that seeks to explain bureaucratic dysfunction. Within this framework, he sets forth a modest agenda for urban policy analysts and planners. Combining elements of centralization and cooperation on the state and federal levels will improve coordination of necessary programs. However, measures must also be taken to develop a large repertoire of administrative strategies that will be flexible enough to respond to the individual citizen and community. (PNS)

VII. Other Policy Areas

1672. Brauer, Carl M. *John F. Kennedy and the Second Reconstruction*. New York: Columbia University Press, 1977.

This thorough history of a major period in recent civil rights development does not pretend to have direct applicability to current policy issues. It is a well-balanced description and assessment of the Kennedy administration approach, which the author sees as a significant acceleration in concern for civil rights. The causes of change are detailed. The long-range impact of the new policies is merely sketched, but the book provides background for those concerned with contemporary issues in this area. (PNS)

1673. Callahan, Raymond E. *Education and the Cult of Efficiency*. Chicago: University of Chicago Press, 1962.

This study traces the rise of business values and practices in educational administration, beginning about 1900. The author sees patterns of local pressure,

building on a dominant value system and extreme vulnerability among school administrators, combining to create predictable reactions in educational policy through the 1970s and, unless change occurs, in the future as well. The tone is critical; the schools have not been doing well because of these modern patterns of control and reaction. The author believes that tracing and evaluating the historical pattern yields some concrete, if complex, policy recommendations for a major overhaul. (PNS)

1674. Chandler, Alfred D., Jr. *The Visible Hand: The Managerial Revolution in American Business.* Cambridge, Mass.: Harvard University Press, 1977.

Adam Smith's "invisible hand" explained a free-market economy with built-in stabilizers, constraints, and incentives that maintained competitive vitality; but Chandler, in his history of American business organization, holds that the nature of the market has changed with new productive and distributive processes. The twentieth century is marked by the ascendency of a managerial structure. Oligopolies inevitably developed because it became more efficient for business to carry on the functions of marketing, coordinating, and regulating distribution than to rely on market forces alone. The development of the railroad and other technologies offered new opportunities for growth. Capital-intensive industries with high energy use were most receptive to change. By 1917, Chandler argues, most firms had acquired their modern structures. Mass production ushered in the complexities of mass distribution, thereby promoting the development of "managerial capitalism." *The Visible Hand* sheds new light on business organization. For too long the business world has been analyzed only in terms of economic, financial, or organizational theory. Chandler clearly places business and the economy in historical perspective. His work is virtually the only historical material currently included in business-school curricula. (PNS)

Chandler, Alfred D., Jr. and Herman Daems, eds. *Managerial Hierarchies: Comparative Perspectives on the Rise of the Modern Industrial Enterprise.* See no. *232.*

The rise and nature of modern management are discussed in this collection of seven essays. The focus of these essays is the transformation of the management structure in advanced industrial economies. A hierarchical system of management developed as a replacement for the market mechanism. In an attempt to uncover managerial trends, the essays consider business in several western industrial nations and some topical issues as well. Managerial hierarchies are rooted in burgeoning economies where technological improvements, first in transportation and communication and then in production, served to outstrip the efficiency of the traditional market mechanism. (PNS)

1675. Donzelot, Jacques. *The Policing of Families.* New York: Pantheon, 1980.

This work is a statement of the social control thesis regarding families, usefully read in conjunction with Lasch (see no. *1688*). Donzelot takes a long and pes-

simistic view of modern family history and its impact on various policy communities and expert approaches from the nineteenth century onward. The book tries to set contemporary debates about the family on a new footing, moving away from a reactionary/feminist-psychiatric reformist dispute. The focus is European, but the implications for contemporary evaluation of the family are sweeping. (PNS)

1676. Dubos, Rene. *Mirage of Health: Utopias, Progress, and Biological Change*. New York: Harper Colophon, 1959.

Dubos offers a wide-ranging examination of the historical context of modern medical attitudes and practices. He dispels or challenges a host of pervasive beliefs about the impact of medical advance as opposed to other factors in health, and he discusses the relevance of this new understanding for the future. (PNS)

1677. Easterlin, Richard A. *Birth and Fortune: The Impact of Numbers on Personal Welfare*. New York: Basic Books, 1980.

Easterlin, a demographer-historian, develops a theory about the relationship between birth rate cohorts and life success, family behavior, and related attitudes for contemporary American society. The book provides an example of a way one kind of historical data can be used for extensive forecasting. (PNS)

1678. Ettling, John. *The Germ of Laziness: Rockefeller Philanthropy and Public Health in the New South*. Cambridge, Mass.: Harvard University Press, 1981.

Ettling studies an early philanthropic effort in medical research and implementation (1909). The case involved efforts to eradicate hookworm disease. The author places the study against a backdrop of the progressive reform mentality and organizational change, and it illuminates some ongoing assumptions, the continuing history of county health organizations, and the formative impact on Rockefeller Foundation approaches in this area. (PNS)

1679. Federal Trade Commission. *National Competition Policy: Historians' Perspective on Antitrust and Government-Business Relationships in the United States*. Washington: Federal Trade Commission, 1981.

The traditional view of antitrust and business relationships in this country has been chiefly a product of lawyers and economists. The Federal Trade Commission promoted a series of seminars on the subject of antitrust policy by five historians: Alfred C. Chandler, Jr., Robert D. Cuff, Louis Galambos, Ellis W. Hawley, and Thomas K. McCraw. This book is an edited transcript of those sessions. A wide range of topics was chosen for discussion in order to permit temporal and cross-national comparisons; consequently, the result was not systematic applied history of a specific policy problem. Rather, two more general purposes were served. First, the historical perspective shows antitrust policy to be a complex issue, exposing misconceptions and what one participant calls "ironies" in the policy. If there was an underlying theme, it was that associationalism has co-

existed with the individual-competitive tradition despite frequent rhetoric to the contrary. Secondly, the study centers on certain issues, trends, and analogies of more specific topics, such as the rise of oligopolies and regulation policy in Japan. (PNS)

1680. Fox, Richard W. *So Far Disordered in Mind: Insanity in California, 1870-1930*. Berkeley: University of California Press, 1979.

The author uses important data about the institutionalization of the insane to condemn current policies in the field. The work links with Rothman (see no. *1696*) in its approach to the issue, in evaluating past policy paradigms, and finding the deficiencies in basic values applicable to current policy issues. The logic of the argument carries the author to advocate de-institutionalization as a basic approach to the mentally ill. (PNS)

1681. Gersuny, Carl. *Work Hazards and Industrial Conflict*. Hanover, N.H.: University Press of New England, 1981.

Gersuny offers an overview of twentieth-century developments in work safety regulation and conflict in the United States, noting specific reference to attacks on the Occupational Safety and Health Act. (PNS)

1682. Greer, Colin. *The Great School Legend: A Revisionist Interpretation of American Education*. New York: Basic Books, 1972.

Greer takes up the rosy picture of achievements in American education—assimilating immigrants and advancing individual and social progress—and debunks it in terms both of intentions and of results of school administration. Considerable attention is given to the role of historians in furthering the "legend" of school success and to the policy implications, for blacks and Chicanos, of this use of educational history. (PNS)

1683. Grob, Gerald N. "Rediscovering Asylums: The Unhistorical History of the Mental Hospital." In Morris J. Vogel and Charles E. Rosenberg, eds. *The Therapeutic Revolution: Essays in the Social History of American Medicine*. Philadelphia: University of Pennsylvania Press, 1979.

Grob advances a major critique of the social-control approach to the history of mental illness and to its policy implications (see Rothman, no. *1696*). Grob argues for the importance of seeing nineteenth-century policy in the light of existing social conditions and real evidence of insanity. (PNS)

1684. Hawley, Ellis. *The New Deal and the Problem of Monopoly*. Princeton, N.J.: Princeton University Press, 1966.

The dynamics of policy issues in the New Deal is the general concern of this book, but, more explicitly, it deals with the "problem of monopoly" as a national concern. Hawley characterizes an ongoing dispute between those who favor individual-competitive incentives and those who advocate planning—antitrust versus regulation. Both views have shaped economic policy and are embedded in the American idea of growth; Americans have not made a choice between them. Hawley argues that programs like the National Recovery Administration, which appear to lack consistency, can be understood only in political terms, in which concessions are made to both approaches. Politically, apparent fluctuations have some consistency and logic. Hawley's historical inquiry provides more than insight into a particular period, for it identifies two trends that have shaped economic policy for most of our industrial history. The relevance of this work to today's policy-maker, according to the author, lies in his demonstration of "the limitations of logical analysis, the difficulty in agreed-upon policy goals" and the need to understand factors such as opinions and political pressure groups. (PNS)

1685. Katz, Michael B. *Class, Bureaucracy, and Schools: The Illusion of Educational Change in America*. New York: Praeger, 1971.

This book is one of the most influential works in the social-control mode, dealing with the history of American education. The focus is on the nineteenth century and the gap between liberal rhetoric and the real intentions of educational policy as schools spread to the masses. But the approach has policy implications in suggesting the desirability of less rigid inclusion of values in contemporary education; and Katz's work has been utilized in discussions of current educational policy. (PNS)

1686. Jeffrey, Julie Roy. *Education for Children of the Poor: A Study of the Origins and Implementation of the Elementary and Secondary Education Act of 1965*. Columbus: Ohio State University Press, 1978.

Jeffrey offers thorough examination of the major Great Society effort in the educational field, intended as a centerpiece for improving the conditions of the poor. She traces the assumptions and political background of the measure and evaluates the outcome. The book makes no precise policy recommendations, but in documenting many failed assumptions and a broader loss of faith in the efficacy of education it has obvious policy implications. (PNS)

1687. Jones, James. *Bad Blood: The Tuskegee Syphilis Experiment*. New York: Macmillan, 1981.

Jones provides an account of medical experimentation on unwitting subjects and of the assumptions that made such experimentation possible. This work is an example of recent policy history for anyone dealing with the realm of medical policy. (PNS)

1688. Lasch, Christopher. *Haven in a Heartless World—The Family Besieged*. New York: Basic Books, 1977.

This book provides a historical approach to policy issues facing the contemporary family. Lasch, who is profoundly pessimistic about the family, argues among other things against the detrimental impact of governmental and expert interference with family functioning. Lasch's sense of a possible modern-to-contemporary family dynamic is an aspect applied historians, dealing more directly in the family policy area, can take into account. The book also provides a recent example of a classic kind of historian-policy linkage—moral outrage at the situation as compared with the past. (PNS)

1689. Mohr, James C. *Abortion in America: The Origin and Evolution of National Policy, 1800-1900.* New York: Oxford University Press, 1978.

This important statement traces the evolution of abortion policy from an attitude of considerable tolerance to one of growing legal rigor. Great emphasis is placed on the role of professional physicians (and the professionalization of physicians) in this evolution. The general pattern of change and its legal manifestations are clearly indicated. A final chapter relates the Supreme Court's Roe decision to the earlier developments. (PNS)

1690. Nadwarny, Milton J. *Scientific Management and the Unions, 1900-1932: A Historical Analysis.* Cambridge, Mass.: Harvard University Press, 1955.

Nadwarny analyzes the impact of Taylorism (scientific management) on the relationship and attitudes of labor and management. In its period of ascent, scientific management posited that given the opportunity for proper implementation, its approach would prove labor unions unnecessary. Taylorism was neither monolithic nor perfect, although it met with early success. Labor, however, was alienated by the anti-union stand and new time-savings methods. Until the 1920s unions rejected the value of scientific management and pursued congressional attention. The evolution of scientific management coupled with labor's weakened position in the 1920s resulted in changing attitudes and a policy of acceptance on both sides. Today policy makers continue to question labor's role in productive efficiency and management. Perspective is gained on many current labor-management questions by understanding the trends and issues that accompanied past innovative methods. (PNS)

1691. Neustadt, Richard, and H. V. Fineberg. *The Swine Flu Affair: Decision-making on a Slippery Disease.* Washington: Department of Health, Education and Welfare, 1978.

The authors offer an unusual kind of commentary history of a domestic policy, done in the mode of studies dealing with management of foreign policy crises. (PNS)

1692. Phelps Brown, E. H. *The Growth of British Industrial Relations.* London: Macmillan, 1959.

The story of the development of industrial relations is entwined with the growth and change of industry. Phelps Brown relates some of this story for Britain by unfolding the economic history and social conditions that help explain the particular nature of British industrial relations. The book focuses on the years 1906 to 1914 because it was a formative period, a time in which management, labor, and government began to discover and define the dynamics of their interrelationship. In that period, the government promoted conciliation rather than handing down strict regulations, and labor and management found it advantageous to bargain on an industry-wide basis. (PNS)

1693. Pierson, Frank C. *Unions in Postwar America: An Economic Assessment.* New York: Random House, 1967.

This book concentrates on a central question: Do union gains in wages and other benefits damage the economy? After analyzing union activities in light of economic conditions over a period of roughly twenty years, Pierson concludes that there is no easy answer. Although unions did not really impede the realization of national goals such as full employment or rapid growth, at times they caused some departure from the competitive norms. Many factors play a role, but the most crucial one is the nature of the industry in question. For Pierson, history indicates that the adverse effects unions may have on the economy depend on a rather complex set of factors. He suggests, however, that the best tack for unions, management, or government is to address the underlying problems in a particular industry. (PNS)

1694. Resnick, Daniel P. "Minimum Competency Testing Historically Considered." *Review of Research in Education*, Vol. VIII (June 1980), pp. 3-29.

Resnick uses clear periodization in the theory and actual implementation of testing to define current testing issues and set context for policy. (PNS)

1695. Resnick, Daniel P., and Lauren B. Resnick. "The Nature of Literacy: An Historical Exploration." *Harvard Educational Review*, Vol. XLVII (April 1977), pp. 370-385.

The authors analyze several major historical cases to determine what has defined literacy: the Protestant-religious (seventeenth-century Sweden), the elite-technical (fifteenth-century France), and the civic national (nineteenth-century France), in terms of criteria, training, and function. They also trace those changes in literacy standards in the early twentieth-century United States. They show that current literacy recommendations represent another upgrading of the literacy standards, with major educational and testing implications. The article constitutes use of history in redefining a current policy problem, showing that historical models, though often invoked, have become inexact. (PNS)

1696. Rothman, David J. *The Discovery of the Asylum: Social Order and Disorder in the New Republic.* Boston: Little, Brown, 1971.

Rothman studies the social-control mentality that developed new forms of institutionalization for the criminal and deviant in the nineteenth century. (PNS)

1697. Temin, Peter. *Taking Your Medicine: Drug Regulation in the United States*. Cambridge, Mass.: Harvard University Press, 1980.

Temin takes a long look at the history of governmental regulation in the area of drug policy. He argues that freedom of choice—by the consumer in the selection of drugs—is a viable alternative to the present systems of regulation offered by the Federal Drug Administration. The author examines the nature of and reasons behind the U.S. regulatory agency and exposes the problems that this type of system creates. In doing so, Temin clarifies the goals of the public policy. *Taking Your Medicine* is applied history in that it analyzes past and current policy and offers a solution. Temin sees the need for intervention by an authoritative body. He acknowledges that the ultimate moral responsibility lies with the people truly in need of help. (PNS)

1698. Tyack, David. *The One Best System: A History of American Urban Education*. Cambridge, Mass.: Harvard University Press, 1974.

Tyack writes a background survey from a policy standpoint and provides a basic text on educational development in its social and institutional context. He is critical of misleading promises and social-control features. (PNS)

1699. Vinovskis, Maris A. "An 'Epidemic' of Adolescent Pregnancy?" *Journal of Family History*, Vol.VI (Summer 1981), pp. 205-230.

Through careful trend analysis the author shows that the concern for rising rates of teenage pregnancy is empirically misplaced and therefore so are policies designed to contend with these rates. The phenomenon became more visible as teenagers become more numerous. (PNS)

1700. Wagner, David. "Clerical Workers: How 'Unorganizable' Are They?" *Labor Center Review*, Vol. II (Spring-Summer 1979), pp. 93-118.

Despite the rapid growth of the white-collar work force and the low rates of organization in the group, organized labor has not developed specific policy toward these workers. Wagner's larger interest is in the organizing of white-collar workers. The problem of white-collar resistance to organization is approached historically and theoretically. Wagner traces the record of organizing in this sector of the work force over most of the century, discerning trends and reaching a number of general conclusions. For example, he finds that despite a recent increase in media attention and union optimism, there has been no real upsurge in the organization of clerical workers. He also notes that large units of white-collar workers continue to resist unionization. (PNS)

AUTHOR INDEX

Note: The numbers in this index refer to entry numbers, *not* page numbers.

ABOUT THE EDITORS

LAWRENCE B. DE GRAAF is Professor of History and Director of the Oral History Program at California State University, Fullerton. He is the author of several articles on Afro-Americans in the western United States and on the teaching of public history. He is a founding director of the National Council on Public History.

ENID H. DOUGLASS is Director of the Oral History Program and Lecturer in History at the Claremont Graduate School in California. She was active in the founding of the national oral history movement and served as president of the Oral History Association, 1979-1980. She was an invited participant at the First National Symposium on Public History sponsored by the Rockefeller Foundation and the University of California, Santa Barbara, in 1979. In 1977 she was appointed by the Governor to the California Heritage Preservation Commission and now serves as its vice-chairman.

GERALD H. HERMAN is Assistant Professor of History and Special Assistant to the Provost at Northeastern University in Boston, in whose graduate Historical Agencies and Archives program he teaches the media production and evaluation course. He has produced two video-based courses in the history of Western Civilization under a Mellon Foundation grant, and he has written and lectured extensively on films and history. A program written by him for public radio in Boston was nominated for a Peabody Award and won the Ohio State Award as best documentary of the year in 1980. He has created several text and multi-media productions in cultural history and is the author of *The Pivotal Conflict* (forthcoming).

SUELLEN HOY is Assistant Director of the North Carolina Division of Archives and History. She was previously Executive Director of the Public Works Historical Society and is coauthor of the recently published annotated bibliography, *Public Works History in the United States: A Guide to the Literature*. A member of the board of the National Council on Public History, she also serves on the editorial board of *The Public Historian*. She is editor of *Institute News*, the newsletter of the North Carolina Institute of Applied History, and was for several years a member of the staff of the *Journal of American History*.

DAVID A. JOHNSON is Associate Professor of History at Portland State University and was formerly Director of the PSU Graduate Program in Public History. In addition to teaching and consulting on history related public projects, he has edited and coauthored *American Culture and the American Frontier*, a special issue of *American Quarterly* (Winter 1982).

THEODORE J. KARAMANSKI is Assistant Professor of History at Loyola University of Chicago where he coordinates the graduate programs in public history. As Director of the Mid-American Research Center, he is active in historic preservation consulting. He is the author of *Fur Trade and Exploration* as well as various journal articles.

RICHARD M. KESNER is Manager of Office Systems and Services for the F. W. Faxon Company, Inc. and was previously the founder and director of the Archives of Appalachia at East Tennessee State University. He is the author of many books and articles dealing with economic and administrative history, archival and library administration, and the new information technologies, including: *Economic Control and Colonial Development* (Greenwood Press, 1981), *Information Management, Machine-Readable Records, and Archival Administration: An Annotated Bibliography*, and *Automating Archival and Records Administration*.

GLEN M. LEONARD is Director of the Museum of Church History and Art of the Church of Jesus Christ of Latter-day Saints in Salt Lake City. He is former Managing Editor of *Utah Historical Quarterly* and former Associate Editor of *Journal of Mormon History*. He is coauthor of *The Story of the Latter-day Saints* and of articles on Utah, Mormon history, and western American history.

ROBERT W. POMEROY III is Deputy Advisor of the Inter-American Development Bank in Washington, D.C., where he has served for more than seventeen years. He is a founding Director of the National Council on Public History and has consulted for a number of programs in public history. He serves on the editorial boards of *The Public Historian* and *OFFICE: Technology and People*. His principal interest is the use of history and of historians by business.

PETER N. STEARNS is Heinz Professor of History at Carnegie-Mellon University and Co-Director of the Program in Applied History/Social Science. He has published numerous books in the field of modern social history and is Editor of the *Journal of Social History*. He has written a number of essays on history and public policy and has conducted several applied-historical studies of retirement and Social Security policies.

BOYD KEITH SWIGGER is Assistant Professor in the School of Library Science, Texas Woman's University, and formerly served on the faculty of the New Center for Learning at East Texas State University. His research includes design of interdisciplinary curricula and the social dimensions of information technologies. He is the author of *A Guide to Resources for the Study of the Recent History of the United States* and studies on the uses of microcomputers in libraries and on preschool children's responses to computer-assisted instruction.

DAVID F. TRASK is the Chief Historian of the U.S. Army Center of Military History in Washington, D.C. He taught at several universities and served as Director of the Office of the Historian at the U.S. State Department before assuming his current position. He is the author of numerous books, including *Victory without Peace: American Foreign Relations in the Twentieth Century; Captains and Cabinets: Anglo-American Naval Relations, 1917-1918*; and *The War with Spain in 1898*. He has published many articles and essays dealing with the history of relations between force and diplomacy. He has just completed a term as President of the Society for History in the Federal Government and is a founding director of the National Council on Public History.

RICHARD HUME WERKING is Director of Libraries and Associate Professor of History at Trinity University in San Antonio. His research interests are in public policy, institutional history, library services and collections, and business-government relations. He is the author of *The Master Architects: Building the United States Foreign Service, 1890-1913* as well as articles in journals such as *The William and Mary Quarterly, Pacific Historical Review, Administrative Science Quarterly, Business History Review*, and *College and Research Libraries*.